FORD

FIESTA, ESCORT, ORION, KA

WORKSHOP MANUAL

by
Lindsay Porter, David Ferguson, Jim Tyler

Ring this number to find your nearest Ford dealer in the UK – 0845 845 111.

CONTENTS

Detailed Contents are shown at the start of each Chapter.

FACT FILE

'LEFT' AND 'RIGHT' SIDES OF THE CAR

• Throughout this manual, we refer to the 'left' and 'right' sides of the car. They refer to the sides of the car that you would see if you were sitting in the driver's seat, looking forward.

First Publishing in 2001 by:
Porter Publishing Ltd.
The Storehouse • Little Hereford Street
Bromyard • Hereford • HR7 4DE • England

Tel: 01885 488 800
Fax: 01885 483 012
www.portermanuals.com

British Library Cataloguing in Publication Data.

A catalogue record for this book is available from the British Library.

ISBN 1-899238-44-1

Series Editor: Lindsay Porter
Layout and Typesetting: TypeMaker Ltd, Birmingham
Printed in England by The Trinity Press, Worcester.

CHAPTER 1: FACTS & FIGURES

*Please read **Chapter 2, Safety First** before carrying out any work on your car.*

This chapter provides you with all the information you will need about your car, especially in connection with servicing and repairing it. First, you'll need to identify the engine type. If you don't know it already, see **Chapter 6, Engine**.

Before buying parts, be sure to take your vehicle's chassis and engine numbers with you.

CONTENTS

IMPORTANT NOTE:
→ Many detail changes have taken place over the years, and there have been many different special editions and options available.
→ The following information will be true of most cases but can only be taken as a general guide.

→ Ford's quoted torque settings and other information sometimes vary between publications. The figures shown here are the latest available to us.
→ If in any doubt, consult your local Ford dealer for confirmation.

Part A: Model Changes

ESCORT and ORION
September 1980: Escort Mk 3 introduced. The first front-wheel drive Escort.

November 1980: Escort estate introduced.

October 1982: Escort Mk 3 XR2i and RS1600i introduced.

December 1983: Escort Cabriolet introduced.

1984: Escort 1.6 diesels introduced.

March 1986: Escort and Orion 'facelift' replaces existing Mk 3 models.

September 1990: Escort Mk 4 hatchback and estate replaces Mk 3 versions. Orion saloon version discontinued.

January 1995: Escort Mk 5 with wide range of minor improvements.

2000: Escort discontinued.

FIESTA
February 1997: Fiesta Mk 1 introduced.

December 1981: Fiesta Mk 1 XR2 introduced.
September 1983: Fiesta Mk 2 replaces Mk 1 versions. Orion models introduced.

1984: Fiesta 1.6 diesels introduced.

April 1989: Fiesta Mk 3 replaces Mk 2 models. CTX constantly-variable auto. transmission available.

October 1989: Fiesta Mk 3 XR2i available.

October 1995: Fiesta Mk 4 replaces Mk 3 models.

October 1999: Fiesta Mk 5 replaces Mk 4 models.

KA
October 1996: KA and KA-2 (with extra 'basics') introduced.

June 1997: KA-3 model introduced.

1: **Fiesta XR2, 1983.**

4: **Escort Mk 4, 1990-1994.**

2: **Fiesta 1.3L, 5-door, 1993.**

5: **Escort Mk 5, 1995-on.**

3: **Fiesta from 1995-on.**

6: **KA, 2001 model.**

7: **Orion.**

Part B: Vital Statistics

Wheels and Tyres

We include here an example of current provision by Dunlop for Ford vehicles. There have been many changes throughout the life of the model range and if you have bought an older model the original specification may have been replaced. We suggest that you check with your Dunlop Tyre station for the correct provision especially with high performance vehicles.

MODEL	RIM WIDTH & TYPE	RADIAL TUBELESS TYRES	TYRE PRESSURES (cold) – first figure = 'bar'; second = p.s.i.			
			FRONT		REAR	
			average load	heavy load	average load	heavy load
KA						
KA	4.5J-13	155/70R13T	2.2/32	2.5/36	1.79/26	2.5/36
KA2	5J-13	165/65R13T	2.1/31	2.5/36	1.79/26	2.5/36
KA3	5.5J-14	165/60R14T	2.1/31	2.5/36	1.79/26	2.5/36
Fiesta						
1.1/1.3 1.1 LX	4.5J-13	155/70R13T	2.1/31	2.5/37	1.79/26	2.9/41
1.3 Cfi Ghia	5J-13	165/65R13S	2.1/31	2.5/37	1.79/26	2.9/41
1.3 Encore	5J-13	155/70R13T	2.4/35	2.5/37	1.79/26	2.9/41
1.3 Finesse	5J-13	165/70R13T	2.1/30	2.5/37	1.79/26	2.9/41
1.3 LX	5J-13	165/65R13S	2.1/30	2.5/36	1.79/26	2.9/41
1.25	4.5J-13	155/70R13T	2.4/35	2.5/36	1.79/26	2.9/41
125 Ghia X	5.5J-13	185/70R13H	2.1/31	2.5/37	1.79/26	2.9/41
1.25Ghia/LX	5J-13	165/70R13T	2.1/31	2.5/37	1.79/26	2.9/41
1.25 Ghia '99 1.25 (Auto)	5.5j-14	185/55R14H	2.1/31	2.5/37	1.79/26	2.9/41
1.4 (Auto)	5J-13	165/70R13T	2.2/32	2.5/36	1.79/26	2.9/41
Endura	5J-13	165/70R13T	2.4/35	2.5/36	1.79/26	2.9/41
1.8D 1995/6	5.5J-13	165/65R13T	2.3/34	2.5/37	1.79/26	2.9/41
1.8 LX D	5J-13	165/65R13S	2.3/33	2.5/36	1.79/26	2.9/41
1.8D 1998	5J-13	165/70R13T	2.4/35	2.5/37	1.79/26	2.9/41
1.8D 1999	5J-14	175/65R14T	2.4/35	2.5/37	1.79/26	2.9/41
1.6 1.6 Si	5J-13	165/65R13S	2.3/33	2.5/36	1.79/26	2.9/41
1.4 Si	5.5J-14	185/55R14H	2.3/34	2.5/37	1.79/26	2.9/41
1.4 Efi Ghia	5J-13	165/65R13S	2.3/34	2.5/37	1.79/26	2.9/41
1.4 Ghia '98	5.5J-14	185/55R14T	2.1/31	2.5/37	1.79/26	2.9/41
1.4 Ghia '99	5.5J-14	185/55R14H	2.1/31	2.5/37	1.79/26	2.9/41
Escort						
1.3/1.4	5J-13	155R13T	2.0/29	2.5/37	1.79/26	2.9/41
1.3/1.4 Est.	5J-13	175/70R13T	2.0/29	2.5/37	1.79/26	2.9/41
1.8D '96/97	5J-13	155R13T	2.3/34	2.5/37	2.0/29	2.9/41
1.6/1.8 L/En	5J-13	175/70R13T	2.3/34	2.5/37	2.0/29	2.9/41
1.6/1.8 LX	5.5J-14	175/65R14H	2.3/34	2.5/37	2.0/29	2.9/41
Ghia/Si	6J-14	185/60R14H	2.3/34	2.5/37	2.0/29	2.9/41

Weights

All weights in kg. All sizes in mm. NB All dimensions when car unladen.
NB Maximum load capacity = (Maximum Laden Weight) minus (Unladen Weight).
Exact unladen weight will vary with model, refer to the VIN plate for details.
The figures quoted below give examples of the ranges likely to be encountered

Maximum roof load: 75 kg (all models)
Maximum weight on towball, when fitted: 50 kg.
Tow Limits: These will vary with each model and will depend on anticipated gradients and altitudes.
We recommend that you refer to your Ford dealer for full details.

MODEL	UNLADEN WEIGHT	MAX. LADEN LADEN WEIGHT
KA		
37Kw	946-998	1265
44Kw	946-1020	1265

MODEL		UNLADEN WEIGHT	MAX. LADEN LADEN WEIGHT
Fiesta			
1.0	3-Door	730-780	1160-1200
	5-Door	795-810	
1.1	3-Door	780-850	1200
	5-Door	810-865	
1.3	3-Door	800-870	1225
	5-Door	845-870	
1.4	3-Door	800-940	1225
	5-Door	840-940	
1.6	3-Door	990-1010	1275
	5-Door	990-1029	
XR2 1.6		890-910	
XR2 1.8		955-974	
Fiesta 1995-on			
Saloon/Van			
Petrol		989-1159	1415-1485
Diesel		1089-1218	1500-1550
Courier/Combi			
Petrol		1112-1203	1625-1630
Diesel		1198-1287	1715
Escort to c.1990			
Hatchback	3-door	845-980	
Hatchback	5-door	870-960	
Estate	3-door	870-970	
Estate	5-door	890-990	
XR3		925-995	
Cabriolet		930-995	
Van		860-995	

MODEL		UNLADEN WEIGHT	MAX. LADEN LADEN WEIGHT
Escort post 1990 examples.			
1.3	Saloon	1000-1055	1475-1500
	Estate	1055	1550
1.4	Saloon	1050-1105	1550-1575
	Estate	1105-1145	1575
	Van	1075	1650-1850
1.6	Saloon	1075-1140	1600-1625
	Estate	1135-1175	1650
	Cabriolet	1175	1650
1.8	Saloon	1085-1140	1600-1625
	Estate	1130-1175	1600-1650
	Cabriolet	1200-1205	1675
1.8D	Saloon	1095-1180	1600-1625
	Estate	1150-1220	1650-1675
	Van	1115	1700-1900
Orion 1983-86			
1.3	Saloon	895	1300
1.6	Saloon	905-945	1325-1350
Orion 1986-90			
1.3/1.4	Saloon	875-880	1325
1.6	Saloon	890-920	1350-1375
Orion 1990-on			
See Escort			

Dimensions

MODELS	OVERALL LENGTH	OVERALL WIDTH*	WHEEL BASE	FRONT TRACK	REAR TRACK	HEIGHT
KA	3620	1639	2448	1395	1411	1385-1413
Fiesta Pre-1983	3718	1580	2296	1331	1321	1371
(13" Wheels)					(1350)	(1331)
Fiesta 1983-89						
Saloon/Van	3468	1585	2288	1367	1321	1334
XR2	3712	1620	2288	1385	1339	1334
Fiesta 1989-1995						
3/5 door	3743	1606	2446	1392	1384	1376
XR2	3801	1630	2446	1406	1376	1365
Courier	4052	1650	2700	1392	1395	1812
Fiesta 1995-on						
Saloon/Van	3833	1634	2446	1429-1434	1373-1378	1334-1337
Courier/Combi	4115	1650	2700			1788-1835
Escort Pre-1986						
Hatchback	3972	1640	2398	1384	1480	1399
Estate	4035	1640	2398	1384	1480	1400
Van	4166	1640				1588
Escort 1986-90						
Hatchback	4049	1834	2400	1404	1427	1371
Estate	4107	1834	2400	1404	1427	1389
XR3/Cabriolet	4061	1834	2402	1423	1439	1349
Van	4181	1834	2501	1404	1384	1594
Escort 1990-94						
Hatchback	4036	1875	2525	1440	1439-1462	1395
Estate	4268	1875	2525	1440	1462	1409
XR3/Cabriolet	4036	1875	2525	1440	1439-1462	1395
Van	4256	1875	2597	1440	1436	1615
Escort 1994 on						
Hatchback	4136	1885	2525	1440	1439-1462	1394
Saloon	4293	1885	2525	1440	1439-1462	1394
Estate	4300	1885	2525	1440	1455-1462	1416-1461
XR3/Cabriolet	4136	1885	2525	1440	1454	1381
Van	4288	1885	2597	1440	1449	1630
Orion1983-93						
Saloon	4229	1834	2400-2525	1404-1440	1427-1462	1385-1395

Part C: Capacities

All fluid figures are given in litres. Manufacturers constantly improve specifications and recommend own brands. Refer to your main dealer if you are in any doubt.

ENGINE OIL: Multi-grade SAE 5W/30 to Ford specification WSS-M2C913-A or better.

MANUAL GEARBOX AND FINAL DRIVE: Hypoid gear oil SAE 80 EP or Synthetic gear oil 75W90 to Ford Specifications SQM-2C 9008-A orWSD-M2C200-C.

AUTOMATIC GEARBOX: ATF to Ford Specification WSS-M2C 202-B.

POWER ASSISTED STEERING: ATF to Ford Specification ESP-M2C 166-H.

BRAKE FLUID: Brake Fluid Dot 4 to Ford Specification SAM-6C 9103-A.

COOLING SYSTEM: Important Note. Do not mix different colour or specification coolants.
Blue/Green coolants to specification ESDM-97B49-A.
Orange coolant to specification WSS-M97B44-D.

FUEL TANK:
KA: 42
Fiesta Pre-1985: 34 (XR2 - 38)
Fiesta 1985-89: 40
Fiesta 1989-on: 42
Escort Pre-1983: 40 (except XR3 and Van)
Escort All other models up to 1990: 48
Escort Van: 50
Escort All Models from 1990: 55
Orion all models: 48

COOLANT CAPACITY INC. HEATER:
KA: 5.25
Fiesta Pre-1984: 5.27
Fiesta 1983-89:
OHV: 5.5
CVH: 6.3
1.6 CVH: 8
Fiesta 1989-95:
HCS: 5.2
CVH and PTE: 7
Zetec: 7
Fiesta 1995-on:
Endura-E: 7.1
Zetec-SE: 6
Diesel: 9.3
Escort up to 1990:
1.1 OHV: 6.7
1.1 CVH (small): 6.2
1.1 CVH (large): 7.2
1.3 OHV and CHV to 1986: 7.1
1.3 and 1.4 CVH: 7.6
1.6 CVH: 7.8 (6.9 up to 1986)
1.8 Diesel: 9.3
Escort from 1990:
1.3 HCS: 7.1
1.4 CVH and PTE: 7.6
1.6 CVH: 7.8
1.6 and 1.8 Zetec: 7
1.8 Diesel: 9.3
2.0: 9.3
Orion 1.3: 7.1
Orion 1.6: 6.9

ENGINE OIL CAPACITY – WITH (WITHOUT) FILTER CHANGE:
KA: 3.25 (2.75)
Fiesta Pre-1983: 3.25 (2.75)
Fiesta 1983-89:
1.0 and 1.1 OHV: 3.25 (2.75)
1.3, 1.4, 1.6, CVH: 3.5 (3.25)
Fiesta 1989-95:
1.0 and 1.1 HCS: 3.25 (2.75)
1.4, 1.6 CVH and PTE: 3.5 (3.25)
Zetec: 4.25 (3.75)
Diesel: 4.5 (4.1)
Fiesta 1995-on:
1.3 Endura: 3.25 (2.75)
1.25 and 1.4 Zetec: 4 (3.5)
1.8 Diesel: 5 (4.5)
Escort up to 1990:
OHV and HCS: 3.25 (2.37)
CVH Pre-1982: 3.75 (3.5)
CVH 1982-on: 3.5 (3.25)
Fuel Injected engines: 3.85 (3.6)
Diesel: 4.5 (4.1)
Escort from 1990:
HCS and Endura: 3.25 (2.75)
CVH and PTE: 3.5 (3.25)
1.6 and 1.8 Zetec: 4.25 (3.75)
1.25 and 1.4 Zetec: 4 (3.5)
1.8 Diesel: 4.5 (4.1)
1.8 Diesel Endura: 5 (4.5)
2.0: 4.5 (4)
Orion: All - 3.5 (3.25)

TRANSMISSION:
Manual:
4-Speed B5: 2.8
5-Speed B5: 3.1
RS 5-Speed: 2.5
5-Speed iB5: 2.8
MTX-75 Type: 2.6
Automatic:
Pre-1990 3-Speed: 7.9
From 1990:
3.5 without fluid cooler
3.6 with fluid cooler
Zetec from 1996: 4.7

STEERING GEAR:
Escort/Fiesta Pre-1983: 90 cc. Semi-Fluid Grease to Specification SAM 1C-9106-AA.
Escort/Fiesta/Orion From1983: 70 cc. Semi-Fluid Grease to Ford Specification SAM 1C-9106-AA.
120cc. Gear oil to Ford Specification SQM 2C 9003-AA

BRAKE FLUID: It is recommended that the brake fluid is changed every three years. Inevitably there will be some additional loss in bleeding but 1 litre of fluid should cover the job on most models.

Part D: Service Data

All settings in mm. unless stated otherwise.

Engine
FIRING ORDER: 1-3-4-2
Except HCS, Endura and OHV Engines 1-2-4-3.

INJECTION ORDER: 1-3-4-2

IGNITION TIMING in degrees Before Top Dead Centre - BTDC:
Petrol engines:
All CVH Engines: 12 (8 Unleaded).
OHV Engines have considerable variation check these guide figures with the manufacturer.
Pre-1884:
1.0, 1.1 litre OHV: 10
1.3 litre OHV: 6
1.6 litre OHV: 10
1984 - 86
1.0 OHV: 12
1.1 OHV: 6
1986–on with unleaded fuel
1.0 OHV: 10
1.1 OHV: 2

SPARK PLUG TYPES AND GAPS

Engine	Motorcraft	Gap (mm)	Champion	Gap (mm)
1.0, 1.1, 1.3 OHV	AGRF 22	1.0	RS9YCC	0.8
1.6 OHV	AGPR 12C	0.6	RC7YC	0.7
1.3 HCS	AGRF 22C	1.0	RC7YC	0.8
1.3, 1.4, 1.6 CVH	AGPR 22C	0.75	RC7YC	0.8
1.6 EFi	AGPR 22CD1	1.0	RC9YCC4	1.0
1.4 CFi and PTE	AGPR 32 C1	1.0	RC9YCC4	1.0
1.1, 1.3 HCS	AGRF 22 C1	1.0	RC7YCC	0.8
1.6 CVH injection	AGPR12CD	0.75	RC6YC	0.7
1.6 RS Turbo	AGPR 901C1	1.0	C61YC	0.6
1.3 Endura	AGFS 22C1	1.0	RS9YCC	0.8
1.6, 1.8 Zetec	AYRF 22P	1.0	RE7PYC5	1.3
2.0	AGPR 22C1	1.0		
1.25, 1.4 Zetec	AYFS 22C	1.3	RE7YCC	1.0

Diesel Engines (Glow Plugs)

	Motorcraft	Champion
1.6		CH79
1.8	EZD6	CH147
1.8 with cat.	EZD8	
1.8 Endura	EZD39	

IDLE SPEED: (RPM) NA = Not adjustable
Petrol Engines
1.0, 1.1, 1.6 OHV	775 to 825
1.3 OHV	700-800
1.0, 1.1 HCS	700-800
1.3 HCS	700-800 (850-950 with catalyst)
1.3, 1.4, 1.6 CVH	750-850
1.6 EFi	850-950
1.4 CFi	850-950
1.4 PTE	870
1.6 CVH injection	850-950
1.6 RS Turbo	920-960
1.3 Endura	825-925
1.6, 1.8 Zetec	825-925
2.0	950
1.25, 1.4 Zetec	825-925
1.6 Diesel	880 30
1.8 Diesel	850 50
1.8 Diesel Endura	930 10

EMISSIONS
	CO	CO_2	O_2	HCppm
Carburated engines	1.0 to 2.0	13-16%	0.5-2.0	300
Cat + fuel injection	NA	14.5-16%	0.1-0.5	100

VALVE CLEARANCES (mm)
(Check when engine cold)
	Inlet	Exhaust
KA 1.3 OHV	0.20	0.30(0.50 from 1996)
Fiesta		
1.0, 1.1 OHV 1976-89	0.22	0.59
1.0, 1.1 OHV 1989-on	0.22	0.32
1.3, 1.6 OHV 1976-84	0.25	0.55
1.3 OHV 1984-99	0.20	0.30
1.25, 1.4 OHV 1995-99	0.17-0.23	0.27-0.33
1.3 Endura	0.20-0.25	0.50-0.55
Escort		
1.1 OHV 1980-88	0.22	0.59
1.1 OHV 1989-90	0.20-0.25	0.30-0.35
1.3, 1.6LX 1984-90	0.15	0.20
Escort/Orion		
1.1/1.3 OHV 1990-97	0.20	0.30-0.35
1.3l	0.20	0.30
Diesel 1.6 All Models	0.24-0.37	0.44-0.57
Diesel 1.8 All Models	0.30-0.40	0.45-0.55

Other Settings
CLUTCH ADJUSTMENT (Pedal Travel)
KA - 37Kw: 120-126 mm
KA - 44Kw: 122-128 mm
Fiesta – 1995-on: 22-128 mm
Escort –1996-on: 145-155 mm
All Previous models are self-adjusting. Nominal Travel:
Fiesta Pre-1995: 145 mm
Escort Pre-1996: 155 mm

BRAKE DISC PAD MINIMUM THICKNESS: All Models 1.5 mm.

BRAKE SHOE FRICTION LINING MINIMUM THICKNESS: All Models 1.0 mm.

Part E: Repair Data 957cc to 1298cc Petrol Engines

Dimensions in mm unless stated otherwise

Engine 'bottom end'

	957cc OHV	999cc OHV, HCS	1117cc OHC, CVH	1117cc OHV	1118cc OHV, HCS	1242 Zetec	1296cc CVH	1297cc OHV, HCS	1297cc OHV	1298/9cc OHV, Endura
BORE:	73.96	68.68	73.96	73.96	68.68	71.8	79.96	73.96	73.96	73.96
STROKE:	55.7	67.4	64.98	64.98	75.48	76.5	64.52	75.48	75.48	75.48

PISTON SIZES:
Petrol: Diesel:

	957cc OHV	999cc OHV, HCS	1117cc OHC, CVH	1117cc OHV	1118cc OHV, HCS	1242 Zetec	1296cc CVH	1297cc OHV, HCS	1297cc OHV	1298/9cc OHV, Endura
Size 1: A:	73.91-73.92	68.65-68.66	73.91-73.92	73.91-73.92	68.65-68.66	71.875-71.885	79.91-79.92	73.91-73.92	73.91-73.92	73.91-73.92
Size 2: B:	73.92-73.93	68.66-68.67	73.92-73.93	73.92-73.93	68.66-68.67	71.885-71.895	79.92-79.93	73.92-73.93	73.92-73.93	73.92-73.93
Size 3: C:	73.93-73.94	68.67-68.68	73.93-73.94	73.93-73.94	68.67-68.68	71.895-71.905	79.93-79.94	73.93-73.94	73.93-73.94	73.93-73.94
Size 4: D:	73.94-73.95	68.67-68.70	74.46-74.49	73.94-73.95	68.67-68.70		79.94-79.95	74.46-74.49	73.94-73.95	
Oversize 0.5 1st Rebore:	74.46-74.49	69.16-69.19	74.46-74.49	74.46-74.49	69.16-69.19		80.43-80.45	74.46-74.49	74.46-74.49	74.46-74.49
Oversize 1.0 2nd Rebore:	74.96-74.99	69.66-69.69		74.96-74.99	69.66-69.69				74.96-74.99	74.96-74.99

PISTON CLEARANCES IN BORE:

	957cc OHV	999cc OHV, HCS	1117cc OHC, CVH	1117cc OHV	1118cc OHV, HCS	1242 Zetec	1296cc CVH	1297cc OHV, HCS	1297cc OHV	1298/9cc OHV, Endura
	0.015-0.050	0.015-0.050	0.01-0.045	0.015-0.050	0.015-0.050		0.01-0.045	0.015-0.050	0.015-0.050	0.05

Diesel Rebore:

PISTON RING CLEARANCES - RING-TO-GROOVE:

	957cc OHV	999cc OHV, HCS	1117cc OHC, CVH	1117cc OHV	1118cc OHV, HCS	1242 Zetec	1296cc CVH	1297cc OHV, HCS	1297cc OHV	1298/9cc OHV, Endura
TOP:		0.2			0.2			0.2		0.2
SECOND:		0.2			0.2			0.2		0.2
BOTTOM:		0.1			0.1			0.1		0.1

PISTON PROJECTION ABOVE BLOCK:

PISTON RING END GAP:

	957cc OHV	999cc OHV, HCS	1117cc OHC, CVH	1117cc OHV	1118cc OHV, HCS	1242 Zetec	1296cc CVH	1297cc OHV, HCS	1297cc OHV	1298/9cc OHV, Endura
TOP:	0.25-0.45	0.25-0.45	0.25-0.45	0.25-0.45	0.25-0.45	0.2-0.3	0.30-0.50	0.25-0.45	0.25-0.45	0.25-0.45
SECOND:	0.25-0.45	0.25-0.45	0.25-0.45	0.25-0.45	0.25-0.45	0.3-0.7	0.30-0.50	0.45-0.75	0.25-0.45	0.45-0.75
BOTTOM:	0.20-0.40	0.20-0.40	0.20-0.40	0.20-0.40	0.20-0.40	0.3-0.7	0.40-1.4	0.20-0.40	0.20-0.40	0.2-0.5

CRANK MAIN JOURNAL DIAMETER:

	957cc OHV	999cc OHV, HCS	1117cc OHC, CVH	1117cc OHV	1118cc OHV, HCS	1242 Zetec	1296cc CVH	1297cc OHV, HCS	1297cc OHV	1298/9cc OHV, Endura
Size 1:	56.99-57.0	56.99-57.0		56.99-57.0	56.99-57.0		57.98-58.0	56.98-57.0	56.99-57.0	56.97-57.0
Size 2:	56.98-56.99	56.98-56.99		56.98-56.99					56.98-56.99	
Size 3:										

CRANK, BIG-END DIAMETER:

	957cc OHV	999cc OHV, HCS	1117cc OHC, CVH	1117cc OHV	1118cc OHV, HCS	1242 Zetec	1296cc CVH	1297cc OHV, HCS	1297cc OHV	1298/9cc OHV, Endura
Size A:	42.99-43.01	40.99-41.01		42.99-43.01	40.99-41.01			47.89-47.91	40.99-41.01	42.99-43.01	40.99-41.01
Size B:										
Size C:										

MAIN BEARING SHELL THICKNESS:
Undersize:

MAIN BEARING CLEARANCE:

	957cc OHV	999cc OHV, HCS	1117cc OHC, CVH	1117cc OHV	1118cc OHV, HCS	1242 Zetec	1296cc CVH	1297cc OHV, HCS	1297cc OHV	1298/9cc OHV, Endura
Size 1:	0.009-0.046	0.009-0.046	0.011-0.058	0.009-0.046	0.009-0.046		0.011-0.058	0.009-0.056	0.009-0.046	0.009-0.056
Size 2:										

MAIN BEARING UNDERSIZES:

	957cc OHV	999cc OHV, HCS	1117cc OHC, CVH	1117cc OHV	1118cc OHV, HCS	1242 Zetec	1296cc CVH	1297cc OHV, HCS	1297cc OHV	1298/9cc OHV, Endura
1: 0.25 mm	56.726-56.746	56.726-56.746	57.73-57.75	56.726-56.746	56.726-56.746		57.73-57.75	56.726-56.746	56.726-56.746	56.726-56.746
2: 0.50 mm	56.472-56.492	56.472-56.492	57.48-57.50	56.472-56.492	56.472-56.492		57.48-57.50	56.472-56.492	56.472-56.492	
3: 0.75 mm	56.218-56.238	56.218-56.238	57.23-57.25	56.218-56.238	56.218-56.238		57.23-57.25	56.218-56.238	56.218-56.238	

BIG-END BEARING SHELL THICKNESS (STANDARD):

Undersize:

BIG-END BEARING CLEARANCE:

	957cc OHV	999cc OHV, HCS	1117cc OHC, CVH	1117cc OHV	1118cc OHV, HCS	1242 Zetec	1296cc CVH	1297cc OHV, HCS	1297cc OHV	1298/9cc OHV, Endura
		0.006-0.6	0.006-0.6		0.006-0.6		0.006-0.6	0.006-0.6		0.006-0.6

BIG-END BEARING UNDERSIZES:

	957cc OHV	999cc OHV, HCS	1117cc OHC, CVH	1117cc OHV	1118cc OHV, HCS	1242 Zetec	1296cc CVH	1297cc OHV, HCS	1297cc OHV	1298/9cc OHV, Endura
1: 0.25 mm	42.74-42.76	40.74-40.76	42.74-42.76	42.74-42.76	40.74-40.76		47.64-47.66	40.74-40.76	42.74-42.76	40.74-40.76
2: 0.50 mm	42.49-42.51	40.49-40.51	42.49-42.51	42.49-42.51	40.49-40.51		47.39-47.41	40.49-40.51	42.49-42.51	40.49-40.51
3: 0.75 mm	42.24-42.26	40.24-40.26	42.24-42.26	42.24-42.26	40.24-40.26		47.14-47.16	40.24-40.26	42.24-42.26	40.24-40.26
4: 1.00mm							46.89-46.91			

THRUST WASHER THICKNESS:

2.80-2.85	2.80-2.85	2.301-2.351	2.80-2.85	2.80-2.85		2.301-2.351	2.80-2.85	2.80-2.85	2.80-2.85

THRUST WASHER OVERSIZE:

2.99-3.04	2.99-3.04	2.491-2.541	2.99-3.04	2.99-3.04		2.491-2.541	2.99-3.04	2.99-3.04	2.99-3.04

CRANKSHAFT END FLOAT:

0.072-0.285	0.10-0.25	0.09-0.30	0.079-0.279	0.10-0.25	0.22-0.43	0.09-0.30	0.10-0.25	0.079-0.279	0.05-0.26

Engine 'top end' and valve gear

CAMSHAFT BEARING JOURNAL DIAMETER:

1:	39.615-39.635	39.615-39.635	45.75		39.615-39.635	39.615-39.635		45.75	39.615-39.635	39.615-39.635	39.615-39.635
2:			45					45			
3:			45.25					45.25			
4:			45.5					45.5			
5:			45.75					45.75			

CAMSHAFT ENDFLOAT:

0.062-0.193	0.02-0.19	0.05-0.15	0.062-0.193	0.02-0.19	0.05-0.13	0.05-0.15	0.02-0.19	0.02-0.19	0.02-0.19

INLET VALVE HEAD SIZE:

32.89-33.15	32.9-33.1	37.9-38.1	32.89-33.15	32.9-33.1		41.9-42.1	34.4-34.6	38.02-38.28	34.4-34.6

EXHAUST VALVE HEAD SIZE:

29.01-29.27	28.9-29.1	32.1-32.3	29.01-29.27	28.9-29.1		33.9-34.1	28.9-29.1	29.01-29.27	28.9-29.1

Part E: Repair Data
1388cc to 1796cc Petrol Engines
1608cc to 1753cc Diesel Engines.

Dimensions in mm unless stated otherwise

Engine 'bottom end'

	1388 Zetec	1392cc CVH/PTE	1597cc CVH	1597cc CVH (var.)	1597cc Zetec	1796cc Zetec	1608cc Diesel	1753cc Diesel
BORE:	75.9	77.24	79.96	Turbo 80.0	76	80.6	80	82.5
STROKE:	76.5	74.3	79.52	Turbo 79.5	88	88	80	82

PISTON SIZES:

Petrol:	Diesel:	1388 Zetec	1392cc CVH/PTE	1597cc CVH	1597cc CVH (var.)	1597cc Zetec	1796cc Zetec	1608cc Diesel	1753cc Diesel
Size 1:	A:		77.19-77.20	79.91-79.92	efi+0.005	75.975-75.985	80.57-80.58	79.96-79.975	82.46-82.475
Size 2:	B:		77.20-77.21	79.92-79.93	efi+0.005	75.985-75.995	80.58-80.59	79.975-79.990	82.475-82.490
Size 3:	C:		77.21-77.22	79.93-79.94	efi+0.005	75.995-76.005	80.59-80.60	80.12-80.135	82.62-82.635
Size 4:	D:		77.22-77.23	79.94-79.95	efi+0.005			80.135-80.15	82.635-82.65
Oversize 0.5	1st Rebore:		77.48-77.49	80.20-80.21	efi+0.005			80.461-80.479	82.961-82.979
Oversize 1.0	2nd Rebore:		77.49-77.50	80.21-80.22	efi+0.005			80.961-80.979	83.461-83.479
			77.50-77.51	80.22-80.23	efi+0.005				

PISTON CLEARANCES IN BORE:

	1388 Zetec	1392cc CVH/PTE	1597cc CVH	1597cc CVH (var.)	1597cc Zetec	1796cc Zetec	1608cc Diesel	1753cc Diesel
		0.01-0.045	0.01-0.045	efi 0.005	Not spec.	Not spec.	0.025-0.055	0.022-0.055
Diesel Rebore:							0.021-0.054	0.021-0.054

PISTON RING CLEARANCES - RING-TO-GROOVE:

	1608cc Diesel	1753cc Diesel
TOP:	0.07-0.102	0.09-0.122
SECOND:	0.05-0.082	0.50-0.082
BOTTOM:	0.03-0.065	0.03-0.065

PISTON PROJECTION ABOVE BLOCK:

	1608cc Diesel	1753cc Diesel
	0.43-0.86	0.5-0.84

PISTON RING END GAP:

	1388 Zetec	1392cc CVH/PTE	1597cc CVH	1597cc CVH (var.)	1597cc Zetec	1796cc Zetec	1608cc Diesel	1753cc Diesel
TOP:	0.2-0.3	0.30-0.50	0.30-0.50		0.30-0.50	0.30-0.50	0.30-0.50	0.35-0.5
SECOND:	0.3-0.7	0.30-0.50	0.30-0.50		0.30-0.50	0.30-0.50	0.20-0.40	0.35-0.5
BOTTOM:	0.15-0.65	0.40-1.4	0.40-1.4	efi 0.25-.40	0.25-1.00	0.38-1.14	0.20-0.45	0.25-0.48

CRANK MAIN JOURNAL DIAMETER:

	1388 Zetec	1392cc CVH/PTE	1597cc CVH	1597cc CVH (var.)	1597cc Zetec	1796cc Zetec	1608cc Diesel	1753cc Diesel
Size 1:		57.98-58.0	57.98-58.0		57.98-58.0	57.98-58.0	53.97-53.99	53.97-53.99
Size 2:								
Size 3:								

CRANK, BIG-END DIAMETER:

	1388 Zetec	1392cc CVH/PTE	1597cc CVH	1597cc CVH (var.)	1597cc Zetec	1796cc Zetec	1608cc Diesel	1753cc Diesel
Size A:		47.89-47.91	47.89-47.91		46.89-46.91	46.89-46.91	48.97-48.99	48.97-48.99
Size B:								
Size C:								

	1388 Zetec	1392cc CVH/PTE	1597cc CVH	1597cc CVH (var.)	1597cc Zetec	1796cc Zetec	1608cc Diesel	1753cc Diesel
MAIN BEARING SHELL THICKNESS:								
Undersize:					0.02-0.25	0.02-0.25		
MAIN BEARING CLEARANCE:								
Size 1:		0.011-0.058	0.011-0.058		0.011-0.058	0.011-0.058	0.015-0.062	0.015-0.062
Size 2:								
MAIN BEARING UNDERSIZES:								
1: 0.25 mm		57.73-57.75	57.73-57.75				53.72-53.74	53.72-53.74
2: 0.50 mm		57.48-57.50	57.48-57.50					53.47-53.49
3: 0.75 mm		57.23-57.25	57.23-57.25					
BIG-END BEARING SHELL THICKNESS (STANDARD):								
Undersize:					0.02-0.25	0.02-0.25		
BIG-END BEARING CLEARANCE:								
		0.006-0.6	0.006-0.6		0.016-0.70	0.016-0.70	0.016-0.70	0.016-0.074
BIG-END BEARING UNDERSIZES:								
1: 0.25 mm		47.64-47.66	47.64-47.66				48.72-48.74	48.72-48.74
2: 0.50 mm		47.39-47.41	47.39-47.41					48.47-48.49
3: 0.75 mm		47.14-47.16	47.14-47.16					
4: 1.00mm		46.89-46.91	46.89-46.91					
THRUST WASHER THICKNESS:		2.301-2.351	2.301-2.351					
THRUST WASHER OVERSIZE:		2.491-2.541	2.491-2.541					
CRANKSHAFT END FLOAT:	0.22-0.43	0.09-0.30	0.09-0.30		0.09-0.31	0.09-0.31	0.093-0.306	0.09-0.37

Engine 'top end' and valve gear

	1388 Zetec	1392cc CVH/PTE	1597cc CVH	1597cc CVH (var.)	1597cc Zetec	1796cc Zetec	1608cc Diesel	1753cc Diesel
CAMSHAFT BEARING JOURNAL DIAMETER:								
1:		45.75	45.75				27.96-27.98	27.96-27.98
2:		45	45					
3:		45.25	45.25					
4:		45.5	45.5					
5:		45.75	45.75					
CAMSHAFT ENDFLOAT:	0.05-0.13	0.05-0.15	0.05-0.15				0.1-0.24	0.1-0.24
INLET VALVE HEAD SIZE:		39.9-40.1	41.9-42.1	26	32		34.8-35.0	36.4-36.6
EXHAUST VALVE HEAD SIZE:		33.9-34.1	36.9-37.1	24.5	28		30.9-31.1	31.9-32.1

Brakes

MINIMUM FRONT DISC THICKNESS:

	Solid	Ventilated
Escort and Orion 1984-90:	8.2	22.2
Escort Diesel to 1989:	8.7	22.7
Fiesta to 1983:	8.7	18.5
All other models:	8	18

MAXIMUM BRAKE DRUM DIAMETER:
Escort/Orion 1984-90 and models fitted with ABS: 204
Fiesta to 1983: 177.8
All other models: 181

There are other variations with high performance vehicles and we advise checking with your main agent.

Cooling System

THERMOSTAT OPENING: (In degrees Celsius).
All models: 85-89 (except Diesel Pre-1990: 86-90)

PRESSURE CAP RATING (bar): These are approximate ranges. Check cap, which should be marked.
Fiesta:
Fiesta pre-1989: 0.9-1.02
Fiesta to 1995: 1.0-1.4
Escort:
Pre-1986:
1.1 litre: 0.9
1.3, 1.6 litre: 0.85-1.1
1986-1991: 0.98-1.2
1991-on: 1.2-1.4
Diesel pre-1990:
1.6 litre: 0.8-1.0
1.8 litre: 1.2-1.5

Clutch

Clutch diameter (mm):
Pre-1988 Fiesta 1.6. and Fiesta 1.0, 1.1, 1.3, 1.4: 190
Pre-1989 Fiesta 1.0, 1.1 and Escort 1.1 Saloon: 165
1.6, 1.8 Fiesta and Escort models: 220 (except 1.8 engine with MTX-75 Transmission: 240)
Fiesta and KA with Endura engine: 180
Fiesta Endura Diesel: 201
Escort 1.1 (Estate and Van) 1.3, 1.4: 190
Pre-1986 Escort 1.6: 200

Clutch lining (mm):
All Models: 3.2 (except Endura engined models: 8.3)

STEERING: (Front adjustable)

Checking tolerances:

	N Toe-out	P Toe-in
Fiesta pre-1984	6	1
Fiesta 1983-89	6	0
Fiesta 1989	3	3
Fiesta from 1990	4.5	0.5
Fiesta New Models from 1995	2.5	2.5
Escort 1980-1983	5.5	1.5
Escort 1983-1986	5.5	0.5
Escort 1.3LX 1984-1989 and KA 1996-1999	1.5	3.5
Escort 1986-1990	3.5	1.5
Escort from 1990	0.5	4.5

Part F: Torque Wrench Settings

Key to Engine Types and Sizes

A: OHV Engines	E: CVH Engines	I: Diesel 1.6
B: 1.0/1.1 1983-89	F: Endura 1.3	J: Diesel 1.8
C: 1.3LX.	G: Zetec 1.25/1.4	K 1.8 D (Torx Head Bolts)
D: HCS Engines	H: Zetec 1.6/1.8	

All figures in Nm except 'mins' = waiting time in minutes, 'deg' = degrees (angle)

Engine

	A	B	C	D	E	F	G	H	I	J	K
Main bearing cap, bolt											
Stage 1	44-51	44-51	32	44	45-50	45	N/A	35	30	(30 Fiesta) (27 Escort)	
Stage 2	88-92	88-92	60-65	88-102	90-100	95		70-90	75 deg	75 deg	
Cylinder head bolts											
Stage 1	40-50	10-15	50-55	30	25	30	15	25	20-30	20-30	10
Stage 2	80-90	40-50	Slack	90 deg	55	90 deg	30	45	76-92	76-92	100
Stage 3	100-110	100-110	60-65	90 deg	90 deg	90 deg	90 deg	105 deg	2 min	3 min	3 min
Stage 4		15 mins			90 deg				90 deg	90 deg	Slack
		100-110									70
Big end, bolts											
Stage 1	13-16	13-16	22	4	15-18	4	8	15-20	20-30	20-30	
Stage 2	26-32	26-32	40-45	90 deg	30-36	90 deg	90 deg	90 deg	55 deg	60 deg	
									23-30deg	20 deg	
Flywheel/Driveshaft bolts	64-70	64-70	45-50	64-70	82-92	67	85	105-117	24-30	15-20	
									35-45deg	35-45 deg	
									35-45deg	35-45 deg	
Clutch - flywheel	24-35	24-35	25-34	25-34	25-34	30	30	25-34	16-20	25-34	
Crankshaft pulley	54-59	54-59	100-115	110-120	54-59	115	40	110-120	20-30	150	
Stage 2 (column H & J) From 1989 (column F).					100-115		90 deg		145 deg	Slack	
Camshaft sprocket bolt	16-20	16-20	16-20	16-20	54-59	28	60	68	27-33	M6-10	
Cam/rocker cover bolt	4-5	4-5	4-5	4-5	6-8	6	6		8-11	4	
Camshaft thrust plate	4-5	4-5	4-5	4-5	9-13	11					
Timing chain/belt Cover	7-10	7-10	7-10	7-10	9-17	10	9	7-10	8-10	8	
Timing chain/belt tensioner	7-9	7-9	7-9	7-9	16-20	8	20	38	27-30	50	
Oil pump - crankcase fixing, bolt	16-20	16-20	16-20	16-20	8-11	18	9	10	7-10	25	
Sump bolts Stage 1	6-8	6-8	6-8	6-8	8-11	7	20	21	6-9	9	
Stage 2	8-11	8-11	8-11	8-11	8-11	10					
Stage 3	8-11	8-11	8-11	8-11		10					
Engine - transmission	35-45	35-45	35-45	35-45	35-40	44	44	40	35-45	40	
Inlet manifold	19	19	19	19	16-20		18	18	18-25	18-25	
Exhaust manifold	16	16	16	16	14-17	23	53	16	18-25	18-25	
Water pump bolts	8	8	8	8	6	9	10	8	23	23	

Engine

	A	B	C	D	E	F	G	H	I	J	K
Water pump pulley bolts	8	8	8	10	10	9	11	10	7-10	7-10	
Thermostat housing	19	19	19	19	9-12	27	18	17-21	18-22	18-22	
Spark plugs/glow plugs	19	19	19	17	25	17	15	15	25-30	25-30	

Bodywork, Steering And Suspension

The selection of Torque settings indicated here vary according to model and year rather than by engine. Many other components also have common settings across the vehicle range.

Figures all in Nm

ITEM	KA	Fiesta '95 on	Fiesta to '95	Escort '90 on	Escort '80-'90
Track rod end	26	39	25-30	25-30	25-30
Front hub	290	290	205-235	235 (1)	205-235
Rear hub	290	270	250-270	250-270 (2)	
Brake caliper/carrier	58	58	20-25	Teves 20-25	20-25
				Bendix 45-55	45-55
Brake caliper/hub	58	58	50-66	50-66	50-66
Road wheels	85	85	70-100	70-100	70-100
Steering wheel nut	45	45	50	50	27-34
				27-34 pre-'90	
Seat mountings	22-25	25	25-32	25	
Seat belt anchors	38	38	25-45	38	29-41
Air bag control unit	4	6			
Air bag fixings	4				

NOTE (1) Detailed figures for 1.8 Diesel quote: M20 x 1.5 bolts: 205-235
M22 x 1.5 bolts 220-250

NOTE (2) A three stage sequence is quoted: 20-25Nm/Slacken off 180deg/Re-tighten finger tight.

Engine Mountings Figures (Nm)
KA

Right-hand engine mounting bracket to body	50
Right-hand engine mounting bracket to engine	68
Left-hand engine mounting	68
Rear roll restraint	120

Escort 1980-1990

	CVH	OHV
Right-hand engine mounting to body	41-58	41-58
Right-hand engine mounting bracket to engine	76-104	54-72
Right-hand engine mounting rubber insulator	41-58	70-95
Pre-1986 front transmission bracket	41-51	41-51
Transmission mounting bolts	52-64	52-64
From 1986 transmission mountings	80-100	80-100
Transmission support crossmember	52	52

Escort 1990-on

	Zetec / CVH	Endura-E
Right-hand engine mounting to cylinder block		120 (Fiesta only)
Right-hand engine mounting bracket to block	90	69
Right-hand engine mounting brace	70	69
Right-hand engine mounting to body	85	84
Left-hand rear bracket to transmission	50	50
Left-hand rear bracket to mounting	68	68
Left-hand front bracket to mounting	68	68
Left-hand front bracket brace	49	49

Fiesta 1995-97
Endura E: See Escort 1990

Endura DE
Front engine mounting bracket
Outer nut	120
Inner nut	70
Engine mounting bracket to cylinder block	33
Front engine mounting bracket	33
Front engine mounting bracket reinforcement	50
Rear engine mounting bracket, bolts	50
Rear engine mounting bracket, nuts	70
Rear engine mounting bracket to cylinder block	50
Rear engine mounting bracket to front sub-frame	70
Right-hand engine mounting bracket	45

Zetec
Engine mounting bracket	55
Left-hand engine mounting bracket, bolt	49
Left-hand engine mounting bracket, nut	69
Rear engine mounting to crossmember	70
Rear engine mounting to engine	50

Fiesta 1989-95
HCS & CVH
Engine mounting bracket bolt to body	41-58
Engine mounting bracket nut to body	41-58
Engine mounting bracket to cylinder block	54-72
Engine mounting rubber insulator	71-95

Zetec
Front right-hand mountings and brackets	58-79
Rear right-hand bracket to cylinder block	76-104
Mounting to cylinder block bracket bolts	71-98
Mounting to body bolt and nut	102-138

Fiesta pre-1989
Apron panel bolt	33-35
Engine mounting bracket to cylinder block	66
Engine bearer to transmission	66
Transmission bearer to chassis	37
Engine mounting to body	66
To side-member or floor pan	35-37
Rubber insulator to bracket	66

Part G: Identification Numbers

Ford have made so many changes and improvements over the years that it's essential to quote your vehicle's VIN (Vehicle Identification Number) when ordering spare parts for your car. It is also helpful to quote the model and year, the body type and the engine size and engine number, if applicable. Another useful number is on the paint code plate. This doesn't just identify the colour, it even enables you to get the shade just right. It's almost alongside the VIN plate.

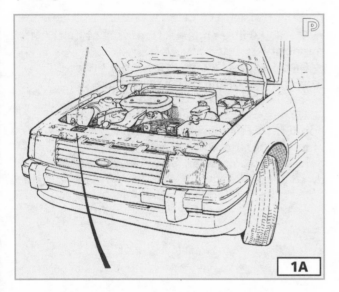

1A

❐ **1A:** The Escort's VIN plate is attached to the top of the front cross-member in the engine bay. It is also helpful to quote the vehicle model, the year the car was made, the body type and engine number if applicable. One useful number on the VIN plate is the paint code. This will make sure you get a perfect paint match if you need to do any bodywork.

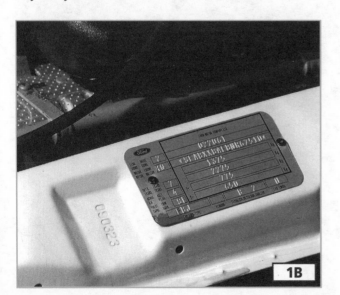

1B

❐ **1B:** The Fiesta and KA's VIN plate/s are in similar locations to the Escort's.

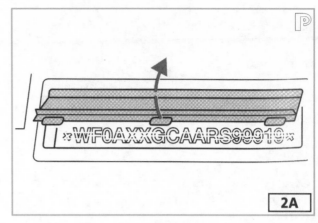

2A

❐ **2A:** The VIN is also stamped on the floor of the car to the right of the driver's seat. It is hidden below a plastic cover – lift the cover and you will see the number.

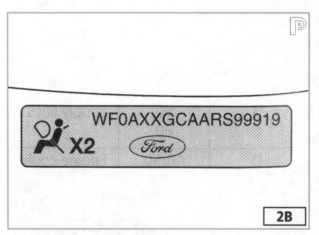

WF0AXXGCAARS99919

2B

❐ **2B:** Where applicable, a symbol on this VIN plate identifies the air bag system.

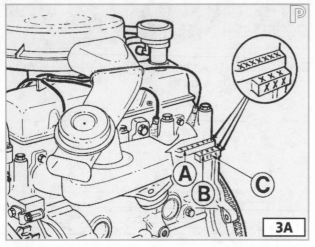

3A

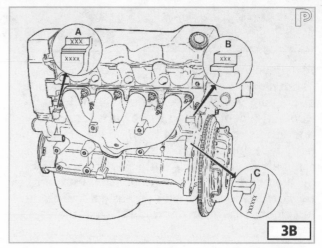

3B

❒ **3:** The engine number is on the cylinder block as follows:

➜ OVH (including HCS) engines – near the gearbox, on the front, facing the radiator, (**3A, item A**).
➜ CVH engines – on the front, next to the alternator bracket, (**3B, item A**).
➜ PT-E engine – front right, under the induction casing.
➜ DOHC 1.6 and 1.8 litre engines – side of the block level with the starter motor, and on the cylinder head (transmission side).

➜ DOHC 2.0 litre engine – front face of block on the right-hand side.
➜ Diesel engines – on the front right (viewed from in front of the car), near the gearbox.

❒ **4:** There is also a tuning decal under the bonnet. This tells you, where applicable, the spark plug gap, ignition timing, idle speed, CO percentage, points gap, valve clearances, and dwell angle.

CHAPTER 2: SAFETY FIRST!

Please read this chapter before carrying out any work on your car.

You must always ensure that safety is the first consideration in any job you carry out. A slight lack of concentration, or a rush to finish the job quickly can easily result in an accident, as can failure to follow the precautions outlined in this manual.

Be sure to consult the suppliers of any materials and equipment you may use, and to obtain and read carefully any operating and health and safety instructions that may be available on packaging or from manufacturers and suppliers.

GENERAL

RAISING THE VEHICLE SAFELY

• ALWAYS ensure that the vehicle is properly supported when raised off the ground. Don't work on, around, or underneath a raised vehicle unless axle stands or hoist lifting pads are positioned under secure, load bearing underbody areas. If the vehicle is driven onto ramps, the wheels remaining on the ground must be securely chocked to prevent movement.

• NEVER work on a vehicle supported on a jack. Jacks are made for lifting the vehicle only, not for holding it off the ground while it is being worked on.

❏ 1: ALWAYS ensure that the safe working load rating of any jack, hoist or lifting gear used is sufficient for the job, and that lifting gear is used only as recommended by the manufacturer.

• NEVER attempt to loosen or tighten nuts that require a lot of force

to turn (e.g. a tight oil drain plug) with the vehicle raised, unless it is safely supported. Take care not to pull the vehicle off its supports when applying force to any part of the vehicle. Wherever possible, initially slacken tight fastenings before raising the vehicle off the ground.

• ALWAYS wear eye protection when working under the vehicle and when using power tools.

• Follow the instructions in **Chapter 4** entitled **Using a Trolley Jack**.

WORKING ON THE VEHICLE

• ALWAYS seek specialist advice from a qualified technician unless you are justifiably confident about your ability to carry out each job. Vehicle safety affects you, your passengers and other road users.

❏ 2: DON'T lean over, or work on, a running engine unless it is strictly necessary, and keep long hair and loose clothing well out of the way of moving mechanical parts.

• Note that it is theoretically possible for fluorescent striplighting to make an engine fan appear to be stationary - double check whether it is spinning or not! This is the sort of error that happens when you're really tired and not thinking straight. So...

• ...DON'T work on a vehicle when you're over tired.

• ALWAYS work in a well ventilated area and don't inhale dust - it may contain asbestos or other harmful substances.

• NEVER run an engine indoors, in a confined space or over a pit.

• REMOVE your wrist watch, rings and all other jewellery before doing any work on the vehicle - and especially when working on the electrical system.

• DON'T remove the radiator or expansion tank filler cap or other openings when the cooling system is hot, or you may get scalded by escaping coolant or steam. Let the system cool down first and even then, if the engine is not completely cold, cover the cap with a cloth and gradually release the pressure.

• NEVER drain oil, coolant or automatic transmission fluid when the engine is hot. Allow time for it to cool sufficiently to avoid scalding you.

• ALWAYS keep antifreeze, brake and clutch fluid away from vehicle paintwork. Wash off any spills immediately.

• TAKE CARE to avoid touching any engine or exhaust system component unless it is cool enough not to burn you.

RUNNING THE VEHICLE

• NEVER start the engine unless the gearbox is in neutral (or 'Park' in the case of automatic transmission) and the parking brake is fully applied.

• NEVER run a vehicle fitted with a catalytic converter without the exhaust system heat shields in place.

• TAKE CARE when parking vehicles fitted with catalytic converters. The 'cat' reaches extremely high temperatures and any combustible materials under the car, such as long dry grass, could be ignited.

PERSONAL SAFETY

• NEVER siphon fuel, antifreeze, brake fluid or other potentially harmful liquids by mouth, or allow contact with your skin. Use a suitable hand pump and wear gloves.

• BEFORE undertaking dirty jobs, use barrier cream on your hands as a protection against infection. Preferably, wear suitable gloves.

• WEAR IMPERVIOUS GLOVES - disposable types are ideal - when there is a risk of used engine oil or any other harmful substance coming into contact with your skin.

❒ 3: Wurth produce a huge range of workshop products, including the safety-related items shown here.

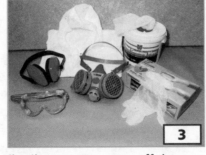

• WIPE UP any spilt oil, grease or water off the floor immediately.

• MAKE SURE that spanners/wrenches and all other tools are the right size for the job and are not likely to slip. Never try to 'double-up' spanners to gain more leverage.

• SEEK HELP if you need to lift something heavy which may be beyond your capability. Don't forget that when lifting a heavy weight, you should keep your back vertical and straight and bend your knees to avoid injuring your back.

• NEVER take risky short-cuts or rush to finish a job. Plan ahead and allow plenty of time.

• BE METICULOUS and keep the work area tidy - you'll avoid frustration, work better and lose less.

• KEEP children and animals well away from the work area and from unattended vehicles.

• ALWAYS tell someone what you're doing and have them regularly check that all is well, especially when working alone on, or under, the vehicle.

HAZARDS

FIRE!

• Petrol (gasoline) is a dangerous and highly flammable liquid requiring special precautions. When working on the fuel system, disconnect the vehicle battery earth (ground) terminal whenever possible and always work outside, or in a very well ventilated area. Any form of spark, such as that caused by an electrical fault, by two metal surfaces striking against each other, by a central heating boiler in the garage 'firing up', or even by static electricity built up in your clothing can, in a confined space, ignite petrol vapour causing an explosion. Take great care not to spill petrol on to the engine or exhaust system, never allow any naked flame anywhere near the work area and don't smoke.

❒ 4: There are several types of fire extinguisher. Take advice from your accredited supplier to make sure that you have the right type for workshop use. Note that water fire extinguishers are not suitable for workshop or automotive use.

PRESSURE

• DON'T disconnect any pipes on a fuel injected engine or on an ABS braking system without releasing residual pressure. The fuel or brake fluid may be under very high pressure - sufficient to cause serious injury. Remember that many systems retain high pressure for sometime after last use. If necessary seek specialist advice.

FUMES

• Vapour which is given off by petrol (gasoline) and many solvents, thinners, and adhesives is potentially very harmful and under certain conditions can lead to unconsciousness or even death, if inhaled. The risks are increased if such fluids are used in a confined space so always ensure adequate ventilation. Always read the supplier's instructions and follow them with care.

• Never drain petrol (gasoline) or use solvents, thinners, adhesives or other toxic substances in an inspection pit. It is also dangerous to park a vehicle for any length of time over an inspection pit. The fumes from even a slight fuel leak can cause an explosion when the engine is started.

MAINS ELECTRICITY

❒ 5: Avoid the use of mains electricity when working on the vehicle, whenever possible. Use rechargeable tools and a DC inspection lamp, powered from a remote 12V battery - both are much safer. However, if you do use mains-powered equipment, ensure that the appliance is connected correctly to its plug, that where necessary it is properly earthed (grounded), and that the fuse is of the correct rating for the appliance. Do not use any mains powered equipment in damp conditions or in the vicinity of fuel, fuel vapour or the vehicle battery. Always use an RCD (Residual Current Device) circuit breaker with mains electricity. Then, if there is a short, the RCD circuit breaker minimises the risk of electrocution by instantly cutting the power supply.

IGNITION SYSTEM

• Never work on the ignition system with the ignition switched on, or with the engine being turned over on the starter, or with the engine running.

❒ 6: Touching certain parts of the ignition system, such as the HT leads, distributor cap, ignition coil etc., can result in a severe electric shock or physical injury as a hand is pulled sharply away. Voltages produced by electronic ignition systems are sometimes very high indeed and could prove fatal, particularly to people with cardiac pacemaker implants. Consult your vehicle's handbook or main dealer if in any doubt.

COOLING FAN

• On many vehicles, the electric cooling fan can switch itself on even with the ignition turned off. This is especially likely after driving the vehicle immediately before turning off, after which heat rises to the top of the engine and turns the fan on, suddenly and without warning. If you intend working in the engine bay, it's best to do so when the engine is cold, to disconnect the battery, or keep away from the fan, if neither of these are possible.

BATTERY

• Never cause a spark, smoke, or allow a naked light near the vehicle's battery, even in a well ventilated area. Highly explosive hydrogen gas is given off as part of the charging process.

• Battery terminals should be shielded, since a spark can be caused by any metal object touching the battery's terminals or connecting straps.

• IMPORTANT NOTE: Before disconnecting the battery earth (ground) terminal read the relevant information in **Chapter 10** regarding saving computer and radio settings. When using a battery charger, switch off the power supply before the battery charger leads are connected or disconnected. If the battery is not of the 'sealed-for-life' type, loosen the filler plugs or remove the cover before charging. For best results the battery should be given a low rate trickle charge. Do not charge at an excessive rate or the battery may burst. Always wear gloves and goggles when carrying or when topping up the battery. Acid electrolyte is extremely corrosive and must not be allowed to contact the eyes, skin or clothes. If it does, wash with copious amounts of water. Seek medical advice if necessary

BRAKES AND ASBESTOS

• Obviously, a vehicle's brakes are among its most important safety related items. ONLY work on your vehicle's braking system if you are trained and competent to do so. If you have not been trained in this work, but wish to carry out the jobs described in this manual, we strongly recommend that you have a garage or qualified mechanic check your work before using the vehicle.

• Whenever you work on the braking system: i) wear an efficient particle mask; ii) wipe off all brake dust from the brakes after spraying on a proprietary brand of brake cleaner (never blow dust off with compressed air); iii) dispose of brake dust and discarded shoes or pads in a sealed plastic bag; iv) wash your hands thoroughly after you have finished working on the brakes and certainly before you eat or smoke; v) replace shoes and pads only with asbestos-free shoes or pads. Note that asbestos brake dust can cause cancer if inhaled; vi) always replace brake pads and/or shoes in complete 'axle' sets - never replace them on one wheel only.

BRAKE FLUID

• Brake fluid absorbs moisture rapidly from the air and this can cause brake failure. Never use a previously opened container of brake fluid.

ENGINE OIL

• Always wear disposable plastic or rubber gloves when draining the oil from your engine. i) Note that the drain plug and the oil are often hotter than you expect. ii) There are very real health hazards associated with used engine oil. Use barrier cream on your hands and try not to get oil on them. Always wear impermeable gloves and wash hands with hand cleaner soon after carrying out the work. Keep oil out of the reach of children; iii) NEVER, EVER dispose of old engine oil into the ground or down a drain.

PLASTIC MATERIALS

• Be aware of dangers in the form of poisonous fumes, skin irritants, and the risk of fire and explosion. Do not allow resin or 2-pack filler or adhesive hardener to come into contact with skin or eyes. Read carefully the safety notes supplied on the can, tube or packaging.

FLUOROELASTOMERS

• Fluoroelastomers are commonly used for oil seals, wiring and cabling, bearing surfaces, gaskets, diaphragms, hoses and 'O' rings. If they are subjected to temperatures greater than 315 degrees Celcius, they will decompose and can be potentially hazardous. Some decomposition may occur when a car has been in a fire or has been dismantled with the assistance of a cutting torch.

• According to the Health and Safety Executive, "Skin contact with this liquid or decomposition residues can cause painful and penetrating burns. Permanent irreversible skin and tissue damage can occur". Damage can also be caused to eyes or by the inhalation of fumes created as fluoroelastomers are burned or heated.

• After a vehicle has been exposed to fire or high temperatures:

1. Do not touch blackened or charred seals or equipment.

2. Preferably, don't handle parts containing decomposed fluoroelastomers, but if you must do so, wear goggles and PVC (polyvinyl chloride) or neoprene protective gloves while doing so. Never handle such parts unless they are completely cool.

3. Contaminated parts, residues, materials and clothing, including protective clothing and gloves, should be disposed of by an approved contractor to currently applicable national or local regulations. Oil seals, gaskets and 'O' rings, along with contaminated material, must not be burned.

WORKSHOP

• Always have a fire extinguisher of the correct type at arm's length when working on anything flammable. If you do have a fire, DON'T PANIC. Direct the extinguisher at the base of the fire.

• NEVER use a naked flame in the workplace.

❐ 7: KEEP your inspection lamp well away from any source of flammable materials.

• NEVER use petrol (gasoline) to clean parts. Use only a proprietary degreaser.

• NO SMOKING. There's a risk of fire or of transferring dangerous substances to your mouth.

• BE METHODICAL in everything you do, use common sense, and think of safety at all times.

ENVIRONMENT FIRST!

• The used oil from the sump of just one car can cover an area of water the size of two football pitches, cutting off the oxygen supply and harming swans, ducks, fish and other river life.

❐ 8: When you drain your engine oil - don't oil the drain! Pouring oil down the drain will cause pollution. It is also an offence.

• Don't mix used oil with other materials, such as paint and solvents, because this makes recycling difficult.

• Take used oil to an oil recycling bank. Telephone FREE in the UK on 0800 663366 to find the location of your nearest oil bank, or contact your local authority recycling officer.

OIL POLLUTES WATER USE YOUR BRAIN - NOT THE DRAIN!

CHAPTER 3: GETTING THROUGH THE ANNUAL TEST

This chapter relates mostly to the UK where vehicles need to pass the 'MoT' test but also has relevance for those in other countries with a similar annual test. Obviously, you won't be able to examine your car to the same degree of thoroughness as the MoT testing station. But you can reduce the risk of being among the four out of 10 who fail the test first time!

The checks shown below are correct for the MoT Test in the UK at the time of writing but they do tend to become stricter! Your local testing station will have the latest information. DON'T BE TURNED AWAY! The vehicle, when presented for test, must be reasonably clean. Testing Stations can refuse to test vehicles that are very dirty and have excessive mud on the underside.

CONTENTS

Part A: Inside the Vehicle

STEERING WHEEL AND COLUMN

❏ 1: Try to move the steering wheel towards and away from you and then from side to side. There should be no appreciable movement or play. Check that the steering wheel is not loose on the column and that there are no breaks or loose components on the steering wheel itself.

❏ 2: Lightly grip the steering wheel between thumb and finger and turn from side to side. Vehicles with a steering rack: free play should not exceed approximately 13 mm (0.5 in.), assuming a 380 mm (15 in.) diameter steering wheel. Vehicles fitted with a steering box: free play should not exceed approximately 75 mm (3.0 in.), assuming a 380 mm (15 in.) diameter steering wheel.

A-2

❏ 3: If there is a universal joint at the bottom of the steering column inside the vehicle, check for movement. Place your hand over the joint while turning the steering wheel to-and-fro a little way with your other hand. If ANY free play can be felt, the joint must be replaced.

❏ 4: Steering security and locking devices (where fitted) must be in working order.

ELECTRICAL EQUIPMENT

❏ 5: With the ignition turned ON, ensure that the horn works okay.

❏ 6: Check that the front wipers work.

❏ 7: Check that the screen washers work.

❏ 8: Check that the internal warnings for the indicator and hazard warning lights work okay. When ABS brakes are fitted: Make sure that there is an ABS warning light that illuminates and that the lamp follows the correct sequence.

CHECKS WITH AN ASSISTANT

❏ 9: Check that the front and rear side lights and number plate lights work and that the lenses and reflectors are secure, clean and undamaged.

☐ 10: Check the operation of the headlights and check that the lenses are undamaged. The reflectors inside the headlights must not be tarnished, nor must there be condensation inside the headlight.

☐ 11: Turn on the ignition and check the direction indicators, front and rear, and the side markers.

☐ 12: Check that the hazard warning lights operate on the outside of the vehicle and at the internal warning light.

☐ 13: Check that the rear fog light/s, including the warning light inside the vehicle, all work correctly.

☐ 14: Check that the rear brake lights work correctly.

☐ 15: Operate the brake lights, side lights and each indicator in turn, then all at the same time. None should affect the operation of the others.

SAFETY FIRST!

• Follow the Safety information in *Chapter 2, Safety First!* but bear in mind that the vehicle needs to be even more stable than usual when raised off the ground.

• There must be no risk of it toppling off its stands or ramps while suspension and steering components are being pushed and pulled in order to test them.

FRONT SCREEN AND MIRRORS

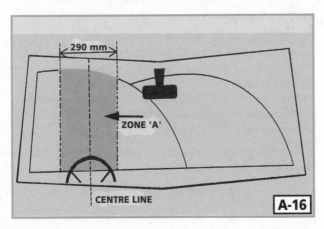

290 mm

ZONE 'A'

CENTRE LINE

A-16

☐ 16: In zone 'A' of the front screen, no items of damage larger than 10 mm in diameter will be allowed. In the rest of the area swept by the screen wipers, no damage greater than 40 mm in diameter will be allowed, nor should stickers or other obstructions encroach on this area.

☐ 17: Check that the exterior mirror on the driver's side is in good condition.

☐ 18: There must be one other mirror in good condition, either inside the vehicle or an external mirror on the passenger's side.

BRAKES

☐ 19: You cannot check the brakes properly without a rolling road brake tester but you can carry out the following checks:

☐ 20: Pull on the parking brake. It should be fully ON before the lever reaches the end of its travel.

☐ 21: Knock the parking brake lever from side to side and check that it does not then release itself.

☐ 22: Check the security of the parking brake lever mountings and check the floor around them for rust or splits.

☐ 23: Check that the front brake pedal is in good condition and that, when you take hold of it and move it from side to side, there is not too much play.

☐ 24: Push the footbrake down hard with your foot. If it creeps slowly down towards the floor, there is probably a problem with the master cylinder. Release the pedal, and after a few seconds, press down again. If the pedal feels spongy or it travels nearly to the floor, there is air in the system or another dangerous fault with the brakes.

☐ 25: Check the servo unit (when fitted) as follows: Pump the brake pedal several times then hold it down hard. Start the engine. As the engine starts, the pedal should move down slightly. If it doesn't the servo or the vacuum hose leading to it may be faulty.

SEAT BELTS AND SEATS

☐ 26: Examine all of the seat belt webbing (pull out the belts from the inertia reel if necessary) for cuts, fraying or deterioration.

☐ 27: Check that each inertia reel belt retracts correctly.

☐ 28: Fasten and unfasten each belt to ensure that the buckles work correctly.

☐ 29: Tug hard on each belt to ensure that the inertia reel locks, and inspect the mountings, as far as possible, to ensure that all are okay.

A-29

IMPORTANT NOTE: Checks apply to rear seat belts as much as to front ones.

☐ 30: Make sure that the seat runners and mountings are secure and that all back rests lock in the upright position.

DOORS AND DOOR LOCKS

☐ 31: Check that doors latch securely when closed and that they can be opened and closed from both outside and inside the vehicle.

Part B: Outside of Vehicle

ELECTRICAL EQUIPMENT

See *Part A: Inside the Vehicle* for checks on the operation of the electrical equipment.

❑ 1: Examine the wiper blades and replace those that show any damage.

VEHICLE IDENTIFICATION NUMBERS (VIN)

❑ 2: The VIN (or chassis number on older vehicles) must be clearly displayed and legible.

❑ 3: Number (licence) plates must be secure, legible and in good condition with correct spacing between letters and numbers which must be of correct size and style.

BRAKING SYSTEM

❑ 4: Inside the engine bay inspect the master cylinder, servo unit (if fitted), brake pipes and mountings. Look for corrosion, loose fitting or leaks.

STEERING AND SUSPENSION

❑ 5: While still in the engine bay, have your assistant turn the steering wheel lightly from side to side and look for play in steering universal joints or steering system mountings and any other steering connections.

❑ 6: If the vehicle is fitted with power steering, check the security and condition of the steering pump, hoses and drivebelt, in the engine bay.

❑ 7: While your assistant turns the steering wheel more vigorously from side to side, place your hand over each track rod end in turn and feel for playing. Inspect all of the steering linkages, joints and attachments for wear.

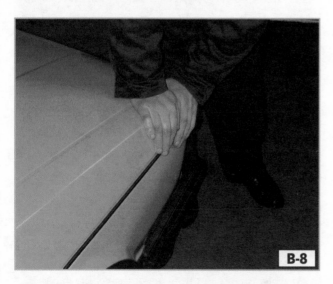

B-8

❑ 8: Go around the vehicle and 'bounce' each corner of the vehicle in turn. Release at the lowest point and the vehicle should rise and settle in its normal position without continuing to 'bounce' of its own accord. If not, a shock absorber is faulty. Always renew in 'axle' pairs or sets.

BODYWORK STRUCTURE

❑ 9: Any sharp edges on the external bodywork, caused by damage or corrosion will cause the vehicle to fail.

❑ 10: Check all load bearing areas for corrosion. Open the doors and check the sills inside and out, above and below. Any corrosion in structural metalwork within 30 cm (12 in.) of seat belt mounting, steering and suspension attachment points will cause the vehicle to fail.

WHEELS AND TYRES

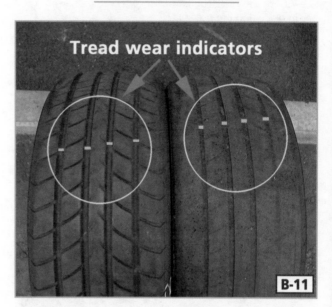

Tread wear indicators

B-11

❑ 11: To pass the test, the tread must be at least 1.6 mm deep throughout a continuous band comprising the central three-quarters of the width of the tread. The Tread Wear Indicators (TWI) will tell you when the limit has been reached, on most tyres. (They are not coloured on 'real' tyres!)

IMPORTANT NOTE: Tyres are past their best, especially in wet conditions, well before this point is reached! (Illustration courtesy of Dunlop)

❑ 12: Check that the front tyres match and that the rear tyres match each other - in terms of size and type but not necessarily make. They must be the correct size for the vehicle and the pressures must be correct.

❑ 13: With each wheel off the ground in turn, check the inside and the outside of the tyre wall for cuts, lumps and bulges and check the wheel for damage. Note that tyres deteriorate progressively over a period of time and if they have degraded noticeably, replace them.

Part C: Under the Vehicle

You will need to support the front of the vehicle off the ground with the rear wheels firmly chocked in both directions.

❑ 1: Have your helper turn the steering from lock to lock and check that the steering turns smoothly and that the brake hoses or pipes do not contact the wheel, tyre or any part of the steering or suspension.

❏ 2: Particular attention should be paid to evidence of corrosion at the steering rack or steering box fixing points.

❏ 3: Have your assistant hold down the brake pedal firmly. Check each brake flexible hose for bulges or leaks. Inspect all the rigid brake pipes underneath the front of the vehicle for corrosion, damage or leaks and also look for signs of fluid leaks at the brake calipers. Rigid fuel pipes also need to be checked for corrosion, damage or leaks.

❏ 4: At each full lock position, check the steering rack rubber gaiters for splits, leaks or loose retaining clips.

❏ 5: Check the track rod end dust covers to make sure they are in place and are not split.

❏ 6: Inspect each constant velocity joint gaiter - both inners and outers - for splits or damage. You will have to rotate each wheel to see the gaiters all the way round.

❏ 7: Check all of the suspension rubber mountings, including the anti-rollbar mountings (when fitted). Take a firm grip on each shock absorber in turn with both hands and try to twist the damper to check for deterioration in the top and bottom mounting bushes.

❏ 8: Check that the shock absorbers are not corroded, that the springs are in good condition and that there are no fluid leaks down the body of the shock absorber. Renew if necessary

❏ 9: Check the front of the exhaust for corrosion and secure fixing at manifold and mounting points.

C-10

❏ 10: Grasp each wheel at 12 o'clock and 6 o'clock positions and try rocking the wheel.
FRONT WHEELS: Look for movement at suspension ball joints, suspension and steering mountings. Repeat while grasping each wheel at 3 o'clock and 9 o'clock.
ALL WHEELS: At the wheel bearing, look for movement between the wheel and hub.

❏ 11: Spin each wheel and check for noise or roughness in the wheel bearing and binding in either the wheel bearing or the brake.

❏ 12: If you suspect wear at any of the suspension points, try levering with a screwdriver to see whether or not you can confirm any movement in that area.

❏ 13: Vehicles fitted with other suspension types such as hydraulic suspension, torsion bar suspension etc. need to be checked in a way that is relevant to the system, with the additional point that there must be no fluid leaks or damaged pipes on vehicles with hydraulic suspension.

❏ 14: Inspect the rear springs for security at their mounting points and for cracks, severe corrosion or damage.

❏ 15: Check the rear shock absorbers in the same way as the checks carried out for the fronts.

❏ 16: Check all rear suspension mounting points, including the rubbers to any locating rods or anti-roll bar that may be fitted.

❏ 17: Check all of the flexible and rigid brake pipes and the fuel pipes just as for the front of the vehicle.

❏ 18: Have your assistant press down firmly on the brake pedal while you check the rear brake flexible hoses for bulges, splits or other deterioration.

❏ 19: Check the fuel tank for leaks or corrosion. Remember also to check the fuel filler cap - a correctly sealing filler cap is a part of the MoT test.

❏ 20: Examine the parking brake mechanism. Frayed or broken cables or worn mounting points, either to the bodywork or in the linkage will all be failure points.

❏ 21: Check each of the rear wheel bearings as for the fronts.

❏ 22: Spin each rear wheel and check that neither the wheel bearings nor the brakes are binding. Pull on and let off the parking brake and check once again to make sure that the parking brake mechanism is releasing.

SAFETY FIRST!

• Only run the car out of doors.
• Beware of burning yourself on a hot exhaust system!

C-23

❏ 23: While you are out from under the vehicle, but with the rear end still raised off the ground, run the engine. Hold a rag over the end of the exhaust pipe and listen for blows or leaks in the system. You can then get back under the vehicle and investigate further if necessary.

☐ 24: Check the exhaust system mountings and check for rust, corrosion or holes in the rear part of the system.

☐ 25: Check the rear brake back plate or calipers (as appropriate) for any signs of fluid leakage.

Part D: Exhaust Emissions

TOP TIP!

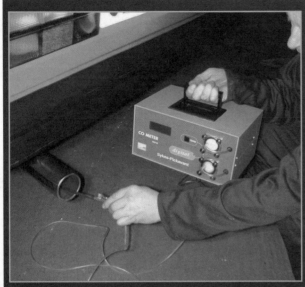

• This is a Sykes-Pickavant CO meter.
• If you don't own a CO meter, you could have your testing station carry out the emission part of the test first so that if it fails, you don't waste money on having the rest of the test carried out.

FACT FILE

FACT FILE: VEHICLE EMISSIONS

The information shown here applies, at the time of writing, to the UK. For information applicable to other territories, or for later amendments, check with the relevant local testing authorities.

PETROL/GASOLINE ENGINED VEHICLES WITHOUT CATALYSER

Vehicles first used before 1 August 1973 - visual smoke check only.

Vehicles first used between 1 August 1973 and 31 July 1986 - 4.5% carbon monoxide and 1,200 parts per million, unburned hydrocarbons.

Vehicles first used between 1 August 1986 and 31 July 1992 - 3.5% carbon monoxide and 1,200 parts per million, unburned hydrocarbons.

PETROL/GASOLINE ENGINED VEHICLES FITTED WITH CATALYTIC CONVERTERS

Vehicles first used from 1 August 1992 (K-registration - on, in the UK)

• All have to be tested at an MoT Testing Station specially equipped to handle vehicles fitted with catalytic converters whether or not the vehicle is fitted with a 'cat'.

• Required maxima are - 3.5% carbon monoxide and 1,200 parts per million, unburned hydrocarbons. There will be a further check to make sure that the catalyst is in working order.

TOP TIP!

• Because 'cats' don't work properly at lower temperatures, ensure that the engine is fully warm!

DIESEL ENGINES' EMISSIONS STANDARDS

• IMPORTANT NOTE: The diesel engine test puts a lot of stress on the engine. It is IMPERATIVE that the vehicle's engine is in good condition before you take it in for the MoT test. The tester is entitled to refuse to test the vehicle if he feels that the engine is not in serviceable condition.

Vehicles first used before 1 August, 1979
• Engine run at normal running temperature; engine speed taken to around 2,500 rpm (or half governed max. speed, if lower) and held for 20 seconds. FAILURE, if engine emits dense blue or black smoke for next 5 seconds, at tick-over.

Vehicles first used on or after 1 August, 1979
• After checking engine condition, and with the engine at normal running temperature, the engine will be run up to full revs between three and six times to see whether the engine passes the prescribed smoke density test. (2.5k for non-turbo vehicles; 3.0k for turbo diesels. An opacity meter probe will be placed in the vehicle's exhaust pipe.) Irrespective of the meter readings, the vehicle will fail if smoke or vapour obscures the view of other road users.

MULTI-FUEL VEHICLES

• Vehicles which run on more than one fuel (eg petrol and LPG) will normally be tested on the fuel they are running on when presented for test.
• There is a slight difficulty with LPG vehicles and unless the testing station analyser has the facility for conversion, the mechanic will have to do a calculation. The machine is set to measure propane, but LPG power gives out hexane. The analyser will have a 'PEF' number shown. This is used as follows: 'propane' reading ÷ PEF no. = hexane value.

CHAPTER 4: WORKSHOP TOP TIPS!

Please read Chapter 2 Safety First! before carrying out any work on your car.

Here are a few *Top Tips!* to help keep things running well in the workshop.

❏ **1:** DON'T LOSE IT! Buy sandwich bags and store small items in them, in groups, as they are removed. Keep the bags in a box or boxes, and keep the box/es in the vehicle if you have to go off and do something else. If you leave stuff lying around you'll lose some of it - right?

LOOK ON THE BRIGHT SIDE! Don't always assume the worst. That misfire - could it be the ECU? Highly unlikely, so try all the small stuff first. Engine running faults in particular are caused, 90% of the time, by failures in simple components such as spark plugs, leads, loose terminals and so on. So don't be a pessimist!

DON'T BE A BLUEBOTTLE! Work methodically; don't whizz around from one thing to another. Make a resolution to finish one thing before starting the next - even when you hit a tough patch, work through it! You'll finish jobs more quickly and you'll lose less stuff!

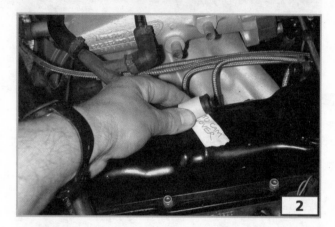

❏ **2:** LABEL IT! Even in a manual like this, it isn't possible to cover every possible variation of wiring and pipework layout. If you assume that you WON'T remember how every single part goes back together - you'll almost certainly be right! Use tags of masking tape stuck on the ends of all removed connections, and label or number the matching parts. You'll save ages when it's time for reassembly!

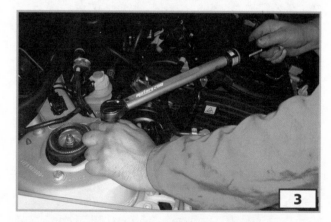

❏ **3:** TIGHTEN RIGHT! Under-torquing and over-torquing threaded fixings is all too common. Some mechanics pride themselves on being able to judge the correct torque 'by feel'. They can't! Yes, they can get closer than a raw amateur, but the demands of modern components leave no room for guessing.

→ Under-torqued fixings can come loose, or allow components to 'work' or chaff; over-torqued fixings can be even worse and can fail catastrophically or distort essential parts. Always check that threads run freely, and use a torque wrench!

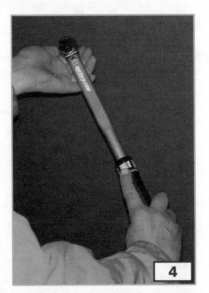

☐ 4: KEEP TORQUING! **Sykes-Pickavant** advise that their torque wrenches - and it actually applies to all makes - will read accurately for much longer if backed-off to the ZERO position before putting away, after each use.

CHOOSING AND USING A HOIST

The best way of raising a vehicle off the ground - almost essential if you intend making your living or part of your income from working on vehicles - is to use a hoist. There are several types available, and the pros and cons are explained here by leading vehicle hoist manufacturer, **Tecalemit**:

→ **FOUR POST:** This type of hoist is the least expensive, it's stable and capable of taking the greatest weights, but it's also the least versatile. With a post in each corner, the vehicle is driven onto ramps which raise the whole of the vehicle off the ground. The ramps do get in the way and the suspension is compressed by the weight of the vehicle. This restricts access in the wheel wells. On the other hand, it is possible to use a cross-beam from which you can jack specific parts of the vehicle - essential when vehicle testing. A four-post hoist is also useful if it's essential to raise a dangerously rusty vehicle off the ground.

→ **TWO POST:** A post each side of the vehicle each carries two legs. The legs are swung so that a foot on the end of each leg is positioned under each end of the vehicle's body, usually under the normal jacking points. The great thing about these hoists is that they are 'wheels free' - the wheels and suspension hang down, providing almost ideal access to the underside of the vehicle. A two-post hoist should never be used on a vehicle that is dangerously rusty, because it will be raised on body parts which may collapse if the corrosion is very severe.

→ **SINGLE POST:** This type has a single post, and swing-out legs reaching right under the vehicle. The advantage gained from the 'loss' of a post is offset by the intrusion of the extra-long support legs. The legs impede under-car access; the second post of a two-post hoist doesn't.

→ **OUR CHOICE:** Without hesitation, we fitted a **Tecalemit** two-post hoist into the Porter Manuals workshop. Excellent service life from this famous-name manufacturer, and easy access for our mechanics, authors and photographers have made the hoist a wise choice!

☐ 5: The legs can only be swung into position when they are fully lowered. They are extended, as necessary and aligned beneath the lifting points of the main body tub of the vehicle. As soon as they begin to raise off the ground, the legs are locked into position.

☐ 6: Access to the vehicle's underside is ideal and, because there are no ramps - and no depressions in the floor, as is often the case with 4-post hoists - there is plenty of room to drive another vehicle beneath the one on the hoist for overnight storage.

☐ 7: These **Tecalemit** hoists can run from 3-phase or 1-phase electrics, and can be fitted with a converter to enable a domestic level of current supply to power the hoist. In such cases, there will be a momentary delay while the converter builds up the power to the level required.

8A: When a vehicle is raised on a hoist, it's perfectly safe, PROVIDED that the hoist has received its regular maintenance check by the suppliers. The **Tecalemit** two-post hoist is raised by screw threads and the legs are locked immovably when the motor is not being operated.

TOP TIP!

8B: • Put a piece of tape on the post when you've established your best working height.
• Now you can raise the vehicle with the legs lined up with this mark every time!

8B

RAISING THE VEHICLE - SAFELY!

Read this section in conjunction with the essential safety notes in *Chapter 2, Safety First!*

For those who don't have access to a pro. hoist:
→ NEVER work beneath a vehicle held solely on a jack, not even a trolley jack. The safest way of raising a vehicle may be to drive one end of it up onto a pair of ramps. Sometimes, however, there is no alternative but to use axle stands because of the nature of the work being carried out.
→ Do not jack-up the vehicle with anyone on board, or when a trailer is connected (it could pull the vehicle off the jack).
→ Pull the parking brake on and engage first (low) gear.
→ WHEELS ON THE GROUND SHOULD BE CHOCKED AFTER THE VEHICLE HAS BEEN RAISED, SO THAT THE VEHICLE CANNOT MOVE.

USING RAMPS

Make absolutely certain that the ramps are parallel to the wheels of the vehicle and that the wheels are exactly central on each ramp. Always have a helper watch both sides of the vehicle as you drive up.
→ Wrap a strip of carpet into a loop around the first 'rung' of the ramps and drive over the doubled-up piece of carpet on the approach to the ramps. This prevents the ramps from skidding away, as they are inclined to do, as the vehicle is driven on to them.

→ Drive up to the end 'stops' on the ramps but never over them!
→ Apply the parking brake firmly and put the vehicle in first or reverse gear (or 'P' in the case of auto).
→ Chock both wheels remaining on the ground, both in front and behind so that the vehicle can't move in either direction.

USING A TROLLEY JACK

On many occasions, you will need to raise the vehicle with a trolley jack - invest in one if you don't already own one. Ensure that the floor is sufficiently clear and smooth for the trolley jack wheels to roll as the vehicle is raised and lowered, otherwise it could slip off the jack.
→ Before raising the vehicle, ENSURE THAT THE PARKING BRAKE IS OFF AND THE TRANSMISSION IS IN NEUTRAL. This is so that the vehicle can move as the jack is raised.
→ Reapply brake and place in gear after the raising is complete and chock each wheel to prevent vehicle movement.
→ Always remember to release brake and gear and remove chocks before lowering again.

9: Axle stands also need to be man enough for the job. These inexpensive **Clarke** stands have an SWL of 3 tonnes. Make sure that the axle stands will each be placed beneath a reinforced part of the body, suitable for jacking from, or a main suspension mounting. Never place the jack or axle stand under a moving suspension part.

9

SAFETY FIRST!

• Whenever you're working beneath a vehicle, have someone primed to keep an eye on you!

• If someone pops out to see how you are getting on at regular intervals, it could be enough to save your life!

• Be especially careful when applying force to a spanner or when pulling hard on anything, when the vehicle is supported off the ground.

• It is all too easy to move the vehicle so that it topples off the axle stand or stands.

TOOLS AND EQUIPMENT

This section shows some of the tools and equipment that we have used while working on the vehicles that have been photographed for this manual.

You'll never have a complete set of tools; there will always be something else that you need! But over the years, if you buy equipment a little at a time, as you need it, you will accumulate a surprisingly large range.

When buying tools, it certainly pays to shop around. Tools that you won't need to use regularly, such as an impact screwdriver or a rubbing block for use with abrasive paper can be picked up for a song.

When it comes to larger and more expensive and specialised items, it pays to stick to a known maker rather than to take a chance with an apparently cheap tool whose make you may never have heard of.

☐ **10:** The **Clarke** 'Strong-Arm' engine hoist has the added advantage of being able to be folded into a really small space for storage.

☐ **11:** This engine stand, from the same manufacturer, is remarkably inexpensive. The engine is held at a comfortable working height and can be turned through 360 degrees. Recommended!

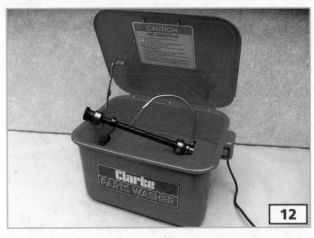

☐ **12:** When you've stripped components down, the most effective way of getting them clean is with a parts washer, this one from **Clarke** again.

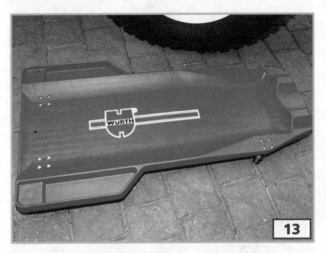

☐ **13:** Sliding beneath the vehicle will be a hundred times easier with a good quality car crawler, such as this plastic moulded crawler from **Wurth**.

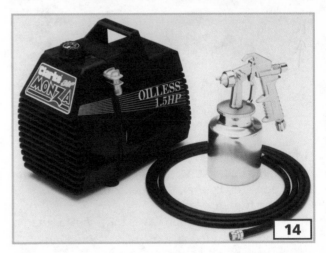

☐ **14:** Another tool that you can scarcely do without is a compressor. At the bottom end of the range, both in terms of price and performance, is a compressor such as the **Clarke** Monza. This tiny compressor will power a spray gun sufficiently for 'blowing-in' a panel and you'll also be able to inflate tyres and carry out all sorts of other lightweight jobs.

15: A compressor such as this 60 c.f.m. unit is the smallest needed by the serious amateur or semi-pro.. It won't run larger air tools, except in shorter bursts, but it's fine for the air wrench, for instance.

16: The Air Kit 400 provides a very useful and remarkably low-cost set of basic air tools capable of being powered by even the smaller compressors. Clockwise from top-left:
→ The engine cleaner gun works much better than a brush.
→ The spray gun is basic but effective.
→ Air hose is suitable for all smaller compressors.
→ Wear goggles when using the invaluable air duster.
→ Double-check tyre pressures with a hand-held gauge when using this tyre inflator and gauge.

17: Another use to which you will be able to put your compressor is spraying cavity protection wax. This **Wurth** injection gun is dual-purpose. It takes disposable **Wurth** screw-on canisters and also has its own large separate canister for injecting any protection wax that you may want to use 'loose'. Hand-powered and cheap-and-cheerful injectors simply don't atomise the protection wax or blast it far enough into nooks and crannies to be useful.

18: Another invaluable tool is an angle grinder. This is the **Bosch** PWS7-115. This piece of equipment is perfect for using with grinding and cutting discs but, when used with this twisted-wire brush (available from bodyshop suppliers), scours paint and rust off steel in seconds. Always wear goggles and gloves with this tool.

19: Another power tool which has a lot of domestic uses as well as being invaluable when working on a vehicle is something like the Jet 3000 Power Washer. It's a marvellous tool for removing mud, oil, grease and grim before stripping down body or mechanical parts and it is also extremely useful around the outside of the house.

□ 20: If your budget – or workshop space – won't run to a stand-alone pillar drill, the **Bosch** drill stand will turn your mains-power drill (this is the **Bosch** PSB with powerful 750W motor) into a perfectly adequate light-user

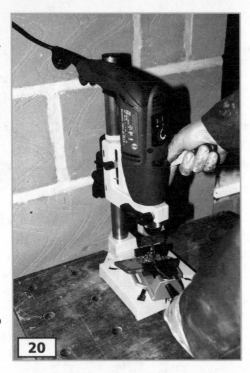

version. The same company also offer the hand vice which is an essential piece of equipment for gripping small pieces.

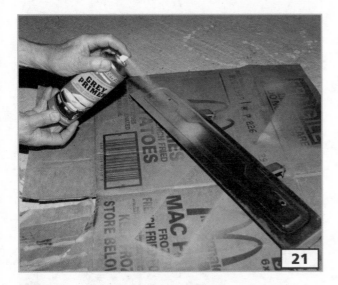

□ 21: Aerosol cans of paint are extremely useful for small items, such as this number plate backing plate, mainly because there's no cleaning up to do afterwards. For large areas, aerosol is prohibitively expensive and you won't find the depth of paint or the quality as good as you would get from a spray gun. There's always a place for aerosol, however, and the **Hycote** range includes all the various types of primer and finish coats that you could want, as well as offering a range of mix-and-match aerosol paints which are mixed to the shade you need.

□ 22: There is a wide range of tool boxes and chests available from **Sykes-Pickavant**. They're made of tough heavy gauge steel, are lockable, and contain separate 'filing cabinet' type drawers for tool storage. Most of the units are stackable.

□ 23. Increasingly, the kind of work described in this manual requires the use of special tools. **Sykes-Pickavant** produce a complete range of regular workshop tools and equipment and also special tools for most purposes.

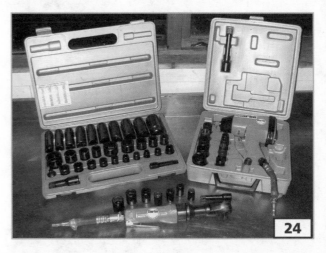

□ 24. An air wrench can save a heck of a lot of time on dismantling and reassembly – although you should always finish off with a torque wrench, where appropriate. The **Clarke** 3/8 in. drive is 'wieldy' enough for engine bay work while the 1/2 in. drive wrench and sockets will cope with most heavy duty jobs. Note the flexible 'tail' we add to each tool to protect the female connector on the air line.

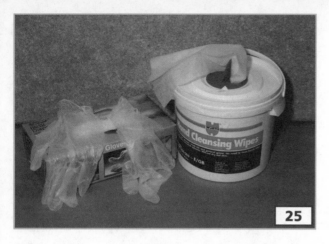

25: You'll need hand cleaner - the sort with granules shifts heavy grease best. **Wurth** also produce these hand wipes - useful if you need to touch upholstery in the middle of a job - and packs of disposable gloves.

26: Wurth produce a huge range of workshop products including electrical connectors and that wonderful 'shrink-fit' wire insulation tubing – slide it on, heat it up, and it 'shrinks' into place and can't come unwrapped.

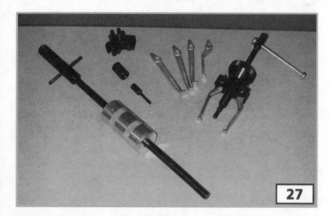

27: It's sometimes necessary to use pullers to remove 'stuck' bearings or other interference fit items. This **Sykes-Pickavant** set includes a variety of arm sizes and types, and a slide hammer to supplement the usual screw-type puller.

28: With these three **Sykes-Pickavant** kits, you can check (from left to right) many of the engine's most basic functions:
→ Cylinder compression tester - essential for a whole range of mechanical diagnostics, without the need for engine dismantling. Different testers are available for Diesel engines with their very high compression pressures.
→ Battery tester - essential for eliminating or confirming the battery as a source of problems.
→ Oil pressure tester. When combined with the cylinder compressions tester, this is capable of providing virtually a complete picture of the 'inner health' of any engine.

29: Last in this Chapter, but first job before carrying out vehicle dismantling: disconnect the battery! Beware of radio sets, alarms and ECUs that need a continuous electricity supply. See *Chapter 10, Electrical, Dash, Instruments* on preserving a battery feed.

CHAPTER 5: SERVICING

PLEASE READ **CHAPTER 2 SAFETY FIRST** BEFORE CARRYING OUT ANY WORK ON YOUR CAR.

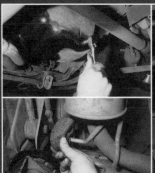

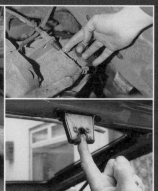

SAFETY FIRST!

• Please read the whole of **Chapter 2, Safety First!** before carrying out any work described here.

HOW TO USE THIS CHAPTER

Note that:
→ Each letter code tells you the Service Interval.
→ Look the code up in the Service Intervals Key.
→ Each Service Job has a Job number.

→ IMPORTANT NOTE: Each service should be carried out at EITHER the recommended mileage OR the recommended time interval, whichever comes first.

SERVICE INTERVALS: KEY
A - Every week, or before every long journey.
B - Every 6 months, or 5,000 miles.
C - Every year or 10,000 miles.
D - Every 2 years, or 20,000 miles.
E - Every 3 years, or 30,000 miles.
F - Every 4 years, or 40,000 miles.
G - Every 5 years or 50,000 miles.
H - Every 6 years or 60,000 miles.

CONTENTS

FACT FILE

ENGINE BAY LAYOUTS

- There are very many different layouts – these are typical of most.
- Not all of the components shown are fitted to all vehicles.

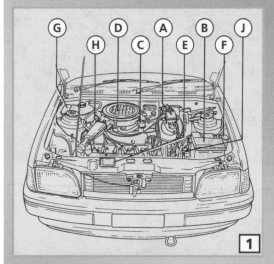

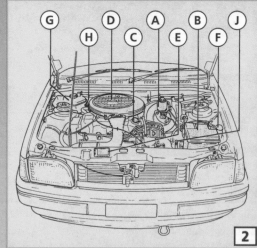

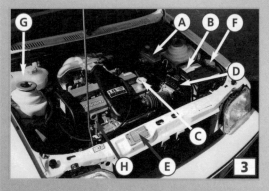

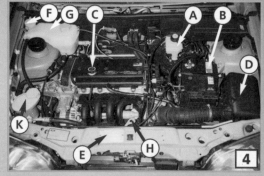

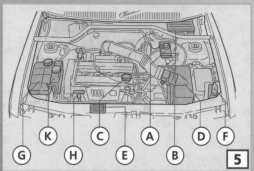

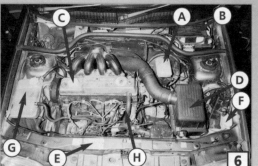

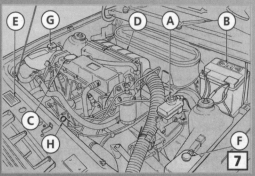

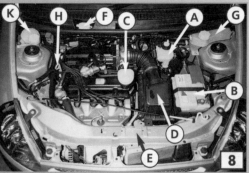

❑ ILLUSTRATION 1: FIESTA - OHV HIGH COMPRESSION SWIRL (HCS) AND ENDURA-E ENGINE.

➔ IMPORTANT NOTE: On pre-1983 Fiestas, the battery was on the right-hand side of the engine compartment with the windscreen washer reservoir on the left.

❑ ILLUSTRATION 2: FIESTA - SINGLE OVERHEAD CAM, COMPOUND VALVE HEMISPHERICAL HEAD (CVH) ENGINE.

❑ ILLUSTRATION 3: FIESTA - EARLY ZETEC DOUBLE OVERHEAD CAM ENGINE.

❑ ILLUSTRATION 4: FIESTA - ZETEC SE ENGINE.

❑ ILLUSTRATION 5: ESCORT - SINGLE OVERHEAD CAM, COMPOUND VALVE HEMI-SPHERICAL HEAD (CVH) ENGINE.

❑ ILLUSTRATION 6: ESCORT - EARLY DIESEL ENGINE MODELS.

❑ ILLUSTRATION 7: ESCORT - LATER DIESEL ENGINE MODELS.

❑ ILLUSTRATION 8: KA - ENDURA E ENGINE.

A - hydraulic fluid reservoir
B - battery
C - engine oil filler cap
D - air cleaner
E - vehicle identification number (VIN) plate
F - screen washer reservoir
G - engine coolant header tank
H - engine oil dipstick
J - automatic transmission dipstick (when fitted)
K - power steering fluid reservoir (when fitted)

JOB 1: ENGINE OIL - *check level.*

❒ 1: Make sure the vehicle is on level ground when you check the dipstick, which on nearly all of these vehicles is coloured yellow.

JOB 2: COOLING SYSTEM - *check level.*

JOB 3: HYDRAULIC FLUID - *check level.*

❒ 3: Wipe the top clean before removing the cap and be careful not to damage the wiring.

Check the brake fluid level warning light.
➜ With the parking brake off - chock the wheels first and place the transmission in first gear (or 'P' in the case of an automatic) - and the ignition switched on, lift the reservoir cap and its float clear of the fluid.
➜ The warning light on the dash should light up.

JOB 4: BATTERY - *check electrolyte level.*

IMPORTANT NOTE: You can't, of course, check the level in a 'sealed for life' battery!

JOB 5: SCREEN/HEADLIGHT WASHER FLUID AND WASHERS - *check level.*

Check the screenwash fluid lever reservoir and top up if necessary.

JOB 6: TYRES - *check pressures and condition (road wheels).*

Pressures should be checked when the tyres are cold - they warm up when a vehicle is driven.
➜ Make sure the tread depth exceeds the legal minimum and look for any signs of uneven wear or damage such as cuts, bulges or objects embedded in the tyres.

JOB 7: LIGHTS - *check/change bulbs.*

See *Chapter 10, Electrical, Dash, Instruments* for bulb replacement information.

JOB 8: ENGINE OIL AND FILTER – *change.*

❒ 8A: This is the location of the oil drain plug on the great majority of these engines.

SAFETY FIRST!

• DON'T pour the old oil down the drain - it's both illegal and irresponsible. Your local council waste disposal site will have special facilities for disposing of it safely. Moreover, don't mix anything else with it, as this will prevent it from being recycled.

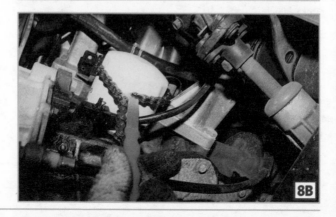

☐ **8B:** Use a strap or chain wrench to remove the filter.

☐ **8C:** Apply clean engine oil to the rubber sealing ring to prevent it buckling as the filter is screwed home.
➜ When the sealing ring contacts the face on the engine, tighten it a further three-quarters of a turn - by hand only.

JOB 9: OIL FILLER CAP - *check*.

EARLY OHV ENGINES: A filter screen inside the oil filler cap separates any oil and moisture from the fumes. Check the cap for signs of blockage.

JOB 10: VALVE CLEARANCES - *check/adjust*.

See *Chapter 6, Engine*.

JOB 11: CAMSHAFT DRIVE BELT - *renew*.

See *Chapter 6, Engine*.

JOB 12: COOLING SYSTEM HOSES - *check*.

Check all the coolant and heater hoses for security and leaks.
➜ Squeeze the larger hoses – with smaller hoses, bend them, listening for cracking sounds, which tell you that the hose needs replacing.

JOB 13: COOLANT - *replace*.

See *Chapter 8: Cooling System*.

JOB 14: TRANSMISSION OIL - *check*.

This check requires the vehicle to be level.

MANUAL TRANSMISSION

☐ **14:** The transmission combined level/filler plug (arrowed) is located on the forward-facing side of the transmission.

TOP TIP!
• The filler can be reached from the engine bay, but it is generally easier to work from beneath.

ATX AND CTX TRANSMISSIONS

With oil at normal operating temperature and engine running apply parking brake and footbrake.
➜ Move gear selector through all positions 3 times.
➜ Move the selector lever to the Park ('P') position and wait for at least one minute.
➜ With engine still running, check the dipstick.

TOP TIP!
• Dark brown or black ATF suggests a worn transmission unit.

JOB 15: TRANSMISSION OIL - *renew*.

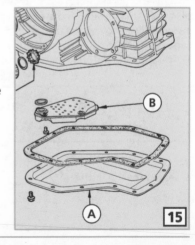

This is not part of Ford's service schedule but common sense suggests that fresh lubricant will allow components to last longer.

MANUAL TRANSMISSION

There is no drain plug fitted to the transmission casing.

> **TOP TIP!**
> • Most transmission oil is lost when a driveshaft gaiter is removed.
> • With the gaiter off, tip the vehicle by raising just one side with a trolley jack, and drain as much oil as possible.

AUTOMATIC TRANSMISSION

❐ **15:** There is no drain plug - you have to unbolt the oil pan (**A**).
➜ Remove all the bolts, except for two adjacent ones, left loose.
➜ Free the plate and allow the oil to drain. This can be messy!
➜ The oil strainer (**B**) should also be removed, washed in white spirit, dried and replaced.
➜ IT IS ABSOLUTELY ESSENTIAL that no trace of dirt - not even fluff from a cloth - is allowed to get into the auto. transmission unit.
➜ Always use a new gasket when re-fitting the plate
➜ **CTX TYPE:** DON'T touch the hydraulic control system found beneath the oil pan.

JOB 16: DRIVE SHAFT GAITERS - *check*.

If any splits are found, replace the gaiters - see **Chapter 11, Steering, Suspension**.

JOB 17: CLUTCH ACTION - *check*.

❐ **17:** If the pedal action feels jerky, 'dry' or heavy, try lubricating the pivots and self-adjusting mechanism located at the top of the pedal with Castrol DWF or releasing fluid.
➜ If the fault persists, the clutch cable probably needs replacing - see **Chapter 7: Transmission, Clutch**.

JOB 18: SPARK PLUGS - *check*.

❐ **18:** On CVH engines, spark plugs are recessed. You'll need an extension bar.

> **TOP TIP!**
> • If a plug which gets tighter as you turn it, there's every possibility that it is cross threaded. Once out, it probably won't go back in again.
> • If the threads can't be cleaned up with a thread chaser, you will have to add a thread insert to the cylinder head.

JOB 19: SPARK PLUGS - *renew*.

Renew the spark plugs irrespective of apparent condition.

JOB 20: CB POINTS/DWELL ANGLE - *check/set*.

See **Chapter 9, Ignition, Fuel, Exhaust**.

> **TOP TIP!**
> • Remove the spark plugs.
> • Apply the parking brake, select second gear and support the right-hand front wheel off the ground - use an axle stand.
> • Now, you can easily turn the engine by turning the road wheel by hand.

JOB 21: CONTACT BREAKER POINTS - *renew*.

See **Chapter 9, Ignition, Fuel, Exhaust**.

JOB 22: IGNITION TIMING - *check*.

See **Chapter 9, Ignition, Fuel, Exhaust**.

JOB 23:   AUXILIARY DRIVE BELT/S - *check*.

See *Chapter 6, Part A* for information on checking and adjusting belts

JOB 24:   IDLE SPEED AND EMISSIONS - *adjust*.

See *Chapter 9, Fuel, Ignition and Exhaust* for all engine types.

JOB 25:   PIPES AND HOSES - *check*.

Make a physical check of all pipework and connections.
→ Bend all flexible brake hoses to show up signs of cracking rubber - if any are found, the hose should be replaced as soon as possible.
→ Hoses should also be free from bulges or chafing marks.

JOB 26:   EXHAUST SYSTEM AND MOUNTINGS - *check*.

❐ 26: Check all the rubber mountings.

TOP TIP!

• If you suspect a leak but it's location isn't obvious, hold a piece of board so that it blocks off the tailpipe. Under pressure, the leak should be more noisy, enabling you to track down its position.

JOB 27:   AIR CLEANER ELEMENT - *renew*.

❐ 27: Remove the top of the air cleaner housing, (screws or clips, depending on model) and unclip the upper 'lid'.
→ Lift out the element and replace it with a new one.

→ On fuel injected petrol and diesel engined cars the air cleaner element is larger and is inside a box at the end of the air inlet trunking.

TOP TIP!

• Many engines with carburetors have a coarse plastic foam filter in the duct leading from the air cleaner housing to the crankcase.
• Lever it out with a screwdriver and renew it.

JOB 28:   DIESEL ENGINES FUEL FILTER - *drain*.

Drain the fuel filter to remove water. See *Chapter 9, Ignition, Fuel, Exhaust*.

JOB 29:   FUEL FILTER - *renew*.

PETROL FUEL INJECTION: On early fuel injection systems the fuel filter is located below the air cleaner housing.
→ Fit the new filter ensuring that the arrows embossed on its casing point in the direction of the fuel flow.
→ Tighten the clamp screw and reconnect the fuel pipe unions.

❐ 29: **DIESEL ENGINE:** See *Chapter 9, Fuel, Ignition and Exhaust*.
→ Use an oil filter strap to release the disposable type.

JOB 30: DIESEL GLOW PLUGS - *check/clean.*

Unscrew each glow plug in turn - see *Chapter 10: Electrical, Dash, Instruments* and clean the carbon off the end with proprietary carburetor cleaner.

JOB 31: FRONT AND REAR WHEEL BEARINGS – *check.*

In order to check for wear, rock the wheel about its centre, feeling for excess bearing play. Also, try spinning each wheel - as far as you can, with driven wheels - feeling for rough rotation.

TOP TIP!

• If a wheel bearing is worn, you will normally hear a noise on the outer, loaded bearing when cornering.

JOB 32: STEERING AND SUSPENSION - *check.*

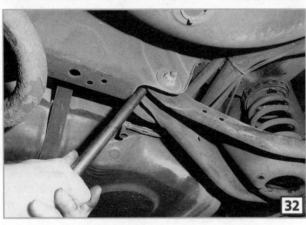

Raise each front wheel just clear of the ground.
→ Put a pry bar under the wheel and try to lever it upwards.
→ Free play suggests wear in suspension bushes or strut.
→ Check the springs for obvious breaks or sagging.
→ Check tie bar bushes for cracking, softness or wear.
→ Check steering rack gaiters.
→ Check steering ball joints.
→ Test the inner suspension arm bush by levering. There should be only a just-perceptible amount of movement.
→ Check all rubber bushes and mountings for distortion, splits or perishing.

JOB 33: SHOCK ABSORBER ACTION - *check.*

See *Chapter 3: The Annual Test* for shock absorber tests.

JOB 34: POWER STEERING FLUID – *check.*

JOB 35: WHEEL NUTS/BOLTS - *check.*

❏ **35:** To 'torque' the wheel nuts/bolts correctly, first slacken each nut or bolt and check that the threads aren't stiff or corroded, then tighten with the wrench.

JOB 36: FRONT AND REAR BRAKE PAD/SHOES - *check/renew.*

See *Chapter 12, Brakes.*

JOB 37: PARKING BRAKE ADJUSTMENT - *check.*

Apply the parking brake. It should lock at between 2 and 4 clicks. If more or less than these figures, the parking brake must be adjusted as described in *Chapter 12, Brakes.*

JOB 38: BRAKE FLUID - *renew.*

If this job is not carried out at the recommended interval, it can result in brakes which fail without warning. See *Chapter 12, Brakes*

JOB 39: SEATS, SEATBELTS AND SEATBELT MOUNTINGS - *check operation and security.*

Check the seats:
→ For secure mounting, by trying to rock them.
→ The seat adjustment mechanism.
→ That the folding seat backs lock securely in the upright position and.

Check the seats belts:
→ Examine seatbelts for signs of damage, such as abrasion, cuts, contamination or frayed stitching.

→ Where inertia-reel seatbelts are fitted, pull the belts out as far as they will go and make sure they fully retract.

→ Make sure the seatbelt anchorage points are secure and the retaining bolts are tight.

→ On older vehicles you should make sure that there is no body corrosion which would weaken the seatbelt mountings.

SAFETY FIRST!

• Some vehicles are fitted with seatbelt pre-tensioners. Special safety precautions are need when this type of seatbelt is being removed or refitted - see *Chapter 14, Interior, Trim*.

JOB 40: SPARE TYRE - *check.*

TOP TIP!

• You should inflate the spare tyre to the maximum pressure recommended for high speed or load running.

• Then, if you have a puncture while on a journey, you'll be okay.

• Just carry a tyre pressure gauge with you and let some air out if necessary.

JOB 41: SCREEN WIPERS - *check.*

JOB 42: HORN - *check.*

JOB 43: LOCKS, CHECK STRAPS AND HINGES (NOT HIGH SECURITY LOCKS) - *lubricate.*

❐ **43:** Apply silicone grease or aerosol spray to the jaws of the lock catches in the edges of the doors and tailgate.

→ Grease hinges and check straps at each door.

→ Apply graphite lock lube to the keyholes of locks unless they are high security locks. THESE SHOULD NOT BE LUBRICATED.

→ Apply grease to the jaws of the bonnet release. Wipe off the surplus.

→ You should also put a blob of grease over the end of the cable where the 'inner' enters the 'outer'.

JOB 44: ALARM SENDER UNIT BATTERIES - *renew.*

JOB 45: ROAD TEST AND FINAL CHECK - *after every service.*

❐ **45:** Before you can claim to have 'finished' working on the vehicle, you must check it and test it. If you are not a qualified mechanic, we strongly recommend having someone who is a properly qualified mechanic inspect all of the vehicle's safety-related items before using it on the road.

→ **WARM-UP:** Run the car for several minutes before setting out then turn off, check fluid levels and check underneath for leaks.

→ **STEERING:** Check that the steering moves freely in both directions and that the car does not 'pull' one way or the other when driving in a straight line - but do bear in mind the effect of the camber on the road.

→ **BRAKES:** Make sure that the brakes work effectively, smoothly and without the need for 'pumping'. There should be no juddering or squealing.

→ **'PULLING'** Check that the car does not 'pull' from one side to the other when you brake firmly from around 40 mph. (Don't cause a skid and don't try this if there is any risk of having an accident.)

→ **CLUTCH OPERATION:** Make sure the clutch pedal operates smoothly and the clutch engages without juddering.

→ **ENGINE PERFORMANCE:** Make sure the engine is operating satisfactorily under load and on the over-run.

→ **TRANSMISSION:** Make sure the gear changes are smooth, and the transmission appears to be working normally

→ **INSTRUMENTS:** Must work and indicate correctly.

CHAPTER 6: ENGINE

PLEASE READ *CHAPTER 2 SAFETY FIRST* BEFORE CARRYING OUT ANY WORK ON YOUR CAR.

Part A: General Procedures

CONTENTS

Many of the skills you will use in rebuilding an engine will be common to all engines. So, to save you time and help the job go more smoothly, those skills are shown right here in *Part A: General Procedures*!

JOB 1: SAFETY FIRST!

Be sure to read and follow the advice in *Chapter 2, Safety First!* before carrying out work on a vehicle. In particular, pay attention to the advice on fuel safety. Remember that there are almost always leaks when disconnecting fuel system components - petrol is highly explosive and rags or paper wipes soaked in diesel fuel are highly inflammable.

In addition, remember that major components may be heavy enough to cause injury if not lifted correctly. See *Job 11* for further important information.

JOB 2: CYLINDER HEAD BOLTS - *tightening, undoing.*

If you get this wrong, you could easily distort the cylinder head - aluminium heads are more prone to distortion than cast iron ones. NEVER remove the head while there is still heat in the engine.

❏ **STEP 1:** MOST IMPORTANT: Don't guess! ALWAYS remove and tighten in the order specified in the relevant section of this manual.

JOB 3: OHC ENGINE BEARING CAPS - *removing.*

❏ **STEP 1:** The camshaft is held down with a number of bearing caps. If they aren't numbered, mark them with a centre punch – it's *essential* that they aren't mixed up. These caps also have arrows to indicate which way they should be fitted. Because of the tension in the valve springs, the caps have to be loosened gradually. You can speed things up by leaving two of the caps tight - such as numbers 2 and 3 in a five-cap set-up - while completely removing the other caps. Now the two remaining caps can be removed. Loosen each nut a turn at a time to gradually release the pressure from the valve springs.

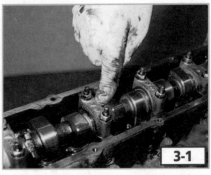

JOB 4: CYLINDER HEAD GASKETS.

❏ **STEP 1:** NEVER re-use a cylinder head gasket - it will almost certainly blow. Fit the new one with the word TOP or OBEN (for German-made gaskets), or sometimes the part number facing **upwards**.

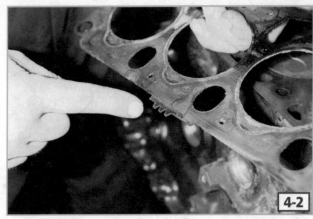

❏ **STEP 2: DIESEL ENGINES:** You will have to select the correct gasket thickness, indicated by notches, because the volume of the combustion chamber is a lot more critical on Diesel engines.

JOB 5: GASKET SEALANT.

• Do NOT use gasket paste on a cylinder head gasket.
• Neoprene (compressible 'rubber') gaskets do not normally need gasket paste. If necessary use silicone sealant.

❏ **STEP 1:** When a joint has to be sealed, make sure that you clean off all of the old sealant first. On a pressed steel sump, use a wire brush.

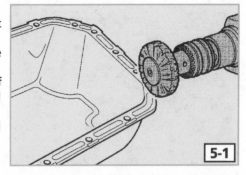

❏ **STEP 2:** Apply silicone sealing compound as follows:
→ Cut off the nozzle on the sealant tube to give the approximate size of bead that you may need. In the case of a sump, it is usually about 3 mm.

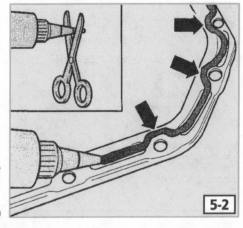

→ Apply the bead about 2 to 3 mm thick.
→ Apply the bead in an unbroken line, going around the *inner* sides of the sump bolt holes.
→ If you cannot avoid a break in the bead, make sure you apply at least a 20 mm overlapping bead at the join.

JOB 6: 'STUCK' CYLINDER HEAD - *freeing.*

Even after all the bolts have been removed, it is sometimes difficult to remove a 'stuck' cylinder head. You must NEVER lever between the mating faces of the head and block. Instead:

→ Look for protrusions or strong brackets on both head and block against which you may be able to lever.

→ Try turning the engine over on the starter motor with spark plugs in place but ignition or Diesel injector pump disconnected, so that the engine can't start. The compression created may shift the head.

→ Extra leverage can be applied by leaving the manifolds in place and pulling on them.

→ You can sometimes use a large, soft-faced mallet on a solid protrusion on the head to try to shock it free. Take very great care not to hammer anywhere that can cause damage.

SAFETY FIRST!

• Make sure that it is safe to spin the engine with HT leads disconnected on your particular engine.

• Some ignition systems may suffer damage if not first completely disconnected.

• Take care not to cause injury or fire from uncontrolled high tension sparks.

JOB 7: CYLINDER HEAD - *lifting, fitting.*

TOP TIP!

☐ **STEP 1:** • When refitting a cylinder head held down with bolts rather than studs fitted in the block – and if there are no alignment dowels fitted by the manufacturer - you may have difficulty in aligning the bolt holes in the gasket with those in the head - and if they're not aligned, you won't be able to screw the bolts into the block.

• Make a pair of guides out of two old cylinder head bolts, or two pieces of plain steel bar of a size that will just slide into the threads in the block.

JOB 8: CYLINDER HEAD AND COMBUSTION CHAMBERS.

☐ **STEP 1:** The cylinder head can be checked for distortion by use of a straight edge and feeler gauge. At the same time, check for excessive corrosion. If you are in

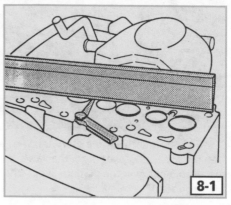

doubt, or if the old gasket had blown, have the cylinder head refaced by an approved Ford dealer or engine specialist.

JOB 9: EXHAUST AND INLET VALVES - *removing, replacing.*

☐ **STEP 1:** Remove the necessary compo-nents to gain access to the valve springs - take care to note or maintain their original positions for reassembly.

☐ **STEP 2:** On some engines, you will need to use a valve-spring compressor with an extension jaw to reach into the recessed valve spring area

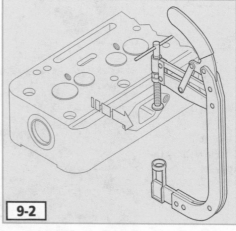

in the head. (Illustration, courtesy Sykes-Pickavant.)

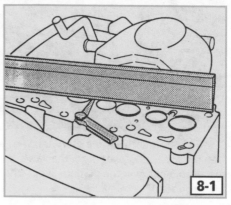

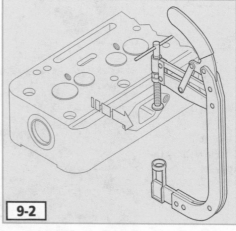

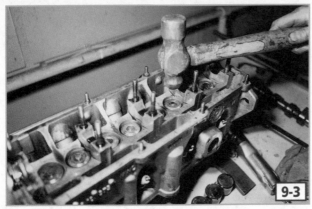

STEP 3: Give each valve a sharp tap with a hammer to free the top spring plate from the valve. You could place a socket spanner over the plate to avoid striking the end of the valve stem.

STEP 4: Compressing the valve springs so that you can reach in and remove the collets from around the heads of the valves.

STEP 5: Slowly and carefully open the spring compressor tool to release the pressure of the valve spring, and remove the upper spring seat...

STEP 6: ...followed by the springs.

STEP 7: Before the valves can be lifted out, the valve seals will have to be removed. This is a Sykes-Pickavant tool – special pliers which grip the seal and lift if off the head of the valve stem.

STEP 8: Slide out the valves, removing the valve seals and discard the old seals; new ones must be used on re-assembly.

TOP TIP!

• The valves should slide freely out of their guides.
• Any resistance may be caused by a build up of carbon, or a slight burr on the stem where the collets engage.
• This can usually be removed by careful use of fine wet-or-dry paper, allowing you to withdraw the valves without scoring their guides.
• Keep the valves in their order temporarily wrapping a numbered piece of masking tape around each stem.

STEP 9: Once all the valves have been removed, clean them up ready for inspection. Remove the carbon deposits with a wire brush and degrease the rest of each

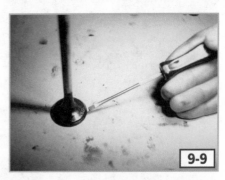

valve. Exhaust valves are prone to burning at their heads, as are their valve seats in the cylinder head. Do not confuse dark 'staining' or marks on the valve heads with burning. Marks are normal and, provided the valve is not worn or damaged, it can be reused - a burnt valve will show signs of physical damage.

❒ **STEP 10:** To install valves, start from one end. Lubricate a valve stem with fresh engine oil and slide it in to its guide.

❒ **STEP 11:** Locate a new valve stem seal over the stem of the valve and push down into contact with the guide. Push the seal onto its seat using a suitable metal tube.

9-10

❒ **STEP 1:** Check for valve guide wear:
→ Lift each valve until the end of the stem is level with the top of the valve guide.
→ Attempt to move the head from side to side.
→ If you feel any noticeable play then you may need new guides.
→ This is a job that has to be carried out by an approved Ford dealer or engine rebuild specialist, who will also have the experience to confirm whether or not wear is acceptable, as well as the special tools needed to replace the valve guides.

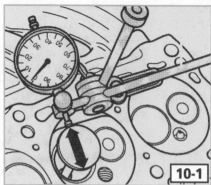

10-1

TOP TIP!

❒ **STEP 12:** • Wrap a short length of insulating tape around the collet grooves at the end of each valve stem.
• This will protect the new valve seals from damage as you slide them over the valve stems.
• When you have pushed the new seal firmly onto the top of the valve guide, remove the tape.

❒ **STEP 13:** Refit the spring seat.

❒ **STEP 14:** Position the springs and the spring cap.

❒ **STEP 15:** Re-apply the valve spring compressor and compress the springs enough to allow you to engage the split collets in the stem grooves. Note that the type of collets, the spring caps and the valves must match each other.

TOP TIP!

• Grease the grooves so that the collets will 'stick' in place.
• Collets are easily fitted by 'sticking' the backs of them onto the end of a screwdriver with some grease and feeding them into position.

❒ **STEP 16:** Carefully release the spring compressor and check that the collets are correctly located. Tap the end of each stem with a hammer to bed them all in.

❒ **STEP 17:** Fit the remaining valves.

JOB 10: EXHAUST AND INLET VALVES - *grinding in.*

TOP TIP!

• Before grinding-in the valves, clean the tops of the valve heads back to shiny metal.
• Now the sucker on the end of your valve grinding stick won't keep falling off when you grind-in the valves!

TOP TIP!

• Modern engines, with hardened valve seats, are not capable of having valves ground in the traditional way, except to remove the smallest of blemishes. If anything more is needed, take the valves and cylinder head to your dealer and have the valves and seats recut to the correct angle by machine.

10-2

❒ **STEP 2:** A power-operated valve grinder, such as this Wurth tool, attaches to the electric drill and makes valve grinding on engines with hardened valve seats a more practicable proposition.

❒ **STEP 3:** Apply a small quantity of coarse grinding paste evenly around the valve seat. Use a valve

10-3

grinding stick tool with a suction cup slightly smaller than the valve face.

STEP 4: Apply a dab of moisture and press the suction pad firmly onto the valve head. Lower the valve stem into the guide and,

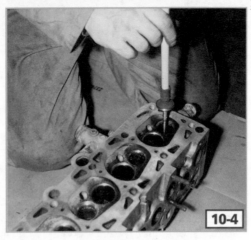

10-4

holding the grinding stick firmly between the palms of your hand, rub back and forth to give rotary grinding action while pressing gently down into the valve seat.

IMPORTANT NOTE: Absolutely NO paste must find its way into the guide, as this will rapidly wear the guide. You must aim to achieve a complete, narrow ring of grey around the valve seat and valve face.

TOP TIP!

• A narrow contact band means high pressure on the seat and longer valve life.
• A wide contact band reduces the contact pressure and induces early valve seat burning.

STEP 5: Now repeat this operation on the remaining valves.

STEP 6: Wash the whole cylinder head

10-5

again using paraffin (kerosene) and an old brush, making sure that all traces of grinding paste are removed, then dry off. Use compressed air if available.

JOB 11: ENGINE - lifting, moving.

STEP 1: Always use suitable lifting equipment, such as the Clarke Strongarm hydraulic engine hoist we show being used.

11-1

JOB 12: CRANKSHAFT BEARINGS, CONNECTING ROD BEARINGS – removing.

FACT FILE
ZETEC MAIN BEARINGS

• Ford do not recommend dismantling the main bearings on the more recent Zetec SE engines.
• If the main bearings and crankshaft need replacing, a new cylinder block, complete with crankshaft must be obtained.

STEP 1: Check that all the connecting rods and their big-end bearing caps are marked with matching numbers.

12-1

STEP 2: If you are to refit the same pistons, mark them to show their position and which way round they face. (The arrow points towards the front of the engine.)

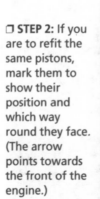

12-2

STEP 3: Undo the securing bolts and remove the caps, keeping them in their correct order.

STEP 4: Use a hammer handle to tap the piston/ connecting rod assemblies carefully out of the bores.

12-4

STEP 5: Keep them in the correct order and keep the matching connecting rods and bearing caps together.

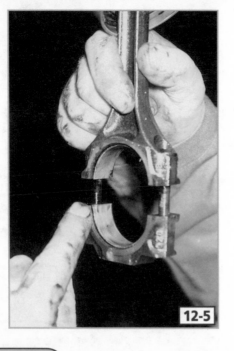

12-5

STEP 6: Check that the crankshaft main bearing caps are correctly marked, starting from the timing cover end. Undo and remove them, keeping them in the correct order.

TOP TIP!

12-7

STEP 7: • If any of the caps are difficult to remove, lever the bolt holes with a bar, or a pair of bars - or a pair of fixing bolts, and tap carefully with a hammer.
• Bearing shells are best removed by sliding them out with your thumbs, pushing the tab-end out first.

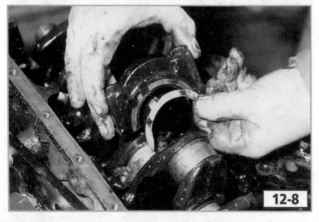

12-8

STEP 8: Retrieve the thrust washers from each side of the centre main bearing cap.

JOB 13: PISTON RINGS - *fitting*.

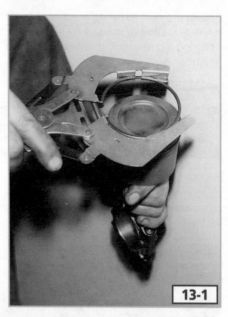

STEP 1: Make sure that the bores and pistons are clean, then fit the rings, preferably using a piston ring spreader. Make sure the rings are fitted with the word 'TOP' facing upwards.

13-1

13-2

STEP 2: If you don't have access to a piston ring spreader, work the rings down a little at a time, using a feeler gauge or gauges to bridge the gaps. Piston rings are very brittle, very easy to break and are expensive to replace!

STEP 3: Arrange the piston ring gaps as specified in the relevant section of this manual.

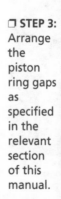
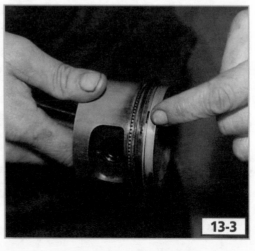

13-3

JOB 14: PISTONS - *removing, refitting.*

Pistons are held to the connecting rods by bolts - see relevant section of manual for tightening procedures. Refitting a piston into its cylinder bore is always as described here:

TOP TIP!

• Wrap insulation tape, or a short piece of plastic tube, over each connecting rod thread, so that it cannot damage the crank as it goes in.

☐ **STEP 1:** Locate a ring clamp over the piston rings and tighten enough to close the ring gaps, but not too tight! Lubricate the rings so that they compress and slide easily within the clamp.

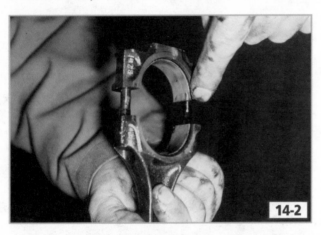

☐ **STEP 2:** Position the assembly in its correct bore with the connecting rod identification marks next to each other and also so that the complete piston/connecting rod assemblies face the right way.

☐ **STEP 3:** With the ring clamp touching the cylinder block, use a hammer shaft to carefully tap the piston through and into the bore.

☐ **STEP 4:** Locate the upper half of the big end shell bearing in the connecting rod, making sure that the mating surfaces are clean. Lubricate the crankpin and the big-end shell and draw the connecting rod down the bore so that the big end locates with the crankpin. Fit the other half of the big-end shell to the bearing cap and lubricate. Offer the

cap to the connecting rod and make sure that the numbers match. Screw in the fixing bolts and tighten progressively to the correct torque.

JOB 15: ENGINE COMPONENTS - *checking, measuring for wear.*

GENERAL

All parts must be thoroughly cleaned before inspection. Keep them in the right order for reassembly in case they are to be re used. Check each component as follows:

CYLINDER BLOCK

☐ **STEP 1:** Look for any cracks or evidence of gas or water blow-by on both sides of the gasket, on the cylinder head and in the block casting, particularly at bolt holes and between cylinders.

☐ **STEP 2:** Check the bores as follows:
➔ Check for score marks, caused by burned pistons or broken rings.

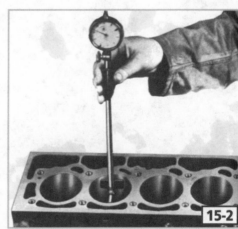

➜ Check for a wear ridge just below the top of the bore where the top piston ring ends its travel.

➜ If you have access to a suitable internal micrometer, measure the bores at the points shown. Otherwise, ask your engine specialist to measure the bores for wear if there is any evidence of a wear ridge.

❏ **STEP 3:** Assuming the bores to be in reasonable condition, it is sometimes possible to 'glaze bust' the bores and fit new piston rings. If not, the cylinders will have to be rebored.

TOP TIP!

❏ **STEP 4:** You can't check for bore ovality like this, but you can gain a good idea of overall wear:

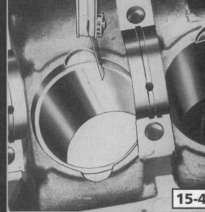

• Push each piston ring squarely into the cylinder until it is about 15 mm from the bottom edge where no wear will have taken place.

• Measure the ring gap with a feeler gauge.

• Now carry out the same check on the most badly worn parts of the bore and see how much wear has taken place.

❏ **STEP 5:** You will need a suitably large external micrometer to measure the pistons. Check about 15 mm from the bottom of the skirt.

❏ **STEP 6:** Check the piston ring clearances with a set of feeler gauges.

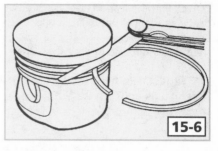

CRANKSHAFT

❏ **STEP 7:** Check the main journals and crankpins:

➜ for any signs of wear ridges round the circumference or scoring of the surface.

➜ for ovality, using a suitable micrometer, although the precision Vernier gauge shown here will give an excellent guide.

❏ **STEP 8:** Check the shell bearings, which should have an even, dull grey finish, like the ones shown here.

STEP 9: If the leaded layer is scored or has worn through to the copper coloured backing, or if the crankshaft has any of the previously mentioned faults, the crankshaft should be reground by your specialist.

STEP 10: Check the crankshaft end float by using a feeler gauge between the thrust washer and the crankshaft.

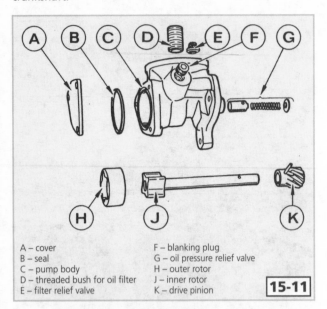

A – cover
B – seal
C – pump body
D – threaded bush for oil filter
E – filter relief valve
F – blanking plug
G – oil pressure relief valve
H – outer rotor
J – inner rotor
K – drive pinion

15-11

STEP 11: If an engine is being rebuilt, a new oil pump should be fitted as a matter of course. This is an oil pump from an overhead valve engine, and it's internal components are typical of the rotor-type oil pump - see *Chapter 1, Facts and Figures* for the clearances on the engine you are working on.

STEP 12: Use feeler gauges to measure the clearance between the inner and outer rotors – for example, 0.051 mm (0.02 in.) to 0.127 mm (0.05 in.) and the outer rotor and body - 0.14 mm (0.055 in.) to 0.26 mm (0.0102 in.).

15-12

STEP 13: Use a straight edge and feeler gauges to measure the axial clearance – for example, 0.025 mm (0.01 in.) to 0.06 mm (0.0024 in.). Check that the bearing face of the cover (illustration *15-11, item A*) is not worn. If in doubt, replace the pump – it's the 'heart' of the engine!

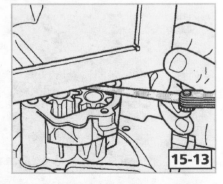

15-13

CAMSHAFT

Check the following:

STEP 14: Check each cam lobe for wear, which can be quite rapid once started. If you replace the camshaft, fit new followers as well.

15-15

STEP 15: Cam followers (bucket tappets) should also be checked, particularly where they contact the cam lobe.

TOP TIP!

This type of tappet can be difficult to remove - use the suction pad on a valve grinding tool.

STEP 16: Check the camshaft journals and their corresponding bearings in the cylinder head or block housing for a smooth, shiny surface without wear ridges.

JOB 16: REASSEMBLING ENGINE COMPONENTS - *lubrication.*

16-1

STEP 1: Apply copious amounts of lubricant to every rotating, rubbing and oil seal surface as the assembly takes place. You CAN'T over-lubricate!

❒ STEP 2: If the engine won't be run straight away, wipe grease onto seal surfaces, so that they won't dry out.

16-2

16-3

❒ STEP 3: Fill the oil pump housing with as much fresh engine oil as it will take, so that the pump itself is lubricated and so that it delivers fresh oil to the engine as quickly as possible.

Before starting the engine, fit a fully charged battery and crank the engine over with spark plugs (or diesel pre-heaters) removed, so that the engine will spin rapidly without starting and without putting strain on the bearings. Turn the engine on the starter for around 30 seconds to circulate oil to the bearings, before starting up.

JOB 17: REASSEMBLING ENGINE COMPONENTS - *clearances.*

Specific assembly details are given in the relevant section of this manual, but it's well worth pointing out some general information, especially with regard to fitting the crankshaft bearings:

17-1

❒ STEP 1: Make sure you have all the necessary gaskets, available in complete sets.

TOP TIP!

• Apply grease to the smooth side of the thrust washers and 'stick' them in position each side of the centre main bearing, before lowering the crank into position.

❒ STEP 2: Make sure all bearing seats are perfectly clean and locate the shells so that their tabs engage with the slots. Once lubricated, a shell can be placed on a journal and pushed around into its correct position.

17-2

❒ STEP 3: Screw bolts in finger tight and check that the crankshaft rotates freely and smoothly.

❒ STEP 4: Tighten each bolt evenly and progressively until the specified torque setting is reached. Check after tightening EACH bearing that the crankshaft rotates smoothly. If it doesn't, remove the bearing cap and shells and investigate as follows:
➜ Check that there is no dirt or debris under a bearing shell – the most likely cause.
➜ The next most likely cause is that there has been a build up of carbon on the rim of a seating and/or cap. Scrape off any that is present.
➜ Check that the shells supplied are the right size for any machining that may have been carried out.

❒ STEP 5: The checks described in *Step 4* will only tell you if a bearing is too tight; it won't tell you if one is too loose.

Part B: Which Engine is Which?

CONTENTS

JOB 1:   UNDERSTAND ENGINE TYPES.

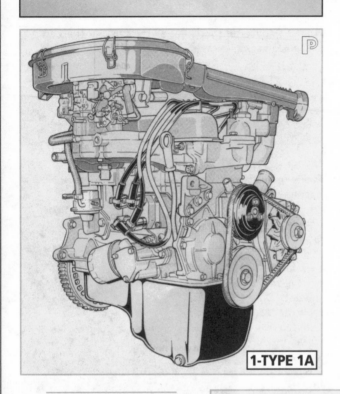

1-TYPE 1A

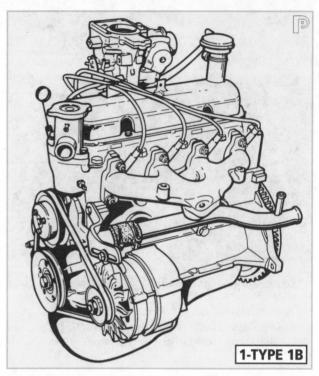

1-TYPE 1B

distributor (3) (where fitted) are driven from gears on the camshaft. This engine can be identified by the pressed steel rocker cover.

OVERHEAD VALVE ENGINES

❏ **TYPE 1A:** The overhead valve engine.

❏ **TYPE 1B:** This is the engine shorn of its ancillaries.

❏ **TYPE 1C:** All versions of this engine have a cast iron cylinder block (**21**) and cast iron cross-flow cylinder head (**20**) - the inlet (**1**) and exhaust manifolds are mounted on opposite sides of the cylinder head. The two valves per cylinder are mounted vertically in the cylinder head and are operated by pushrods (**2**) and rocker arms from a camshaft (**13**) running in the cylinder block - valve clearances are manually adjusted. The camshaft is chain driven (**16**) from the front end of the crankshaft and the oil pump (**8**) (which has a full-flow oil filter) and

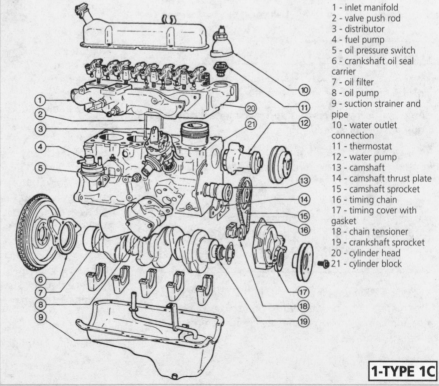

1 - inlet manifold
2 - valve push rod
3 - distributor
4 - fuel pump
5 - oil pressure switch
6 - crankshaft oil seal carrier
7 - oil filter
8 - oil pump
9 - suction strainer and pipe
10 - water outlet connection
11 - thermostat
12 - water pump
13 - camshaft
14 - camshaft thrust plate
15 - camshaft sprocket
16 - timing chain
17 - timing cover with gasket
18 - chain tensioner
19 - crankshaft sprocket
20 - cylinder head
21 - cylinder block

1-TYPE 1C

❏ **TYPE 1D:** The engines fitted to 1.0 and 1.1 litre models have three main bearings; all other OHV engines have five main bearings.

SINGLE OVERHEAD CAMSHAFT ENGINES

❏ **TYPE 2A:** The single overhead camshaft engine was known as the CVH (Compound Valve angle, Hemispherical head) when first introduced. The PTE (Pent roof, high Torque, low Emission) version was introduced in the mid-1990s.

A – fresh air pipe
B – pipe to inlet manifold
C – blanked off connection
D – location of control orifice
1 – oil filler cap
2 – air cleaner
3 – vacuum pipe and diaphragm unit
4 – hot air duct
5 – hot air box
6 – cold air intake
7 – thermostat
8 – belt tension adjuster
9 – alternator
10 – belt tension check point
11 – coolant pump
12 – camshaft skew gear
13 – pulley
14 – camshaft drive chain
15 – chain tensioner
16 – dipstick
17 – drain plug
18 – oil intake strainer
19 – camshaft
20 – relief valve
21 – oil pump
22 – oil filter
23 – distributor vacuum pipe
24 – tappet
25 – flywheel
26 – fuel pump
27 – pushrod
28 – Ford VV carberetor
29, 30 – coolant pipes to and from automatic choke control
31 – anti run-on valve
32 – distributor
33 – inlet valve
34 – exhaust valve
35 – piston
36 – gudgeon pin

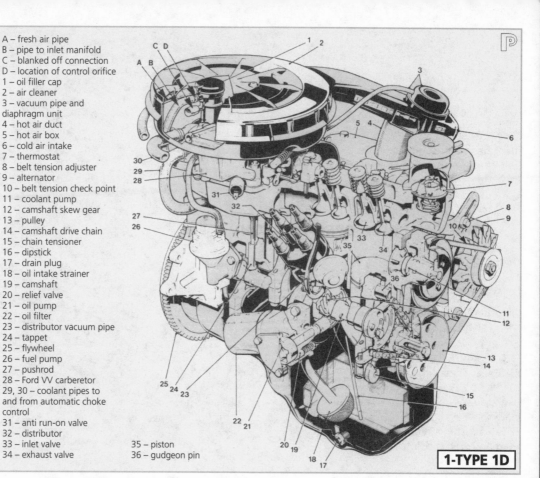

1-TYPE 1D

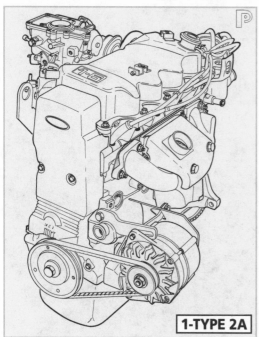

1-TYPE 2A

❏ **TYPE 2B:** All versions of this engine have a light alloy cross-flow cylinder head (**19**), cast iron cylinder block (**20**) and five main bearing crankshaft. Each cylinder has two valves, fitted at an angle either side of the single, centrally mounted camshaft (**4**) and operated by rocker arms direct from the camshaft. The camshaft is driven from the crankshaft by a toothed rubber timing belt (**13**) and the distributor (**3**) is fitted at the rear of the engine (left-hand side of the vehicle).

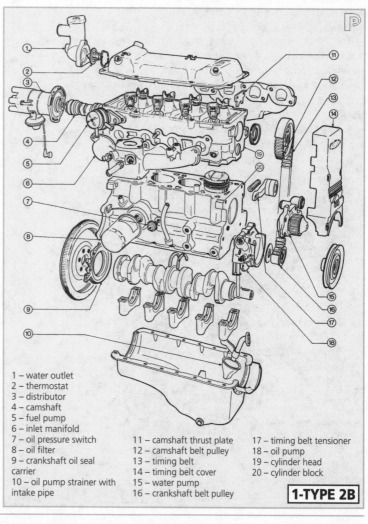

1 – water outlet
2 – thermostat
3 – distributor
4 – camshaft
5 – fuel pump
6 – inlet manifold
7 – oil pressure switch
8 – oil filter
9 – crankshaft oil seal carrier
10 – oil pump strainer with intake pipe
11 – camshaft thrust plate
12 – camshaft belt pulley
13 – timing belt
14 – timing belt cover
15 – water pump
16 – crankshaft belt pulley
17 – timing belt tensioner
18 – oil pump
19 – cylinder head
20 – cylinder block

1-TYPE 2B

☐ **TYPE 2C:** The engine can be identified by the light alloy cam cover and narrow plastic box-like timing belt cover.

DOUBLE OVERHEAD CAMSHAFT ENGINES

☐ **STEP 3A: ZETEC AND ZETEC E ENGINES:** These have a cast iron cylinder block with conventional main bearing caps and five main bearing crankshaft.

➜ Self adjusting hydraulic tappets are used on Zetec and Zetec E engines.

☐ **STEP 3B: ZETEC SE ENGINES:** These have a light alloy cylinder block with a 'ladder'-type main bearing assembly.

➜ The Zetec SE's main bearings must not be dismantled - if the big end journals or main bearings are damaged or worn, a new cylinder block complete with crankshaft must be obtained.

➜ Bucket tappets with adjusting shims are used on Zetec SE engines.

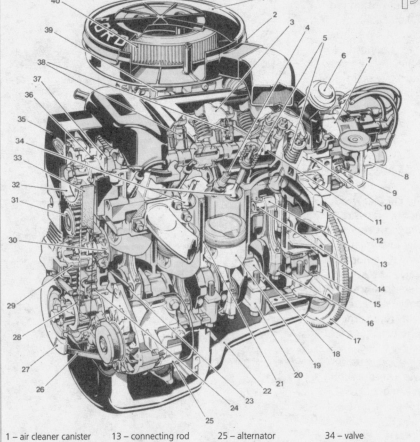

1 – air cleaner canister cover
2 – air cleaner canister
3 – rocker
4 – spark plug
5 – valve spring
6 – oil filler cap
7 – distributor
8 – coolant outlet housing
9 – thermostat valve
10 – cylinder head
11 – camshaft
12 – exhaust manifold
13 – connecting rod
14 – gudgeon pin
15 – left-hand oil seal
16 – big-end cap
17 – flywheel and ring gear
18 – crankshaft journal
19 – piston
20 – main bearing cap
21 – crankcase
22 – sump
23 – alternator drive belt tensioner strut
24 – oil pump
25 – alternator
26 – alternator drive belt
27 – crankshaft pulley
28 – crankshaft toothed pulley
29 – coolant pump toothed pulley
30 – coolant pump
31 – tensioner pulley
32 – camshaft toothed pulley
33 – camshaft drive belt
34 – valve
35 – cover
36 – camshaft oil seal
37 – camshaft thrust plate
38 – hydraulic tappet
39 – carburetor
40 – air cleaner element

1-TYPE 2C

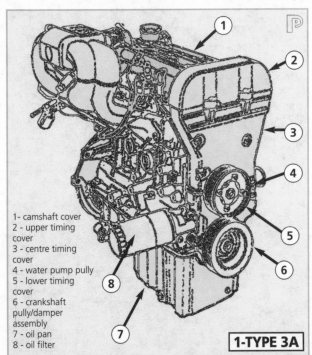

1- camshaft cover
2 - upper timing cover
3 - centre timing cover
4 - water pump pully
5 - lower timing cover
6 - crankshaft pully/damper assembly
7 - oil pan
8 - oil filter

1-TYPE 3A

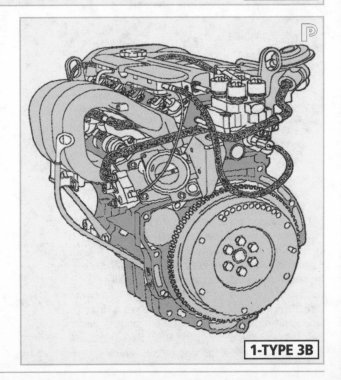

1-TYPE 3B

DIESEL ENGINES

❑ **TYPE 4A:** The diesel engines fitted to Fiesta, Escort and Orion models are 1.6 (1608cc) litre or 1.8 litre (1753cc) capacity. Both engines are conventional water cooled, four cylinder, in-line types with a five main bearing crankshaft and single camshaft mounted in the cylinder head. The cylinder head and block are made from cast iron.

Unlike the petrol engines described previously, the camshaft bearing shells are renewable.

1.6 LITRE ENGINES: On this type, the diesel injection pump is driven from the crankshaft via an idler gear, the gear housing also contains the oil pump components. The toothed rubber belt drive to the camshaft is taken from the injection pump and protected by a plastic cover.

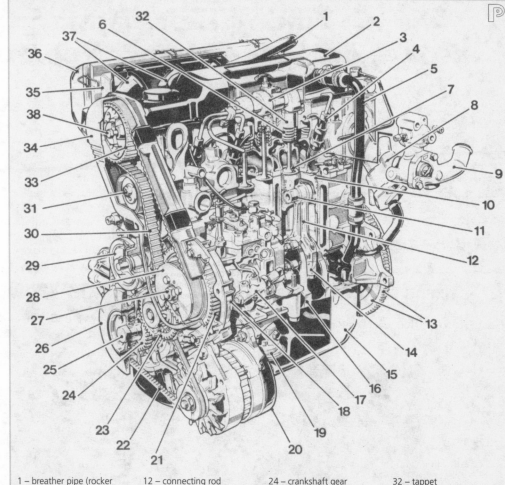

1 – breather pipe (rocker cover to inlet manifold housing)
2 – rocker cover
3 – camshaft
4 – injector
5 – breather pipe (crankcase to rocker cover)
6 – valve spring
7 – valve
8 – vacuum pump
9 – thermostat housing
10 – piston
11 – gudgeon pin
12 – connecting rod
13 – flywheel and ring gear
14 – big-end cap
15 – sump
16 – crankshaft
17 – injection pump
18 – timing casing
19 – gauze strainer
20 – alternator
21 – injection pump drive gear
22 – alternator and coolant pump drive belt
23 – idler (two-piece) gear
24 – crankshaft gear
25 – crankshaft pulley retaining bolt
26 – 'V' belt pulley
27 – injection pump drive nut
28 – camshaft driving toothed pulley
29 – coolant pump drive pulley
30 – camshaft drive toothed belt
31 – tensioner pulley torx bolt
32 – tappet
33 – camshaft driven toothed pulley
34 – toothed belt cover
35 – inlet manifold housing
36 – intake silencer/cleaner cover
37 – intake horn
38 – camshaft pulley retaining bolt

1-TYPE 4A

❑ **TYPE 4B:** The major differences on the 1.8 litre engine are the use of two toothed belts, again protected by plastic covers (**a**), and the external oil pump, driven by the auxiliary shaft.

➔ During production, the most significant change has been the replacement of the imperial threaded cylinder head bolts (hexagon heads) with metric thread cylinder head bolts (Torx heads). Another significant change was the introduction of a light alloy sump as on this Turbo version.

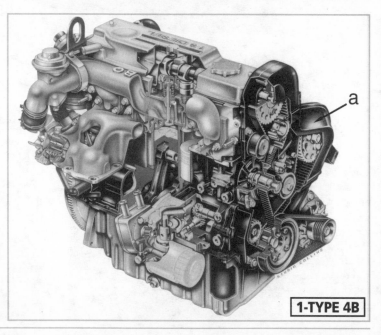

1-TYPE 4B

Part C: Timing Belt, Timing Chain Inspection, Adjustment, Replacement

CONTENTS

JOB 1: TIMING BELT - *check*.

TIMING BELT REPLACEMENT

→ It is ESSENTIAL that you renew the timing belt at the recommended interval. See *Chapter 5, Servicing* for replacement intervals - *Job 2* explains how to carry out the work.

☐ **STEP 1:** Before dismantling, disconnect the battery negative (-) earth/ground terminal. See *Chapter 10, Electrical, Dash, Instruments, Fact File: Disconnecting the Battery* BEFORE doing so!

1-2

☐ **STEP 2:** Remove the timing belt cover - see *Job 2*.
→ Replace the belt immediately if there are any signs of cuts, cracks, rubbing or contamination.
→ You should also make sure the teeth are in good condition.

1-3

☐ **STEP 3:** Turn the crankshaft in the normal direction of rotation so that you can inspect the entire belt length.
→ IMPORTANT NOTE: Do not attempt to turn the engine via the camshaft pulleys, always turn the crankshaft.

1-4

☐ **STEP 4:** You can carry out an approximate check of belt tension by twisting the belt through 90 degrees on the longest run between the crankshaft and camshaft pulleys.
→ This is only a very rough guide to belt tension and Ford recommend the use of a gauge (Part No 21-113) for checking the tension on Single Overhead Camshaft and 1.6 litre Diesel engines.
→ Belt tension on Double Overhead Camshaft and 1.8 litre Diesel engines is set by spring pressure.
→ See the relevant section of *Job 2* for all types.

JOB 2: TIMING BELT - *replacement, adjustment*.

ENGINE SAFETY FIRST!

• Serious engine damage can be caused if the camshaft or crankshaft are turned with an incorrectly fitted belt or without a belt fitted. Take extreme care during removal and refitting to ensure that neither the crankshaft nor camshaft is rotated and that the belt is fitted with the correct valve timing.

• If a belt has failed while the engine was running there is a very high probability of piston and valve damage. The cylinder head should be removed so that the pistons and valves can be inspected. Even if no damage is apparent, you should carry out a compression test of all cylinders to confirm that the valves are seating correctly.

Section A: Single Overhead Camshaft engine.

STEP A1: This is the layout of the timing belt on both CVH and PTE single overhead camshaft engines.

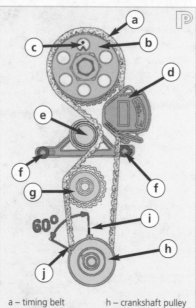

a – timing belt
b – camshaft pulley
c – TDC mark
d – Ford timing belt tension gauge
e – tensioner pulley
f – tensioner adjustment bolts
g – idler pulley

h – crankshaft pulley
i – TDC mark and position
j – mark on crankshaft pulley when turned back 60 degrees – see text

2-A1

STEP A2: Before dismantling, disconnect the battery negative (-) earth/ground terminal. See *Chapter 10, Electrical, Dash, Instruments, Fact File: Disconnecting the Battery* BEFORE doing so!

STEP A3: Remove the following:
➔ The air filter housing and air intake pipe.
➔ The alternator drive belt, idle air control valve and vacuum hose.
➔ The lower splash guard from inside the right-hand wheel arch.

2-A3

STEP A4: Take out the screws holding the timing belt cover in place.
➔ Depending on model, you might need to remove the washer bottle, coolant reservoir or other obstructions to reach the cover and work on the timing belt.

2-A4

STEP A5: Remove the timing belt upper cover.

2-A5

TOP TIP!

• Turning the crankshaft will be easier if you remove the spark plugs.

STEP A6: Turn the crankshaft in the normal direction of rotation so that No 1 piston is at TDC and the timing marks, being pointed out here, are aligned.
➔ Also, see illustration *2-A1*.
➔ Turn ONLY using the crankshaft pulley bolt (arrowed).

2-A6

STEP A7: Remove the crankshaft pulley – see *Part K*.

2-A7

2-A8

STEP A8: On later vehicles, remove the lower cover (screws arrowed).

STEP A9: Slacken the timing belt tensioner bolts, release the tension in the belt...

STEP A10: ...and lift the belt off the pulleys.

2-A9

2-A10

TOP TIP!

• Ford modified the tensioner pulley during production.
• Engines with the early pulley (pre-April 1988) should have the modified pulley fitted during reassembly.

STEP A11: Check the water pump (a) and tensioner (b) for signs of bearing wear or deterioration.
➔ The bearings should rotate without any signs of freeplay, binding or excessive noise.
➔ Replacing any suspect components now can save extra work in the future and the possibility of belt failure, which could result in serious engine damage.

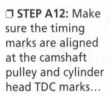

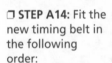

2-A11

STEP A12: Make sure the timing marks are aligned at the camshaft pulley and cylinder head TDC marks...

STEP A13: ...and at the camshaft drive belt pulley (A).

2-A12

STEP A14: Fit the new timing belt in the following order:
➔ First, to the crankshaft pulley, making sure the teeth engage correctly.
➔ Next, pull the belt vertically upwards on the side opposite the tensioner side.
➔ Make sure there is no slack and fit the belt around the camshaft pulley with the teeth correctly engaged.
➔ Fit the belt around the tensioner and water pump.

2-A13

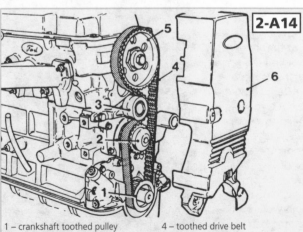

2-A14

1 – crankshaft toothed pulley
2 – coolant pump pulley
3 – tensioner pulley
4 – toothed drive belt
5 – camshaft pulley
6 – belt cover (one-piece shown)

□ **STEP A15:** To tension the camshaft belt note the following:

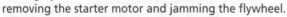

➜ Only tension the belt when the engine is cold.

➜ Prevent the crankshaft from turning by removing the starter motor and jamming the flywheel.

➜ Place a 41 mm socket extension and torque wrench on the camshaft pulley bolt.

➜ **CAMSHAFT:** Apply and maintain the following torque in an anti-clockwise direction. **1.3 LITRE CVH ENGINE:** 62 Nm; **1.6 LITRE CVH ENGINE:** 48 Nm

2-A16

□ **STEP A16:** With the torque figures given in *Step A15* maintained, tighten the tensioner bolts (arrowed).

➜ Check the alignment of the camshaft and crankshaft pulleys and if they are not properly aligned remove the belt and repeat the fitting sequence.

□ **STEP A17:** Some versions have a tensioner which has to be rotated in the direction of the curved arrow with an Allen key until the required tension is achieved at which point the tensioner adjustment (a) can be retightened.

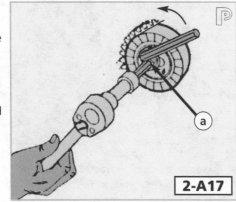

2-A17

□ **STEP A18:** These are the components of the camshaft timing belt (a) and fuel pump drive/timing belt (b) for diesel models with separate belts.

➜ Both belts will need to be adjusted – see *Sections D, E and F* for adjustment of diesel pump belt.

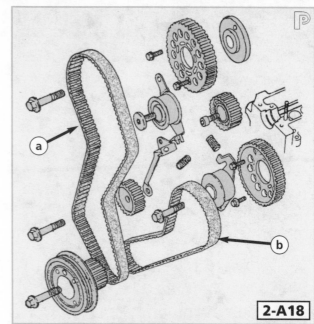

2-A18

□ **STEP A19:** For all models from the mid '80s Ford specify the use of a tension gauge (Part No 21-113) to ensure correct belt tension – see illustration *2-A1*. This is the Sykes-Pickavant timing belt tension checking tool – used with the belt *in situ* of course!

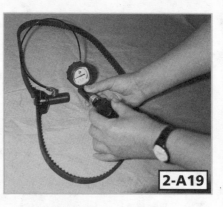

2-A19

□ **STEP A20:** Temporarily refit the crankshaft pulley nut.

➜ IMPORTANT NOTE: Turn the engine slowly and stop immediately if any resistance is felt. Investigate and resolve any resistance before proceeding.

➜ Turn the crankshaft slowly two full turns in the normal direction of rotation.

□ **STEP A21:** Now turn the crankshaft about 60 degrees in the opposite to the normal direction of rotation (approximately three teeth on the camshaft pulley) – see *Step A1*.

➜ Fit the tension gauge to the belt – see *Step A19*.

➜ A new belt should give a reading of 10-11 units (on the Ford gauge).

➜ IMPORTANT NOTE: Ford recommend that you do not refit a used belt.

□ **STEP A22:** Repeat *Steps A19 to A21*, slackening the bolts (*2-A16,* arrowed) and adjusting the tensioner position, until the timing belt is at the correct tension.

□ **STEP A23:** From now on reassembly is the reverse of the removal process.

➜ Make sure all nuts and bolts, particularly the crankshaft auxiliary drive pulley bolt, are tightened to the correct torque - see *Chapter 1, Facts and Figures*.

Section B: 1.25 and 1.4 litre Double Overhead Camshaft engine.

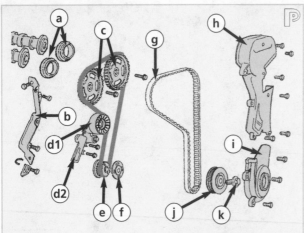

a – seals
b – cover bracket
c – camshaft pulleys
d1 – camshaft tensioner pulley
d2 – hydraulic tensioner – different types fitted – see Step B13
e – timing belt crankshaft pulley
f – attachment ring
g – timing belt
h – upper timing belt cover
i – lower timing belt cover
j – ancillary belt crankshaft pulley
k – crankshaft pulley bolt

2-B1

❐ **STEP B1:** These are the relevant components of the 1.2 and 1.4 litre engines.

❐ **STEP B2:** Before dismantling, disconnect the battery negative (-) earth/ground terminal. See *Chapter 10, Electrical, Dash, Instruments, Fact File: Disconnecting the Battery* BEFORE doing so!
➔ Remove the spark plugs or glow plugs so that the engine can be turned without compression.

❐ **STEP B3:** If necessary, depending on model, remove the washer bottle, coolant reservoir and any other obstructions.

❐ **STEP B4:** Support the engine:
➔ EITHER: From above with an engine hoist or engine-bay frame.
➔ OR: From beneath with a trolley jack or axle stands.

2-B4

2-B5

❐ **STEP B5:** Remove the following:
➔ The alternator/ mounting bracket.
➔ Camshaft position sensor multi-plug (when fitted)
➔ Injector multi-plug (when fitted).

2-B6

❐ **STEP B6:** Slacken the bolts holding the right-hand engine mounting in place and make sure that the engine support holds the engine in position.

❐ **STEP B7:** Remove the engine mounting bracket.

❐ **STEP B8:** Remove the upper timing belt cover.
➔ On later Zetec engines, the camshaft cover gasket is bonded to the camshaft cover.
➔ If you damage the gasket, you will have to obtain a new cover.
➔ Temporarily refit the crankshaft pulley bolt.
➔ IMPORTANT NOTE: Ford recommend that you do not refit a used belt.
➔ Remove the lower timing belt and auxiliary pulley cover (illustration *Step 2-B1, item i*).
➔ Take out the crankshaft pulley bolt (*2-B1, item k*) and remove the auxiliary pulley (*2-B1, item j*) with a suitable puller.

2-B7

2-B8

❐ **STEP B9:** You will now need to set the engine to Top Dead Centre (TDC):
➔ If you have the Ford timing

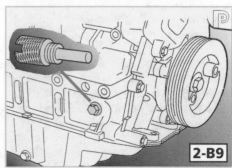

2-B9

pin (Part No. 21-210 – see inset) or an accessory alternative, such as the one available from Sykes-Pickavant, you can follow this approach.

➔ Remove the blanking plug from the right-hand rear of the cylinder block and fully screw in the timing pin.

➔ Slowly turn the crankshaft in the normal direction until the crankshaft rests against the timing pin.

❑ **STEP B10:** An alternative way of identifying TDC is to use a dial gauge.

➔ Remove the spark plug from No. 1 cylinder and rotate the engine in the normal direction of rotation until the piston is shown on the dial gauge to be at TDC.

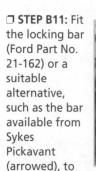
2-B10

❑ **STEP B11:** Fit the locking bar (Ford Part No. 21-162) or a suitable alternative, such as the bar available from Sykes Pickavant (arrowed), to the slots in the camshaft.

2-B11

➔ If the bar does not fit easily, first check that the slots in the camshaft are aligned correctly.

TOP TIP!

• Because the camshafts rotate at half the crankshaft speed it may be necessary to remove the timing pin or locking bar, turn the crankshaft a further complete rotation until it is once again at TDC and then refit the locking bar.

❑ **STEP B12:** On some versions, a different type of locking bar (arrowed) fits at the rear of the cylinder head in slots in the ends of the camshafts.

2-B12

❑ **STEP B13A:** If a hydraulic tensioner is fitted, use a clamp placed across the tensioner in the positions indicated and compress the tensioner until the holes in the tensioner are aligned.

➔ Insert a pin, such as a 1.5 mm drill bit, into the holes to lock the tensioner pushrod and remove the clamp.

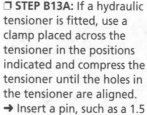

2-B13A

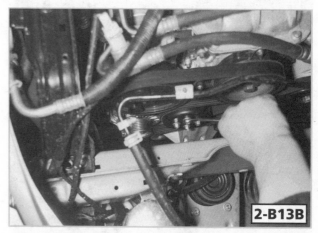
2-B13B

❑ **STEP B13B:** On other versions, you undo the fixing bolts and then turn the tensioner anti-clockwise to release the tension.

❑ **STEP B13C:** Some types have a single bolt for holding the tensioner tight and an Allen key hole in the tensioner – either 6 mm or 8 mm, depending on model.

2-B13C

➔ You slacken the centre bolt and use an Allen key to turn the tensioner anti-clockwise to release the tension.

➔ On all versions you can now slide the belt off the pulleys...

❑ **STEP B14:** ...and remove it from the vehicle.

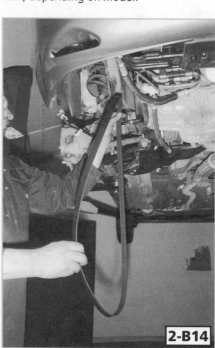
2-B14

TOP TIP!

• If you try to fit a new belt now, chances are that the teeth on the belt won't align with the pulleys on the camshaft.
• Place a bar through each pulley and, taking GREAT CARE not to put any strain on the camshaft and/or camshaft locking bar, and/or crankshaft locking pin, slacken the camshaft pulley bolts.
• FROM 1997: The camshafts each have a hexagon section on them so that you can hold them to prevent them from turning while you slacken the camshaft pulley bolts.
• Gently tap each pulley to break the taper but do not remove the pulley – the bolts should have remained in place.
• Each pulley should now rotate freely and enable you to locate the teeth on the timing belt.
• It is MOST IMPORTANT that you do not use the locking bar or TDC locating pin to prevent the engine from turning while the pulley bolts are being loosened.

2-B15

☐ **STEP B15:** Make sure that the tensioner is backed off and fit the timing belt.
→ Always start with the crankshaft pulley and work anti-clockwise fitting the timing belt to each pulley in turn.
→ With the belt correctly positioned, allow the tensioner to take up the slack in the belt.

☐ **STEP B16:** Setting the tensioner:
→ **HYDRAULIC TENSIONER:** No setting is necessary.
→ **SEMI-AUTOMATIC TENSIONER, 8 MM ALLEN KEY:** Turn the tensioner clockwise until the indicator is central with the rectangular recess. Tighten the tensioner bolt to the correct torque.
→ **SEMI-AUTOMATIC TENSIONER, 6 MM ALLEN KEY:** Turn the tensioner cam anti-clockwise until the cam is in the centre of the window. Tighten the tensioner bolt to the correct torque.

☐ **STEP B17:** Fit the following items:
→ The thrust washer and bolt guide (when fitted).
→ Timing belt lower cover and crankshaft auxiliary drive pulley. To fit the auxiliary drive pulley, use the old pulley bolt and a suitable washer and make sure that the pulley is fully seated against the thrust washer.
→ Fit a new crankshaft pulley bolt but don't tighten it at this stage until the timing location bar and/or pin have been removed.

IMPORTANT NOTE: The crankshaft pulley bolt should only be used once on these engines and once removed, should be replaced with a new bolt.

☐ **STEP B18:** Prevent the camshafts from turning (see *Top Tip!* after *Step B14*) and tighten the camshaft sprocket to the specified torque.

☐ **STEP B19:** Remove the timing pin and/or locking bar and turn the crankshaft just short of two complete turns.
→ Insert the timing pin and carefully rotate the crankshaft until it is against the timing pin once again.
→ Now make sure that you can refit the camshaft locking bar.
→ If the locking bar does not fit, loosen the camshaft pulley bolts and readjust the camshaft positions.
→ Repeat the check, rotating the crankshaft another two complete turns and when the adjustment is correct, finally remove the timing pin and locking bar.
→ Reassemble the remaining components dismantled earlier.

ENGINE SAFETY FIRST!

• Before starting the engine, turn the crankshaft through two more complete revolutions to make sure that there is no valve/piston interference.

• It is vital that you turn the engine slowly and stop immediately if any resistance is felt.

• Investigate and resolve any resistance before proceeding.

Section C: 1.6 and 1.8 litre Double Overhead Camshaft engines.

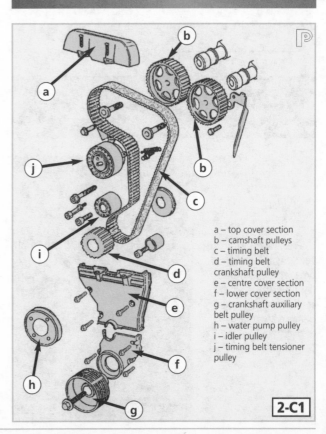

a – top cover section
b – camshaft pulleys
c – timing belt
d – timing belt crankshaft pulley
e – centre cover section
f – lower cover section
g – crankshaft auxiliary belt pulley
h – water pump pulley
i – idler pulley
j – timing belt tensioner pulley

2-C1

IMPORTANT NOTE: This section must be followed in conjunction with *Section B*. Most of the stages described in *Section B* are also applicable to this section, except where described here.

Before dismantling, disconnect the battery negative (-) earth/ground terminal. See *Chapter 10, Electrical, Dash, Instruments, Fact File: Disconnecting the Battery* BEFORE doing so!

☐ **STEP C1:** These are the relevant components of the camshaft belt assembly.

☐ **STEP C2:** Remove the following items:
→ Air intake pipe from the volume air flow sensor (VAF).
→ Coolant expansion tank.
→ Crankshaft pulley cover.

☐ **STEP C3:** Disconnect the following items:
→ Power steering sensor plug.
→ Power steering pump hoses.
→ Throttle cable.

☐ **STEP C4:** When dismantling, you will have to remove the water pump pulley (see *2-C1, item h*) after taking off the auxiliary belt crankshaft pulley.

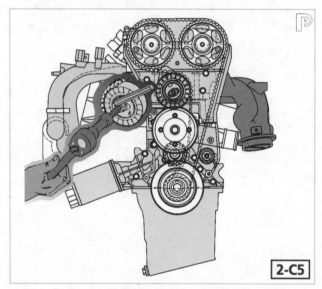

2-C5

☐ **STEP C5:** The timing belt tensioner (inset) is similar to that as described for the 1.25 and 1.4 litre engines using a 6 mm or 8 mm Allen key.
→ The timing belt also passes around an idler pulley, not fitted to the smaller engine - see (*2-C1, item i*).

☐ **STEP C6:** In September 1992, Ford introduced a modified crankshaft pulley with tensioner spring (arrowed) and bolt.
→ If the engine you are working on does not have the modified parts and suffers from an excessively noisy timing belt, you should obtain the necessary amended parts from your Ford dealership.

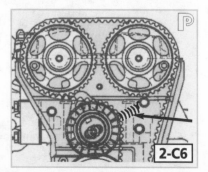

2-C6

Section D: 1.6 Litre Diesel engine.

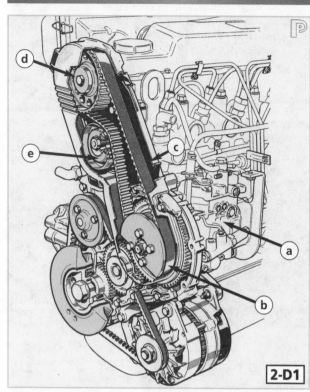

2-D1

☐ **STEP D1:** These are the relevant components of the 1.6 diesel engine. The injection pump (**a**) is gear driven by the engine. The drive sprocket (**b**) on the pump drives the timing belt (**c**) which rotates the camshaft sprocket (**d**). The belt adjuster (**e**) is dealt with later in the text.

☐ **STEP D2:** Before dismantling, disconnect the battery negative (-) earth/ground terminal. See *Chapter 10, Electrical, Dash, Instruments, Fact File: Disconnecting the Battery* BEFORE doing so!

☐ **STEP D3:** Remove the camshaft cover and the timing belt cover.

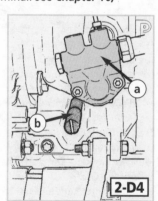

2-D4

☐ **STEP D4:** To align the injection pump timing marks:
→ Remove the blanking plug and screw the timing pin Part No 21-104 (**b**) into the cylinder block below the injection pump (**a**).
→ Slowly turn the crankshaft in the normal direction of rotation, about 50 degrees, until it contacts the timing pin.

☐ **STEP D5:** Make sure that the injection pump sprocket timing mark (**b**) is 25 degrees clockwise from the TDC timing cover mark (**a**).

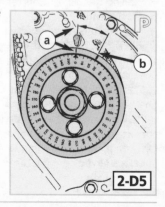

2-D5

❏ **STEP D6:** Make sure the slot (arrowed) in the rear of the camshaft is parallel with the cylinder head.

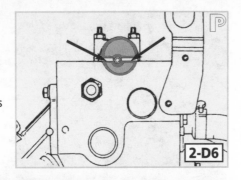

2-D6

2-D7

❏ **STEP D7:** Slacken the camshaft pulley bolt (**a**). Slacken the Torx headed tensioner bolt (**b**). Remove the timing belt.

❏ **STEP D8:** Before fitting a new belt, insert the camshaft locking bar (Part No 21-105) into the slot in the rear of the camshaft.

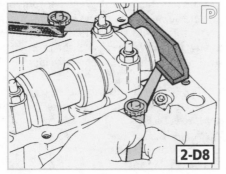

2-D8

→ Use a pair of feeler gauges to make sure the camshaft is centralised on the locking bar.
→ Check that the crankshaft is against the timing pin.

❏ **STEP D9:** Fit the new belt, making sure the teeth are correctly seated.
→ Make sure the camshaft pulley can turn freely on its taper freeplay.
→ Tighten the Torx headed tensioner bolt finger tight.
→ IMPORTANT NOTE: Belt tension should be checked when the engine is cold.
→ Attach a tension gauge to the belt midway between the crankshaft and camshaft pulleys on the side opposite the tensioner – see *Job 2, Section B*.

❏ **STEP D10:** Use an Allen key (**a**) to rotate the tensioner anti-clockwise until the tension gauge indicates 8.5 to 10.5 units. Tighten the Torx headed tensioner bolt to the correct torque - see *Chapter 1, Facts and Figures*.

❏ **STEP D11:** Tighten the camshaft pulley bolt to the correct torque.

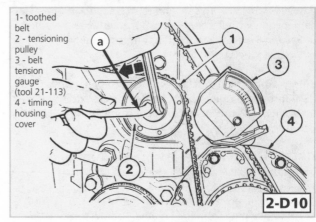

1- toothed belt
2 - tensioning pulley
3 - belt tension gauge (tool 21-113)
4 - timing housing cover

2-D10

❏ **STEP D12:** Remove the timing pin and camshaft locking bar.

❏ **STEP D13:** Check and adjust the injection pump timing - see *Chapter 9, Fuel, Ignition, Exhaust*.

❏ **STEP D14:** Fit the timing belt and camshaft covers. See *ENGINE SAFETY FIRST!* after *Step B19*

Section E: 1.8 Litre Diesel engine - camshaft timing belt.

FACT FILE

TENSIONER TYPES

• Depending on model and date of manufacture, the 1.8 litre diesel engine will either have an automatic or a semi-automatic belt tensioner.
• The semi-automatic layout has a tensioner pulley and guide sprocket while the automatic layout has a tensioner pulley and tensioner sprocket.

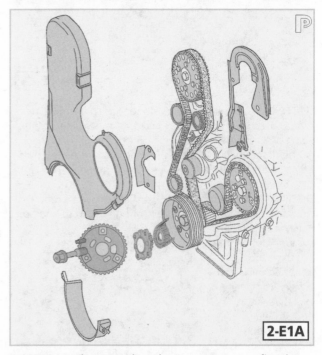

2-E1A

❏ **STEP E1A:** These are the relevant components fitted to the diesel turbo engine.

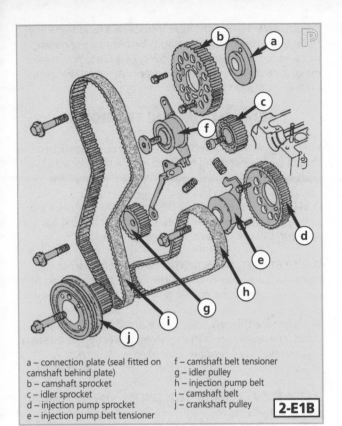

a – connection plate (seal fitted on camshaft behind plate)
b – camshaft sprocket
c – idler sprocket
d – injection pump sprocket
e – injection pump belt tensioner
f – camshaft belt tensioner
g – idler pulley
h – injection pump belt
i – camshaft belt
j – crankshaft pulley

2-E1B

❐ **STEP E1B:** These are the non-turbo engine components relevant to this section.

ENGINE SAFETY FIRST!

• **The camshaft and injection pump timing belts should not be removed until the engine is thoroughly cold.**

❐ **STEP E2:** Remove the following components.
➔ **ESCORT, ORION PRE-1996:** Remove the coolant expansion tank - see *Chapter 8, Cooling and Ventilation System* and, where appropriate, the power steering reservoir - see *Chapter 11, Steering, Suspension* - only disconnect the return hose.
➔ **ALL MODELS:** Auxiliary drive belts and tensioners - see *Part D*.
➔ Alternator cover (if fitted).
➔ Alternator and bracket (if necessary for easier access).
➔ Power steering pump pulley (if fitted to injection pump).
➔ Power steering pump (if necessary for easier access) - see *Chapter 11, Steering, Suspension*. The pipes and hoses can be left connected.

❐ **STEP E3: FIESTA FROM 1996:** Support the engine and remove the following components.
➔ The right-hand engine mounting.
➔ The crankshaft pulley bolts and the crankshaft pulley.

❐ **STEP E4:** Remove the upper timing belt cover...

❐ **STEP E5:** ...and the lower timing belt cover.

❐ **STEP E6: FIESTA FROM 1996:** Remove the injection pump timing belt cover.

❐ **STEP E7: ALL MODELS FROM 1996:** Remove the camshaft cover.

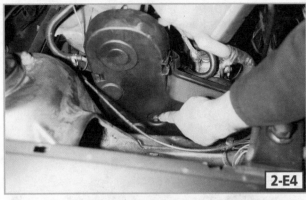

2-E4

2-E5

❐ **STEP E8:** Turn the crankshaft clockwise until the slot in the injection pump pulley (**a**) is in the 11 o'clock position (**b**) when compared with the TDC pointer (**c**).

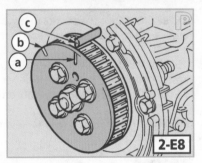

2-E8

❐ **STEP E9:** Remove the blanking plug from the cylinder block and insert the timing pin (Part No 21-104). See *Section D, Step D4*.

❐ **STEP E10:** Continue rotating the crankshaft until it stops against the timing pin.

2-E11

❐ **STEP E11: SEMI-AUTOMATIC TENSIONER:** Insert the timing pin (**a**) into the hole in the camshaft pulley.
➔ Insert the timing pin (**b**) into the hole in the injection pump pulley.
➔ On engines fitted with a CAV injection pump, insert a 6 mm drill. These are Sykes-Pickavant timing pins.

❒ **STEP E12: AUTOMATIC TENSIONER:** Hold the camshaft pulley to prevent it from turning (Ford recommend a special tool Part No 15-030-A), and loosen the camshaft bolt.
➔ Do NOT put any pressure on the timing pin.

❒ **STEP E13: AUTOMATIC TENSIONER:** Fit a locking bar (Part No 21-162B) into the slot in the rear of the camshaft and insert a 6 mm drill into the hole in the injection pump pulley. See *Section D, Step D6*.

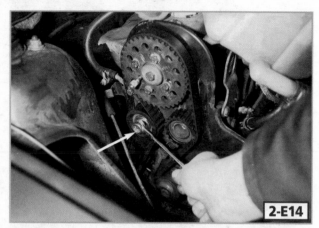

2-E14

❒ **STEP E14: SEMI-AUTOMATIC TENSIONER:** Slacken the tensioner bolts (arrowed) - one has a hexagon head, the other is a Torx type.

❒ **STEP E15:** Move the tensioner away from the belt and finger tighten the hexagon head bolt.

❒ **STEP E16: AUTOMATIC TENSIONER:** Slacken the tensioner bolt and turn the tensioner anti-clockwise.
❒ **STEP E17:** Remove the camshaft timing belt.

IMPORTANT NOTE: Ford recommend that you do not refit a used belt.

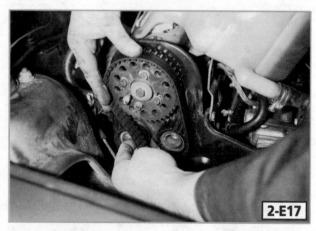

2-E17

❒ **STEP E18:** If necessary you can now remove the injection pump timing belt.

❒ **STEP E19:** Examine the guide sprocket or tensioner sprocket, as appropriate, and the tensioner pulley for cracks chips or other damage.
➔ Rotate these components, checking for bearing noise and smooth running.
➔ Check the tensioner components for any signs of damage resulting from earlier removal.
➔ Replace any suspect components.

IMPORTANT NOTE: Ford have introduce a modified lower timing belt cover which prolongs belt life by preventing dirt and debris entering the timing belt area. You should make sure that the improved cover is fitted by checking with an approved Ford dealer.

SEMI-AUTOMATIC TENSIONER

If the engine is equipped with a plastic guide sprocket, this should be removed and replaced with a steel sprocket (Part No 7053802).

❒ **STEP E20:** Make sure that the crankshaft is against the timing pin and the timing pins, drill bits or locking bar (as appropriate) are in place.

❒ **STEP E21: SEMI-AUTOMATIC TENSIONER:** Start at the crankshaft and, working anti-clockwise, fit the timing belt over the water pump pulley, guide sprocket and camshaft pulley.
➔ Make sure the belt is tight, any arrows or direction of rotation markers point in the normal direction of rotation and the teeth are properly seated.
➔ All the slack should be on the tensioner side of the belt.

❒ **STEP E22: AUTOMATIC TENSIONER:** Loosen the camshaft pulley from its taper.
➔ Use a drift through the hole in the timing belt rear cover or, if there is no hole, place a tight fitting metal spacer between the cover and the pulley and gently tap the cover with a soft hammer to loosen the pulley.

❒ **STEP E23: AUTOMATIC TENSIONER:** Start at the crankshaft and fit the timing belt over the water pump pulley, tensioner sprocket, camshaft pulley, tensioner pulley and auxiliary shaft sprocket.
➔ Make sure that any arrows or direction of rotation markers point in the normal direction of rotation and the teeth are properly seated.

❒ **STEP E24: SEMI-AUTOMATIC TENSIONER:** Slacken the camshaft pulley bolts, injection pump pulley bolts and the tensioner bolt by half a turn.
➔ Allow the tensioner to operate then tighten the camshaft and injection pump pulley bolts making sure the bolts are not at the ends of the slots.
➔ Tighten the tensioner bolts.

❒ **STEP E25: AUTOMATIC TENSIONER:** Use a suitable Allen key to turn the tensioner adjusting cam clockwise to the 9 o'clock position and tighten the tensioner bolt.
➔ Hold the camshaft pulley and tighten the camshaft bolt.

❒ **STEP E26:** Remove the timing pins, drill bits or locking bar as appropriate.

❒ **STEP E27: SEMI-AUTOMATIC TENSIONER:** Turn the crankshaft two turns clockwise until the injection pump pulley slot is in the 12 o'clock position.
➔ Now turn the crankshaft back until the slot is at 11 o'clock, insert the crankshaft timing pin and turn the crankshaft clockwise until it meets the pin.
➔ Insert the pins or drill bit in the camshaft and injection pump pulleys.
➔ Loosen the camshaft pulley bolts, injection pump pulley

bolts and tensioner bolts. Push the tensioner firmly against the belt and release.
→ Tighten the camshaft pulley bolts, injection pump pulley bolts and tensioner bolts to the specified torque.

☐ **STEP E28: AUTOMATIC TENSIONER:** Turn the crankshaft six turns clockwise until the injection pump pulley slot is at the 11 o'clock position.
→ Insert the crankshaft timing pin and continue turning the crankshaft clockwise until it meets the pin.
→ Slacken the camshaft pulley bolt, fit the locking bar to the slot in the rear of the camshaft and insert a 6 mm drill bit in the injection pump pulley.
→ Loosen the camshaft pulley from its taper.
→ Slacken the tensioner bolt and use a suitable Allen key to turn the tensioner adjusting cam clockwise until the arrows on the automatic tensioner pulley are aligned.
→ Tighten the tensioner bolt to the specified torque.
→ Hold the camshaft pulley and tighten the camshaft bolt to the specified torque.

☐ **STEP E29:** Remove the timing pins, drill bits or locking bar as appropriate.

☐ **STEP E30: AUTOMATIC TENSIONER:** Turn the crankshaft four turns clockwise until the injection pump pulley slot is in the 11 o'clock position.
→ Insert the crankshaft timing pin and continue turning the crankshaft clockwise until it meets the pin.
→ Make sure that the camshaft locking bar fits into the slot in the rear of the camshaft, the 6 mm drill bit fits into the hole in the injection pump pulley and the arrows on the automatic tensioner pulley are offset by less than 3 mm - repeat the tensioning procedure if necessary.
→ Remove the timing pin, drill bit and locking bar.

☐ **STEP E31:** Refitting the removed components is the reverse of the removal process. Make sure that nuts and bolts are tightened to the specified torque.

IMPORTANT NOTE:
• Before starting the engine, turn the crankshaft through two complete revolutions to make sure you have set everything correctly and there is no valve/piston interference.
• It is vital that you turn the engine slowly and stop immediately if any resistance is felt.
• Investigate and resolve any resistance before proceeding.

Section F: 1.8 Litre Diesel engine - injection pump timing belt.

☐ **STEP F1:** See *Section E, Step E1* for the components referred to here.
→ Before dismantling, disconnect the battery negative (-) earth/ground terminal. See *Chapter 10, Electrical, Dash, Instruments, Fact File: Disconnecting the Battery* BEFORE doing so!

☐ **STEP F2:** Make sure a timing pin (Part No 23-019) (arrowed) or 6 mm drill bit is inserted correctly in the injection pump pulley.
→ Remove the camshaft timing belt - see *Section E*.

2-F2

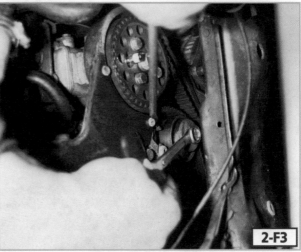
2-F3

☐ **STEP F3:** Slacken the tensioner bolt, lift the tensioner against spring pressure and tighten the bolt.

2-F4

☐ **STEP F4:** Remove the injection pump belt.

☐ **STEP F5:** Slacken the injection pump pulley bolts.

☐ **STEP F6:** Make sure the timing pin or 6 mm drill bit is fitted correctly in the injection pump pulley and the crankshaft is against the timing pin.

☐ **STEP F7:** Start at the crankshaft and work anti-clockwise fitting the timing belt. Make sure the slack is on the tensioner side and teeth are correctly seated.

☐ **STEP F8:** Slacken the tensioner bolt and allow the tensioner to operate. Tighten the tensioner bolt to the specified torque - see *Chapter 1, Facts and Figures*.

STEP F9: Tighten the injection pump pulley bolts to the specified torque - see *Chapter 1, Facts and Figures*, making sure the bolts are not at the ends of the slots in the pulley.

STEP F10: Fit the camshaft timing belt - see *Section D*.

JOB 3: TIMING CHAIN (OHV ENGINES) – *removal, replacement.*

It is well worth fitting a replacement timing chain and tensioner whenever an engine rebuild is being carried out.

Before dismantling, disconnect the battery negative (-) earth/ground terminal. See *Chapter 10, Electrical, Dash, Instruments, Fact File: Disconnecting the Battery* BEFORE doing so!

3-1

STEP 1: Remove the timing chain cover - see *Part J*.
➡ From the crankshaft, remove the woodroof key (a) followed by the oil slinger (b), noting the way it is fitted.

TOP TIP!

• During manufacture, Ford use a one-piece gasket for the water pump and timing chain cover.
• If the water pump is not being removed you can trim the original gasket back to the water pump and use a new gasket just for the timing chain cover.

3-2

STEP 2: Lever the chain tensioner (arrowed) back against its cam and slide the tensioner arm from its pivot.
➡ Turn the crankshaft so that the timing dots being pointed out here, on the crankshaft and camshaft sprockets, are next to each other.

TOP TIP!

• Aligning the timing marks at this stage is not essential but saves turning the camshaft and crankshaft separately later.
• Obviously, if the engine is being completely dismantled there is no benefit in aligning the timing marks at this stage.

STEP 3: Unbolt and remove the tensioner (engine now inverted).

STEP 4: On the relevant vehicles, note the way the camshaft position sender plate is fitted.

STEP 5: Hold the camshaft sprocket stationary.
➡ Bend back the lock tabs where appropriate.
➡ Remove the camshaft sprocket attachment bolts and, where fitted, the camshaft position sender plate.

3-3

STEP 6: Pull the camshaft sprocket away from the cylinder block and unhook the timing chain from the crankshaft sprocket.

STEP 7: Alternatively, pull the crankshaft sprocket off the crankshaft.
➡ The sprocket may be tight so you might have to use a suitable puller.
➡ You can also remove the Woodruff key (arrowed) from the crankshaft at this stage.

3-5

STEP 8: Thoroughly clean the timing chain and sprockets and inspect them for signs of wear or damage. Look for the following points.
➡ Check the profile of the teeth on both sprockets. The profile should be the same on both sides of each tooth. Replace the sprockets if the teeth are worn.
➡ Inspect the chain and sprockets for any signs of damage such as bent links or cracked teeth.
➡ Check the rubber on the tensioner spring and replace if grooved or showing signs of deterioration.

STEP 9: If there is the slightest doubt about the condition of the timing chain or sprockets we recommend that a new ones are fitted.

3-7

☐ **STEP 10:** If removed, fit the Woodruff key to the crankshaft. Make sure it is parallel or you may have difficulty fitting the crankshaft sprocket.

☐ **STEP 11:** Slide the crankshaft sprocket onto the crankshaft.
➔ Make sure the timing dot faces outwards.
➔ If the sprocket does not slide on easily, make sure the Woodruff key is fitted correctly - you can use the crankshaft bolt and suitable washers to pull the sprocket on.

☐ **STEP 12:** Fit the timing chain tensioner and tighten the mounting bolts to the specified torque.

☐ **STEP 13:** The face of the tensioner cam should be parallel with the block - Ideally, use a dial gauge to check that the cam is no more than 0.16 mm out of parallel at points 20 mm apart. Slacken and re-tighten the mounting bolts as necessary.

☐ **STEP 14:** Turn the crankshaft so that the timing mark is in line with the centre of the camshaft sprocket mounting flange.

☐ **STEP 15:** Fit the timing chain to the camshaft sprocket and then the crankshaft sprocket. Push the camshaft sprocket onto its mounting flange. If you are lucky, the timing marks and camshaft sprocket retaining bolt holes will line up.

You may have to remove and refit the camshaft sprocket several times, adjusting its position relative to the crankshaft sprocket slightly each time, to get the timing marks into alignment. As long as the timing marks align you can turn the camshaft slightly to align the bolt holes.

☐ **STEP 16:** On relevant vehicles, fit the camshaft position sensor plate to the sprocket.

☐ **STEP 17:** Fit the camshaft sprocket bolts and tighten to the specified torque.

☐ **STEP 18:** Turn the tensioner cam so that the tensioner arm can be slid onto its pivot - release the cam so that it presses the arm against the chain.

☐ **STEP 19:** Fit the oil slinger to the front of the crankshaft with the convex (domed) side facing the sprocket.

☐ **STEP 20:** Lightly oil the front of the crankshaft and the oil seal lip. Use a new gasket and refit the timing chain cover. Make sure that the sump mating surface of the cylinder block and cover are in line with each other and use the crankshaft pulley to help centre the cover while it is bolted on to the correct bolt torque.

Part D: Auxiliary Drive Belts Inspection, Removal, Refitting

CONTENTS

JOB 1:   'V'-TYPE DRIVE BELTS - *check*.

☐ **STEP 1:** Before dismantling, disconnect the battery negative (-) earth/ground terminal. See *Chapter 10, Electrical, Dash, Instruments, Fact File: Disconnecting the Battery* BEFORE doing so!

☐ **STEP 2:** Turn the engine slowly by hand and examine the complete length of the belt.
➔ Replace any belt that shows signs of cracking, 'polishing' on the surfaces of the 'V', fraying or severe wear on the inner faces - see *Job 2*.

TOP TIP!

• Turning the engine will be easier if the spark plugs or glow plugs are removed.

IMPORTANT NOTE: Ford recommend the use of a tension gauge for checking belt tension. The method given here is adequate for setting approximate belt tension - you should have the tension checked using the correct equipment as soon as possible.

❐ STEP 3: Check belt tension on the longest section of belt. Without using excessive force, the belt should

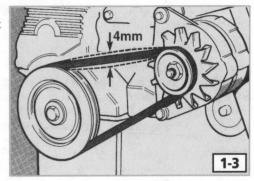

4mm

1-3

deflect 4 mm under finger pressure. If necessary, adjust the tension - see *Job 2*.

JOB 2:   'V'-TYPE DRIVE BELTS - *remove, refit, adjust.*

IMPORTANT NOTE: Do not overtighten the belt. Too much tension in the belt will result in premature bearing wear.

❐ STEP 1: Before dismantling, disconnect the battery negative (-) earth/ground terminal. See *Chapter 10, Electrical, Dash, Instruments, Fact File: Disconnecting the Battery* BEFORE doing so!

❐ STEP 2: 1.6 LITRE DIESEL ENGINES: Raise and support the front of the vehicle on suitable stands. Where fitted, remove the alternator splash shield.

❐ STEP 3: SLIDING ADJUSTER: Loosen the alternator pivot and adjuster nuts and bolts and push the alternator towards the engine.

❐ STEP 4: RACK AND PINION ADJUSTER: Loosen the alternator pivot bolts, adjuster mounting bolt and the pinion locking nut (arrowed). Turn the

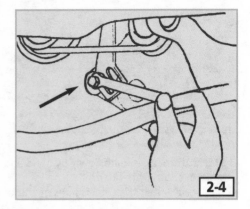

2-4

pinion nut to release the tension in the belt.

❐ STEP 5: Slip the belt from the pulleys.
➜ On some models it may be necessary to completely remove the adjuster to obtain sufficient movement of the alternator.

❐ STEP 6: Refitting the belt is the reverse of the removal process. You should be able to slip the belt easily over the pulleys.
➜ If the belt has marks indicating direction of rotation, make sure it is fitted correctly.

2-5

❐ STEP 7: SLIDING ADJUSTER: Adjustment will be easier if you partly tighten the alternator pivot and adjuster nuts and bolts - just enough to allow the alternator to be moved without being loose.
➜ If necessary you can use a lever to push the alternator away from the engine but take care not to damage the alternator case.
➜ Hold the alternator in position when the belt is at the correct tension - see *Job 1, Step 3* - and tighten the alternator pivot and adjuster nuts and bolts.
➜ Re-check and re-adjust the tension if necessary.

❐ STEP 8: To avoid the chance of damage to the alternator case you should tighten bolt (D) after tightening bolts (A), (B) and (C).

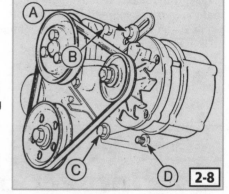

2-8

❐ STEP 9: RACK AND PINION ADJUSTER:
Rotate the pinion to take up the tension in the belt - see *Job 1, Step 3*. Tighten the nuts and bolts to the specified torque. Re-check and re-adjust the tension if necessary.

❐ STEP 10: New 'V'-belts stretch in use, so re-check and re-adjust the tension, if necessary, after 5-10 minutes of engine running and, ideally, again after 200 miles.

JOB 3:   'POLY' V-BELTS – *check.*

FACT FILE

• 'Poly' V-belts will be found on models manufactured after 1989/90. The length and routing of the belt depends on the engine type and whether the model is equipped with power steering and air conditioning.
• If a 'Poly' V-belt is slipping, the tensioner must be replaced - see *Part J*.

Follow *Job 1: 'V'-type Drive Belts, Check*, except for:

❏ **STEP 1:** While the engine is being turned, examine the drive belt pulleys.
➔ Check for security and replace any pulleys that are damaged or excessively corroded - see *Part J*.
➔ Make sure the pulleys are clean and free from dirt or debris - use a wooden or plastic scraper to clean out the grooves, do not use a wire brush.
➔ Make sure the belt is running centrally and evenly on the pulleys.

❏ **STEP 2:** On models with adjustable tensioners, check belt tension on the longest section of belt.
➔ Without using excessive force, the belt should deflect 4.0 mm under finger pressure.
➔ If necessary, adjust the tension - see *Job 4*.

JOB 4: 'POLY' V-BELTS – *remove, refit, adjust.*

IMPORTANT NOTE: Do not overtighten the belt. Too much tension in the belt will result in premature bearing wear.

TOP TIP!

• KA: On Ka models access to the belt is very limited and you will have to remove the right-hand headlight to gain access to the tensioner and pulleys.
• You may wish to raise the front of the vehicle to improve access the crankshaft pulley.

❏ **STEP 1:** Before dismantling, disconnect the battery negative (-) earth/ground terminal. See *Chapter 10, Electrical, Dash, Instruments, Fact File: Disconnecting the Battery* BEFORE doing so!

❏ **STEP 2: KA:** Remove the right-hand headlight - see *Chapter 10, Electrical, Instruments, Dash*.
➔ If necessary, raise and support the front of the vehicle.
➔ Where necessary, remove the crankshaft pulley cover.

❏ **STEP 3: FIESTA, ESCORT:** Raise and support the front of the vehicle, remove the right-hand front wheel and the auxiliary drive belt lower cover.

IMPORTANT NOTE: On some Fiesta models from 1989 to 1995, with the HCS overhead valve engine and power steering, you will have to remove the power steering pump drive belt before you can remove the alternator/water pump drive belt.

4-4

❏ **STEP 4:** The route of 'Poly' V-belts can be quite complicated, especially when air conditioning and power steering are fitted, so make a careful note or sketch of the belt routing.
➔ If you are refitting the old belt, you should also note any markings that can be used to indicate direction of rotation - alternatively, mark the belt with typists' correcting fluid.

❏ **STEP 5: MANUAL TENSIONER:** Loosen the tensioner centre bolt and turn the bolt on the adjuster bracket to remove the tension in the belt and lift the belt off the pulleys.

❏ **STEP 6: AUTOMATIC TENSIONER:** Using a suitable spanner, rotate the tensioner clockwise to release the tension in the belt and lift the belt off the pulleys.
➔ On some models, the tensioner will lock in the 'no tension' position.

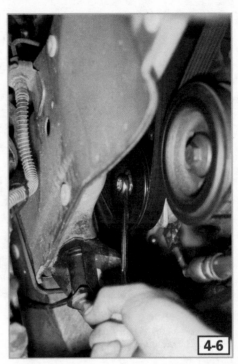
4-6

❏ **STEP 7:** Examine the pulleys.

❏ **STEP 8: AUTOMATIC TENSIONER:** Check that the tensioner appears to be working correctly.
➔ Where appropriate, unlock the tensioner by rotating anti-clockwise. Spring pressure should be strong and the pulley should move smoothly throughout its travel.

❏ **STEP 9:** Refer to your notes or sketch and fit the belt to the pulleys - if you are refitting the old belt refer to the markings indicating the direction of rotation. Make sure the belt seats correctly and evenly on each pulley.

❏ **STEP 10: AUTOMATIC TENSIONER:** If the engine has a locking tensioner, simply rotate the tensioner anti-clockwise, making sure the belt seats correctly then release the tensioner.
➔ Where a non-locking tensioner is fitted, rotate the tensioner clockwise and release the tensioner.

❏ **STEP 11: MANUAL TENSIONER:** Turn the bolt on the adjuster bracket to tension the belt - see *Job 3, Step 2* for the correct tension.
➔ Tighten the tensioner centre bolt to the specified torque.

☐ **STEP 12:** Use a suitable spanner on the crankshaft and turn the engine through several revolutions. Check that the belt is centred on the pulleys.

☐ **STEP 13: MANUAL ADJUSTER:** Run the engine for 5-10 minutes and re-check the tension.

☐ **STEP 14:** Refit the components that have been removed for access, tightening nuts and bolts to the specified torque.

Part E: Valve Clearances Checking, Adjusting

CONTENTS

JOB 1: VALVE CLEARANCES – *checking, adjusting.*

> **TOP TIP!**
>
> • If the rocker cover or camshaft cover sticks - which it frequently does - DON'T lever off the cover or you could easily damage the cover, gasket or cylinder head, particularly on Zetec SE engines where the gasket is bonded to the camshaft cover. Work the cover free, carefully.
> • Where the camshaft cover has a replaceable gasket, renew it every time the cover is refitted.

☐ **STEP 1:** Before dismantling, disconnect the battery negative (-) earth/ground terminal. See *Chapter 10, Electrical, Dash, Instruments, Fact File: Disconnecting the Battery* BEFORE doing so!

> **TOP TIP!**
>
> • Turning the engine will be much easier if you remove the spark plugs or glow plugs.

1-2

☐ **STEP 2: OVERHEAD VALVE ENGINES:** Remove the components listed below, undo the four screws and remove the rocker cover.
➔ **FIESTA AND ESCORT CARBURETOR MODELS:** Remove the air cleaner - see *Chapter 9, Fuel, Ignition, Exhaust.*

➔ **FIESTA FUEL INJECTION MODELS, KA:** Disconnect the crankcase ventilation hose, remove the oil filler cap and place it out of the way.
➔ **FIESTA FUEL INJECTION MODELS:** Remove the air inlet duct from between the throttle housing and air cleaner.

☐ **STEP 3: 1.6 LITRE DIESEL ENGINES:** Disconnect the crankcase ventilation hoses, undo the ten bolts and remove the camshaft cover. Note the location of the reinforcing strips.

1-4

☐ **STEP 4: 1.8 LITRE DIESEL ENGINES:** Disconnect the crankcase ventilation hoses, undo the ten bolts and remove the camshaft cover.
➔ On later engines, you will have to remove the oil baffle that is fitted over the camshaft.
➔ Undo the retaining nuts, remove the baffle and replace the nuts, tightening them to the specified torque.

1-5

→ Replacing the nuts is important as they also secure the camshaft bearing caps.

❑ **STEP 5: ZETEC SE ENGINES:** Lift the plastic flap and disconnect the crankcase breather - see *Chapter 9, Fuel, Ignition, Exhaust*. Undo the screws and remove the plastic cover which fits over the camshaft cover. Remove the camshaft position sensor wiring from the channel in the camshaft cover, undo the four bolts and remove the camshaft cover.

FACT FILE
ZETEC SE ENGINES

• The camshaft cover gasket on Zetec SE engines is bonded to the camshaft cover. If the gasket is damaged, you will have to obtain a new camshaft cover.

• The four rubber plugs fit over extensions on the camshaft bearing caps and care should be taken when refitting the cover. Damaged plugs can be replaced using a special installer provided with the replacement plugs.

❑ **STEP 6:** Use a suitable spanner on the crankshaft pulley nut (arrowed) to turn the engine in the normal direction of rotation and measure the maximum valve clearance as follows.

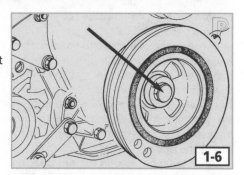
1-6

❑ **STEP 7: OVERHEAD VALVE ENGINES - CHECKING:** Turn the crankshaft until the timing mark on the crankshaft pulley aligns with the timing mark on the timing chain cover (arrowed)…

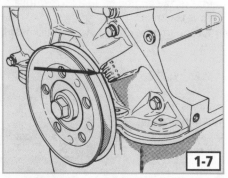
1-7

❑ **STEP 8:** …and the rocker arms on No. 4 cylinder are rocking – i.e.

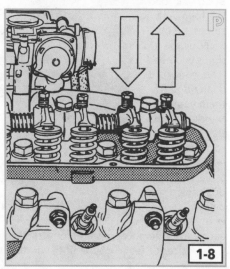
1-8

when rotation of the crankshaft in either direction will start the rockers moving in opposite directions.
→ If the rocker arms on No. 1 cylinder are rocking, turn the crankshaft through a further 360 degrees. Note that No. 1 cylinder is at the crankshaft pulley end.
→ Check the valve clearances in the following sequence:

Cylinder Valves	Moving Valves to Check
No. 4	No. 1
No. 3	No. 2
No. 1	No. 4
No. 2	No. 3

FACT FILE
WHICH VALVE IS WHICH?

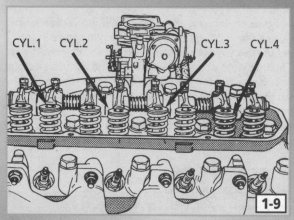
CYL.1 CYL.2 CYL.3 CYL.4
1-9

❑ **STEP 9:** • Make sure you use the correct clearance figure - the valve arrangement depends on the engine. Starting from the front (No 1 cylinder) end:
957 cc and 1117 cc Engines
CYL 1. Exhaust-Inlet; **CYL 2.** Exhaust-Inlet; **CYL 3.** Exhaust-Inlet; **CYL 4.** Exhaust- Inlet
1298 cc and 1598 cc non-HCS Engines pre-1989
CYL 1. Exhaust-Inlet; **CYL 2.** Inlet-Exhaust; **CYL 3.** Exhaust-Inlet; **CYL 4.** Inlet- Exhaust
1118 cc and 1297 cc HCS Engines from 1989
CYL 1. Exhaust-Inlet; **CYL 2.** Exhaust-Inlet; **CYL 3.** Inlet-Exhaust; **CYL 4.** Inlet-Exhaust

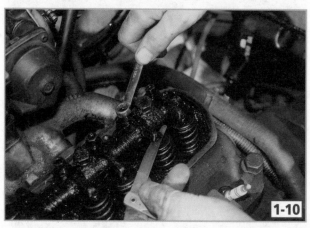
1-10

❑ **STEP 10: OHV ENGINES – ADJUSTING:** Insert a feeler gauge of the correct thickness (see *Chapter 1, Facts and Figures*), between the valve stem and rocker arm - the feeler gauge should slide in and out without being too tight or loose.

→ Repeat the procedure, making sure you check each valve and use the correct feeler gauge thickness.

☐ **STEP 11: DIESEL ENGINES - CHECKING:** The valve clearance is measured directly beneath the cam and must be checked when the high point of the cam (cam lobe) is pointing away from the cam follower.

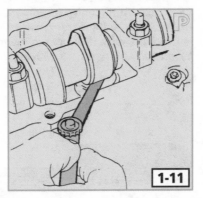

1-11

→ Turn the engine in the normal direction until the cam lobe on any valve is pointing vertically up.
→ Use a feeler gauge to measure the gap between the heel of the cam and the shim.
→ Make a note of the measurement and continue turning the engine until the next cam lobe is vertically up - this may be on a different cylinder so it is important that you make a note of the measurement.
→ Compare the measured values with the specified values - see *Chapter 1, Facts and Figures*.

FACT FILE

WHICH VALVE IS WHICH?

• From the No. 1 cylinder (crankshaft pulley) the valve arrangement is as follows:
Inlet-Exhaust; Inlet-Exhaust; Inlet-Exhaust; Inlet-Exhaust

IMPORTANT NOTE: If valve clearances have to be adjusted, turn the engine so that the pistons are well clear of the TDC position - this will prevent any risk of the valves contacting the pistons during the adjusting procedure.

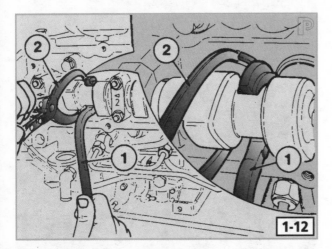

1-12

☐ **STEP 12: DIESEL ENGINES - ADJUSTING:** The valve clearances can be adjusted without removing the camshaft by pressing on the tappet to compress the valve spring and levering out the shim.
→ Ford have special tools - Part Nos 21-106 (1) and 21-107 (2) but it is possible to use a screwdriver and spanner.
→ Check the shim's thickness and select a replacement with a suitable thickness to give the correct clearance.

→ Some arithmetic is required to arrive at the correct shim thickness and it is worth checking your calculations - bear in mind that you reduce valve clearance with a thicker shim and increase clearance with a thinner shim.
→ See *Step 15* for an example of the process used to select the correct shim.
→ After adjusting all the clearances, turn the crankshaft through two complete turns and re-check the clearances.
→ Each shim has its thickness etched onto one of the surfaces.

☐ **STEP 13: ZETEC SE ENGINES - CHECKING:** The procedure used to check the valve clearances on Zetec SE engines is similar to the one used for diesel engines.
→ However, the cam lobes will not be vertically upwards because the valves are angled in the cylinder head - make sure the cam lobe is diametrically opposite the shim during checking and adjusting.
→ Note that there are two inlet and two exhaust valves per cylinder, each valve having its own cam.

☐ **STEP 14: ZETEC SE ENGINES - ADJUSTING:** Again the procedure is similar to the one used for diesel engines but, although it is possible to compress the valve springs and remove the shim without the correct tool (Part No 21-218) it is much more difficult.
→ The special tool bolts to the camshaft mounting bolts and a lever system used to press on the tappet. If the special tool is not available and you wish to avoid the chance of damage through using inappropriate tools, you can always remove the camshaft but this means removing the camshaft drive belt and re-timing the cams - see *Part C*. Bear in mind the following points when removing and fitting the shims.
→ Turn the tappet so that the slot is facing towards the centre of the engine - a small screwdriver can be used to lift out the shim.
→ Fit the shims with the etched thickness figures facing down.

☐ **STEP 15:** The following assumes that you don't have the luxury of a full set of shims in your garage. But if you follow the following stages, go out and buy the shims you need from your Ford dealer and fit them yourself, the clearances should be correct:
→ **a.** Make up a table, like the one shown below.
→ **b.** Measure

1-15

each valve clearance, pushing, or attempting to push in various sizes of feeler gauge until you find the right one.

→ **c.** You can now fill in the first column of the table, writing down all the 'Actual Clearance' figures you measure. You can also fill in the second column, using the information given in *Chapter 1, Facts and Figures* for your particular engine.

→ **d.** Write down the difference you will need to achieve the correct figure. (Go for the 'mid-point' when a 'plus or minus' figure is given. In other words, 50 mm plus or minus 5 mm, means 45 to 55 mm: use 50 as your 'target'.)

→ **e.** Take out each shim and write down its thickness in the 'Old Shim' column. The thickness should be shown on the shim; if invisible you will need to measure the shim with a micrometer.

→ **f.** You can now calculate the figure required to reach the recommended figure. If you need to achieve a different clearance, you will have to replace an existing shim.

Valve	Actual Clearance	Required Clearance	Difference	Old Shim size	Required Shim size	New Clearance
No 1 Exhaust	.43mm	.50mm ±.05mm	.07mm too small			
No 1 Inlet	.32mm	0.35mm ±0.05mm	Within tolerance			
No 2 Exhaust	.48mm					
...and so on:-						

Part F: Cylinder Head Removal

CONTENTS

Even in a manual of this size it is not possible to illustrate in detail every cylinder head variation. However, the basic principles of cylinder head removal are the same for all types and we have highlighted the differences between cylinder heads from the different engine families.

JOB 1:   CYLINDER HEAD – *removal*.

☐ **STEP 1:** Before dismantling, disconnect the battery negative (-) earth/ground terminal. See *Chapter 10, Electrical, Dash, Instruments, Fact File: Disconnecting the Battery* BEFORE doing so!

☐ **STEP 2:** Remove the spark plugs or glow plugs and rotate the crankshaft so that No. 1 cylinder is at TDC on the firing stroke - see *Part C*.

☐ **STEP 3: FUEL INJECTION MODELS:** Depressurise the fuel system - see *Chapter 9, Fuel, Ignition, Exhaust*.

☐ **STEP 4:** Remove/dismantle the following:
→ The HT leads.
→ The coolant and coolant hoses from the thermostat housing.
→ The rocker cover or cam covers and the timing belt as appropriate - see *Part E*.
→ The front of the exhaust system.
→ Note the positions and disconnect the electrical connections from the various sensors and switches fitted to cylinder head.
→ Where appropriate, remove sections of the wiring loom attached to the cylinder head noting the routing and method of attachment.
→ Disconnect fuel line connections, where necessary. See *Chapter 2, Safety First!*

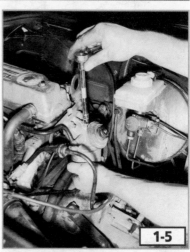

1-5

☐ **STEP 5:** If necessary, remove the fuel filter on diesel engines.

☐ **STEP 6:** The distributor on overhead camshaft engines.

1-6

❏ **STEP 7:** Where fitted, disconnect the oxygen (Lambda) sensor wiring and remove the heat shield from the exhaust manifold.

TOP TIP!

• On most vehicles you can remove the cylinder head either with the manifolds attached, or removed, according to choice.

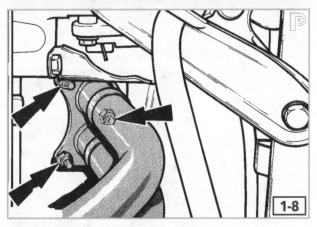

❏ **STEP 8: FIESTA, ESCORT, ORION:** Separate the exhaust downpipe from the manifold and support the exhaust pipe.

❏ **STEP 9:** If necessary and, where fitted, you can remove the warm air box from the exhaust manifold.

❏ **STEP 10: KA:** Disconnect the flange bolts attaching the catalytic converter to the exhaust system and remove the mounting bolt attaching the catalytic converter to the transmission. Support the exhaust pipe.

IMPORTANT NOTE:
• Exhaust flange gaskets and self locking nuts should be discarded and new items fitted during re-assembly.
• Where a flexible section is fitted in the exhaust pipe, make sure that the exhaust pipe is properly supported and the flexible section does not bend excessively

❏ **STEP 11:** Remove the securing nuts...

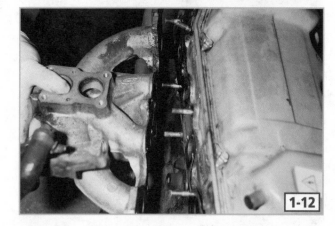

❏ **STEP 12:** ...and slide the exhaust manifold (attached to the catalytic converter where appropriate) off the cylinder head studs.

❏ **STEP 13: FIESTA - FROM 1995: KA:** Remove the support bolt (arrowed) and move the dipstick away from the cylinder head.

❏ **STEP 14: FIESTA, ESCORT - PULSE AIR SYSTEM:** On vehicles fitted with a pulse air system, remove the piping and filter. See *Chapter 9, Fuel, Ignition, Exhaust* for details.

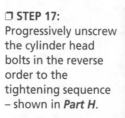

☐ **STEP 17:** Progressively unscrew the cylinder head bolts in the reverse order to the tightening sequence – shown in *Part H*.

☐ **STEP 15: FIESTA - FROM 1995, KA:** Support the engine so that the weight is removed from the right-hand mounting.
→ Disconnect the wiring, where necessary, remove the alternator and separate the mounting.

☐ **STEP 16: OVERHEAD VALVE ENGINES:** Remove the four bolts (arrowed) and lift the rocker assembly away from the cylinder head. Lift out the pushrods and mark or store them so that they can be refitted in their original positions.

ENGINE SAFETY FIRST!

• Light alloy cylinder heads distort if the cylinder head bolts are loosened before the engine is completely cold.

• Cylinder head bolts may be re-used once. You should mark the bolts with paint or, more permanently, with a punch to indicate that they have been used.

☐ **STEP 18:** Lift the cylinder head clear of the engine.
→ If the cylinder head is 'stuck' do not use a lever between the cylinder head and block. See *Part A, Job 6* for useful information on separating cylinder heads.

☐ **STEP 19:** Clean all traces of the old cylinder head gasket, scraping from the top face of the cylinder block and head.
→ Take care not to gouge or damage either face.

Part G: Cylinder Head Dismantling, Overhaul

CONTENTS

TOP TIP!

• If you decide to fit an exchange cylinder head, remember to remove all the ancillary components such as temperature sensors and even studs from the old one. They will be needed on the new cylinder head.

VALVES AND VALVE GUIDES

• Some cylinder heads have replaceable valve guides while on others, Ford have specified the use of valves with oversize stems.

• Where Ford have specified the use of oversize valves, it is necessary to ream the valve guides to accept the new valves and then re-cut the valve seats. On certain early overhead valve cylinder heads, replacement valve guides are available but special boring equipment is needed to prepare the cylinder head. In all cases where valve guides are replaceable, specialist press equipment is needed to fit the valve guides to the cylinder head, the valve seats will also have to be re-cut.

JOB 1:   OVERHEAD VALVE CYLINDER HEAD.

DISMANTLING

1-1

☐ **STEP 1:** If not already removed, separate the inlet and exhaust manifolds - see *Chapter 9, Fuel, Ignition, Exhaust* for specific information.
➜ Take off the four nuts holding the rocker gear in place.

1-2

☐ **STEP 2:** Remove the rocker gear - see *Part F, Job 1, Step 16.*
➜ If necessary, the rocker shaft can be dismantled for checking - make sure you can identify the components so they can be refitted in their original locations, if serviceable.
➜ Remove the split pin, spring and washer at one end (**a**) and slide the components off the shaft.

➜ Tight rocker supports should be removed by tapping with a soft-faced hammer.
➜ Check the rocker shaft and rocker bores for wear.
➜ Check the pads on the rockers (**b**) where they bear against the valves. They should be smooth - replace any rockers that show signs of unevenness.

OVERHAUL

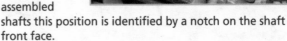

☐ **STEP 3:** Reassembling the rocker shaft is the reverse of the removal process.
➜ Make sure that the components are thoroughly lubricated.
➜ Check that the oil bores for rocker lubrication face downwards to the front - on assembled

1-3

shafts this position is identified by a notch on the shaft front face.
➜ Make sure that new rocker shafts are fitted with end plugs.

☐ **STEP 4:** Thoroughly clean the cylinder head removing all traces of oil, gasket and carbon deposit - see *Part A* for general guidance on cleaning.

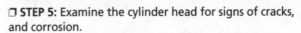

1-5

☐ **STEP 5:** Examine the cylinder head for signs of cracks, and corrosion.
➜ Cracks can sometimes be repaired but we recommend replacement.
➜ Corrosion will weaken the cylinder head and can occur from the inside out, especially if corrosion inhibiting anti-freeze has not been used.
➜ Look for signs of leakage at core plugs - these can be replaced but corrosion may have damaged the seats.

☐ **STEP 6:** Remove the valves - keep them in their original sequence until you have decided whether to re-use or replace.
➜ The procedure is similar to the single overhead camshaft cylinder head - see *Job 2, Steps 15 and 16.*

➜ Check the valves and valve guides for wear, check the condition of the valve seats and the mating surfaces on the valves - see *Part A*.

☐ **STEP 7:** Check the valve springs - see *Part A*. Fit new valve springs if the engine has covered more than 50,000 miles.

☐ **STEP 8:** Check the face of the cylinder head for distortion - see *Part A*.

☐ **STEP 9:** Check the straightness of the pushrods by rolling each rod along a flat surface - straight rods should roll evenly. Replace any that show the slightest sign of being bent.

☐ **STEP 10:** Reassembly is the reverse of the removal process. Fit new valve stem oil seals taking care to prevent damage to the seals during reassembly.
➜ If new valves/valve guides have been fitted, re-cut the valve seats and grind in the valves - see *Part A*. Tighten all nuts and bolts to the specified torque.

JOB 2: SINGLE OVERHEAD CAMSHAFT CYLINDER HEAD.

☐ **STEP 1:** If not already removed, separate the inlet and exhaust manifolds - see *Chapter 9, Fuel, Ignition, Exhaust* for specific information.

☐ **STEP 2:** Remove the camshaft pulley.

☐ **STEP 3:** Undo the bolts...

☐ **STEP 4:** ...and remove the camshaft thrust plate.

☐ **STEP 5:** Remove the distributor, if not already removed. See *Part F, Step 10*.

☐ **STEP 6:** Remove the fuel pump - see *Chapter 9, Fuel, Ignition, Exhaust*.

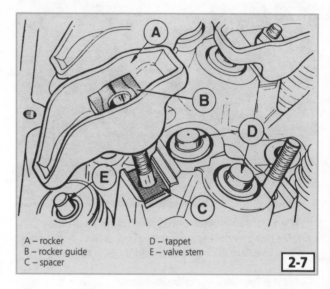

A – rocker
B – rocker guide
C – spacer
D – tappet
E – valve stem

2-7

☐ **STEP 7:** Unbolt the rocker arms.

☐ **STEP 8:** Remove the rocker arms.

STEP 9: Remove the hydraulic tappets. Keep these in order until they have been cleaned and checked for wear.

STEP 10: Remove the camshaft oil seal. The seal will be damaged during removal so make sure you have a new seal available.
➜ Slide out the camshaft, taking care to prevent the cams damaging the bearing surfaces in the cylinder head.

2-9

2-10

STEP 11: If not already done, thoroughly clean the cylinder head removing all traces of oil, gasket and carbon deposit. See *Part A* for general guidance on cleaning.

STEP 12: Examine the cylinder head for signs of cracks, and corrosion - see *Job 1, Step 5*.

STEP 13: Check the face of the cylinder head for distortion - see *Part A*.

STEP 14: Check the camshaft bearings and cams for wear - see *Chapter 1, Facts and Figures*.

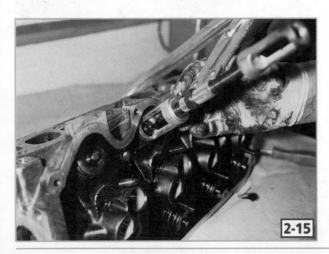
2-15

STEP 15: Remove and check the valves and valve springs.
➜ You will need to use a valve spring compressor with a long reach, such as this Sykes-Pickavant type.

STEP 16: Remove the valves and springs...

2-16

STEP 17: ...and the valve seat inserts.

STEP 18: Reassembly is the reverse of the dismantling process.

2-17

JOB 3:   DOUBLE OVERHEAD CAMSHAFT CYLINDER HEAD.

TOP TIP!

• **MANUALLY ADJUSTED TAPPETS:** Before removing the camshafts, check and record the valve clearances.
• If the camshafts and bearings are found to be serviceable, you will have saved yourself the effort of reassembling these components later, just to check the clearances.

STEP 1: If not already removed, separate the inlet and exhaust manifolds - see *Chapter 9, Fuel, Ignition, Exhaust* for specific information.

STEP 2: Remove the camshaft pulleys. Hold each pulley and undo

3-2

the Torx headed centre bolt. The pulleys are interchangeable.

3-3

□ **STEP 3:** Remove the camshaft bearing caps:
→ Take off caps 1, 3 and 5 without undoing 2 or 4.
→ You can now undo the remaining four bolts, progressively by half a turn at a time.
→ Slacken these four camshaft bearing caps progressively to release the tension in the valve springs.

□ **STEP 4:** Note the markings and remove the bearing caps.
→ Each cap should be marked with a number and letter, 'I' for inlet and 'E' for exhaust, but the markings may not be clear so you may have to make your own marks.
→ The camshafts run directly in the bearing caps and cylinder head so it is important to make sure the caps can be refitted in their correct location.

> ## TOP TIP!
> □ **STEP 5: ZETEC SE ENGINES:** • Note the depth of the oil seal so that the replacement can be fitted in the same position.
> • You can lever out the oil seal, taking care not to damage the camshaft or oil seal mating surfaces or remove the seal once the bearing cap has been removed - new seals should be fitted during reassembly.

□ **STEP 6:** Remove the oil seals (arrowed).

□ **STEP 7:** Lift off the camshafts. The camshafts can be identified by the lugs for the camshaft position sensor - exhaust camshaft on Zetec SE and inlet camshaft on Zetec and Zetec E.

□ **STEP 8:** Use a rubber sucker, such as a valve grinding tool (see *Job 4, Step 8*), and remove the tappets.

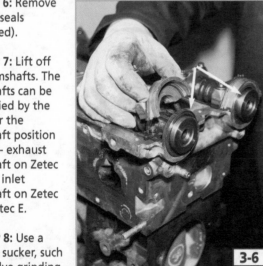

3-6

→ Store them in such a way that they can be refitted to their original location.

3-7

□ **STEP 9:** Examine each camshaft and tappet for signs of damage such as scoring, pitting or overheating.
→ Measure the tappets, checking for signs of ovality, and the camshaft lobes and bearings, checking for wear – replace if necessary.

□ **STEP 10:** Thoroughly clean the cylinder head removing all traces of oil, gasket and carbon deposit - see *Part A* for general guidance on cleaning.

□ **STEP 11:** Check the face of the cylinder head for distortion - see *Part A*.

□ **STEP 12:** Examine the camshaft bearing surfaces in the cylinder head, refit the bearing caps and check the bearing dimensions. If the bearing surfaces are damaged or worn, a new cylinder head must be obtained.

□ **STEP 13:** Remove the valves – see *Job 2, Step 15*.
→ Check the valves for wear - see *Job 1, Steps 6 and 7*.

> ## TOP TIP!
> • Ford specify a special tool (Part No 21-160), which allows easy removal of the lower valve spring seats and oil seals without damaging the cylinder head.
> • A suitable diameter spring can be used as an alternative.

□ **STEP 14:** You can now check camshaft end float by refitting the camshafts and bearing caps.
→ Tighten the cap bolts to the specified torque and push the camshaft as far as it will go in one direction.
→ Fit a dial gauge to the cylinder head with its pointer on one end of the camshaft.
→ Push the camshaft in the opposite direction and check the change of reading on the dial gauge - if the endfloat is greater than specified, fit a new camshaft and recheck.
→ Excessive clearance with a new camshaft head means a new cylinder head is needed.

□ **STEP 15:** Where appropriate, if the valve clearances were incorrect, check the relevant shim thickness and obtain a replacement shim that will give the correct clearance - see *Part D*.

□ **STEP 16:** Reassembly is the reverse of the dismantling process, bearing in mind the points in *Job 2, Step 18*, plus the following:

→ **MANUALLY ADJUSTED TAPPETS:** Fit the tappets and shims to their original bores. The tappets are a tight fit and must be square to the bore - do not use too much force.

→ **HYDRAULIC TAPPETS:** Make sure the tappets are fully charged with oil and they are fitted the correct way up. They are a tight fit and must be square to the bore - do not use too much force.

→ **ZETEC SE:** Apply a thin bead of sealant (Ford recommend WSK-M2G348-A5) to the mating surface of the No. 1 camshaft bearing caps at the oil seal end.

→ **ZETEC AND ZETEC E:** Apply a thin film of sealant (Ford recommend 'Loctite' 518) to the mating surface of the No 1 camshaft bearing caps. Fit the new camshaft seals at this stage - lubricate the seal lips and fit the seals into position with the outer edges flush with the bearing cap outer faces.

→ Fit Nos. 2 and 4 bearing caps and progressively tighten the bolts until the caps just contact the cylinder head surfaces.

→ You can now fit the other caps. Make sure the bearing caps fit squarely over the dowels and the seals are not distorted when the bearing caps are tightened. Wipe away any surplus sealant.

→ **ZETEC SE ENGINES:** Thoroughly lubricate the seals. Fit them over the camshafts and into the bearing cap with the closed end facing outwards. Using a suitable hollow drift, such as socket, press the seal into position to the previously noted depth.

→ Apply thread locking compound to the camshaft pulley bolt threads, fit the pulleys and timing belt, making sure the cams are correctly timed with the crankshaft - see **Part C.**

JOB 4:   DIESEL ENGINE CYLINDER HEAD.

❏ **STEP 1:** These are the components of the 1.6 diesel engine cylinder head.

→ If you have not already done so, remove the fuel injectors and glow plugs, vacuum pump and the inlet and exhaust manifolds. See **Chapter 9, Fuel, Ignition, Exhaust** for specific information.

❏ **STEP 2:** Undo the camshaft bolt and remove the bolt, washer and camshaft pulley.

→ You will have to gently tap the pulley with a soft hammer to 'break' the taper.

→ On 1.8 litre engines, the pulley is keyed to the camshaft so must be pulled straight off.

❏ **STEP 3: 1.8 LITRE ENGINE:** If still fitted, remove the baffle plate - see **Part E.**

❏ **STEP 4:** • Check and record the valve clearances.
• If the camshafts and bearings are found to be serviceable, you will have saved yourself the effort of reassembling these components later, just to check the clearances.

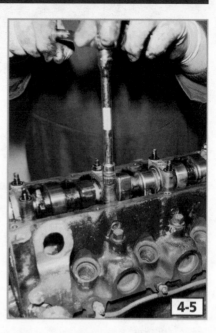

4-5

❏ **STEP 5:** Remove Nos. 1, 3 and 5 bearing caps and the upper bearing shells.

❏ **STEP 6:** Now you can undo the No. 2 and No. 4 bearing caps progressively, half a turn at a time to release the tension in the valve springs.

→ All the caps should be numbered and have arrows pointing to the front (pulley) end of the engine.

→ Remove the caps and store the caps and relevant shell so that they can be refitted in the correct location, if reusable.

❏ **STEP 7:** Lift off the camshaft together with its oil seal.
→ Remove the lower bearing shells and store them with the caps and upper shells.

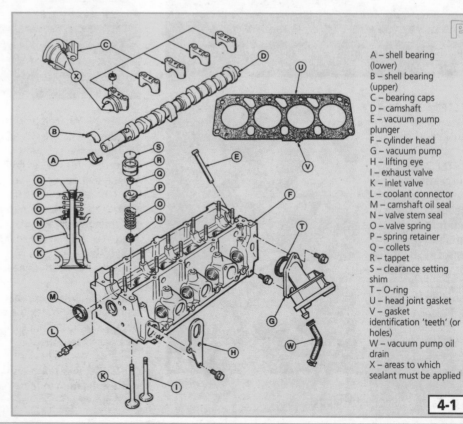

A – shell bearing (lower)
B – shell bearing (upper)
C – bearing caps
D – camshaft
E – vacuum pump plunger
F – cylinder head
G – vacuum pump
H – lifting eye
I – exhaust valve
K – inlet valve
L – coolant connector
M – camshaft oil seal
N – valve stem seal
O – valve spring
P – spring retainer
Q – collets
R – tappet
S – clearance setting shim
T – O-ring
U – head joint gasket
V – gasket identification 'teeth' (or holes)
W – vacuum pump oil drain
X – areas to which sealant must be applied

4-1

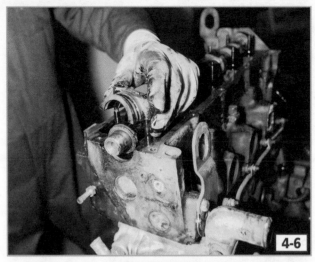

→ Replace any components that are damaged or found to be outside their tolerances.

□ **STEP 11:** If not already done, thoroughly clean the cylinder head removing all traces of oil, gasket and carbon deposit - see *Part A* for general guidance on cleaning.

□ **STEP 12:** Remove and check the valves for wear. See *Job 2, Steps 15 and 16*. You will need to use a valve spring compressor with a long reach.

□ **STEP 13:** Check the face of the cylinder head for distortion (see *Part A*), but note that the head cannot be refaced - a distorted head must be replaced.

□ **STEP 8:** Use a valve grinding tool, and remove the tappets.
→ Store them in such a way that they can be refitted to their original location.
→ If any valve clearances were incorrect when you checked them earlier, you will need to check the thickness of the relevant shim so that an appropriate replacement can be fitted - see *Part D*.

□ **STEP 14:** Check the valve seats and swirl chambers for burning and make sure the swirl chamber projection is within limits.
→ Valve seats and swirl chambers can be replaced but this is specialist work.

□ **STEP 15:** Refit the bearing shells, camshaft and bearing caps and check the camshaft endfloat - see *Job 3, Step 14*. If endfloat is excessive, fit a new camshaft and re-check the endfloat - a new cylinder head must be obtained if endfloat is still excessive.

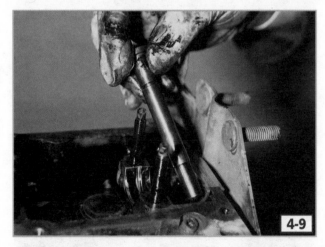

□ **STEP 9:** Remove the vacuum pump plunger and other ancillary components as necessary.

□ **STEP 10:** Examine the camshaft and tappets for signs of damage such as scoring, pitting or overheating.
→ Measure the tappets, checking for signs of ovality, and the camshaft lobes and bearings, checking for wear.
→ Note that standard or oversize tappets and shells may have been fitted during production - oversize shells have a green mark but tappets must be identified by measuring.

□ **STEP 16:** Reassembly is the reverse of the removal process, bearing in mind the points described in *Job 2, Step 18*, where appropriate.

Part H: Cylinder Head Refitting

CONTENTS

FACT FILE

GET YOUR HEAD STRAIGHT!

• Make sure the cylinder head and cylinder block mating surfaces are perfectly clean and flat.
• Even if the cylinder head appears to be within limits, it is a good idea to have it lightly skimmed (not diesels),by an engine overhaul specialist before reassembly.
• Refitting a head that has not been skimmed is likely to lead to a blowing head gasket.
• Distorted diesel engine cylinder heads must be replaced as the compression ratio will be raised too high if it is skimmed.

OVERHEAD VALVE ENGINES

➜ The rocker gear can be fitted to the cylinder head before or after the cylinder head is fitted to the cylinder block. There is no danger of the valves contacting the pistons, even if the camshaft is not connected to the crankshaft.

OVERHEAD CAMSHAFT ENGINES

➜ Camshafts can be fitted to the cylinder heads before or after the cylinder heads are fitted to the cylinder block but note the following.
➜ Make sure the pistons and camshafts are positioned so that valves do not contact the pistons when the bearing caps (diesel engines and double overhead camshaft engines) or rockers (single overhead camshaft engines) are fitted.
➜ SINGLE OVERHEAD CAMSHAFT: If the engine is fitted in the vehicle, you must fit the camshaft before the cylinder head is fitted to the cylinder block as there is not enough room to insert the camshaft with the engine in the vehicle.

JOB 1:   CYLINDER HEAD – *refitting*.

The following precautions will ensure that the cylinder head is fitted in such a way that the valves do not contact the pistons and the minimum adjustment is need to refit the timing belt.
➜ Turn the crankshaft so that No. 1 piston is approaching, but is still about 12 mm (1/2 in.) short, of TDC. On diesel engines, if you have not removed the injection pump make sure the No. 1 piston is approaching TDC on the firing stroke.
➜ If fitted, turn the camshafts so that they correspond to No. 1 piston TDC on the firing stroke. Place the cylinder head in position, and slowly rotate the crankshaft to the timing position, see *Part C* - no resistance should be felt.

Should you wish to fit the cylinder head without the camshafts, make sure they are fitted and tightened down in the position corresponding to No. 1 cylinder TDC.
➜ After fitting the cylinder head and timing belt, turn the crankshaft slowly by hand through two complete rotations. Stop immediately if any resistance is felt and re-check the settings.

FACT FILE

GASKETS AND BOLTS

• A cylinder head gasket may only be compressed once. After tightening, it loses its resilience and will not seal properly again. So, if you need to remove the head a second time, even if you have just fitted a new gasket and have torqued the head down, you will need to use yet another new gasket.

• Use all new gaskets for all applicable items, such as the cam or rocker cover, manifolds and so on. Note that on Zetec SE engines the gasket is bonded to the cam cover and is re-useable provided it is undamaged. On this engine, a damaged gasket means a replacement cam cover.

• Ford have specified different tightening procedures and limited the number of times that cylinder head bolts can be used. See *Chapter 1, Facts and Figures* for torque settings and *Step 8* for further information.

• Check the tightening procedure - some bolts have to be re-tightened after a period of running the engine while others, those that are tightened through a specified angle, do not.

• On diesel engines you will have to measure piston protrusion and select a gasket of a suitable thickness to give the correct compression ratio.

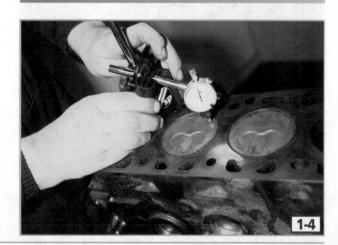

1-4

STEP 1: Check the cylinder head for cracks, especially around and between valve seats, and for distortion, using a straight edge and feeler gauges.

STEP 2: Check that all the cylinder head mating surfaces are thoroughly clean.
→ Ensure that the bolt holes in the block are free of debris and that the threads are free running.
→ Check that the pistons are cleaned and that there is no loose debris in the cylinders.
→ It is vitally important that the oilways are clean.

STEP 3: On one side of the cylinder head gasket is the part number, or the word "OBEN" or "TOP". This must be placed upwards, facing the cylinder head.

STEP 4: DIESEL ENGINES: Piston protrusion above the block at TDC must be measured.
→ In place of the Sykes-Pickavant dial gauge shown here, you could use a perfectly straight steel bar placed over the piston crown, and use a pair of feeler gauge sets to measure the parallel clearances between the block face and each side of the bar.
→ Measure maximum protrusion of each piston. If the values differ greatly, discuss the supply of a better matched set of pistons with your supplier and/or check connecting rods.

STEP 5: DIESEL ENGINES: Select and fit a Diesel engine gasket as follows:
→ The number of notches or holes indicates gasket thickness, which is selected to match piston protrusion. See FACT FILE right.

1-5

STEP 6: Make sure that the locating dowels (arrowed) are fitted to the cylinder head or block

STEP 7: OVERHEAD VALVE ENGINES: If you are fitting the cylinder head with the rocker gear in place, make sure you fit the pushrods before fitting the cylinder head.

1-6

TOP TIP!

• The cylinder head gaskets used on Zetec and Zetec E engines have teeth, similar to those used on diesel engine cylinder head gaskets, but in this case, they indicate engine size.
• Do not confuse the two completely different gaskets!

FACT FILE

GASKET - DIESEL ENGINE PISTON PROTRUSION

• Gaskets for engines with standard bores have notches, those for engines with oversize bores have holes.

1.6 LITRE ENGINE

Piston Protrusion (mm)	No. of Notches or Holes
0.430 - 0.620	1
0.621 - 0.680	2
0.681 - 0.740	3
0.741 - 0.800	4
0.801 - 0.860	5

1.8 LITRE ENGINE

Piston Protrusion (mm)	No. of Notches or Holes
0.500 - 0.680	2
0.681 - 0.740	3
0.741 - 0.840	4

TOP TIP!

Correctly aligning the cylinder head as it is lowered into place can be difficult, even where dowels are fitted. The following simple alternatives can make the job easier.
• Two old cylinder head bolts with the heads cut off, OR
• Two pieces of steel bar about 200 mm (8 in.) long and an easy sliding fit into the threaded cylinder head bolt holes, in the block.
• They will act as guides when you lower the cylinder head into position and keep the gasket in the correct place at the same time.

STEP 8: Refer to *Chapter 1, Facts and Figures* for the correct torque stages and settings for your particular model. Tighten the head bolts to their correct settings in the specified sequence, starting with the LOWEST NUMBER and working upwards, as follows:

OVERHEAD VALVE ENGINES

STEP 9: The tightening sequence is the same for all overhead valve engines but the tightening procedure varies.

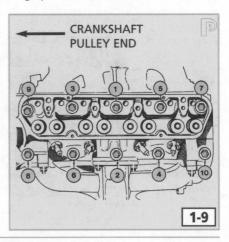

CRANKSHAFT PULLEY END

1-9

☐ **STEP 10A: UP TO 1989/90:** Cylinder head bolts should be tightened to specified torque figures in four stages with a wait of 10-20 minutes between the third and fourth stages.

☐ **STEP 10B: AFTER 1989/90:** A revised type of cylinder head bolt was used and this should be tightened in three stages - an initial torque loading followed by two tightening stages where the bolt is turned through a specified angle, see *Chapter 1, Facts and Figures* for torque figures and angles.

→ The revised type of bolt can be identified by the reduced diameter section between the bolt head and threaded portion.

→ Early torque tightened bolts can be used many times but later, angle tightened bolts, can only be re-used once.

SINGLE OVERHEAD CAMSHAFT ENGINES

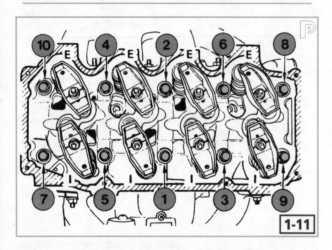

1-11

☐ **STEP 11:** The tightening sequence is the same for all single overhead camshaft valve engines and the bolts are tightened in four stages - the first two stages are to a specified torque followed by two stages of 90 degrees each. See *Chapter 1, Facts and Figures* for the correct torque figures.

→ These bolts must not be re-used, new bolts should be used during reassembly.

DOUBLE OVERHEAD CAMSHAFT ENGINES

☐ **STEP 12:** The cylinder head bolts used on all double overhead camshaft Zetec engines should be used once only, new bolts should be used during reassembly.

→ Three tightening stages are specified, the first two stages are to a specified torque and the final stage is through a specified angle, the figures vary so check *Chapter 1, Facts and Figures.*

☐ **STEP 13: ZETEC AND ZETEC E:** Tighten the cylinder head bolts in the order shown.

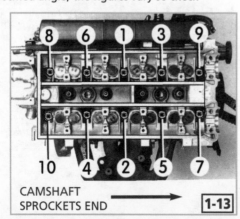

CAMSHAFT SPROCKETS END

1-13

☐ **STEP 14: ZETEC SE:** Tighten the cylinder head bolts in the order shown.

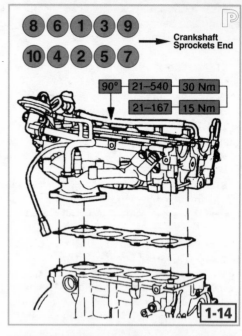

Crankshaft Sprockets End

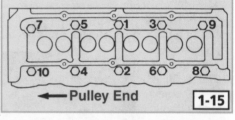

DIESEL ENGINES

☐ **STEP 15:** The cylinder head bolts on all diesel engines should be used once only. Three tightening stages are specified for 1.8 litre engines with imperial threaded bolts and 1.6 litre engines. The procedure for later 1.8 litre engines with metric bolts is complex and you should check the procedure in *Chapter 1, Facts and Figures*. However, the tightening sequence is the same for both engines.

1-14

Pulley End   1-15

☐ **STEP 16:** If the engine is fitted in a vehicle, you can refit the following:

→ Using new gaskets place the exhaust and inlet manifolds onto their studs and tighten to the specified torque, see *Chapter 1, Facts and Figures*.

→ The exhaust down pipe can now be reconnected.

→ Replace the carburetor or injection components.

→ Fit a new timing belt. See *Part C*

→ Reconnect all the remaining hoses, cables and wires to the cylinder head.

☐ **STEP 17:** Apply lots of fresh engine oil to each of the valve tappets, then replace the end seals and rocker or camshaft cover, where a cork gasket is used - DON'T re-use the old compressed one!

☐ **STEP 18:** With spark or glow plugs out, turn the engine by hand, slowly and with care, to check that there are no collisions between valves and pistons.

☐ **STEP 19:** Refill the cooling system with the correct solution of fresh anti-freeze solution. Check the engine oil level and top up if necessary.

☐ **STEP 20:** If the earlier type of cylinder head bolts are used (the ones that are tightened to a given torque figure, and not to the multi-stage torque-plus-angular tightening process) the head bolts should be re-tightened to the correct torque after about 250 miles of running.

Part I: Engine and Transmission Removal, Separation, Refitting

CONTENTS

JOB 1:   ENGINE AND TRANSMISSION – *removal.*

FACT FILE
WHICH WAY OUT?

• Most of the engines on most models covered by this manual are intended to be removed from underneath the vehicle with the engine attached to the transmission.
• Fiesta models from 1989 to 1995 and Escort models fitted with the HCS engine are the exception.
• This means that in most cases you will need to be able to raise the vehicle to allow room for the engine and transmission to be manoeuvred from under the raised vehicle. If you have limited equipment the main difficulty will be in raising the front of the vehicle high enough.

Section A: All engine types.

☐ **STEP A1:** Before dismantling, disconnect the battery negative (-) earth/ground terminal. See *Chapter 10, Electrical, Dash, Instruments, Fact File: Disconnecting the Battery* BEFORE doing so!

☐ **STEP A2:** Drain the engine and transmission oil.

☐ **STEP A3: BONNET/HOOD REMOVAL:**
→ Fiesta models from 1976 to 1989 have a forward opening bonnet and access for engine removal will be far easier if you remove it.
→ On Fiesta models from 1989 to 1995 and Escort models fitted with the HCS engine the engine can be removed from above, so the bonnet must be removed.
→ See *Chapter 13, Bodywork* for information on bonnet removal.

☐ **STEP A4:** Apply the parking brake and chock the rear wheels.
→ Raise and support the front of the vehicle so that you have access to disconnect and remove components from underneath.

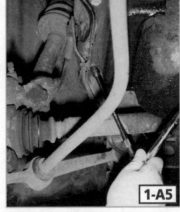

☐ **STEP A5:** On vehicles where engines and transmissions are to be lowered, remove the under-engine splash shields and drive belt covers as necessary.
→ Here we show the right-hand engine splash guard being removed from an Orion.

1-A5

1-A6

☐ **STEP A6: MANUAL TRANSMISSION MODELS:** Disconnect the clutch cable or the hydraulic connection (arrowed) from the clutch slave cylinder and the support bracket - the hose has a quick release connector.
→ Use a suitable hose clamp to reduce hydraulic fluid loss.

□ STEP A7: Separate the gear shift mechanism and stabiliser.

➔ MANUAL TRANSMISSION MODELS: Before disconnection, select the appropriate gear to ensure correct reassembly - see *Chapter 7, Clutch, Transmission, Driveshafts*.

➔ AUTOMATIC TRANSMISSION MODELS: Separate the electrical connector from the starter inhibitor switch (on the transmission).

➔ Disconnect the selector mechanism and disconnect the oil cooler feed and return pipes - see *Chapter 7, Clutch, Transmission, Driveshafts*.

➔ Use a suitable container to collect the hydraulic fluid spillage and plug the open ends of the connections to prevent the ingress of dirt or other contamination.

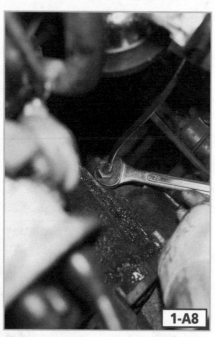
1-A8

□ STEP A8: Disconnect the speedometer drive cable from the transmission.

TOP TIP!
• We have indicated in the appropriate *Steps* where radiator removal is necessary for engine removal.
• Where radiator removal is not necessary, removing the radiator and cooling fan will improve access and reduce the chances of damage to the radiator and cooling fan.
• See *Chapter 8, Cooling, Ventilation System* for specific information on radiator removal.

SAFETY FIRST!
AIR CONDITIONING
• Do not, under any circumstances, attempt to separate or open any air conditioning hoses.

• If necessary, have an air conditioning specialist empty the gas from the system, then have them check and refill it when the work is complete.

□ STEP A9: AIR CONDITIONING: You don't always have to empty the system!

➔ FIESTA AND ESCORT MODELS: You can avoid disconnecting air conditioning components, and the need to extract refrigerant from the system, by separating the relevant components from the engine and securing them out of the way.

➔ KA MODELS: Ford recommend that you have the refrigerant extracted by a specialist and remove the dehydrator.

□ STEP A10: Drain the cooling system and separate the coolant hoses from the engine - see *Chapter 8, Cooling, Ventilation System*.

➔ The number, location and method of attaching the coolant hoses depends on the model and engine.

□ STEP A11: Disconnect the fuel pipes at the engine - see *Chapter 9, Ignition, Fuel, Exhaust*. See *Chapter 2, Safety First!*

➔ Again, the number location and method of attaching the fuel pipes depends on the model and engine.

➔ These are the quick release connectors on a Zetec SE engine in a Fiesta.

1-A11

□ STEP A12: CARBURETOR MODELS: Disconnect and/or remove the following:

➔ The air cleaner assembly.

➔ Disconnect the accelerator cable, choke cable (on vehicles with a manual choke), vacuum and breather hoses (where appropriate) and the electrical cables. See *Chapter 9, Ignition, Fuel, Exhaust* for specific details.

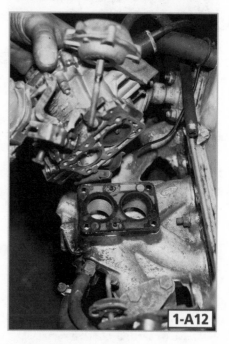
1-A12

➔ Although removing the carburetor is not essential, removal will reduce the chances of damage and improve clearance during engine removal.

□ STEP A13: FUEL INJECTION MODELS - PETROL AND DIESEL: De-pressurise the fuel system, where appropriate and disconnect the accelerator cable - see *Chapter 9, Ignition, Fuel, Exhaust*. On vehicles fitted with Central Fuel injection (CFi), removing the CFi unit is not essential but will reduce the chances of damage during engine removal.

STEP A14: B5 AND iB5 TRANSMISSION: Remove or disengage the transmission breather from the recess in the body - see *Chapter 7, Clutch, Transmission, Driveshafts*.

STEP A15: Disconnect the cables from the starter motor and alternator - see *Chapter 10, Electrical, Instruments*.
→ On some models, such as diesels, the alternator is reached from beneath.

STEP A16: Separate the driveshafts from the transmission - see *Chapter 7, Clutch, Transmission, Driveshafts*.

STEP A17: Disconnect and remove the additional model specific components detailed in the following sections. (See *Chapter 9, Ignition, Fuel, Exhaust* for specific details on ignition, fuel and exhaust system component removal.)

IMPORTANT NOTE: The number and location of the various pipes, cables and electrical connectors varies, depending on model, engine and year of manufacture. The following *Steps* are a guide and variations may occur.

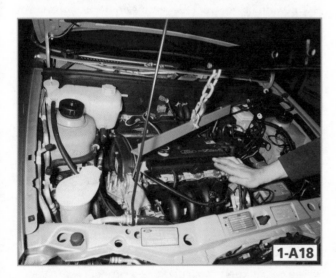

STEP A18: Attach a suitable hoist to the engine and support the weight of the engine and transmission on the hoist. This, for illustration, is the Clarke 'Strongarm' hoist attached to a Fiesta Zetec SE engine.

STEP A19: Unbolt the engine and transmission mountings - see *Part K*.

STEP A20: Have a final check around the engine and transmission to make sure that all the necessary components have been separated and there is enough space to manoeuvre the engine/transmission assembly clear of the vehicle.

STEP A21: Fiesta models from 1989 to 1995 and Escort models fitted with the HCS engine, lower the engine/transmission assembly then raise the front of the vehicle sufficiently to allow the engine/transmission unit to be manoeuvred clear.

STEP A22: Where appropriate, the engine and transmission are easily separated after removal - see the relevant *Steps* in *Chapter 7, Clutch, Transmission, Driveshafts*.

Section B: Fiesta 1976 - 1989.

Read *Section A* as well as this Section, and carry out the relevant work described there.

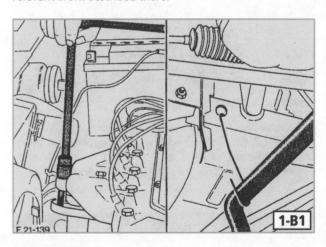

STEP B1: Separate the exhaust pipe from the manifold and its mountings.
→ Support the exhaust system so that it's out of the way or remove it completely - see *Chapter 9, Ignition, Fuel, Exhaust*.

STEP B2: Where fitted, remove the warm air box from the exhaust manifold - see *Part F, Step 12*.

☐ **STEP B3:** Disconnect the following electrical leads - see *Chapter 10, Electrical, Instruments* for specific information.
→ The oil pressure switch (below the distributor).
→ The temperature sender unit (below the thermostat housing).
→ On vehicles with temperature activated fans, the temperature sensor (at the thermostat housing).

☐ **STEP B4: FIESTA 1983 - 1989:** Remove the radiator and fan unit - see *Chapter 8, Cooling, Ventilation System*.

☐ **STEP B5:**
Disconnect the ignition coil negative leads - see *Chapter 9, Ignition, Fuel, Exhaust*.

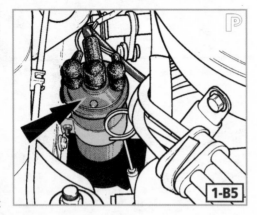

☐ **STEP B6:**
Disconnect the engine earth/ground strap from the front of the cylinder block.

☐ **STEP B7:** Separate the vacuum hose (vehicles with servo assisted brakes) and breather hose from the inlet manifold - see *Chapter 9, Ignition, Fuel, Exhaust*.

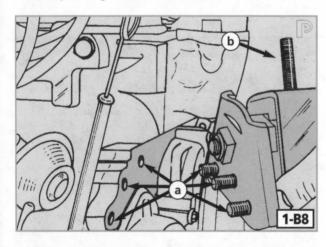

☐ **STEP B8:** This front mounting would normally have its studs (a) still fitted to the engine but be unbolted at the stud (b) from the vehicle.
→ See *Part K, Job 1* for full details on engine mountings.

Section C: Fiesta 1989 - 1995 with HCS engine.

Read *Section A* as well as this Section, and carry out the relevant work described there.

☐ **STEP C1:** Remove the air cleaner, if not already removed - see *Chapter 9, Ignition, Fuel, Exhaust*.
→ Disconnect the accelerator cable at the engine.

☐ **STEP C2:** Disconnect the brake servo and fuel trap vacuum hoses from the inlet manifold. The brake servo hose has a sleeve type quick release connector – see *Chapter 12, Brakes*.

☐ **STEP C3:** Disconnect the fuel supply and return pipes from the fuel pump or CFi unit. Release the pipes by pressing on the sides of the couplings and pulling the pipes away - see *Chapter 9, Ignition, Fuel, Exhaust* - watch out for fuel spillage. Plug or cover the open connections to prevent the ingress of dirt or contamination.

☐ **STEP C4:** Disconnect the following electrical leads - see *Chapter 9, Ignition, Fuel, Exhaust* for information on Fuel, Exhaust and Emission components and *Chapter 10, Electrical, Instruments* for general information on electrical components. (See illustration on page 6-51.)
→ The engine coolant temperature gauge sender unit (**ELEMENT 3**).
→ The cooling fan thermostatic switch.
→ The oil pressure switch.
→ The idle cut-off valve (**ELEMENT 4**).
→ The crankshaft position sensor (**ELEMENT 1**).
→ The DIS ignition coil (**ELEMENT 2**).
→ The radio earth/ground lead.
→ The wiring plugs from the sensors on the inlet manifold and the oxygen (Lambda) sensor on the exhaust system.

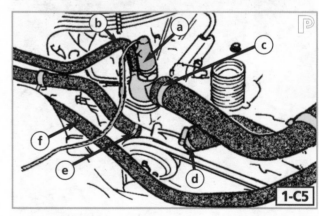

☐ **STEP C5:** Also, disconnect:
→ The engine coolant temperature sensor (a).
→ The hoses to/from expansion tank to thermostat (b); radiator top (c); radiator bottom (d); heater (e) and hose from expansion tank to radiator (f).

☐ **STEP C6:** Separate the exhaust downpipe from the manifold and remove the manifold heat shield - see *Chapter 9, Ignition, Fuel, Exhaust*.

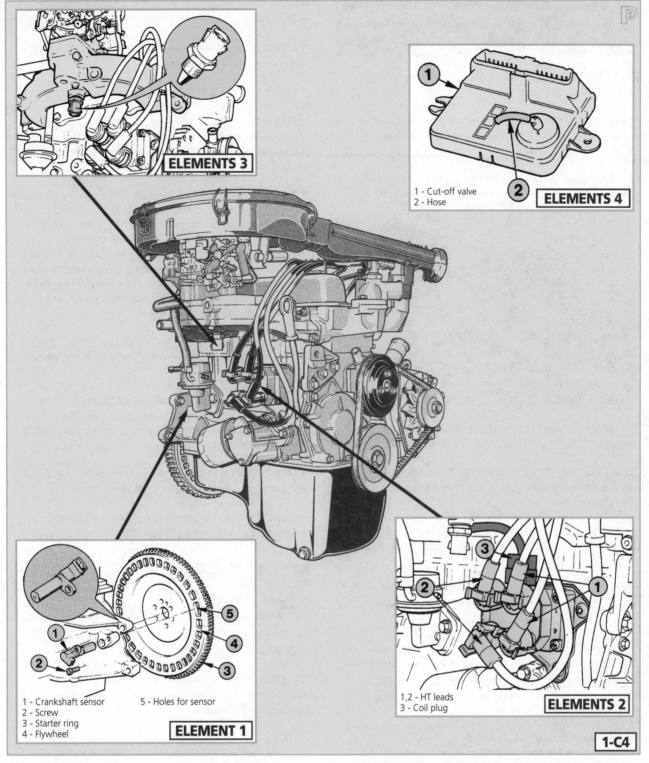

ELEMENTS 3

ELEMENTS 4

1 - Cut-off valve
2 - Hose

ELEMENT 1

1 - Crankshaft sensor   5 - Holes for sensor
2 - Screw
3 - Starter ring
4 - Flywheel

ELEMENTS 2

1,2 - HT leads
3 - Coil plug

1-C4

☐ **STEP C7:** Remove the starter motor - see *Chapter 10, Electrical, Instruments*.

☐ **STEP C8:** Remove the engine to transmission attachment bolts and the clutch lower cover plate - see *Chapter 7, Clutch, Transmission, Driveshafts*.

☐ **STEP C9:** Attach a suitable hoist to the engine and support the transmission, either from below using a jack, or from above using a bridge.

☐ **STEP C10:** Take the weight of the engine on the hoist and undo the engine mounting bolts. See *Part K*.

☐ **STEP C11:** Have a final check around the engine and transmission to make sure that all the necessary components have been separated and there is enough space to lift the engine clear.

☐ **STEP C12:** Carefully separate the engine from the transmission - see *Chapter 7, Clutch, Transmission, Driveshafts*, and lift the engine clear.
➜ Make sure that the transmission input shaft does not support the weight of the engine or transmission during removal.

Section D: Fiesta 1989 - 1995 with CVH and PTE engines.

Read *Section A* as well as this Section, and carry out the relevant work described there.

❏ **STEP D1:** Remove the air cleaner and air inlet duct components, if not already removed - see *Chapter 9, Ignition, Fuel, Exhaust*.

❏ **STEP D2: 1.4 MODELS WITH CFi:** Make sure you disconnect the coolant hose from the injection unit.

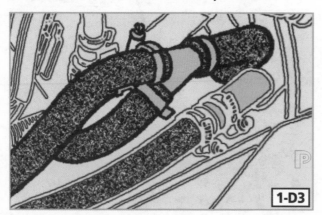

1-D3

❏ **STEP D3: EFi AND SEFi MODELS:** Make sure you disconnect the heater hose from the 'Y' connector.

❏ **STEP D4: TURBOCHARGER MODELS:** Make sure you disconnect the coolant return hose from the turbocharger connection pipe.

❏ **STEP D5:** Disconnect the brake servo hose from the inlet manifold. The brake servo hose has a sleeve type quick release connector.

❏ **STEP D6: CFi AND EFi MODELS:** Disconnect the vacuum hose from the MAP sensor and the hose between the carbon canister and injection unit.

❏ **STEP D7:** Disconnect the following electrical leads - see *Chapter 9, Ignition, Fuel, Exhaust* for information on Fuel, Exhaust and Emission components and *Chapter 10, Electrical, Instruments* for general information on electrical components.
➜ The coolant temperature sender unit.
➜ The coolant temperature sensor.
➜ The cooling fan thermostatic switch.
➜ The oil pressure switch.
➜ The carburetor.
➜ The distributor or E-DIS unit as appropriate.
➜ The earth leads from the transmission and engine.
➜ The reversing light switch (on the transmission).
➜ The crankshaft position sensor.

❏ **STEP D8: INJECTION MODELS:** Disconnect the electrical leads from the following components.
➜ The inlet air temperature sensor.
➜ The vehicle speed sensor.
➜ The throttle position sensor.
➜ The throttle plate control motor (CFi models).

➜ The idle speed control valve (EFi and SEFi models)
➜ The injector harness connector.

❏ **STEP D9:** Separate the wiring and coolant pipe bracket from above the transmission.

❏ **STEP D10:** Remove the starter motor and alternator.

❏ **STEP D11: MODULATOR TYPE ANTI-LOCK BRAKES:** Separate the modulator units and support them out of the way - see *Chapter 12, Brakes*. It is not necessary to disconnect the hydraulic connections.

❏ **STEP D12:** Where fitted, separate the multi-plug from the support bracket and disconnect the electrical cable from the oxygen (Lambda) sensor on the exhaust downpipe.

❏ **STEP D13:** Separate the exhaust downpipe from the manifold and the downpipe from the remainder of the exhaust system. Alternatively, separate the downpipe from the manifold and remove the complete system. See *Chapter 9, Ignition, Fuel, Exhaust*.

❏ **STEP D14:** Where fitted, and where necessary to allow engine and transmission removal, remove the exhaust heat shield.

❏ **STEP D15: POWER STEERING MODELS:** Separate the power steering pump from the engine - see *Chapter 11, Steering, Suspension*. It is not necessary to disconnect the hydraulic pipes.

❏ **STEP D16: XR2i MODELS:** Remove the front suspension crossmember - see *Chapter 11, Steering, Suspension*.

❏ **STEP D17:** Remove the auxiliary drive belt cover from under the crankshaft pulley - see *Part D*.

Section E: Fiesta 1989 - 1995 with Zetec engine.

Read *Section A* as well as this Section, and carry out the relevant work described there.

❏ **STEP E1:** Remove the air cleaner and air inlet duct components, if not already removed - see *Chapter 9, Ignition, Fuel, Exhaust*.

❏ **STEP E2: POWER STEERING MODELS:** Separate the electrical connector from the power steering pressure switch.

❏ **STEP E3:** Separate the earth cable from the engine lifting eye and refit the bolt.

❏ **STEP E4:** Disconnect the vacuum hoses from the inlet manifold and the vacuum hose from the pulse-air solenoid valve.

1-E5

❏ **STEP E5:** Disconnect the following electrical leads - see *Chapter 9, Ignition, Fuel, Exhaust* for information on Fuel, Exhaust and Emission components and *Chapter 10, Electrical, Instruments* for general information on electrical components.
→ The engine/transmission earth leads.
→ The oil pressure switch.
→ The multi-plug from the E-DIS ignition coil and the engine main wiring loom multi-plug behind the E-DIS ignition coil.
→ The multi-plugs from the reversing light switch (on the transmission).
→ The crankshaft speed/position sensor and VSS.
→ The multi-plug from the oxygen (Lambda) sensor.
→ The interference suppressor from the ignition coil.

❏ **STEP E6: MODULATOR TYPE ANTI-LOCK BRAKES:** Separate the modulator units and support them out of the way- see *Chapter 12, Brakes.* It is not necessary to disconnect the hydraulic connections.

❏ **STEP E7:** Remove the exhaust manifold heat shield.

❏ **STEP E8:** Remove the auxiliary drive belt.

❏ **STEP E9: POWER STEERING:** Disconnect the power steering pressure and return lines. Use a suitable container to collect hydraulic fluid spillage. Plug or cover the open connections to prevent the ingress of dirt or contamination.

❏ **STEP E10: XR2i MODELS:** Remove the front suspension crossmember - see *Chapter 11, Steering, Suspension.*

❏ **STEP E11:** Separate the exhaust system downpipe from the manifold and the catalytic converter from the rear section of the exhaust system. Remove the downpipe and catalytic converter from the vehicle.

❏ **STEP E12:** Remove the oil filter.

Section F: Fiesta from 1995 with Endura E engine.

Read *Section A* as well as this Section, and carry out the relevant work described there.

❏ **STEP F1:** Remove the battery and battery box.
❏ **STEP F2:** Remove the air duct from the throttle housing and air flow meter.

❏ **STEP F3:** Disconnect the following electrical leads - see *Chapter 9, Ignition, Fuel, Exhaust* for information on Fuel, Exhaust and Emission components and *Chapter 10, Electrical, Instruments* for general information on electrical components.
→ The Vehicle Speed Sensor (VSS) wiring at the bulkhead or on the rear of the transmission
→ The oxygen (Lambda) sensor connector.
→ The two engine wiring loom connectors at the bulkhead, unclip the support bracket.
→ The engine coolant temperature (ECT) sensor wiring.
→ The fan motor thermoswitch plug.
→ The HT leads.
→ The engine/transmission earth leads.

❏ **STEP F4:** If not already disconnected, separate the coolant line from the heat exchanger.

❏ **STEP F5:** Disconnect the vacuum line from the evaporative emission control (EVAP) valve.

❏ **STEP F6:** Disconnect the vacuum hoses from the inlet manifold.

❏ **STEP F7:** Remove the oil filler cap, disconnect the crankcase breather hose and refit the oil filler cap.

❏ **STEP F8:** Remove the auxiliary drive belt and, if necessary, the drive belt tensioner. See *Part D.*

❏ **STEP F9: POWER STEERING MODELS:** Disconnect the feed and pressure connections from the power steering pump. Use a hose clamp to reduce fluid loss and collect the spillage in a suitable container - see *Chapter 11, Steering, Suspension.*

❏ **STEP F10:** Remove the crankshaft lower pulley cover.

❏ **STEP F11:** Remove the radiator air guide and fan - see *Chapter 8, Cooling, Ventilation System* - complete radiator removal is not necessary. On models with air conditioning, the condenser does not have to be completely removed - unbolt it and tie it to one side.

❏ **STEP F12: AIR CONDITIONING MODELS:** Disconnect the electrical connector from air conditioning compressor, unbolt the compressor and tie it to one side.

❏ **STEP F13:** Remove the exhaust manifold heat shield, separate and remove the exhaust -downpipe from the manifold and the catalytic converter from the remainder of the exhaust system - see *Chapter 9, Ignition, Fuel, Exhaust.*

❏ **STEP F14:** Support the engine to remove the tension from the rear engine mounting link. Remove the through bolt and the link.

Section G: Fiesta from 1995 with Zetec SE engines.

Read **Section A** as well as this Section, and carry out the relevant work described there.

IMPORTANT NOTE: The procedure used to remove the Zetec SE engine is similar to the one used for removing the Endura E engine. We have highlighted here the **Steps** that are only applicable to Zetec SE engine removal - note that not all **Steps** relating to Endura E engine removal are applicable and the location of some components may vary.

1-G1

❒ **STEP G1:** Lift the flap at the front of the cover on top of the engine and disconnect the crankcase breather.

❒ **STEP G2:** Remove the oil filler cap, remove the cover on top of the engine and refit the oil filler cap.

❒ **STEP G3:** In addition to the items in **Section F, Step E2**, disconnect the following electrical leads - see **Chapter 9, Ignition, Fuel, Exhaust** for information on Fuel, Exhaust and Emission components and **Chapter 10, Electrical, Instruments** for general information on electrical components.
→ The engine wiring harness.
→ The throttle position sensor.
→ The EI ignition coil.
→ Camshaft position sensor.
→ The injectors.
→ The idle air control valve.
→ Remove the hoses from the exhaust gas recirculation valve, the inlet manifold, throttle body housing and all other associated sensors and components.

Section H: Escort with OHV engine to 1989.

Read **Section A** as well as this Section, and carry out the relevant work described there.

❒ **STEP H1:** Disconnect the following electrical leads - see **Chapter 9, Ignition, Fuel, Exhaust** for information on Fuel, Exhaust and Emission components and **Chapter 10, Electrical, Instruments** for general information on electrical components.
→ The coolant temperature sender
→ The oil pressure switch.
→ The engine earth strap.
→ The cooling fan switch.
→ The reversing lamp switch.
→ The HT and LT connections at the ignition coil.

❒ **STEP H2:** Disconnect the vacuum servo hose from the inlet manifold (vehicles with power assisted brakes).

❒ **STEP H3:** Separate the warm air box (where fitted) from the exhaust manifold - see **Chapter 9, Ignition, Fuel, Exhaust**.

❒ **STEP H4:** Disconnect the exhaust downpipe from the manifold, unhook the exhaust system from its mountings and remove the exhaust system from the vehicle - see **Chapter 9, Ignition, Fuel, Exhaust**.

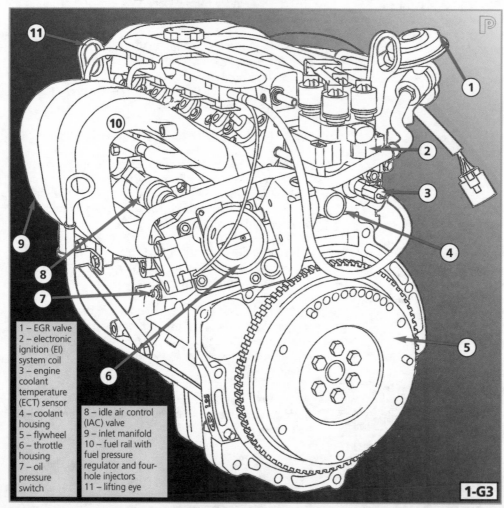

1 – EGR valve
2 – electronic ignition (EI) system coil
3 – engine coolant temperature (ECT) sensor
4 – coolant housing
5 – flywheel
6 – throttle housing
7 – oil pressure switch
8 – idle air control (IAC) valve
9 – inlet manifold
10 – fuel rail with fuel pressure regulator and four-hole injectors
11 – lifting eye

1-G3

STEP H5: When you separate the driveshafts from the transmission on pre-1986 models fitted with an anti-roll bar, the right-hand mounting clamp should be removed and the anti-roll bar lowered with the driveshafts.

Section I: Escort and Orion with HCS and Endura E engine from 1989.

Read *Section A* as well as this Section, and carry out the relevant work described there.

IMPORTANT NOTE:
• The engine can be lifted out of the engine bay with or without the transmission attached. While it is possible to remove the engine with the radiator in place, it is easily damaged and we recommend removal.
• Preparatory dismantling for engine removal is similar to the earlier models with the OHV engine - see *Section H* - the differences are as follows.

STEP I1: Remove the radiator - see *Chapter 8, Cooling, Ventilation System*.

STEP I2: Disconnect the following vacuum hoses from the inlet manifold.
➔ Brake servo - on later models the vacuum servo pipe has a sleeve type quick release connection.
➔ Pulse air hose.
➔ Fuel separator hose.
➔ MAP sensor (where fitted).

STEP I3: Disconnect the fresh air pipes from the pulse air system. Remove the pulse air filter and silencer.

STEP I4: Disconnect the following electrical connections.
➔ The engine coolant temperature sensor.
➔ The temperature gauge sender unit.
➔ The oil pressure switch.
➔ The cooling fan switch.
➔ The reversing lamp switch.
➔ The EI coil.
➔ The throttle valve stepper.
➔ The throttle position sensor.
➔ The throttle body assembly.
➔ The intake air temperature sensor.
➔ The crankshaft position sensor.
➔ The oxygen (Lambda) sensor at the exhaust manifold or downpipe.
➔ **ENDURA E ENGINES:** Undo the wire clips and separate the four fuel injector multi-plugs.
➔ The engine/transmission earth leads, including the earth lead from inlet manifold

STEP I5: It is only necessary to separate the exhaust downpipe from the manifold and remove the exhaust pipe bracket under the engine. The exhaust system can be left in place but support the downpipe to avoid straining the mountings.

STEP I6: Separate the starter lead support bracket from the transmission housing (where fitted).

STEP I7: Remove the starter motor and alternator cover.

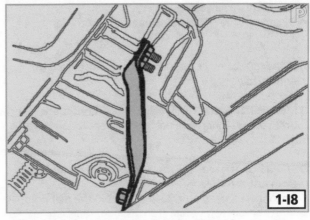

1-18

STEP I8: Remove the rear right-hand and front engine mounting braces, the engine to transmission attachment bolts and the clutch lower cover plate.

STEP I9: Lower the vehicle.

STEP I10: Attach a suitable hoist to the engine and support the transmission, either from below using a jack or from above using a bridge.

STEP I11: Take the weight of the engine on the hoist and undo the engine mounting bolts. See *Part K*.

STEP I12: Carefully separate the engine from the transmission - see *Chapter 7, Clutch, Transmission, Driveshafts*, and lift the engine clear. Make sure that the transmission input shaft does not support the weight of the engine or transmission during removal.

Section J: Escort and Orion with CVH engine to 1989.

Read *Section A* as well as this Section, and carry out the relevant work described there.

STEP J1: FUEL INJECTION MODELS: Separate the air intake duct from the fuel distributor and manifold. Remove the air duct from the vehicle.

STEP J2: Disconnect the following electrical leads - see *Chapter 9, Ignition, Fuel, Exhaust* for information on Fuel, Exhaust and Emission components and *Chapter 10, Electrical, Instruments* for general information on electrical components.
➔ The engine/transmission earth leads.
➔ The coolant temperature sender.
➔ The oil pressure sender.
➔ The cooling fan.
➔ The engine oil dipstick (where applicable).
➔ The reversing light switch.

STEP J3: FUEL INJECTION MODELS: Additionally, disconnect the following electrical components.
➔ The earth lead from the throttle valve stop.
➔ The cold start valve.
➔ The warm-up regulator.
➔ The thermo-time switch.

→ The auxiliary air valve.
→ Disconnect the HT and LT connections at the ignition coil.

❑ **STEP J4:** Disconnect the vacuum servo hose from the inlet manifold.

❑ **STEP J5: FUEL INJECTION MODELS:** Disconnect the fuel cut-off valve vacuum hose and engine ventilation valve hose.

❑ **STEP J6:** Separate the warm air box (where fitted) from the exhaust manifold.
→ Disconnect the exhaust downpipe from the manifold, unhook the exhaust system from its mountings and remove the exhaust system from the vehicle - see *Chapter 9, Ignition, Fuel, Exhaust*.

❑ **STEP J7:** Separate the driveshafts from the transmission - see *Chapter 7, Clutch, Transmission, Driveshafts*, and release the anti-roll bar at each side - the anti-roll bar should be lowered along with the suspension lower arms.

Section K: Escort and Orion with CVH and PTE engines from 1990.

Read *Section A* as well as this Section, and carry out the relevant work described there.

❑ **STEP K1: FUEL INJECTION MODELS:** On 1.4 litre models with CFi, make sure you also disconnect the coolant hose from the injection unit. On EFi and SEFi models make sure you separate the heater hose 'Y' connector - see *Step D3*. Where applicable, remove the air intake duct between the air cleaner and engine.

❑ **STEP K2: CARBURETTOR MODELS:** Make sure you separate the fuel supply hose from the fuel pump and the return hose from the carburettor.

❑ **STEP K3: FUEL INJECTION MODELS:** CFi models have quick release fuel connectors which are operated by compressing the couplings while pulling the hoses from the couplings - disconnect the fuel hose at the injector/pressure regulator unit and the return line. On EFi and SEFi models, detach the fuel line from the fuel rail by unscrewing the union. Plug or cover the open connections to prevent the ingress of dirt or contamination.

❑ **STEP K4:** Disconnect the brake servo vacuum pipe from the inlet manifold - the vacuum servo pipe has a sleeve type quick release connection.

❑ **STEP K5: FUEL INJECTION MODELS:** On CFi and EFi models, disconnect the vacuum hose from the MAP sensor and the hose between the fuel injection unit and carbon canister.

❑ **STEP K6:** Disconnect the following electrical leads - see *Chapter 9, Ignition, Fuel, Exhaust* for information on Fuel, Exhaust and Emission components and *Chapter 10, Electrical, Instruments* for general information on electrical components.

→ The temperature gauge sender.
→ The engine coolant temperature sensor.
→ The ignition coil unit.
→ The oil pressure switch.
→ The crankshaft position sensor.
→ The engine/transmission earth leads.
→ The cooling fan switch.
→ The reversing lamp switch.
→ The crankshaft position sensor.

❑ **STEP K7: FUEL INJECTION MODELS:** Additionally on fuel injection models, disconnect the following electrical components.
→ The inlet air temperature sensor.
→ The vehicle speed sensor.
→ The throttle plate control motor.
→ The throttle position sensor.
→ The heater plate for pre-heating.
→ The injectors and the injector harness connector.
→ The idle speed control valve.
→ Mass Air Flow (MAF) sensor.
→ Power steering pressure switch.
→ Radio interference suppressor.
→ **POWER STEERING:** Remove the earth lead and bracket from the power steering pipe. Disconnect the plug from the power steering pressure switch.

❑ **STEP K8: POWER STEERING:** Disconnect the power steering pump hydraulic lines - see *Chapter 11, Steering, Suspension*. Use a suitable container to collect fluid spillage and plug or cover the open connection to prevent the ingress of dirt or contamination. Pull out the reservoir and push to one side.

❑ **STEP K9:** Remove the wiring and coolant hose bracket above the transmission.

❑ **STEP K10:** Remove the starter motor.

❑ **STEP K11:** Remove the two bolts and disconnect the engine transmission mounting from the mounting bracket.

❑ **STEP K12:** On the appropriate catalytic converter equipped vehicles, disconnect the electrical wiring from the oxygen (Lambda) sensor.

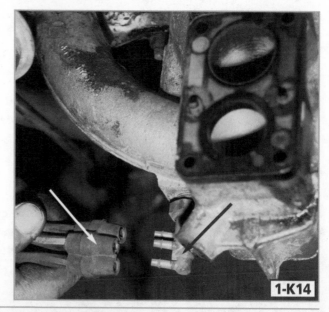

1-K14

STEP K13: Disconnect the exhaust downpipe from the manifold and the remainder of the system. Remove the exhaust downpipe and the exhaust heat shield from the vehicle.

STEP K14: On the appropriate vehicles, disconnect the pulse-air supply hose from the check valve and separate the system (arrowed) at the three port vacuum switch (PVS) under the inlet manifold.

STEP K15: Remove the transverse brace from the transmission and the brace from the right-hand engine mount.

STEP K16: Remove the auxiliary drive belt cover from below the crankshaft pulley.

STEP K17: AIR CONDITIONING: Remove the auxiliary drive belt - see *Part D*, and the air conditioning compressor - do not undo the refrigerant hose connections - see *SAFETY FIRST: AIR CONDITIONING*.

STEP K18: FUEL INJECTION MODELS: On models with EFi, remove the screws (positions arrowed) holding the MAP sensor to the right-hand engine mounting bracket.

1-K18

Section L: Escort and Orion with Zetec and Zetec E engines from 1992.

Read *Section A* as well as this Section, and carry out the relevant work described there.

STEP L1: Detach the air inlet duct from the manifold.

STEP L2: Disconnect the following electrical leads - see *Chapter 9, Ignition, Fuel, Exhaust* for information on Fuel, Exhaust and Emission components and *Chapter 10, Electrical, Instruments* for general information on electrical components.
→ The EI ignition coil multi-plug.
→ The main engine wiring loom multi-plug.
→ The radio interference suppressor.
→ The oxygen (Lambda) sensor.
→ The crankshaft position/speed sensor and vehicle speed sensor multi-plugs.
→ The oil pressure switch.
→ The reversing light switch.
→ The cooling fan.
→ The blower motor.
→ **POWER STEERING:** The power steering pressure switch.
→ The engine/transmission earth leads. Refit the attachment bolt at the engine lifting eye.

STEP L3: Disconnect the following vacuum hoses.
→ The brake servo vacuum pipe from the inlet manifold.
→ The evaporative emission (EVAP) hose.
→ The vacuum line from the pulse-air solenoid and filter.

STEP L4: Remove the exhaust manifold heat shield - see *Chapter 9, Ignition, Fuel, Exhaust*.

STEP L5: POWER STEERING: Remove the brackets from the power steering high pressure pipes, the pulley cover from the power steering pump and the power steering fluid reservoir. Loosen the power steering pump pulley bolts, remove the auxiliary drive belt - see *Part D*, the power steering pump pulley and separate the power steering pump from the engine. Tie the power steering pump out of the way.

STEP L6: Separate and remove the exhaust downpipe from the manifold and the catalytic converter from the remainder of the exhaust system - see *Chapter 9, Ignition, Fuel, Exhaust*. On vehicles with B5 and iB5 transmissions, remove the exhaust heat shield.

STEP L7: AIR CONDITIONING MODELS: It is not necessary to dismantle the air conditioning system but some components will have to be removed to allow engine and transmission lowering. Unbolt the components as necessary but do not undo the refrigerant hose connections - see *SAFETY FIRST: AIR CONDITIONING*.

STEP L8: Remove the bolts and the right-hand engine support brace.

Section M: Diesel engine models.

Read *Section A* as well as this Section, and carry out the relevant work described there.

IMPORTANT NOTE: The procedure used to remove the 1.6 litre and 1.8 litre diesel engines is similar on both Fiesta and Escort models - we have illustrated engine removal from a 1.8 litre Escort diesel.

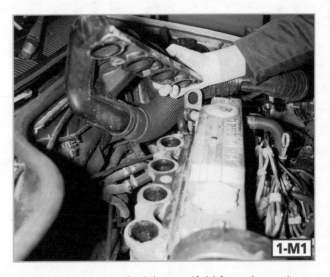

1-M1

STEP M1: Separate the inlet manifold from the engine...

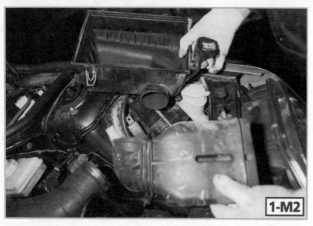

1-M2

❏ **STEP M2:** …and remove the remainder of the air inlet components.

1-M3

❏ **STEP M3:** Blocking the inlet ports with old rags or covering with tape (arrowed) will prevent objects falling into the openings.

❏ **STEP M4: FIESTA:** Remove the battery and battery box.

❏ **STEP M5:** Disconnect the following electrical leads - see *Chapter 9, Ignition, Fuel, Exhaust* for information on Fuel, Exhaust and Emission components and *Chapter 10, Electrical, Instruments* for general information on electrical components.
→ The injection pump wiring loom.
→ The glow plug wiring.
→ The diesel fuel heater.
→ The exhaust gas recirculation valve.
→ The temperature gauge sender unit.
→ The engine coolant temperature (ECT) sensor.
→ The oil pressure switch.
→ The multi-function switch or reversing light switch on the transmission.
→ The crankshaft position sensor.
→ The engine/transmission earth leads.

❏ **STEP M6:** Disconnect the brake servo vacuum pipe from the vacuum pump - see *Chapter 12, Brakes*.

❏ **STEP M7: POWER STEERING MODELS:** Ford recommend that the power steering hose and pressure pipe are disconnected from the power steering pump. Remove the auxiliary drive belt and support brackets as necessary to allow disconnection. Use a suitable container to collect fluid spillage. See *Chapter 11, Steering, Suspension*.

❏ **STEP M8: FIESTA:** Remove the radiator - see *Chapter 8, Cooling, Ventilation System*.

❏ **STEP M9: AIR CONDITIONING MODELS:** It is not necessary to dismantle the air conditioning system but the air conditioning condenser and compressor will have to be unbolted to allow engine and transmission lowering - tie these components out of the way. Do not undo the refrigerant hose connections - see *SAFETY FIRST: AIR CONDITIONING*.

❏ **STEP M10:** Separate and remove the exhaust downpipe from the exhaust manifold and intermediate section.

Section N: Ka.

Read *Section A* as well as this Section, and carry out the relevant work described there.

❏ **STEP N1:** Where fitted, remove the drive belt lower cover.

❏ **STEP N2:** Remove the air inlet duct as follows.
→ **VEHICLES WITH MASS AIR FLOW (MAF) SENSOR, TO 1999:** Separate the air inlet duct from the throttle housing. Disconnect the plugs from the Intake Air Temperature (IAT) and MAF sensors.
→ **VEHICLES WITH TEMPERATURE MANIFOLD ABSOLUTE PRESSURE (TMAP) SENSOR, FROM 1999:** Separate the air inlet duct from the throttle housing and the air cleaner.

❏ **STEP N3:** Pull the air cleaner housing up from its mounting and disconnect the crankcase ventilation hose. On vehicles fitted with a MAF, remove the air duct and MAF sensor.

❏ **STEP N4:** Disconnect the engine wiring harness at the right-hand rear of the engine.

❏ **STEP N5:** Disconnect the brake vacuum hose from the inlet manifold - see *Chapter 12, Brakes*.

❏ **STEP N6: VEHICLES WITH MASS AIR FLOW (MAF) SENSOR, TO 1999:** Unclip the engine wiring loom and the two connectors from the bulkhead cover. Open the connector covers and separate the connectors. The covers must be prised open and will probably be damaged - new connector covers should be used during reassembly.

❏ **STEP N7: VEHICLES WITH (TMAP) SENSOR, FROM 1999:** Unclip the engine wiring loom and disconnect the connectors at the left-hand side of the bulkhead. Separate the TMAP sensor plug and remove the alternator wiring cover.

❏ **STEP N8:** Disconnect the vacuum line from the evaporative emission control canister purge solenoid valve.

❏ **STEP N9:** If not already disconnected, separate the coolant line from the heat exchanger.

☐ **STEP N10:** Disconnect the following electrical leads - see *Chapter 9, Ignition, Fuel, Exhaust* for information on Fuel, Exhaust and Emission components and *Chapter 10, Electrical, Instruments* for general information on electrical components.

→ On the bulkhead, disconnect the wiring from the Vehicle Speed Sensor (VSS) and, at the right-hand side, the engine wiring harness plug.

→ Disconnect the engine wiring loom connector.

→ Disconnect the oxygen (Lambda) sensor connector, located on the bonnet lock panel.

→ Disconnect the wiring from the multi-function switch (to-1999) or reversing light switch (from-1999) on the front of the transmission.

→ Engine/transmission earth leads

☐ **STEP N11:** Separate the catalytic converter from the exhaust system and unhook the exhaust system from the flexible supports. Use a splint to prevent excessive bending of the flexible section. See *Chapter 9, Ignition, Fuel, Exhaust*. Lower the exhaust system and position it so that it will not be damaged when the engine and transmission are lowered.

☐ **STEP N12:** Remove the exhaust heat shield from the underbody.

TOP TIP!

• As a precaution against damage during removal, you should remove the camshaft position sensor - tape or plug the opening to prevent the ingress of dirt and contamination.
• For greater clearance, remove the stud from the rear left-hand side of the transmission.

☐ **STEP N13: POWER STEERING MODELS:** Clamp the fluid reservoir supply hose and disconnect the hose at the pump. Separate the power steering pipes from the crossmember at the bottom of the radiator and disconnect

the couplings at the left-hand side and the coupling at the right-hand side - see *Chapter 11, Steering, Suspension*. Use a suitable container to collect fluid spillage. The pressure pipe from the pump remains with the engine but the other pipes can be removed.

☐ **STEP N14: AIR CONDITIONING MODELS:** Disconnect the refrigerant line from the top right-hand side of the condenser - access is via the aperture in the engine compartment front crossmember. See **SAFETY FIRST: AIR CONDITIONING**.

JOB 2: ENGINE AND TRANSMISSION – *installation*.

☐ **STEP 1:** Installation is generally carried out in the reverse order to removal.

☐ **STEP 2: FIESTA 1983 - 1989:** Use new bolts when fitting the engine crossmember.

☐ **STEP 3: OHV, HCS, CVH, PTE AND DIESEL ENGINES:** Make sure that the engine back plate (also known as the adapter plate) is correctly located on its dowels before refitting the transmission.

☐ **STEP 4: KA ENGINE MOUNTS:** Fit a 10 mm thick metal plate between the vehicle body and the bracket on the right-hand side of the engine. With the plate held against the engine, tighten the two nuts and single bolt. Leave the plate in place and fit another 10 mm thick plate between the transmission and mounting bracket. Hold the plate against the engine and tighten the left-hand engine mounting nuts. Remove the plates after tightening the nuts and bolt to the specified torque - see *Chapter 1, Facts and Figures*.

Part J: Cylinder Block Dismantling, Rebuilding

CONTENTS

FACT FILE

DISMANTLING RESTRICTIONS

• The big difference with the Zetec SE engine is the way in which the crankshaft and main bearings are assembled - because of the very closely toleranced bearing clearances and bearing shells, Ford do not recommend dismantling the main bearing assembly. If there are any problems in this area, Ford have specified that a new cylinder block complete with crankshaft and main bearings is obtained. See *Job 1, Step 1* for the layout of the Zetec SE bottom end.

• For more information on the differences between engine types - see *Part B, Which Engine is Which*.

JOB 1: CYLINDER BLOCK – *layouts.*

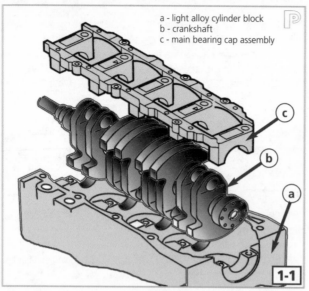

a - light alloy cylinder block
b - crankshaft
c - main bearing cap assembly

1-1

❐ **STEP 1:** This is the layout of the Zetec SE bottom end. You will see that there is a 'ladder' type main bearing cap assembly, which provides greater rigidity when the engine is running, but is not so 'mechanic friendly'.

❐ **STEP 2:** These are the block assembly components for the Overhead Valve (OHV), engines with five main bearings and distributor ignition.
→ Note that some early 1.0 and 1.1 litre Fiesta engines have only three main bearings.
→ On later engines with distributorless ignition (DIS), the distributor's main functions take place within the computerised Powertrain Control Module, the HT spark coming from a remote coil unit. See *Chapter 9, Ignition, Fuel, Exhaust* for more information on ignition systems.

❐ **STEP 3:** These are the cylinder block and timing gear components for the single overhead camshaft, CVH and PTE engine types.

❐ **STEP 4:** The layout of the double overhead cam Zetec engines, except for the Zetec SE, and the diesel engine cylinder blocks is similar to the CVH and PTE types. See the relevant section for specific information on component location and other minor differences.

IMPORTANT NOTE:
• Do not attempt to remove the bearing cap assembly and crankshaft from Zetec SE engines. Just loosening the main bearing cap bolts can result in incorrect tolerances and Ford do not specify a torque figure for re-tightening.
• If the bearing cap bolts on Zetec SE engines are loosened, the cylinder block must be replaced complete with the crankshaft.

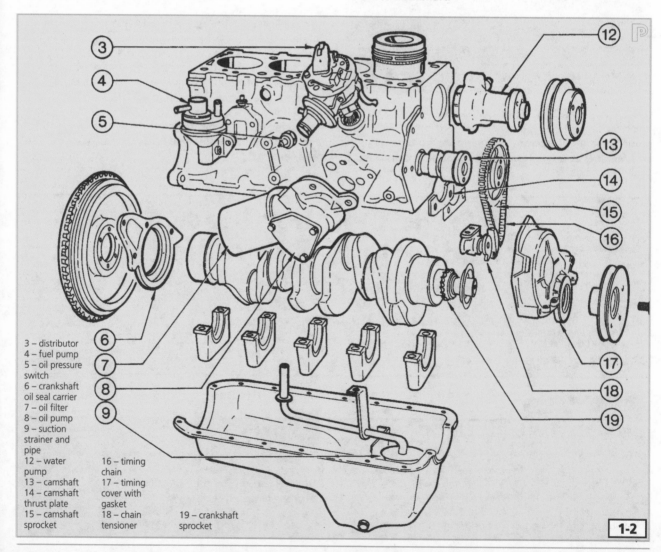

3 – distributor
4 – fuel pump
5 – oil pressure switch
6 – crankshaft oil seal carrier
7 – oil filter
8 – oil pump
9 – suction strainer and pipe
12 – water pump
13 – camshaft
14 – camshaft thrust plate
15 – camshaft sprocket
16 – timing chain
17 – timing cover with gasket
18 – chain tensioner
19 – crankshaft sprocket

1-2

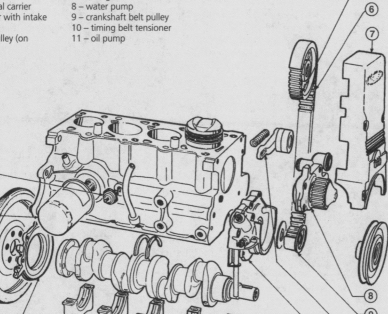

1 – oil pressure switch
2 – oil filter
3 – crankshaft oil seal carrier
4 – oil pump strainer with intake pipe
5 – camshaft belt pulley (on cylinder head)
6 – timing belt
7 – timing belt cover
8 – water pump
9 – crankshaft belt pulley
10 – timing belt tensioner
11 – oil pump

`1-3`

☐ **STEP A3:** Remove the clutch - see *Chapter 7, Transmission, Clutch, Driveshafts*, and the flywheel.

IMPORTANT NOTE:
• On models with alloy sumps, the sump is bolted direct to the clutch bellhousing and the rear oil seal carrier may be bolted to the sump - the clutch, flywheel and rear oil seal carrier bolts have to be removed, before the sump can be separated.

☐ **STEP A4:** Remove the spacer fitted between the engine and transmission.

☐ **STEP A5:** Remove the rear oil seal carrier.
→ The design of the rear oil seal carrier varies between engine types
→ This shows the carrier being removed from a diesel engine.

JOB 2: CYLINDER BLOCK – *dismantling*.

Section A: General Information

The dismantling procedure is essentially the same for each engine type but there are many minor differences which should be born in mind. We have given the general guidance first and provided separate sections specific to each engine type where there are important differences. You should combine the information here with the general procedures in *Part B*.

☐ **STEP A1:** Remove the cylinder head, (see *Part F*), if still fitted.

☐ **STEP A2:** Remove all ancillary components and also remove the power steering and air conditioning pumps (if fitted).
→ For specific information - see *Part D* for drive belts, *Chapter 8, Cooling, Ventilation System* for cooling and air conditioning system components; *Chapter 9, Ignition, Fuel, Exhaust* for ignition fuel and exhaust system components and *Chapter 11, Steering, Suspension* for power steering system components.

`2-A3`

`2-A5`

STEP A6: Turn the engine on its side (or upside-down) and remove the oil sump pan and gasket.

→ Steel sumps fitted to cast iron cylinder blocks can be levered off but levering is not recommended for alloy sumps and alloy cylinder blocks.

→ Gently tap around the flange with a soft faced hammer.

2-A6

TOP TIP!

• Completely inverting the engine before the sump is removed can allow any debris and sludge in the bottom of the sump to enter the oilways. This can result in problems later - a blockage at worst or prolonged cleaning at least.

FACT FILE

CRANKSHAFT OIL SEALS

• FRONT SEAL: On overhead valve engines, the seal is fitted to the timing chain cover. All other petrol and 1.6 litre diesel engines have the oil seal fitted to the oil pump. The seal on 1.8 litre diesel engines is fitted to the inner timing belt cover.

• REAR SEAL: On all engines, the seal is held in a carrier which can only be removed after the flywheel has been removed.

Section B: Overhead valve engines.

2-B1

2-B2

STEP B1: Unbolt and remove the oil pump. Remove the dipstick tube (arrowed).

STEP B2: Remove the crankshaft pulley and the timing chain cover.

STEP B3: Remove the timing chain tensioner.

STEP B4: Unbolt the camshaft drive sprocket...

2-B3

2-B4

2-B5

STEP B5: ...and slide the timing chain and sprockets off their shafts. Check the chain and sprockets for signs of wear and replace as necessary - see *Part C*.

2-B6

STEP B6: Unbolt and remove the camshaft retainer plate.

STEP B7: Invert the engine so that the tappets fall clear of the camshaft and remove the camshaft from the block, taking extreme care to ensure that the camshaft lobes do not score the bearing surfaces in the block.

2-B7

TOP TIP!

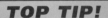

2-B8

STEP B8: Remove the tappets - a magnetic probe (as shown here) or rubber sucker, such as the end of a valve grinding tool, can be used to extract the tappets.

STEP B9: If necessary, remove the oil pick-up pipe and strainer but bear in mind that on engines where the pick-up pipe is a simple push fit, Ford specify the use of a special adhesive during refitting and the flat on the flange must align as shown.

STEP B10: Removing the pistons, connecting rods and crankshaft is standard - see *Section F*.

Section C: Single overhead cam engines.

STEP C1: If not already removed, take off the timing belt - see *Part C*...

STEP C2: ...and the cylinder head - see *Part F*.

2-C1

STEP C3: Remove the crankshaft pulley bolt.

STEP C4: You can now remove the timing belt tensioner. Here, it's being removed before the cylinder head but the sequence is not critical.

2-C2

2-C3

2-C4

☐ **STEP C5:** Remove the water pump complete with timing belt idler sprocket.

☐ **STEP C6:** Remove the crankshaft timing belt sprocket, noting the spacer which must be retained for use during reassembly.

☐ **STEP C7:** If you haven't already done so, remove the sump so that you can separate the oil pick-up pipe bracket (fixings arrowed) from the cylinder block.

☐ **STEP C8:** You can now remove the oil pump, with the oil pick-up pipe still attached.

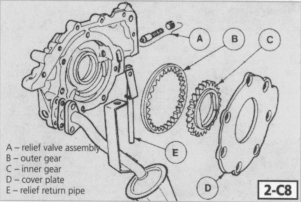

A – relief valve assembly
B – outer gear
C – inner gear
D – cover plate
E – relief return pipe

☐ **STEP C9:** Here, the oil seal and carrier have been taken off (to allow the crankshaft to come away when the time comes), and the big-end caps are being removed. Note that they are numbered for correct refitting.

☐ **STEP C10:** This piston has been very badly scored down the side.

☐ **STEP C11:** With the engine once again inverted, the main bearing cap bolts can be undone and removed which allows...

☐ **STEP C12:** ...the crankshaft to be lifted out.

☐ **STEP C13:** You should now remove the baffle. Remove the oil gallery plug and core plugs so that the block can be cleaned thoroughly.

2-C13

Section D: DOHC cast-iron Zetec engine.

The cast-iron Zetec engine is relatively conventional, except as described in the following:

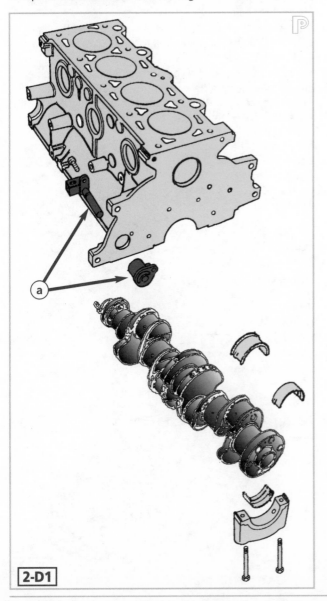

2-D1

☐ **STEP D1:** These are the (conventional) crank and block components, with the flywheel sensor components **(a)** shown each side of the end plate.

☐ **STEP D2:** Some versions have oil sprays bolted to the block, seen here with crankshaft removed.
→ Other versions have blanking plugs where the sprays are otherwise fitted.

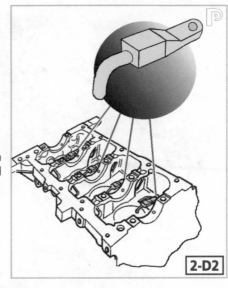

2-D2

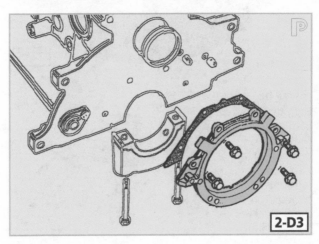

2-D3

☐ **STEP D3:** The transmission-end crankshaft oil seal is held in place with a retainer.
→ The seal can be changed when the engine is not dismantled by levering the old one out, then feeding the replacement over the crank end by wrapping a piece of thin plastic sheet over the end of the crank and sliding the seal over it.

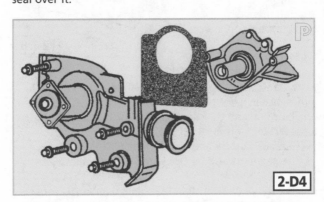

2-D4

☐ **STEP D4:** The water pump bolts simply to the block.

☐ **STEP D5:** The oil pump - removed with sump taken off - is bolted to the block with six bolts (positions, **a**).

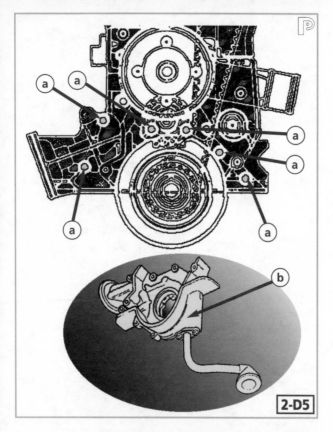

2-D5

IMPORTANT NOTE: The sump MUST be fitted so that the crankshaft-end of the sump is precisely lined up with end of the block. Use a straight edge to ensure that they are aligned before finally tightening the sump bolts to the correct torque.

Section E: DOHC light alloy Zetec engine.

The light alloy version of the Zetec engine is completely different at its bottom end from the iron-block engine.

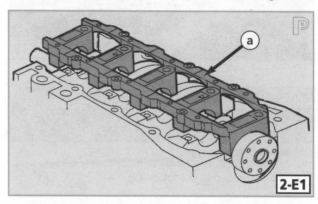

2-E1

☐ **STEP E1:** The crankshaft and bearing are held in place with a ladder-frame arrangement of main bearing caps (**a**).
→ Ford recommend that the bottom end of this engine cannot be rebuilt in the conventional way.
→ If the bearings and/or crankshaft need replacement, the entire block assembly needs to be replaced.

☐ **STEP D6:** Both the oil pump (**1**) and the oil seal retainer (**2**) have some movement in them before the bolts are tightened up. It is ESSENTIAL that each is fitted correctly, or the sump pan will leak oil:
→ Fit the bolts but not fully tighten them; you must be able to just move the pump or seal retainer.

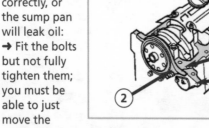

2-D6

→ Use a straight edge and feeler gauge and measure the difference in height between the sump pan-sealing face of the block (**a**) and the sump pan-sealing face of the pump or seal retainer (**b**).
→ The gap must be between 0.3 and 0.5 mm.
→ The gap must also be THE SAME on both sides.

☐ **STEP D7:** Before refitting the sump, be sure to properly locate the gasket in the sump flange.
→ Always use a new sump gasket.
→ Put a bead of silicone sealer on the sump pan-sealing faces of the pump and seal retainer (illustration *2-D6, positions a and b*).

☐ **STEP E2:** The water pump bolts on the side of the block.

☐ **STEP E3:** The crankshaft seal can be replaced after removing the end plate.

2-E2

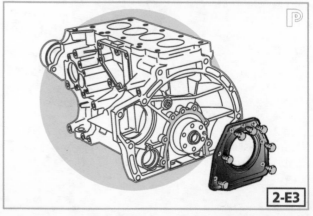

2-E3

STEP E4: At the other end of the engine, the oil pump (**a**) can be unbolted and removed but only after the oil pick-up pipe and strainer (**b**) have been removed.
→ The strainer assembly is bolted (**c**) to the block.
→ The pick-up pipe is pushed into the block (**d**) and has a seal on the end of the pipe.

STEP E5: Before refitting the sump:
→ Use a straight edge and feeler gauge and measure the difference in height between the sump pan-sealing face of the block (illustration **2-D6, item a**) and the sump pan-sealing face of the pump or seal retainer (**b**).
→ Place a bead of silicone sealer all along the face of the support (illustration **2-E4, position 1**) and along the joints (**position 2**).

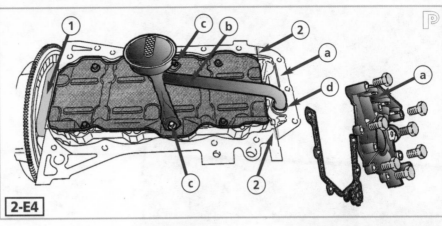

2-E4

Section F: 1.8 litre diesel engines.

2-F1

STEP F1: If still fitted, remove the camshaft drive belt (see **Part C**), the cylinder head, see (**Part F**), and the upper belt backing plate.

STEP F2: If still fitted, remove the fuel pump drive belt (see **Part C**), the fuel pump bracket and the fuel pump - see **Chapter 9, Ignition, Fuel, Exhaust**.

STEP F3: TURBOCHARGED ENGINES: Remove the turbocharger (see **Chapter 9, Ignition, Fuel, Exhaust**), disconnect the oil feed pipe from the turbocharger, the oil cooler coolant hoses, remove the turbocharger mounting plate from the cylinder block and the crankshaft position sensor.

STEP F4: Unbolt and remove the crankshaft vibration damper - note the locating pegs. A new bolt should be used during reassembly.

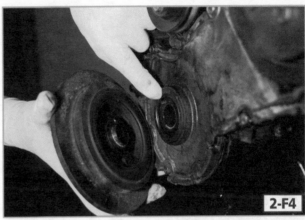

2-F4

STEP F5: Unbolt and remove the oil pump from the cylinder block. This is the oil pump fitted to a normally aspirated engine.

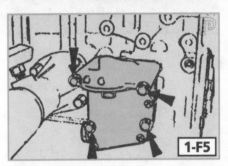

1-F5

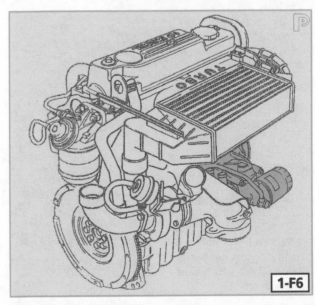

1-F6

STEP F6: TURBOCHARGED ENGINES: Engines fitted with a turbocharger and oil cooler have additional components, although the location is similar.

2-F7

❏ **STEP F7:** The coolant inlet (arrowed) can be separated from the pump...

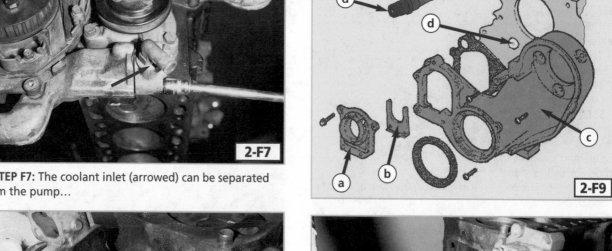

2-F9

2-F8

❏ **STEP F8:** ...or removed along with the pump.

❏ **STEP F9:** Hold the auxiliary shaft sprocket and undo the centre bolt. Remove the following:
➜ The seal retainer (**a**) – four bolts
➜ The thrust plate (**b**) – remove two screws, lift clear of the recess in the end of the auxiliary shaft.
➜ The complete housing assembly (**c**).
➜ You can now withdraw the auxiliary shaft (**d**).

❏ **STEP F10:** Remove the following:
➜ The engine front plate.
➜ The drive belt sprocket from the crankshaft.
➜ The oil pick-up pipe.

❏ **STEP F11:** Removing the pistons, connecting rods and crankshaft is standard, see *Section F*, but note that this engine has piston cooling oil jets which must be removed if the lubrication system is to be thoroughly cleaned.

2-F10

Section G: 1.6 litre Diesel Engines.

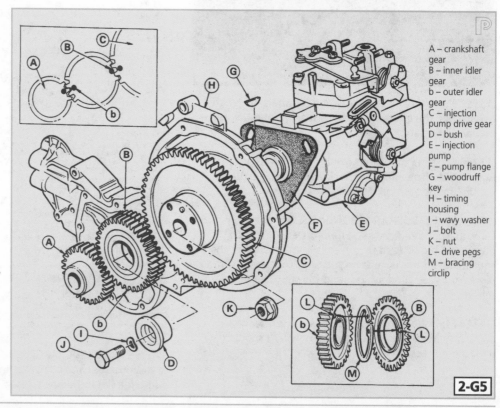

A – crankshaft gear
B – inner idler gear
b – outer idler gear
C – injection pump drive gear
D – bush
E – injection pump
F – pump flange
G – woodruff key
H – timing housing
I – wavy washer
J – bolt
K – nut
L – drive pegs
M – bracing circlip

2-G5

STEP G1: If still fitted, remove the camshaft drive belt (see *Part C*) and the cylinder head - see *Part F*.

STEP G2: Unbolt and remove the crankshaft vibration damper. Note the locating pegs - see *Step F4*.

STEP G3: Remove the fuel pump drive sprocket – see *Part C*.

STEP G4: Remove the coolant pump along with the coolant inlet - see *Steps F7 and F8*.

STEP G5: Remove the bolt (**J**) from the end of the injection pump shaft and the three nuts attaching the fuel pump flange (**F**) to the timing case.
➡ Slacken the bolt holding the pump bracket to the engine block.
➡ Use a suitable puller to break the taper between the pump shaft and the gear.
➡ Remove the fuel pump bracket and the fuel pump - see *Chapter 9, Ignition, Fuel, Exhaust*.

STEP G6: Unbolt and remove the front section of the timing cover.

STEP G7: Remove the fuel pump gear (**1**) and pull the crankshaft gear (**2**) from the crankshaft. The fuel pump gear fits to the fuel pump shaft and we have used a substitute bolt to hold this gear in place so that you can see the correct gear arrangement. Note the locating pins (arrowed).

2-G7

STEP G8: Unbolt and remove the idler gear.

2-G8

2-G9

STEP G9: Remove the oil pump pick-up pipe.

STEP G10: Unbolt and remove the rear section of the timing cover, complete with the oil pump.

STEP G11: Removing the pistons, connecting rods and crankshaft is standard procedure - see *Section H*.

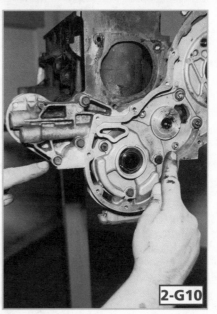

2-G10

Section H: Piston, Connecting rod and Crankshaft Removal.

TOP TIP!

2-H1

STEP H1: • Before dismantling the big-end and crankshaft main bearings, make sure the bearing caps and connecting rods are marked so that they can be fitted in the correct locations - similarly, if you are refitting the same pistons, mark them to show their position and which way round they face (the arrow points towards the front of the engine).

❑ **STEP H2:** Undo the big-end securing bolts (also see illustration *3-B8*) and remove the caps, keeping them in their correct order.
→ Remove the pistons complete with connecting rods.

TOP TIP!
• Use a hammer handle to tap the piston/connecting rod assemblies carefully out of the bores.
• Inspect the top of each cylinder bore - there may be a small ring of carbon build-up which can make it difficult to remove the pistons. If so, scrape it carefully away.

❑ **STEP H3:** Keep the pistons in the correct order and the matching connecting rods, bearing shells and bearing caps together.

TOP TIP!
• If any of the caps are difficult to remove, lever the bolt holes with a bar, or a pair of bars - or a pair of fixing bolts, and tap carefully with a hammer.

❑ **STEP H4:** Check that the five (or three) crankshaft main bearing caps are correctly marked, starting from the timing cover end.
→ Undo and remove them, keeping them in the correct order.
→ Do not dismantle the main bearing caps on Zetec SE engines - see *FACT FILE, ENGINE DISMANTLING*.

❑ **STEP H5:** Retrieve the thrust bearings from each side of the centre main bearing cap.

❑ **STEP H6:** Lift the crankshaft clear of the cylinder block.

2-H4

2-H5

2-H6

❑ **STEP H7: 1.8 LITRE DIESEL:** Remove the oil spray nozzles from inside the block and check that each is clear before putting it ready for refitting.

❑ **STEP H8:** Thoroughly clean and check all components. Pay particular attention to cleaning oilways and coolant ducts.

JOB 3: ENGINE – *reassembly*.

Engine reassembly is, generally, the reversal of dismantling but not in every respect. This job must be read in conjunction with *Part A: General Procedures*.
→ All bearings, shells, piston rings and ALL seals that bear on moving parts MUST be copiously lubricated with fresh engine oil as the engine is being reassembled.
→ Use new gaskets and seals throughout. Note that on Diesel engines, an exhaust manifold gasket was not used during manufacture but a new gasket must be used after any subsequent dismantling and reassembly.

Section A: Crankshaft.

IMPORTANT NOTE:
This section does not relate to Zetec SE engines. The main bearing and crankshaft assembly used on this engine should not be dismantled.
→ On both diesel engines and single overhead cam engines (CVH and PTE), the plain shells are fitted to the main bearing caps except for No 1 bearing which has a grooved shell fitted to both the main bearing cap and the cylinder block. All other engines have grooved shells fitted to the cylinder block and plain shells fitted to main bearing caps.
→ Make sure the oilways have been thoroughly cleaned - any dirt left in the oilways will go straight to the new bearings shells as soon as oil starts flow!
→ The thrust bearings on Zetec and Zetec E engines are integral with the No 3 upper main bearing shell.
→ On 1.8 litre diesel engines, make sure the piston-cooling oil jets are correctly fitted.

❑ **STEP A1:** Make sure the bearing seating areas in the caps and block are perfectly clean.
→ Locate the shells so that their tabs engage with the slots - check to make sure that the oil holes in the block are aligned with the holes in the bearing shells.

3-A1

→ Lubricate the shells liberally with fresh engine oil and lower the crankshaft into position.

☐ **STEP A2:** Fit the remaining halves of the shells into the bearing caps.
→ Lubricate them and position the caps the right way round and

3-A2

in the correct order - any arrows on the main bearing caps should face towards the front (crankshaft pulley) end of the engine.
→ Fit any new seals that may be required in the main bearing end caps.

☐ **STEP A3:** Lightly lubricate the bolt threads with engine oil. Screw the bolts in finger tight and check that the crankshaft rotates freely and smoothly.

TOP TIP!

• Where the correct torque is achieved by turning the main bearing cap bolts through a specified angle, the bolts should only be tightened to the specified torque once - new bolts should be used every time the crankshaft assembly is dismantled and reassembled.
• On diesel engines, the No 1 bearing cap must be flush with the front face of the cylinder block.

☐ **STEP A4:** Check crankshaft end float and make sure this is within the specified limits - if necessary, select and fit thrust bearings of the appropriate thickness. See illustration **2-H4**.

☐ **STEP A5:** Tighten the bolts evenly and progressively until the specified torque setting is reached - see **Chapter 1, Facts and Figures**.

3-A5

Again, make sure the crankshaft rotates freely and smoothly.

TOP TIP!

ZETEC SE ENGINES
• The rear oil seal and carrier are manufactured as a single unit and incorporate a bonded gasket - the seal is not available separately.

☐ **STEP A6:** Using a suitable hook or lever, remove the old oil seal from the crankshaft rear oil seal carrier. Clean the oil seal recess in the carrier and carefully press the new seal into position completely evenly all round - the lip of the seal facing in towards the block. Lubricate the seal with copious amounts of fresh engine oil.

TOP TIP!

• On diesel engines, you should apply a smear of sealant (Ford Spec SM 4G 4644 AA/AB) to the threads of the rear oil seal carrier bolts.

☐ **STEP A7:** Refit the housing with a new gasket and tighten the bolts. Where appropriate, ensure that the carrier is flush with the lower surface of the cylinder block or, Zetec and Zetec E engines, 0.3 mm to 0.8 mm below the level of the crankcase - the measurement must be exactly the same on each side. Make sure the carrier and oil seal are centred on the crankshaft.

☐ **STEP A8:** The front crankshaft oil seal is removed and fitted to the timing chain cover, oil pump housing or inner timing belt cover, as appropriate, in the same way as the rear oil seal.

☐ **STEP A9:** **SINGLE OVERHEAD CAM, DOUBLE OVERHEAD CAM AND 1.6 LITRE DIESEL ENGINES:** We recommend that you fit a new oil pump, the mark on the gear indicates which way round it

3-A9

should be fitted. Bolt the oil pump to the housing.

☐ **STEP A10:** Fit the oil pump housing or inner timing belt cover, as appropriate, making sure that flats on the pump and crankshaft engage correctly, the lower surface of the cylinder block is flush and the oil seal is centred on the crankshaft. Thoroughly lubricate the pump with engine oil.

Section B: Piston/connecting rod assemblies.

☐ **STEP B1:** The pistons and connecting rods on diesel engines are easily separated - the gudgeon pins are held in place by circlips. On all other engines the gudgeon pins are a tight press fit and can only be removed or refitted using specialist equipment - a job for a Ford dealer or specialist engine builder.

3-B1

STEP B2: DIESEL ENGINES: Push in the gudgeon pins and fit the circlips. Make sure the marks on the piston and connecting rod pin are

3-B2

fitted correctly, the marks on the piston indicating front should correspond with those on the connecting rod - the letter 'F' indicates front.

TOP TIP!

• If the gudgeon pins are a tight fit, heat the pistons to 60 degrees Celsius (140 degrees Fahrenheit), which is equivalent to hot, but NOT boiling water, and the pin should go straight in.
• DON'T apply direct heat!

STEP B3: Make sure that the bores and pistons are thoroughly clean, especially the piston ring grooves and oilways.
→ If you have not had the block re-bored, make sure you 'glaze bust' (hone) the cylinders.
→ Fit the rings, using a piston ring spreader, if possible.
→ Fit the piston ring gaps at equal intervals round the pistons circumference and lubricate them well.
→ Make sure the rings are fitted with the word 'TOP' facing upwards.

3-B4

STEP B4: Lubricate the piston rings and locate a ring clamp over the piston rings.

STEP B5: Position the assembly in its correct bore with the connecting rod identification marks facing the intermediate shaft.

STEP B6: With the piston ring clamp touching the cylinder block, use a hammer shaft to carefully tap the piston through and into the bore.

IMPORTANT NOTE:
• New big-end bolts should be used when reassembling all overhead valve engines - we recommend that new big-end bolts are used on all engines.
• Zetec SE engines do not have a tab for locating the big-end bearing shells. Make sure the ends of each shell are flush with the connecting rod or big-end cap.

STEP B7: Locate the upper half of the big end shell bearing in the connecting rod, making sure that the mating surfaces are clean.

→ Lubricate the crankpin and the big-end shell and draw the connecting rod down the bore so that the big end locates with the crankpin.
→ Fit the other half of the big-end shell to the bearing cap and lubricate.
→ Offer the cap to the connecting rod and make sure that the numbers match.
→ Screw in the fixing bolts and tighten progressively to the correct torque.

3-B8

STEP B8: Fit the remaining piston/connecting rod assemblies and stand the engine upside down on a clean surface.

STEP B9: 1.8 LITRE DIESEL ENGINES: Lubricate the auxiliary shaft bearings and position the shaft in the cylinder block. Fit the auxiliary shaft seal assembly, thrust plate (with oil grooves visible) and the housing assembly. New oil seal assemblies are supplied with a retainer and plastic installer which should be used to prevent seal damage during installation.

STEP B10: OVERHEAD VALVE AND 1.8 LITRE DIESEL ENGINES: Thoroughly lubricate and refit the oil pump.

STEP B11: Refit the oil pick-up pipe and strainer.

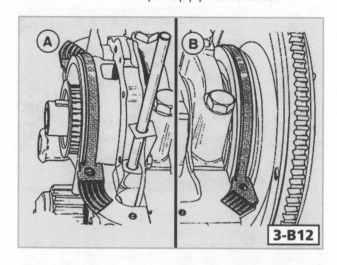

3-B12

STEP B12: Refit the baffle (where appropriate) and sump.
→ Where appropriate, note the location of the sump gaskets at front (**A**) and rear (**B**) main bearings.

STEP B13: If the engine isn't mounted on a stand, you can now turn it over and carry out the following operations, referring to the relevant sections of this manual.

→ Fit the coolant pump.
→ Refit the flywheel and clutch.
→ Refit the cylinder head.
→ Fit the crankshaft, auxiliary and camshaft sprockets. On 1.6 litre diesel engines, fit the fuel pump drive gears.
→ On overhead valve engines, fit the tappets, camshaft, timing gear and chain.
→ Refit the fuel pump.

→ Fit the camshaft and, on 1.8 litre diesel engines the fuel pump, timing belts.
→ Fit the crankshaft pulley/vibration damper and tighten the bolt.
→ Lubricate the sealing ring and screw on a new oil filter.
→ Refit the engine mounted ignition and fuel components.
→ Refit all remaining auxiliary components using new gaskets as necessary.
→ Reconnect the engine to the transmission and refit the complete unit to the vehicle.

Part K: Engine Mountings Replacement

CONTENTS

JOB 1: ENGINE/TRANSMISSION MOUNTINGS – *removal, replacement.*

1-1

STEP 1: On all models you will need to do the following:
→ Disconnect the battery negative terminal. Before dismantling, disconnect the battery negative (-) earth/ground terminal. See *Chapter 10, Electrical, Dash, Instruments, Fact File: Disconnecting the Battery* BEFORE doing so!
→ Support the engine/transmission unit so that the weight is taken off the mounting. Take care not to strain the mountings in an upward direction!

FIESTA XR2i MODELS: You will first have to remove the front suspension crossmember – see *Chapter 11, Steering, Suspension.*

STEP 2: The right-hand mounting is unbolted beneath the wheelarch (**A**) and inside the engine bay (**B**).

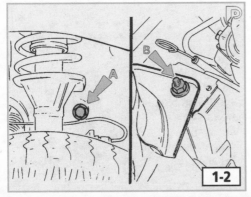

1-2

STEP 3: The lower mounting insulator nuts (**a**) would normally be left connected while the bracket bolts (**b**) are removed from the vehicle.

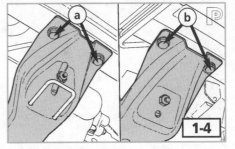

1-3

STEP 4: The lower bracket – the engine bearer – is unbolted from the body at the front (**a**) and the rear (**b**) and can be lowered with the engine/ transmission unit.

1-4

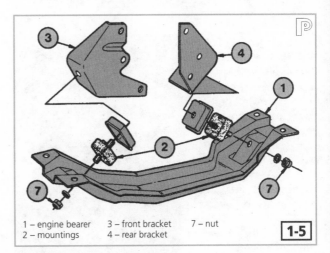

1 – engine bearer   3 – front bracket   7 – nut
2 – mountings   4 – rear bracket

1-5

STEP 5: These are the components of the engine bearer and associated brackets.

STEP 6: The rear end of the early type of Fiesta mounting is unbolted from the body.

STEP 7: The central stud at the front end of the mounting holds the rubber mounting block to the support bracket.

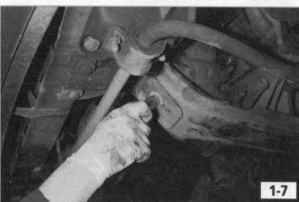

STEP 8: Even if you are just replacing the rubber mounting, you will still need to release the front end of the support bracket so that the bracket can be lowered sufficiently to remove the rubber.

STEP 9: 1.8 DIESEL ENGINED MODELS: These vehicles have an additional anti-vibration block (arrowed) bolted to the mounting.
→ The anti-vibration block can come loose within its mounting and create a 'clonking' noise as the vehicle is started away in first or reverse gear.
→ You will then have to replace the block. It cannot be repaired.

STEP 10: This is typical of a rear mounting of the later type, especially where 1.25 and 1.4 Zetec engines are fitted.

STEP 11: This is a typical right-hand mounting and is a pendulum type of mounting used to connect the engine to the suspension strut area.

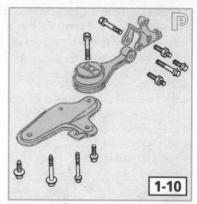

STEP 12: As with the earlier type of mounting, these later mountings are simply unbolted even though, by definition, there are usually more ancillary components to remove before they can be properly reached.

STEP 13: This is a typical left-hand engine mounting used on vehicles with manual transmission.

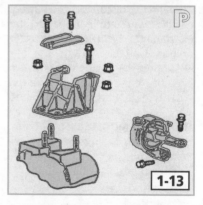

STEP 14: Vehicles with automatic transmission typically have this type of mounting arrangement on the left-hand side.

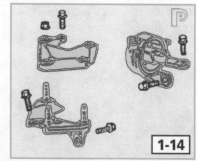

CHAPTER 7: CLUTCH, TRANSMISSION, DRIVESHAFTS

*PLEASE READ **CHAPTER 2 SAFETY FIRST** BEFORE CARRYING OUT ANY WORK ON YOUR CAR.*

Part A: Clutch, Transmission and Driveshafts General Information

CONTENTS

JOB 1:   SYSTEMS EXPLAINED.

HYDRAULIC CLUTCH

❏ **POINT 1:** Fiesta models from 1995 and all Ka models have a hydraulically operated clutch.
➜ The slave cylinder (3) is integral with the clutch bellhousing.
➜ The clutch shares the hydraulic fluid reservoir (4) with the braking system but feeds through a supply tube (5) from a separate compartment.

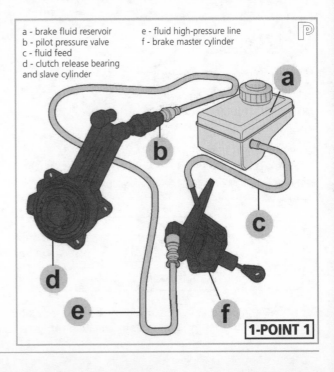

a - brake fluid reservoir
b - pilot pressure valve
c - fluid feed
d - clutch release bearing and slave cylinder
e - fluid high-pressure line
f - brake master cylinder

1-POINT 1

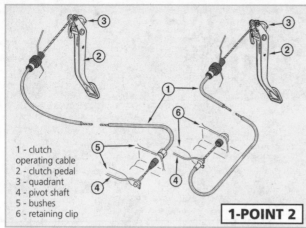

1 - clutch
operating cable
2 - clutch pedal
3 - quadrant
4 - pivot shaft
5 - bushes
6 - retaining clip

1-POINT 2

CABLE OPERATED CLUTCH

❐ **POINT 2:** All other vehicles covered by this manual have a cable operated clutch. Note the different arrangements between right-hand (**5**) and left-hand (**6**) drive vehicles.

❐ **POINT 3:** Except on Escort models from 1996 which have manual clutch cable adjustment (**1**), the clutch is adjusted automatically by a pawl (**2**) and toothed quadrant (**3**) fitted to the clutch pedal.

1-POINT 3

MANUAL TRANSMISSION

❐ **POINT 4:** Depending on age and specification, vehicles with manual transmissions will have a four or five-speed transmission, with most models having a B5 or iB5 (improved B5) type or the MTX 75 transmission, fitted to more recent Escorts with higher powered Zetec SE engines.

➜ Externally, the transmissions are similar - the five speed B5 and iB5 units can be identified by an additional housing (arrowed).

1-POINT 4

AUTO. TRANSMISSION

❐ **POINT 5:** Up to 1989, Escort models with automatic transmission were fitted with the ATX system - a three speed automatic gearbox.

❐ **POINT 6:** All automatic Fiesta models and Escort models from 1989 have been fitted with the CTX system, shown here, which provides continuously variable gear ratios.

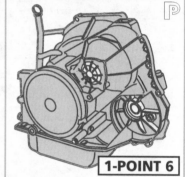

1-POINT 6

Part B: Clutch Components – Inspection, Removal, Replacement

CONTENTS

JOB 1:   CLUTCH FRICTION PLATE - *removal, inspection, replacement.*

To remove and replace the clutch you will have to separate the transmission from the engine. You can either remove the transmission, leaving the engine in place, or remove the engine and transmission as a unit and separate them after removal.

➜ Unless the engine has to be removed for other work, it is easier and quicker to leave the engine in place. See *Chapter 6, Engine* if you wish to remove the engine and transmission as a unit.

STEP 1: Separate the transmission from the engine so that you have access to the clutch - see *Part C*.

STEP 2: Remove the six bolts (arrowed) attaching the pressure plate to the flywheel.

1-2

TOP TIP!

To prevent damage to the clutch assembly, unscrew bolts no more than a turn at a time and in a diagonal pattern until the pressure if released.

STEP 3: Carefully lift the pressure plate off its locating dowels and away from the flywheel.
→ Be ready to catch the friction plate, which will drop away as the pressure plate is removed.

STEP 4: Examine the friction plate (**a**), pressure plate (**b**) and flywheel (**c**) for signs of wear, overheating or contamination. Check the thickness of the friction material and the friction plate for cracks, loose springs or loose rivets.

1-4

TOP TIP!

• Some friction plates will be marked 'FLYWHEEL SIDE' but if this marking is not present, look for the word 'SCHWUNGRADSEITE' which is stamped on the flywheel side of the friction plate.
• In the absence of any markings, you should take a careful note of the way in which the old friction plate was fitted so that the new plate can be fitted the same way.

STEP 5: Finger tighten the six cover plate attachment bolts and use a clutch aligning tool to centralise the friction plate. Fully tighten the attachment bolts, evenly and in a diagonal pattern, to the specified torque - see *Chapter 1, Facts and Figures*.

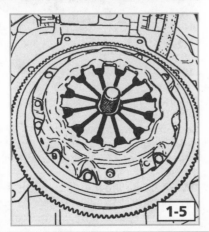

1-5

STEP 6: Make sure the release bearing guide shaft, input shaft splines and friction disc splines are clean. Apply a very light smear of high melting point grease to these areas - do not use too much grease!

JOB 2: CLUTCH RELEASE BEARING - *removal, replacement.*

→ On early cable operated clutches, the release fork is bolted to the operating shaft which allows the shaft and fork to be separated.
→ This design was modified on later models, the release fork being permanently attached to the shaft so that the two components cannot be separated.
→ On hydraulically operated clutches, the release bearing is mounted directly onto the slave cylinder.

TOP TIP!

• A worn bearing feels rough and noisy when spun.

Section A: Bolted release fork.

STEP A1: Remove the release fork attachment bolt (arrowed)…

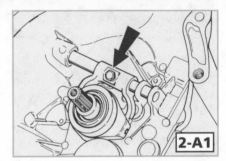

2-A1

STEP A2: …and withdraw the operating shaft (**a**) in the direction of the arrow.
→ Withdraw the release fork and bearing from the transmission input shaft.

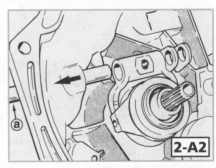

2-A2

STEP A3: With the release fork and bearing clear of the transmission input shaft (**a**) you can manoeuvre the release bearing (**b**) clear of the pegs (**c**) on the release fork.

STEP A4: Refitting is the reverse of the removal process.

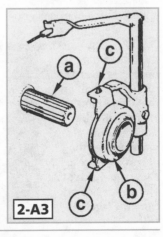

2-A3

Section B: Fixed release fork.

❑ **STEP B1:** Slide the release bearing (**a**) along the transmission input shaft so that it is clear of the input shaft sleeve (**b**). Some manoeuvring of the release bearing will now be necessary to unhook it from the release fork (**c**).

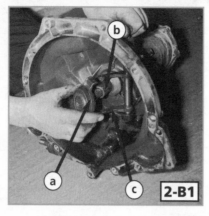

2-B1

❑ **STEP B2:** Refitting is the reverse of the removal process.

Section C: Hydraulic clutch.

❑ **STEP C1:** Lever the release bearing away from the slave cylinder.

❑ **STEP C2:** Refit the release bearing (**a**) by aligning the tag (**b**) with the cut-out in the slave cylinder (**c**) and sliding the release bearing into position.

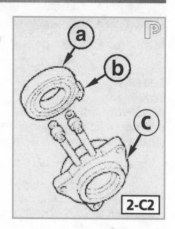

2-C2

JOB 3:   CLUTCH CABLE - *removal, replacement.*

Escort models from 1996 have a manually adjusted clutch.
➔ Apart from minor differences to the clutch pedal to cable attachment, the manually and automatically adjusted cables are similar.

❑ **STEP 1:** Disconnect the cable from the operating lever and support bracket on the bellhousing. There should be sufficient free movement of the operating lever to allow the clutch cable end to be released from the lever.

3-1

❑ **STEP 2:** These are typical arrangements for LHD (**A**) and RHD vehicles (**B**).

IMPORTANT NOTE: On some models it will be necessary to remove lower dash trim panels.

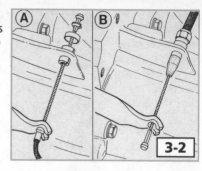

3-2

❑ **STEP 3:** Move the clutch pedal upwards to disengage the pawl (**A**) and rotate the toothed quadrant (**B**) forwards against the pull of the tension spring (**C**).
➔ Disconnect the clutch cable from the toothed quadrant.
➔ After disconnecting the cable, carefully allow the tension spring to rotate the toothed quadrant back.
➔ **ESCORT ADJUSTABLE TYPE:** Attach cable to quadrant (**a**) and adjust pedal free-play (see *Chapter 1, Facts and Figures*) with an Allen key on screw (**b**).

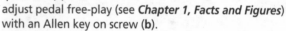
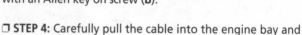

3-3

❑ **STEP 4:** Carefully pull the cable into the engine bay and remove the cable from the vehicle.

❑ **STEP 5:** When refitting the clutch cable:
➔ Feed the new cable into the passenger compartment from the engine bay and through the gap between the pedal and the adjuster.

❑ **STEP 6:** Connect the cable to the toothed quadrant and operating lever:
➔ **A.** Lift the pawl (**a**) and turn the quadrant (**b**) in the direction of the arrow...
➔ **B.** ...setting the pawl so that it is in contact with the smooth section of the adjuster mechanism.

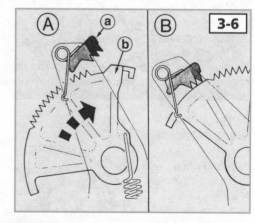

3-6

❑ **STEP 7:** Operate the clutch pedal several times to make sure that the auto adjuster is working correctly and the clutch disengages. Refit any trim panels.

JOB 4: CLUTCH PEDAL - *removal, replacement.*

Section A: Cable operated clutch.

❑ **STEP A1:** Disconnect the clutch cable from the pedal - see *Job 3*.

❑ **STEP A2:** Remove the brake pedal-to-servo linkage retaining clip - see *Chapter 12, Brakes.*

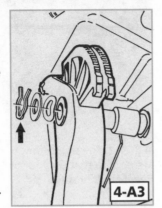

❑ **STEP A3:** Remove the pivot shaft retaining clip:
➜ The clip (arrowed) may be on the left-or right hand side.
➜ Note the position of the washers and spacers.

4-A3

❑ **STEP A4:** Slide out the pivot shaft and lift away the pedals.

❑ **STEP A5:** Dismantle the pedal as far as necessary to replace any worn or damaged components.

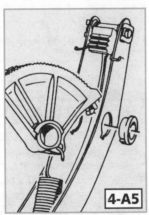

❑ **STEP A6:** Refitting the pedal is the reverse of the removal process but first set the pawl so that it is in

4-A5

contact with the smooth section of the toothed adjuster mechanism - see *Job 3*. Bear in mind the following points during refitting.
➜ Apply a smear of multi-purpose grease to the pivot shaft before refitting the pedals.
➜ Fit the washers and spacers in their original positions.
➜ After reconnecting the clutch cable, operate the clutch several times to check for correct operation and set the adjuster.

Section B: Fiesta and Ka hydraulic clutch.

❑ **STEP B1:** These are the relevant components of the clutch assembly.
➜ All of the following Steps refer to this drawing.

❑ **STEP B2:** Before dismantling, disconnect the battery negative (-) earth/ground terminal. See *Chapter 10, Electrical, Dash, Instruments, Fact File: Disconnecting the Battery* BEFORE doing so!

❑ **STEP B3: KA:** Remove the steering column - see *Chapter 11, Steering, Suspension.*

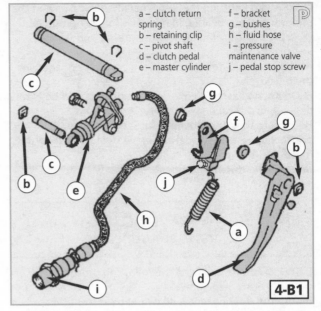

a – clutch return spring
b – retaining clip
c – pivot shaft
d – clutch pedal
e – master cylinder
f – bracket
g – bushes
h – fluid hose
i – pressure maintenance valve
j – pedal stop screw

4-B1

❑ **STEP B4:** Disconnect and remove the clutch return spring (a).

❑ **STEP B5: KA:** Disconnect the accelerator cable and remove the accelerator pedal - see *Chapter 9, Ignition, Fuel and Exhaust.* Disconnect the cable and remove the stop light switch - see *Chapter 12, Brakes.*

❑ **STEP B6:** Disconnect the cable and remove the clutch switch. This switch is removed and fitted in the same way as the brake stop light switch - see *Chapter 12, Brakes.*

❑ **STEP B7: KA:** Disconnect the servo linkage pushrod from the brake pedal - see *Chapter 12, Brakes.*
➜ If necessary, move the bonnet release cable as necessary to gain access.

❑ **STEP B8:** Remove the retaining clips and master cylinder pushrod to pedal pin. You may need to use a punch to drive out the pin.

❑ **STEP B9: FIESTA:** Separate the pedal from the master cylinder pushrod by lifting the pedal.
➜ Remove the retaining clip from the left-hand end of the pedal pivot shaft.
➜ Push the pedal pivot shaft to the right until it clears the clutch pedal and withdraw the pedal from the bracket.
❑ **STEP B10: KA:** Remove the pedal bracket mounting nuts from the left and right-hand side of the bracket followed by the upper pedal bracket mounting bolts.
➜ Remove the retaining clip from the right-hand end of the pivot shaft and push the pivot shaft to the left, withdrawing the brake pedal and then the clutch pedal.
➜ Note the location of the bushes and spring.

❑ **STEP B11:** Examine the pedal bushes and replace if worn. You should also check the pivot shafts, fitting new if there are any signs of wear.

TOP TIP!

• The bushes used on the brake pedals are different from those used on the clutch pedal and are not interchangeable.

CHAPTER 7 Part B - Job 4

7-5

❏ **STEP B12:** Refitting the clutch pedal is the reverse of the removal process, bearing in mind the following points.
➜ Apply a smear of multi purpose grease to the bushes and pivot shaft.
➜ Make sure the retaining clips are properly engaged in their grooves.
➜ On Ka models, tighten the mounting nuts and bolts to the specified torque - see *Chapter 1, Facts and Figures*.
➜ Operate the clutch to make sure there are no obstructions and the pedal can move freely throughout its travel.
➜ Check the clutch adjustment - see *Job 5*.

JOB 5: HYDRAULIC CLUTCH - *pedal travel adjustment.*

❏ **STEP 1:** Ford recommend the following procedure for checking clutch pedal travel.
➜ Turn the steering wheel 30 degrees left from the straight ahead position then tighten a cable-tie around the clutch pedal at the second groove from the bottom.
➜ Hook an expanding steel rule onto the cable-tie and extend the rule over the steering wheel rim.
➜ Press down on the clutch pedal and check the travel, making sure pedal movement is not restricted by the carpet.
➜ Correct travel is as follows.
• Fiesta and 44 kW engined Ka models 122 mm to 128 mm
• 37 kW engined Ka models 121 mm to 125 mm
• IMPORTANT NOTE: The clutch master cylinder may be damaged if pedal travel is excessive.

❏ **STEP 2:** If necessary, adjust pedal travel by loosening the pedal stop screw locknut and turning the stop screw (see illustration *4-B1, item j*) until the pedal travel is within specification. Tighten the locknut.

❏ **STEP 3:** Check for any sponginess when the clutch is operated and bleed the system as necessary - see *Job 6*.

❏ **STEP 4:** Check that the clutch pedal moves freely throughout its travel and there are no obstructions. In particular, make sure that movement of the pedal is not obstructed by floor carpet or mats.

JOB 6: HYDRAULIC CLUTCH - *bleeding.*

SAFETY FIRST!

• **Make sure that it is safe to spin the engine with HT leads disconnected on your particular engine.**

• **Some ignition systems may suffer damage if not first completely disconnected.**

• **Take care not to cause injury from uncontrolled high tension sparks, or from diesel injection spray.**

❏ **STEP 1:** The bleed screw is located on top of the transmission bellhousing, beside the hydraulic fluid connection to the slave cylinder.

➜ This is the bleed screw location on a Fiesta (arrowed).
➜ On Ka models you will have to remove the air cleaner assembly to gain access to the bleed screw.

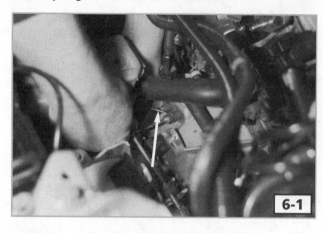

6-1

❏ **STEP 2:** The procedure for bleeding the system is identical to that used for bleeding the brakes - see *Chapter 12, Brakes*.

JOB 7: HYDRAULIC CLUTCH HOSES - *inspection, removal, refitting.*

FACT FILE

PRE-LOADING VALVE

• A pre-loading valve is used to maintain a pressure around 1.0 bar in the slave cylinder.
• This pressure ensures that the release bearing is always kept in contact with the pressure plate.
• The valve is fitted to the slave cylinder inlet, on the outside of the bellhousing. See illustration *4-B1, item i*.

❏ **STEP 1:** Examine the clutch hydraulic pipes and hoses (arrowed and *4-B1, item h*), replace any that show signs of deterioration, cuts or chafing. Check the connections and replace any hoses that have insecure or damaged connections.

7-1

❏ **STEP 2:** To reduce spillage when removing hoses, you should remove sufficient fluid from the hydraulic reservoir to bring the fluid level below the inlet to the clutch master cylinder. For information on draining the reservoir, see *Chapter 12, Brakes*.

❏ **STEP 3:** Clean all dirt or contamination from the reservoir and master cylinder.
➜ Remove the clips and disconnect the supply hose from the reservoir and the master cylinder.

❏ **STEP 4:** Clean all dirt or contamination from the reservoir, pre-loading valve and bleed valve.

→ Remove the clips and disconnect the high pressure hose from the master cylinder and the pre-loading valve.

☐ **STEP 5:** Refitting the hoses is the reverse of the removal process. Bleed the clutch hydraulic system after re-fitting the hoses - see *Job 6*.

JOB 8:	**CLUTCH MASTER CYLINDER -** *removal, refitting.*

For the location of the master cylinder – see *4-B1, item e*.

IMPORTANT NOTE: Ford do not supply repair kit for the clutch master cylinder. If the master cylinder is unserviceable, a new master cylinder must be fitted.

☐ **STEP 1:** Drain the hydraulic reservoir - see *Job 7*.

☐ **STEP 2:** Disconnect the supply hose and high pressure hose from the master cylinder - see *Job 6*. Plug or cover the open connections to prevent contamination and reduce fluid loss.

☐ **STEP 3:** Separate the pedal from the master cylinder pushrod - see *Job 4*. Then undo the bolts attaching the master cylinder to the pedal mounting bracket.
→ On Ka models Ford recommend separating the pedal mounting bracket from the bulkhead so that you can access the master cylinder attachment bolts - see *Job 4*.

☐ **STEP 4:** Remove the master cylinder from the bracket. Use absorbent paper or rags to collect hydraulic fluid spillage as the master cylinder is removed. Retrieve the sponge rubber padding from the outlets for re-use during reassembly.

☐ **STEP 5:** Refitting is the reverse of the removal process, bearing in mind the following points.
→ Smear grease on the pushrod pin before refitting.
→ Check the adjustment of the clutch pedal - see *Job 5*.
→ Bleed the clutch hydraulic system - see *Job 6*.

JOB 9:	**CLUTCH SLAVE CYLINDER -** *removal, refitting.*

☐ **STEP 1:** Separate the transmission from the engine - see *Part C*.

9-2

☐ **STEP 2:** To reduce hydraulic fluid loss, fit a hydraulic hose clamp to the clutch high pressure hose near to the slave cylinder.

☐ **STEP 3:** Remove the clip and disconnect the hose from the pre-loading valve – see illustration *4-B1, item i*.

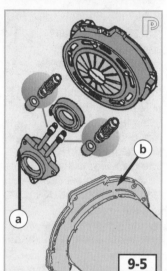
9-5

☐ **STEP 4:** Slowly unscrew and remove the bleed screw to release residual pressure.
→ You can now remove the pre-loading valve.

☐ **STEP 5:** Remove the slave cylinder mounting bolts and withdraw the slave cylinder (a) from the bellhousing (b).

☐ **STEP 6:** Refitting the slave cylinder is the reverse of the removal process, bearing in mind the following points.
→ Do not overtighten the pre-loading valve when re-fitting. If the valve is tightened beyond the specified torque, it may not work properly.
→ Bleed the hydraulic clutch system - see *Job 6*.

Part C: Manual Transmission Inspection, Removal, Replacement

CONTENTS

JOB 1:	**TRANSMISSION OIL AND FLUID SEALS** - *removal, replacement.*

The transmission oil and fluid seal replacement procedure is the same for manual and automatic transmissions.

→ The driveshaft seals can be replaced without removing the transmission from the vehicle but the input shaft seal can only be replaced with the transmission separated from the engine.

Section A: Input shaft seal.

❏ **STEP A1:** Separate the transmission from the engine - see *Job 2*.

❏ **STEP A2:** Remove the release bearing (cable clutch) or slave cylinder (hydraulic clutch) - see *Part B*.

❏ **STEP A3:** Lever out the old seal, taking care not to damage the input shaft or transmission casing.

❏ **STEP A4:** Clean the input shaft and seal seating recess.

❏ **STEP A5:** Smear oil around the sealing lip and lightly press the seal into the recess in the transmission casing.
➜ Make sure the seal is fitted the right way round - the open side (arrowed) should face into the transmission.

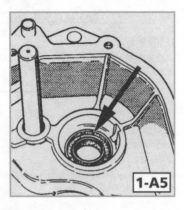

1-A5

❏ **STEP A6: HYDRAULIC CLUTCH MODELS:** Refit the slave cylinder - see *Part B*.
➜ Evenly tightening the slave cylinder attachment bolts to the specified torque will press the seal into place.

❏ **STEP A7: CABLE CLUTCH AND AUTOMATIC TRANSMISSION MODELS:** Use a suitable diameter tube and gently tap the seal into place, making sure it is square in the transmission recess at all times.

❏ **STEP A8: CABLE CLUTCH MODELS:** Refit the release bearing.

❏ **STEP A9:** Refit the transmission to the engine - see *Job 2*.

Section B: Driveshaft seals.

❏ **STEP B1:** Remove and support the inner end of the relevant driveshaft - see *Part E*. Have a suitable container ready to collect any oil spillage.

TOP TIP!

The driveshaft must be supported because the CV joints will be damaged if the inner joint is out of alignment by more than 18 degrees and the outer joint by more than 45 degrees.
• If you remove both driveshafts at the same time, use a suitable plug to prevent the differential rotating within the transmission - see *Part E*.
• It is only necessary to separate the inner ends of the driveshaft, the outer ends can remain attached to the hubs.

❏ **STEP B2:** Clean the seal and surrounding area. Measure the depth between the face of the transmission and the seal.
➜ The new seal must be fitted into the recess (arrowed) to the same depth - around 5 mm.

1-B2

❏ **STEP B3:** Lever the old seal out of the transmission, taking care not to damage the transmission casing.
➜ The seal is a tight fit and you might need to apply some force to remove the old seal.

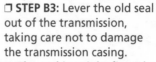

1-B3

❏ **STEP B4:** Clean the recess in the transmission casing and lightly press the new seal into place.
➜ Make sure the seal is fitted the right way round - the open side should face into the transmission - see *Step A5*.

❏ **STEP B5:** Use a suitable diameter tube or drift and gently tap the seal into place, making sure it is square in the transmission casing at all times. The new seal must be fitted to the same depth as the old seal.

❏ **STEP B6:** Smear oil around the sealing lip and refit the relevant driveshaft - see *Part D*.

Section C: Selector shaft seal.

❏ **STEP C1:** Fully apply the handbrake and chock the rear wheels. Raise and support the front of the vehicle on stands.

❏ **STEP C2:** Disconnect the gearshift rod and remove the rubber boot (arrowed).

1-C2

❏ **STEP C3:** Lever the seal from its recess in the transmission - see Illustration *1-B3*.

TOP TIP!

• This seal can be particularly difficult to remove and you will probably have to make hole in the seal to allow enough purchase to lever it from the recess.

❏ **STEP C4:** Smear oil around the sealing lip and lightly press the new seal into the recess in the transmission casing. Make sure the seal is fitted the right way round - the open side should face into the transmission - see *Step A5*.

☐ **STEP C5:** Use a suitable diameter tube and gently tap the seal into place, making sure it is square in the transmission recess at all times.

☐ **STEP C6:** Refit the rubber boot, reconnect and adjust the gearshift rod - see *Job 4*.

JOB 2: MANUAL TRANSMISSION - *removal, refitting.*

TOP TIP!

• To make reassembly of the gearshift mechanism easier, Ford recommend that a gear - the one specified below - is engaged before the transmission is fitted to the vehicle. You will then know which positions to put the selector mechanism and gear lever in when they are being reconnected.

The gears to be engaged before refitting are as follows:
➜ Four speed transmissions up to February 1987 - engage 4th gear.
➜ Five speed transmissions up to February 1987 - engage reverse gear.
➜ Four speed transmission from February 1987 - engage 2nd gear.
➜ Five speed transmissions from February 1987 - engage 4th gear.
➜ MTX 75 transmissions – place mechanism in neutral.

VEHICLES WITH ELECTRONIC ENGINE MANAGEMENT SYSTEMS AND SECURITY CODED RADIOS

IMPORTANT NOTE: • Disconnecting the battery may affect the engine management system and prevent the radio working until a security code has been re-entered. Check the vehicle handbook, if available, for any precautions or warnings before disconnecting the battery.
– see *Chapter 10, Electrical, Instruments, FACT FILE: DISCONNECTING THE BATTERY*.

☐ **STEP 1:** Disconnect the battery negative connection. Before dismantling, disconnect the battery negative (-) earth/ground terminal. See *Chapter 10, Electrical, Dash, Instruments, Fact File: Disconnecting the Battery* BEFORE doing so!

☐ **STEP 2:** Carry out the additional preparatory work shown here on the following models:
➜ **FIESTA FROM 1995 AND KA:** Remove the battery.
➜ **FIESTA FROM 1995:** Remove the battery tray.
➜ **ESCORT AND FIESTA FROM 1989, KA:** Remove the air cleaner and inlet duct as far as necessary to gain access to the top of the transmission, but also noting the following where relevant:
➜ **FIESTA FROM 1995, ZETEC SE ENGINE:** It is only necessary to remove the air inlet duct between the throttle housing and the air mass flow sensor on the air cleaner.
➜ **FIESTA FROM 1995, ENDURA E ENGINE:** Only the air inlet duct needs to be removed.

➜ **FIESTA FROM 1995, ENDURA DE ENGINE:** Only the air inlet duct between the inlet manifold and resonator needs to be removed but you will also have to remove the mounting bolts and resonator.

☐ **STEP 3:** Where fitted, remove the transmission earth/ground lead from the top of the transmission.
➜ This is a different lead from the battery earth strap mentioned later.

☐ **STEP 4: MODELS WITH CABLE CLUTCH:** Disconnect the clutch cable from the clutch release lever - see *Part B*.

☐ **STEP 5: MODELS WITH HYDRAULIC CLUTCH:** To reduce hydraulic fluid loss, fit a hydraulic hose clamp to the clutch hydraulic hose.
➜ Pull out the clip and disconnect the quick release connector from the slave cylinder - see *Part B*.
➜ Replace the clip after disconnection.
➜ Plug or cover the open connections to reduce further fluid loss and prevent contamination.
➜ Release the clutch hydraulic line from the support on the transmission.

☐ **STEP 6:** Unscrew the retaining nut and remove the speedometer drive cable from the transmission or, where fitted, the speed sensor.

☐ **STEP 7:** Where fitted, disconnect the plug from the vehicle speed sensor.

☐ **STEP 8:** At the front of the transmission, disconnect the wiring from the reversing light switch or, on later models, the multi-function switch (arrowed).

2-8

☐ **STEP 9:** Where possible you should drain the oil from the transmission, bearing in mind the following points:
➜ Fiesta models from 1995 have a transmission drain plug. All other models with the B5 and iB5 transmission can be drained via the selector shaft cap nut (**A**).
➜ The nut is under tension from the spring (**B**) which fits over the interlock pin (**C**).
➜ On Escort and Orion models from 1986, there is insufficient room to remove the selector shaft cap nut - the transmission can only be drained after removal.
➜ Refit the drain plug or selector shaft cap nut after draining. Use a sealant on the threads of the cap nut.

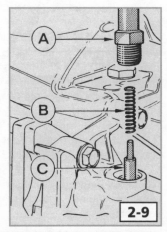

☐ **STEP 10:** Fully apply the parking brake, chock the rear wheels, jack up and support the front of the vehicle.

2-9

STEP 11: Where applicable, remove any protective splash shields or undertrays.

STEP 12: Support the weight of the engine.

STEP 13: B5 AND IB5 TRANSMISSION BREATHER: Depending on model, the transmission breather is removed from its location in the transmission or chassis side member - see *Steps 14 to 16*, for particular information.

STEP 14: ESCORT AND PRE-1995 FIESTA: Pull out the breather tube from the chassis side member.

STEP 15: FIESTA FROM 1995 WITH ENDURA-E AND DE ENGINES: Pull out the breather from the transmission.

STEP 16: FIESTA FROM 1995 WITH ZETEC SE ENGINE: Remove the reinforcement bar and pull out the breather from the transmission.

STEP 17: FIESTA FROM 1995: Remove the nuts from the left-hand engine mounting.

STEP 18: FIESTA FROM 1995 WITH ENDURA DE ENGINE: Remove the right-hand engine mounting bracket.

2-18

STEP 19: Unscrew and remove all the engine to bellhousing attachment bolts that are accessible from above - on Fiesta models from 1995, access is limited and removal of the engine to bellhousing bolts is best left until the transmission is lowered - see *Step 52*.
→ The number of bolts and their location varies, depending on vehicle model and transmission type.
→ Make a note of any cables, clips, supports and brackets that are fitted to these bolts.

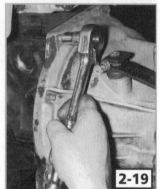

2-19

STEP 20: FIESTA FROM 1995 WITH ENDURA E ENGINE AND ESCORT FROM 1991 WITH ZETEC OR ZETEC E ENGINES AND MTX 75 TRANSMISSION: Disconnect the oxygen sensor multi-plug and, on Escort models, release the cable from the tie - see *Chapter 9, Ignition, Fuel and Exhaust*.

STEP 21: Tie any hoses, cables or pipes out of the way to prevent them from getting in the way and being damaged.

STEP 22: Detach the exhaust from the engine as you would for engine removal - see *Chapter 9, Ignition, Fuel and Exhaust*.

TOP TIP!

• To separate the engine from the gearbox, it is necessary to lower the engine at the left-hand side.
• This will be much easier if the exhaust is first separated from the engine.
• On models with a flexible section in the exhaust pipe, make sure the flexible section is not bent excessively. Strap a splint to the flexible section.

STEP 23: Where necessary, remove the starter motor.
→ On Escort models with the MTX 75 transmission, the top bolt is also used to attach an earth/ground cable.

TOP TIP!

• Removing the starter motor is not essential on all models but removal is not difficult and access will be easier if it is out of the way.

STEP 24: MODELS EQUIPPED WITH THE MODULATOR TYPE ABS: On the relevant Fiesta models you will have to remove the left-hand ABS modulator unit from its mounting bracket - leave the hydraulic pipe and hose connected - see *Chapter 12, Brakes*.
→ Relevant Escort and Orion models just need to have the modulator drive belt removed – again, see *Chapter 12, Brakes*.

TOP TIP!

• Complete removal of the driveshafts from the vehicle is not necessary.
• The driveshafts can be left attached to the hubs, provided the hubs can be swung out of the way to allow separation of the driveshafts from the transmission.

STEP 25: Remove the driveshafts from the transmission - see *Part D*.

IMPORTANT NOTE: Make sure you support the driveshafts so that the inner joint is not bent at more than 18 degrees and the outer joint at not more than 45 degrees.

STEP 26: ESCORT AND ORION PRE-1990 EQUIPPED WITH ANTI-ROLL BAR: Disconnect the anti-roll bar from the body - see *Chapter 11, Steering and Suspension*.

STEP 27: FIESTA FROM 1989 TO 1995: Remove the lower engine adapter plate and, where fitted, engine/ transmission adapter plate.

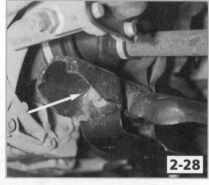

2-28

STEP 28: FIESTA FROM 1995 WITH ZETEC SE ENGINE: If fitted, remove the small bracket (arrowed) from the front of the left-hand subframe.

☐ **STEP 29:** Where fitted, remove the exhaust heatshields so that you have access to the gearshift mechanism.

☐ **STEP 30:** Remove the bolt attaching the gearshift stabiliser rod to the transmission and secure the rod to one side - see *Job 3*. Note the location of any washers.

☐ **STEP 31:** Remove the clamp bolt and disconnect the gearshift rod from the transmission shaft. On B5 transmissions, unhook the selector rod tension spring - see *Job 3*. Secure the rod to one side.

TOP TIP!

• Before disconnecting the gearshift rod, put alignment marks on the rod and shaft so that they can be reconnected in the correct position.

☐ **STEP 32:** Where fitted, unbolt and remove the lower flywheel cover plate. The shape of the plate, number of bolts and their location varies, depending on engine type.

2-32

☐ **STEP 33:** Support the transmission assembly. Use a suitable jack from below or attach the transmission to the engine hoist or support bar.

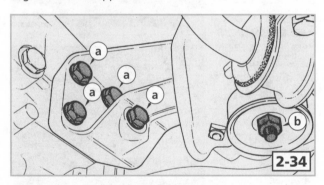

2-34

☐ **STEP 34: ESCORT AND ORION PRE-1986:** Remove the following:
→ The four bolts (**a**) attaching the front mounting bracket to the transmission.
→ The nut (**b**) attaching the mounting to the body.

☐ **STEP 35:** Remove the three bolts (arrowed) attaching the rear mounting body bracket to the body.

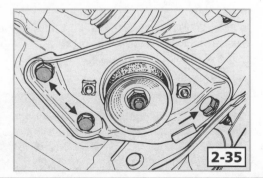

2-35

☐ **STEP 36: ESCORT AND ORION FROM 1986 TO 1990 AND FIESTA TO 1995:** Where fitted, unbolt and remove the transmission support member from the body and transmission.

2-36

☐ **STEP 37: ESCORT AND ORION FROM 1990 IB5 TRANSMISSION:** Remove the left-hand rear engine/ transmission mounting bracket...

☐ **STEP 38:** ...and the left-hand front engine/transmission mounting bracket.

2-38

IMPORTANT NOTE: For further information relating to *Steps 39 to 46*, see *Chapter 6, Engine*.

☐ **STEP 39: ESCORT AND ORION FROM 1990 WITH 1.6 LITRE CVH ENGINE:** Unscrew the seven bolts and remove the engine/transmission bracing plate from each side.

☐ **STEP 40: ESCORT AND ORION FROM 1990 WITH 1.3, 1.4 OR 1.6 LITRE ENGINES AND B5 OR IB5 TRANSMISSION:** Remove the engine/transmission adapter plates.

☐ **STEP 41: ESCORT FROM 1991 WITH ZETEC OR ZETEC E ENGINES AND MTX 75 TRANSMISSION:** Detach the front left-hand engine mounting from the body.

☐ **STEP 42: ESCORT FROM 1991 WITH ZETEC OR ZETEC E ENGINES AND MTX 75 TRANSMISSION:** Disconnect the crankshaft position sensor multi-plug and remove the bolt attaching the pulse air system filter housing.

☐ **STEP 43: ESCORT FROM 1991 WITH ZETEC OR ZETEC E ENGINES AND MTX 75 TRANSMISSION:** Remove left-hand rear engine/transmission mounting. Lower the engine/transmission so that you have access to the six bolts attaching the left-hand mounting brackets to the transmission and remove the brackets.

☐ **STEP 44: FIESTA FROM 1995 WITH ZETEC SE ENGINE:** Remove the plastic cover that fits below the crankshaft pulley. If the cover is left in place it will be damaged when the right-hand side of the engine is lowered.

☐ **STEP 45: FIESTA FROM 1995 WITH ENDURA E ENGINE:** Remove the auxiliary drive belt lower cover.

SAFETY FIRST!

• There is likely to be tension in the link so make sure the engine is properly supported and make sure that tension will not cause the components to part suddenly.

☐ **STEP 46: FIESTA FROM 1995:** Remove the rear engine mounting link.

❒ **STEP 47: FIESTA FROM 1995 WITH ZETEC SE ENGINE:** Disconnect the vacuum hose from the exhaust gas recirculation valve.
➔ Lower the engine/transmission so that the left-hand mounting is clear of the mounting studs and remove the bracket from the throttle housing.

❒ **STEP 48: FIESTA FROM 1995 WITH ENDURA E ENGINE:** Make a note of the locations and disconnect the fuel supply and return lines at the fuel supply rail.
➔ Be ready to catch a small amount of fuel spillage - see *Chapter 9, Ignition, Fuel and Exhaust*.

❒ **STEP 49: KA:** Remove the centre bolt from the rear roll restrictor and remove the mounting brackets from the transmission and vehicle body.

❒ **STEP 50: KA:** Remove the left-hand engine/transmission support bracket from the battery support bracket and transmission.

❒ **STEP 51: KA:** Remove the wiring supports from the right-hand engine mounting.
➔ Unscrew the two nuts and a bolt and remove the engine mounting upper bracket.

❒ **STEP 52:** Lower the engine/transmission so that there is sufficient room for the bellhousing to engine attachment bolts to be removed and remove them.

❒ **STEP 53: FIESTA FROM 1989 TO 1995:** Remove the three nuts attaching the rear transmission mounting bracket to the transmission. Remove the bracket and unscrew the three studs from the transmission.

❒ **STEP 54: FIESTA FROM 1995 WITH ENDURA E ENGINE:** Move the cable guide out of the way when you remove the bolts at the top of the bellhousing and remove the adapter plate.

❒ **STEP 55: FIESTA FROM 1995 WITH ZETEC SE ENGINE:** Note the transmission earth/ground lead is attached by the top bolt.

❒ **STEP 56: ESCORT FROM 1990 WITH B5 AND IB5 TRANSMISSION:** Note that two bolts at the rear attach the mounting bracket stay.

SAFETY FIRST!

• The transmission is heavy! Make sure it is adequately supported and, if possible, have an assistant help out.

❒ **STEP 57:** Pull the transmission away from the engine, until the input shaft is clear of the clutch, and lower the transmission away from the vehicle.

❒ **STEP 58:** Refitting the transmission is the reverse of the removal process, bearing in mind the following points.
➔ Put a very thin smear of high melting point grease on the transmission input shaft splines.
➔ Adjust and check the operation of the gearshift linkage - see *Job 3*.
➔ Make sure all engine, transmission and exhaust mountings are aligned correctly.
➔ Check the operation of the clutch - see *Part B*.
➔ Refill the transmission with the specified oil.

JOB 3: GEARSHIFT LINKAGE - *removal, refitting.*

To ensure that correct reassembly of the gearshift mechanism will be possible on B5 and iB5 transmissions - see *Part C, Job 2*.

❒ **STEP 1: VEHICLES WITH B5 AND IB5 TRANSMISSIONS:** Engage the relevant gear – see *Part C, Job 2*.

3-2

❒ **STEP 2:** Remove the knob from the gear lever.

❒ **STEP 3:** Remove the outer gear lever gaiter.
➔ On vehicles with a centre console, you will have to release the outer gaiter from the console.

3-3

❒ **STEP 4:** Where appropriate, remove the central console - see *Chapter 14, Interior, Trim*

❒ **STEP 5: ESCORT AND ORION FROM 1984, FIESTA FROM 1989:** Where possible, remove the rubber cover from the base of the gear lever. On some Fiesta models this cover is fixed and cannot be removed.

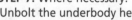
3-5

❒ **STEP 6:** Fully apply the handbrake, chock the rear wheels, raise the front of the vehicle.

❒ **STEP 7:** Where necessary:
➔ Unbolt the underbody heatshields.
➔ Release or disconnect the exhaust pipe, so that you have access to the gearshift linkage.

TOP TIP!

On models with a flexible section in the exhaust pipe, make sure the flexible section is not bent excessively.
• Strap a splint to the flexible section whenever the exhaust system is released from its mountings.

STEP 8: Remove the bolt (**a**) attaching the gearshift stabiliser rod to the transmission and secure the rod to one side. Note the location of any washers.

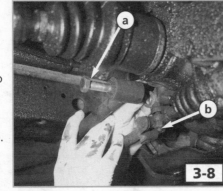
3-8

STEP 9: Remove the clamp bolt (illustration, *Step 8, Item B*) and disconnect the gearshift rod from the transmission shaft.
➔ On B5 transmissions, unhook the selector rod tension spring.
➔ Secure the rod to one side.

TOP TIP!

• Before disconnecting the gearshift rod, put alignment marks on the rod and shaft so that they can be reconnected in the correct position.

STEP 10: Remove the nuts attaching the gear lever baseplate to the floor.
➔ Depending on model and date of manufacture, these will either be accessible from inside the vehicle, or from underneath.

3-10

STEP 11: Release the gearshift rod and stabiliser rod, and withdraw the complete gearshift mechanism downwards and away from the vehicle.

STEP 12: Refitting is the reverse of the removal process, bearing in mind the following points.
➔ On vehicles with the MTX 75 transmission, fit the clamp bolt over the selector shaft and make sure that the gear lever housing is lined up satisfactorily with the transmission and not stressed. Loosen the attachment nuts and retighten if necessary.
➔ Check and adjust the operation of the gearshift linkage - see *Job 4*.

JOB 4: GEARSHIFT LINKAGE - *adjusting.*

STEP 1: Fully apply the handbrake, chock the rear wheels, jack up and support the front of the vehicle.

STEP 2: Where necessary, remove the underbody heatshields and release or disconnect the exhaust pipe, so that you have access to the gearshift linkage.

TOP TIP!

• On models with a flexible section in the exhaust pipe, make sure the flexible section is not bent excessively. Strap a splint to the flexible section.

STEP 3: Put the gear lever into the appropriate position for the gearbox type.

TOP TIP!

• Ford specify the use of a special tool (16-064) to hold the gear lever in the neutral position while the MTX 75 linkage is connected.
➔ It is possible to adjust and connect the linkage without this tool, provided an assistant can hold the gear lever rigidly in the centre of the neutral section of the gate.

STEP 4: B5 TRANSMISSION: Make sure the shift rod tension spring is disconnected.

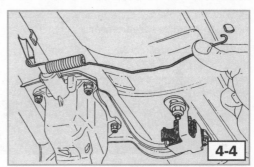
4-4

STEP 5: B5 AND IB5 TRANSMISSION: Put a suitable diameter lock pin (arrowed) into the hole in the gear lever housing.
➔ The pin must be long enough and large enough in diameter to lock the gear lever in position.
➔ It may be necessary to move the gear lever around a little to allow the pin to fit.

4-5

STEP 6:B5 AND IB5 TRANSMISSION: Make sure the transmission is in the correct gear.
➔ Use a suitable drift through the hole (arrowed) in the transmission shaft and rotate the transmission input shaft as far as it will go, first clockwise and then anticlockwise.
➔ Turn the input shaft back halfway between the two extremes and push it as far forward as possible, to take up the freeplay in the transmission.
➔ Reconnect the selector shaft and tighten the clamp bolt.
➔ Remove the drift and lockpin, check the operation of the gearshift mechanism re-adjust if necessary.

4-6

❏ **STEP 7: MTX 75 TRANSMISSION:** Fit the special tool to the gear lever, or have an assistant hold the gear lever centralised in the neutral position.
→ Make sure the transmission is in neutral.
→ Reconnect the selector shaft.
→ Tighten the clamp bolt.
→ Check the operation of the gearshift mechanism and re-adjust if necessary.

JOB 5: SPEEDOMETER DRIVE – *removal, refitting.*

❏ **STEP 1:** Before dismantling, disconnect the battery negative (-) earth/ground terminal. See *Chapter 10, Electrical, Dash, Instruments, Fact File: Disconnecting the Battery* BEFORE doing so!

❏ **STEP 2:** Remove the speedometer drive cable and, where fitted, the vehicle speed sensor.

TOP TIP!
• The pin will probably be tight so do not be half hearted.
• If you do not grip the pin very tightly, you will probably damage the pin and have to use a suitable drift to knock it out.

❏ **STEP 3:** Pull the speedometer drive retaining pin from the side of the transmission casing (arrowed).

5-3

❏ **STEP 4:** Pull the speedometer drive and bearing out of the transmission.
→ Take care, as the drive (a) and bearing (b) are easily separated.
→ Hook out the 'O' ring seal (c) from the bearing.
→ The position of the drive location pin hole (d) can now be seen.

❏ **STEP 5:** Refitting is the reverse of the removal process, bearing in mind the following points.
→ Use a new 'O' ring seal and lightly oil the seal before refitting.
→ Tap the retaining pin into place with a hammer.

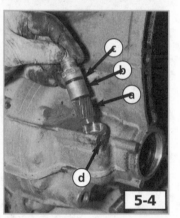

5-4

Part D: Automatic Transmission Inspection, Removal, Replacement

CONTENTS

JOB 1: TRANSMISSION OIL AND FLUID SEALS - *removal, replacement.*

See *Part C, Job 1*.

JOB 2: AUTOMATIC TRANSMISSION - *removal, refitting.*

• The ATX (automatic transaxle) transmission, fitted to Escorts and Orions up to 1989, has three separate forward gears.
• The CTX (continuously variable transaxle) is a gearless transmission providing infinite 'gear' positions.

TOP TIP!
• If you suspect that an automatic transmission is faulty, you should first check the level and condition of the fluid. Topping up or draining and replacing the fluid can sometimes cure problems, provided no permanent damage has been caused to the transmission.

• See *Chapter 2, Safety First* for further specific information about the handling and disposal of harmful fluids.

• Whenever checks are carried out that need the engine to be running always make sure the selector is in the park position and, ideally, have an assistant in the driving seat who can, in an emergency, apply the brakes and stop the engine.

Section A: Escort and Orion (to 1990) with ATX transmission.

☐ **STEP A1:** Before dismantling, disconnect the battery negative (-) earth/ground terminal. See *Chapter 10, Electrical, Dash, Instruments, Fact File: Disconnecting the Battery* BEFORE doing so!

☐ **STEP A2:** Remove the air cleaner.

☐ **STEP A3:** Drain the transmission fluid into a suitable container. Clean and replace the drain plug when all the fluid has stopped draining.

☐ **STEP A4:** Disconnect the inhibitor switch by separating the multi-plug (**A**) at the switch.
→ Put the selector in the 'D' (Drive) position.
→ Disconnect the selector cable (**B**) from the selector shaft lever by removing one nut. Also, see *Job 3*.
→ Take care not to damage the cable as the pin will rotate as the nut is removed.

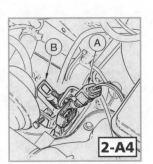
2-A4

• Transmission fluid can get hot enough to cause injury. Allow time for hot fluid to cool before draining.

☐ **STEP A5:** Removal and refitting of the downshift linkage will be easier if you remove the two bolts attaching the throttle cable mounting bracket to the right-hand side of the engine - see *Job 3 Step A5*.

☐ **STEP A6:** Disconnect the downshift linkage (**A**) from the downshift/throttle valve shaft:
→ Slacken the downshift linkage adjuster screw (**B**) and unscrew the retaining nut (**C**).

2-A6

☐ **STEP A7:** Remove the two engine-to-transmission top attachment bolts - see *Part C*.

☐ **STEP A8:** Fully apply the handbrake and chock the rear wheels. Raise and support the front of the vehicle on stands, making sure you have sufficient room to lower and withdraw the transmission.

☐ **STEP A9:** Support the weight of the engine.

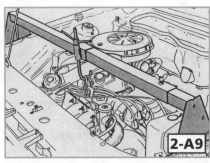
2-A9

☐ **STEP A10:** Unscrew the retaining nut and remove the speedometer drive cable (**A**) from the transmission. Remove the bolts (arrowed) and separate the selector cable bracket from the transmission unit.

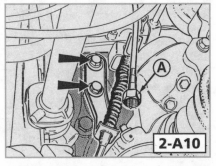
2-A10

☐ **STEP A11:** Remove the starter motor - see *Chapter 6, Engine*.

☐ **STEP A12:** Unscrew the bolts (arrowed) and remove the torque converter cover plate.

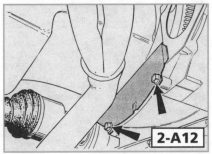
2-A12

☐ **STEP A13:** Remove the driveshafts - see *Part E*.

TOP TIP!

• Complete removal of the driveshafts from the vehicle is not necessary.
• The driveshafts can be left attached to the hubs, provided there is room for the hubs to be swung out of the way to allow separation of the driveshafts from the transmission.
• IMPORTANT NOTE: Make sure you support the driveshafts so that the inner joint is not bent at more than 18 degrees and the outer joint at not more than 45 degrees.

☐ **STEP A14:** Remove the nut (**A**) attaching the front transmission mounting to the support plate and the four bolts (arrowed) attaching the support plate to the vehicle.

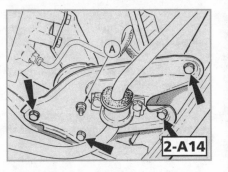
2-A14

□ **STEP A15:** Disconnect the transmission fluid cooler pipes (a) at the transmission and remove the pipes.
➜ Plug or cover the open connections to prevent contamination.

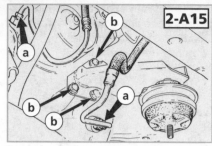

2-A15

□ **STEP A16:** Remove the three attachment bolts (see illustration *2-A15, item* b) and the front mounting bracket from the transmission.

□ **STEP A17:** Remove the bolts (arrowed) and the rear support plate, complete with mounting bracket, from the transmission and vehicle.

2-A17

□ **STEP A18:** Remove the four torque converter retaining nuts.
➜ Turn the flywheel (a) so that each nut (arrowed) is accessible, in turn, through the cover plate aperture.
➜ Undo the nuts evenly, a couple of turns at time until they are all undone.

2-A18

□ **STEP A19:** Support the transmission assembly.

2-A19

➜ Use a suitable jack (**B**) and block of wood or other insulator (**A**) from below or attach the transmission to the engine hoist or support bar.

□ **STEP A20:** Remove the remaining engine-to-transmission attachment bolts. These are similar to manual transmissions - see *Part C*.

□ **STEP A21:** Have a final check around the transmission to ensure that all cables and linkages have been removed.
➜ Carefully pull the transmission away from the engine.
➜ Hold the torque converter against the transmission and lower the transmission.
➜ IMPORTANT NOTE: The torque converter is only loosely attached so it must be held in place.

□ **STEP A22:** Refitting is the reverse of the removal process, bearing in mind the following.
➜ Make sure that the mating surfaces between the transmission and engine are clean.
➜ Make sure all engine and transmission mountings are aligned correctly.
➜ Tighten the mounting nuts and bolts finger tight initially, fully tightening to the specified torque when all have been installed.
➜ Adjust and check the operation of the selector mechanism - see *Job 4*.
➜ Refill the transmission with the specified fluid, (see *Chapter 1, Facts and Figures*), making sure the fluid is at the correct level.

Section B: Escort and Orion (from 1990), Fiesta with CTX transmission.

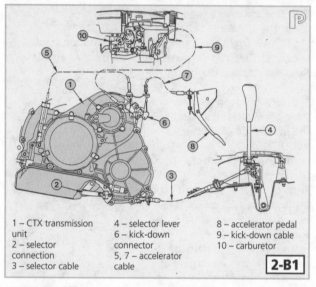

1 – CTX transmission unit	4 – selector lever	8 – accelerator pedal
2 – selector connection	6 – kick-down connector	9 – kick-down cable
3 – selector cable	5, 7 – accelerator cable	10 – carburetor

2-B1

□ **STEP B1:** These are the locations of the external selector, throttle and kick-down components.

□ **STEP B2:** Before dismantling, disconnect the battery negative (-) earth/ground terminal. See *Chapter 10, Electrical, Dash, Instruments, Fact File: Disconnecting the Battery* BEFORE doing so!
➜ FIESTA FROM 1995: Remove the battery and battery tray.

□ **STEP B3:** Remove the air cleaner and inlet duct as far as necessary to gain access to the top of the transmission.

□ **STEP B4:** Unscrew the retaining nut and remove the speedometer drive cable from the transmission (position arrowed) or, where fitted, the speed sensor.
➜ This, for reference, shows the major components of the CTX transmission, viewed from the bellhousing-end.

□ **STEP B5:** Where fitted, disconnect the lead from the vehicle speed sensor.

□ **STEP B6:** Disconnect and unclip the starter inhibitor switch and reversing light wiring from the transmission.

□ **STEP B7: FIESTA FROM 1989 TO 1995:** Remove the two securing bolts, disconnect the throttle valve cable from the assembly and secure the bracket out of the way.

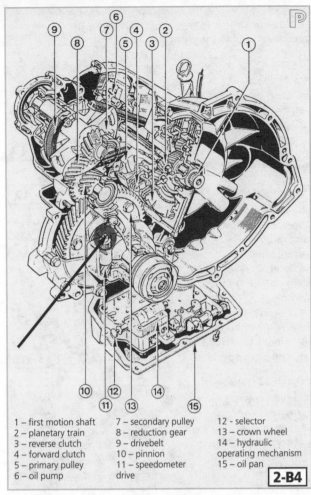

1 – first motion shaft
2 – planetary train
3 – reverse clutch
4 – forward clutch
5 – primary pulley
6 – oil pump
7 – secondary pulley
8 – reduction gear
9 – drivebelt
10 – pinnion
11 – speedometer drive
12 - selector
13 – crown wheel
14 – hydraulic operating mechanism
15 – oil pan

2-B4

❐ **STEP B8: FIESTA FROM 1995:** Separate the accelerator cable from the throttle housing - see *Chapter 6, Engine*.

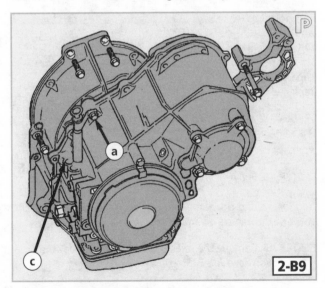

2-B9

❐ **STEP B9: ESCORT AND ORION:** To disconnect the cam plate cable – see inset - from the throttle linkage:
➔ Remove the attachment bolt (**a**) and separate the cable support bracket from the transmission.
➔ Pull the tube (**b**) from out of the casting (**c**), just in front of the dipstick tube.

❐ **STEP B10: ESCORT AND ORION:** You can now separate the cam plate cable link – see illustration *2-B9, item d*.

❐ **STEP B11:** Drain the transmission fluid into a suitable container. Clean and replace the drain plug when all the fluid has stopped draining.

❐ **STEP B12: FIESTA FROM 1995:** Disconnect the hoses from the exhaust gas recirculation valve.

❐ **STEP B13: FIESTA FROM 1995:** Remove the radiator grille - see *Chapter 13, Bodywork*.

❐ **STEP B14:** Remove the top engine-to-transmission attachment bolts.
➔ Note the position of any earth/ground leads and cable support brackets.

❐ **STEP B15:** Fully apply the handbrake and chock the rear wheels. Raise and support the front of the vehicle on stands, making sure you have sufficient room to lower and withdraw the transmission.

❐ **STEP B16: FIESTA FROM 1995:** Remove the screws and the lower radiator cover.

❐ **STEP B17:** Disconnect the transmission fluid cooler pipes at the transmission.

❐ **STEP B18: FIESTA FROM 1995:** Disconnect and unclip the electric cooling fan wiring from the radiator.

❐ **STEP B19: FIESTA FROM 1995:** Secure the radiator to the top crossmember.

❐ **STEP B20: FIESTA FROM 1995:** Unscrew the radiator lower support crossmember attachment bolts and withdraw the support crossmember and fan.

❐ **STEP B21: FIESTA FROM 1995 WITH POWER STEERING:** Remove the auxiliary drivebelt.
➔ Unbolt the power steering pump along with its bracket and secure the pump out of the way - see *Chapter 11, Steering and Suspension*.

❐ **STEP B22:** Disconnect the selector cable at the transmission - see *Job 3*.

❐ **STEP B23:** Remove the starter motor.

❐ **STEP B24: FIESTA TO 1995, ESCORT AND ORION:** Remove the lower flywheel cover plate.

❐ **STEP B25: FIESTA FROM 1995:** Separate the exhaust front downpipe from the intermediate pipe - see *Chapter 9, Ignition, Fuel and Exhaust*.

TOP TIP!
• On models with a flexible section in the exhaust pipe, make sure the flexible section is not bent excessively. Strap a splint to the flexible section whenever the exhaust system is released from its mountings.

❐ **STEP B26: FIESTA FROM 1995:** Remove the rear engine mounting roll restrictor.
➔ There will be tension in the restrictor so support the engine – hold it stationary - while removing the bolts.

❑ **STEP B27:** Support the weight of the engine.

❑ **STEP B28: ESCORT AND ORION:** Remove the three bolts attaching the front transmission mounting bracket to the transmission and the two bolts attaching the bracket to the vehicle body - remove the mounting bracket.

❑ **STEP B29: ESCORT AND ORION:** Lower the engine slightly, remove the retaining bolts and the rear support bracket from the transmission.

❑ **STEP B30: FIESTA TO 1995:** Remove the four bolts attaching the transmission support to the vehicle.
➜ Lower the engine and transmission until there is sufficient room to separate and withdraw the transmission.

❑ **STEP B31: FIESTA FROM 1995:** Remove the left-hand mounting bracket from the transmission.

❑ **STEP B32: FIESTA FROM 1995:** Remove the right-hand engine/transmission mounting upper bracket.

❑ **STEP B33: FIESTA FROM 1995:** Lower the engine and transmission until the left-hand mounting is clear of the studs.

❑ **STEP B34:** Support the transmission on a suitable jack, making sure the engine is still supported, and remove the remaining engine-to-transmission attachment bolts.
➜ Note the position of the earth/ground strap on Escort and Orion models and the location of the wiring support brackets on Fiesta models from 1995.

❑ **STEP B35:** Pull the transmission away from the engine, manoeuvre it down and withdraw it from the vehicle.

❑ **STEP B36:** Refitting is the reverse of the removal process, bearing in mind the following points.
➜ Refit the torsional vibration damper to the flywheel.
➜ Do not apply any lubricant to the input shaft splines.
➜ Check the operation of the selector mechanism and, if necessary adjust the cable.
➜ Refill the transmission with the specified fluid.
➜ Check the operation of the accelerator cable and, where fitted, the choke cable - adjust if necessary. See *Chapter 6, Engine* and *Chapter 9, Ignition, Fuel and Exhaust*.

JOB 3:	AUTOMATIC TRANSMISSION SELECTOR CABLE - *removal, refitting, adjustment*.

Section A: Escort and Orion (to 1990) with ATX transmission.

❑ **STEP A1:** Put the selector lever in the 'D' (Drive) position.

IMPORTANT NOTE:
• For correct adjustment of the cable, the selector lever and selector linkage must be in the correct positions relative to each other.

• Selecting the 'D' (Drive) position at this stage ensures that the linkage is in the correct position when reconnecting the selector cable.

❑ **STEP A2:** At the transmission, unscrew the nut (arrowed) that attaches the selector cable to the selector shaft lever.

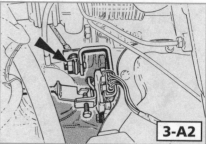
3-A2

❑ **STEP A3:** Inside the vehicle, undo the screws (arrowed) and remove the console unit:
➜ Carefully lever the gate cover from the console.
➜ Unscrew the selector lever knob.
➜ Remove the screws attaching the console.

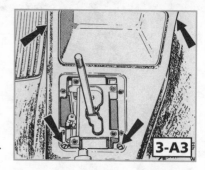
3-A3

❑ **STEP A4:** Take out the two screws (arrowed) and remove the selector gate and stop plate.

❑ **STEP A5:** Separate the selector lever from the cable by removing the securing clips (A) and (B).
➜ On some models, the pin held in by clip (A) was replaced with a ball and socket joint. In these cases, lever the ball and socket type apart.

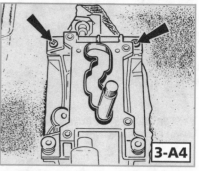
3-A4

3-A5

❑ **STEP A6:** Fully apply the handbrake and chock the rear wheels. Raise and support the front of the vehicle on stands.

❑ **STEP A7:** Remove the selector cable bracket from the transmission - see *Job 2, Step A10*.

❑ **STEP A8:** Pull the rubber seal (a) from its seating (b) and withdraw the cable from under the vehicle.

❑ **STEP A9:** Refitting is the reverse of the removal process.
➜ For correct adjustment you must make sure that selector lever and selector linkage remain in the 'D' (Drive) position.

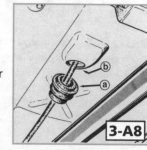
3-A8

Section B: Escort and Orion (from 1990), Fiesta with CTX transmission.

❏ **STEP B1:** Before dismantling, disconnect the battery negative (-) earth/ground terminal. See *Chapter 10, Electrical, Dash, Instruments, Fact File: Disconnecting the Battery* BEFORE doing so!

❏ **STEP B2:** Remove the centre console - see *Chapter 14, Interior and Trim*.

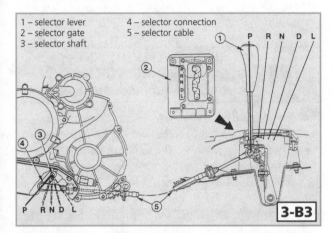

1 – selector lever
2 – selector gate
3 – selector shaft
4 – selector connection
5 – selector cable

`3-B3`

❏ **STEP B3:** These are the components of the selector mechanism.
➔ Put the selector lever (1) in the 'P' (Park) position.

IMPORTANT NOTE: For correct adjustment of the cable, the selector lever and selector linkage must be in the correct positions relative to each other. Selecting the 'P' (Park) position at this stage ensures that the linkage is in the correct position when reconnecting the selector cable.

❏ **STEP B4:** Remove the selector lever gate from the selector lever housing.

❏ **STEP B5:** You may now have to cut the carpet at the front to gain sufficient access.
➔ Lever the cable from the plastic connector on the selector lever.
➔ Lever free the cable retaining clip.
➔ Remove the cable from the cable housing.

❏ **STEP B6:** Fully apply the handbrake and chock the rear wheels. Raise and support the front of the vehicle on stands.

❏ **STEP B7:** At the transmission, pull out the clip and disconnect the cable from the lever and transmission bracket.

❏ **STEP B8:** Pull the rubber seal from its seating and withdraw the cable from under the vehicle.

❏ **STEP B9:** Refitting is the reverse of the removal process, bearing in mind the following points.
➔ Reconnect the cable to the selector lever. Make sure the annular bead on the cable eye faces the end of the pin.
➔ Put the selector lever in the 'P' (Park) position, reconnect the cable to the transmission and check the adjustment.

TOP TIP!

• Before adjusting the selector cable, make sure the selector lever is in the 'P' (Park) position, the parking pawl is engaged and the transmission is locked.

❏ **STEP B10:** Working underneath the vehicle check that the cable yoke and lever/selector shaft drilling are in alignment and the connecting pin fits easily.
➔ If the pin is not an easy fit, pull back the gaiter and turn the yoke in the appropriate direction until the pin fits.
➔ Fit the pin, clip and reposition the gaiter.

JOB 4: AUTOMATIC TRANSMISSION SELECTOR MECHANISM - *removal, refitting.*

❏ **STEP 1:** Disconnect the selector cable from the selector lever - see *Job 3*.

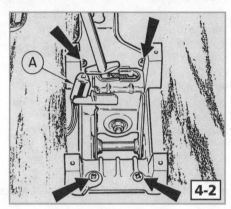

`4-2`

❏ **STEP 2:** Remove the light holder (A) from the lever housing, unscrew the retaining screws (arrowed) and lift the housing away.

❏ **STEP 3:** Refitting is the reverse of the removal process, bearing in mind the following points.
➔ Tighten the retaining screws/bolts to the specified torque.
➔ Reconnect and adjust the selector cable - see *Job 5*.

JOB 5: DOWNSHIFT LINKAGE - *removal, refitting.*

The downshift linkage is only fitted to Escort and Orion models up to 1989.

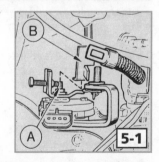

`5-1`

❏ **STEP 1:** Disconnect the downshift linkage (B) from the throttle valve shaft (A).

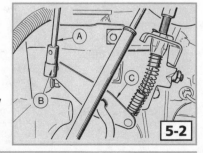

`5-2`

❏ **STEP 2:** Remove the securing clip (B) and disconnect the throttle linkage (A) from the linkage pivot lever (C) below the inlet manifold.

☐ **STEP 3:** Remove the two bolts (arrowed) securing the throttle cable mounting bracket. Remove the linkage and bracket.

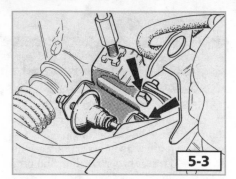

5-3

☐ **STEP 4:** Remove the clip (**C**) and disconnect the throttle cable (**A**) from the downshift linkage (**B**). Remove the nut and clamp bolt (**F**).
➜ Separate the control lever (**E**) from the downshift linkage (**B**).
➜ Remove the downshift linkage.
➜ Item (**D**) is the damper.

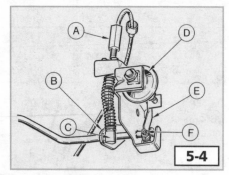

5-4

☐ **STEP 5:** Refitting is the reverse of the removal process, bearing in mind the following points.
➜ When you retighten the clamp bolt, make sure the lever can move.
➜ Tighten the throttle cable mounting brackets to the specified torque.
➜ Adjust the downshift linkage - see **Job 6**.

JOB 6: DOWNSHIFT LINKAGE - *adjusting*.

☐ **STEP 1:** Make sure of the following before making any adjustments.
➜ The engine is running correctly.
➜ The transmission fluid is at the correct level.
➜ The engine is at normal operating temperature.

☐ **STEP 2:** Slacken the adjuster screw so that there is a clearance of 2 mm to 3 mm (0.079 in. to 0.118 in.) between the adjuster screw and the abutment.

☐ **STEP 3:** Fully apply the parking brake and chock the rear wheels.
➜ Start the engine and check that the idle speed is correct.

☐ **STEP 4:** Tighten the adjusting screw:
➜ Leave a maximum gap of 0.1 mm between the screw and stop.

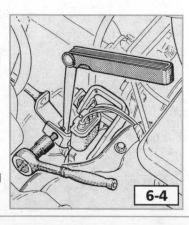

6-4

➜ Use a feeler gauge to measure the gap.

☐ **STEP 5:** Pivot the downshift lever on the downshift linkage so that the damper rod (**A**) is pressed in 5 mm.

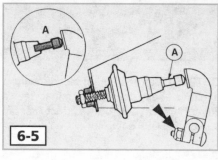

6-5

➜ Tighten the clamp bolt (arrowed) in this position.

JOB 7: REVERSING LIGHT AND STARTER INHIBITOR SWITCH - *testing, removal, replacement*.

Models equipped with automatic transmission have a combined reversing light and inhibitor switch, located on the rear of the transmission. The inhibitor switch should only allow the engine to be started when the selector is in the park ('P') or neutral ('N') positions.

Section A: Escort and Orion (to 1990) with ATX transmission.

☐ **STEP A1:** Using a ratchet wrench:
➜ Remove the nut (position **b**)
➜ Detach the downshift linkage from the downshift/ throttle valve shaft on the transmission.
➜ Detach the

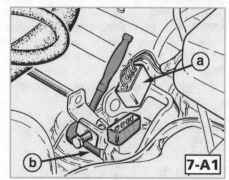

7-A1

multi-plug (**a**) from the inhibitor switch.

☐ **STEP A2:** Separate the downshift linkage mounting bracket from the engine - see **Job 5, Step 3**.

☐ **STEP A3:** To complete the dismantling:
➜ Remove the downshift/ throttle valve shaft lever (**A**) along with the stepped washer (**B**).
➜ Disconnect the return spring (**C**).
➜ Remove the two screws and withdraw the starter inhibitor switch (**D**).

☐ **STEP A4:**
Refitting is the reverse of the removal process but adjust the inhibitor switch before tightening the attachment screws, as follows:

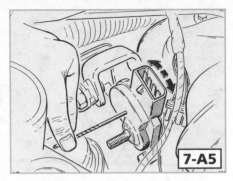

7-A5

☐ **STEP A5:** After checking that the selector lever remains in position 'D':
→ Insert a 2.3 mm drill bit into the hole in the inhibitor switch.
→ Move the switch (see directional arrows) until the drilling in the switch casing lines up with inner drilling of the inhibitor switch.
→ Push the drill bit in further to immobilise the switch.
→ Tighten the attachment screws with the switch in this position.

☐ **STEP A6:** Reassemble and adjust the downshift linkage - see *Jobs 5 and 6*.

Section B: Escort and Orion (from 1990), Fiesta with CTX transmission.

☐ **STEP B1:** Remove the electrical connector and identify the reversing light contacts.
→ Check the continuity of the reversing light switch in all selector positions.
→ If there is no continuity when reverse is selected, or there is continuity in any other position, the switch is faulty and should be replaced.

SAFETY FIRST!

• Take extreme care when carrying out these tests. The inhibitor switch is a safety device and a faulty switch may allow the engine to start when drive or reverse is engaged - a potentially dangerous situation.

• When this test is being carried out, make sure there is a qualified driver in the driving seat and remember that you are only checking to see whether the starter motor will turn when you try to start the engine.

• Do not press on the accelerator during this test and, if the starter motor works in any position other than 'P' or 'N', switch the ignition off immediately.

• Make sure there are no people, animals or obstructions in front of, or behind the vehicle during this test.

☐ **STEP B2: TO CHECK THE STARTER INHIBITOR SWITCH:**
Raise both of the driven wheels off the ground and fully apply the parking brake.
→ Move the selector to each position and try to start the engine.
→ The starter motor should only work when park ('P') or neutral ('N') are selected.

→ If the starter motor works with any other position selected, or does not work at all, you will have to check switch continuity.
→ Remove the electrical connector from the switch and identify the inhibitor switch connectors - see *Chapter 10, Electrical, Dash and Instruments*.
→ There should be continuity across the switch when park ('P') or neutral ('N') are selected. In all other positions the switch should be open circuit.
→ Replace the switch, if faulty, or check the wiring (see *Chapter 10, Electrical, Dash and Instruments*), if the switch itself is satisfactory.

☐ **STEP B3:** If switch replacement is necessary, raise and support the front of the vehicle.
→ Have a suitable container ready to collect any oil or fluid spillage.
→ Remove the electrical connector and unscrew the switch.

☐ **STEP B4:** Screw in the new switch, tighten to the specified torque, and refit the electrical connector.

☐ **STEP B5:** Check the operation of the new switch and, if necessary because of fluid leakage, check the level of the transmission oil or fluid.

JOB 8: ATX TRANSMISSION FILTER – *remove, replace.*

☐ **STEP 1:**
With the transmission in its normal, installed attitude (oil pan facing downwards) Remove

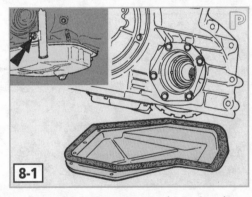

8-1

oil filler pipe and dipstick (1 screw, arrowed - see inset).
→ Remove oil pan downwards, (13 bolts) so that no metal particles can get inside the transmission.
→ IMPORTANT NOTE: Don't forget that the oil pan is still full of oil!

☐ **STEP 2:**
Remove the three bolts (arrowed) and take the filter from the transmission.
→ Wash out the

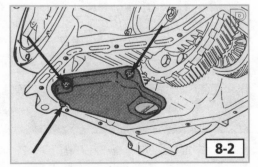

8-2

filter in solvent (see *Chapter 2, Safety First!*).

❏ **STEP 3:** Clean all transmission components thoroughly before reassembling.

➜ If metal particles are found, flush out oil cooler and replace torque converter - see *Job 9*.

❏ **STEP 4:** Refit as the reverse of removal, but use all new gaskets and seals.

JOB 9:	**ATX TRANSMISSION TORQUE CONVERTER** – *remove, replace.*

❏ **STEP 1:** Remove the oil sump pan - see *Job 8*.

❏ **STEP 2:** Lift out torque converter.
➜ Two threaded sleeves can be used as aids (one arrowed).
➜ These must be made up

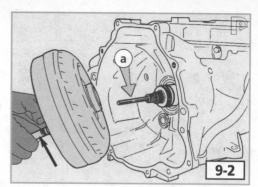

to match the threads of the torque converter bolts.
➜ IMPORTANT NOTE: Torque converter is full of oil!
➜ Remove oil pump driveshaft (**a**) if required.

Part E: Driveshafts Removal, Replacement

CONTENTS

FACT FILE

• When the CV joints do need replacing, it may be necessary to replace the complete driveshaft because, on some models, the CV joints are not available as separate components. You should check availability of parts before starting work.

• Vehicles with two section driveshafts have bolted-on inner CV joints.

• Other significant differences to watch out for are i) the change from cage-type CV joints to the tripod type after 1989, and; ii) the torsional vibration damper fitted to the longer drive shaft on some vehicles; iii) Vehicles with modulator-type ABS have special inner CV joints, with teeth for the modulator drivebelts.

• During driveshaft removal, you should support the driveshaft so that the inner joint does not deflect more than 18 degrees or the outer joint more than 45 degrees.

JOB 1:	**DRIVESHAFTS** - *removal, refitting.*

TOP TIP!

• The front hub nut is very tight and you should loosen this nut before raising up the vehicle off the ground.

❏ **STEP 1:** Fully apply the parking brake, chock the rear wheels, loosen the appropriate wheel nuts/bolts, raise and support the front of the vehicle.

❏ **STEP 2:** Remove the front brake caliper - see *Chapter 12, Brakes*.

❏ **STEP 3:** Disengage the hub from the outer end of the driveshaft - see *Chapter 11, Steering and Suspension*.

TOP TIP!

• Complete removal of the hub from the vehicle is not essential. You only have to remove the hub far enough to disengage the driveshaft.
• On vehicles manufactured before 1989, take care not to dislodge the bearings when removing the hub.
• On vehicles with a central, single nut top suspension strut mounting, you should loosen the nut five to six turns before dismantling the lower end of the strut - this prevents damage to the top mounting.

❏ **STEP 4:** Where necessary, remove splash guards and undertrays.

❏ **STEP 5: VEHICLES WITH MODULATOR TYPE ABS:** Slacken the modulator belt - see *Chapter 9, Fuel, Ignition and Exhaust*.

NON BOLTED CV JOINT

❏ **STEP 6: LEFT-HAND DRIVESHAFT:** Lever out the left-hand driveshaft at the point shown here (arrowed), taking care not to damage the transmission casing.
→ Withdraw the driveshaft from the vehicle and use a suitable container to collect the transmission oil/fluid spillage.

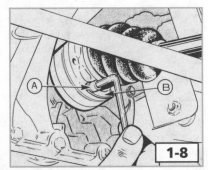

1-6

❏ **STEP 7: ONE-PIECE RIGHT-HAND DRIVESHAFT:** Use a suitable drift and tap out the right-hand driveshaft from the transmission in the direction shown here (arrowed).
→ Withdraw the driveshaft from the vehicle and use a suitable container to collect the transmission oil/fluid spillage.

1-7

BOLTED CV JOINT

❏ **STEP 8: LEFT-HAND DRIVESHAFT:** Remove the six Allen key type bolts (**A**) and the three linked washers (**B**).
→ Separate the driveshaft from the transmission stub shaft and withdraw the driveshaft from the vehicle.

1-8

❏ **STEP 9: LEFT-HAND DRIVESHAFT:** The transmission output shaft (**A**) can be levered (**B**) out from the transmission.

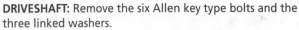

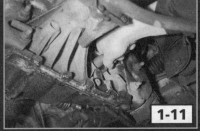

1-9

❏ **STEP 10: RIGHT-HAND TWO-PIECE DRIVESHAFT:** Remove the six Allen key type bolts and the three linked washers.
→ Separate the driveshaft from the intermediate shaft and withdraw the driveshaft from the vehicle.
→ If necessary, the intermediate shaft can also be removed from the engine and transmission - see *Job 3*.

BOTH CV JOINT TYPES

TOP TIP!

❏ **STEP 11:** If both driveshafts - or on vehicles with bolted CV joints, the output shaft - are being removed at the same time, insert a suitable dummy shaft into the transmission as soon as possible to prevent displacement of the differential gears.

1-11

IMPORTANT NOTE:
• You should ALWAYS use a new front hub nut when reassembling the hub.
• Where 'Nyloc' type nuts are fitted, new nuts should be used when reassembling components.

❏ **STEP 12:** Refitting the driveshafts is the reversal of the removal process, bearing in mind the following points.
→ Ford recommend that you fit

1-12

new snap rings to the splines on the driveshafts and CV joints.
→ Before refitting, lubricate the splines at the inboard end of the non-bolted CV driveshaft with transmission oil/fluid.
→ Make sure that the snap ring on the non-bolted CV engages when the inner end of the drive shaft is fitted into the transmission - you should hear or feel it click into place and it should not be possible to pull the driveshaft out by hand.
→ On the bolted-CV driveshaft, tighten the bolts in a diagonal pattern and to the specified torque.

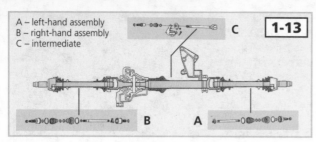

A – left-hand assembly
B – right-hand assembly
C – intermediate

C 1-13

❏ **STEP 13:** This, for reference, is a typical drive shaft layout, when the type with intermediate shaft is fitted.

JOB 2: DRIVESHAFT GAITERS - *removal, refitting.*

FACT FILE
ESSENTIAL INFORMATION

• Make sure the outer joint is not allowed to deflect more than 45 degrees at any time and the inner joint is not deflected by more than 18 degrees at any time.

• Make sure you do not pull the inner CV joint apart when separating the outer joint.

TOP TIP!

• It is possible to replace the inner and outer gaiters without removing the driveshafts from the vehicle. However, if you need to thoroughly clean and inspect the CV joint, (the outer joint in particular), it is better to remove the driveshaft and work on a bench.
• Wear disposable gloves – CV grease stains the skin!

Section A: Inner and Outer and Gaiters.

❏ **STEP A1:** Fully apply the parking brake, chock the rear wheels, loosen the appropriate wheel nuts/bolts, raise and support the front of the vehicle.

❏ **STEP A2:** Remove the appropriate front wheel.

❏ **STEP A3:** Where necessary, remove splash guards and undertrays.

❏ **STEP A4: INNER GAITERS - VEHICLES WITH MODULATOR TYPE ABS:** Slacken the modulator drivebelt - see *Chapter 9, Fuel, Ignition and Exhaust.*

❏ **STEP A5:** Disconnect the hub carrier from the steering and suspension, but do not disconnect the strut or driveshaft - see *Chapter 11, Steering and Suspension.*

❏ **STEP A6: INNER GAITERS - NON BOLTED CV JOINT:** Separate the relevant inner CV joint from the transmission - see *Job 1, Steps 6 to 10.*

❏ **STEP A7: INNER GAITERS - BOLTED CV JOINT:** Remove the six Allen key type bolts and the three linked washers. Separate the driveshaft from the transmission stub shaft (left-hand) or intermediate shaft (right-hand) - see *Job 1, Steps 8 to 10.*

❏ **STEP A8:**
Note the way the gaiter clips are fitted before removal. Here we are using side cutters to remove the old clip.

2-A8

→ Slide the gaiter along the driveshaft so that you have access to the CV joint or, if the gaiter is unserviceable, it can be cut off.
→ Note the location of any nylon washers when removing the outer CV joints.

❏ **STEP A9: BALL AND CAGE TYPE JOINT:** Clean the grease away so that you can see the retaining snap ring (arrowed).

2-A9

→ See illustration *1-12* for details of the snap ring in the CV joint.
→ Expand the snap ring and pull the CV joint off the driveshaft.

❏ **STEP A10: TRIPOD TYPE JOINT:** Pull the joint apart, remove the snap ring and slide the spider off the driveshaft, taking care to prevent the roller bearings from falling off. Check for alignment markings on the end of the driveshaft and spider.

❏ **STEP A11:** Clean and inspect the CV joint for any signs of damage or wear. Clean away all old grease.

❏ **STEP A12:** Before refitting a new or cleaned CV joint:
→ Work new CV grease, of the correct specification, over the CV joint bearing surfaces and into the ball and cage assembly. If a grease pack was supplied with the new gaiter, use all of the grease contained in the pack.

❏ **STEP A13:** Slide the new gaiter and retaining clips (and nylon washer where appropriate) onto the driveshaft, reassemble the CV joint and refit the driveshaft, bearing in mind the following points.
→ On tripod type CV joints, make sure the marks on the spider and driveshaft are aligned.
→ Check for chamfered splines on the spider or cage - the driveshaft should be refitted from the chamfered side.
→ Ford recommend that new snap rings are fitted before reassembly.
→ Make sure the gaiter is not twisted and is located correctly on the driveshaft and CV joint. If there are no seating grooves on the driveshaft, set the gaiter so that dimension 'A' corresponds to the relevant illustration.

➜ A special tool should be used to compress the clips but, with care, woodworker's pincers can be used - nylon cable ties are an alternative. Do not overtighten the clips as this will damage the gaiters.

➜ Reconnect the driveshaft to the transmission or intermediate shaft - see **Job 1**.

FACT FILE

CHECK DIMENSIONS

❐ STEP A14A: INNER CV GAITER FIESTA 1.0 AND 1.1 MODELS: With the inner CV joint fully contracted

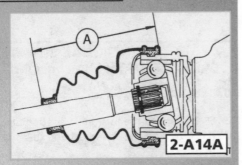

2-A14A

and at an angle of 10 degrees to 20 degrees, dimension 'A' should be 95 mm (3.7 in).

❐ STEP A14B: INNER CV GAITER FIESTA 1.3 MODELS: With the inner CV joint fully contracted and straight,

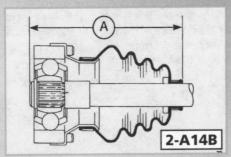

2-A14B

dimension 'A' should be 144 mm (5.67 in).

❐ STEP A14C: ESCORT: With the outer CV joint fully contracted and at an angle of 10 degrees to 20 degrees:

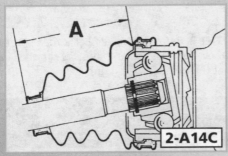

2-A14C

➜ Dimension 'A' should be 127 mm (5.0 in) on 1.1 models...
➜ ...and 132 mm (5.19 in) on 1.3 and 1.6 models.

❐ STEP A14D: FIESTA: With the outer CV joint fully contracted and

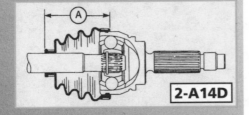

2-A14D

straight, dimension 'A' should be 95 mm (3.7 in).

❐ STEP A15: Re-assemble the components – see relevant Job.

Section B: Intermediate shaft gaiter - Fiesta with two-section right-hand driveshaft.

The transmission end of the intermediate shaft on very early Fiesta models was fitted with a universal joint. This type of shaft does not have a gaiter.

❐ **STEP B1:** Separate the right-hand inner CV joint from the intermediate shaft - see **Job 1**.

❐ **STEP B2:** Remove the clip attaching the gaiter to the transmission output shaft.

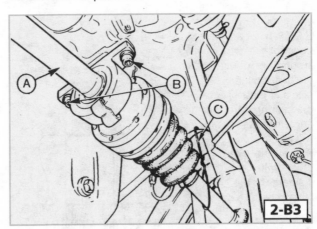

2-B3

❐ **STEP B3:** Support the driveshaft (**A**) and intermediate shaft (**C**). Remove bolts (**B**) and separate the bearing housing from the support bracket.

❐ **STEP B4:** Slide the intermediate shaft off the transmission shaft, remove the clip attaching the gaiter to the intermediate shaft and remove the gaiter.

❐ **STEP B5:** Refitting is the reverse of the removal process, bearing in mind the following points.
➜ Make sure the end of the driveshaft, the transmission output shaft splines and the inside of the gaiter (if being reused) are clean and free from dirt.
➜ Lightly lubricate the transmission output shaft splines with molybdenum disulphide grease.
➜ Make sure the gaiter is not twisted and is seated correctly.
➜ Use new clips when securing the gaiter.

JOB 3: INTERMEDIATE DRIVESHAFT BEARING - *removal, refitting.*

❐ **STEP 1:** Remove the intermediate driveshaft - see **Jobs 1 and 2**.

❐ **STEP 2:** Check that the bearing rotates freely without excessive freeplay or roughness.

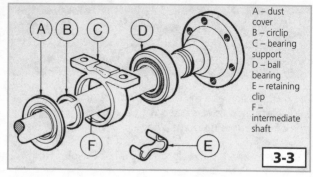

A – dust cover
B – circlip
C – bearing support
D – ball bearing
E – retaining clip
F – intermediate shaft

3-3

❏ **STEP 3:** If the bearing has to be replaced:
→ Dismantle the bearing.
→ Use a suitable long-reach puller to separate the bearing from the intermediate driveshaft.

❏ **STEP 4:** Put a smear of grease around the inside of the bearing inner race and press or tap the bearing onto the driveshaft as far as it will go.
→ Use a piece of tube, similar in diameter to the inner race, as a drift.

❏ **STEP 5:** Make sure the bearing rotates freely, reassemble the bearing and refit the driveshaft - see *Jobs 2 and 3*.

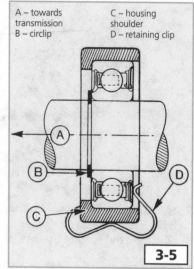

A – towards transmission
B – circlip
C – housing shoulder
D – retaining clip

3-5

JOB 4:	LUBRICANT SEEPAGE FROM BOLTED CV JOINTS – *rectification*.

TOP TIP!

• On Fiesta models, up to 1989, transmission oil may seep from the inner bolted CV joints.
• This can be rectified by the application of sealant to the CV joint.

❏ **STEP 1:** Separate the inner bolted CV joint from the transmission output shaft - see *Job 1*.

❏ **STEP 2:** Remove the CV joint from the end of the driveshaft - see *Job 1*.

❏ **STEP 3:** Clean the mating surfaces on the joint and metal cap.
→ Apply non-hardening jointing compound to the metal cap.
→ Reassemble the CV joint.

JOB 5:	TORSIONAL VIBRATION DAMPER - *checking, removal, refitting*.

❏ **STEP 1:** Examine the torsional vibration damper. Make sure it is secure on the driveshaft and that the locking bolt is tight.
→ The dimension (**5-3,A**) should be between 288 and 302 mm (1.8 in. ± 0.08 in.)

❏ **STEP 2:** To remove the torsional vibration damper:
→ Separate the driveshaft at the outer CV joint.
→ Make a note of the damper position on the driveshaft.
→ Loosen the damper locking bolt.
→ Slide the damper from the driveshaft.

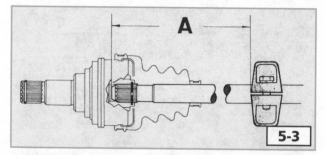

A

5-3

❏ **STEP 3:** Refitting the damper is the reverse of the removal process, making sure it is correctly located and that the locking bolt is tight.

CHAPTER 8: COOLING, VENTILATION SYSTEM

*PLEASE READ **CHAPTER 2 SAFETY FIRST** BEFORE CARRYING OUT ANY WORK ON YOUR CAR.*

CONTENTS

JOB 1:	COOLING SYSTEMS EXPLAINED.

❏ **STEP 1:** This is a typical overhead valve engine cooling system layout.

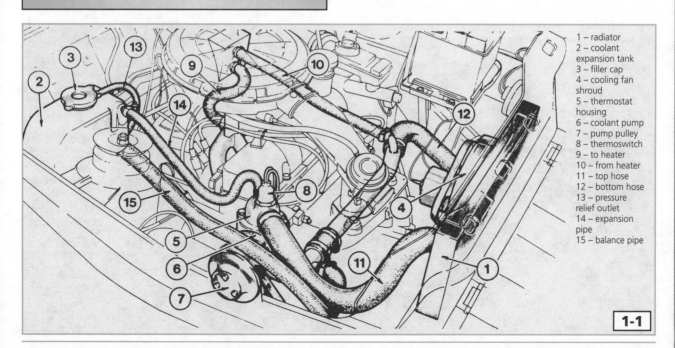

1 – radiator
2 – coolant expansion tank
3 – filler cap
4 – cooling fan shroud
5 – thermostat housing
6 – coolant pump
7 – pump pulley
8 – thermoswitch
9 – to heater
10 – from heater
11 – top hose
12 – bottom hose
13 – pressure relief outlet
14 – expansion pipe
15 – balance pipe

1-1

SAFETY FIRST!

• Read the general safety notes in *Chapter 2, Safety First!*

• Except on some pre-1982 Fiesta models, where the cooling fan is switched on and off by the ignition switch, the electric cooling fan can start at any time. Disconnect the battery before attempting to remove the radiator or cooling fan.

AIR CONDITIONING
• DO NOT open the pressurised pipework on the air conditioning system.

• If air conditioning units are in the way of carrying out other work, whenever possible move units to one side with pipes still attached.

• Otherwise, have an air conditioning specialist de-pressurise the system so that you can dismantle it.

❏ **STEP 2:** This is a typical layout of the CVH and iron-block Zetec engines' cooling system.
➔ Note that on later models, the reservoir (3), thermostat housing (5) and thermoswitch (8) may be in different locations as indicated here.

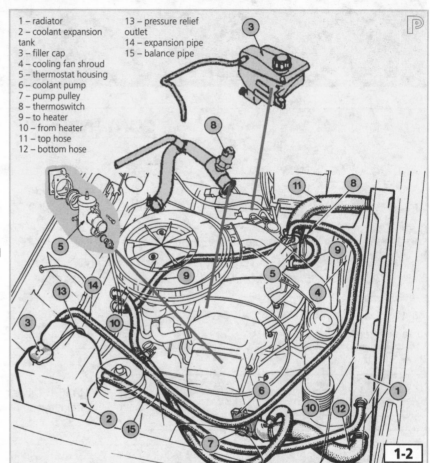

1 – radiator
2 – coolant expansion tank
3 – filler cap
4 – cooling fan shroud
5 – thermostat housing
6 – coolant pump
7 – pump pulley
8 – thermoswitch
9 – to heater
10 – from heater
11 – top hose
12 – bottom hose
13 – pressure relief outlet
14 – expansion pipe
15 – balance pipe

1-2

❏ **STEP 3:** These are typical locations of the diesel engine's cooling system.

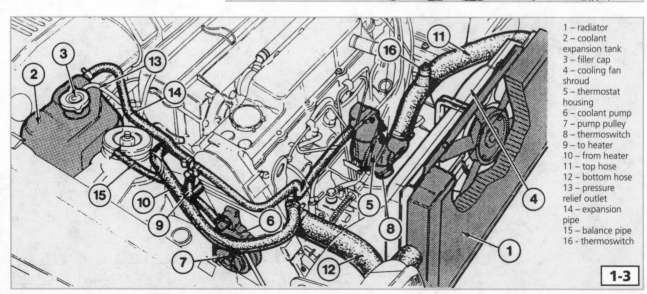

1 – radiator
2 – coolant expansion tank
3 – filler cap
4 – cooling fan shroud
5 – thermostat housing
6 – coolant pump
7 – pump pulley
8 – thermoswitch
9 – to heater
10 – from heater
11 – top hose
12 – bottom hose
13 – pressure relief outlet
14 – expansion pipe
15 – balance pipe
16 - thermoswitch

1-3

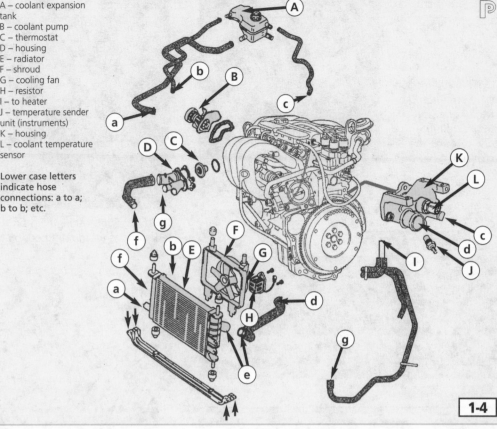

A – coolant expansion tank
B – coolant pump
C – thermostat
D – housing
E – radiator
F – shroud
G – cooling fan
H – resistor
I – to heater
J – temperature sender unit (instruments)
K – housing
L – coolant temperature sensor

Lower case letters indicate hose connections: a to a; b to b; etc.

❒ **STEP 4:** These are typical coolant system components layouts for the Zeta SE engines, with light alloy block.

1-4

JOB 2: COOLING SYSTEM - *draining, refilling.*

❒ **STEP 1:**
Wait until the engine is cold and remove the filler cap.
➜ The cap is on the radiator on early Fiesta models
➜ It is on the coolant expansion tank on all other models.

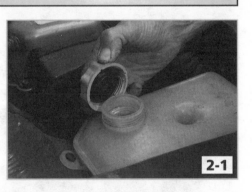

2-1

❒ **STEP 2:**
Undo the clamp and separate the bottom hose from the radiator.

❒ **STEP 3:**
You can also remove the cylinder block drain plug (arrowed) and allow the coolant to drain into a suitable container.
➜ The plug location is similar on all engines, except the Zetec SE where it is on the opposite side to that shown here.

2-2

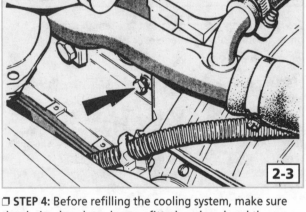

2-3

❒ **STEP 4:** Before refilling the cooling system, make sure the drain plugs have been refitted or closed and the heater control is in the 'HOT' position.

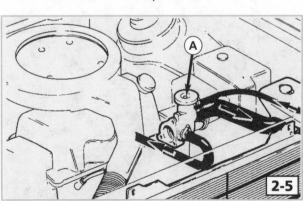

2-5

❒ **STEP 5:** On early engines with bayonet-type caps to the expansion tank, refill the system through the cap (**A**) on the thermostat housing.

STEP 6: On models with a screw-on cap to the expansion tank, all filling is done through the expansion tank.

2-6

TOP TIP!

• Signs of overheating - assume there is an air lock in the first instance. Stop the engine and allow it to cool before venting the system.
• To avoid or attempt to rectify an air lock, detach the heater supply hose at its highest connection, hold the hose at or just above the level of the connection. Top up with coolant and reconnect as soon as coolant flows from the end.

JOB 3: THERMOSTAT - *removal, checking, refitting.*

STEP 1: Partly drain the cooling system to prevent unnecessary coolant spillage over the engine and ancillaries. See *Job 2*.

STEP 2: Remove the coolant hose and, where fitted, the electrical leads from the temperature sensor (4) on the thermostat cover.
→ On overhead valve engines the thermostat is located at the crankshaft pulley end of the cylinder head.
→ Note the different types of thermostat cover (1) that may be encountered.

1 - thermostat cover.
2 - thermostat
3 - gasket
4 - temperature sensor

3-2

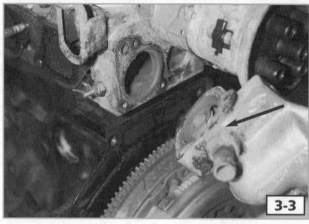

3-3

STEP 3: Remove the thermostat cover or, on CVH engines, separate the thermostat housing (arrowed) from the cylinder head.

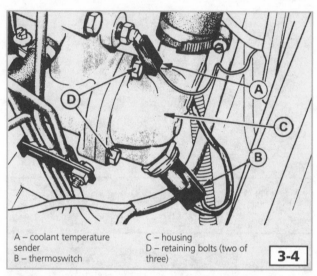

A – coolant temperature sender
B – thermoswitch
C – housing
D – retaining bolts (two of three)

3-4

STEP 4: DIESEL ENGINES: The thermostat is fitted in a housing (C) that is bolted to the side of the cylinder head.
→ To reach the thermostat, remove the bolts (D).

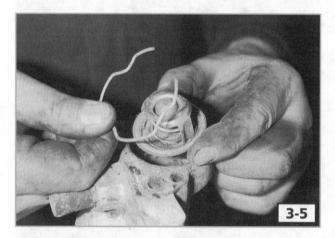

3-5

STEP 5: SINGLE OVERHEAD CAMSHAFT (CVH AND PTE) ENGINES: Remove the thermostat retaining clip.

STEP 6: SINGLE OVERHEAD CAMSHAFT (CVH AND PTE) ENGINES, ALL ZETEC ENGINES AND DIESEL ENGINES: Remove the sealing ring (3).
→ These are the different arrangements used on Zetec engines.

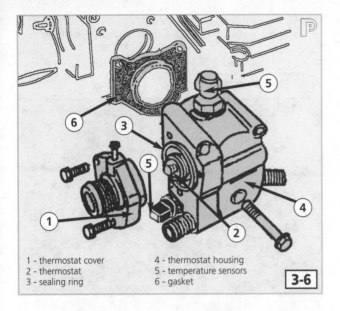

1 - thermostat cover
2 - thermostat
3 - sealing ring
4 - thermostat housing
5 - temperature sensors
6 - gasket

3-6

□ **STEP 7:** Refitting the thermostat is the reverse of the removal process.

□ **STEP 8: SINGLE OVERHEAD CAMSHAFT (CVH AND PTE) ENGINES, ALL ZETEC ENGINES AND DIESEL ENGINES:** Make sure the sealing ring and (CVH and PTE engines) retaining clip are fitted.
→ Make sure that the bleed hole (arrowed) is fitted at the top.
→ Always use a new gasket with a light smear of sealant.

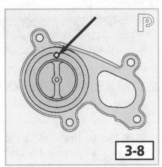

3-8

JOB 4: RADIATOR, RADIATOR FAN - *removal, replacement.*

□ **STEP 1:** Disconnect the battery negative (-) earth/ground terminal. See *Chapter 10, Electrical, Dash, Instruments, Fact File: Disconnecting the Battery* BEFORE doing so!

□ **STEP 2:** If necessary, remove the fan assembly.
→ Separate the cooling fan plug and, where necessary, cut the ties attaching the electrical cable to the fan shroud.
→ On most models, the fan can be separated from the motor by removing the retaining clip and pulling the fan from the shaft on the motor.

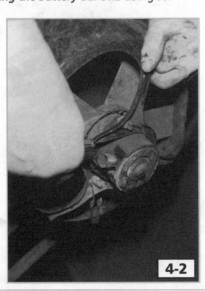

4-2

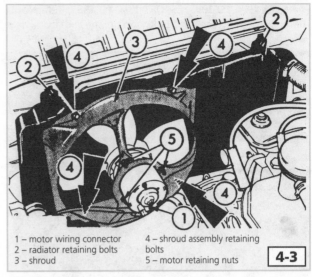

1 – motor wiring connector
2 – radiator retaining bolts
3 – shroud
4 – shroud assembly retaining bolts
5 – motor retaining nuts

4-3

□ **STEP 3:** This is a typical method of radiator attachment.

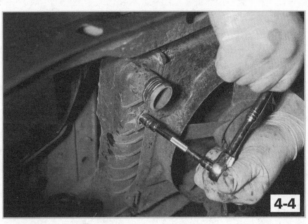

4-4

□ **STEP 4:** Remove the bolts, or single top bolt where appropriate, and separate the radiator fan shroud assembly from the radiator.
→ Locations of top bolts vary between models.
→ Some models also have bottom bolts; others have push-in pegs.

4-5

□ **STEP 5:** On later models, such as this 1999 Fiesta, the shroud is held in place by pegs at the top and bottom.

□ **STEP 6:** To remove the radiator:
→ First drain the cooling system.
→ Disconnect all the hoses from the radiator.
→ On models with automatic transmission you will have to disconnect the transmission cooler pipes - see *Chapter 7, Transmission, Clutch, Driveshafts.*

➜ **FIESTA 1976 TO 1995, ESCORT 1980 TO 1985:** Remove the two upper attachment bolts and lift the radiator away.

4-7

❒ **STEP 7: ESCORT 1985 TO 1990:** Remove the two lower attachment bolts (right-hand arrowed). Pull the bottom of the radiator to the rear and lower it to disengage the upper locating pins.

❒ **STEP 8: FIESTA FROM 1995:** Refer to illustration *1-4*. Raise and support the front of the vehicle.
➜ Where fitted, remove the shield from under the radiator.
➜ Remove the four bolts (1-4, positions arrowed).
➜ Carefully lower the radiator and radiator support member from the vehicle.

❒ **STEP 9: ESCORT AND ORION FROM 1990:** Also check the following.
➜ On carburetor models, remove the air cleaner.
➜ Where fitted, remove the wheel arch liner extension.
➜ On models with air conditioning, remove the splash shield and undo the three nuts attaching the air conditioning condenser from the side of the radiator deflector.

❒ **STEP 10: KA:** Also check the following.
➜ Remove the front wheel arch liners and front bumper - see *Chapter 13, Bodywork*.
➜ Remove the screws and shield from under the radiator.
➜ Remove the air intake ducting from the left-hand side of the engine compartment and release the oxygen sensor wiring from the fan support.
➜ On models with power steering, unbolt the power steering hydraulic line supports from the valence below the radiator.
➜ On models with air conditioning, remove the air conditioning condenser from the front of the radiator.

❒ **STEP 11:** Refitting the radiator is the reverse of the removal process, making sure the rubber insulators are fitted and the locating lugs are in their correct position.

JOB 5:   COOLANT HOSES - *removal, replacement.*

❒ **STEP 1:** Allow the engine to cool down before removing hoses - see *Chapter 2, Safety First!*

❒ **STEP 2:** Drain the cooling system.
➜ Undo the relevant hose clips and pull the hose from the connection.

TOP TIP!

5-3

❒ **STEP 3:** • If you are renewing the hose, cut through the old one with a craft knife.
➜ Use soapy water as a lubricant, to stop the blade from binding.
➜ The same lubricant helps when fitting new hoses.

JOB 6:   COOLANT EXPANSION TANK - *removal, replacement.*

❒ **STEP 1:** Disconnect the battery negative (-) earth/ground terminal. See *Chapter 10, Electrical, Dash, Instruments, Fact File: Disconnecting the Battery* BEFORE doing so!

❒ **STEP 2:** When cold, drain the cooling system.
➜ Separate the hoses from the expansion tank.

❒ **STEP 3: ESCORT AND ORION FROM 1990:** On models with power steering, separate the power steering fluid reservoir from the expansion tank.

❒ **STEP 4:** Remove the attachment screws.
➜ This is the expansion tank on an Escort 1.8 diesel.
➜ You can now remove the expansion tank.
➜ Refitting is the reversal of the removal process.

6-4

JOB 7: WATER PUMP - *checking, removal, replacement.*

7-1

❏ **STEP 1:** Checking a fitted water pump (**a**) is restricted to making sure the pump is not leaking and the bearings are in good condition.
➜ Look for leaks beneath where the pump mates with the cylinder block (**b**) and at the water pump shaft (**c**).
➜ A leak could be just a failing gasket (**d**) but unlikely.
➜ To check the pump, slacken the auxiliary drive belt - see *Chapter 6, Engine, Part D*.
➜ Hold the water pump pulley (**e**) and check for freeplay in the bearings.
➜ Rotate the pulley, making sure the bearings rotate freely without roughness or unusual noises.
➜ Worn bearings will mean pump replacement - see *Chapter 6, Engine, Part J*.

JOB 8: TEMPERATURE SENDERS AND SENSORS - *checking, removal, replacement.*

Section A: Temperature senders.

❏ **STEP A1:** A basic check of the temperature gauge and sender can be carried out as follows.
➜ Remove the connector from the temperature sender, make sure the cable end is not touching an earth and switch on the ignition - the temperature gauge should be fully at the cold end of the scale.
➜ Now, have an assistant watch the temperature gauge while you touch the cable end to a good earth/ground - the temperature gauge should move to the hot end of the scale.
➜ If the gauge works when tested like this, the sensor is probably faulty and should be replaced - see *Chapter 6, Engine*.
➜ Should the gauge show no signs of life when tested like this, the gauge itself is probably faulty and should be replaced - see *Chapter 10, Electrical, Instruments*.
➜ Ideally, you should thoroughly test the components but substitution is often quicker.

IMPORTANT NOTE: Do not attempt to use the methods given here to test the temperature sensors fitted to vehicles with Powertrain Control Modules - see *FACT FILE: COOLANT SENSORS AND SENDERS* at the start of this Job.

Section B: Temperature sensors.

❏ **STEP B1: COOLING FAN SENSOR:** Switch off the ignition and remove the electrical connection from the sensor.
➜ Use a suitable wire to short circuit the cable connections and switch on the ignition.
➜ If the fan operates, the sensor is at fault and should be replaced.

❏ **STEP B2: ENGINE COOLANT TEMPERATURE (ECT) SENSOR:**
➜ The test itself is theoretically quite simple and all you have to do is note the coolant temperature while measuring the electrical resistance between the sensor electrical contacts, though in practice, it may be difficult to achieve an accurate temperature reading.
➜ A fault with the ECT sensor is best resolved via a diagnostic check – see *Chapter 9, Ignition, Fuel, Exhaust*.

FACT FILE

COOLANT SENSORS AND SENDERS

• The COOLANT TEMPERATURE SENSOR provides coolant temperature information for the coolant fan and, where appropriate, engine management purposes.

• The COOLANT TEMPERATURE SENDER UNIT provides a signal for the dashboard temperature gauge.

• On recent vehicles (after 1995) with electronic engine management (Power Train Control module), the appropriate coolant temperature sensor (sometimes known as ECT – Engine Coolant Temperature-sensor) must be checked with suitable diagnostic equipment. It must NOT be checked by any other means!

JOB 9: HEATER ASSEMBLY - *removal, replacement.*

FACT FILE

HEATER ASSEMBLY

• Removing the heater assembly can only be achieved by removing part of the dashboard

• It may be necessary to remove the central console.

• It is usually possible to remove the heater matrix without completely removing the heater assembly although the work involved is only slightly less than complete heater assembly removable.

Section A: Fiesta 76-95, Escort 80-90, Orion 83-90.

Before dismantling, disconnect the battery negative (-) earth/ground terminal. See *Chapter 10, Electrical, Dash, Instruments, Fact File: Disconnecting the Battery* BEFORE doing so!

TOP TIP!

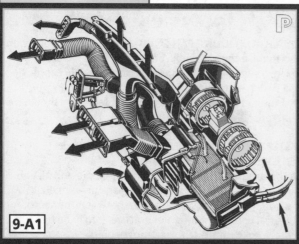

9-A1

❑ **STEP 1:** • The heater assembly is removed from inside the vehicle and there is a considerable risk of coolant spilling onto the vehicle carpets. Plug the heater inlet and outlet pipes (arrowed) before removal.

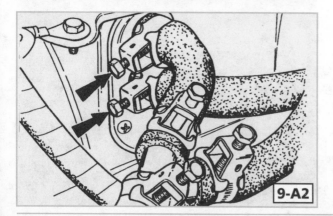

9-A2

❑ **STEP A2:** Put the heater controls in the hot position.
➜ Working in the engine compartment, disconnect the heater inlet and outlet hoses (arrowed).

❑ **STEP A3:** On the engine compartment bulkhead, remove the plate (**a**) and gasket (**b**) that fit around the heater inlet (**c**) and outlet pipes (**d**).

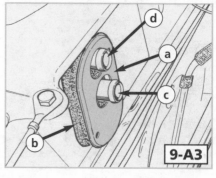

9-A3

❑ **STEP A4: FIESTA 83-89:** At the rear of the engine compartment, remove the ventilation air inlet cover plate (**1**). Move the plate, complete with bonnet lock (**2**) out of the way so that you can reach in and disconnect the fan motor electrical connector.

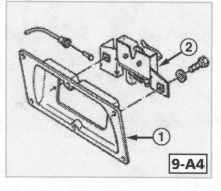

9-A4

❑ **STEP A5:** Remove the dashboard or dashboard trim sufficient to gain access to the heater assembly. See *Chapter 14, Interior, Trim, Job 3*.

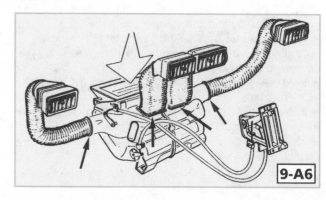

9-A6

❑ **STEP A6:** Remove the ventilation ducts (arrowed) from the heater assembly.
➜ On some models these are a push fit while others are held by screws.

❑ **STEP A7:** Disconnect the control cables from the heater assembly. Also see illustration *9-A10, items a*.

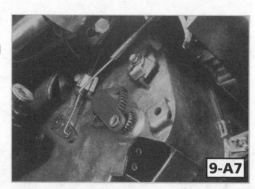

9-A7

❏ **STEP A8: FIESTA 76-83:** Remove the heater retaining bracket.

❏ **STEP A9: ESCORT FROM 1990:** Where fitted, unbolt the two heater assembly support brackets.

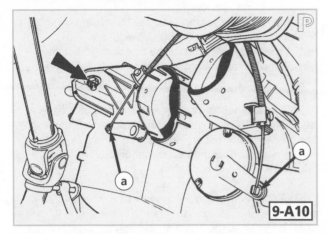

9-A10

❏ **STEP A10:** Disconnect the cables (**a**). Remove the heater assembly to bulkhead attachment nuts (arrowed).

9-A11

❏ **STEP A11:** Pull the heater assembly away from the bulkhead, disconnect the electrical connection from the blower motor, if still fitted, and manoeuvre the heater assembly from under the dashboard.

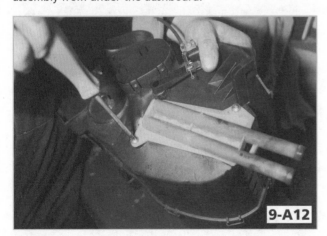

9-A12

❏ **STEP A12:** The heater matrix is quite easily removed but the method varies.
➜ **FIESTA 83-95:** Lever open the clips and separate the lower cover, complete with heater matrix, from the heater assembly.
➜ **ALL OTHER MODELS:** Remove the attachment screws.

9-A13

❏ **STEP A13: ALL MODELS:** Slide the matrix from the heater assembly.

❏ **STEP A14: BLOWER MOTOR, FIESTA 89-95:** The fan motor is removed from the engine compartment, following the steps here.

9-A14

➜ Remove the air cleaner.
➜ Remove the coolant reservoir.
➜ Remove the wheel brace and jack.
➜ Disconnect the electronic modules on the bulkhead panel.
➜ Separate the wiring loom, connectors, cable ties and hoses from the bulkhead panel.
➜ Remove the bulkhead panel rubber seal and the bulkhead panel - this panel is in two sections, held by screws with a nut at each side.
➜ Remove the cover from the blower, disconnect the wiring from the motor and resistor.
➜ Undo the two nuts and remove the blower assembly.
➜ If necessary you can separate the blower motor by releasing the two clips and removing the blower cover, releasing the blower retaining strap and withdrawing the blower motor.

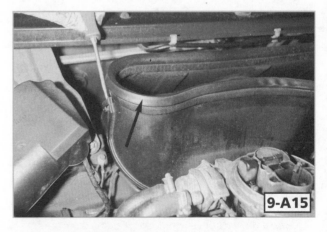

9-A15

❏ **STEP A15: BLOWER MOTOR, ESCORT 80-90, ORION 83-90:** The fan motor is removed from the engine compartment:

→ Pull off the rubber seal (arrowed) from the ventilation air inlet, lever off the spring clips and separate the cover at the front.
→ Disconnect the wiring multi-plug and earth lead - located close to the heater inlet and outlet pipes on the bulkhead.

9-A16

❏ **STEP A16: BLOWER MOTOR, ESCORT 80-90, ORION 83-90 - CONTINUED:**
→ Undo the nuts and remove the blower housing from the vehicle.
→ If necessary, lever open the clips (arrowed) and remove the fan covers. Remove the resistors and the blower motor.

❏ **STEP A17: BLOWER MOTOR AND EVAPORATOR, ESCORT FROM 1990:** The blower motor and evaporator (models with air conditioning) are removed from the engine compartment:
→ Where applicable, remove the air cleaner and battery.
→ Remove the seal, separate the hose and wiring loom from bulkhead.
→ Undo the six bolts and remove the cover from the air chamber.
→ Release the heater blower cover from its guides and pull it away.
→ On models without air conditioning, you can disconnect the blower motor electrical connections, undo the two retaining nuts and lift the blower motor from the vehicle. If necessary, lever open the locking clips and separate the motor from the housing. Separate the resistor from the motor.

MODELS WITH AIR CONDITIONING:
→ Undo the three bolts and separate the air conditioning pipe gasket plate and gasket from the bulkhead.
→ Remove the bolt and disconnect the compressor low-pressure pipe and the dehydrator liquid pipe from the front of the expansion valve.
→ Disconnect the multi-plugs from the vacuum motor and anti-ice switches and separate the two vacuum hoses from the vacuum reservoir. Remove the vacuum reservoir assembly and disconnect the two condensation hoses from the evaporator housing. If necessary you can separate the vacuum motor switch from the vacuum reservoir.
→ You can now undo the two bolts and nuts and remove the evaporator housing from the vehicle.
→ Release the vacuum motor linkage clamp screw from the side of the evaporator housing, undo the two nuts and remove the vacuum motor. If necessary you can also remove the anti-ice switch and vacuum reservoir from the

evaporator housing.
→ Disconnect the blower motor resistor wiring plug, remove the screws and the evaporator housing cover.
→ Remove the screws and disengage the evaporator housing upper and lower half retaining clips so that you can separate the housing.
→ Remove the screws and separate the expansion valve from the evaporator. Keep the valve seals.
→ Lift the evaporator out of the housing, release the blower motor retaining strap and remove the blower motor.

❏ **STEP A18:** If necessary you can dismantle the heater assembly, by levering off the spring clips and lifting out the blower motor (where applicable).
→ You may have to undo clips and remove the valves, which are twist-and-push fit.

❏ **STEP A19:** Refitting is the reverse of the removal process.
→ Make sure the foam gaskets are correctly located.

Section B: Fiesta from 1995.

❏ **STEP B1:** Disconnect the battery negative (-) earth/ground terminal. See *Chapter 10, Electrical, Dash, Instruments, Fact File: Disconnecting the Battery* BEFORE doing so.
→ Drain the cooling system.

❏ **STEP B2:** Remove the dashboard - see *Chapter 14, Interior, Trim*.

❏ **STEP B3:** Remove the engine compartment bulkhead (scuttle) panel. Follow the steps here.
→ Move the coolant expansion tank clear of the bulkhead - do not strain the hoses.
→ Remove the bulkhead panel rubber seal and the cover from the fusebox on the left-hand side on the engine compartment.
→ Where applicable, remove the MAP sensor bracket and Lambda sensor connector from the bulkhead panel.
→ Remove the windscreen washer hoses from the right-hand side of the panel.
→ Remove the bulkhead panel to fusebox attachment screw.
→ Remove the screws and clips and withdraw the bulkhead panel

❏ **STEP B4: MODELS WITH AIR CONDITIONING:** Have an air conditioning specialist remove the air conditioning refrigerant - see *Job 10, Safety First!*
→ This is a typical air conditioning layout.
→ Disconnect the refrigerant lines from the evaporator (located in the scuttle).

❏ **STEP B5:** Disconnect the heater coolant valve wiring plug and the coolant hoses from the heater matrix pipes. Disconnect the air conditioning refrigerant hoses when fitted. You can now continue with complete heater assembly removal or you can remove the heater matrix on its own:
→ Disconnect the screen wiper motor wiring plug, separate the wiring loom and move it clear of the heater matrix housing.

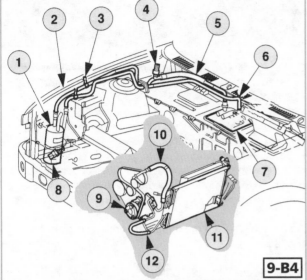

1 - accumulator
2 - high-pressure side service port
3 - low pressure side service port
4 - cycling switch
5 - suction hose
6 - liquid line
7 - evaporator cover plate
8 - high pressure switch
9 - a/c compressor
10 - suction and discharge line
11 - condenser
12 - suction and discharge line

9-B4

→ Slide the heater coolant valve from the top of the heater matrix housing.
→ Undo the four screws and separate the heater matrix housing cover from the scuttle. On models with air conditioning, separate the evaporator from the heater housing.
→ Carefully pull the heater matrix from the heater housing.

☐ **STEP B6:** Inside the passenger compartment:
→ Disconnect the blower resistor in the footwell and remove the attachment screw and the resistor.
→ Undo the two screws and remove the pollen filter housing. Undo the two screws and remove the blower motor cover then undo the two screws attaching the blower motor to the heater housing.
→ In the footwell, disconnect the blower motor wiring plug, separate the wiring grommet from the motor housing and withdraw the motor from the scuttle.
→ After disconnecting the air recirculation valve control motor, remove the three attachment screws and the control motor.

☐ **STEP B7: AIR CONDITIONING:** Disconnect the condenser drain hose.

☐ **STEP B8:** Undo the three nuts, pull the assembly away from the bulkhead and withdraw the heater assembly from the vehicle.

Section C: Ka.

On models equipped with air conditioning, have an air conditioning specialist remove the refrigerant from the system..

☐ **STEP C1:** Before dismantling, disconnect the battery negative (-) earth/ground terminal. See *Chapter 10,*

Electrical, Dash, Instruments, Fact File: Disconnecting the Battery BEFORE doing so!

☐ **STEP C2: BLOWER MOTOR RESISTOR:** Disconnect the wiring plug from the resistor - located in the footwell, on the side of the heater assembly. Remove the attachment screw and withdraw the resistor.

☐ **STEP C3: AIR CIRCULATION CONTROL VALVE MOTOR:** Remove the dashboard - see *Chapter 14, Interior, Trim*.
→ Disconnect the motor wiring plug, remove the three attachment screws and withdraw the motor.

☐ **STEP C4: HEATER ASSEMBLY AND HEATER MATRIX:**
→ Heater assembly only - remove the dashboard - see *Chapter 14, Interior, Trim*.
→ Move the coolant expansion tank clear of the bulkhead - do not strain the hoses.
→ Remove the screen wiper arms and the grille panel over the wiper mechanism.
→ Undo the bolts and pull the bulkhead trim panel clear of the scuttle.
→ Disconnect the hoses from the coolant valve.
→ Where appropriate, disconnect the refrigerant lines from the evaporator.
→ **HEATER MATRIX ONLY:** Remove the heater housing cover from the bulkhead and carefully pull the matrix from its housing. On models equipped with air conditioning, also pull the evaporator from the housing.
→ **HEATER ASSEMBLY ONLY:** Disconnect the wiring from the heater control panel, blower motor resistor, air recirculation control valve motor and blower motor. Remove the nuts and pull the heater assembly from the bracket. Separate the air ducts from the heater unit and, on models with air conditioning, the evaporator condensation tube from the floor.

☐ **STEP C5: BLOWER MOTOR AND COOLANT VALVE:**
→ Move the coolant expansion tank clear of the bulkhead - do not strain the hoses.
→ Remove the screen wiper arms and the grille panel over the wiper mechanism, *Chapter 10, Electrical, Instruments*.
→ Undo the bolts and pull the bulkhead trim panel clear of the scuttle.
→ **BLOWER MOTOR ONLY:** Inside the vehicle, disconnect the blower motor wiring. Remove the pollen filter housing and the blower motor cover, remove the screws and lift out the blower motor along with the wiring and grommet.
→ **COOLANT VALVE ONLY:** Disconnect the wiring plug and the coolant hoses. Slide the valve from the heater matrix housing.

JOB 10:	AIR CONDITIONING COMPONENTS - *removal, replacement*.

You will need to have the refrigerant extracted from the system, which can only be done by an air conditioning specialist.
→ However, Ford specify the use of a special tool for separating connectors - Tool N0 34-001 for Fiesta and Escort/Orion vehicles and Tool No 34-003 on Ka vehicles.
→ Although suitable alternative methods can be used, we recommend the use of the correct tools.

→ Evaporator removal is covered in *Job 9*, along with heater matrix and blower motor removal.
→ Cover or plug the opens connections immediately to prevent the ingress of dirt or debris.
→ Use new seals during reassembly and have the system recharged by an air conditioning specialist.

SAFETY FIRST!

• DO NOT open the pressurised pipework on the air conditioning system.

• The air conditioning system contains pressurised gas and specialist equipment is needed to extract it. It is illegal to discharge the gas to the atmosphere.

• The gas used in air conditioning systems is extremely harmful to the environment and may cause injury to the person carrying out the work if released in an uncontrolled manner.

• If air conditioning units are in the way of carrying out other work, whenever possible move units to one side with pipes still attached.

• If this is not possible, or there is a risk of damage to pipes or connections, have an air conditioning specialist de-pressurise the system so that you can dismantle it.

10-1

❑ **STEP A1:** • If the system needs to be drained for any reason, or if you suspect a leak, take the vehicle to a Vauxhall dealer or an air-conditioning specialist.

• After it has been re-assempled, the system will have to be tested (usually with inert nitrogen) and recharged by a specialist such as Autoclimate.

Section A: Compressor.

IMPORTANT NOTE:
Before dismantling, disconnect the battery negative (-) earth/ground terminal. See *Chapter 10, Electrical, Dash, Instruments, Fact File: Disconnecting the Battery* BEFORE doing so!

❑ **STEP A1:** Remove the auxiliary drive belt (see *Chapter 6, Part D*) and any components that prevent access to the compressor.

❑ **STEP A2:** Disconnect the compressor multi-plug and the refrigerant pipes.

❑ **STEP A3:** Remove the attachment bolts and separate the compressor from the engine. Watch out for a possible spillage of lubricating oil replace the 'lost' oil during reassembly

Section B: Condenser.

❑ **STEP B1: FIESTA:** Remove the right-hand headlight for access to disconnect the refrigerant lines - see *Chapter 10, Electrical, Instruments*.

❑ **STEP B2:** Remove the shields from below the condenser/radiator mounting bracket. Move and support the radiator and, where appropriate, power steering pipes out of the way so that you have access to the condenser. See *Job 4* for radiator removal. On Ka models you may have to remove the fan assembly from the radiator.

❑ **STEP B3:** Separate the refrigerant lines from the condenser.

❑ **STEP B4: ESCORT AND ORION:** Separate the dehydrator from the condenser/dehydrator mounting bracket, move the dehydrator to one side and separate the mounting bracket from the body.

❑ **STEP B5:** You can now remove the necessary attachment or clamp bolts and manoeuvre the condenser from the vehicle.

Section C: Dehydrator.

❑ **STEP C1: ESCORT AND ORION:** See *Section B* and separate the dehydrator from the condenser/dehydrator mounting bracket.

❑ **STEP C2: FIESTA:** Remove the dehydrator upper attachment bolt at the right-hand side of the engine compartment.

❑ **STEP C3: KA:** Disconnect the wiring from the low pressure switch on the dehydrator at the right-hand rear corner of the engine compartment.

❑ **STEP C4:** Disconnect the refrigerant pipes at the dehydrator.

❑ **STEP C5: ESCORT AND ORION:** Disconnect the high pressure switch multi-plug and remove the high pressure switch - you can now remove the dehydrator from the vehicle.

❑ **STEP C6: FIESTA:** Release the right-hand wheel arch liner sufficiently to gain access to the dehydrator attachment bolts.
→ You can now remove the bolts and lower the dehydrator from under the front of the vehicle.

❑ **STEP C7: KA:** Remove the mounting nuts and lower the dehydrator from the vehicle.

CHAPTER 9: IGNITION, FUEL, EXHAUST

*PLEASE READ **CHAPTER 2 SAFETY FIRST** BEFORE CARRYING OUT ANY WORK ON YOUR CAR.*

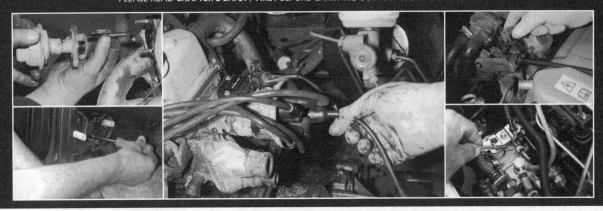

CONTENTS

We have placed both Ignition and Fuel systems in this, the same chapter. In the old days, the two areas could be treated separately, but that is no longer the case, and with today's electronic devices, ignition and fuel systems are inter-related.

TOP TIP!

READ THIS FIRST!
Before carrying out any adjustments, checks or dismantling of the fuel system, note the following:
• Never disconnect the battery with the engine running.
• Do not disconnect the ECU with the ignition switch in the ON position.
• Disconnect the battery before carrying out any work on the ignition or fuel systems. Both the radio and the ECU will loose their stored 'memories' - make sure that you first have the radio code
• Many injection systems cannot be adjusted. Their elements can be tested as described here, or by a fully equipped injection specialist or main dealer.

SAFETY FIRST!

IGNITION SYSTEMS

• When working on engines with electronic ignition systems, note the following, to avoid personal injury or damage to the ignition system:

• ELECTRONIC IGNITION SYSTEMS MAY INVOLVE VERY HIGH VOLTAGES! All manufacturers recommend that only trained personnel should go near the high-tension circuit (coil, distributor and HT wiring) and it is ESSENTIAL that anyone wearing a medical pacemaker device does not go near the ignition system.

• Do NOT touch ignition wires while the engine is running or being turned on the starter.

• Make sure the ignition is switched off before removing any wires from the ignition system.

• If the engine is to be turned on the starter without starting:

NON ELECTRONIC IGNITION: Disconnect the HT and LT leads from the ignition coil.

ELECTRONIC IGNITION: Disconnect the multi-pin plug from the distributor or ignition transformer (i.e. whichever one has the HT spark plug leads connected to it.)

FUEL SYSTEMS

Where fuel injectors are fitted with electrical plugs, disconnect the plug from each of the four injectors.

• Never work on the fuel system unless the engine is completely cool.

• Some fuel injection systems inject fuel at extremely high pressure.

• Pressure must be released in a controlled fashion to avoid any risk of a pressurised spray of fuel being produced.

• Residual pressure can remain in the fuel system for some considerable time, even the engine has been switched off.

• IMPORTANT NOTE: Removing pressure from the fuel lines, as described below, will not necessarily remove pressure from each of the components - they may still be pressurised.

• Before working on any part of the injection system it is necessary to remove the pressure from the system, as described in the FACT FILE: RELIEVING THE PRESSURE before the start of Job 1.

RELIEVING THE PRESSURE

Fuel injection systems can retain a dangerously high pressure for a considerable time after an engine is turned off. Before starting to dismantle any part of the fuel injection or fuel inlet system, and to remove the risk of severe injury:

1. Disconnect the battery negative terminal. See *FACT FILE: DISCONNECTING THE BATTERY* in *Chapter 10, Electrical, Instruments*.
2. Work out of doors and away from any sources of flame or ignition. Wear rubber or plastic gloves and goggles. Have a large rag ready.

3. Place a container beneath the filter to catch the fuel that is likely to be spilt.
4. Place your spanner/wrench on the first connection to be undone. Before undoing the connection, wrap the rag, folded to give several thicknesses, over the joint.
5. Undo the connection very slowly and carefully, allowing the pressure within the pipework to be let out without causing a dangerous jet of fuel.
6. Release the pressure from each of the pipes in the same way.
7. Mop up all traces of fuel and allow to dry thoroughly before reconnecting the battery, starting the car or taking it back indoors.

Part A: Petrol/Gasoline Engines

CONTENTS

JOB 1:   SYSTEMS – *explained*.

WHICH SYSTEM IS WHICH? - PETROL ENGINES

• To ensure correct testing procedures, settings and replacement parts you need to identify the precise system fitted. The following list gives an idea of which vehicles you can expect to find equipped with the various systems. See *Chapter 6, Part B, Which Engine is Which?* for engine details.

Section A: Ignition systems.

FIESTA

→ Fiesta models up to 1981 had contact breaker type ignition systems. In September 1981, 1.3 litre and XR2 models were equipped with breakerless distributor ignition. Except for 1.0 litre and 1.1 litre models, all other models were equipped with breakerless distributor ignition from 1983. The 1.0 litre and 1.1 litre models retained the contact breaker system until 1986.
→ All models from 1986 to 1989 had breakerless distributor ignition.
→ From 1989, the breakerless distributor ignition system was fitted to 1.1 litre CVH engines with Central Fuel injection (CFi) systems.
→ All other models from 1989 have been fitted with distributorless ignition systems (DIS).

ESCORT AND ORION

➜ 1.1 litre CVH engines, up to 1986, had contact breaker type ignition systems.
➜ 1.1 litre CVH engines from 1986, all 1.3 litre OHV and CVH engines, 1.4 litre and 1.6 litre CVH carburetor engines, and the 1.6 litre engines with the Bosch K-Jetronic fuel injection system had breakerless distributor ignition systems.
➜ 1.4 litre CVH engines with CFi type fuel injection had a version of the breakerless distributor ignition system.
➜ 1.1 litre and 1.3 litre HCS engines, from 1989, and 1.6 litre engines with EFi systems had distributorless ignition systems.
➜ From 1990, all models had versions of the distributorless DIS system.

KA

➜ All Ka models have DIS.

Section B: Fuel systems.

FACT FILE
FUEL INJECTION SYSTEMS

• Several fuel injection systems have been fitted to the vehicles covered here. CFi is a single point system. EFi and Sequential Electronic Fuel injection (SEFi) are similar, more sophisticated multi-point systems. All three systems are controlled by Ford's EEC IV engine management module or, on later models, the EEC V engine management module also known as the Powertrain Control Module.
• The Bosch K-Jetronic, fitted to some Orion 1.6i models is a continuous injection multi-point system. It is completely different from the Ford systems described above.

FIESTA

➜ All models up to 1989 had carburetors: Ford (Motorcraft) single or variable venturi (VV) types or Weber single (1V TLM) or double venturi types (2V, 2V DFTM or 2V TLD).
➜ From 1989, 1.1 litre and 1.3 litre HCS engines and some 1.4 litre CVH engines were fitted with the CFi system. All other models retained carburetors.
➜ All models from 1995 were fitted with the SEFi system.

ESCORT AND ORION

➜ All pre-1990 models, except as detailed below, had carburetors: (Ford Motorcraft) variable venturi (VV) types or Weber double venturi types (2V TLDM, 2V DFTM, 2V TLD or 2V DFT).
➜ 1.3 litre HCS engines and 1.4 litre CVH engines from 1990 had the CFi system.
➜ 1.6 litre CVH engines from 1990 had the EFi system

➜ XR3i and some Orion 1.6i models had the Bosch K-Jetronic fuel injection system.
➜ 1.3 litre Endura E, 1.4 litre PTE engines, 1.6 litre and 1.8 litre Zetec and Zetec E engines had the SEFi system.

KA

➜ All Ka models have the SEFi system.

Section C: Emission control components.

Ever more stringent controls on vehicle emissions have led to the introduction of various devices to reduce exhaust, crankcase and fuel tank emissions. Depending on model and territory, you may encounter the following.
➜ **POSITIVE CRANKCASE VENTILATION (PCV):** The PCV system mixes air with the blow-by gases that escape past the piston into the crankcase and draws this mixture into the combustion chamber via an oil separator and PCV valve.
➜ **TEMPERATURE CONTROLLED INLET AIR:** A temperature sensitive valve in the air cleaner blends fresh air with air from a heater box fitted to the exhaust manifold to maintain a constant inlet air temperature.
➜ **EXHAUST GAS RECIRCULATION (EGR):** A small amount of exhaust gas is bled into the fresh mixture entering the combustion chamber which reduces peak combustion temperatures and the production of harmful nitrogen oxides.
➜ **DECELERATION VALVE:** The deceleration valve maintains sufficient mixture flow to allow complete combustion during deceleration, which prevents erratic combustion and the resulting excessive hydro-carbon (unburned fuel) emissions.
➜ **SPARK DELAY VALVE (SDV):** A Spark Delay Valve slows down the vacuum advance system to match the rate at which the mixture changes.
➜ **PORTED VACUUM SWITCH (PVS):** This valve is used to control the EGR system (two port type) and deceleration valve or spark delay valve (three port type), ensuring that these emission control devices only operate once the engine has warmed up.
➜ **EVAPORATIVE EMISSION CONTROL:** Fuel vapours from the fuel tank are not vented in to the atmosphere but to a canister containing carbon. The carbon absorbs the vapour when the engine is stationary but releases it into the inlet system once the engine is running.
➜ **PULSE AIR SYSTEM:** The pulse air system performs two functions during engine warm-up; firstly, filtered air is fed into the exhaust ports burning any unburned hydrocarbons or carbon monoxide reducing emissions of these two substances; secondly, the heat from the burning helps to warm-up the catalytic converter, reducing the time it takes to reach normal operating temperature.
➜ **CATALYTIC CONVERTER:** A catalytic converter reduces emissions of hydrocarbons and carbon monoxide (two-way oxidation type) and, additionally, harmful oxides of nitrogen (three-way reduction type).

UNLEADED FUEL

Vehicles manufactured before the mid-1980s should be safe with unleaded fuel. Check the vehicle handbook or contact an approved Ford dealer if you are not sure.

➔ As a basic guide, the following petrol engines are suitable for continuous use with unleaded petrol:

➔ 957cc and 1117cc engines up to the end of January 1986 with VG or VL stamped on the flywheel end of the cylinder head.

➔ 957cc and 1117cc OHV engines from February 1986 and 1296cc OHV engines from October 1985.

➔ Single overhead camshaft CVH engines up to the end of 1984 with LPG stamped on the cylinder head above No. 1 cylinder exhaust port.

➔ All single overhead camshaft CVH engines from the end of 1984.

➔ All Zetec, Zetec E and Zetec SE engines.

JOB 2: DIAGNOSTICS - *carry out checks.*

Section A: Background.

Vehicles are becoming increasingly dependent on electronics. When things are going well, this has great advantages for the driver, including:
➔ Greater efficiency.
➔ Better reliability.
➔ Less maintenance.

Of course, almost everything has its downside, and vehicle electronics are no exception. Features often seen as 'problems' include:
➔ The need for special tools - mainly electronic diagnostic stuff.
➔ The need for knowledge and information not found in traditional manuals.
➔ The fact that it's impossible to see faults with electronic systems.

However, the problems presented by vehicle electronics are 'overcome-able' - and indeed, such problems can be turned on their heads. Then, instead of appearing as problems, they can be seen as a set of extra advantages for the mechanic, such as:
➔ Rapid fault diagnosis.
➔ Less guesswork.
➔ Fewer 'grey' areas caused by wear - electronics tend to work or not-work, and they don't usually wear out in a mechanical sense.

Turning the minuses into pluses is a matter of knowing where to obtain information and how to use it. It is not possible to fault-find many areas affected by electronics on an old-fashioned common-sense basis. But fortunately, the information is not too difficult to put to use - and it's even easier to find, if you know where to look!

☐STEP A1:
It is not possible - even in a manual of this size - to cover diagnostics in specific detail; there's no room, and no need. We will describe how to use diagnostic test equipment and the equipment itself will do the rest. Or at

2-A1

least, that's the theory! What diagnostic test equipment, such as the Sykes-Pickavant ACR System Tester, is good at is identifying specific fault areas:

➔ If a component such as the engine knock sensor, the hall sender unit, or the Lambda sensor is failing to give a reading, the tester can tell you, almost instantly.

➔ If you want to fool a component into working without the engine running, an advanced unit such as this one can simulate a signal to the component, so that you listen and feel for a solenoid clicking, a flap opening and closing, or the buzz of an EGR valve working.

What it can't always tell you is the source of the fault. Before fitting an expensive replacement, you will want to know:
➔ Is the wiring to or from the component at fault?
➔ Is it a corroded plug or socket?
➔ Has someone else connected it up incorrectly?

TOP TIP!
• Check the basics before assuming that anything more complex is at fault.
• See *Chapter 4, Workshop Notes* and in particular Workshop Top Tips! and Pic 28 in that Chapter.

To analyse the results, you will need to go a step further. You will still need a wiring diagram, to check circuits and connections. And you will need extra diagnostics information to know how to check out potential faults. Most of the information you will need is in this manual - but if all of it had been printed here, the book would have been too thick to carry!

TOP TIP!
• It's a myth that only the manufacturers' own diagnostics gear can do the job! But you will need a plug-in diagnostics tester to interrogate electronic-based systems.
• There are several makes of tester on the market. We feature the pro-oriented Sykes-Pickavant ACR System Tester. It's typical of the best of the testers available.

2-A2

STEP A2: Detailed diagnostic information is available from a number of sources:

➜ You can order the manufacturer's own data, although some of it may be restricted information and not widely available. Try your local Ford dealer's parts department.

➜ There are several companies who specialise in producing detailed data of this sort. The one shown here is produced by CAPS (Computer Aided Problem Solving). It covers, as do all of them, a very wide range of manufacturers and models. All of these data compilations are expensive, typically costing many times the price of this manual!

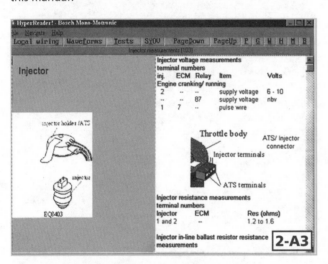

2-A3

STEP A3: CAPS lists an immense amount of data on each disk, including:

➜ ECU pin settings.

➜ Values expected for various test readings using, for instance, a standard test meter.

➜ Waveforms for oscilloscope component testing.

➜ Virtually everything you may need in order to carry out extensive diagnostic testing, in conjunction with a fault code reader.

STEP A4: A good quality multi-meter will be an essential tool for the diagnosis of the more basic faults, such as continuity and correct connections. This Sykes-Pickavant multi-meter comes complete with full instructions for use and is both versatile and accurate. We have come across cheaper tools that are most inaccurate, which makes them next to useless. How can you tell if there is a fault with the level of current (for instance) if the meter reads inaccurately?

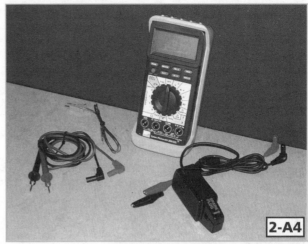

2-A4

STEP A5: We look later at a more comprehensive and complete diagnostic tool from Sykes-Pickavant, but this sensor simulator and tester is an extremely useful piece of kit in its own right. Although it is not designed to actually drive solenoids and actuators (it will test them both to see if they are

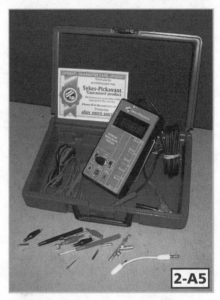

2-A5

receiving a control signal), it will test the following: Camshaft sensor; Crankshaft sensor; Mass Air Flow Meter; Manifold absolute pressure sensors; Oxygen sensor; Power steering pressure switch; Temperature sensors; Throttle position sensor.

2-A6

STEP A6: An efficient Lambda sensor is essential for protecting the catalytic converter, allowing the vehicle to run efficiently and enabling the engine to pass the emissions laws. The Sykes-Pickavant tester can be used to check the sensor while it is in situ.

DIAGNOSTIC TESTING

BACKGROUND INFORMATION FROM SYKES-PICKAVANT
Electronic fuel injection and ignition systems on modern vehicles have a computer (called an ECU) to provide the proper control of the fuel-air mixture. The ECU works by measuring many different characteristics of the car then, using this information, it calculates the correct quantity of fuel, the time of the fuel injection and the time for the ignition spark.

The ECU is a computer, like any other you could buy from a High Street shop, but instead of a keyboard it has SENSORS as inputs, and instead of a TV screen, it has ACTUATORS. These are the output of the computer; for example the ECU controls the fuel injectors by opening and closing them for a few thousandths of a second. During this time fuel is sprayed into the inlet manifold (near the inlet valves) in the exact proportions required for efficient combustion. The ECU also controls the engine's idle speed with the "idle speed control valve".

Sensors are prone to failure, mainly due to being exposed to the harsh engine environment where harness connections can easily deteriorate over a few years. When this kind of fault occurs the ECU can be misled by the information being sent from the sensor, this results in the wrong quantity of fuel or timing for the sparks. Soon, the car allows too much of the wrong exhaust gases to escape, becomes difficult to drive or even does not start at all.

ECUs are able to detect faults in sensor signals by comparing the value with a range of values which are programmed by the designer of the ECU. If a signal is outside the expected range then something is wrong. The ECU does not "know" what exactly is wrong but is can sense that the signal is not in the range it expects to receive. This detected fault is stored as a code number in the memory of the ECU and it is this code which is known as a "fault-code". ECU designers have built-in limited number of such fault-codes into most modern systems. Each manufacturer has a different coding system and a different way of reading the codes, but they have some basic similarities.

Somewhere on the car's harness is a diagnostic socket which connects directly to the ECU. By connecting a second computer (the ACR Systems Tester, in this instance) to this socket we can send messages back and forth between the two computers and read the stored codes.

A simple code reader will show only the two or three digit code numbers which you then need to look up in a book to find out what they mean. The Sykes-Pickavant

ACR Systems Tester does much more, by READING, CLEARING, ACTUATOR TESTS, and COMPONENT TESTS.

READ CODES

The ACR System Tester is able to read codes and display the meaning of each code. For example if the coolant temperature sensor is faulty then on some Bosch ECU's the fault-code stored is "15". The ACR System Tester shows the following on its two line display:

15 COOLANT SENS
VOLTAGE LOW

CLEAR CODES

When this problem has been corrected (perhaps by replacing the sensor) the stored fault code (15) must be removed from the ECU, otherwise the ECU will still think something is wrong. This is what the Clear Codes function is for. After clearing codes, the engine should be started and a final check for any stored fault codes made, just to be certain that nothing else has occurred.

ACTUATOR TEST

This feature is a method of testing the ECU outputs when the engine is turned off. For example to test the injectors involves sending a signal from the ACR System Tester to trigger a special program in the ECU which, in turn, causes the injectors to open and close every second. The injectors can be heard quite clearly "ticking" like a clock every second. With this we have clear proof that a signal is able to reach the injectors, we DO NOT KNOW if the injectors are blocked or gummed, so we do not know if any fuel can get into the engine...there are other ways of testing for that.

The final group of tests are components, (this is another way of saying sensors) where we can show the voltage, time or angle of various sensors which provide input to the ECU.

IMPORTANT NOTES:
• The ECU can only measure what is happening to the car using the sensors it is connected to. If there is no sensor it cannot be measured. This may seem obvious but some people seem to think computers are all-powerful.
• The ECU calculates the value that the ACR System Tester displays; the Tester is NOT connected directly to the sensor. The display you see is what the ECU "thinks" is the correct value. So if you see "Coolant Temperature 79 degrees Celsius" and the engine is stone-cold, you know something is wrong, but the ECU doesn't. This is a vital point to understand about code-readers which connect to the diagnostic socket; they can only display what the ECU is programmed to show and what the ECU calculates from its input.

Section B: The ACR tester – using.

❏ **STEP B1:** Find the location of the diagnostic socket - the Sykes-Pickavant/Facom Diagnostics mini-manual will tell you where to look. Some typical ones are:

➔ **EARLY FORDS WITH DIAGNOSTICS:** 2 sockets - a 3-pin (triangular) and 5-pin (sometimes 'church window') shaped sockets; one white (**a**), one black (**b**).

2-B1

□ **STEP B2: 'INTER-MEDIATE':** Single socket in similar location to illustration *2-B1*. Different numbers of pins on different models.

2-B2

□ **STEP B3: LATER:** Models with EEC V system. 16-pin OBD (On Board Diagnostics) socket within driver's reach - in this case, behind trim panel.

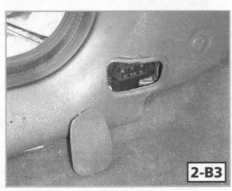
2-B3

□ **STEP B4:** With the ignition OFF, push the plug/s into the relevant socket/s and follow the instructions with the ACR kit.

□ **STEP B5:** Each ROM pod (and there are several - each one covering a range of makes and models) comes with its own small manual which 'walks' you through the setting up and running procedure.

→ When the unit comes to life, you select the type of system on the menu offered on the read-out. The ACR then communicates with the vehicle's ECU.

→ You then select from the menu which type of test you want to carry out, such as 'Read Errors', 'Clear Errors' or 'Test Actuators'.

2-B5

→ If you selected 'Test Actuators' for instance, the next menu allows you to choose which one - say, 'Fuel Injector'.

→ The ACR then interrogates the system for errors.

→ If an error is found, the error code number appears AND (unlike many testers) an abbreviated description of the error, such as **"0522: COOLANT TEMP SENSOR"** appears on the screen.

→ Pressing the **'OK'** button on the ACR applications can expand abbreviations. **"INJ P/W"**, for example, becomes **"INJECTOR PULSE WIDTH"** - useful until you are able to memorise the abbreviations.

□ **STEP B6:** A similar approach is followed - a walk-through by the manual, combined with step-by-step on-screen prompts and menus -

2-B6

allows the user to carry out most of the other functions that would normally only be carried out by the main dealer. Depending on the system, the SP ACR has the following capabilities:

→ Identifying ECU number and type.

→ Reads and clears fault codes.

→ Drives actuators e.g. coil, injectors etc..

→ Shows 'live engine data' e.g. throttle potentiometer, Lambda switching etc..

→ CO timing and base idle adjustment.

→ Service light reset.

→ Instrument panel codes and actuators (gauges, warning lights) on some Ford vehicles.

IMPORTANT NOTES:

• Fault code readers that only display code numbers can be misleading. 'Live engine data' is far more useful.

• A fault code will only be logged by a system if the component has failed open circuit or short to ground. If the component is working but incorrectly, like the hot engine showing a coolant reading of 20 degrees Celsius, this would only be seen using the component 'live data' option.

• Also it is highly recommended that any fault code is read, then deleted. The car should then be driven and re-tested to see if the code has returned, if it does then treat is as real.

TOP TIP!

• Many fault codes are introduced by people simply unplugging components – double-check before assuming a component fault!

We have dealt in outline with the type of ACR pods and cables used for the vehicles covered by this manual. Other vehicles and other manufacturer's vehicle groups require their own modules and their own specific setting-up approaches. In each case, the set-up is described in the Sykes-Pickavant manual supplied with the relevant ROM pod.

JOB 3: CONTACT BREAKER POINTS (EARLY VEHICLES ONLY) - *check, replace.*

❏ **STEP 1:** Switch off the ignition and remove the distributor cap.

❏ **STEP 2:** Bosch and Ford (Motorcraft) Distributors: Use a flat bladed screwdriver to release the clips from the distributor cap.

3-2

❏ **STEP 3:** **LUCAS DISTRIBUTOR:** The distributor cap is held in place with two cross-headed screws.

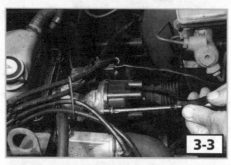

3-3

❏ **STEP 4:** **SINGLE OVERHEAD CAMSHAFT (CVH) ENGINES:** Before you can remove the distributor cap, you will need to pull off this metal cover.

3-4

❏ **STEP 5:** Dirt, dampness and light deposits on the studs inside the cap can be cleaned off but replace the

3-5

distributor cap if there is excessive deposit build-up or wear on the four studs inside the cap, cracks or a badly worn or insecure central carbon contact.

❏ **STEP 6:** Check that the rotor arm is a secure fit on the distributor shaft and not cracked.

❏ **STEP 7:** Gently prise apart the contact breaker points and check for burning or pitting.

3-8

❏ **STEP 8:** Assuming there are no signs of burning or pitting, turn the engine so that the points are at their maximum opening - the heel of the pivoting section (**B**) is at the highest point on one of the cam lobes (**C**). Insert a feeler gauge of the appropriate thickness into the gap - the feeler gauge should be a sliding fit with a little resistance felt as it is moved in and out. The correct gap (**A**) is as follows.
➔ Ford (Motorcraft) 0.64 mm (0.025 in.)
➔ Bosch 0.45 mm (0.018 in.)
➔ Lucas 0.5 mm (0.020 in.)

❏ **STEP 9:** If adjustment is necessary, loosen the single screw (arrowed) (Bosch and Lucas distributors) or...

3-9

❏ **STEP 10:** ...loosen two screws (arrowed) on Ford distributors.

❏ **STEP 11:** Use a wide bladed screwdriver in the adjusting notch on the

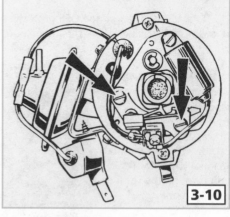

3-10

baseplate to open/close the points gap as necessary. Check the gap after tightening the screw(s) and readjust if necessary.
➔ You can check the points gap more accurately using a dwell angle meter.

TOP TIP!

• Only loosen the screws enough to be able to make the adjustment.

STEP 12: If you are changing the contact breaker points, completely remove the attachment screw(s) - (**B**).
➔ Separate the low tension feed (**A**) at the connector (Bosch distributors)...

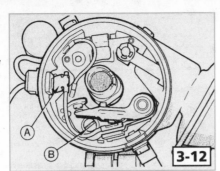

3-12

STEP 13 ...or at the screwed connection (Ford distributor shown here)...

STEP 14: ...or at the connection (*3-15, item C*) on the Lucas distributor – see *Step 15*.

3-13

STEP 15: Refitting is the reverse of removal, bearing in mind the following points.
➔ On Lucas distributors, make sure the forked cam is located on the pin (**A**).
➔ The securing screw is item (**B**).
➔ Set the contact breaker points - see *Step 8* to *Step 11*.
➔ Apply a very thin smear of grease to the cam lobes.
➔ We recommend checking the points after a few hundred miles.

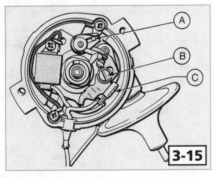

3-15

JOB 4:   IGNITION TIMING - *checking, setting*.

On models equipped with distributor systems, it is possible to set the ignition timing with the engine stationary (static timing). However, we recommend only doing this when setting the initial timing after engine reassembly.
➔ Dynamic timing, using a stroboscope with the engine running, is much more accurate.
➔ On more recent models, with DIS, ignition timing is controlled by the engine management system. It can only be checked using specialist test equipment. If you suspect a fault with the ignition timing, we recommend that you have an approved Ford dealer test the system on their dedicated diagnostic equipment.

IMPORTANT NOTE:
• You must check and, if necessary, adjust the contact breaker gap before setting the ignition timing.

• The timing values in *Chapter 1, Facts and Figures*, are the manufacturer's original values. On older vehicles, which were intended for use with leaded fuel, these timing values may have been amended to allow the vehicles to run on unleaded fuel. If you have any doubt about the correct values, you should check with an approved Ford dealer.

Section A: Static ignition timing.

STEP A1: Turn the engine until the notch (**A**) in the crankshaft pulley is in line with the appropriate mark (**B**) on the front cover and No. 1 cylinder is

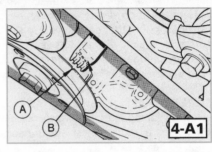

4-A1

approaching TDC on the firing stroke - see *Chapter 1, Facts and Figures* for the static advance figure - each mark is equivalent to 4 degrees advance.
➔ When the engine is set correctly, the rotor arm should be pointing to the No. 1 cylinder stud on the distributor cap.

STEP A2: CONTACT BREAKER TYPE DISTRIBUTORS: Slacken the clamp bolt/attachment bolts at the base of the distributor, see *Job 6*, and turn the distributor until the points just open.
➔ Hold the distributor in this position and tighten the clamp bolt/attachment bolts.

STEP A3: BREAKERLESS DISTRIBUTORS PRE-1983: Slacken the clamp at the base of the distributor and rotate the distributor until the appropriate tooth (**B**) on the

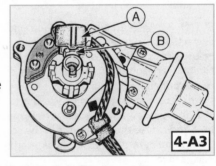

4-A3

trigger wheel is exactly aligned with the stator.
➔ You will have to judge the exact position - some later distributors had two lines marked (**A**) on the ignition coil to help with the alignment.

STEP A4: BREAKERLESS DISTRIBUTORS, CVH CARBURETOR ENGINES 1989 TO 1995: During manufacture marks (arrowed) were punched on the cylinder head and distributor flange - ignition timing is correct when these marks are aligned. If these marks are not present, set the distributor so that the clamp bolts are in the mid-slot position then carry out a dynamic timing check - see *Section B*.

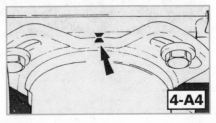

4-A4

☐ STEP A5:
BREAKERLESS
DISTRIBUTORS,
CVH ENGINES
WITH CFI PRE-
SEPTEMBER
1990: The
ignition timing
is correct when
the punch
marks on the
cylinder head

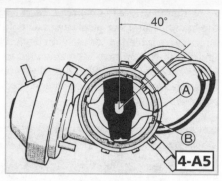

and distributor flange are aligned. If punch marks are not present the approximate timing can be set by rotating the distributor until the centre line through the multi-plug connector is at 40 degrees to the vertical. Accurate ignition timing setting must be carried our by an approved Ford dealer with the necessary specialist equipment.

☐ STEP A6: Refit the distributor cap and any other removed components, such as spark plugs. Ideally, carry out a dynamic timing check and, if necessary, adjust the engine idle speed.

Section B: Dynamic (Stroboscopic) ignition timing.

SAFETY FIRST!

• The dynamic timing is checked with the engine running. Do not wear loose clothing and keep well clear of rotating components and drive belts. Watch out for the thermostatically controlled fan starting at any time.

☐ STEP B1: Refer to *Chapter 1, Facts and Figures* for the correct engine speed/advance figures.
→ Use white paint or correcting fluid to highlight the timing marks on the crankshaft pulley and cover.
→ Disconnect the vacuum advance line from the distributor and block the line leading to the manifold.
→ If the ignition advance is incorrect, slacken the clamp bolt and rotate the distributor in the correct direction to advance or retard the ignition. Tighten the clamp bolt(s) and recheck the advance.
→ If you have a vacuum pump and gauge, you can check the operation of the vacuum advance. Refer to *Chapter 1, Facts and Figures* for the vacuum/advance figures.

TOP TIP!

• If the advance does not change with engine speed, the mechanical advance mechanism is not working correctly and should be overhauled or a replacement distributor fitted - see *Job 6*.
• If the advance is erratic, the distributor is worn and a replacement should be fitted - see *Job 6*.

JOB 5: IGNITION COIL - *replacement.*

Section A: Distributor ignition systems.

The ignition coil is designed to work on a voltage lower than that from the battery or charging circuit.
→ When the engine is running, a ballast resistor reduces the system voltage.
→ During starting, battery voltage drops and the ballast resistor is switched out of the circuit so that the lower battery voltage is supplied direct to the coil.
→ It is vital that you fit a coil of the correct voltage for a ballast resistor.

☐ STEP A1: Locate the coil (arrowed).
→ The position varies depending on vehicle model, engine type and year of manufacture - this is an Escort.

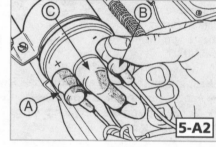

☐ STEP A2: Make sure the ignition is switched off and disconnect the low tension (**LT**) wires from the coil - make a note of the way they are connected.
→ It is important that the positive (+) (**A**) and negative (-) (**B**) terminals on the coil are connected correctly.
→ Disconnect the high tension (**HT**) lead (**C**). Undo the mountings and remove the coil.

☐ STEP A3: Mount the new coil and remake all the connections.

Section B: Distributorless ignition systems (DIS).

☐ STEP B1:
Locate the coil as follows:
→ **CVH, PTE AND ZETEC ENGINES:** On the cylinder head at the left-hand end (arrowed).

→ HCS ENGINES: On the engine bulkhead side of the cylinder block, close to the oil filter. Access may be difficult, especially on Ka models.

☐ **STEP B2:** Disconnect the battery negative lead, the main electrical connector to the coil and, where fitted, the suppressor connector.

☐ **STEP B3:** Make sure the HT leads and their locations on the coil are clearly marked so that they can be refitted in the correct locations. Press in the retaining clips on each connector and pull the leads away.

☐ **STEP B4:** Remove the Torx type screws and lift away the coil complete with mounting bracket.

☐ **STEP B5:** Refitting is the reverse of removal.

JOB 6: DISTRIBUTOR - *removal, refitting*.

Section A: Overhead valve engines.

☐ **STEP A1:** Make sure the ignition is switched off.

☐ **STEP A2:** Remove the distributor cap.
→ Pull the vacuum pipe from the vacuum advance

6-A2

mechanism and disconnect the low tension lead.

☐ **STEP A3:** Turn the crankshaft in the normal direction of rotation until No. 1 piston is at top dead centre on the firing stroke - see *Job 4, Step A1*.

TOP TIP!

DISTRIBUTOR REFITTING - OVERHEAD VALVE ENGINES
• Before removal, mark the position of the distributor in relation to the cylinder block and the position of the rotor arm in relation to the distributor - this will save time during refitting.
• Do not loosen the mounting plate clamp when removing the distributor, because refitting will be much easier if you remove the mounting plate and distributor as a unit.
• The rotor arm will rotate anti-clockwise as the worm gear on the camshaft meshes with the gear on the distributor shaft. You will have to anticipate the amount of rotation and compensate by turning the rotor arm through a small clockwise angle. It may take several attempts to find the right angle.

☐ **STEP A4:** Mark the position of the distributor relative to the cylinder block and the position of the rotor arm relative to the distributor.

☐ **STEP A5:** Undo the single bolt (a) attaching the clamp plate to the cylinder block and lift the distributor away.
→ The horizontal hexagon (large arrow) is the clamp plate bolt.

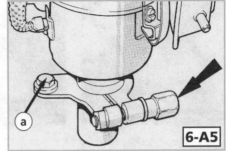
6-A5

☐ **STEP A6:** Refitting is the reverse of removal - if you are fitting a new distributor, transfer the alignment markings. Check the static timing, where possible, before starting the engine and the dynamic timing once the engine is running - see *Job 4*.

Section B: Single overhead camshaft engines.

IMPORTANT NOTE:
PRE-1990 CVH ENGINE MODELS WITH CFi
• If the alignment marks are not present on the cylinder head or distributor, for example when new components are being fitted – see *Step B5*.
• If marks are lost - see *Job 4, Step A5*.

☐ **STEP B1:** Make sure the ignition is switched off.

☐ **STEP B2:** Remove the distributor cap or remove the HT leads.
→ Disconnect the low tension supply and, where fitted, the vacuum advance tube.

6-B2

☐ **STEP B3:** A revised distributor with two

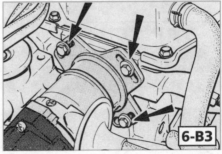
6-B3

attachment bolts, similar to the type used on Fiestas, was fitted to Escort and Orion models with CVH engines from early 1985 - the previous distributor – shown here - had three attachment bolts.

☐ **STEP B4:** The earlier design is no longer available but the later design can be used on earlier models without modification. However, the low tension wiring is different

6-B4

6-B5

and a new assembly, Ford Part No. 84AG-12045-BA should be used with the later distributor.

❒ **STEP B5:** Check that there are alignment marks punched on the distributor and cylinder head - see *Step B1*.
➜ If no marks are present, you should make your own alignment marks (arrowed).
➜ Remove the two or three distributor attachment bolts and lift the distributor away.

❒ **STEP B6:** Refitting is the reverse of removal, bearing in mind the following points.
➜ See *Important Note, Pre-1990 CVG Engine Models with CFi* for information relevant to these models.
➜ Check the condition of the distributor 'O'-ring seal and replace if necessary.
➜ If you are fitting a new distributor, which does not have an alignment mark, insert the distributor in the approximately correct position and tighten the attachment bolts so that they are centrally positioned in the alignment slots. Check the timing - see *Job 4*. When the timing is correct, punch alignment marks on the distributor and cylinder head.

JOB 7:   LAMBDA SENSOR (CAT. ENGINES) - *test, replace.*

The Lambda sensor is also known as the oxygen sensor or heated oxygen sensor and is only found on vehicles with catalytic convertors.

TOP TIP!

• The Lambda sensor is fragile and will be damaged if dropped, or even knocked.

Section A: Removal and replacement.

❒ **STEP A1:** The Lambda sensor is either screwed into the exhaust manifold...

❒ **STEP A2:** ...or the exhaust down pipe.

❒ **STEP A3:** Remove the exhaust heatshields as necessary for access - see *Part C*.

❒ **STEP A4:** Trace the electrical wiring (**a**) back from the Lambda sensor and separate the multi-plug.
➜ You can now unscrew the Lambda sensor (**b**), noting the following.

❒ **STEP A5:** Refitting is the reverse of removal, bearing in mind the following points.
➜ Use a new sealing washer.
➜ Apply a very light smear of anti-seize grease to the threads to make any subsequent removal easier.

7-A5

Section B: Testing.

❒ **STEP B1:** You will need a Lambda sensor tester, such as this Sykes-Pickavant unit which is simply connected to the sensor wiring as described in the tester manual.

7-B1

❒ **STEP B2:** Prepare for the test as follows.
➜ Run the engine until it is thoroughly warm (fan turns on and off twice).
➜ When the engine is hot, run for 30 seconds at 3,000 rpm to heat the Lambda sensor.
➜ Let the engine speed return to normal tick-over - if testing is prolonged, run the engine up to 3,000 rpm for 30 seconds at intervals.

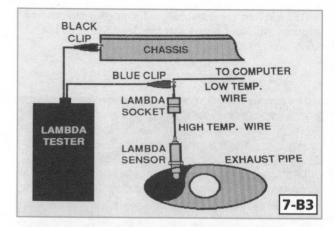

7-B3

❒ **STEP B3:** Check the voltage at the sensor.
➜ The average should be about 0.45 volts to 0.5 volts but the sensor is okay if the voltage fluctuates between 0.2 volts and 0.8 volts.
➜ Alternatively, use the diagnostics functions on the Lambda tester.

STEP B4: If the readings are outside these limits, try the following.
→ If the reading is consistently too high (mixture too rich), snap open the throttle several times and see if the level readjusts to within the correct range.
→ If the reading is too low (mixture too lean), try running without the air cleaner element to see if the level adjusts to within the correct range.
→ If you cannot obtain a reading within the acceptable range, the sensor is probably faulty and should be replaced - see *Section A*.

STEP B5: More recent Lambda sensors have a heating element.
→ Typically the supply is from the fuel system relay - check wiring diagrams - and the earth/ground will be via a separate cable, either to the ECU or direct to an earth/ground point.
→ To check the heating element, disconnect the plug and check the resistance across the heating element wires.
→ A typical resistance is 5 ohms to 10 ohms.
→ A faulty element usually gives no reading (short circuit) or a very high reading (open circuit).

JOB 8:   CARBURETOR - *adjustment.*

The same type of carburetor may have been fitted to more than one model but that does not mean the carburetors are interchangeable.
→ We have restricted ourselves to describing the basic tune-up adjustments. If you do wish to overhaul a carburetor you should check the availability of the necessary parts with an approved Ford dealer or carburetor specialist and follow the instructions supplied with overhaul kits.

Section A: Common procedures.

STEP A1: Before adjusting the carburetor make sure that all other engine settings have been checked and adjusted - carburetor adjustment should be the last tuning job on the list.

STEP A2: The engine should be at normal operating temperature before you make any checks or adjustments.

STEP A3: Check and adjust the idle speed first.
→ On some carburetors, Ford specify that the engine must be stabilised by running it at 3000 rpm for 30 seconds then releasing the throttle to let the engine idle.

STEP A4: Check the idle speed mixture. We recommend that you use an exhaust gas analyser to check the CO% - follow the manufacturer's instructions and make sure the choke is in the off position.

STEP A5: Once you have correctly set the idle speed and mixture you can go on to check the fast idle speed and choke operation.

STEP A6: CHOKE PULL-DOWN: Some type of carburetor have an automatic choke which is partly controlled by manifold vacuum. Satisfactory choke operation is dependent on correct setting of the vacuum pull-down.

STEP A7: THROTTLE KICKER: A throttle kicker is fitted on some carburetors. This device automatically increases engine idle speed when certain high load accessories, such as air conditioning, are switched on.

Section B: Ford (Motorcraft) single venturi (1V) carburetor, Fiesta 1.0 litre models to 1989 and 1.1 litre models to 1983.

STEP B1: IDLE SPEED ADJUSTMENT: The idle speed limits are:
→ 1.0 litre models 775 rpm to 825 rpm
→ 1.1 litre models 750 rpm to 850 rpm.

STEP B2: IDLE MIXTURE SETTING: The correct CO% reading is between 0.75% and 1.75%.

STEP B3: FAST IDLE SPEED ADJUSTMENT:
Hold the choke butterfly (3) in the fully open position.
→ Operate the choke linkage as far as it will go and check that the fast idle speed is within the range 1000 rpm to 1200 rpm or 1400 rpm on models from 1983.
→ If necessary, bend the tag (4) to bring the speed within limits.
→ **CHOKE BUTTERFLY PULL DOWN:** Turn the choke operating lever on the carburetor until the choke butterfly (3) is fully closed then open the plate against spring pressure until you reach the stop.
→ Adjustment is correct when there is a 2.75 mm (0.11 in.) to 3.25 mm (0.13 in.) gap, 3.5 mm (0.14 in.) on models from 1983, between the choke butterfly and carburetor.
→ Adjust the tag (5) as necessary to obtain the correct gap.

1 - mixture adjusting screw
2 - idle speed adjusting screw.
3 - choke butterfly
4 - fast idle speed adjusting tag
5 - choke butterfly adjusting tag

8-B3

Section C: Weber double venturi (2V) carburetor, Fiesta 1.3 litre to 1983 and 1.6 litre models to 1986.

STEP C1: IDLE SPEED SETTING: Ford recommend that the idle speed is set with the cooling fan running - you can keep the fan running continuously by pulling the two wires from the sensor and connecting them with a jumper lead.

➜ The correct idle speed is between 775 rpm and 825 rpm.
➜ These are the idle speed and mixture adjusting screws.

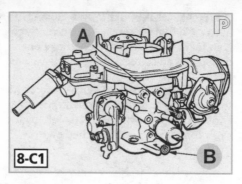

8-C1

❏ **STEP C2: IDLE MIXTURE SETTING:** The correct CO% readings are as follows:
➜ 1.3 litre models 1.25% to 1.75%
➜ 1.6 litre models 1.0% to 1.50%

❏ **STEP C3: FAST IDLE SPEED ADJUSTMENT:** Hold the throttle (**1**) partly open, close the choke butterflies (**2**) by hand and release the throttle - the throttle mechanism will hold the choke mechanism at the fast idle position.

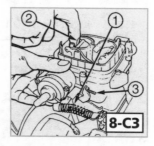

8-C3

➜ Release the choke butterflies - if they do not return to the fully open position the engine is either below normal operating temperature or the automatic choke is faulty.

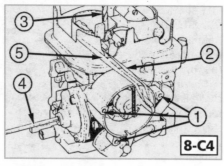

8-C4

➜ Without touching the throttle, start the engine and check that the fast idle speed is as follows:
• 1.3 litre models 2000 rpm
• 1.6 litre models (pre-1983) 1800 rpm
• 1.6 litre models (1983 to 1986) 2700 rpm
➜ Adjust the fast-idle screw (**3**) as necessary.

❏ **STEP C4: CHOKE VACUUM PULL-DOWN:**
Disconnect the wire from the electric choke.
➜ Remove the three screws (**1**), lift off the automatic choke outer housing and bi-metal spring followed by the internal heat shield.
➜ Open the throttle to let the choke butterflies close fully then hold the choke butterfly lever (**2**) so that the choke butterfly is kept closed - a rubber band (**5**) is used here.
➜ Push the choke diaphragm open to its stop.
➜ Use a spacer, such as a twist drill (**3**) to check that the clearance between the choke butterfly and carburetor body is as follows:
➜ 1.3 litre and 1.6 litre models (1983 to 1989) 5.2 mm (0.21 in.) to 5.8 mm (0.23 in.).
➜ 1.6 litre models (pre-1983) 4.5 mm (0.18 in.) to 5.5 mm (0.22 in.)
➜ If necessary, adjust the clearance with the adjusting screw (**4**).

❏ **STEP C5:** Use the alignment marks on the carburetor and outer housing to correctly position the automatic choke mechanism.

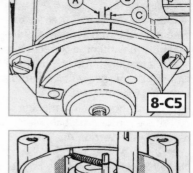

8-C5

❏ **STEP C6: CHOKE PHASING:** Adjust the vacuum pull-down before adjusting the choke phasing - see *Step C4*.
➜ Part-open the throttle and position the fast idle adjusting screw on the centre step of the fast idle

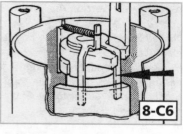

8-C6

cam - release the throttle and the cam should remain in this position.
➜ Push the choke butterflies down until the cam stops against the fast idle screw.
➜ Check that the gap between the choke butterfly and carburetor body is as follows:
• 1.3 litre models 2.25 mm (0.09 in.) to 2.75 mm (0.11 in.)
• 1.6 litre models (pre-1983) 1.75 mm (0.07 in.) to 2.25 mm (0.09 in.)
• 1.6 litre models (1983 to 1986) 1.5 mm (0.06 in.) to 2.5 mm (0.01 in.)
➜ Adjust the gap as necessary by bending the tag (arrowed).
➜ Refit the removed components.

> ## Section D: Ford (Motorcraft) variable venturi (VV) carburetor, Fiesta 1.1, 1.3 litre models 1983 to 1989, Escort 1.1, 1.3 litre OHV, Escort, Orion 1.3 litre CVH engine models, Escort, Orion 1.6 litre models (except XR3) pre 1986.

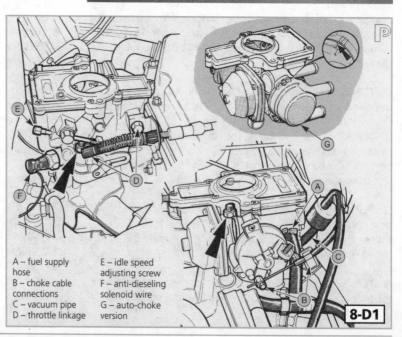

A – fuel supply hose
B – choke cable connections
C – vacuum pipe
D – throttle linkage
E – idle speed adjusting screw
F – anti-dieseling solenoid wire
G – auto-choke version

8-D1

❏ **STEP D1: IDLE SPEED SETTING:** Ford recommend that the idle speed is set with the cooling fan running - see *Step C1*.

➜ Stabilise the engine - see *Step A3*.

➜ Check that the idle speed is as follows:

• Manual transmission, 750 rpm to 850 rpm

• Automatic transmission, 850 rpm to 950 rpm

❏ **STEP D2: MIXTURE SETTING:** The CO% should be in the range 1.0% to 2.0%.

➜ These are the idle speed (**A**) and the mixture (**B**) setting screw beneath a 'tamper-proof' cap.

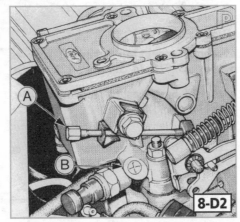

8-D2

Section E: Weber single venturi (1V and 2V TLM) carburetors, Fiesta 1.0 litre models from 1989 to 1991.

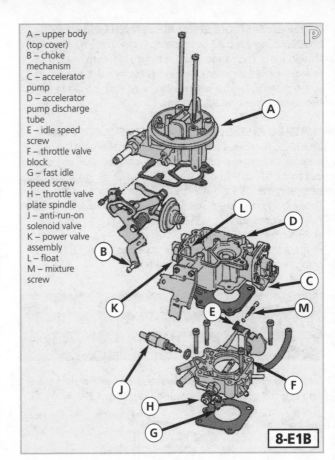

A – upper body (top cover)
B – choke mechanism
C – accelerator pump
D – accelerator pump discharge tube
E – idle speed screw
F – throttle valve block
G – fast idle speed screw
H – throttle valve plate spindle
J – anti-run-on solenoid valve
K – power valve assembly
L – float
M – mixture screw

8-E1B

❏ **STEP E1A: IDLE SPEED SETTING:** These are the components of the 1V TLM carburetor.

➜ Stabilise the engine - see *Step A3*.

➜ Check that the idle speed is as follows:

• Pre-1989 models, 775 rpm to 825 rpm.

• From 1989 models, 700 rpm to 800 rpm

❏ **STEP E1B:** ...and these are the components of the 2V TLM carburetor.

❏ **STEP E2: IDLE MIXTURE SETTING:** The CO% reading should be as follows:

• Pre-1989 models, 1.2% to 1.3%.

• From 1989 models, 0.5% to 1.5%.

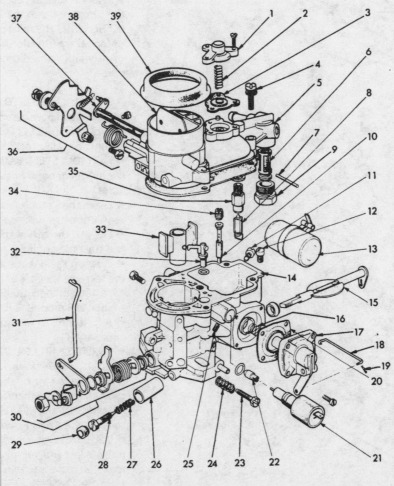

1 - power valve cover
2 - spring
3 - power valve diaphragm
4 - screw
5 - upper body
6 - filter
7 - float pivot pin
8 - needle valve
9 - plug
10 - emulsion tube
11 - main jet
12 - accelerator pump one-way valve
13 - float
14 - carburetor body
15 - throttle valve
16 - spring
17 - accelerator pump cover
18 - link rod
19 - spring clip
20 - accelerator pump diaphragm
21 - anti-run-on valve
22 - idle jet
23 - idle speed adjuster
24 - spring
25 - grub screw
26 - tamper proof plug housing
27 - spring
28 - idle mixture adjuster
29 - tamperproof plug
30 - throttle spindle assembly components
31 - link rod
32 - accelerator pump delivery nozzle
33 - auxiliary venturi
34 - air corrector jet
35 - needle valve housing
36 - choke cam assembly components
37 - choke spindle
38 - choke butterfly
39 - seal

8-E1A

☐ **STEP E3: FAST IDLE SPEED ADJUSTMENT, PRE-1989 MODELS:** See *Step B3* but note that the fast idle speed should be in the range: 3100 rpm to 3300 rpm.
→ Adjust the fast idle speed as necessary - the adjusting screw may be locked with sealant and you should re-seal the screw after any adjustment.

☐ **STEP E4: FAST IDLE SPEED ADJUSTMENT, POST-1989 MODELS:** Remove the air cleaner and make sure the engine is at normal operating temperature. Pull the choke out to its full extent and use a 5.0 mm (0.20 in.) spacer between the choke butterfly and venturi to hold the choke butterfly open. The fast idle speed should be in the following range:
→ 3300 rpm to 3500 rpm.
→ If necessary, use the fast idle speed adjusting screw to bring the speed within these limits.

Section F: Weber double venturi (2V DFTM) carburetor, Fiesta, Escort and Orion 1.4 litre models.

Ford recommend that the idle speed *and* idle mixture are set with the cooling fan running - see *Step C1*.

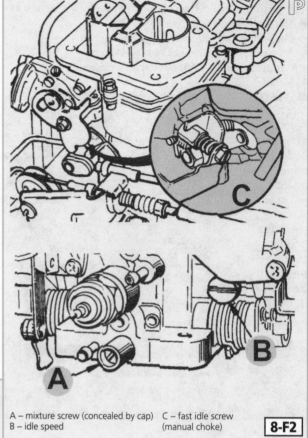

A – mixture screw (concealed by cap)   C – fast idle screw
B – idle speed   (manual choke)

8-F2

A – idle control screw
B – mixture screw
2 – gasket
3 – nut
5 – choke body
6 – diaphragm
8 – gasket
11 – fuel shut off valve
12 - solenoid
14 – fuel inlet valve
17 – throttle controller

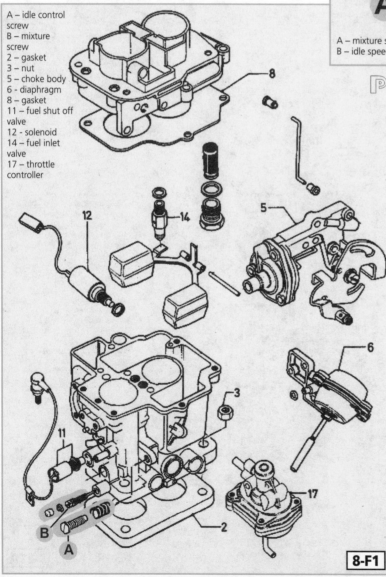

8-F1

☐ **STEP F1: IDLE SPEED SETTING:** These are the components of the 2V DFTM carburetor.
→ Check that the idle speed is as follows:
• Manual transmission, 750 rpm to 850 rpm.
• Automatic transmission, 800 rpm to 900 rpm.

☐ **STEP F2: CARBURETOR SETTINGS:** These are the relevant adjustment points.
→ **IDLE MIXTURE SETTING:** The CO reading should be 1.25% to 1.75%.
→ **FAST IDLE SPEED ADJUSTMENT:** Remove the air cleaner and hot and cold air inlet hoses.
→ Leave the vacuum and crankcase ventilation hoses connected - where fitted.
→ Pull out the choke knob to its full extent and start the engine.
→ Press on the linkage lever and check that the fast idle speed is as follows:
• Pre-1989 models, 2600 rpm to 2800 rpm.
• Post-1989 models, 2700 rpm to 2900 rpm.
→ Adjust the fast idle speed screw as necessary (**C**).
→ **THROTTLE KICKER (WHERE FITTED):** See illustration *8-G4, item 1.*
→ Remove the air cleaner and plug the vacuum from the manifold.
→ Make sure the idle speed and mixture are correct - see *Steps F1 and F2.*
→ With the engine is running, lift the throttle kicker lever up and check that the speed increase is within the following range:
• pre-1989 models: 1250 rpm to 1350 rpm.

• post-1989 models: Manual transmission, 1250 rpm to 1350 rpm.
• post-1989 models: Automatic transmission, 1050 rpm to 1150 rpm.
→ If necessary, remove the tamperproof plug on the top of the kicker body and adjust the unit to give a speed within the correct range.

Section G: Weber double venturi (2V TLD) carburetor, Fiesta (from 1991), Escort (from 1986) – except XR3 – 1.1 and 1.3 Litre HCS engine models and Orion 1.3 litre HCS engine models.

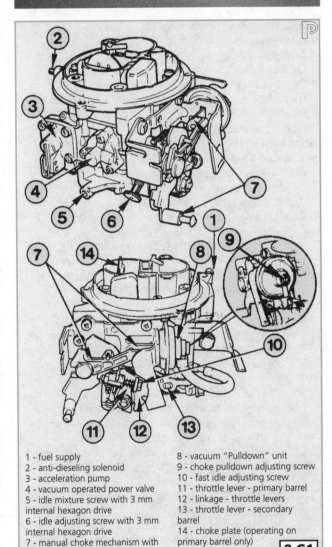

1 - fuel supply
2 - anti-dieseling solenoid
3 - acceleration pump
4 - vacuum operated power valve
5 - idle mixture screw with 3 mm internal hexagon drive
6 - idle adjusting screw with 3 mm internal hexagon drive
7 - manual choke mechanism with pulldown diaphragm
8 - vacuum "Pulldown" unit
9 - choke pulldown adjusting screw
10 - fast idle adjusting screw
11 - throttle lever - primary barrel
12 - linkage - throttle levers
13 - throttle lever - secondary barrel
14 - choke plate (operating on primary barrel only)

8-G1

❑ **STEP G1:** These are the carburetor components.

❑ **STEP G2: IDLE SPEED SETTING:** Ford recommend that the idle speed is set with the cooling fan running - see *Step C1.*
→ Check that the idle speed is between 700 rpm and 800 rpm.
→ Disconnect the throttle kicker vacuum tube when a throttle kicker is fitted – all auto. models. Reconnect.

❑ **STEP G3: IDLE MIXTURE SETTING:** Ford recommend that the idle mixture is set with the cooling fan running - see *Step C1.*
→ The CO% reading should be 0.5% to 1.5%.

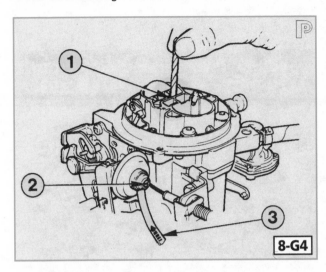

8-G4

❑ **STEP G4: FAST IDLE SPEED ADJUSTMENT:** Note that the fast idle speed should be as follows:
• 1.1 litre engines manual transmission, 2800 rpm.
• 1.1 litre engines automatic transmission, 2600 rpm.
• 1.3 litre engines, 2500 rpm.
→ Fully open the choke.
→ With the engine running, the pulldown diaphragm rod should now be up to the stop – check that it is.
→ Measure the gap between the butterfly plate and the carburettor wall using a 2 mm drill (**1**).
→ Adjust the screw (**2**) until the gap is correctly set.

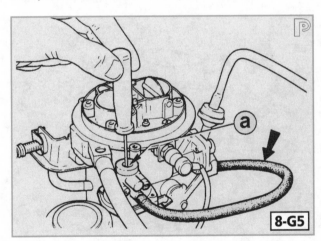

8-G5

❑ **STEP G5: THROTTLE KICKER (WHERE FITTED):** Make sure the idle speed and mixture are correct - see *Steps F1 and F2.*
→ Remove the air cleaner and detach the vacuum tube from the inlet manifold to the throttle kicker - do not disconnect the vacuum connection to the ignition module.
→ Connect a tube (arrowed) directly between the manifold and kicker unit, by-passing the kicker vacuum switch.
→ Start the engine and make sure the engine speed is in the following range:
• 1.1 litre engines manual transmission, 1250 rpm to 1350 rpm.

• 1.1 litre engines automatic transmission, 1050 rpm to 1150 rpm.

• 1.3 litre engines, 1800 rpm to 2000 rpm.

→ If necessary, remove the tamperproof plug on the top of the kicker body and adjust the unit (a) to give a speed within the correct range.

Section H: Weber double venturi (2V DFT) carburetor, Escort XR3.

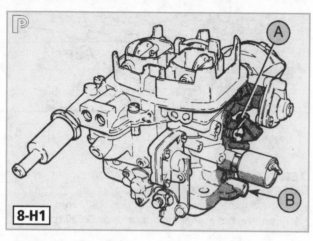

8-H1

❏ **STEP H1:** These are the positions of the adjustment screws.

→ **IDLE SPEED SETTING (A):** See *Step F1*.

→ **MIXTURE SETTING (B):** Ford recommend that the idle speed is set with the cooling fan running - see *Step C1*.

→ The CO reading should be 1.0% to 1.5%.

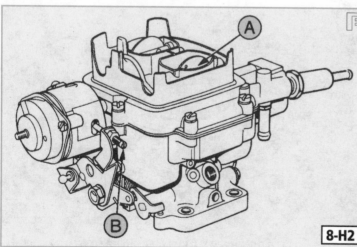

8-H2

❏ **STEP H2: FAST IDLE SPEED ADJUSTMENT:** See *Step G2* but note that the fast idle screw (B) should be resting on the high cam and the fast idle speed should be as follows:

• 2600 rpm to 2800 rpm.

→ Item (A) is the choke butterfly.

❏ **STEP H3: CHOKE PULL-DOWN:** See *Step G3*. The clearance should be as follows:

→ 5.2 mm (0.21 in.) to 5.8 mm (0.23 in.).

JOB 9: CARBURETOR - *removal, replacement.*

❏ **STEP 1:** The following Steps are applicable to all types.

→ Be sure to read *Step 8* to see if there is any information relating to the carburetor you are working on.

→ See illustrations in *Job 8*, where relevant.

SAFETY FIRST!

• The carburetor float chamber contains fuel so be ready for some spillage. Read *SAFETY FIRST* at the beginning of this Chapter and the general notes relating to fuel handling in *Chapter 2, Safety First*.

❏ **STEP 2:** Refer to the appropriate Chapters or Jobs and remove the following components.

→ Air cleaner.

→ Throttle cable.

→ Choke cable.

→ Distributor vacuum tube.

→ Fuel inlet hose and, where appropriate, any fuel vent pipes and the fuel return hose.

❏ **STEP 3:** During manufacture, crimp type clamps were used to attach the fuel hoses. These clamps will be destroyed during removal and the fuel hoses should be refitted with screw type clamps.

❏ **STEP 4:** Disconnect the electrical connections from the fuel cut-off solenoid valves on the carburetor body.

❏ **STEP 5: AUTOMATIC CHOKE:** On carburetors with an automatic choke, allow the coolant temperature to fall and depressurise the cooling system.

→ Disconnect the coolant hoses from the carburetor.

❏ **STEP 6:** Depending on type, the carburetor will be attached to the manifold by nuts at the flange, or screws through the carburetor body.

❏ **STEP 7:** Refitting is the reverse of removal, bearing in mind the following points:

→ Clean away all traces of the old carburetor to manifold gasket and use a new gasket.

→ Adjust the throttle and choke cables and check the carburetor settings - see *Job 8*.

❏ **STEP 8:** The following Steps are specific to the carburetor types listed below.

→ If there are no notes here you can take it that everything has been covered in *Steps 1 to 7*.

→ **WEBER DOUBLE VENTURI (2V) CARBURETOR, FIESTA 1.3 LITRE TO 1983 AND 1.6 LITRE MODELS TO 1986:** This carburetor has an electric choke and, therefore, no manual choke cable. Disconnect the choke electrical connection.

JOB 10: FUEL INJECTION SYSTEMS - *adjustment.*

A diagnostic tester can be used to carry out most tests on the equipment shown here although some, such as fuel pressure measurement, must still be tested separately. See *Job 2* for information on diagnostic testing.

Section A: Central fuel injection (CFi).

❏ **STEP A1:** This is the arrangement of the fuel-side of the single-point CFi system.
→ The CFi unit replaces the carburetor on the inlet manifold – hence 'single-point'.

❏ **STEP A2:** A single centrally mounted solenoid controlled fuel valve (injector) injects fuel into the inlet airstream.
→ The fuel valve is controlled by the EEC IV engine management control unit.

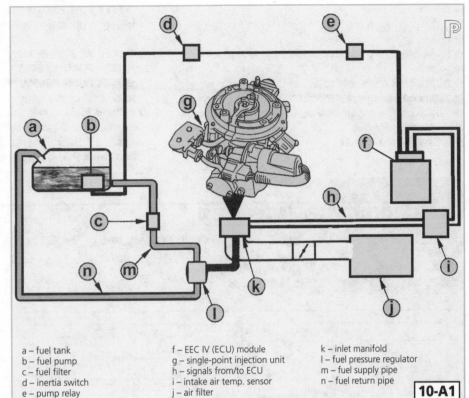

a – fuel tank	f – EEC IV (ECU) module	k – inlet manifold
b – fuel pump	g – single-point injection unit	l – fuel pressure regulator
c – fuel filter	h – signals from/to ECU	m – fuel supply pipe
d – inertia switch	i – intake air temp. sensor	n – fuel return pipe
e – pump relay	j – air filter	

10-A1

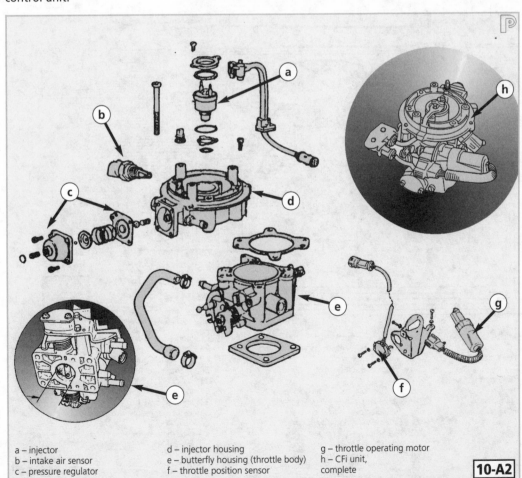

a – injector	d – injector housing	g – throttle operating motor
b – intake air sensor	e – butterfly housing (throttle body)	h – CFi unit, complete
c – pressure regulator	f – throttle position sensor	

10-A2

SYSTEM CHECKS

❏ **STEP A3: FUEL PUMP OPERATION:** Make sure there is sufficient fuel in the tank and switch on the ignition. You should be able to hear the fuel pump run for a few seconds then switch off - this should happen every time the ignition is switched on.
→ A pump that runs continuously indicates that the engine management system is operating in Limited Operation Strategy (LOS).
→ This is a back up state and indicates a system fault - you should carry out a diagnostic check, see *Job 2* - or have a test carried out by an approved Ford dealer.

□ **STEP A4: FUEL PUMP PRESSURE:** Connect a suitable pressure gauge to the fuel line between the CFi unit and fuel filter - follow the gauge manufacturer's instructions. The fuel pressure, with the engine idling, should be within the following limits:
→ 0.9 bar to 1.1 bar.
→ If the pressure is too high, suspect a blockage in the fuel lines.
→ If the pressure is too low, suspect the fuel pressure regulator.
→ Although it is possible to adjust the regulator we recommend fitting a replacement - see *Job 11, Step A5*.
→ Switch off the engine and check that fuel pressure is maintained as follows:
→ 0.5 bar after 1 minute.

Section B: Electronic fuel injection (EFi).

□ **STEP B1:** These are the components of the EEC IV fuel injection operating system.

□ **STEP B2: FUEL PUMP:**
→ **FUEL PUMP OPERATION:** See *Step A1*.
→ **FUEL PUMP PRESSURE - STATIC CHECK:** Connect a suitable pressure gauge to the fuel line between the fuel rail and fuel filter - follow the gauge manufacturer's instructions. Disconnect the wiring from the fuel injectors and the E-DIS coil. Switch the ignition on and off twice and check that the pump pressure is at least 3 bar.

FACT FILE

ELECTRONIC FUEL INJECTION

• Signals from engine sensors, see *FACT FILE: CFi OPERATION*, are used by the EEC IV unit to decide how much fuel should be injected.
• It is possible to adjust fuel mixture and idle speed.
• The remainder of the EFi fuel system is similar to the CFi fuel system.

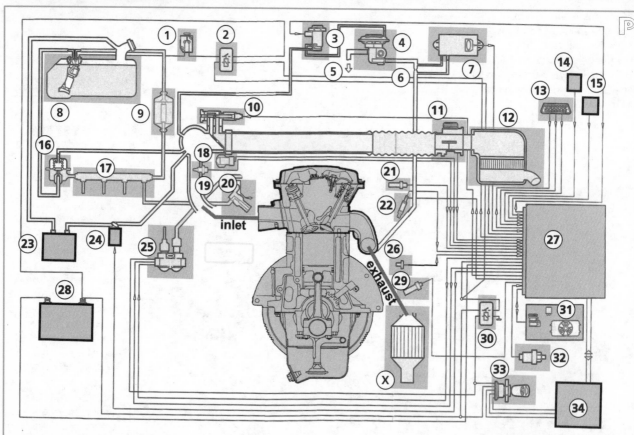

1 - inertia fuel shut-off (IFS) switch
2 - fuel pump relay (FPR)
3 - exhaust gas recirculation (EGR) vacuum regulator
4 - exhaust gas recirculation (EGR) valve
5 - to inlet manifold
6 - differential pressure measuring point
7 - exhaust gas recirculation (EGR) pressure transducer
8 - intake fuel pump (FP)
9 - fuel filter
10 - idle air control (IAC) valve
11 - mass air flow (MAF) sensor
12 - air cleaner assembly
13 - data link connector (DLC)
14 - octane adjust service connector (OAI)
15 - air conditioning clutch
16 - fuel pressure regulator
17 - fuel rail
18 - throttle position (TP) sensor
19 - intake air temperature (IAT) sensor
20 - fuel injector
21 - camshaft position (CMP) sensor
22 - heated oxygen sensor (HO2S)
23 - carbon evaporative emission (EVAP) canister
24 - EVAP canister purge valve
25 - electronic ignition (EI) system coil
26 - engine coolant temperature (ECT) sensor
27 - powertrain control module (PCM)
28 - battery
29 - crankshaft position (CKP) sensor
30 - power supply relay
31 - air conditioning/cooling fan circuit
32 - power steering pressure (PSP) switch
33 - ignition switch
34 - vehicle immobiliser or passive anti-theft system (PATS)
X – catalytic converter

10-B1

➔ **FUEL PUMP PRESSURE - ENGINE RUNNING:** Connect a suitable pressure gauge. With the engine at idle speed, disconnect the vacuum hose at the fuel pressure regulator-plug the hose. Check that the fuel pressure is as follows:
• **FIESTA:** 2.3 to 2.5 bar.
• **ESCORT AND ORION:** 2.9 bar to 3.1 bar.
➔ If necessary, remove the plug from the top of the fuel pressure regulator and use a suitable Allen key to adjust the pressure.
➔ Switch off the engine and check that pressure is maintained as follows:
• No less than 0.8 bar below regulated pressure after 2 minutes.

❑ **STEP B3: FUEL MIXTURE:** Follow the manufacturer's instructions and use a suitable exhaust gas analyser to check the CO reading - the correct settings are as follows:
➔ Non-turbo models, 0.55 % to 1.05%.
➔ Turbo models, 1.25 % to 1.75%.
➔ If necessary, lever out the tamper proof cap from the fuel mixture potentiometer (located on the engine bulkhead) and adjust the screw as necessary - clockwise to increase CO% and anti-clockwise to decrease CO%.

❑ **STEP B4: POTENTIOMETER:** If you have difficulty obtaining the correct CO% and you believe the mixture control potentiometer to be faulty, it can be checked as follows.
➔ Check the resistance between one of the outer pins and the centre pin, the reading should be in the range 448 to 5993 ohms.
➔ Carry out a full diagnostic and wiring check and, if no other faults are found, replace the potentiometer.

FACT FILE

IDLE SPEED

• The normal engine idle speed is 850 rpm to 950 rpm and is controlled by the EEC IV unit via an idle speed control valve. However, the EEC IV unit uses a base idle speed of 700 rpm to 800 rpm as a datum for maintaining the normal idle speed.

• Two types of idle control valve have been used.
➔ Early models have a Weber valve mounted on the air cleaner. This unit requires cleaning at 20,000 mile intervals - see *Job 11, Step B6*.
➔ Later models have a Hitachi valve, mounted on the engine compartment bulkhead or inlet manifold, which does not require regular cleaning.

• Idle speed checks should be carried out with all electrical components, including the fan, switched off.

❑ **STEP B5: BASE IDLE SPEED CHECK AND ADJUSTMENT - BULKHEAD OR AIR CLEANER MOUNTED VALVE:** With the engine at normal operating temperature, disconnect the multi-plug from the idle speed control valve.
➔ Hold the engine speed at 2000 rpm for 30 seconds, release the throttle and check that the base idle speed is within the setting range 725 rpm to 775 rpm.
➔ If necessary, lever out the tamperproof screw in the throttle body and adjust the screw (clockwise to increase) to bring the base idle speed within the correct range.

➔ Again, hold the engine speed at 2000 rpm for 30 seconds and re-check the base idle speed, adjusting if necessary.
➔ When the base idle speed is correct, reconnect the idle speed control valve multi-plug, and check that the idle speed rises above 900 rpm before falling back to the normal idle speed.
➔ Keep the engine running for five minutes to allow the EEC IV unit to 'learn' the new settings.

❑ **STEP B6: BASE IDLE SPEED CHECK AND ADJUSTMENT - INLET MANIFOLD MOUNTED VALVE:** Drive the vehicle for several miles to make sure the engine is thoroughly warm.
➔ Disconnect the idle speed control valve multi-plug - if the engine continues to run, the setting is correct.
➔ Refit the idle speed control valve immediately and keep the engine running for five minutes to allow the EEC IV unit to learn the new settings.
➔ If the engine stalls, we recommend that you reconnect the idle speed control valve and have the base idle speed checked by an approved Ford dealer.

Section C: Sequential electronic fuel injection (SEFi).

FACT FILE

SEQUENTIAL ELECTRONIC FUEL INJECTION

• The SEFi system is similar in layout and operation to the EFi system except that the SEFi system injects fuel sequentially to each inlet port to correspond to the firing order.

• The EEC IV or EEC V module uses information from the various engine sensors to determine the exact amount of fuel to be injected. Except for the following, the sensors are the same as those used with the CFi system:
➔ A camshaft position sensor is now used as well as a crankshaft position sensor. This allows the EEC IV or EEC V module to determine firing order.
➔ A mass airflow (MAF)sensor replaces the MAP sensor.

• Apart from diagnostic checks, see *Job 2*, and component inspection, the only other check to carry out is a fuel pump operation and pressure check.

❑ **STEP C1:** These are typical locations of the components referred to here.

❑ **STEP C2: FUEL PUMP:**
➔ **FUEL PUMP OPERATION:** See *Step A1*.
➔ **FUEL PUMP PRESSURE:** Connect a suitable pressure gauge to the fuel line between the fuel rail and fuel filter - follow the gauge manufacturer's instructions. On Zetec engines a Schrader type valve (blue cap) is fitted at the fuel rail/fuel feed junction and should be used for connecting the pressure gauge - Ford supply an adapter (Part No. 29-033) which allows an ordinary pressure gauge to be used. With the engine at idling speed, the fuel pressure readings should be as follows:
➔ 1.9 to 2.3 bar.

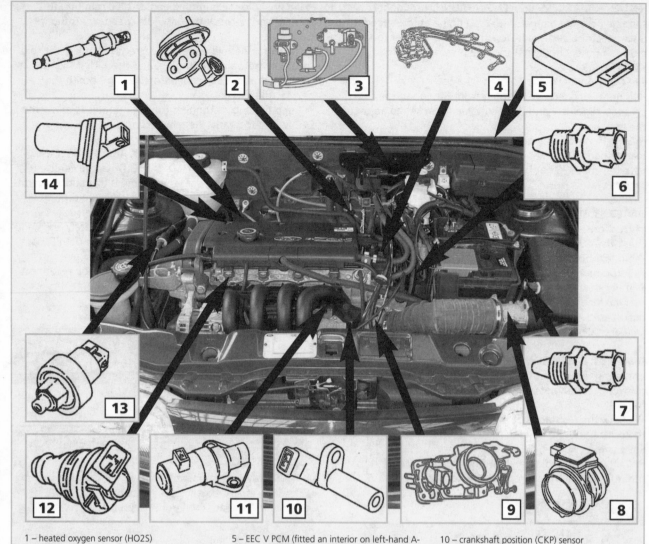

1 – heated oxygen sensor (HO2S)
2 – EGR valve
3 – bracket with EGR vacuum regulator, EVAP canister purge valve and EGR pressure transducer (from left to right)
4 – electronic ignition (EI) system coil with HT leads

5 – EEC V PCM (fitted an interior on left-hand A-pillar behind footwell trim panel)
6 – engine coolant temperature (ECT) sensor
7 – intake air temperature (IAT) sensor
8 – mass air flow (MAF) sensor
9 – throttle housing

10 – crankshaft position (CKP) sensor
11 – idle air control (IAC) valve
12 – fuel injector
13 – power steering pressure (PSP) switch
14 – camshaft position (CMP) sensor

10-C1

→ Disconnect the vacuum hose from the pressure regulator and check that the pressure rises as follows:

→ 2.5 bar to 2.9 bar.

→ If the pressures are too high, check for a blocked fuel return line first before replacing the pressure regulator.

→ If the pressures are too low, compress the fuel return line - an increase in pressure indicates a faulty regulator which should be replaced. No change in pressure indicates a blockage or fault between the tank and gauge.

→ Reconnect the vacuum hose and switch the engine off. Check that at least 1.8 bar is maintained for five minutes.

Section D: Bosch K-Jetronic fuel injection.

❏ **STEP D1:** This is a typical K-Jetronic injection layout.

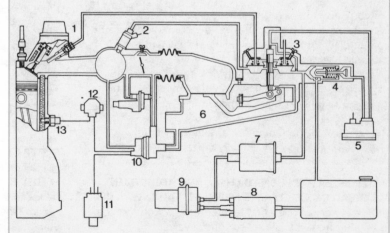

1 – injector
2 – cold start valve
3 – fuel distributor
4 – pressure regulator
5 – warm up regulator
6 – air sensor
7 – fuel filter

8 – fuel pump
9 – fuel accumulator
10 – decel fuel cut-off valve
11 – speed sensor
12 – throttle switch
13 – temperature switch

10-D1

❏ **STEP D2: FUEL PUMP DELIVERY RATE:** Disconnect the main return hose from the end of the pressure regulator. Attach a suitable hose (2) to the connection (1) and use a graduated container (3) to collect the fuel -

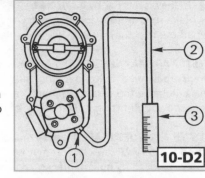

10-D2

remove the fuel pump relay from its holder and bridge terminals 30 and 87 on the holder (this will allow the fuel pump to run with the engine stationary). Check that the quantity of fuel delivered in 30 seconds and is greater than 750 ml. Replace the pump if the quantity is less.

❏ **STEP D3: FUEL SYSTEM PRESSURE CHECK:** Disconnect the fuel pipe between the top of the metering head and the cold start injector. Connect one end of a suitable pressure gauge to the

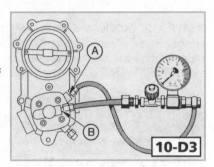

10-D3

connector on top of the metering head (B), remove the blanking test connector plug from the side of the metering head and connect the other end of the pressure gauge to the exposed port (A). Run the fuel pump. The pressure should be 5.6 bar to 6.0 bar.
➔ If the pressure is too low, and the fuel pump delivery rate is good, suspect a faulty pressure regulator.
➔ If the pressure is too high, disconnect the return from the pressure regulator - if the pressure is now within limits, suspect a blockage in the fuel return line. If the pressure remains too high, suspect a faulty regulator.

❏ **STEP D4: FUEL MIXTURE:** Follow the manufacturer's instructions and use a suitable exhaust gas analyser to check the CO% is within the range 1.0% to 1.5%. Adjust the CO% if necessary, using a 3 mm Allen key (arrowed).

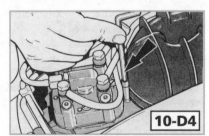

10-D4

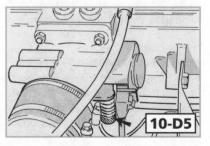

10-D5

❏ **STEP D5: IDLE SPEED:** On early models the adjuster (arrowed) is located on the rear of the throttle housing and you may have to remove the heater plenum chamber for access - on later models the screw is on top of the throttle housing, under a tamperproof cap. The correct idle speed is 750 rpm to 850 rpm.

JOB 11: **FUEL INJECTION COMPONENTS** - *removal, replacement.*

SAFETY FIRST!

• Depressurise the fuel system before disconnecting any fuel line components.

Section A: Multi-point systems.

❏ **STEP A1: FUEL CUT-OFF SWITCH:**
➔ **FIESTA:** Remove the left-hand sill scuff plate - see *Chapter 14, Interior, Trim*. Remove the bracket attachment and

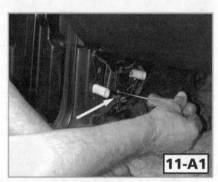

11-A1

withdraw the switch complete with bracket - separate the multi-connector. If necessary, remove the attachment screws and separate the bracket from the switch.
➔ **ESCORT AND ORION:** Remove the left-hand front footwell side trim – see *Chapter 14, Interior, Trim*. Remove the attachment screws and withdraw the switch - separate the multi-connector (arrowed).
➔ Refitting is the reverse of removal - when the switch is securely in place press down on the top button to make sure it is reset.

❏ **STEP A2: EEC IV ENGINE MANAGEMENT MODULE - FIESTA:** Remove the two module cover nuts in the engine compartment and remove the cover. Undo the multi-plug retaining bolt and separate the multi-plug from the module. Press in the retaining tags while an assistant withdraws the module into the passenger compartment - the module is fragile and easily damaged if dropped or knocked.

❏ **STEP A3: EEC IV ENGINE MANAGEMENT MODULE - ESCORT AND ORION:** Remove the side cowl kick panel in the left-hand footwell. Release the module from its retaining bracket - the module is fragile and easily damaged if dropped or knocked. Undo the multi-plug retaining bolt and separate the multi-plug from the module.

❏ **STEP A4: CFi UNIT:** Remove the air cleaner. Allow the coolant temperature to fall and depressurise the cooling system, disconnect the coolant hoses from the CFi unit - use a suitable container to collect spillage. Depressurise the fuel system and disconnect the fuel lines from the CFi unit. Disconnect the accelerator cable and vacuum tube from the CFi unit and the following multi-plugs:
➔ Inlet air temperature sensor (1).
➔ Throttle plate control motor (2).

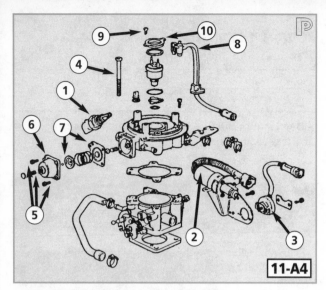

11-A4

→ Throttle position sensor (**3**).
→ Undo the four attachment screws, lift the CFi unit and gasket from the manifold (**4**). (Refitting is the reverse of removal.
→ Repressurise the system by switching the ignition on and off several times - start the engine and check for fuel leaks.

❑ **STEP A5: FUEL PRESSURE REGULATOR:** Remove the CFi unit, see **Step A4** and the four regulator cover screws (**5**). Remove the cover (**6**) carefully and note the orientation of the springs, ball, diaphragm and cup (**7**) as they are removed - do not alter the position of the screw in the centre of the housing or, if no screw is fitted, lever out the plug. Refitting is the reverse of removal, start the engine and check for fuel leaks.

❑ **STEP A6: THROTTLE PLATE CONTROL MOTOR:** Remove the air cleaner. Refer to **Step A4** and separate the multi-plugs from the throttle position sensor (**3**) and throttle plate control motor (**2**) and release the retaining clips on the bracket. Remove the motor support bracket screws and the bracket complete with motor from the CFi unit. Refitting is the reverse of removal, bearing in mind the following points:
→ The throttle position sensor must locate on the accelerator linkage and the bracket must align with the pegs.
→ After reassembly, check the idle speed.

❑ **STEP A7: THROTTLE POSITION SENSOR:** Remove the air cleaner assembly. Release the clip and separate the wiring connector. Remove the two attachment screws and separate the sensor from the throttle plate control motor bracket - take care not to force the sensor's centre to turn past its normal operating range, this will seriously damage the sensor. Refitting is the reverse of removal, make sure the sensor operating arm is correctly engaged.

❑ **STEP A8: FUEL INJECTOR:** Refer to **Step A4**. Depressurise the fuel system and remove the air cleaner. Release the injector multi-plug and pull the plug from the injector - do not pull on the cable. Bend back the injector screw locking tabs and remove the screws. Remove the injector retaining collar (**11-A4, item 10**), the injector (note the way it is fitted) and the seals. Refitting is the reverse of removal, bearing in mind the following points:

→ Use new seals lightly lubricated.
→ Make sure that the locating peg engages correctly when the injector is fitted.

❑ **STEP A9: MAP SENSOR:** The sensor is located on the engine bulkhead. Disconnect the multi-plug and vacuum hose. Remove the two attachment screws and lift the sensor away. Refitting is the reverse of removal.

❑ **STEP A10: FUEL TRAP:** On some models a fuel trap is fitted to the MAP sensor vacuum hose. The fuel trap is easily removed by pulling off the vacuum hoses.

❑ **STEP A11: INLET AIR TEMPERATURE SENSOR:** Remove the air cleaner assembly, release the clip and disconnect the sensor's electrical connection. Unscrew the sensor from the CFi unit. Refitting is the reverse of removal - do not overtighten, the sensor has a tapered thread and the recommended torque is only 20 -25 Nm (15 -18 ft lbs).

❑ **STEP A12: KNOCK SENSOR:** Where fitted, the knock sensor is screwed into the cylinder block close to the oil filter. Remove the electrical connection and unscrew the sensor. Refitting is the reverse of removal.

Section B: Electronic fuel injection (EFi).

❑ **STEP B1: THROTTLE HOUSING:** Where necessary on Fiesta models, disconnect the HT leads from the spark plugs,- release the HT leads from the retaining slots in the air inlet ducting and secure them out of the way.
→ Remove the air inlet components as necessary for access.
→ Disconnect the throttle cable at the throttle linkage.
→ **FIESTA, ESCORT AND ORION WITH PTE ENGINES:** Remove the attachment nuts and bolt - separate the accelerator cable support bracket at the throttle housing.
→ Disconnect the multi-plug from the throttle position sensor and, where applicable, any vacuum hoses.
→ Remove the four attachment bolts and lift the throttle housing, and gasket away.
→ Refit is the reverse of removal - you should use a new gasket.

❑ **STEP B2: THROTTLE POSITION SENSOR:** See **Step A7** for removal details. Refitting is the reverse of removal, bearing in mind the following points:
→ With the throttle closed, locate the sensor on the 'D' shaped shaft and align the body so that the bolts holes are aligned with the throttle housing.

IMPORTANT NOTE:
FUEL INJECTORS AND FUEL RAIL
• We have detailed the removal and refitting of the fuel injectors in one STEP although it is possible to remove components individually. If you wish to remove individual components, refer to the appropriate points detailed in **Step B3**.

❑ **STEP B3: FUEL INJECTORS AND FUEL RAIL:** Depressurise the fuel system and remove the throttle housing - see **Step B1**. Disconnect and remove components as follows:

→ Disconnect the multi-plugs from the engine coolant temperature sensor, inlet air temperature sensor and fuel injectors.

→ Remove the two nuts and separate the wiring harness from the fuel rail.

→ Split the fuel supply pipe at the fuel rail and disconnect the fuel return and vacuum pipes from the fuel pressure regulator - watch out for fuel spillage and plug the open connections to prevent the entry of dirt or other contaminants.

→ Remove the fuel rail attachment bolts and lift the rail, along with the injectors, from the engine.

→ You can now remove the injectors from the fuel rail - the two seals fitted to each injector should be removed and new seals fitted during reassembly.

→ Refitting is the reverse of removal - lightly lubricate the seals and check that the injectors are correctly seated before tightening the fuel rail bolts to the specified torque - see *Chapter 1, Facts and Figures*.

❒ **STEP B4: FUEL PRESSURE REGULATOR:** Depressurise the fuel system.

→ Separate the fuel return and vacuum pipes from the regulator.

→ Remove the two retaining bolts, the regulator and the sealing ring - a new ring should be fitted during reassembly.

→ Refitting is the reverse of removal, bearing in mind the following points:

→ Lightly lubricate the new seal.

→ Pressurise the fuel system by switching the ignition on and off several times before starting the engine and check for fuel leaks.

❒ **STEP B5: IDLE SPEED CONTROL VALVE:** See *Job 10, FACT FILE, IDLE SPEED* for valve type and location details. Disconnect the valve multi-plug and, where applicable the air hoses from the valve. Depending on type, remove the two or four bolts and lift the valve away from the manifold, air cleaner or bulkhead. Refitting is the reverse of removal, bearing in mind the following points:

→ Start the engine and check for air leaks.

❒ **STEP B6: AIR CLEANER MOUNTED WEBER VALVE - CLEANING:** Remove the valve from the air cleaner, see *Step B5* for removal and refit details. Submerge the valvehead in clean petrol for at least three minutes, then clean the valve bore, slots and piston with petrol using a lint-free cloth. Use a suitable tool to gently move the piston up and down in its bore - do not use the slots to move the piston. Rinse the valve again and dry with compressed air. Clean the mating surfaces on the valve and air cleaner and refit the valve.

❒ **STEP B7: MAP SENSOR:** See *Step A9*.

❒ **STEP B8: INLET AIR TEMPERATURE SENSOR:** See *Step A11* but note that the sensor is fitted to the inlet manifold.

❒ **STEP B9: FUEL MIXTURE ADJUSTING POTENTIOMETER:** The potentiometer is on the engine bulkhead below the ignition module. Disconnect the battery negative lead and the potentiometer multi-plug. Remove the attachment screw and remove the potentiometer. Refitting is the reverse of removal.

❒ **STEP B10: FUEL CUT-OFF SWITCH:** See *Step A1*.

❒ **STEP B11: EEC IV ENGINE MANAGEMENT MODULE:** See *Steps A2 and A3*.

Section C: Sequential electronic fuel injection (SEFi), Fiesta pre-1995.

❒ **STEP C1: THROTTLE HOUSING:** See *Step B1*.

❒ **STEP C2: THROTTLE POSITION SENSOR:** See *Step A7* for removal details. Refitting is the reverse of removal, bearing in mind the following points:

→ With the throttle closed, locate the sensor on the 'D' shaped shaft and align the body so that the bolts holes are aligned with the throttle housing.

❒ **STEP C3: FUEL INJECTORS AND FUEL RAIL:** Depressurise the fuel system and remove the throttle housing - see *Step B1*. Disconnect and remove components as follows:

→ Disconnect the fuel pressure regulator vacuum hose from the inlet manifold and the crankcase breather hose from the cylinder head cover.

→ Disconnect the multi-plugs from the inlet air temperature sensor and fuel injectors.

→ Disconnect the fuel supply and return quick release connectors, be ready for some fuel spillage, then separate the fuel hoses from the inlet manifold.

→ Remove the fuel rail attachment bolts and lift the rail, along with the injectors, from the engine.

→ Secure the fuel rail and remove the two bolts attaching each injector - the injector rail nose seals and the two seals fitted to each injector should be removed and new seals fitted during reassembly.

→ Refitting is the reverse of removal - lightly lubricate the injector seals and check that the injectors are correctly seated in the fuel rail recess - the tab on the injector should fit into the slot in the rail, before tightening the injector attachment bolts to the specified torque - see *Chapter 1, Facts and Figures*.

→ Make sure the new nose seals are not dislodged as the rail is fitted and fully seat the rail in the manifold before tightening the attachment bolts to the specified torque - see *Chapter 1, Facts and Figures*.

→ Make sure all the hoses and wiring have been routed and supported correctly. Adjust the throttle cable and pressurise the fuel system by switching the ignition on and off several times - check for fuel leaks before staring the engine.

❒ **STEP C4: FUEL PRESSURE REGULATOR:** Depressurise the fuel system and separate the vacuum pipe from the regulator. Remove the two retaining bolts, the regulator and the sealing ring - be ready for some fuel spillage. Refitting is the reverse of removal, bearing in mind the following points:

→ Use a new sealing ring which should be lightly lubricated before the regulator is refitted.

→ Pressurise the fuel system by switching the ignition on and off several times before starting the engine and check for fuel leaks.

❒ **STEP C5: IDLE SPEED CONTROL VALVE:** See *Step B5*.

☐ **STEP C6: MAF SENSOR:** Undo the clip and separate the multi-plug from the sensor. Release the two clips and separate the sensor from the air cleaner cover then separate the sensor from the air inlet hose. Refitting is the reverse of removal - make sure the sensor is properly seated and there are no air leaks.

☐ **STEP C7: FUEL CUT-OFF SWITCH:** See *Step A1*.

☐ **STEP C8: EEC IV ENGINE MANAGEMENT MODULE:** See *Steps A2 and A3*.

☐ **STEP C9: INLET AIR TEMPERATURE SENSOR:** See *Step A11* but note that the sensor is fitted as follows:
➜ **ESCORT AND ORION WITH PTE AND ZETEC ENGINES, FIESTA:** The inlet manifold.
➜ **ESCORT AND ORION WITH ENDURA E ENGINES:** The air cleaner casing.
➜ **ESCORT AND ORION WITH ZETEC E ENGINES:** The air inlet hose.

Section D: Sequential electronic fuel injection (SEFi), Fiesta from 1995, Ka.

☐ **STEP D1: THROTTLE HOUSING:** Remove the air inlet duct as necessary. Disconnect the throttle cable from the lever on the throttle housing and the multi-plug from the throttle position sensor. Remove the attachment bolts and, on Zetec SE engines, the support bracket. Refitting is the reverse of removal, bearing in mind the following points:
➜ Use a new gasket.
➜ Adjust the throttle cable.

☐ **STEP D2: THROTTLE POSITION SENSOR:** See *Step A7* for removal details and *Step C2* for refitting details.

☐ **STEP D3: FUEL INJECTORS AND FUEL RAIL - ENDURA E ENGINES:** Depressurise the fuel system, disconnect and remove components as follows:
➜ Remove the idle air control valve - see *Step D6*.
➜ Disconnect the throttle cable at the throttle housing. Undo the single bolt and remove the throttle cable retaining bracket.
➜ Remove the air inlet duct.
➜ Disconnect the crankcase breather hose from the inlet manifold.
➜ Separate the HT leads from the spark plugs and lead supports, position the leads out of the way.
➜ Disconnect the multi-plug at the throttle position sensor.
➜ Disconnect the fuel injector and injector loom plugs.
➜ Remove the injector loom attachment screws and position the loom out of the way.
➜ Disconnect the vacuum hose from the fuel pressure regulator.
➜ Disconnect the fuel inlet and return pipes at the quick release connectors, be ready for some fuel spillage.
➜ On models manufactured before the middle of 1998, undo the single screw and remove the fuel inlet and return pipe bracket.
➜ Remove the fuel rail mounting bolts, pull the injectors from the manifold and remove the fuel rail complete with injectors. If necessary, remove the clips and separate the injectors from the fuel rail.

➜ Refitting is the reverse of removal, use new 'O' seals on the injectors and lightly lubricate them before inserting them into the cylinder head.
➜ Make sure all the hoses and wiring have been routed and supported correctly.
➜ Adjust the throttle cable and pressurise the fuel system by switching the ignition on and off several times - check for fuel leaks before starting the engine.

☐ **STEP D4: FUEL INJECTORS AND FUEL RAIL - ZETEC SE ENGINES:** Depressurise the fuel system, disconnect and remove components as follows:
➜ Lift the cover and disconnect the vent hose.
➜ Disconnect the wiring loom adapter from the injectors - press down the retaining clips and ease the adapter away from the injectors. Position the adapter out of the way.
➜ Disconnect the fuel inlet and return pipes at the quick release connectors, be ready for some fuel spillage.
➜ Remove the attachment bolts and lift the fuel rail, complete with injectors, from the cylinder head - recover the bolt hole adapters from the cylinder head and the seals from the inner end of the fuel rail.
➜ If necessary, remove the two bolts attaching each injector and carefully lever the injectors from the fuel rail - they may be tight.
➜ Refitting is the reverse of removal, use new 'O' seals on the injectors and lightly lubricate them before inserting them into the cylinder head.
➜ Make sure all the hoses and wiring have been routed and supported correctly.

☐ **STEP D5: FUEL PRESSURE REGULATOR:** Depressurise the fuel system, disconnect and remove components as follows - note the additional actions which are only necessary on Endura E engines:
➜ **ENDURA E ENGINES:** Disconnect the air inlet duct from the throttle housing. On models manufactured before the middle of 1998, undo the single screw and remove the fuel inlet and return pipe retaining bracket. Disconnect the fuel return pipe at the quick release fitting - be ready for some fuel spillage.
➜ Disconnect the vacuum pipe from the fuel pressure regulator. Undo the two screws and remove the fuel pressure regulator from the fuel rail. Refitting is the reverse of removal, fit a new 'O' seal which should be lightly lubricated before the regulator is refitted.

☐ **STEP D6: IDLE AIR CONTROL VALVE:** The valve is fitted on the inlet manifold - see *Step B5* for details.

☐ **STEP D7: MAF SENSOR:** Undo the clip and separate the air inlet duct from the MAF sensor on the air cleaner cover. Disconnect the multi-plug from the sensor, remove the attachment screws and separate the sensor from the air cleaner cover. Refitting is the reverse of removal.

IMPORTANT NOTE: The fuel cut-off switch can be reset by removing the plug in the left-hand footwell trim and pressing the button on top of the switch.

☐ **STEP D8: FUEL CUT-OFF SWITCH:**
➜ **FIESTA:** Pull the weatherstrip away from the lower front of the right-hand door aperture. Remove the trim clips - on five door models you will also have to lever out the cover and remove the retaining screw at the rear.

→ **KA:** Remove the trim panel from the right-hand footwell.
→ Remove the switch attachment screws and separate the multi-plug as you withdraw the switch.

☐ **STEP D9: EEC V MODULE:**
→ **FIESTA:** Remove the fuel cut-off switch - see *Step D8*.
→ **KA:** Pull back the floor covering for access to the module, located behind the front left-hand footwell side trim.
→ Remove the rivets and the security shield covering the module.
→ Release the module from its bracket and manoeuvre it clear - take care, the module is fragile and easily damaged if dropped or knocked.
→ Remove the attachment screw and separate the multi-plug from the module.
→ Refitting is the reverse of removal.

☐ **STEP D10: INLET AIR TEMPERATURE SENSOR:** Disconnect the plug from the sensor which is mounted on the air cleaner. Turn the sensor through 90 degrees and remove it. Refitting is the reverse of removal.

Section E: Bosch K-Jetronic fuel injection.

☐ **STEP E1: FUEL PUMP:** See *Job 16*.

☐ **STEP E2: FUEL ACCUMULATOR:** See *Job 16*.

☐ **STEP E3: FUEL FILTER:** Disconnect the fuel inlet (**A**) and outlet (**C**) connections, be ready for fuel spillage and cover the open connections to prevent the entry of dirt or other contaminants.

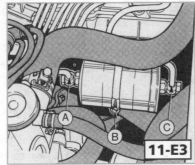

11-E3

Loosen the clamp bracket screw (**B**) and remove the filter. Refit is the reversal of removal.

☐ **STEP E4: FUEL DISTRIBUTOR:** Disconnect the fuel inlet (**E**) and injector outlet (**A**) banjo unions and the warm-up regulator feed (**F**). Remove the three attachment screws (arrowed) from the upper face and lift the unit from the vehicle - DO NOT disturb the four screws beside

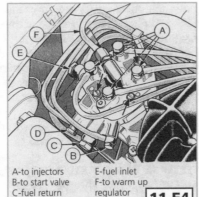

A-to injectors   E-fuel inlet
B-to start valve   F-to warm up
C-fuel return   regulator
D-from regulator   11-E4

each injector outlet. Refit is the reverse of removal - you should use new banjo sealing washers.

☐ **STEP E5: THROTTLE HOUSING:** Disconnect or remove the following components:
→ Separate the air inlet hose from the throttle housing.
→ Disconnect the throttle cable from the linkage at the throttle.
→ Disconnect the vacuum hose and auxiliary air hose from underneath the throttle housing.
→ Remove the four attachment nuts and the throttle housing.
→ Refitting is the reverse of removal - check the idle speed.

☐ **STEP E6: INJECTORS AND DELIVERY PIPES:** Disconnect or remove the following components:
→ Undo the nuts and separate the supply pipes from the injectors.
→ Remove the bracket bolts and the injectors, complete with their 'O' seals.
→ If you need to remove the injector supply pipes, disconnect the banjo unions at the fuel distributor - see *Step D4* - label the connections for later identification. Remove the pipes complete with injector harness and plastic hoses - you should not separate the pipes or hoses from the harness.
→ Refit is the reverse of removal - you should use new banjo washers and 'O' seals.
→ Start the engine and check for fuel leaks.

☐ **STEP E7: WARM-UP REGULATOR:** Disconnect the warm-up regulator inlet (**B**) and outlet (**C**) pipes. Separate the electrical connection (**A**) from the regulator, remove the two Torx type screws

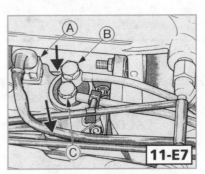

11-E7

each side (arrowed) of the regulator. Refit as the reverse of removal - you should use new banjo washers and thread-locking compound on the screw threads.

☐ **STEP E8: AUXILIARY AIR DEVICE:** The auxiliary air device is located below the cold start valve. Disconnect the two air hoses (**A** and **B**) and the multi-plug (**C**), remove the two

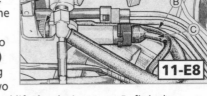

11-E8

Torx type screws and lift the device away. Refit is the reverse of removal.

☐ **STEP E9: COLD START VALVE:** Separate the multi-plug (**A**) from the unit and disconnect the fuel supply banjo connector (**C**) - if you haven't already depressurised the

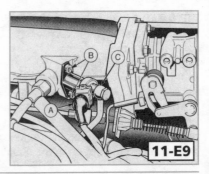

11-E9

system, undo the connection slowly and use a cloth to collect escaping fuel. Remove the two attachment bolts - Allen type on early models, Torx type (B) on later models. Refitting is the reversal of removal - you should use new banjo washers.

❒ **STEP E10: THERMO-TIME SWITCH:** Drain the cooling system, raise and support the front of the vehicle - the switch (arrowed) is fitted to the inlet manifold

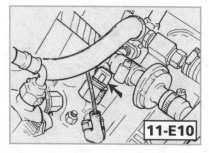

intermediate flange and access is from below. Disconnect the multi-plug and unscrew the switch.

❒ **STEP E11: IDLE SPEED COMPENSATOR FROM 1986:** Disconnect the air hoses and the multi-plug from the unit - located at the centre of the engine compartment bulkhead. Remove the two screws and the lift the unit away.

JOB 12: ACCELERATOR CABLE - *adjustment, replacement.*

❒ **STEP 1:** Depending on model, remove the lower dashboard trim as necessary for access to the top of the throttle pedal - see *Chapter 13, Bodywork*.

ESCORT AND ORION PRE-1990

❒ **STEP 2:** Disconnect the cable from the pedal:
→ **RHD VERSIONS:** Slide off the spring clip to release the cable from the ball stud (B, arrowed).

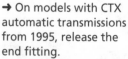

→ **LHD VERSIONS:** Remove the pin holding the end of the cable to the pedal (A, arrowed).

❒ **STEP 3: AUTOMATIC VERSIONS:** The cable goes to the downshift damper bracket.
→ This is the cable adjuster (arrowed) viewed from beneath.

❒ **STEP 4: FIESTA, ESCORT AND ORION FROM 1990, KA:** Lever the grommet (A) free from the top of the throttle pedal, release the tension in the cable and manoeuvre the cable through the slot (B) in the pedal.

❒ **STEP 5:** Free the throttle cable grommet from the bulkhead.

❒ **STEP 6:** Remove the air cleaner components as necessary for access to the throttle cable connection at the carburetor or throttle housing.

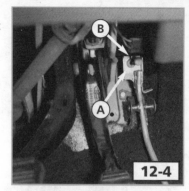

❒ **STEP 7: CARBURETOR:** Remove the clip and lever the inner cable end (arrowed) from the throttle lever on the carburetor.

❒ **STEP 8: FUEL INJECTION:** On manual transmission models, remove the clip (A) pivot the throttle cable quadrant (B) to slacken the throttle cable and detach the cable nipple (C) from the mechanism.
→ On models with CTX automatic transmissions from 1995, release the end fitting.
→ See *Job 11, Section D* for the arrangement on models with the Bosch K-Jetronic injection system.

❒ **STEP 9: EARLY CARBURETOR CABLE WITH ADJUSTER SLEEVE:** Carefully prise out the outer cable retaining clip, press in the retaining tags and pull the outer cable end from the mounting bracket. You can now remove the throttle cable from the vehicle.

❒ **STEP 10: CAM PLATE CABLE - ESCORT AND ORION FROM 1990 WITH CTX TRANSMISSION:** Press the red or orange button on the auto adjuster mechanism to release the cable. You should here a click and the cable shoulder should protrude about 20 mm. Turn the throttle cam plate to the open position and then release it - the automatic adjuster should do its work and you should here a click as the cable automatically adjusts. The shoulder should now protrude about 10 mm. Adjust the throttle cable - see *Step 12*.

❒ **STEP 11:** Refitting is the reverse of removal but note the different adjustment methods.

❒ **STEP 12: EARLY CARBURETOR CABLE WITH ADJUSTER SLEEVE:** Adjust the throttle cable by holding the throttle pedal in the fully open position and winding the adjusting sleeve at the carburetor until the carburetor linkage is just in the fully open position.

STEP 13: LATER CARBURETOR AND FUEL INJECTION CABLE WITH ADJUSTER CLIP: Adjust the throttle cable by holding the throttle pedal in the fully open position. Without moving the inner or outer cables, slide the grommet so that it can be fitted to the mounting bracket, insert the retaining clip.

JOB 13: THROTTLE PEDAL - *removal replacement*.

❐ **STEP 1:** Disconnect the throttle cable from throttle pedal - see *Job 12*.

❐ **STEP 2: FIESTA 1976 TO 1983, ESCORT AND ORION PRE-1990:** See illustration *12-2*.
→ Remove the two nuts (Fiesta), two bolts (Escort and Orion RHD models) or three nuts (Escort and Orion LHD models) and pull the throttle pedal away from the bulkhead. The nuts and bolts are located as follows:
→ **FIESTA RHD AND LHD MODELS, ESCORT AND ORION RHD MODELS:** In the footwell at the throttle pedal.
→ **ESCORT AND ORION LHD MODELS:** Two nuts on the left-hand side of the bulkhead in the engine compartment and one nut in the footwell at the throttle pedal.

❐ **STEP 3: FIESTA 1983 TO 1989:** Removal is similar to earlier models but the nut/bolt location are different. Remove the throttle pedal bracket bolt and ...
→ **RHD MODELS:** The bracket retaining nut from inside the right-hand wheelarch.
→ **LHD MODELS:** The bracket retaining nut from the left-hand side of the bulkhead in the engine compartment.

❐ **STEP 4: FIESTA FROM 1989, ESCORT AND ORION FROM 1990, KA:** Prise the clip (arrowed) from the throttle pedal pivot shaft and remove the pedal.

13-4

❐ **STEP 5:** Refitting is the reverse of removal - check the throttle cable adjustment - see *Job 12*.

JOB 14: CHOKE CABLE (MANUAL CHOKE) - *adjustment, replacement*.

❐ **STEP 1:** Remove the air cleaner components as necessary for access.

❐ **STEP 2:** Working at the carburetor, remove the spring clip (A) attaching the outer choke

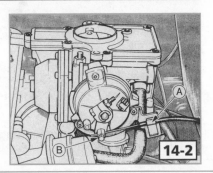

14-2

---

cable and unscrew the inner cable locking screw (B) except for ...
→ **FIESTA FROM-1989, ESCORT 1.1 LITRE AND 1.3 LITRE MODELS WITH HCS ENGINES FROM 1986:** Simply unhook the inner cable from the operating lever.

❐ **STEP 3:** Remove the interior trim as necessary for access to the choke mounting inside the vehicle.

❐ **STEP 4: FIESTA 1976 TO 1983:** Loosen the single clamp bolt (arrowed), separate the choke cable from the steering column and pull the choke cable into the vehicle.

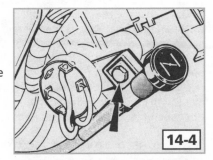

14-4

❐ **STEP 5: FIESTA 1983 TO 1989, ESCORT AND ORION PRE-1986:** Remove the single screw and the cable shroud (Fiesta) or coin box (E) (Escort).
→ Lever off the knob retaining clip (C) and pull the choke knob (D) from the cable (B).

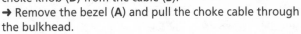

14-5

→ Remove the bezel (A) and pull the choke cable through the bulkhead.

❐ **STEP 6: FIESTA FROM 1989, ESCORT AND ORION FROM 1986:** Push in the pin on the side of the choke operating knob and remove the knob.
→ Disconnect the choke warning light multi-plug and unscrew the collar attaching the choke cable assembly to the lower shroud.
→ Push the bulkhead panel grommet out of its location and pull the choke cable through the bulkhead.

❐ **STEP 7:** Refitting is the reverse of removal. Refer to the following *Steps* for choke cable adjustment.

❐ **STEP 8: FIESTA 1976 TO 1983:** Adjust the choke cable by pulling the slack from the outer cable and clamping it in place with the attachment clip.
→ Pull the choke knob out by 6 mm (0.25 in) and remove the slack from the inner cable.
→ Hold the choke butterfly in the fully open position while you reconnect the inner cable.

❐ **STEP 9: FIESTA 1983 TO 1989, ESCORT AND ORION PRE-1986:** Pull out the choke knob so that X is 37 mm (1.45 in) - ideally make up a

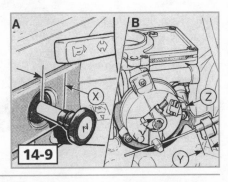

14-9

spacer so that the setting is not disturbed while you are working on the other end of the cable.

→ At the carburetor end, make a mark on the inner cable 22 mm (0.87 in) Z from the end of the inner cable - some cables have a ferrule and others may be kinked at this point.

→ Position the inner cable in its attachment clamp, distance Y should not exceed 4.5 mm (0.18 in), pull on the outer cable so that the operating lever is against the full-open stop and fit the attachment clip.

→ Check that the choke knob is still out by 37 mm with the operating lever against the full-open stop - reset if necessary.

→ Remove the spacer, if fitted, and make sure the choke opens and closes fully.

→ FORD VV CARBURETOR: Make sure there is a gap of 1 mm (0.040 in) between the operating lever and fully-off stop when the choke knob is pushed fully in.

❏ STEP 10: FIESTA FROM 1989, ESCORT AND ORION FROM 1986: Before connecting the choke cable at the carburetor end, pull the choke knob fully out. Now connect the choke inner and outer cables with the choke valve in the fully on position - valve closed. Push the operating knob fully in and make sure the choke valve plate is fully open - it should be a 90 degrees to the venturi. Readjust inner and outer cables as necessary.

JOB 15: MECHANICAL FUEL PUMP - *replacement.*

On the overhead valve family of engines (OHV, HCS and Endura E), the mechanical fuel pump is mounted on the cylinder block on the engine bulkhead side.

→ On the single overhead camshaft family of engines (CVH and PTE), the mechanical fuel pump is mounted on the cylinder head on the engine bulkhead side.

❏ STEP 1: Disconnect the fuel hoses (arrowed) from the fuel pump and, where fitted, the fuel vapour separator - plug or cover the open connections to prevent the entry of dirt or other contaminants.

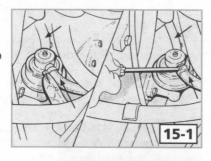
15-1

❏ STEP 2: Remove the two attachment bolts and the washers. Separate the pump and, where fitted, fuel vapour separator from the engine block, recover any insulating spacers for re-use. On single overhead camshaft engines, remove the pushrod.

15-2

❏ STEP 3: Refitting is the reverse of removal.

JOB 16: ELECTRIC FUEL PUMP AND ACCUMULATOR - *replacement.*

SAFETY FIRST!

• See *Chapter 2, Safety First!*

All Fiesta, Escort, Ka and most Orion models equipped with Central Fuel injection (CFi), Electronic Fuel injection (EFi) and Sequential Fuel injection (SEFi) systems have a fuel pump combined with the fuel tank sender unit and both are removed as a combined unit - see *Part B, Job 3*. Orion 1.4 litre models with CFi may have a fuel pump, similar to the one used on XR3i and some Orion 1.6i models, mounted on the underside of the vehicle.

→ Escort and some Orion 1.6i models are equipped with the Bosch K-Jetronic fuel injection system which has a separate fuel pump mounted at the rear of the fuel tank. This system also has a fuel accumulator, which dampens fuel flow pulsations and maintains pressure in the system when the engine is switched off. We have covered these components in the Sections here.

Section A: Fuel pump - Bosch K-Jetronic system.

❏ STEP A1: Relieve fuel system pressure by slowly loosening the fuel inlet union (arrowed) at the warm-up regulator. Be prepared for some fuel leakage.

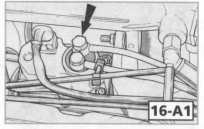
16-A1

❏ STEP A2: Raise and support the rear of the vehicle - see *Chapter 2, Safety First.*

❏ STEP A3: To prevent leakage

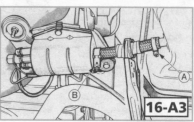
16-A3

from the tank, use a brake hose clamp on the fuel hose between the tank and fuel pump. Disconnect the fuel inlet and outlet hoses (arrowed A and B) from the pump. Be prepared for some fuel spillage.

❏ STEP A4: Note the way they are connected and disconnect the electrical connections to the pump.

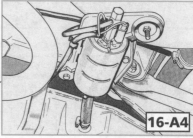
16-A4

❏ STEP A5: Undo the pump bracket attachment bolt and separate the pump from the vehicle.

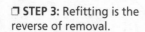

STEP A6: Refitting is the reverse of removal, bearing in mind the following points.
→ Check the fuel hoses and replace any that are damaged or deteriorating.
→ Make sure the rubber protector is correctly fitted around the pump before tightening the clamp bolt.

Section B: Fuel accumulator - Bosch K-Jetronic system.

On pre-1986 models, the fuel accumulator is mounted above the left-hand rear suspension arm, near the fuel pump.
→ On post 1986 models, the fuel accumulator is mounted in the engine compartment, behind the fuel distributor.

STEP B1: PRE-1986 MODELS: Raise and support the rear of the vehicle.

STEP B2: POST 1986 MODELS: Remove the air cleaner.

STEP B3: Depressurise the fuel system - see *Step A1*.

STEP B4:
Disconnect the fuel outlet (**A**) and inlet (**B**) pipes from the accumulator, be ready for some fuel spillage.

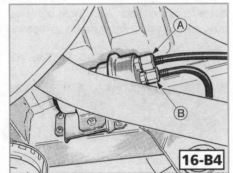

STEP B5:
Remove the clamp screw and the accumulator.

JOB 17: EMISSION CONTROL COMPONENTS - *checking, replacement*.

No periodic maintenance is specified for many of the components detailed here, see *Chapter 5, Servicing* for routine service schedules. The need for checking usually follows from other faults, such as excessive emissions or poor fuel consumption.

STEP 1: EXHAUST GAS RECIRCULATION (EGR) COMPONENTS: See *Part B, Job 12*.

STEP 2: POSITIVE CRANKCASE VENTILATION (PCV): Maintenance is restricted to cleaning components, use a suitable solvent cleaner, and examine components for damage. Check the servicing schedules - see *Chapter 5, Servicing* for maintenance intervals.

STEP 3: TEMPERATURE CONTROLLED INLET AIR: With the engine cold and switched off, the control valve should be open.
→ Make sure the ambient temperature is at least 16 degrees C (60 degrees F). Start the engine and allow it to idle - the valve should close. Within five minutes of starting the engine the control valve should open.
→ A more precise check means reading the temperature inside the air cleaner - above 24 degrees C (75 degrees F) the valve should be open and below 24 degrees C (75 degrees F) the valve should be partly opening, the exact position depending on the temperature.
→ If the valve does not operate as detailed, you should replace the components.

STEP 4: DECELERATION VALVE: Disconnect the PVS hose, see *Step 6*, and plug the connection. Connect a vacuum gauge to the line between the deceleration valve and inlet manifold - you will have to make up a special line with a 'T' piece connector.
→ Run the engine for a few seconds at 3,000 rpm for a few seconds then note the vacuum gauge readings as the throttle is released - the reading should rise then fall to zero within 2.5 seconds to 3.5 seconds.
→ If necessary, you can adjust the valve. Remove the plug from the top of the valve and turn the adjuster - screw in to increase and screw out to decrease recovery time.
→ If you cannot adjust the valve to obtain the correct recovery time, carry out the following checks which should identify the source of the problem.
→ **RECOVERY TIME TOO SHORT:** Insert a suitable tool through the bottom cover and raise the diaphragm. No change in engine speed indicates that you should check the metering jets in the carburetor and the hose to the carburetor for blockage. An increase in engine speed to around 1500 rpm indicates a fault with the valve, which should be replaced.
→ **RECOVERY TIME TOO LONG:** If the recovery time is too long and the idle speed is too high, disconnect the inlet hose and plug the inlet. The valve is faulty and should be replaced if the idle speed falls to normal. No fall in idle speed means a serviceable valve - you will have to check other related components.

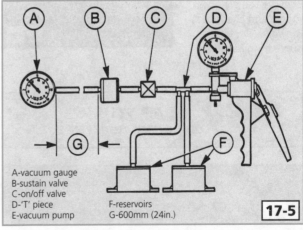

A-vacuum gauge
B-sustain valve
C-on/off valve
D-'T' piece
E-vacuum pump
F-reservoirs
G-600mm (24in.)

17-5

STEP 5: SPARK DELAY VALVE (SDV): You will need to make up a test rig similar to the one shown here. Fit the spark delay valve (**B**) to the test rig with the black section or 'CARB' mark towards the vacuum pump. Close the on/off valve (**C**) and build up a vacuum of 33 kPa (250 mm Hg), open the valve (**C**) and note the time taken for the vacuum to fall to 27 kPa (203 mm Hg) - replace the spark delay valve if the time taken is not between 6 seconds and 14 seconds. Make sure the valve is fitted correctly when refitting.

☐ **STEP 6: PORTED VACUUM SWITCH (PVS):** Two port or three port switches have been fitted to the vehicles covered by this manual - the testing methods are similar and the vacuum readings should hold for at least 10 seconds.

→ Connect a vacuum pump to the lower port (two port type) or centre port (three port type) and a vacuum gauge to the other ports.

→ With the engine cold, operate the pump to give a vacuum of 33 kPa (250 mm Hg). If the switch is operating correctly, the following readings should be obtained.

→ 33 kPa (250 mm Hg) at the upper port of a three port switch. Zero at the lower port of a three port switch and upper port of a two port switch.

→ Run the engine until normal operating temperature is reached. With the pump set as above, the following readings should be obtained.

→ 33 kPa (250 mm Hg) at the lower port of the three port switch and the upper port of the two port switch. Zero at the upper port of the three port switch.

☐ **STEP 7: EVAPORATIVE EMISSION CONTROL:** No tests are specified for the charcoal canister. To remove the canister, pull of the hoses and undo the attachment nuts. Refitting is the reverse of removal.

☐ **STEP 8: PULSE AIR SYSTEM - CHECKING:** See *Job 18* for Pulse Air System component replacement.

→ You can test the solenoid valve as follows - energise the solenoid and check that air can flow through the valve. Remove the electrical supply and check that the valve closes, preventing air flow.

17-8

JOB 18: PULSE AIR SYSTEM - *component replacement.*

Section A: HCS engines.

☐ **STEP A1: PULSE AIR VALVE, FILTER AND HOUSING:** Disconnect the vacuum hose at the rear of the valve unit, undo the screws and separate the unit from the mounting bracket. If necessary, you can remove the top (four screws) and foam filter, which can be cleaned in a suitable solvent. Replace the complete unit if there are any signs of damage or wear.

☐ **STEP A2: PULSE AIR PIPING:** Remove air cleaner components as necessary for access and disconnect the vacuum hose from the valve unit. Pipe removal and refitting is as follows.

→ Separate the air tube from its attachments, undo the nuts attaching the delivery pipes to the cylinder head and remove the pipes as a complete unit. Take care not to distort the pipes or damage the pipe ends.

Section B: CVH engines.

☐ **STEP B1: PULSE AIR FILTER HOUSING:** You can unclip the lid and lift out the filter for cleaning, or detach the air hoses and completely remove the filter housing. Refitting is reverse of removal.

☐ **STEP B2: PULSE AIR VALVE:** Separate the vacuum and air hoses from the valve, and lift the valve away. You should note the location of the hoses and the orientation of the valve to ensure correct refitting.

☐ **STEP B3: PULSE AIR CHECK VALVE:** Separate the air hoses from the check valve. Hold the lower tube and unscrew the valve. Refitting is the reverse of removal.

☐ **STEP B4: PULSE AIR PIPING:** See *Step A2.*

Section C: Zetec engines.

☐ **STEP C1: PULSE AIR VALVE, FILTER AND HOUSING:** Jack up and support the front of the vehicle - see *Chapter 2, Safety First.* Remove air cleaner components as necessary for access. Disconnect the vacuum hose from the base of the filter unit, remove the piping to filter unit screws and the mounting bolt. See *Step A1* for filter unit dismantling and examination.

☐ **STEP C2: PULSE AIR SOLENOID VALVE:** Separate the electrical connector from the valve (it's held in place by a spring clip) and release the valve from its mounting bracket. Disconnect the vacuum hoses, you should note the location of the hoses and the orientation of the valve to ensure correct refitting.

☐ **STEP C3: PULSE AIR PIPING:** Jack up and support the front of the vehicle. Remove air cleaner components as necessary for access and the exhaust manifold heat shield. Disconnect the vacuum hose at the base of the filter unit, remove the two support bracket bolts and the pipe to manifold nuts. The remainder of the removal, examination and refitting procedure is detailed in *Step A2.*

Part B: Diesel Engines

CONTENTS

JOB 1: GENERAL AND SAFETY – *read this first*!

SAFETY FIRST!

• Never open the fuel system unless the engine is completely cold.

• All Diesel fuel injection systems inject fuel at extremely high pressure.

• Pressure must be released in a controlled fashion to avoid risk of a pressurised spray of fuel being released.

• We strongly recommend that injectors are tested only with specialised test equipment, such as by an approved Ford dealer or fuel injection specialist.

• Residual pressure can remain in the fuel system for some time after the engine has been switched off.

• Removing pressure from the fuel lines will not necessarily remove pressure from each of the components - they may still be pressurised.

• Before working on any part of the system it is necessary to relieve the pressure – see FACT FILE: DEPRESSURISE THE SYSTEM!

Apart from the differences between Bosch or CAV RotoDiesel fuel injection pumps, the basic fuel systems are similar on all types of engine.

➜ The process of carrying out diagnostic electronic tests on the appropriate Diesel versions of these cars is exactly the same as for petrol/gasoline versions - see *Part A, Job 2: Diagnostics - carry out checks.*

JOB 2: FUEL SYSTEM - *bleeding.*

FACT FILE

• The Bosch pump is self bleeding but it may take some time for the pump to deliver fuel, especially if components have been replaced. You can save considerable wear and tear on the battery if you bleed as much air as possible from the system before trying to start the engine - see *Section A.*

• The CAV RotoDiesel pump does have a priming pump (the black button on top of the filter). If air has entered the fuel system, you should bleed and prime the system as far as practical before trying to start the engine - see *Section B.*

IMPORTANT NOTE: During the bleeding and priming process use a container or absorbent material to catch fuel spillage.

FACT FILE

DEPRESSURISE THE SYSTEM

• Before working on any part of the system it is necessary to relieve the pressure as follows:

1. Disconnect the battery negative terminal.

2. Work out of doors and away from sources of flame or ignition. Wear rubber or plastic gloves and goggles. Have a large cloth ready.

3. Place a container beneath the filter to collect fuel spillage.

4. Wrap several turns of cloth around each connector as you very slowly undo the connection. This allows the release of pressure without causing a dangerous jet of fuel.

5. Release the pressure from each of the pipes in the same way.

6. Mop up all traces of fuel before continuing with other work and especially before reconnecting the battery or moving the vehicle indoors.

Section A: Bosch fuel pump bleeding.

☐ **STEP A1:** The recommended method for bleeding the system is to crank the engine on the starter motor until it starts.

→ Use the starter motor in bursts of 10 to 15 seconds and allow the battery to rest for at least twice this time between bursts.

TOP TIP!

☐ **STEP A2:** If the system has been extensively dismantled, you can reduce the priming time, and the strain on the battery, by filling the filter through its vent screw (**a**) and priming the pump through the inlet and outlet connections (**b** and **c**).

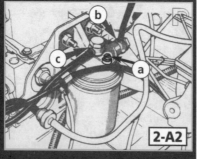

2-A2

☐ **STEP A3:** It is possible to prime more of the system by drawing fuel through with a suction pump.

Section B: CAV RotoDiesel pump bleeding.

IMPORTANT NOTE: The correct bleeding sequence is as follows.
1. Bleed from the filter.
2. Bleed from the fuel pump return union.

☐ **STEP B1:** Slacken the bleed nipple on the fuel filter and operate the priming button until the fuel coming out is free from air.

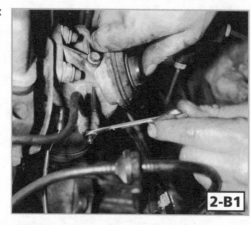

2-B1

→ Tighten the nipple and continue pumping until resistance is felt.

☐ **STEP B2:** Switch the ignition on so that the fuel cut-off solenoid will open and allow fuel to flow through the fuel pump.

→ Loosen the fuel return union and operate the priming button until the fuel coming out is free from air.

→ Fully tighten the union and operate the priming button until resistance is felt.

JOB 3: FUEL INJECTION PUMP – *speed settings*.

Section A: All pump types - maximum speed checking and

SAFETY FIRST!

• There are potential risks associated with running the engine at maximum speed. Make sure the engine and, vitally important, the cam drive belt is in good condition before carrying out this test.

☐ **STEP A1:** Accelerate the engine to maximum speed and check the reading on the rev counter. Do not hold maximum speed for more than 5 seconds. The maximum no load speeds are as follows.

→ 1.6 Litre and 1.8 Litre (Non Turbo) Engine - 5300 rev/min to 5400 rev/min.

→ 1.8 Litre (Turbo) Engine - 5150 rev/min to 5250 rev/min.

☐ **STEP A2:** Let the engine decelerate and make sure the speed reduces to idle speed in less than 5 seconds.

→ Adjust the deceleration time as necessary - see *Section E*.

☐ **STEP A3:** If the maximum speed is not within the specified limits, you can use the maximum speed adjusting screw to alter the speed.

→ This screw is sealed during production and if you don't know what you are doing there is a considerable risk of destroying the engine through over-revving it.

→ If necessary, have the work carried out by an approved Ford dealer or diesel fuel system specialist.

→ See the illustrations in other parts of this Job for the location of the maximum speed adjustment screw – if fitted - on the type of pump you are working on.

Section B: 1.6 litre engine with Bosch pump.

IDLE SPEED SETTING

☐ **STEP B1:** Run the engine until normal operating temperature is reached.

☐ **STEP B2:** Check that the idle speed is in the range 850 to 910 rpm.

☐ **STEP B3:** If the idle speed is incorrect, slacken the idle speed screw locknut and turn the idle speed

3-B3

screw (**A**) - clockwise to increase speed and anti-clockwise to reduce speed.

→ Tighten the locknut and make sure the engine speed does not change.

→ Do not attempt to adjust screw (**B**) which is the maximum speed governor.

MAXIMUM SPEED SETTING

☐ **STEP B4:** DO NOT adjust the screw (illustration *3-B3, item B*) without reading *Section A*.

Section C: Idle speed and anti-stall settings - 1.6 and 1.8 litre engine with CAV RotoDiesel pump.

☐ **STEP C1:** These are the relevant components of the CAV RotoDiesel pump.

IMPORTANT NOTE: Illustrated in the following sequence is Ford special tool Part No. 23-016. This is a 3 mm spacer designed to 'stay-put' by itself.

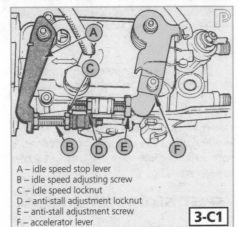

A – idle speed stop lever
B – idle speed adjusting screw
C – idle speed locknut
D – anti-stall adjustment locknut
E – anti-stall adjustment screw
F – accelerator lever

3-C1

IDLE SPEED ADJUSTMENT

☐ **STEP C2: CHECK EXISTING IDLE SPEED:** There are different procedures depending on the existing idle speed:

→ Make sure that the engine is at normal operating temperature and check the idle speed with a diesel engine tachometer.

→ Now go to the next relevant step depending on the level of the existing idle speed.

☐ **STEP C3: IF EXISTING IDLE SPEED IS LESS THAN 850 RPM:** Place a 2 mm thick spacer (**a**) between the idle speed stop lever (**A**) and idle speed adjusting screw (**B**).

→ IF ENGINE SPEED DOES NOT ALTER: Set the anti-stall adjustment – see *Steps C5* to *C7*.

→ IF ENGINE SPEED DOES ALTER: Set the idle speed – see *Step C4*.

☐ **STEP C4: IF EITHER EXISTING IDLE SPEED EXCEEDS 910 RPM OR ENGINE SPEED ALTERS AS DESCRIBED IN STEP C3:** Slacken the idle speed screw locknut (*3-C1, item C*).

→ Adjust the idle speed screw (**B**) until the engine idle speed is between 850 and 910 rpm.

→ Tighten the idle speed screw locknut without allowing the engine idle speed to change.

ANTI-STALL SPEED ADJUSTMENT

☐ **STEP C5:** With the engine at normal operating temperature:

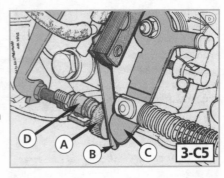

3-C5

→ Fit the special tool (**A**) plus an additional 1 mm feeler gauge or spacer (**B**) – or simply a 4 mm spacer in place of (**A**) and (**B**) – between the accelerator lever (**C**) and anti-stall speed adjusting screw (**D**).

→ Now insert a 3 mm thick spacer in position (**a**) as described in *Step C3*.

→ Release the anti-stall adjustment screw locknut (*3-C1, item D*).

→ Start the engine.

→ Turn the anti-stall adjustment screw (*3-C1, item E*) until the engine idle speed is between 890 and 910 rpm.

→ Remove the 4 mm thickness of spacers (**A** and **B**) from between the accelerator lever and anti-stall speed screw.

→ Remove the 3 mm spacer that was previously fitted in the position shown in (*3-C3, position a*) and make sure that the stop lever is tight against the head of the adjuster screw.

→ With the engine still running, release the locknut on the idle speed adjusting screw (*3-C1, item C*) and turn the screw (*3-C1, item B*) until the engine idle speed is between 850 and 910 rpm.

☐ **STEP C6: CHECK FOR SLOW DECELERATION:** If the engine is slow to decelerate, turn the anti-stall adjusting screw in an anti-clockwise direction by a maximum of a 1/4 of a turn so that deceleration takes place more promptly.

☐ **STEP C7: CHECK ENGINE STALLING:** If the engine continues to stall, turn the anti-stall adjusting screw in a clockwise direction by no more than 1/4 of a turn so that the engine no longer continues to stall.

If stalling and slow deceleration persist after the pump has been correctly set, there must be some other engine or fuel system fault that will need to be rectified.

Section D: 1.8 litre engine Bosch pump (Non Turbo).

IDLE SPEED SETTING

☐ **STEP D1:** Run the engine until normal operating temperature is reached.

☐ **STEP D2:** Connect the rev counter and check the idle speed - the idle speed is acceptable if in the range 800 to 900 rpm.

☐ **STEP D3:** If the idle speed is incorrect or erratic you should carry out the following setting procedure.

☐ **STEP D4:** To set the pump, carry out the following:

CHECK IDLE SPEED: Use the idle speed adjusting screw (**b**) to bring the idle speed to 850 rpm.

→ Insert a 0.5 mm spacer between the accelerator lever and the residual capacity adjusting screw (**a**).

→ If the idle speed changes, follow the basic setting procedure – see *Step D5*.

→ Assuming the idle speed has not changed, replace the 5.0 mm spacer with a 1.0 mm spacer.

→ The idle speed should now increase by up to 20 rev/min. If the idle speed still does not change, follow the basic setting procedure.

→ If the idle speed increases, check the fast idle speed - see below.

2. BASIC IDLE SPEED SETTING:

→ Use the idle speed adjusting screw (**b**) to bring the idle speed to 850 rpm.

→ Release the end stop on the waxstat fast idle cable so that it cannot affect the idle speed.

→ Fit a 0.5 mm spacer between the accelerator lever and the residual capacity adjusting screw (**a**).

→ Slacken the locknut and turn the residual capacity screw one full turn anti-clockwise.

→ Reset the idle speed to 850 rev/min using the idle speed adjusting screw.

→ Repeat this procedure until the residual capacity screw does not affect the idle speed.

→ Remove the 0.5 mm spacer and fit a 1.0 mm spacer.

→ Adjust the residual capacity adjusting screw (**a**) to give an engine speed between 860 rev/min and 870 rev/min. Tighten the locknut and remove the spacer.

→ Check the idle speed is within limits and fit the 0.5 mm spacer - the idle speed should not change.

→ Repeat the procedure if the idle speed changes.

☐ **STEP D5: 3. FAST IDLE SETTING:** Reset the fast idle waxstat cable stop so that there is a 1.0 mm gap between the fast idle adjuster screw (*3-D4, item c*) and the idle lever when the engine is at normal operating temperature.

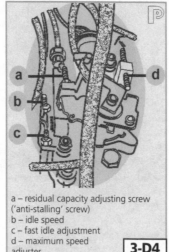

a – residual capacity adjusting screw ('anti-stalling' screw)
b – idle speed
c – fast idle adjustment
d – maximum speed adjuster

3-D4

Section E: 1.8 litre turbo engine - idle speed, speed slow-down time and cold-start cable adjustment.

☐ **STEP E1:** These are the components of the Lucas DPC pump used on these engines.

→ All of the illustration numbers used in this Job relate to this drawing.

IDLE SPEED ADJUSTMENT

☐ **STEP E2:** Push the stop lever (**2**) at the dual idle speed lever to one side and insert a 3 mm pin (**11**) into the hole of the idle lever.

☐ **STEP E3:** Fit the special tool Part No. 23-016 onto the fuel lever adjustment screw (**6**) and add a 1 mm feeler gauge.

→ Alternatively, use a 4 mm spacer but make sure that it stays in place!

☐ **STEP E4:** Adjust the idle speed to between 800 and 1000 rpm using the fuel lever adjustment screw (**6**).

☐ **STEP E5:** Remove the special tool and feeler gauge (or 4 mm spacer) and the 3 mm pin (**5**).

→ Now adjust the idle speed to between 800 and 1000 rpm using the idle speed adjustment screw at the dual idle speed lever (**3**).

SPEED SLOW-DOWN TIME ADJUSTMENT

FACT FILE

SPEED SLOW-DOWN TIME

• The 'speed slow-down time' is the time it takes for the engine speed to drop from its maximum to its correct idle speed.

• The time interval should be 3 - 4 seconds.

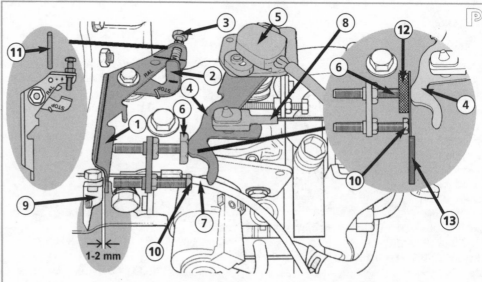

1 – cold-start lever
2 – stop lever
3 – idle adjustment screw
4 – fuel lever
5 – fuel lever position sensor
6 – fuel lever stop screw
7 – cold start cable
8 – throttle cable
9 – cold-start stop
10 – FLVR sensor adjustment screw
(NOT for service adjustment)
11 – 3 mm pin
12 – special tool 23-016
13 – feeler gauge

3-E1

STEP E6: Raise the engine speed to its maximum allowed (5150 rpm).
➜ DO NOT exceed this figure.
➜ Release the accelerator control and measure the time it takes to drop from maximum speed down to the correct idle speed.

STEP E7A: If the time interval is greater than 4 seconds, the fuel lever stop screw has to be adjusted by turning the screw clockwise by a maximum of 1/4 turn.

STEP E7B: If the time interval is less than 4 seconds, the fuel lever stop screw has to be adjusted by turning the screw anti-clockwise by a maximum of 1/4 turn.

COLD-START CABLE ADJUSTMENT

STEP E8: With the engine at normal running temperature:
➜ Adjust the cold-start cable so that there is a clearance of between 1 and 2 mm at the idle lever (**9**).

Section F: Idle speed increase (Idle Up) control.

Certain Escort and Orion models may have an idle speed increase (also known as Idle Up) control. This device increases the idle speed when reverse gear is selected.
➜ The idle speed control unit is mounted on the left-hand side of the engine bay and the glow plug relay is attached to the mounting bracket.
➜ The system control unit has inputs from the reversing light circuit and vacuum pump.

STEP F1: Start the engine and let it idle for at least 5 minutes.
➜ Select reverse gear and check that the idle speed increases and steadies within 3 seconds.
➜ Deselect reverse gear and check that the idle speed returns to normal within 3 seconds of deselection.
➜ If the system does not operate correctly, carry out adjustments as follows.

STEP F2: BOSCH FUEL PUMP: Switch the ignition to position 'II' for at least 3 minutes so that the waxstat operating cable is fully extended.
➜ Check that there is a 0.5 mm clearance between the cable idle lever and cable clamp. Adjust the clamp as necessary – see **Section D**.
➜ Re-check the operation of the system - see **Step F1**.

STEP F3: CAV ROTODIESEL PUMP: Make sure there is no vacuum in the servo and the idle operating cable is fully released.
➜ Check that there is a 0.5 mm to 1.0 mm clearance between the idle speed increase lever and idle speed increase cable clamp – see **Section E**.
➜ Adjust the clamp as necessary and re-check the operation of the system - see **Step F1**.

STEP F4: If the system still does not operate correctly:
➜ Check that the vacuum connection at the control unit is working.

➜ Check all electrical connections.
➜ If necessary, run a diagnostic check for correct operation of electronic controls.

JOB 4: FUEL INJECTION PUMP - *remove, refit.*

STEP 1: Before dismantling, disconnect the battery negative (-) earth/ground terminal. See *Chapter 10, Electrical, Dash, Instruments, Fact File: Disconnecting the Battery* BEFORE doing so!
➜ **TURBO ENGINES:** Drain the cooling system.

STEP 2: With the engine cold, depressurise the fuel system – see *Job 1*.

STEP 3: Set the engine to TDC - see *Chapter 6, Part C.*

STEP 4: 1.8 LITRE ENGINE: Remove the pump drivebelt from the pump sprocket - see *Chapter 6, Part C.*

STEP 5: Disconnect from the pump:
➜ The accelerator cable and, where necessary, remove the cable bracket - see *Job 10*.
➜ The injector pipes – see *Job 6*.
➜ Plug or cover the open connections to prevent the ingress of dirt and contamination.

STEP 6: Separate all electrical connections from the pump – label them for ease of reassembly.

STEP 7: EGR SYSTEM: On an engine fitted with an exhaust gas recirculation (EGR) system, locate and disconnect the two hoses from the vacuum regulator valve - see *Job 12*.

STEP 8: Where fitted, remove the alternator shield - see *Chapter 10, Electrical, Instruments*.

STEP 9: TURBO ENGINES: Remove the following:
➜ The alternator - see *Chapter 10, Electrical, Instruments*.
➜ Where applicable, the air conditioning compressor drivebelt - see *Chapter 6, Part D*.
➜ Disconnect the hose and pipe from the power steering pump, remove the drivebelt and pump pulley - see *Chapter 11, Steering, Suspension*.
➜ Support the engine and remove the right-hand mounting - see *Chapter 6, Part K*.

TOP TIP!

STEP 10: If you are going to refit the original pump, make a suitable alignment mark on the pump attachment flange (**a**) and the timing gear/belt case (**b**).
➜ You will still have to accurately set the timing after refitting the pump but this alignment mark will allow you to fit the pump close to the correct position.

4-10

1.6 LITRE ENGINE DRIVE GEAR

• On these engines, the fuel injection pump is driven by gears from the crankshaft. As part of the pump removal process, therefore, the gearing has to be removed as follows:

❑ **STEP FF1:** Turn the engine to TDC.

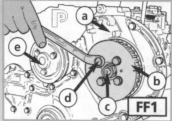

→ When the engine is at TDC, the lug on the engine (**a**) and the mark on the pulley (**b**) will be in these positions.

→ The pulley mark is meant to be aligned with the lug before fitting the TDC pin and the mark will be in the position shown here when the engine is at TDC: mark **b** will have advanced 25 degrees from position **a**.

→ With pump pulley locked so that it cannot move, undo and remove the pump shaft nut (**c**).

→ Remove the four bolts (**d**) and take off the pulley.

→ Remove the water pump (**e**) complete from the engine.

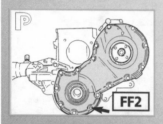

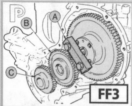

❑ **STEP FF2:** Remove the ring of bolts (one bolt arrowed) and take off the timing gear cover (shaded area).

❑ **STEP FF3:** Use a puller (**A**) to draw the injection pump drive gear off the injection pump shaft.

→ The inner idler gear (**B**) and crankshaft gear (**C**) are left in place.

1.6 LITRE ENGINE

❑ **STEP 11:** IMPORTANT NOTE: Once the pump is removed, the drive gear (inside the timing cover) and cam belt drive sprocket are not positively engaged.

→ If the mesh between the timing gear (**a**) and idler (**b**) (shown here with the timing cover removed) is lost you will have to remove the cover to re-engage the gear.

❑ **STEP 12: CAV ROTODIESEL PUMP:** Remove the mounting bracket.

→ **BOTH TYPES:** Loosen but do not remove the belt drive sprocket bolts.

→ Use a suitable puller to break the taper and lock the sprocket in position without allowing it to rotate.

→ Now remove the pump driveshaft nut.

→ **BOSCH PUMP:** Remove the pump mounting bracket nut and bolt. Retrieve the Woodruff key (**k**) as it becomes accessible.

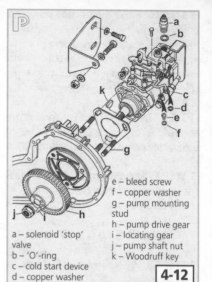

a – solenoid 'stop' valve
b – 'O'-ring
c – cold start device
d – copper washer
e – bleed screw
f – copper washer
g – pump mounting stud
h – pump drive gear
i – locating gear
j – pump shaft nut
k – Woodruff key

4-12

❑ **STEP 13: 1.8 LITRE ENGINE:** Remove the injection pump drivebelt sprocket and the injection pump to attachment bracket bolts.

→ **BOSCH PUMP:** Loosen the cylinder block to attachment bracket bolts.

→ **CAV ROTODIESEL PUMP:** Completely remove the mounting bracket.

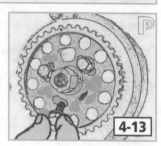

4-13

❑ **STEP 14:** Remove the three pump attachment nuts (one arrowed) (1.6 litre engines) or Torx screws (1.8 litre engines). You can now remove the pump from the engine.

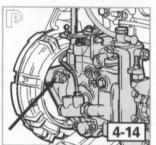

4-14

BOTH ENGINE SIZES

❑ **STEP 15:** Refitting is the reverse of removal.

→ If a new pump is being fitted, prime it by filling it with diesel fuel through the fuel return outlet.

❑ **STEP 16: 1.6 LITRE ENGINE:** Fit a new gasket between the pump and timing case.

→ Align the key on the pump shaft with the keyway on the timing gear and carefully insert the driveshaft. Make sure the timing gear is not pushed out of mesh - see *Step 11*.

→ Finger tighten the three attachment nuts.

→ **BOSCH PUMPS:** The rear support bracket nuts and bolts.

→ **CAV ROTODIESEL PUMPS:** Do not fit the rear support bracket until the pump timing has been set.

→ **BOTH TYPES:** Apply sealant to the pump driveshaft threads and tighten the nut to draw the shaft taper into the gear. Finally tighten the nut to the correct torque.

→ Refit the sprocket and tighten the sprocket attachment nuts to the correct torque.

❑ **STEP 17: 1.8 LITRE ENGINE:** Align the drive flange and pump body timing holes and fit a timing peg or 5.5 mm drill bit.

→ Fit the pump and tighten the Torx screws to the correct torque.

→ Attach the drive sprocket making sure that the timing holes are aligned (the timing peg should pass through all three holes) and the bolts (finger tight only) are in the middle of the slots.
→ Refit the drivebelt - see *Chapter 6, Part C*.

❑ **STEP 18: BOTH ENGINE TYPES:**
→ Set the pump timing - see *Job 5*.
→ **CAV ROTODIESEL PUMPS:** Remember to fit the rear support bracket after the pump has been timed.
→ Bleed the fuel system - see *Job 2*.
→ Refit the remainder of the disconnected/removed components.
→ Start the engine - this may take some time - and allow it to run for a few minutes to purge remaining air from the system.
→ Check for fuel, coolant or oil leaks.
→ Check the idle speed and, where fitted, the adjustment of the EGR vacuum regulator valve.

JOB 5: FUEL INJECTION PUMP – *set timing*.

❑ **STEP 1:** Loosen the attachment nuts or bolts just enough to be able to rotate the pump within the limits of the mounting slots - see *Job 4, Step 14*.

❑ **STEP 2:** Set the engine to TDC – see *Chapter 6, Engine*.

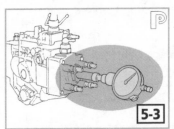 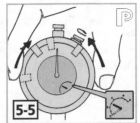

❑ **STEP 3:** Mount a dial test indicator on the pump so that the shaft contacts the plunger in the centre hole. - it may be necessary to remove the injector pipes.
→ The Sykes-Pickavant unit is fitted with its own adapter.

❑ **STEP 4:** You now need to measure the amount of lift on the plunger in the pump:
→ Turn the engine crankshaft anti-clockwise until the reading on the dial test indicator stops moving.

❑ **STEP 5:** Set the dial test indicator to zero.

❑ **STEP 6:** Now turn the engine clockwise and back to its TDC setting
→ **BOSCH PUMP:** The pump is correctly timed when the reading on the dial test indicator is between 0.91 mm and 0.93 mm.
→ **CAV ROTODIESEL PUMP:** The reading should be between 1.33 and 1.47 mm.

❑ **STEP 7:** If necessary adjust the pump.

❑ **STEP 8A: 1.6 ENGINES:** Loosen the pump mountings and rotate the pump until the reading is correct.

❑ **STEP 8B: 1.8 ENGINES:** Loosen the injection pump sprocket bolts and rotate the pump shaft until the reading is correct.

❑ **STEP 9:** Retighten the mountings or sprocket bolts and repeat the test to make sure the reading has not changed.

❑ **STEP B10:** Refit the disconnected/removed components.

JOB 6: FUEL INJECTION PIPES - *removal, refitting*.

Although similar in appearance, the pipes used with Bosch injection pumps have a 2.0 mm internal bore and those used with CAV RotoDiesel pumps have a 2.5 mm internal bore. Make sure you have the correct pipes for the pump and injectors.

❑ **STEP 1:** Before dismantling, disconnect the battery negative (-) earth/ground terminal. See *Chapter 10, Electrical, Dash, Instruments, Fact File: Disconnecting the Battery* BEFORE doing so!

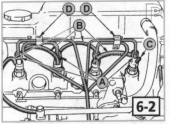 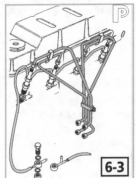

❑ **STEP 2:** Thoroughly clean the areas around the pipe unions at both ends of the pipes (**A**) and disconnect them.
→ Disconnect the return (or 'spill') pipes (**B**) and the end-plug (**C**).
→ Plug or cover the open connections immediately to prevent the ingress of dirt or contamination.
→ If necessary you can now remove the anti-vibration clips (**D**) and separate the pipes.

❑ **STEP 3:** Refitting is the reverse of the removal process, bearing in mind the following points.
→ Blow through the pipes with compressed air – wear goggles! - to make sure they are thoroughly clean inside.
→ Start the engine - it may take some time - and allow it to run for a few minutes to purge all air from the system.
→ Check all connections for leaks.

JOB 7: FUEL INJECTORS - *removal, checking, refitting*.

SAFETY FIRST!

• The high pressure spray from the injectors is dangerous.

• Suspect injectors must be tested by an approved Ford dealer or fuel injection specialist with the necessary equipment.

• See also *SAFETY FIRST!* at the beginning of this section.

INJECTOR TYPES AND REPAIRS

• Different designs of injector are used, depending on whether a Bosch or CAV RotoDiesel pump is fitted.

• **CAV ROTODIESEL:** The injector has a conical section just below the pipe attachment thread.

• **BOSCH:** The injector body is cylindrical.

• The different injectors are not interchangeable.

• Depending on the fault, a defective injector can be repaired but this is a job for a specialist.

• It is usually cheaper, and sometimes more reliable, to fit new ones.

❏ **STEP 1:** Before dismantling, disconnect the battery negative (-) earth/ground terminal. See *Chapter 10, Electrical, Dash, Instruments, Fact File: Disconnecting the Battery* BEFORE doing so!

❏ **STEP 2:** Remove any loose dirt, pull the fuel return hoses from the relevant injectors and separate the injection pipe or pipes (arrowed) - see *Job 6*.

❏ **STEP 3:** Remove the injectors - a 27 mm deep socket will be needed.

❏ **STEP 4:** Each insulating washer (arrowed) can now be removed.

❏ **STEP 5:** Examine the injector for build up of carbon deposits and any signs of physical damage. Reconnecting the injector to the fuel

supply pipe and watching the spray pattern while the engine is cranked on the starter motor is potentially highly dangerous - see *Safety First!* at the beginning of this *Job*.
➜ It also does not give any information about the actual fuel pressure within the injector.

❏ **STEP 6:** Refitting the injectors is the reverse of the removal process, bearing in mind the following points.
➜ Always fit new insulating washers with the convex (domed) face away from the injector. Make sure the washer is fully inserted and seated correctly.
➜ Tighten the injectors to the specified torque - see *Chapter 1, Facts and Figures*.
➜ Reconnect the fuel supply pipes and the fuel return hoses – see *Job 6*.
➜ Start and run the engine for a few minutes to purge air. Check that there are no fuel leaks.

JOB 8: FUEL SHUT-OFF SOLENOID - *remove, refit.*

❏ **STEP 1:** Disconnect the battery negative lead and locate the solenoid on top of the fuel pump, at the injector pipe end.
➜ You should be able to pull the electrical lead from the solenoid spade connector or, as shown here, remove the connector nut (position arrowed).

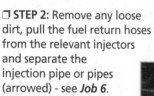

❏ **STEP 2:** Thoroughly clean around the solenoid and, using a deep socket, unscrew the solenoid.
➜ Note that the spring and plunger are separate.

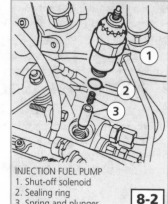

INJECTION FUEL PUMP
1. Shut-off solenoid
2. Sealing ring
3. Spring and plunger

❏ **STEP 3:** Refitting the solenoid is the reverse of the removal process, bearing in mind the following points.
➜ Use a new 'O' seal.
➜ **SOLENOID ON BOSCH PUMP:** Tighten sufficiently to provide a good seal and prevent fuel leaks when the engine is running - do not overtighten.
➜ **SOLENOID ON CAV ROTODIESEL PUMP:** Tighten to a torque of 16 Nm to 20 Nm.
➜ Start and run the engine for a few minutes, to make sure the solenoid is working, that there are no fuel leaks and to purge air from the system.
➜ Switch off the engine and make sure it stops!.

JOB 9: TURBOCHARGER AND INTERCOOLER - *remove, replace.*

Several different turbocharger designs have been used on the Escort and Orion diesel models covered here. The turbocharger design depends on the age of the vehicle and whether an intercooler is fitted.

❏ **STEP 1:** Before dismantling, disconnect the battery negative (-) earth/ground terminal. See *Chapter 10, Electrical, Dash, Instruments, Fact File: Disconnecting the Battery* BEFORE doing so!

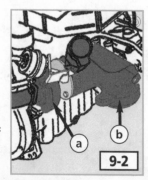

❏ **STEP 2:** This is the location of the turbocharger (a), adjacent to the exhaust manifold (b).

→ Systematically separate all pipes, hoses and electrical connectors, labelling them for ease of re-assembly.
→ Separate the rubber inlet pipe from the intercooler (when fitted).
→ Separate the exhaust downpipe from the manifold.
→ Separate the fuel filter from the engine and secure it out of the way - see *Job 11*.
→ Remove the nuts attaching the turbocharger to the support bracket and the turbocharger to the exhaust manifold.
→ Lift the turbocharger away from the engine.

❏ **STEP 3: INTERCOOLER:** Where fitted, the intercooler (arrowed) is easily removed.

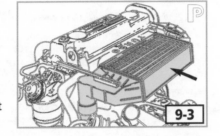
9-3

→ Loosen the hose clamps on the right and left of the intercooler.
→ Remove the retaining nuts and support washers, and lift the intercooler clear of the engine.
→ If necessary, you can separate the intercooler duct seal.

❏ **STEP 4:** Refitting is the reverse of the removal process, bearing in mind the following points.
→ Renew all 'O' rings, gaskets and sealing washers.
→ Make sure that all hoses are properly aligned (any alignment marks should be together) and not twisted or strained.

JOB 10: ACCELERATOR CABLE AND DAMPER - *adjust, replace.*

We have covered disconnection at the fuel pump here - cable disconnection at the accelerator pedal and complete cable removal are covered in *Chapter 9, Part A*.

❏ **STEP 1:** Before dismantling, disconnect the battery negative (-) earth/ground terminal. See *Chapter 10, Electrical, Dash, Instruments, Fact File: Disconnecting the Battery* BEFORE doing so!

❏ **STEP 2:** Working at the pump, carefully lever off the inner cable retaining clip (arrowed) and free the inner cable from the operating arm on the pump.

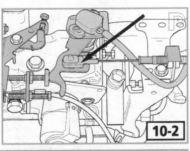
10-2

❏ **STEP 3:** Release the outer cable clip (a) from the bracket on the pump.
→ On early versions, press in the retaining tangs (b) and pull the retainer from the bracket.

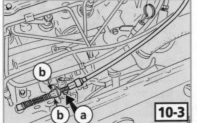
10-3

→ Later versions have a simple metal clip which is pulled off to free the cable.

❏ **STEP 4:** Refitting is the reverse of the removal procedure, bearing in mind the following points.
→ There should be a small amount of slack in the cable when the pedal is released.
→ Check that the throttle lever on the pump moves through its full range, contacting the idle and maximum speed screws, when the accelerator pedal is operated.

❏ **STEP 5:** Where appropriate, adjust the cable as follows.
→ Working at the fuel pump, remove the adjustment clip from the outer cable and lubricate the adjuster with silicone lubricant,
→ Pull the cable as far out of the adjuster as possible to remove slack then have an assistant press the accelerator pedal fully down. Refit the adjustment clip.
→ Check that the accelerator lever on the fuel pump moves smoothly over its full range.

JOB 11: FUEL FILTER - *replace.*

Before staring work, thoroughly clean the area around the filter and drain the fuel from the filter or filter housing through the drain screw at the base.

There are three main designs of diesel fuel filter.

❏ **STEP 1:** There is a removable canister type, with a disposable inner element and sealing ring.

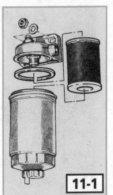
11-1

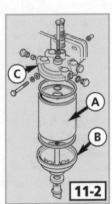
11-2

❏ **STEP 2:** This type has a disposable filter body (**A**) sandwiched between water bowl (**B**) and filter head (**C**).

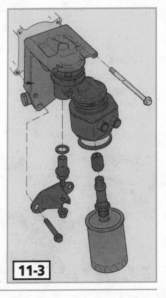

❏ **STEP 3:** The third type has a fully disposable filter cartridge, being attached to the pump and oil cooler connections.

11-3

☐ **STEP 4:** If the filter is of the one-piece cartridge type, it is removed by unscrewing by hand, or if too tight, with the aid of an oil filter wrench.

11-4

☐ **STEP 5:** Alternatively, removal is a question of undoing the centre nut/bolt. Note the sealing rings.
→ Ensure that the small one is in the filter box when you buy the replacement cartridge.

☐ **STEP 6:** The rubber sealing ring at the top of the filter element or cartridge should be smeared with diesel fuel prior to fitting so that it doesn't grip and prevent proper tightening.

11-5

☐ **STEP 7:** Note that the Bosch type shown here has a small diameter inner seal as well as a larger outer one, plus a plastic retainer to secure it prior to fitting the filter.

11-6

☐ **STEP 8:** The new filter is screwed firmly into place by hand only, or, if of the bolt-retained type as shown here, tightened – though not with excessive force!

11-8

11-7

JOB 12: EXHAUST GAS RECIRCULATION SYSTEM COMPONENTS - *check, replace.*

Section A: Checking.

The following checks will only be necessary if emissions are excessive or the fuel injection pump has been refitted.

☐ **STEP A1:** Run the engine until it reaches normal operating temperature.
→ With the engine idling, disconnect and reconnect the vacuum pipe on the top of the exhaust gas recirculation (EGR) valve.
→ Listen for the sound of the valve operating.
☐ **STEP A2:** If the valve fails to operate but there is a vacuum at the pipe end, check the vacuum regulator valve - see *Section B*.
→ If there is no vacuum at the pipe end, check back through the system to find the blockage.
→ The presence of a vacuum at the pipe end combined with satisfactory operation of the vacuum regulator valve means there is probably a faulty EGR valve.
→ Cleaning carbon deposits from the EGR valve may solve the problem but replacement is usually necessary.

Section B: Vacuum regulator valve.

You will need a vacuum pump and gauge to check/adjust the vacuum regulator valve.
→ Make a note of the vacuum pipe connections before disconnecting them so that they can be refitted correctly. The inlet pipe is nearest the engine and the outlet, which connects to the EGR, is nearest the radiator. On later models the outlet pipe may have a yellow tracer.

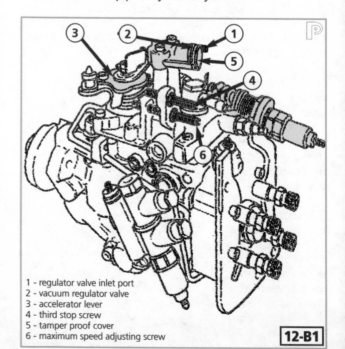

1 - regulator valve inlet port
2 - vacuum regulator valve
3 - accelerator lever
4 - third stop screw
5 - tamper proof cover
6 - maximum speed adjusting screw

12-B1

STEP B1: Connect a vacuum pump to the inlet port (**1**); it's the port nearest the engine, of the vacuum regulator valve (**2**).
→ Hold the accelerator lever in the fully open position and operate the vacuum pump. The reading on the gauge should be approximately 0.6 bar.
→ Now fit an 11.8 mm spacer between the accelerator lever (**3**) and the third stop screw (**4**). With the accelerator lever pushed against the spacer, operate the vacuum pump. The reading on the gauge should be approximately 0.6 bar.
→ Replace the 11.8 mm spacer with a 12.1 mm spacer so that the regulator valve is held open and no vacuum is obtained when the pump is operated.
→ If the vacuum readings are different from those here, the vacuum regulator valve should be adjusted.
→ Remove the tamperproof cover (**5**), and hold the accelerator lever against the maximum speed adjusting screw (**6**) and operate the vacuum pump. The reading on the gauge should be between 0.6 bar and 0.7 bar.
→ Now fit a 12.0 mm spacer between the accelerator lever and the third stop lever and operate the vacuum pump. Adjust the regulator valve adjuster until the reading on the gauge is 0.35 bar.
→ Recheck the vacuum with the 11.8 mm and 12.1 mm spacers fitted.

STEP B2: Fit a new tamperproof cover when the vacuum readings are correct.

STEP B3: The vacuum regulator valve may need to be replaced if it cannot be adjusted to give the correct readings.

Section C: Thermal-Operated vacuum switch.

No checks are specified for the thermal operated vacuum switch. The switch should be replaced if faulty.

STEP C1: Drain the cooling system so that the coolant level is below the thermostat housing.

STEP C2: Locate the thermal operated vacuum switch (arrowed) on the vacuum pump side of the thermostat housing.
→ Disconnect the vacuum pipes and unscrew the switch from the thermostat housing.

STEP C3: When you fit the replacement switch, use a new sealing washer or apply sealant to the threads as necessary.

Section D: Exhaust gas recirculation valve.

STEP D1: Before dismantling, disconnect the battery negative (-) earth/ground terminal. See *Chapter 10, Electrical, Dash, Instruments, Fact File: Disconnecting the Battery* BEFORE doing so!

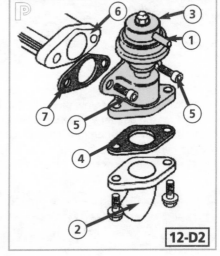

STEP D2: To remove the EGR valve:
→ Pull-off the vacuum pipe (**1**) and separate the supply pipe (**2**) from the EGR valve (**3**).
→ Discard the gasket (**4**) between the supply pipe and EGR valve.
→ Remove the bolts (**5**) and separate the EGR valve from the inlet manifold (**6**).
→ Discard the gasket (**7**).

STEP D3: Refitting is the reverse of the removal process, bearing in mind the following points.
→ Use new gaskets. If you have separated both ends of the supply pipe, fit gaskets at both ends.
→ Tighten the attachment bolts to the correct torque.
→ Start the engine and check the operation of the EGR - see *Section A*.

JOB 13: GLOW PLUGS - *removal, replacement.*

Section A: Glow plug testing.

STEP A1: Connect a suitable voltmeter, or test lamp, between any glow plug terminal and earth/ground.
→ Switch on the 'ignition' and note the indication.
→ The voltmeter should indicate a nominal 12V for a few seconds then drop to zero, or the lamp should illuminate and then go out.
→ If there is no indication, check the system fuse first.
→ If the fuse is intact, the glow plug relay is probably faulty and should be replaced - see *Section C*.

STEP A2: Connect a suitable ammeter in series between the glow plug feed and busbar.
→ Switch on the 'ignition' and check the current.
→ If all glow plugs are working, the current should be approximately 32A.

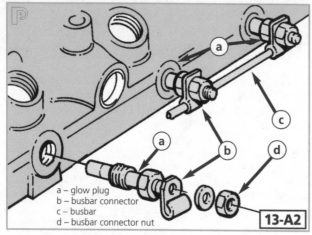

a – glow plug
b – busbar connector
c – busbar
d – busbar connector nut

13-A2

→ A much lower reading indicates a faulty glow plug.
→ You can check each glow plug individually by connecting the ammeter in series with each glow plug in turn - the reading for an individual plug should be approximately 4A.
→ Replace faulty glow plugs as necessary - see *Section B*.

Section B: Glow plug removal and refitting.

☐ **STEP B1:** Before dismantling, disconnect the battery negative (-) earth/ground terminal and the busbar feed cable. See *Chapter 10, Electrical, Dash, Instruments, Fact File: Disconnecting the Battery* BEFORE doing so!

☐ **STEP B2:** Remove the terminal nut (arrowed) from each glow plug and the busbar.

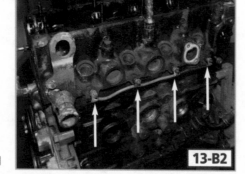

13-B2

☐ **STEP B3:** Thoroughly clean around each glow plug before removing it.

☐ **STEP B4:** Refitting is the reverse of the removal process, bearing in mind the following points.
→ Later removal will be easier if anti-seize grease is smeared on the threads.

Section C: Glow plug relay removal and refitting.

FACT FILE

GLOW PLUG LOCATION

• Depending on model the glow plug relay is located:
• EITHER: On the left-hand side of the engine bay, under the jack stowage position;
• OR: Or attached to the idle speed controller bracket.

☐ **STEP C1:** Before dismantling, disconnect the battery negative (-) earth/ground terminal. See *Chapter 10, Electrical, Dash, Instruments, Fact File: Disconnecting the Battery* BEFORE doing so!

☐ **STEP C2:** Separate the electrical connector from the relay and remove the attachment screws. Lift the relay from the vehicle.

☐ **STEP C3:** Refitting is the reverse of the removal process.

JOB 14: FUEL HEATER - *removal, refitting.*

☐ **STEP 1:** Before dismantling, disconnect the battery negative (-) earth/ground terminal. See *Chapter 10, Electrical, Dash, Instruments, Fact File: Disconnecting the Battery* BEFORE doing so!

☐ **STEP 2: 1.6 LITRE ENGINE:** The fuel heater on these engines is integral with the fuel filter mounting.
→ Disconnect the fuel heater electrical multi-plug and remove the complete fuel filter mounting.

14-2

☐ **STEP 3: 1.8 LITRE ENGINE LUCAS CAV:** Disconnect the electrical multi-plug from the base of the fuel heater (a).
→ Release any pipe support clips and separate the fuel pipe quick release connections (b) from the filter and supply pipe.
→ Collect any fuel spillage in a suitable container.

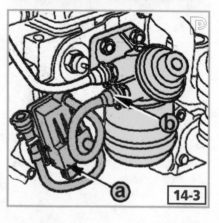

14-3

☐ **STEP 4: 1.8 LITRE ENGINE - BOSCH:** Undo the single retaining bolt and separate the bracket complete with fuel heater from the engine.
→ If necessary, you can remove the plastic rivets and separate the heater from the bracket.

☐ **STEP 5:** Refitting is the reverse of the removal process. Bleed the fuel system - see *Job 2*.

Part C: Both Engine Types

CONTENTS

JOB 1: FUEL TANK AND FUEL PIPES - removal, refitting.

SAFETY FIRST!

• We strongly recommend that you carry out all of this work out of doors.

• Read *Chapter 2, Safety First!* before carrying out this work.

• Store drained fuel in an approved, safe container or containers and not near a house.

• Wear gloves or goggles - petrol and diesel fuel can be harmful to the skin and is always harmful to the eyes. Avoid prolonged inhalation of fuel vapour.

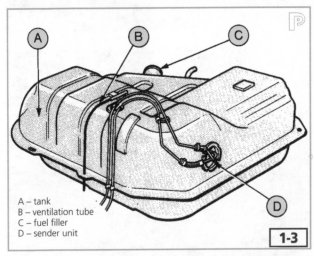

A – tank
B – ventilation tube
C – fuel filler
D – sender unit

1-3

☐ **STEP 1:** Before dismantling, disconnect the battery negative (-) earth/ground terminal. See *Chapter 10, Electrical, Dash, Instruments, Fact File: Disconnecting the Battery* BEFORE doing so!

☐ **STEP 2:** These are typical tank assembly components - earlier models are less complicated than later models.
➜ Start by draining the tank.

☐ **STEP 3:** On models with side mounted sender units you can disconnect the fuel lines and sender electrical connectors at this stage.
➜ Make sure the fuel level is below the outlet!
➜ Where the sender is mounted on top of the tank you will have to lower the tank first.

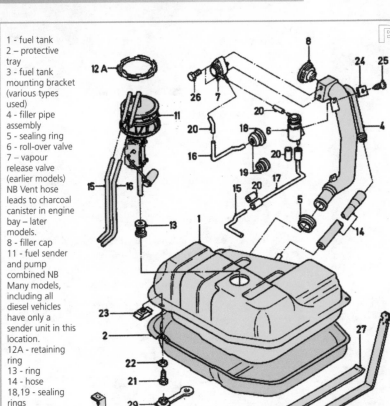

1 - fuel tank
2 – protective tray
3 - fuel tank mounting bracket (various types used)
4 - filler pipe assembly
5 - sealing ring
6 - roll-over valve
7 – vapour release valve (earlier models) NB Vent hose leads to charcoal canister in engine bay – later models.
8 - filler cap
11 - fuel sender and pump combined NB Many models, including all diesel vehicles have only a sender unit in this location.
12A - retaining ring
13 - ring
14 - hose
18,19 - sealing rings
15, 16, 17, 20 - vapour vent hose
21, 22 – tank mounting screw, when fitted
27 – rubber pad
28, 29 – spacer, special screw, when fitted

1-2

1-4

☐ **STEP 4:** Remove the filler pipe attachment screws.

STEP 5: Disengage the filler pipe at the filler and separate the filler pipe from the tank.

STEP 6: On more recent models the filler pipe is secured to the tank by a clip (arrowed).

1-5

1-6

1-7

STEP 7: Earlier models are a push fit.

STEP 8: FIESTA FROM 1995: You will have to peel back the wheel arch liner.

1-8

1-9

STEP 9: Disconnect any remaining hoses, pipes and components such as this fuel filter in the pipe leading from the tank.

STEP 10: Support the weight of the tank, remove the attachment screws - some models have a strap or straps - and carefully lower the tank.
→ As the tank is slowly lowered, check to make sure that you have disconnected all the pipes, hoses and electrical leads.

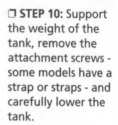

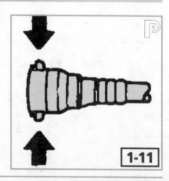

1-10

SAFETY FIRST!

FUEL TANK SAFETY
• You must NEVER just leave the fuel tank at this stage!

• If you are only planning to store the tank for a very short time, the aperture must be thoroughly sealed.

• The biggest danger in a fuel tank comes from the fumes within it. Petrol/gasoline fumes are highly flammable and a tank full of fumes is a bomb waiting to go off if any sparks or cigarette ends get near it.

• If the tank is to be stored for more than a few days, it should be steam cleaned internally to remove all traces of fuel but do not assume that a steam cleaned tank is completely safe.

STEP 11: If necessary, you can unclip and disconnect the fuel pipes and related components.
→ Later models have these push-on connectors on the pipe ends.
→ Push in the clips (arrowed) while pulling the connector off its stub.

1-11

☐ **STEP 12:** Refitting the tank, pipes and hoses is the reverse of the removal process.

JOB 2: FUEL GAUGE SENDER UNIT - *replacement.*

SAFETY FIRST!

• **Ideally drain the tank before removing the sender but, at least make sure that any fuel in the tank is below the level of the sender.**

☐ **STEP 1:** Disconnect the fuel lines and electrical connector/s from the sender unit.

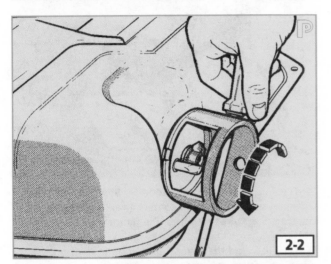

2-2

☐ **STEP 2:** Ford specify special tools for fuel gauge sender removal and refitting. Tool no 23-026 is specified for later top mounted senders and 23-014 for earlier side mounted senders.

2-3

→ It may be possible to drift the sealing ring round, although there is a strong risk of damaging it.
→ Use ONLY a wooden or plastic drift – DO NOT risk causing a spark!
→ Rotate the sender anti-clockwise to remove.
→ Recover seals and take care to prevent dirt falling into the tank.

☐ **STEP 3:** Refitting is the reverse of removal but make sure the seals are in good condition or, ideally, use new seals.

JOB 3: EXHAUST SYSTEM - *replacement.*

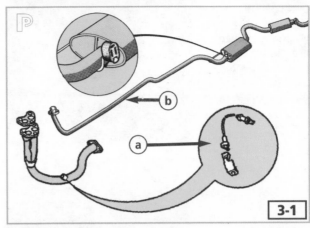

3-1

☐ **STEP 1:** The variety of exhaust systems fitted to the vehicles covered here is enormous. However, apart from cat (**a**) and non-cat (**b**) systems, the differences are mainly in appearance.

FACT FILE
REPLACING THE 'CAT'

• If you have to replace an exhaust tailpipe or the catalytic converter on some models, note that the system fitted during manufacture has to be cut and the new section clamped to the existing pipe.
• Although Ford provide cutting measurements, using the new components is a more reliable method, especially if 'pattern' parts are being used.
• On some models, as shown here, the catalytic converter is part of the downpipe and is not replaceable separately.

☐ **STEP 2:** Removing the old exhaust system is relatively easy, provided of course that attachment bolts and clamps are not excessively corroded and difficult to undo.
→ Clamps and flange attachment bolt can be cut off but be particularly careful with manifold studs.

☐ **STEP 3:** Gaining access to the downpipe on many models involves removing the heatshield.

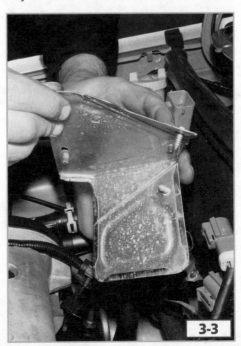

3-3

❏ **STEP 4:** The flexible section (arrowed) fitted to more recent systems is easily damaged - use a splint to prevent it bending too far.

❏ **STEP 5:** Check the condition of the rubber supports and replace any that have deteriorated. Note the special support here that has an outer 'emergency' section.

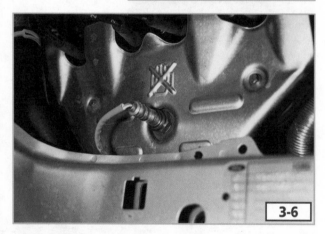

❏ **STEP 6:** If necessary, the Lambda sensor (petrol cat. models) can be removed.

REASSEMBLY

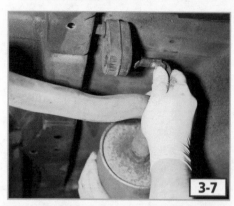

❏ **STEP 7:** Refit the components into place starting at the manifold end.

❏ **STEP 8:** Mount the exhaust on its supports...

❏ **STEP 9:** ...and only when properly aligned, with sufficient space to prevent contact or excessive heat transference, start to tighten the flange bolts...

❏ **STEP 10:** ...and the clamps - just enough to grip the pipes while allowing you to make final adjustments.
➜ Make sure the exhaust is mounted evenly, with adequate clearances and no supports are under more tension than others - only then should you fully tighten the clamps.
➜ Start and run the engine to ensure nothing rattles!

CHAPTER 10: ELECTRICAL, INSTRUMENTS

PLEASE READ CHAPTER 2 SAFETY FIRST BEFORE CARRYING OUT ANY WORK ON YOUR CAR.

CONTENTS

SAFETY FIRST!

- Never smoke, use a naked flame or allow a spark near the battery.
- Never disconnect the battery with battery caps removed – or with engine running, which will damage electronic components.
- **BATTERY TERMINALS: ALWAYS** disconnect earth/ground FIRST and reconnect LAST.
- If battery acid comes into contact with skin or eyes, flood with cold water and seek medical advice.
- Don't top up the battery within half an hour of charging it – electrolyte may flood out.

FACT FILE

DISCONNECTING THE BATTERY

- If you disconnect the battery, you might find the alarm goes off, the ECU loses its 'memory', or the radio needs its security code.
- You can ensure a constant electrical supply with a separate battery, protected with a 1 amp fuse.
- In some cases, you might need to disconnect the battery completely. For instance, if you need to disable the air bays.
- When the battery DOES need to be disconnected, you MUST make sure that you've got the radio security code before disconnecting it.
- This is the Sykes-Pickavant Computer Saver. Clip the cables to your spare battery and plug into your cigar lighter before disconnecting the vehicle battery.

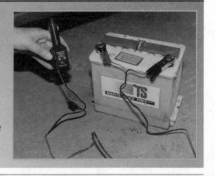

JOB 1:   SYSTEM CHECKS.

See *SAFETY FIRST!* at the start of this chapter.

❒ **STEP 1:** Decide whether you have enough knowledge or information to do this work yourself, or whether to consult your Ford dealer or auto-electrician.
PORTER MANUALS *Auto-Electrics Manual* explains everything in a simple-to-follow style and has won the coveted *'BEST BUY!'* award from Auto-Express magazine.

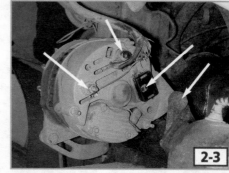

❒ **STEP 2:** Before assuming that a flat battery is 'dead', check the charging system. This Sykes-Pickavant electronic battery tester is more accurate - and a lot safer! - than the old-fashioned type of battery drop tester, which has been known to cause a battery to explode! See *Chapter 2, Safety First* for important safety precautions relating to batteries and battery charging.

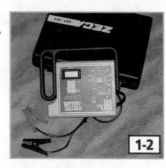

JOB 2:   ALTERNATOR - *remove, replace.*

IMPORTANT NOTES:
• For specific details relating to the different drive belts - see *Chapter 6, Engine, Part D*.
• For specific details on power steering - see *Chapter 11, Steering, Suspension*.
• Where an automatic belt tensioner is fitted, you will have to release the belt tension and remove the belt before unbolting the alternator.

> **TOP TIP!**
> • If any of the leads are capable of being replaced the wrong way round, label them as you remove them.

❒ **STEP 1:** Before dismantling, disconnect the battery negative (-) earth/ground terminal. See *Fact File: Disconnecting the Battery* at the start of this chapter BEFORE doing so!

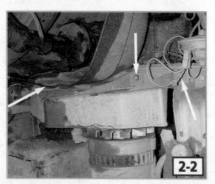

❒ **STEP 2:** Where necessary, remove the protective shield (bolts arrowed) to give access to the retaining bolts.

❒ **STEP 3:** Disconnect the plug or multi-pin connector on the back of the alternator and any other leads (arrowed), clearly labelling them.

❒ **STEP 4:** Slacken and remove the drive belt from the alternator pulley - see *Chapter 6, Engine, Part D*.

❒ **STEP 5:** Undo the retaining bolts and remove the alternator from its mountings.
→ Note the location of any spacer washers so that these can be fitted in the correct position during refitting.

❒ **STEP 6:** Refitting is the reverse of removal. It is very important the alternator bolts and washers are fitted correctly. Make sure you tighten the alternator bolts in the following order:
→ adjuster
→ front mounting
→ rear mounting.

JOB 3:   STARTER MOTOR – *remove, replace.*

> **FACT FILE**
> ### STARTER MOTOR TYPES
>
> • Two different types of starter motor may be found on the models covered by this manual - the inertia type and the pre-engaged type. Removal and refitting is similar for both types.
>
> • The pre-engaged type is easily identified by the solenoid mounted on top of the starter motor.

❒ **STEP 1:** Before dismantling, disconnect the battery negative (-) earth/ground terminal. See *Fact File: Disconnecting the Battery* at the start of this chapter BEFORE doing so!

❏ **STEP 2:** Disconnect and label the cables (arrowed) from the rear of the starter motor (inertia type) or solenoid (pre-engaged type).

3-2

❏ **STEP 3: ALL TYPES:** Undo the two or three - according to model - mounting bolts (**a**) at clutch/transmission end and remove bolts and washer...

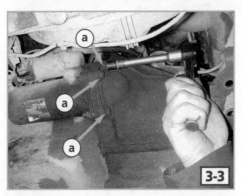

3-3

❏ **STEP 4:** ...and - where fitted - remove the additional support bracket mounting bolt (arrowed) above the solenoid.

3-4

❏ **STEP 5:** You can now remove the starter motor.

3-5

❏ **STEP 6:** Refit in the reverse order bearing in mind the following:
➜ Make sure the pre-engaged type does engage and both types are correctly seated.

JOB 4: INSTRUMENT PANEL – *remove, replace.*

FACT FILE
INSTRUMENT PANEL TYPES

• You will come across several different types of instrument panel and a variety of fittings. We have given here general principles that can be applied to all models.

❏ **STEP 1:** Before dismantling, disconnect the battery negative (-) earth/ground terminal. See *Fact File: Disconnecting the Battery* at the start of this chapter BEFORE doing so!

❏ **STEP 2:** Remove the upper and lower steering column shrouds.
➜ Removal of the steering wheel is not essential on any model but may give better access especially on Escorts and early model Fiestas. If necessary - see *Chapter 14, Interior, Trim*.

❏ **STEP 3: PRE-1983 FIESTA:** It will be necessary to lever off the heater control knobs at the side of the fascia.

❏ **STEP 4: KA MODELS:**
➜ It will be necessary to remove the heater control panel (**a**) by undoing

4-4

the screws and clips and then disconnecting the control cable and wiring plugs.
➜ Remove the radio and surround panel (**b**).

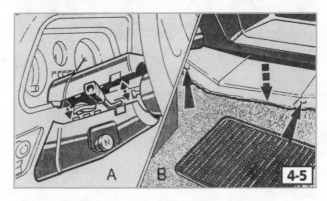

4-5

❏ **STEP 5:** On some models it is possible to undo the lower panel (**B**) and reach up behind the instrument panel to disconnect the speedometer cable - press the grooved section sideways and pull off the cable.
➜ If disconnection is difficult, this step can be delayed until the instrument panel is free - see *Step 8*.
➜ Part (**A**) shows the top of the steering column shroud being removed.

**STEP 6A:
OLDER FIESTA
MODELS:** Hold the instrument panel at the cut-outs (**a**) and pull the bezel from the instrument panel.

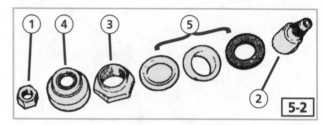

4-6A

**STEP 6B:
MOST
MODELS:**
Remove the two (or four, depending on version) instrument panel bezel attachment screws (arrowed) and remove the bezel.

4-6B

STEP 7:
With the bezel removed, take out the four instrument panel attachment screws (arrowed).

4-7

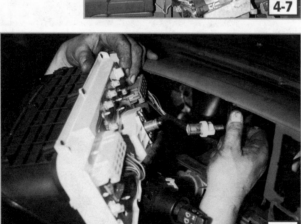

4-8

STEP 8: Pull the instrument panel forward from the dashboard.
→ If the speedometer cable has not already been disconnected, release it - see **Step 5**.

STEP 9: Disconnect the multi-plug and, where fitted, the indicator and brake warning lights. Withdraw the instrument panel.

STEP 10: Refitting is the reverse of the removal process.

JOB 5: FRONT WIPER ASSEMBLY - *replace.*

TOP TIP!
• Use tape or a marker pen to mark the position of the wiper blades on the screen before removal.

STEP 1: Before dismantling, disconnect the battery negative (-) earth/ground terminal. See *Fact File: Disconnecting the Battery* at the start of this chapter BEFORE doing so!

5-2

STEP 2: Remove the windscreen wiper arms:
→ Lift the cover, undo the retaining nut (**1**) and carefully pulling the wiper arm off the splined shaft (**2**) - it may be very tight.
→ Undo the spindle retaining nut (**3**) which may be underneath a plastic cover (**4**).
→ Note the location of the remaining components (**5**).

EARLIEST VEHICLES

STEP 3: To remove the wiper motor:
→ Remove the trim cover, when fitted, to access the motor assembly.
→ Remove the electrical connectors (**B**) from the motor.

5-3

→ Undo the attachment bolts (**A**) - two shown here.
→ If necessary - on some models - you can alternatively remove the bolts and remove the motor with the mounting plate.
→ Lift the motor out of the way so that you have access to separate the linkage from the operating arm.
→ See **Step 9** for windscreen wiper motor removal on post-1989 models.

OTHER FIESTAS PRE-1989

STEP 4: To remove the wiper linkage.
→ Remove the bonnet lock assembly - see **Chapter 13, Bodywork**. You may need to

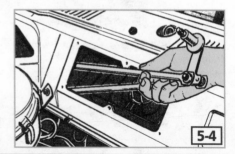

5-4

move the coil bracket out of the way.
→ Remove the heater blower motor from its recess - see *Chapter 8, Cooling System*.
→ Push the wiper arm spindles downwards, clear of the bulkhead, and manoeuvre the linkage assembly out through the bonnet lock aperture.

OTHER ESCORT AND ORION PRE-1990

☐ STEP 5: Remove the cover from the wiper motor, where fitted.

☐ STEP 6: Disconnect the wiper motor multi-plug and remove the two mounting plate attachment bolts (arrowed).

☐ STEP 7: Push the wiper arm spindles downwards and withdraw the motor complete with linkage from the engine compartment.

☐ STEP 8: If necessary you can undo the crank nut (**a**) to separate the motor from the linkage and the motor attachment bolts (**b**) to separate the motor from the mounting plate.

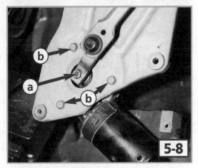

FIESTA FROM 1989, ESCORT AND ORION FROM 1990

☐ STEP 9: Unscrew the nut (**1**) on the windscreen motor drive shaft and pull the crank and linkage (**2**) from the driving shaft taper.
→ Access on Escort and Orion models may be easier if you remove the scuttle grille panel (**3**) and on some Fiesta models, you may need to remove the following items for access.

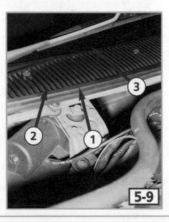

→ The air cleaner components - so that you have access to the bulkhead panel.
→ The cooling system reservoir, electrical and cooling systems components from the bulkhead panel.
→ The rubber seal from the bulkhead panel along with the attachment screws.

☐ STEP 10: Undo the three windscreen wiper attachment bolts (**1**).

☐ STEP 11: Manoeuvre the motor so you can remove the cover (**a**) and disconnect the multi-plug.
→ You can now remove the motor and, if necessary, the operating linkage from the vehicle.

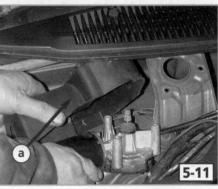

→ Manoeuvre the linkage into a suitable position, push the wiper arm spindles down through the scuttle panel and remove the linkage.

KA MODELS

☐ STEP 12: PREPARATION: Remove the screws and move the scuttle grill panel forward so that you have access to the windscreen wiper arm attachment nuts.
→ Completely remove the grille panel if you are going to remove the windscreen wiper motor and linkage - remember to disconnect the washer hose if you are removing the panel.

☐ STEP 13: Move the coolant reservoir and, where appropriate, the power steering fluid reservoir to one side.
→ Remove the electrical components from the bulkhead panel, undo the attachment screws and move the bulkhead panel forward.

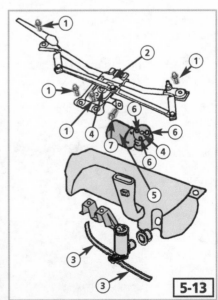

→ Disconnect the multi-plugs from the wiper motor and screen washer pump.

→ Remove the four wiper assembly motor attachment bolts (1), manoeuvre the complete assembly (2) from the bulkhead and disconnect the washer hoses (3) - be ready for some spillage and drain the reservoir into a suitable container as quickly as possible.

→ If necessary you can now dismantle the assembly - a single nut (position 4) attaches the linkage operating crank to the wiper motor (position 5) and three bolts (positions 6) attach the wiper motor.

→ A single bolt (7) attaches to the reservoir.

→ You can separate the reservoir by undoing the single bolt and, if necessary removing the remainder of the screen washer components.

ALL MODELS

☐ STEP 13: Re-assembly is the reverse of removal.

→ If you have removed the mounting plate on pre-1989 Fiesta models, make sure the sealing strip is replaced and is in good condition.

TOP TIP!

• Before reconnecting the wiper arms, reconnect the electrical connectors to the wiper motor. You can now make sure the wiper arms are in the parked position.

☐ STEP 14: Reconnect the wiper arms.

→ KA MODELS: The linkage operating crank locates in a slot in the motor spindle. Ford specify the use of a special tool (32-006) to check wiper blade angle but checking should only be necessary if you suspect that the wiper arm has been bent.

JOB 6: TAILGATE WIPER MOTOR - *replacement.*

☐ STEP 1: Disconnect the battery negative (-) earth/ground terminal. See *Fact File: Disconnecting the Battery* at the start of this chapter BEFORE doing so!

☐ STEP 2: Remove the wiper arm and spindle retaining nuts - see *Job 5, Step 2*.

☐ STEP 3: Carefully remove the tailgate trim panel. See *Chapter 13, Bodywork*.

☐ STEP 4: Withdraw and disconnect the multi-plug (a) and undo the earth/ground lead attachment screw (b).

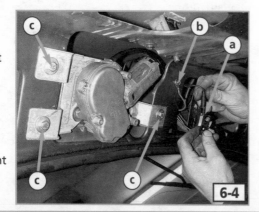

6-4

☐ STEP 5: Depending on model, undo two or three bracket attachment bolts (*6-4, items c*) and withdraw the motor from the vehicle - these are the attachment bolts on a 1990-model Escort.

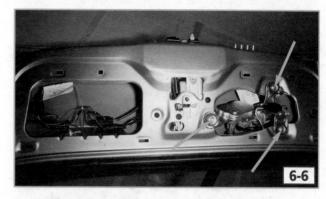

6-6

☐ STEP 6: These are the bolts on a 1999 Fiesta. Once removed, the bracket and motor can be separated by undoing the three attachment bolts - note the location of any washers, spacers and bushes.

☐ STEP 7: Refit in reverse order, making sure the motor and arm are in the parked position.

JOB 7: SCREEN AND HEADLIGHT WASHER PUMPS - *replacement.*

Depending on model, there will either be separate reservoirs for the windscreen and tailgate washers or a single reservoir.

Section A: Washer nozzles.

FRONT SCREEN WASHERS NOZZLES

☐ STEP A1: FIESTA TO 1989: Push the nozzle rearwards and lift up the front edge until it can be lifted clear, sufficient to separate the washer tube.

☐ STEP A2: ESCORT AND ORION TO 1990: Where a single jet is fitted, the nozzle is removed easily by pushing it to one side so that the locating tag is released.

☐ STEP A3: FIESTA FROM 1989, ESCORT AND ORION FROM 1990: Where fitted, remove the under bonnet insulation sufficient for access to the windscreen washer nozzles.

→ Disconnect the washer pipes and press in the washer jet retaining lugs so that you can pull the jet from the bonnet.

☐ STEP A4: KA MODELS: Remove the scuttle grille panel. As the scuttle panel is lifted away you can release the washer nozzle.

REAR SCREEN WASHERS NOZZLES

☐ STEP A5: FIESTA TO 1989: Remove the weatherstrip and headlining trim so that you can access the underside of the nozzle.

→ Pull off the washer tube, undo the retaining nut and remove the nozzle.

☐ **STEP A6: ESCORT TO 1990:** Remove the tailgate wiper motor - see *Job 6*.

→ Separate the washer nozzle from the wiper motor shaft, disconnect the supply tube and remove the nozzle.

☐ **STEP A7: FIESTA FROM 1989, ESCORT FROM 1990, KA:** On XR2i models, remove the tailgate spoiler - see *Chapter 13, Bodywork*.

→ It may be possible to lever the nozzle from the top of the tailgate - take care not to damage the paintwork.

→ Alternatively, remove the blanking plug from the centre of the tailgate upper section, press in the retaining lugs and pull the jet from the tailgate, noting the location of the seal.

HEADLIGHT WASHER NOZZLES

TOP TIP!

• Where the headlight washers are integral with the bumper over-rider (see *Chapter 13, Bodywork*) they cannot be replaced separately.

☐ **STEP A8: HEADLIGHT WASHERS NOZZLE, ORION TO 1990:** Remove the front bumper - see *Chapter 13, Bodywork*.

→ Disconnect the supply tube connector and undo the nozzle retainer screw.

→ Pull the nozzle assembly up through the bumper.

☐ **STEP A9: HEADLIGHT WASHERS NOZZLE, ESCORT AND ORION FROM 1990:** Undo the screws and remove the cover from the nozzle assembly below the headlight.

→ Pull the nozzle and mounting bracket out from under the bumper and separate the washer supply tube.

☐ **STEP A10: FIESTA PRE 1989:** There are several different fittings, depending on model and front bumper type.

→ Reach up behind the bumper and undo the screw or nut so that you can pull the nozzle assembly away from the supply tube, valve assembly or 'T' piece.

→ Alternatively you can pull the nozzle assembly away and remove the screw to free the holder.

☐ **STEP A11: FIESTA 1989 TO 1995:** Reach up behind the bumper and loosen the nut so that you can pull the nozzle assembly forward from the bumper and release the valve assembly.

☐ **STEP A12: FIESTA FROM 1995:** Carefully remove the cover so that you can free the nozzle assembly from the 'T'-connector.

Section B: washer pumps and reservoirs.

Depending on model, a front mounted reservoir will either supply the windscreen and headlight washers only or may supply the rear washer as well.

→ A front mounted washer may be located in the engine compartment or, on later vehicles, in one of the front wheel arches.

→ Where a separate rear screen washer reservoir is fitted, this is located in the luggage compartment, usually behind a trim panel.

☐ **STEP B1:** Before dismantling, disconnect the battery negative (-) earth/ground terminal. See *Fact File: Disconnecting the Battery* at the start of this chapter BEFORE doing so!

☐ **STEP B2:** Locate the washer reservoir:

→ **RESERVOIR UNDER WHEEL ARCH:** Remove the left-hand front wheel and wheelarch liner.

→ **RESERVOIR IN ENGINE BAY:** Move any adjacent components that might prevent you from reaching the retaining bolts.

☐ **STEP B3:** Drain the reservoir, if possible. This is simpler when the reservoir is mounted beneath the wheelarch.

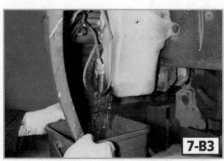
7-B3

☐ **STEP B4:** Disconnect the electrical connection/s from the washer pump.

☐ **STEP B5A: RESERVOIR UNDER WHEEL ARCH:** Remove the fixing screw (arrowed) and move the washer reservoir to one side.

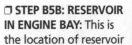

☐ **STEP B5B: RESERVOIR IN ENGINE BAY:** This is the location of reservoir and screws in a typical engine-bay location.

7-B5A

☐ **STEP B6:** Remove the tubes from the pump and remove it.

7-B5B

☐ **STEP B7: REAR MOUNTED RESERVOIRS:**

→ Before dismantling, disconnect the battery negative (-) earth/ground terminal. See *Fact File: Disconnecting the Battery* at the start of this chapter BEFORE doing so!

→ Remove the trim, as necessary, and the restraining strap or screws.

→ Disconnect as for front-mounted reservoirs.

→ **KA MODELS:** The screenwasher reservoir on the Ka is located with the windscreen wiper motor linkage - see *Job 5, Step 14*.

JOB 8: HEADLIGHT UNITS AND BULBS – *replacement, alignment.*

SAFETY FIRST!

• Read **SAFETY FIRST** at the beginning of this Chapter before starting work.

Proper headlight beam alignment requires specialist equipment.

Before starting work, read through the relevant section here. In many cases, replacing bulbs and headlight units requires dismantling and removal of other components.

Section A: Fiesta to 1995, Escort and Orion to 1990.

☐ **STEP A1:** Pull off the electrical plug (**1**) and rubber cover (**2**) from the rear of the headlight.
→ Depending on type, squeeze together the two sections of the spring clip (**3**) and remove the clip or rotate the securing clip to release the bulb (**4**).

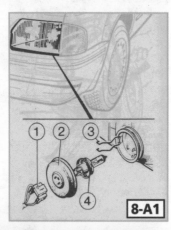

8-A1

☐ **STEP A2:** Lift out the headlight bulb, taking care not to touch the glass with bare skin.

☐ **STEP A3:** Before removing the headlight unit, first remove the sidelight bulb. See illustrations *8-A4, 8-A5 and 8-A6*.

8-A2

☐ **STEP A4: FIESTA, EXCEPT XR2 PRE-1983:** Remove the securing screw (**2**) at the top of the headlight unit and remove the headlight unit by rotating it forward and lifting up to disengage the lower locating lugs.

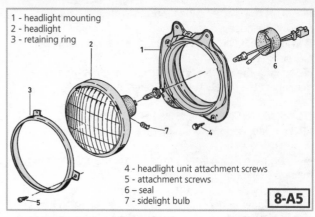

1 - headlight mounting
2 - headlight
3 - retaining ring
4 - headlight unit attachment screws
5 - attachment screws
6 – seal
7 - sidelight bulb

8-A5

☐ **STEP A5: FIESTA - XR2 PRE-1983:** A round headlight assembly is fitted to these vehicles but bulb removal is the same as for the rectangular type - see *Steps A1 and A2*. To remove the round headlight (**2**), undo the following:
→ Remove the three screws attaching the front surround to the bodywork.
→ Take out the four screws (**4**) attaching the headlight mounting (**1**).
→ Disconnect the rubber boot (**6**) and electrical multi-plug and pull the headlight unit from the vehicle.
→ If necessary, you can undo the three screws (**5**) and separate the retaining ring (**3**).

☐ **STEP A6: ESCORT AND ORION:** These are the headlight

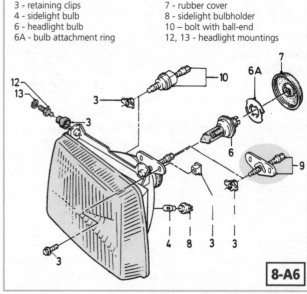

3 - retaining clips
4 - sidelight bulb
6 - headlight bulb
6A - bulb attachment ring
7 - rubber cover
8 - sidelight bulbholder
10 – bolt with ball-end
12, 13 - headlight mountings

8-A6

components.
→ Remove the radiator grille on pre-1986 models - see *Chapter 13, Bodywork.*

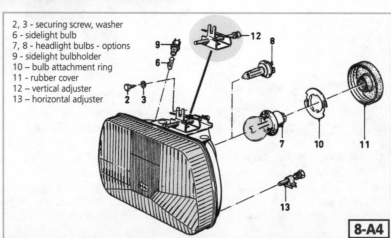

2, 3 - securing screw, washer
6 - sidelight bulb
7, 8 - headlight bulbs - options
9 - sidelight bulbholder
10 – bulb attachment ring
11 - rubber cover
12 – vertical adjuster
13 – horizontal adjuster

8-A4

☐ STEP A7:
Release the headlight mountings by rotating the side retaining clip through 90 degrees.

8-A7

☐ STEP A8:
Release the headlight from the upper adjuster fixing bolt (**A**) and pull the headlight forward from the ball stud (**C**) and remove it from the vehicle.
➜ For reference, the side fixing clip is item (**B**) and the indicator light support is item (**D**).

8-A8

☐ STEP A9: Refitting is the reverse of removal, bearing in mind the following points.
➜ The headlight beam must be checked and adjusted with beam-setting equipment.

Section B: Fiesta from 1995.

☐ STEP B1: Remove the radiator grille - see *Chapter 13, Bodywork*.

☐ STEP B2:
Remove the single attachment screw located at the top, outboard end of the headlight unit (**a**) and the two screws located at the inboard end of the headlight unit (**b**).

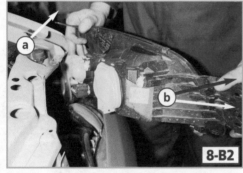

8-B2

☐ STEP B3:
Remove the headlight unit by sliding it towards the centre of the vehicle and pulling forward.

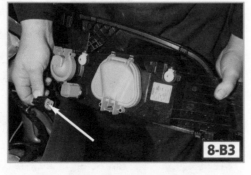

8-B3

➜ Disconnect the multi-plug (arrowed) and withdraw the headlight unit from the vehicle.

☐ STEP B4:
Release the clips (**a**) and remove the bulb covers (**b**).

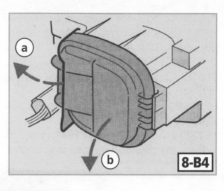

8-B4

TOP TIP!

• Separate main and dipped bulbs are fitted so make sure you identify the correct bulb.

8-B5

☐ STEP B5: Remove the electrical connector from the appropriate bulb, release the spring clip and remove the bulb – see *Section A*.
➜ If necessary, you can undo the clips (**a**) and remove the glass lens (**b**) and seal (**c**).
➜ If necessary you can now remove the headlight beam adjuster motor (**d**) if fitted. See *Section E, Step E10*.

☐ STEP B6: Refitting is the reverse of removal.

Section C: Escort and Orion, 1990 to 1996.

☐ STEP C1:
Remove the electrical connector and rubber cover from the rear of the headlight.

8-C1

STEP C2: Squeeze together the two sections of the spring clip and remove the clip to release the bulb – see *Section A, Step A1*.

STEP C3: Remove the headlight as follows, noting the difference between models:
→ **PRE-1993 MODELS:** Remove the radiator grille - see *Chapter 13, Bodywork*.
→ **XR3i MODELS, 1993 TO 1996:** Remove the four screws, release the clips and remove the support bracket above the radiator.

STEP C4: Remove the front direction indicator - see *Job 9*.

8-C5

STEP C5: Remove the sidelight, where appropriate, at the rear of the headlight unit.

STEP C6: Undo the two upper and one lower attachment screws, noting the washer arrangement.

8-C6

STEP C7: If a new headlight unit is being fitted, transfer the headlight and sidelight bulbholders to the new unit.

STEP C8: Refitting is the reverse of removal.

8-C7

Section D: Escort, from 1996.

STEP D1: See *Section C* for headlight bulb removal/replacement.

STEP D2: Remove the radiator grille and front bumper - see *Chapter 13, Bodywork*.

---

a - headlight attachment unit screws
b - headlight levelling motor
c - headlight bulb
d - sidelight bulb
e - indicator bulb and holder
f - rear cover
g - clips

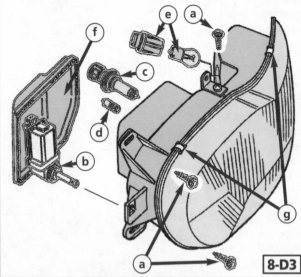

8-D3

STEP D3: To remove the unit from the vehicle:
→ Remove the three headlight unit attachment screws (a).
→ Disconnect the electrical connectors and remove the headlight unit from the vehicle.
→ If necessary, you can remove the headlight levelling motor (b).
→ The glass can be removed after removing the clips (f).

STEP D4: Refitting is the reverse of removal - have the headlight beam checked and aligned with beam-setting equipment.

Section E: Ka.

STEP E1: Release the retaining clip and remove the plastic cover from the rear of the headlight.
→ Separate main (bottom) and dipped (top) bulbs are fitted so make sure you identify the correct bulb.

STEP E2: Disconnect the electrical connector from appropriate bulb, release the spring clip and remove the bulb.

8-E1

STEP E3: Refit is the reverse of removal. Make sure the bulb is correctly fitted in the headlight unit - the locating tabs should fit in the cut-outs.

TOP TIP!

• Removing the headlight unit means releasing the bumper around the wheelarch.
• The clips used to attach the bumper are very brittle and easily broken.

☐ **STEP E4:** Release the bumper from around the wheelarch - see *Chapter 13, Bodywork*.

☐ **STEP E5:** Remove the side and centre screws attaching the bumper/grille assembly to the crossmember.

☐ **STEP E6:** Remove the headlight upper mounting bolt.
➔ You will have to carefully hold the bumper/grille attachment lug out of the way, without causing damage.

8-E6

☐ **STEP E7:** Release the front indicator bulbholder from the side of the headlight unit. Reach in through the access hole in the front crossmember and release the bulbholder by turning it anti-clockwise.

☐ **STEP E8:** Remove the lower headlight unit mounting bolt and the side mounting bolt.

8-E8

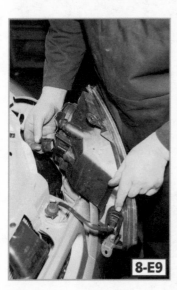

8-E9

☐ **STEP E9:** Separate the multi-plugs and carefully pull the headlight unit from the vehicle noting the location of the guide pin.

☐ **STEP E10:** If necessary you can now remove the headlight beam leveller motor by:
➔ Removing the cover from the rear of the headlight.
➔ Disconnecting the wiring connector.
➔ Twisting the control motor anti-clockwise to release it from the headlight unit.

☐ **STEP E11:** Refitting is the reversal of removal.

JOB 9: FRONT SIDELIGHTS AND INDICATOR LIGHTS – *remove, refit, bulb replacement.*

SAFETY FIRST!

• Read *SAFETY FIRST* at the beginning of this Chapter before starting work.

Section A: Front sidelights.

IMPORTANT NOTES:
• On all models, except Escort XR3i from 1990, the front sidelight is incorporated into the headlight unit so removal and refitting the bulbholder should be a very simple job. However, access on some later models is restricted.
• Where the sidelight is incorporated into the headlight - see *Job 8* for illustrations.

☐ **STEP A1: FIESTA TO 1995, ESCORT AND ORION TO 1990:** Remove the bulbholder from the rear of the headlight unit by twisting anti-clockwise.

☐ **STEP A2: FIESTA FROM 1995:** Remove the headlight and the headlight rear cover - see *Job 8, Section B*. Pull the bulbholder from the headlight assembly and the bulb from the bulbholder.

☐ **STEP A3: ESCORT (EXCEPT XR3i) AND ORION FROM 1990:** Pull the bulbholder from the headlight unit and the bulb from the bulbholder. On models from 1996, you will first have to remove the cover from the rear of the headlight.

☐ **STEP A4: ESCORT XR3i FROM 1990:** Unhook the retaining spring from the rear of the sidelight and release the sidelight by moving it forward.
➔ Twist the bulbholder and pull it free from the sidelight.
➔ You can now remove the sidelight unit from the vehicle or replace the bulb, by pressing and twisting.

☐ **STEP A5: KA** Remove the plastic cover and bulbholder from the rear of the headlight unit and pull the bulb from the holder.

Section B: Front indicators.

☐ **STEP B1: MOST EARLY MODELS:** The connections are reached from inside the engine bay, alongside the headlights.
➔ Turn the bulb socket (A) anti-clockwise and pull out.
➔ Remove the bulb (B) by pressing in, twisting and pulling out, in the normal way.

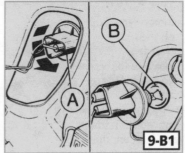

9-B1

☐ **STEP B2: SOME EARLY FIESTAS:** The lens is removed by taking out the two screws (**a**). The bulb is beneath.

➔ The unit is removed by taking out two screws (**b**).

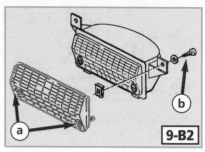

9-B2

☐ **STEP B3: LATER VEHICLES:** Release the spring retainer (**A**) from inside the engine bay, remove the light unit (**B**) from outside the car, and disconnect the bulbholder (**C**) and bulb.

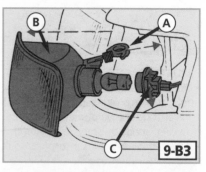

9-B3

Section C: Front Direction Indicator Repeaters.

Three types of fixing are used for the side repeater indicator lights.

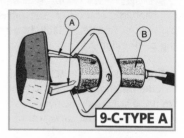

9-C-TYPE A

☐ **TYPE A:** With this type, you have to turn the complete assembly to the right-hand or left-hand side and pull it out.

➔ You may have to reach into the wheelarch and squeeze the tabs (**A**) to release the bulbholder.

➔ Disconnect the bulbholder (**B**).

☐ **TYPE B:** On later types shown here, all you do is twist the bulbholder clockwise and pull it out. Then turn the bulbholder anti-clockwise to get at the bulb.

9-C-TYPE B

☐ **TYPE C:** With this common type, you push the unit forwards or backwards (direction **a**) to release the catch (**b**).

➔ The unit is removed from the vehicle far enough to unclip the bulbholder (**c**) and remove the bulb.

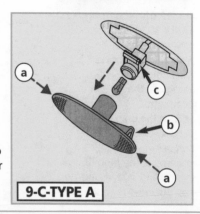

9-C-TYPE A

JOB 10: FRONT AUXILIARY LIGHTS – *remove, replace.*

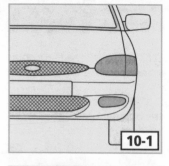

10-1

☐ **STEP 1:** Latest cars have front fog lights mounted within the bumper.

☐ **STEP 2:** To replace the bulb, remove the rubber cap from behind the bumper, push the clip outwards, pull out the bulb and disconnect it from the cable.

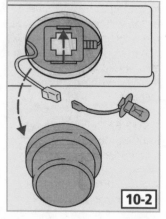

10-2

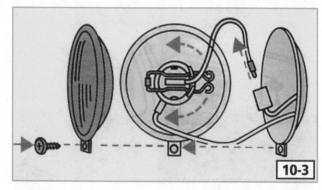

10-3

☐ **STEP 3:** Where separate Ford driving lights are fitted, you loosen the screw to remove the lens reflector unit, then unplug the wiring connector.

➔ Release both sides of the spring clip to release the bulb.

JOB 11: REAR LIGHTS, NUMBER PLATE LIGHTS AND HIGH LEVEL BRAKE LIGHTS – *removal, refitting, bulb replacement.*

SAFETY FIRST!

• Read *SAFETY FIRST* at the beginning of this Chapter before starting work.

Check each of the rear lights in turn. In most cases, tail light, indicator, reversing light and fog light bulbs are grouped together within the same bulbholder, except where shown in the following.

ESCORT HATCHBACK AND KA

On all hatchback models the light cluster is reached from inside the luggage compartment.

❏ **STEP 1: EARLIER MODELS:** The bulbholder can be released by pushing in the plastic catch at the inner edge.
→ To replace the bulbholder, feed the tab at the outer end into its

socket and push the inner end firmly into position.

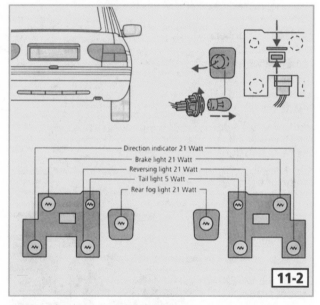

❏ **STEP 2: LATER MODELS:** Squeeze-in the locking tabs (arrowed), remove the entire bulbholder and you can then replace whichever bulb is required.

❏ **STEP 3: LATER MODEL FOG LIGHTS:** On these models, the fog lights are in the tailgate. Remove the cover and turn the bulbholder anti-clockwise to remove it, which gives you access to the bulb.

ORION AND ESCORT SALOON MODELS

❏ **STEP 4:** As with most other models, the entire bulbholder assembly is removed to give access to the bulbs.

→ Unlike later hatchbacks, there are no separate fog lights in the luggage bay lid.

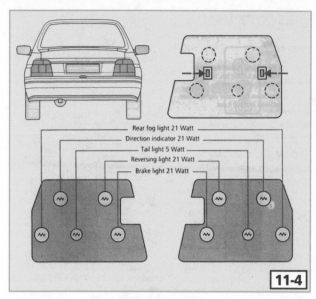

→ Press in the locking tabs (arrowed) to release the assembly and give access to the bulbs.

ESTATE MODELS

❏ **STEP 5: EARLIER ESTATE MODELS:** First remove the fibreboard cover by turning the four plastic screws a quarter of a turn with a broad bladed screwdriver or coin.
→ The bulbholder (3) is now exposed.
→ It is lifted out, complete with all the bulbs, after releasing two plastic tabs, one at the top (1) and the other at the bottom (2).
→ To replace it, feed the bulbs into their apertures and push the bulbholder firmly home.

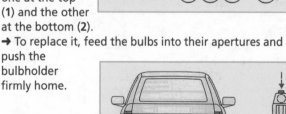

4 – stop/tail light bulb (12 volt, 21/5 watt)
5 – tail light bulb (12 volt, 5 watt)
6 – indicator bulb (12 volt, 21 watt)
7 – reversing light bulb (12 volt, 21 watt)
8 – rear fog light bulb (12 volt, 21 watt)

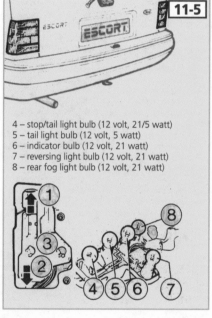

❏ **STEP 6: LATER ESTATE MODELS:** The rear cover just pulls off. A single locking tab (arrowed) releases the bulbholder once you have pressed it down.

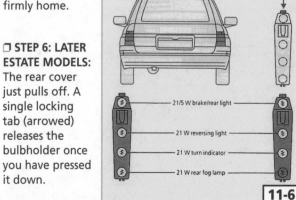

ESCORT VAN

☐ **STEP 7:** All of the vans' rear lights are set vertically, each side of the door.

➜ There is no cover inside the load area, and each bulbholder can be lifted out by turning it anti-clockwise, giving access to each separate bulb in turn.

➜ This is the bulb layout on the early models...

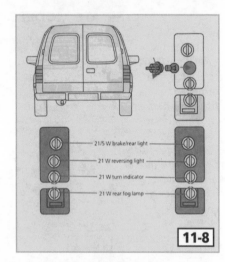

1 – indicator bulb (12 volt, 21 watt)
2 – stop/tail light bulb (12 volt, 21/5 watt)
3 – reversing light bulb (12 volt, 21 watt)
4 – rear fog light bulb (12 volt, 21 watt)

11-7

☐ **STEP 8:** ...and this is how they appear on later vans.

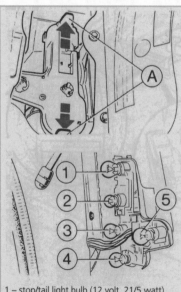

21/5 W brake/rear light
21 W reversing light
21 W turn indicator
21 W rear fog lamp

11-8

CABRIOLETS

☐ **STEP 9:** These models have a push-on trim cover over the light clusters.

➜ After removing the cover, push the retaining tabs (A) apart and lift out the bulbholder.

➜ To replace it, feed the bulbs into their apertures and push the holder firmly home.

1 – stop/tail light bulb (12 volt, 21/5 watt)
2 – tail light bulb (12 volt, 5 watt)
3 – indicator bulb (12 volt, 21 watt)
4 – rear fog light bulb (12 volt, 21 watt)
5 – reversing light bulb (12 volt, 21 watt)

11-9

FIESTA

☐ **STEP 10: SOME EARLY MODELS:** After removing the trim side panel, you can pull each bulbholder out individually to replace the bulb.

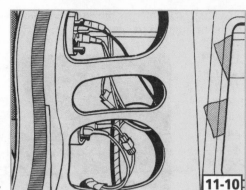

11-10

☐ **STEP 11: OTHER EARLY MODELS:** To get to the bulbs on some models, first remove a fibreboard cover by undoing a screw (A) with a broad bladed screwdriver.

➜ The bulbholder, complete with all the bulbs, lifts out after releasing a plastic tab (B). In our illustration, **1** is the stop/tail, **2** is the reversing light and **3** is the indicator light.

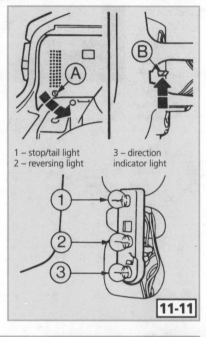

1 – stop/tail light
2 – reversing light
3 – direction indicator light

11-11

☐ **STEP 12: LATER MODELS:** The bulbholder unit is removed from inside the luggage compartment by pressing together two plastic tabs.

11-12

COURIER VANS

☐ **STEP 13:** On Courier vans, the complete light unit lifts out from outside the vehicle after undoing two plastic screws inside the load compartment. Then the backplate can be separated from the lens and individual bulbs changed as necessary.

REAR FOG LIGHTS

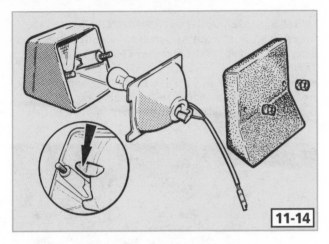

11-14

☐ **STEP 14:** Access to rear fog lights on all vehicles, where fitted, is by undoing two nuts inside the luggage compartment and lifting the light away from under the rear bumper.
➔ The reflector and bulbholder lift out after depressing two tabs (arrowed).

NUMBER PLATE LIGHT

11-15

☐ **STEP 15:** On all passenger models the number plate light is a push fit in the rear bumper. You may have to use a screwdriver to lever it out.
➔ After lifting out the number plate light you get to the bulb by releasing two catches (pushing them outwards) one catch each side of the light.

☐ **STEP 16:** The van number plate light is removed by prising out carefully with a screwdriver. Turn the bulb socket anti-clockwise to remove the bulb.

11-16

HIGH LEVEL BRAKE LIGHTS

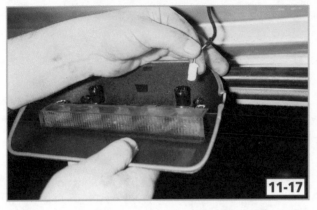

11-17

☐ **STEP 17:** Remove the screws and disconnect the electrical connection as you remove the complete light unit.

11-18

☐ **STEP 18:** Ease the housing outwards to unclip the bulbholder and remove the reflector.

11-19

☐ **STEP 19:** The bulbs are a push fit. Refit is the reverse of removal.

JOB 12: INTERIOR LIGHTS.

SAFETY FIRST!

• Read *SAFETY FIRST* at the beginning of this Chapter before starting work.

IMPORTANT NOTE: There are many different styles of interior light unit. The examples illustrated here can be used as guides to the other types.

12-1

☐ **STEP 1: COURTESY LIGHTS:** For access to the bulb, carefully lever the lens away from the roof panel (most models) or light unit.
➜ Look out for the recess (arrowed) in the light unit.
➜ If necessary, you can disconnect the electrical cables and remove the light unit.

TOP TIP!

• On most models, where the switch is at one side, you should lever at the opposite end to the switch.

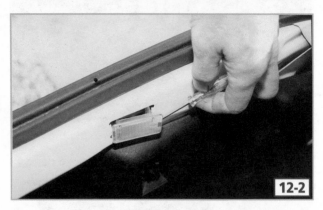

12-2

☐ **STEP 2: LUGGAGE COMPARTMENT LIGHTS:** For access to the bulb and light unit, carefully lever the lens/light unit away from the trim panel.

☐ **STEP 3: GLOVEBOX LIGHT:** It should be possible to pull the bulb from the bulbholder.
➜ If this is difficult, press the bulbholder from the latch unit so that you have better access to remove the bulb.

☐ **STEP 4: INSTRUMENT PANEL LIGHTS:** Remove the instrument panel sufficient to gain access to the rear face - see *Job 4*.
➜ The bulbholders are removed

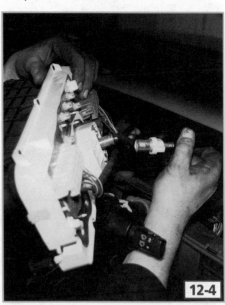

12-4

by twisting and pulling free - the bulbs are a push fit in the holders.

☐ **STEP 5: HEATER CONTROL PANEL LIGHTS:** Remove the heater controls and control panels sufficiently to gain access to the bulbs at the rear - see *Chapter 14, Interior, Trim*.
➜ The bulbholders are removed by twisting and pulling free - depending on model, the bulbs are a push fit in the holder or integral with the bulbholders.

12-6

☐ **STEP 6: INSTRUMENT LIGHTS:** Where instruments are fitted to the dashboard, as with the clock shown here, you generally have to lever the instrument out so that you can gain access to change the bulb.
➜ Take care to avoid damage to the dashboard and instrument!

JOB 13: CHECK/CHANGE FUSES.

Fuses are colour coded: Red for 10 amp, blue for 15 amp, yellow for 20 amp, neutral or clear for 25 amp and green for 30 amp. A blown fuse is clearly identified by a break in the wire.

13-TYPE A

☐ **TYPE A:** On early vehicles, the main fuse box is located on the bulkhead/ firewall.

☐ **TYPE B:** On later vehicles, the fuse and relay box is on the right of the instrument panel, under the steering wheel.
➜ Pull off the cover and use the fuse grip fitted to the inside of the cover to remove a broken fuse.

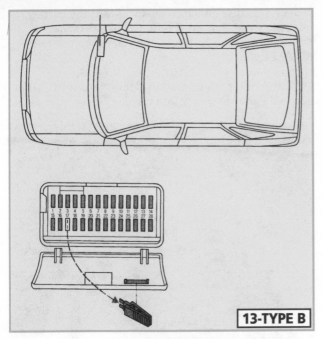

13-TYPE B

→ The fuses are numbered and the circuits protected by each fuse are indicated by international symbols on the fuse box cover. They are also given in the owner's handbook.

→ IMPORTANT NOTE: The numbers allocated by Ford to each circuit may differ from model to model and also change with the age of the car. Make sure you identify the correct fuse for the circuit which has failed.

→ Some circuits, such as the radio, may have a separate line fuse in the wiring to them.

SAFETY FIRST!

• Make sure that the ignition and all the electrical circuits are switched off before removing or replacing a fuse. NEVER try to 'cure' a fault by fitting a fuse with a higher amperage rating then the one specified.

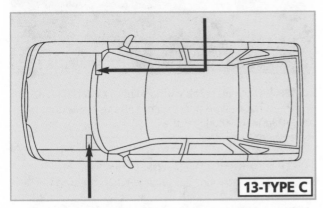

13-TYPE C

❏ **TYPE C:** Some models have a second auxiliary fuse box on the opposite side of the car next to the battery. This contains six 'box' fuses labelled A, B, C, D, E and F. Fuses D, E and F, all 50 amp, protect the engine cooling fan, heated windscreen and diesel engine glow plugs respectively. These can be replaced without removing the fuse box.

→ Fuses A, B and C, 80 amp, 60 amp, and 60 amp respectively, are in the supply lines to the main fuse box. Before these can be removed, the battery has to be

---

disconnected and the box has to be removed from the bulkhead.

→ If a whole group of circuits in the main fuse box does not work, it may be that one of the feed line fuses has failed but these rarely fail unless there is a short circuit. If this happens, you should disconnect the battery and you may need to seek specialist advice from a qualified auto. electrician or your Ford dealer.

JOB 14: ELECTRIC WINDOW MOTORS - *replacement.*

See **Chapter 13, Bodywork** and **Chapter 14, Interior**.

JOB 15: INDICATOR AND STEERING COLUMN SWITCHES - *remove/refit.*

SAFETY FIRST!

• On vehicles equipped with air bags, refer to the safety instructions in **Chapter 11, Steering, Suspension** before removing the steering wheel.

15-1

❏ **STEP 1:** Before dismantling, disconnect the battery negative (-) earth/ground terminal. See **Fact File: Disconnecting the Battery** at the start of this chapter BEFORE doing so!

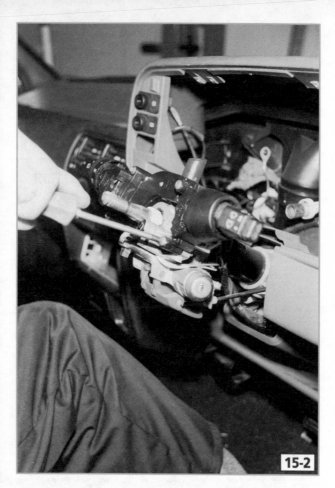

15-2

❏ **STEP 2:** Remove the steering wheel and steering column shrouds - see *Chapter 11, Steering, Suspension*.

❏ **STEP 3:** Undo the attachment screws (indicated by the screwdriver) and lift the switch unit away.

❏ **STEP 4:** Disconnect the electrical connections.

❏ **STEP 5:** Refit is the reverse of removal.

JOB 16: RADIO - *remove/refit.*

The removal of the radio is a standard procedure in most cars using DIN removal tools. The chief variations include:
→ Differing wiring plugs.
→ Other switches or lights integral to the radio panel.
→ Some vehicles may require partial dismantling of the dash or removal of masking covers to access retaining screws or nuts.
→ Older radios may require the removal of the control knobs to access the nuts beneath.

❏ **STEP 1:** Before dismantling, disconnect the battery negative (-) earth/ground terminal. See *Fact File: Disconnecting the Battery* at the start of this chapter BEFORE doing so!

❏ **STEP 2:** Insert the DIN removal tools into the holes on each side until they click into place.

16-3

❏ **STEP 3:** Having released the locks, gently pull the radio from the fascia.

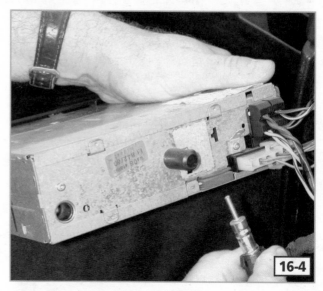

16-4

❏ **STEP 4:** Disconnect the wiring plugs and aerial lead.
→ Where the radio is part of a bigger panel disconnect any other leads and label them.
→ Remove the unit.

❏ **STEP 5:** Refitting is the reversal of removal.
→ Ensure the securing clips engage when the unit is pushed home.
→ Reconnect the battery and enter the security code if applicable.

CHAPTER 11: STEERING, SUSPENSION

*PLEASE READ **CHAPTER 2 SAFETY FIRST** BEFORE CARRYING OUT ANY WORK ON YOUR CAR.*

CONTENTS

Part A: Steering and Suspension

JOB 1:   SYSTEMS EXPLAINED.

STEERING

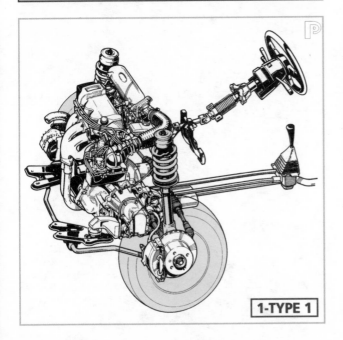

❏ **TYPE 1: ESCORT AND ORION MODELS PRE-1990:** This is the front suspension, steering and drive train set up on these models.

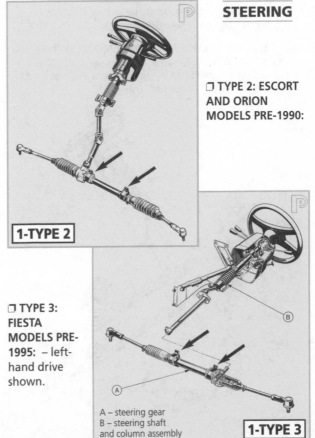

❏ **TYPE 2: ESCORT AND ORION MODELS PRE-1990:**

1-TYPE 2

❏ **TYPE 3: FIESTA MODELS PRE-1995:** – left-hand drive shown.

A – steering gear
B – steering shaft and column assembly

1-TYPE 3

1-TYPE 1

REAR SUSPENSION

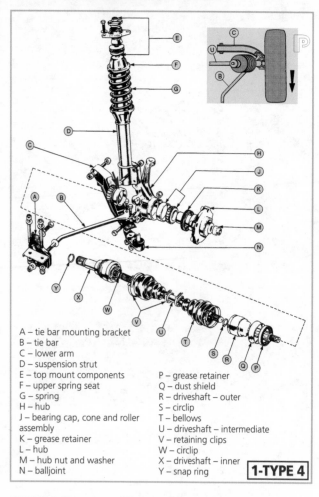

A – tie bar mounting bracket
B – tie bar
C – lower arm
D – suspension strut
E – top mount components
F – upper spring seat
G – spring
H – hub
J – bearing cap, cone and roller assembly
K – grease retainer
L – hub
M – hub nut and washer
N – balljoint

P – grease retainer
Q – dust shield
R – driveshaft – outer
S – circlip
T – bellows
U – driveshaft – intermediate
V – retaining clips
W – circlip
X – driveshaft – inner
Y – snap ring

1-TYPE 4

❒ **TYPE 4:** The general layout of the earlier Fiesta suspension is shown in the inset.

❒ **TYPE 5: EARLY ESCORT AND ORION MODELS:** The early Escort and Orion models had a front suspension system similar to that of the Fiesta in that there is a lower arm (**a**) with a single inboard mounting (**b**).

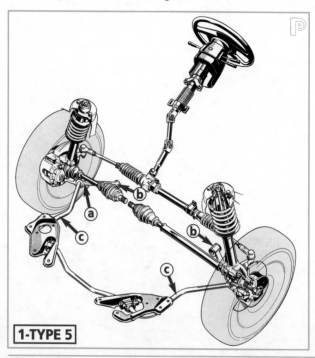

1-TYPE 5

➙ The arm is prevented from having excessive backwards and forwards movement by an anti-roll bar (**c**).

a – wishbone
b – wishbone mounting panel
c – front wishbone mounting
d – rear wishbone mounting
e – driveshaft
f – strut

g – steering rack (lhd shown)

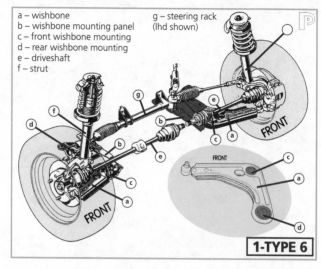

1-TYPE 6

❒ **TYPE 6: FIESTAS 1989-ON AND KA MODELS:** Fiestas from 1989-on and Ka models have a 'proper' wishbone (**a**).
➙ The Fiesta type (main illustration) has a horizontal mounting pin through the rear wishbone mount.
➙ Ka models (see inset) have vertical mountings for both front and rear wishbone mounts.
➙ For models with anti-roll bar - see illustration *1-Type 9*.

❒ **TYPE 7: ESCORT MODELS 1990-ON:**

a – wishbone
b – strut
c – subframe
d – front wishbone mounting
e – rear wishbone mounting
f – anti-roll bar

❒ **TYPE 8: FIESTA MODELS 1996-ON:**

1-TYPE 7

a – subframe
b – wishbone
c – wishbone front mount
d – wishbone rear mount

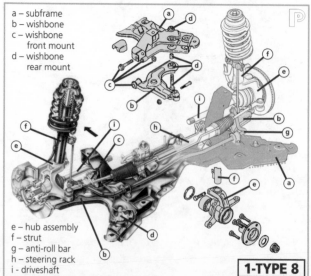

e – hub assembly
f – strut
g – anti-roll bar
h – steering rack
i - driveshaft

1-TYPE 8

REAR SUSPENSION

❒ **TYPE 9: KA MODELS:**
➜ This illustration includes the anti-roll bar not shown in illustration *1-Type 6*.

1-TYPE 9

❒ **TYPE 10: FIESTA MODELS UP TO 1989:**

A – trailing arms
B – spring insulator pads
C – shock absorbers
D – anti-roll bar (where fitted)
E – springs
F – bump rubbers
G – axle
H – panhard rod
I – parking brake cable
J – integral hub and brake drum

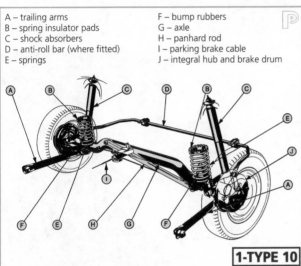

1-TYPE 10

❒ **TYPE 11: ESCORT AND ORION MODELS UP TO 1990:**
These models also have coil springs (**a**) mounted separately from the shock absorbers (**b**).
➜ A pair of trailing arms (**c**) locates the outer ends of the wishbones (**d**).
➜ When a rear anti-roll bar (**f**) is fitted, it is connected to the wishbones via link arms (**e**).

1-TYPE 11

❒ **TYPE 12: ESCORT AND ORION MODELS UP TO 1990:**
➜ **VEHICLES BUILT BEFORE MAY 1983:** The lower arm fixing point (**Y**) is lowered by 25 mm. The tie bar fixing point (**X**) is raised by 30 mm.

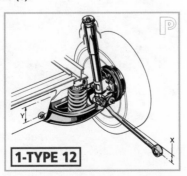

1-TYPE 12

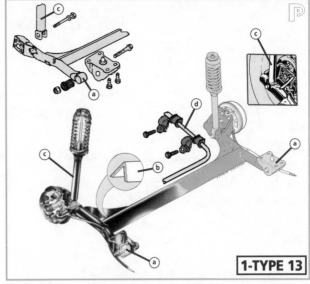

1-TYPE 13

❒ **TYPE 13: FIESTA FROM 1989, ESCORT FROM 1990, KA MODELS:** All use the same type of 'twist beam (**b**) axle' rear suspension.
➜ On later versions, an anti-roll bar (**d**) became available, clamped to the trailing arm, as shown.
➜ All versions have the front end of the trailing arm (**a**) attached to the vehicle's body.
➜ The strut (**c**) is bolted to the trailing arm, although there are detail differences.

❒ **TYPE 14: ESCORT VAN:** This is the rear suspension for Escort Van with leaf spring suspension.

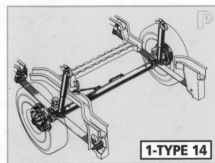

1-TYPE 14

❒ **TYPE 15: ESCORT ESTATE AND VAN:** The coil spring and shock absorber are mounted separately.

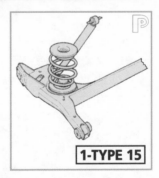

1-TYPE 15

❒ **TYPE 16: FIESTA VAN AND COURIER:** These models are fitted with this unique torsion bar suspension.

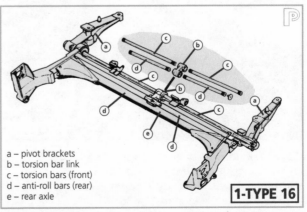

a – pivot brackets
b – torsion bar link
c – torsion bars (front)
d – anti-roll bars (rear)
e – rear axle

1-TYPE 16

Part B: Steering
Inspection, Removal, Replacement

CONTENTS

JOB 1: TRACK ROD ENDS (TREs) - *inspection.*

❐ **STEP 1:** If there is any movement between the track rod end and the steering arm, the track rod end should be replaced - see *Job 2*.

❐ **STEP 2:** Straighten the split pin (arrowed) then extract with a pair of pliers. You can now loosen the retaining nut.

JOB 2: TRACK ROD ENDS (TREs) - *replacement.*

❐ **STEP 1:** Before disconnecting the TRE at the balljoint, loosen the locknut by one complete turn.
➜ Use an adjustable wrench to grip the trackrod (arrowed) while the locknut is undone.

TOP TIP!

• On some versions, Ford use a split pin to prevent the retaining nut working loose, but some track rod ends may use a Nyloc type nut as an alternative.
• Once undone, a Nyloc nut should be discarded and a new Nyloc nut used.
• On Fiesta models manufactured from 1989, the end of the balljoint pin has an Allen key socket which can be used to prevent the ball joint rotating.

❐ **STEP 3:** Use a ball joint separator to release the tapered section of the ball joint from the steering arm.

STEP 4: Undo the nut, if it is still fitted, and remove the track rod end from the steering arm.

STEP 5: Unscrew the track rod end from the track rod. Make a note of the number of turns it takes to unscrew.

STEP 6: Screw the new track rod end onto the track rod the same number of turns it took to unscrew the old track rod.

STEP 7: Fit the tapered section of the track rod end into the steering arm and tighten the ball joint nut to the correct torque.

STEP 8: Tighten the locknut against the track rod end.

STEP 9: Have the steering alignment adjusted with tracking equipment.

JOB 3: STEERING RACK GAITERS - *inspection.*

STEP 1: If the gaiter is split, holed or showing any signs of imminent failure - such as cracks, it should be replaced - see *Job 4*.

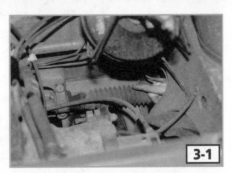

JOB 4: STEERING RACK GAITERS - *replacement.*

STEP 1: Remove the track rod end and lock nut - see *Job 2*.

STEP 2: Undo the clips at each end of the gaiter, and slide the gaiter off the steering rack and track rod.

STEP 3: FIESTA TO 1989, ESCORT AND ORION TO 1990 and all others with oil in the rack: If the rack contains grease, the lubricant should not need replacing.
→ You should expel old oil from the steering rack (when used) and refill with new fluid.
→ The old lubricant should be expelled from the pinion-end of the rack. So, if you are only replacing the gaiter on the left-hand side, you will need to remove and peel back the gaiter from the pinion-side.
→ Slowly turn the steering wheel from side to side until no more lubricant is expelled.

STEP 4: Wipe clean and apply a very light smear of grease to the gaiter seating areas on the rack and track rod. Slide on the gaiter and make sure it seats correctly.
→ If the gaiter is twisted, parts of it will collapse (arrowed).
→ Lighten one end of each gaiter.

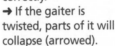

STEP 5: Replace oil in the rack, as necessary, through the open end of the gaiter.

STEP 6: Refit the track rod ends.

JOB 5: NON-POWER STEERING RACK - *removal, replacement.*

See *Part A* for exploded drawings relevant to this Job.
→ Access is obviously more difficult when – as is usual – you have to work around the back of the engine!
Before dismantling, disconnect the battery negative (-) earth/ground terminal. See *Chapter 10, Electrical, Dash, Instruments, Fact File: Disconnecting the Battery* BEFORE doing so!

STEP 1: Disconnect the track rod ends from the steering arms - see *Job 2*.

STEP 2A: Unscrew and remove the steering column to pinion clamp bolt (arrowed).
→ On Escort/Orion models from

1990 and Fiesta models from 1995, the steering column pinch bolt is at the base of the steering column, in the driver's footwell.

☐ **STEP 2B:** On all other models covered by this manual, access to this bolt is reached via the engine compartment (shown with the engine removed).

5-2B

TOP TIP!

ESCORT AND ORION - FROM 1990
• Complete removal of the subframe should not be necessary. If the subframe is carefully lowered you should have sufficient access to separate the rack from the subframe.

☐ **STEP 3: ESCORT AND ORION - FROM 1990:** Prepare to lower the front subframe. See *Part C, Job 8, Steps 1 to 9*.

☐ **STEP 4: FIESTA - 1989 TO 1995:** Remove the one piece undertray and, on XR2i models, the front suspension crossmember - see *Part C*.

FIESTA - FROM 1995
→ On Fiesta models from 1995, Ford specify the use of special tools (15-097) to align the crossmember. Have the work carried out by an approved Ford dealer.

☐ **STEP 5: FIESTA - FROM 1995:** Lower the front suspension crossmember, see (*Part C*), bearing in mind the following points.
→ It is only necessary to lower the front suspension crossmember sufficiently to allow removal of the steering rack.
→ There is no need to disconnect the anti-roll bar link on the suspension struts or the hub carriers from the lower suspension arm ball joints.

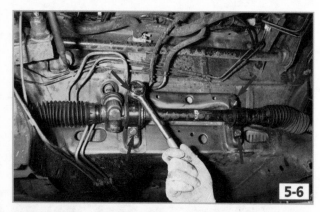

5-6

☐ **STEP 6: ALL MODELS - PRE 1990:** Knock back the locking tabs (arrowed) on the four steering rack securing bolts. Unscrew and remove the bolts and the two U-shaped clamp brackets.

☐ **STEP 7: ALL MODELS - POST 1990:** Unscrew and remove the two steering rack securing bolts.

☐ **STEP 8:** Separate the pinion from the steering column.

☐ **STEP 9A:** Withdraw the steering rack from the side of the vehicle.
→ Generally - but not always - it is easier to remove the steering rack from the right-hand side.

5-8

5-9A

5-9B

☐ **STEP 9B: ESCORT DIESEL FROM 1990:** It is possible to remove the rack from the engine compartment.

☐ **STEP 10:** Before refitting the steering rack, make sure the rack, wheels and steering wheel are all in the straight ahead position.
→ You can check the rack position by measuring the distance between the ends of the track rods and the steering rack body - the rack is in the straight ahead position when these distances are equal.

☐ **STEP 11:** Refitting the steering rack is the reversal of the removal process, bearing in mind the following points.
→ On racks with U-shaped brackets you should use new lock tabs when refitting.
→ Tighten all bolts to the specified torque.
→ Have the steering alignment checked and set as soon as possible.

JOB 6: POWER STEERING RACK -
removal, replacement.

See *Part A* for exploded drawings relevant to this Job.

Before dismantling, disconnect the battery negative (-) earth/ground terminal. See *Chapter 10, Electrical, Dash, Instruments, Fact File: Disconnecting the Battery* BEFORE doing so!

Section A: Applies to all types.

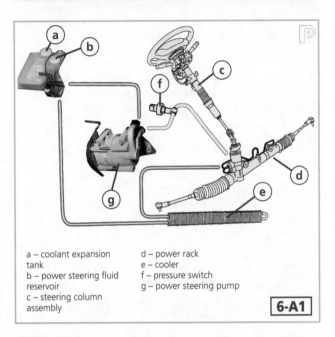

a – coolant expansion tank
b – power steering fluid reservoir
c – steering column assembly
d – power rack
e – cooler
f – pressure switch
g – power steering pump

6-A1

☐ **STEP A1:** These are typical power steering components.
→ You will need to start by draining the power steering fluid.
→ Clamp the fluid supply pipe from the reservoir.
→ Disconnect the pipework from its lowest point and drain the fluid into a container.

Section B: Fiesta from 1995.

IMPORTANT NOTE:
On Fiesta models from 1995, Ford specify the use of special tools (15-097) to align the crossmember. Have the work carried out by an approved Ford dealer.

☐ **STEP B1:** Lower the crossmember far enough to allow access to the power steering pipe connections on the steering rack.

☐ **STEP B2:** Undo the unions and release the power steering fluid pipes from the rack.

☐ **STEP B3:** Separate the power steering rack from the crossmember - see *Job 5*.

Section C: Ka.

☐ **STEP C1:** On the left-hand side of the engine compartment, disconnect the union (arrowed) in the hydraulic fluid pressure line.

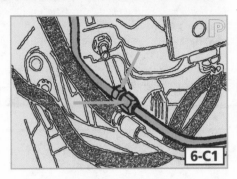

6-C1

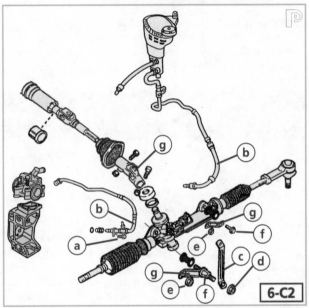

6-C2

☐ **STEP C2:** Note the location of the hydraulic pipes at the steering rack.
→ Remove the screw (**a**) and release the hydraulic pipes (**b**) from the inside of the engine bay.
→ Unscrew the hydraulic pipe unions.

☐ **STEP C3:** Disconnect the anti-roll bar. See illustrations in *Part A*.

☐ **STEP C4:** On the drivers side of the vehicle, unscrew – but DO NOT fully remove - the rearmost bolt from the lower suspension arm mounting bracket.

☐ **STEP C5:** Now follow the Step in connection with illustration *6-C2*.
→ If the vehicle has a brake servo support stay (**c**) fitted adjacent to the steering rack, unscrew the nut (**d**) from the steering rack mounting bolt and move the stay away from the steering rack.
→ Remove the upper steering rack support bracket nuts (**e**) and the two bolts (**f**) attaching the brackets (**g**) to the steering rack and swing the brackets out of the way.
→ Detach the steering rack – there are hooks on the back of the rack.
→ Make sure the steering column to pinion clamp (**g**) is disengaged.
→ Withdraw the steering rack from the drivers side of the vehicle.

Section D: Refit – all types.

❒ **STEP D1:** Refitting the steering rack is the reversal of the removal process.
➝ Where Nyloc type nuts are used, fit new nuts.
➝ Use new 'O'-ring seals where appropriate.
➝ Refill and bleed the hydraulic system - see *Job 7*.
➝ Check the steering alignment before using the vehicle on the road.

JOB 7:   POWER STEERING SYSTEM – *bleeding.*

The steering hydraulic system is, to a certain extent, self bleeding. Topping up the reservoir and operating the steering will generally purge the system of air. If this method does not remove all air, you will have to use a vacuum pump.

Section A: Normal bleeding.

❒ **STEP A1:** Raise the front of the vehicle so that the wheels are clear of the ground.

❒ **STEP A2:** Check the level of the fluid in the power steering reservoir and top up to the maximum mark.

❒ **STEP A3:** Turn the steering smoothly from side to side several times and check the level in the reservoir, topping up if necessary.
➝ Do not be over enthusiastic as turning the steering too rapidly from side to side can raise the pressure in the rack, causing damage to the gaiters.

❒ **STEP A4:** Start the engine and, with the engine at idling speed, slowly turn the steering several times from one lock to the other.
➝ Do not hold the steering at full lock for more than 15 seconds.

❒ **STEP A5:** Check the fluid in the reservoir and repeat *Steps A2 to A4* if there are signs of air bubbles.
➝ See *Section B* if, after several attempts at normal bleeding, there is still air in the system.

❒ **STEP A6:** Top up the reservoir, if necessary, and lower the front of the vehicle.

Section B: Vacuum bleeding.

TOP TIP!

• During the bleeding process, the initial vacuum will decrease, so check regularly to make sure that the correct level is maintained.
• A very rapid decrease in vacuum, more than 0.07 bar in 5 minutes, indicates a leak in the system. Check and rectify the leak before continuing.

❒ **STEP B1:** Raise the front of the vehicle so that the front wheels are clear of the ground.

❒ **STEP B2:** Remove the reservoir filler cap and fit an adapter (Ford Part No. 15-097) to the reservoir. Connect a suitable vacuum pump to the adapter.

❒ **STEP B3:** Start the engine and, with the engine at idling speed, turn the steering until it is just short of full right-lock.

❒ **STEP B4:** Stop the engine and apply a vacuum of 0.51 bar. Maintain the vacuum while the air is purged from the system - this will take longer than 5 minutes.

❒ **STEP B5:** Release the vacuum and repeat *Steps B3 and B4* but this time with the steering just short of full left-lock.

❒ **STEP B6:** Release the vacuum, remove the adapter, top up the fluid level and refit the reservoir filler cap.

❒ **STEP B7:** Start the engine and turn the steering from one lock to the other. If there are still signs of air in the system, such as excessive noise, repeat the bleeding process.

❒ **STEP B8:** Top up the reservoir, if necessary, and lower the front of the vehicle.

❒ **STEP B9:** If, after repeating the vacuum bleeding process there is still evidence of air in the system, try leaving the vehicle for at least 12 hours and then repeating the bleeding process.

JOB 8:   POWER STEERING PUMP - *removal, replacement.*

Section A: Pump removal and replacement – all models

❒ **STEP A1:** Before dismantling, disconnect the battery negative (-) earth/ground terminal. See *Chapter 10, Electrical, Dash, Instruments, Fact File: Disconnecting the Battery* BEFORE doing so!

❒ **STEP A2:** Start by draining the power steering fluid. See *Job 6, Step A1*

❒ **STEP A3:** Remove the power steering pump drivebelt (arrowed) – see *Chapter 6, Engine.*

8-A3

☐ **STEP A4:** Remove the three or four bolts holding the pump to the engine and remove it.
→ On some models it is simpler to unbolt the bracket from the engine, take off the pump and bracket together and then remove the bracket from the pump when off the vehicle.

☐ **STEP A5:** If the pump is being replaced, you will have to remove the pulley from the pump using a suitable puller.

REFITTING THE PUMP

Bear in mind the following points:
→ On some versions, the pulley must be pressed on to the pump shaft before the mounting bracket is attached. It needs to be pressed on until it is flush with the end of the shaft. In other cases, the bracket is attached first.
→ The pulley can usually be pressed on to the shaft using a suitable bolt, nut and washer in place of the Ford special tool Part No. 21-192.
→ Always fit new high pressure pipe 'O'-rings.

Section B: Notes relevant to specific models.

FIESTA WITH ENDURA E ENGINE

You will need to remove the upper grille panel – see *Chapter 13, Bodywork* – and the right-hand headlight – see *Chapter 10, Electrical, Instruments*.

ESCORT AND ORION WITH ZETEC ENGINE

PUMP PULLEY: To remove the pulley, hold the steering pump shaft with a 9 mm Allen key while the three pulley retaining bolts are removed.

FIESTA WITH ENDURA DE ENGINE, WITH AIR CONDITIONING

You will have to remove the following components:
→ The power steering fluid reservoir.
→ The right-hand headlight.
→ The high pressure pipe support bracket.

REFITTING: When refitting the pump to the engine, the front bolts should be tightened first.

VEHICLES WITH ZETEC SE ENGINE

You will have to remove the following items:
→ The exhaust manifold heat shield.
→ The drivebelt tensioner bolt – see *Chapter 6, Engine*.
→ The coolant tank attachments and unclip the coolant pipe from the throttle cable so that the coolant expansion tank can be moved out of the way.

KA MODELS

You will have to remove the following:
→ The right-hand bumper/wheel arch trim.
→ The right-hand headlight.

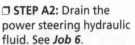

JOB 9: POWER STEERING HYDRAULIC FLUID COOLER - *removal, replacement.*

Many models fitted with power assisted steering have a cooler consisting of plain or finned pipes fitted alongside the radiator.

Section A: All types.

☐ **STEP A1:** Before dismantling, disconnect the battery negative (-) earth/ground terminal. See *Chapter 10, Electrical, Dash, Instruments, Fact File: Disconnecting the Battery* BEFORE doing so!

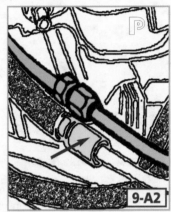

☐ **STEP A2:** Drain the power steering hydraulic fluid. See *Job 6*.
→ Separating the quick-release type of unions (arrow) can be difficult and Ford specify a special tool (Part No. 17-049).

9-A2

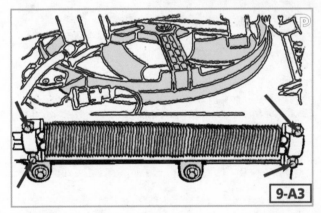

9-A3

☐ **STEP A3:** The cooler is held to the side of the radiator with clamps and bolts (arrowed).

☐ **STEP A4:** Refitting the cooler is the reverse of the removal process.
→ Use new O-ring seals where appropriate.
→ Bleed the steering hydraulic system – see *Job 7*.

Section B: Specific information.

Read and follow the specific information that relates to the vehicle that you are working on.

FIESTA MODELS

Where fitted, remove the shield from under the radiator and engine.

FIESTA TO 1995

Remove and/or disconnect the following:
→ The front bumper and bonnet lock assembly – see *Chapter 13, Bodywork*.
→ Remove the two bolts and separate the bonnet lock stay from the cooler - support the bonnet separately.

KA MODELS

Remove and/or disconnect the following components:
→ The right-hand headlight unit.
→ Release the drivebelt from the pulley and remove the power steering pump pulley. See *Job 8*.

JOB 10: POWER STEERING HYDRAULIC FLUID PRESSURE SWITCH - *removal, replacement.*

FACT FILE
SWITCH FUNCTIONS

• **FIESTA MODELS FROM 1995 AND KA:** When the engine is at idle speed, turning the steering wheel causes the engine to slow down. The pressure switch sends a signal to the ECU which increases engine speed.

• **ESCORT:** The pressure sensing switch sends a signal which reduces engine speed when the pressure is too high.

❑ **STEP 1:** Before dismantling, disconnect the battery negative (-) earth/ground terminal. See *Chapter 10, Electrical, Dash, Instruments, Fact File: Disconnecting the Battery* BEFORE doing so!

❑ **STEP 2:** Disconnect the electrical plug from the switch and unscrew the switch from the high pressure fluid pipe.

❑ **STEP 3:** Refitting is the reversal of the removal process.
→ Bleed the steering hydraulic system - see *Job 7*.

JOB 11: STEERING WHEEL - *removal, replacement.*

SAFETY FIRST!

VEHICLES WITH AIR BAGS AND SEAT BELT TENSIONERS - READ CHAPTER 14, JOBS 13 & 14 BEFORE STARTING WORK

❑ **STEP 1:** Before dismantling, disconnect the battery negative (-) earth/ground terminal. See *Chapter 10, Electrical, Dash, Instruments, Fact File: Disconnecting the Battery* BEFORE doing so!

❑ **STEP 2:** Remove the steering column shrouds - see *Chapter 14, Interior, Trim*.

❑ **STEP 3: VEHICLES WITH AIRBAGS:** Remove the airbag unit from the vehicle - see *Chapter 14, Interior, Trim*.

❑ **STEP 4: VEHICLES WITHOUT AIRBAGS:** Carefully lever the central trim from the steering wheel or remove horn push assembly - see *Chapter 14, Interior, Trim*.

❑ **STEP 5:** Make sure that the front road wheels are in the straight-ahead position.

❑ **STEP 6: VEHICLES WITH ANTI-THEFT IMMOBILISERS:**
Disconnect the electrical plug, remove the attachment screw (arrowed) and withdraw the anti-theft immobiliser transceiver unit from the ignition switch assembly.

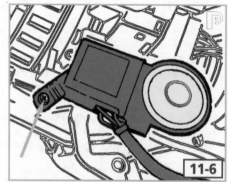
11-6

❑ **STEP 7: VEHICLES WITH AIRBAGS:** Separate the airbag module wiring connector from the steering column wiring harness.

❑ **STEP 8:** Unscrew the steering wheel nut or bolt, as appropriate to somewhere near the end of its thread but DO NOT yet remove it.

11-8

TOP TIP!

• To aid correct refitting, you should make an alignment mark on the end of the steering column and steering wheel.

❑ **STEP 9:** Grip each side of the steering wheel and pull it from the steering column shaft.
→ If necessary, bang the wheel towards you using both hands.
→ The nut or bolt left in position will stop the wheel from flying off and hitting you in the face!

FACT FILE
WHEEL-TO-COLUMN FIXINGS

• **FIESTAS 1976 TO 1983 AND MODELS MANUFACTURED AFTER 1990:** Splines are used to fix the position of the steering wheel on the steering column.
• **OTHER MODELS:** The steering column has a hexagonal end-section.

STEP 10: Turn the ignition key to lock the steering.

STEP 11: VEHICLES WITH AIRBAGS: If necessary, transfer the airbag clockspring assembly to the new steering wheel - see *Chapter 14, Interior, Trim*.

STEP 12: Refitting the steering wheel is the reversal of the removal process.
→ Make sure the front wheels are in the straight-ahead position.
→ On vehicles with airbags, make sure the airbag clock spring assembly is centralised and the clockspring tabs engage correctly over the steering lock plunger assembly – see *Chapter 14, Interior, Trim*.
→ Make sure the indicator stalk is in the central position to avoid damage from the tag on the steering wheel.
→ Where a bolt is used to secure the steering wheel, thoroughly clean the bolt threads and coat with a thread locking compound before refitting. Fit the bolt and tighten to the correct torque.

JOB 12: STEERING COLUMN - *removal, replacement.*

SAFETY FIRST!

VEHICLES WITH AIR BAGS AND SEAT BELT TENSIONERS

• READ *CHAPTER 14, JOBS 13 & 14, BEFORE STARTING WORK*.

IMPORTANT NOTE:
If the steering wheel is not removed from the steering column on vehicles equipped with air bags, you should make

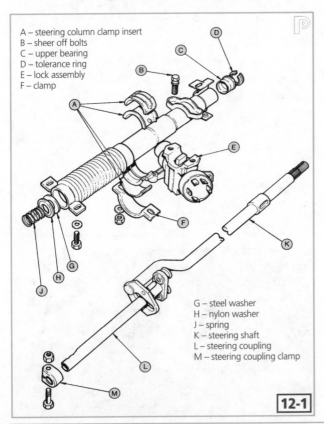

A – steering column clamp insert
B – sheer off bolts
C – upper bearing
D – tolerance ring
E – lock assembly
F – clamp

G – steel washer
H – nylon washer
J – spring
K – steering shaft
L – steering coupling
M – steering coupling clamp

12-1

---

sure that the steering wheel remains in the central position. Allowing the steering wheel to rotate can damage the airbag clockspring.

STEP 1: These are the components of the early Fiesta's steering column.

STEP 2: Before dismantling, disconnect the battery negative (-) earth/ground terminal. See *Chapter 10, Electrical, Dash, Instruments, Fact File: Disconnecting the Battery* BEFORE doing so!
→ Ensure the front wheels are in the straight ahead position and engage the steering lock.

STEP 3: FIESTA - 1989 TO 1995: Where fitted, remove the manual choke operating knob. Press in the securing lug and pull the knob from the shaft.

STEP 4: ESCORT AND ORION - 1980 TO 1990: Remove the steering wheel - see *Job 11*.
→ Remove the direction indicator cam from the top end of the steering shaft.

STEP 5: Remove the steering column shrouds - see *Chapter 14, Interior, Trim*.

STEP 6: FIESTA - 1989 TO 1995: Where a manual choke is fitted, remove the choke warning light switch assembly from the lower shroud.
→ Unscrew the retaining collar.

ESCORT AND ORION - 1980 TO 1990

STEP 7: Remove the insulation panel from the lower part of the dash.

12-8

STEP 8: Disconnect the bonnet release cable from the operating lever...

12-9

STEP 9: ...and from underneath the steering column.

OTHER SPECIFIC MODELS

❏ **STEP 10: ESCORT AND ORION - 1980 TO 1990:** Undo the retaining screw (**E**) and remove the bonnet release lever (**D**) from the steering lock mounting (**H**).

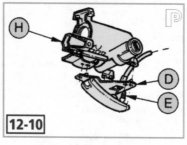

12-10

❏ **STEP 11: FIESTA - 1989 TO 1995, ESCORT AND ORION - 1980 TO 1990:** Remove the multi-function switch from the steering column - see *Chapter 10, Electrical, Instruments*.

❏ **STEP 12: ESCORT AND ORION - 1990 ON:** Remove the steering wheel and the multi- function switch from the steering column - see *Job 11 and Chapter 10, Electrical, Instruments*.

❏ **STEP 13: FIESTA - 1989 TO 1995:** Remove the loom plate from the left-hand side of the steering column.

ALL MODELS

❏ **STEP 14:** Disconnect all electrical connections to the steering column..

❏ **STEP 15:** Unscrew and remove the steering column to pinion clamp bolt - see *Job 6*.

→ Unbolt all steering column retaining fixings and/or clamps and withdraw the steering column.

12-15

❏ **STEP 16:** Refitting is the reversal of removal:
→ Ensure that the lower end of the column shroud is pushed down against the spring (**B**) – locate the peg (**A**) in the slot (**C**) in the collar.

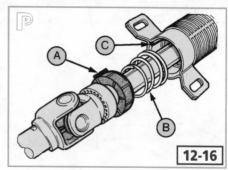

12-16

→ Use new steering column nuts when self-locking nuts are fitted.
→ Ensure that the steering rack and steering column are aligned with the wheels in the straight-ahead position.
→ Tighten all nuts and bolts to the correct torque.

Part C: Front Suspension Inspection, Removal, Replacement

CONTENTS

JOB 1:   FRONT WHEEL BEARINGS - *checking*.

❏ **STEP 1:** Rotate the wheel backwards and forwards several turns each way. The wheel should rotate freely and smoothly. Replace the bearing if there are any grating or rubbing noises.

1-1

JOB 2: FRONT HUB (SPINDLE) CARRIER - *removal, replacement*.

IMPORTANT NOTE:
• The hub carrier and suspension strut can be removed:
➔ **EITHER:** Together as a complete unit.
➔ **OR:** Independently of each other.
➔ If you wish to remove them as a complete unit, you can ignore *Steps 10 to 12*.

TOP TIP!

HUB RETAINING NUT
• The hub retaining nut is tight and loosening it requires considerable force.
• Loosen it before raising the vehicle.

❏ **STEP 1:** Use a suitable tool to lever or drive the staked portion out of the slot in the driveshaft and loosen - but don't remove - the hub retaining nut.

2-1

❏ **STEP 2:** Safely support the front of the vehicle and remove the appropriate front wheel.

❏ **STEP 3:** Remove the brake caliper and brake disc - see *Chapter 12, Brakes*.

❏ **STEP 4: FIESTA AND ESCORT AFTER 1989 AND KA MODELS:** On models fitted with an anti-roll bar, disconnect the link rod from the bracket on the strut (arrowed).

2-4

❏ **STEP 5:** Remove the hub retaining nut and washer.

❏ **STEP 6:** Remove the track rod end from the steering arm - see *Part B*.

❏ **STEP 7:** Unscrew and remove the pinch bolt at the base of the hub carrier.

2-7

❏ **STEP 8:** Use a suitable lever to carefully lever apart the split in the clamp at the base of the hub carrier and, at the same time, push down on the track control or lower suspension arm to separate the balljoint from the hub carrier.

2-8

TOP TIP!

• If you are removing the hub carrier and strut as a separate unit you can go straight to *Step 13*.

❏ **STEP 9: FIESTA - 1976 TO 1983:** Unscrew and remove the one or two bolts, according to model (C) attaching the hub carrier (B) to the strut (A).

❏ **STEP 10: FIESTA - 1976 TO 1983 - SPECIAL CLOSE-TOLERANCE BOLTS:** During manufacture, Ford used a jig to ensure correct alignment of the strut and hub carrier, normal bolts being used to attach the hub carrier to the strut.
➔ During subsequent dismantling and reassembly, the normal bolts should be discarded and special close-tolerance bolts fitted.
➔ These bolts will ensure correct alignment.
➔ The special bolts, which are reusable, can be recognised by two knurled sections (arrowed) on the shank.

2-9

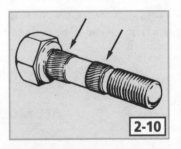
2-10

❏ **STEP 11: ALL OTHER MODELS:** Note the way the bolt is fitted then unscrew and remove the pinch bolts at the top of the hub carrier.

2-11

STEP 12: Carefully lever apart the clamp at the top of the hub carrier.
→ Push down on the hub carrier and separate the hub carrier from the strut - some force may be necessary.

2-12

STEP 13:
MODELS WITH ELECTRONIC ABS: Unbolt and remove the wheel sensor. Support the sensor clear of the hub to reduce the chance of damage. See *Chapter 12, Brakes*.

STEP 14: If the hub carrier does not easily come away from the driveshaft, use a suitable puller such as the Sykes-Pickavant puller shown here. On pre-1989 models, make sure the hub does not separate from the hub carrier at this stage unless, of course, you are removing the hub carrier to replace the bearings and the old bearings will be discarded.
→ If there is room to remove the hub, the brake caliper carrier can stay in place. If not, it must be removed.

2-14

PRE-1989 MODELS

→ On pre-1989 models, the hub and hub carrier separate easily but care must be taken to prevent damage to the bearings

→ On models manufactured after 1989, the hub is an interference fit on the bearings.

ALL MODELS

→ When you remove the hub from the driveshaft, make sure that the inner CV joint does not separate from the driveshaft.

→ Support the driveshaft, making sure that the inner CV joint is not moved more than 18 degrees out of alignment and the outer CV joint not moved more than 45 degrees out of alignment. The CV joints will be damaged if these angles are exceeded.

STEP 15: Note the location of any cut-outs (C) and remove the dust shield (A) from the recess on the inside of the hub carrier (B).

2-15

STEP 16: Refitting is the reverse of the removal process, bearing in mind the following points.
→ **FIESTA 1976 TO 1983:** Make sure that the correct special bolts are used to attach the hub carrier to the suspension strut.
→ Clean all mating surfaces before reassembly.
→ Apply a smear of grease to the hub splines before refitting the driveshaft.
→ Take care not to dislodge or damage the bearings and seals when fitting the driveshaft through the hub.
→ If necessary, use the old hub retaining nut to pull the driveshaft through the hub during reassembly. Do not knock the hub carrier onto the driveshaft - this will damage the CV joint.
→ Use a new hub retaining nut for final assembly and rotate the wheel as this is being tightened to ensure correct bearing seating.
→ **TWO BOLT LOWER STRUT FIXINGS:** Make sure that the strut and tapered shaft from the lower balljoint are fully located before inserting and tightening the pinch bolts. It is vital that the lower pinch bolt passes through the cut-out in the taper section of the balljoint shaft and the upper pinch bolt passes through the flange on the strut.
→ Tighten all nut and bolts to the specified torque. Remember to fully tighten the hub retaining nut when the wheels are on the ground.

STEP 17: Use a narrow punch to stake the hub retaining nut into the cut-out in the driveshaft.

2-17

STEP 18: This is the correct location of the balljoint stud in the base of the hub carrier.
→ The bolt (C) MUST locate correctly in the groove in the stud (D).

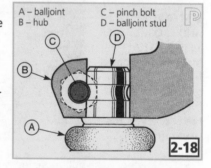
A – balljoint C – pinch bolt
B – hub D – balljoint stud
2-18

JOB 3: FRONT WHEEL BEARINGS - *removal, replacement.*

Section A: Applies to all types.

IMPORTANT NOTE:
• On models manufactured after 1989, the wheel bearings cannot be re-used once they have been dismantled. New bearings must be fitted.

• Always replace the bearings as a set - on each hub there are two bearings always replace them both at the same time.
• On models with a single upper mounting bolt, you should undo the nut by five complete turns before disconnecting the lower end of the strut. If this is not done, the upper mounting can be damaged by strut movement.

❏ **STEP A1:** Remove the hub (spindle) carrier - see *Job 2*.

❏ **STEP A2:** Mount the hub (spindle) carrier securely on the bench.

❏ **STEP A3:** If still fitted, remove the dust shield (arrowed). See also, *Job 2, Step 17*.

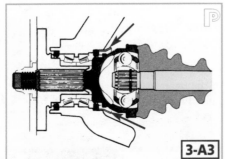

❏ **STEP A4:** Lever out the two grease seals - one is on the hub carrier, the other on the hub.
→ The seals will be damaged during removal and new seals must be used during reassembly.

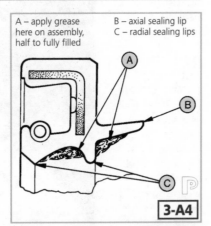

A – apply grease here on assembly, half to fully filled
B – axial sealing lip
C – radial sealing lips

Section B: Pre-1989 models.

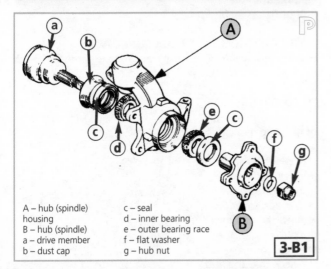

A – hub (spindle) housing
B – hub (spindle)
a – drive member
b – dust cap
c – seal
d – inner bearing
e – outer bearing race
f – flat washer
g – hub nut

❏ **STEP B1:** With the seals (**c**) removed, lift out the bearings, (**d**) and (**e**), and check the bearings and bearing cones for any signs of wear, damage or deterioration.

❏ **STEP B2:** Clean all traces of old grease from the bearings, hub and hub carrier before refitting.

❏ **STEP B3:** If new bearings are to be fitted, press or drift out the bearing cones (or 'cups') from the hub carrier.
→ Clean all traces of old grease from the hub and hub carrier.
→ Check the cone seats for any signs of damage. Carefully remove any burrs with a file.

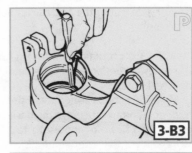

❏ **STEP B4:** Press or drift the new bearing cones (**B**) into the hub carrier (**C**).
→ Take care not to damage the cones and make sure they are fully seated.

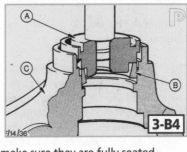

→ Ideally, use a press and suitable tool (**A**) for bearing on the cones. A socket of the right size is fine.

❏ **STEP B5:** Work new grease fully into the bearings and ensure the bearings are fully packed with grease. Insert the bearings into the hub carrier.

❏ **STEP B6:** Smear grease around the lips of each seal (**B**) – see *Step A4* - and press the seals into the hub (**C**).
→ Ideally, the grease seals should be pressed into the hub carrier with the correct tool (**A**).

→ Alternatively, you can use a suitably sized socket or block of wood and carefully tap the grease seals into position - make sure the seals are square to the bore at all times.

❏ **STEP B7:** Refit the hub carrier - see *Job 2*.

Section C: Models produced between 1989 and June 1990.

IMPORTANT NOTE:
The bearings are made unserviceable by the removal process so, only remove the bearings from the hub carrier if they are to be renewed.

FACT FILE

• **ON MODELS MANUFACTURED BEFORE JUNE 1990**, it is possible to drift the bearing assemblies from the hub carrier.
• **AFTER JUNE 1990**, the bearings are an interference fit on the hub. The inner sections of the outer bearing will remain fitted to the hub during removal. A knife-edged puller is needed to remove this section of bearing from the hub.

❏ **STEP C1:** Remove the hub carrier - see *Job 2*.

❏ **STEP C2:** Remove the hub from the hub carrier - the hub should slide out of the hub carrier but a puller may be necessary.

❏ **STEP C3:** Drift the outer bearing from the hub - tap on the outer circumference of the bearing at diametrically opposed points.
➜ Make sure the bearing remains square to the hub carrier bore at all times otherwise the bore can be damaged, making it difficult or impossible to fit the new bearings.
➜ Repeat for the inner bearing.

❏ **STEP C4:** Thoroughly clean the hub and the bore in the hub carrier.

❏ **STEP C5:** Press the outer bearing into the hub carrier - use a section of tube with an outer diameter just less than the internal diameter of the hub carrier bore or a long threaded rod with suitable large diameter flat washers. Repeat for the inner bearing. Make sure the bearings fully seat on the shoulders in the hub carrier.

IMPORTANT NOTE:
You must only press on the outer circumference of the bearing - do not press on the centre section of the bearing as this will cause permanent damage.

❏ **STEP C6:** Refit the hub into the hub carrier.
➜ If you have to press the hub in place, the inner section of the inner bearing must be supported - use a section of tube with an appropriate diameter.

❏ **STEP C7:** Check that the hub rotates freely and refit the hub carrier to the vehicle - see *Job 2*.

Section D: Models manufactured after June 1990.

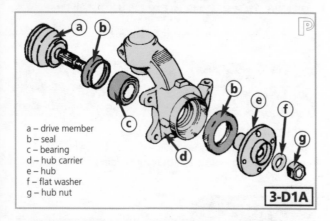

a – drive member
b – seal
c – bearing
d – hub carrier
e – hub
f – flat washer
g – hub nut

3-D1A

❏ **STEP D1A:** There are several different bearing types, according to model, but replacement procedures are similar.
➜ After June 1990, the bearings are an interference fit on the hub. The inner sections of the outer bearing will remain fitted to the hub during removal. A knife-edged puller is needed to remove this section of bearing from the hub.

❏ **STEP D1B:** The major difference is that, on some models, the bearing (a) is located in the hub carrier (b) with a circlip (c).

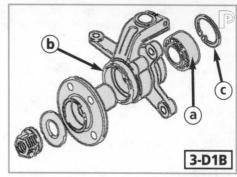

3-D1B

❏ **STEP D2:** Remove the hub carrier - see *Job 2*.

❏ **STEP D3:** Remove the inner section of the bearing (arrowed) from the hub using a suitable knife-edged puller.

3-D3

❏ **STEP D4:** Press or drift the outer bearing from the hub carrier.

❏ **STEP D5: FIESTA AND ESCORT MODELS AFTER 1995 AND KA MODELS:** Remove the bearing circlip from the inner face of the hub carrier. See illustration *3-D1B*. Refit with a new circlip fitted during reassembly.

3-D5

❏ **STEP D6:** Press or drift the inner bearing from the hub carrier - see *Step D4*.

❏ **STEP D7: MODELS WITH ELECTRONIC ABS:** During bearing removal from the hub carrier, take care to prevent damage to the ABS wheel sensors.

❏ **STEP D8:** Thoroughly clean the hub and the bore in the hub carrier.

❏ **STEP D9:** Use a press (b) to push the outer bearing (a) into the hub carrier. See *Step C5*.
➜ Press the hub into the hub carrier. See *Step C6*.
➜ Check that the hub rotates freely and refit the hub carrier to the vehicle - see *Job 2*.

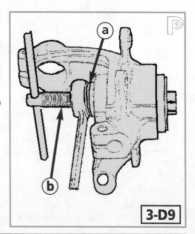

3-D9

JOB 4: FRONT SUSPENSION STRUTS - *remove, dismantle, replace.*

SAFETY FIRST!

• To fully dismantle the front suspension struts, the coil spring must be compressed.

• Considerable energy is stored in the compressed spring and damage or injury can be caused if a spring suddenly expands - only use coil spring compressing tools designed for this job.

The front suspension struts can be removed separately or as an assembly with the hub carrier. Unless you have reasons for removing the hub carrier it is easier to remove the strut separately.

FACT FILE

STRUT TYPES

❏ **STEP 1:** There are two types of strut top mountings:

→ **TYPE A:** Two or three bolts, according to model.

→ **TYPE B:** One central nut.

• On

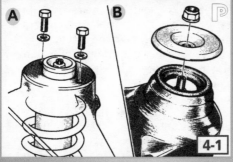

models with a single upper mounting bolt, you should undo the nut by five complete turns before disconnecting the lower end of the strut. If this is not done, the upper mounting can be damaged by strut movement.

❏ **STEP 2:** Where appropriate, disconnect the brake line connector (**a**) and the anti-roll bar connections (**b**) from the strut.

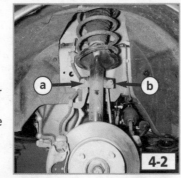

❏ **STEP 3:** To disconnect the lower end of the strut from the hub carrier.

→ Remove the pinch bolt or bolts.

❏ **STEP 4:** Open up the clamp at the rear of the hub...

❏ **STEP 5:** and separate the two - see *Job 2, Steps 12 and 13*.

→ Support the hub to prevent excessive mis-alignment of the CV joints.

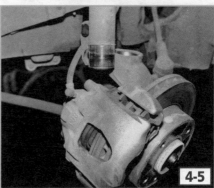

SAFETY FIRST!

• Where two nuts are used to attach the strut, the central nut holds the spring in compression. Do not attempt to remove the central nut in order to remove the strut. The nut is restraining the great force within the coil spring.

SINGLE CENTRAL NUT

❏ **STEP 6:** If fitted, remove the plastic protective cap from the central nut

❏ **STEP 7:** Use a suitable Allen key to prevent the strut from turning and loosen the retaining nut.

→ Support the strut before the nut is fully undone.

STEP 8: Lift off the top plate and lower the strut from the vehicle.

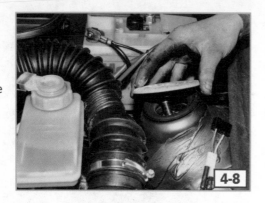
4-8

TWO ATTACHMENT NUTS

STEP 9: Undo the nuts and, before they are fully undone, support the strut.

4-9

STEP 10: Completely remove the nuts and lower the strut from the vehicle.

4-10

TOP TIP!

• On pre-1989 Fiesta models, special lower attachment bolts must be used during reassembly. These bolts can be recognised by knurled sections on the bolt shank. If these bolts have already been fitted, they can be re-used.

BOTH TYPES

STEP 11: Compress the spring with a suitable spring compressor.

4-11

STEP 12: Undo and remove the central retaining nut while preventing the central shaft from turning with an Allen key.

4-12

STEP 13: Dismantle the strut, making a careful note of the location and order of assembly of the top mounting components.

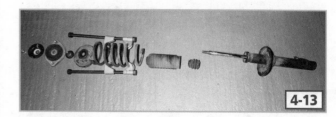
4-13

STEP 14: Reassembly is the reverse of removal:
➜ Fully tighten the central retaining nut before releasing the tension in the spring.
➜ Make sure that the springs are seated correctly in their seats as tension is released from the spring compressor.

STEP 15: SINGLE PINCH-BOLT TYPES: Make sure that the strut is fully seated in the hub. Drift the hub up from beneath to be sure.

JOB 5:   FRONT ANTI-ROLL BAR - removal, replacement.

IMPORTANT NOTE:
• On Fiesta models from 1995, Ford recommend that the front suspension crossmember is removed before attempting to remove the front anti-roll bar. When the crossmember is being refitted, Ford specify the use of a special aligning tool (Tool No 15-097). The work should be entrusted to a suitably equipped Ford dealer.

Section A: Fiesta, Escort and Orion from 1989 and Ka models.

STEP A1A: FIESTA MODELS - 1989 TO 1995: Where fitted, remove the undertray.
➜ XR2i MODELS: Ford also recommend that the front suspension crossmember is removed.

STEP A1B: KA MODELS: Disconnect the lower suspension arm from the hub carrier - see *Job 2, Steps 9 and 10*

STEP A2:
To remove the anti-roll bar:
→ Undo the nut (a) and disconnect the lower end of the connecting link from the anti-roll bar.

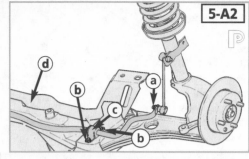

→ Remove the four bolts - two each side (b) - attaching the anti-roll bar brackets (c) to the lower suspension arm mounting brackets (Fiesta and Ka) or subframe (d -Escort and Orion).

STEP A3: KA MODELS: Unbolt and remove the lower suspension arm mounting brackets (arrowed). Remove the brackets complete with the lower suspension arms – see *Job 6*.

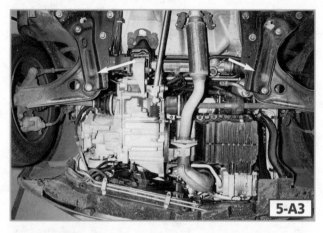

STEP A4: Remove the anti-roll bar brackets and withdraw the anti-roll bar from the vehicle.

STEP A5: Refitting is the reversal of the removal process. Where 'Nyloc' type nuts are used, new nuts should be used during reassembly.

Section B: Escort and Orion – pre-1989 models.

STEP B1: Bend back the lock tabs, where fitted, and unscrew the four bolts or nuts (arrowed) securing the anti-roll bar clamp brackets.

STEP B2:
Unscrew the nuts, remove the washers and bushes from each end of the anti roll bar.
→

IMPORTANT NOTE: The nut on the right-hand side of the anti-roll bar has a left-hand thread and unscrews in a clockwise direction.

STEP B3: Undo the nut and remove the pivot bolt from the inner end of one lower suspension arm.

STEP B4: Manoeuvre the anti-roll bar from the lower suspension arms and withdraw the anti-roll bar from the vehicle.
→ If necessary, you may have to separate the track control arm from the hub carrier.

TOP TIP!

STEP B5: When you are replacing the anti-roll bar bushes, leave all the nuts slightly loose, lower the vehicle onto its wheels and bounce the front a few times to settle the bushes.
• Tighten the nuts and bolts to the correct torque with the vehicle weight on the wheels.

STEP B6: Refitting is the reverse of removal:
→ Make sure the end of the anti-roll bar with the left-hand thread is fitted to the right-hand side of the vehicle.
→ Fit the dished washers with the hollow side away from the bushes.

JOB 6:	FRONT SUSPENSION LOWER ARM - *removal, overhaul, replacement.*

Section A: Fiesta, Escort and Orion pre-1989.

STEP A1: Note that pre-1983 1.1 litre Escort models had a pressed steel lower suspension arm similar to the one used on the Fiesta.
All other pre-1989 Escort and Orion models had a forged lower suspension arm.
→ Disconnect and remove the track control arm (C) from the lower arm (D).

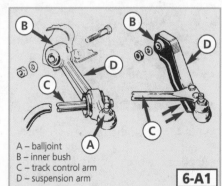

A – balljoint
B – inner bush
C – track control arm
D – suspension arm

☐ **STEP A2:** Loosen the front wheel bolts/nuts and raise the front of the vehicle.
→ Remove the front wheels.

☐ **STEP A3:**
Once the track control arm, which is also the anti-roll bar in this instance (a) has
been removed, disconnect the following:

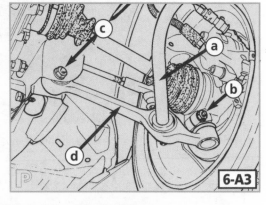
6-A3

→ The outer end of the track control arm from the hub carrier (b) - see *Job 2*.
→ Undo the nut and remove the pivot bolt from the inner end of the track control arm (c).
→ Remove the lower arm (d).

PRESSED STEEL TYPE

☐ **STEP A4:** See illustration *6-A1*.
→ Undo the nuts and withdraw the two bolts (arrowed) attaching the track control arm (C).
→ Disconnect the balljoint and inner mounting and remove the track control arm.

FACT FILE
EARLY MODELS

1.1 LITRE ESCORT MODELS PRE - 1983 AND FIESTA: The bolts attaching the tie bar to the track control arm also attach the balljoint to the track control suspension arm.

• When these bolts are removed to disconnect the tie bar, the balljoint is also detached from the track control arm.

6-A5

☐ **STEP A5:** Check the condition of the inner pivot bush (*6-A6, item C*).
→ Replace the bush if there are any signs of cracks, splits or deterioration.

☐ **STEP A6:**
The old bush can be pressed out of the arm (B) using a vice and suitably sized sections of tube or sockets (A and D).

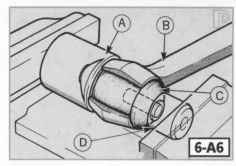
6-A6

TOP TIP!

• Some new bushes have to be fitted in a specific location, depending on type.
• Before removing the old bushes, make alignment marks and refit to the marks.

☐ **STEP A7:**
Reassembly is the reverse of the dismantling process.

6-A7

Section B: Fiesta, Escort, Orion after 1989 and Ka.

☐ **STEP B1:** Disconnect the lower balljoint at the base of the hub carrier. See *Job 2, Step 10*.

☐ **STEP B2:** Unscrew and remove the two lower suspension arm retaining bolts on the subframe (Escort and Orion) or mounting brackets (Fiesta and Ka).

☐ **STEP B3:** Withdraw the lower suspension arms from the vehicle.

6-B2

☐ **STEP B4:** Reassembly is the reverse of removal:
➔ The lower suspension arm mounting bolt should be fitted from below and finger tightened.
➔ Final tightening should be done with the vehicle weight back on the wheels.
➔ It is vital that the hub carrier clamp bolt engages correctly with the cut-out in the balljoint shaft - see *Job 2, Step 21*.

<table>
<tr><td>

JOB 7:

</td><td>

FRONT SUSPENSION TIE BAR, PRE-1983 1.1 LITRE ESCORT AND PRE-1989 FIESTA - *removal, replacement.*

</td></tr>
</table>

☐ **STEP 1:** Disconnect the outer end of the tie bar from the lower arm. See *Job 6*.

☐ **STEP 2:**
To remove the tie bar:
➔ Remove the nut (**B**) and remove the outer bush (**D**).
➔ Pull the tie bar (**C**) out of the bracket (**A**).

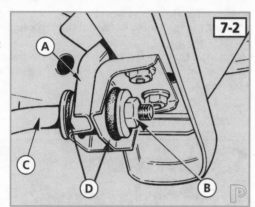

☐ **STEP 3:** Reassembly is the reversal of removal.

<table>
<tr><td>

JOB 8:

</td><td>

FRONT SUSPENSION SUBFRAME - *removal, replacement.*

</td></tr>
</table>

ESCORT, ORION 1989-ON

☐ **STEP 1:** Before dismantling, disconnect the battery negative (-) earth/ground terminal. See *Chapter 10, Electrical, Dash, Instruments, Fact File: Disconnecting the Battery* BEFORE doing so!

☐ **STEP 2:** Support the engine - see *Chapter 6, Engine*.

☐ **STEP 3:** Centralise the steering and remove the steering column to pinion clamp bolt - see *Part B*.

☐ **STEP 4:** Remove the engine/transmission mounting bracket bolts at the subframe.

☐ **STEP 5: MODELS WITH LAMBDA SENSORS:** Disconnect the Lambda sensor multi-plug.

☐ **STEP 6:** Detach the exhaust downpipe - see *Chapter 6, Engine*.

☐ **STEP 7:** Disconnect the gear change linkage (arrowed) at the transmission. If necessary, remove the exhaust heat shields to gain access.

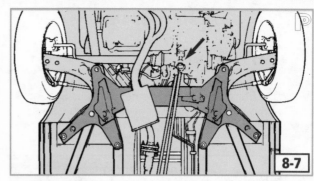

☐ **STEP 8:** Disconnect the track rod ends from the steering arms - see *Part B*.

☐ **STEP 9:** Disconnect the lower suspension arm balljoint from the hub carrier - see *Job 2*.

☐ **STEP 10:** Unscrew the attachment bolt and detach the right-hand engine support bar from the subframe followed by the second engine/transmission mounting bolt.

☐ **STEP 11: MODELS WITH ANTI-ROLL BARS:** Detach the anti-roll bar link rods from the suspension strut.

☐ **STEP 12: POWER STEERING MODELS:** Detach the hydraulic lines from the steering rack - see *Part B*.

☐ **STEP 13:** Support the subframe on a trolley jack and unscrew the eight subframe retaining bolts – four per side (arrowed).
➔ **XR2i MODELS:** Undo the four attachment bolts.
➔ Carefully lower the subframe, disconnecting the pinion from the steering column as the subframe comes away from the vehicle.

☐ **STEP 14:** Reassembly is the reversal of removal:
➔ Make sure all mating surfaces are clean.
➔ Make sure that the steering rack and steering wheel are in the straight ahead position.
➔ Engage the pinion in the steering column.
➔ Ensure that the subframe locating dowels engage in the guide recesses in the floorpan.
➔ It is vital that the attachment bolt engages with the cut out in the lower suspension balljoint - see *Job 2*.
➔ Check the steering alignment.

FIESTA 1995-ON

JOB 9: LOWER SUSPENSION ARM MOUNTING BRACKETS, KA - *removal, replacement.*

IMPORTANT NOTE:
See the illustrations in *Part A* in connection with this Job.

❏ **STEP 1:** Before dismantling, disconnect the battery negative (-) earth/ground terminal. See *Chapter 10, Electrical, Dash, Instruments, Fact File: Disconnecting the Battery* BEFORE doing so!

❏ **STEP 2:** Disconnect the lower suspension arm from the hub carrier - see *Job 2.*

❏ **STEP 3:** Disconnect the anti-roll bar from the connecting link.

❏ **STEP 4:** Remove the bolts attaching the anti-roll bar to the lower suspension arm mounting bracket.

❏ **STEP 5:** Unbolt and withdraw the lower arm mounting bracket, complete with lower arm, from the vehicle.
➜ The shorter attachment bolt is an alignment bolt.
➜ Undo the bolts and separate the lower arm from the mounting bracket.

❏ **STEP 6:** Reassembly is the reversal of removal:
➜ Make sure the heads of the lower arm to mounting bracket bolts face downward. Tighten to the correct torque in two stages - see *Chapter 1, Facts and Figures.*
➜ Offer up the mounting bracket so that the peg is central in its locating hole. Insert and finger tighten the alignment bolt.
➜ Insert the remaining bolts and tighten evenly to the correct torque.
➜ It is vital that the lower hub carrier attachment bolt engages with the cut out in the lower suspension balljoint - see *Job 2.*

Part D: Rear Suspension Inspection, Removal, Replacement

CONTENTS

JOB 1: REAR WHEEL BEARINGS - *checking.*

See *Part C, Job 1* for details of how to check bearings.

Unlike the front bearings, the rear bearings are adjustable. If there appears to be excessive freeplay in the rear bearings, resetting the bearings may cure the problem – see *Job 2.*

JOB 2: REAR HUB – *remove, replace.*

On all versions except Escort Van, removing the rear hub is the same as:
➜ **DRUM BRAKE MODELS:** Rear brake drum removal.
➜ **REAR DISC BRAKE MODELS:** Rear disc removal.

❏ **STEP 1:**
ESCORT VAN: Remove the brake drum – see *Chapter 12, Brakes.*
➜ Remove dust cap, the split pin and the retainer and undo the hub nut.

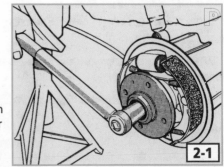

2-1

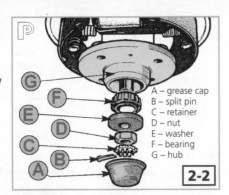

❏ **STEP 2:** Pull off the hub complete with bearing and washer. You may need to use a hub puller in which case take care not to damage the thread on the hub spindle.

A – grease cap
B – split pin
C – retainer
D – nut
E – washer
F – bearing
G – hub

2-2

JOB 3:	REAR WHEEL BEARINGS - *replace*.

FACT FILE

FIESTA COURIER AND COMBI: On these models the bearings cannot be replaced.
• If bearings are worn, a new hub complete with bearings will have to be fitted.

❏ **STEP 1:** Remove the hub – see *Job 2*.
➜ IMPORTANT NOTE: **MODELS WITH ELECTRONIC ABS:** Remove the sensor ring from the hub – see *Chapter 12, Brakes, Part I*.

❏ **STEP 2:** Use a screwdriver to lever the inner seal out of the inside of the hub.

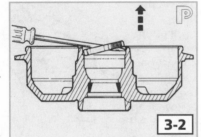

3-2

❏ **STEP 3:** Turn the hub or drum over remove the bearing race and drift the cone out of the drum, evenly.

❏ **STEP 4:** The other bearing and cone can now be removed in the same way.
➜ Clean out the hub removing all traces of grease and dirt before fitting the new bearing.

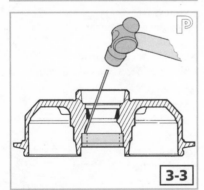

3-3

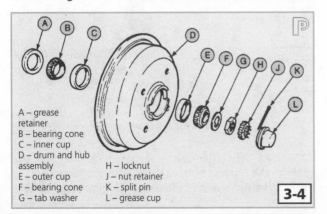

A – grease retainer
B – bearing cone
C – inner cup
D – drum and hub assembly
E – outer cup
F – bearing cone
G – tab washer
H – locknut
J – nut retainer
K – split pin
L – grease cup

3-4

❏ **STEP 5:** Fit both bearing cones (**C**) to the hub.
➜ The best way of doing so is to use a press (**A**) and stepped tool (**B**) to push each cup in evenly.

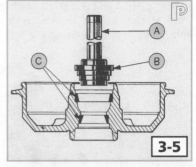

3-5

❏ **STEP 6:** Insert the new inner bearing (see illustration *3-4, item B*) and then fit the seal (*item A*).
➜ It is essential that the seal is fitted evenly and that when in place, it is flush with the inner face of the hub.

3-6

❏ **STEP 7:** While holding the outer bearing race (see illustration *3-4, item F*) in place in the hub, refit the hub to the stub axle. See *Chapter 12, Brakes*.

❏ **STEP 8: ESCORT BEFORE 1990:** Refit the hub and adjust as follows:
➜ Tighten the hub nut to 20-25 Nm (15-18 lb. ft.) while rotating the hub.
➜ Now slacken the nut off 180 degrees (1/2 turn).
➜ Retighten the nut finger-tight.
➜ Fit the nut retainer so that a slot lines up with the split pin hole without moving the nut.
➜ Fit a new split pin, bending the ends back in opposite directions and fit the grease cap.
➜ **FIESTA UP TO 1989:** Tighten the hub nut to a torque of 36 Nm (27 lb. ft.) while rotating the hub.
➜ Back off the hub nut by 90 degrees.
➜ Retighten the nut finger-tight.
➜ Fit the nut retainer so that a slot lines up with the split pin hole without moving the nut.
➜ Fit a new split pin, bending the ends back in opposite directions and fit the grease cap.
➜ **ESCORT VAN:** Refit the brake drum and adjust the brakes – see *Chapter 12, Brakes*.

JOB 4:	REAR SHOCK ABSORBER – VEHICLES WITHOUT INTEGRAL STRUT – *remove, replace*.

RAISING THE VEHICLE: You must never place a jack or axle stand beneath the crossbeam.

Section A: Fiesta 1976 to 1989.

❏ **STEP A1:** Support the vehicle off the ground so that the rear suspension is hanging down under its own weight.

→ Now place a jack under the rear suspension on the side from which the shock absorber is to be removed – just enough to slightly compress the rear springs.

❐ **STEP A2:** Working inside the vehicle, remove the plastic cap from the top of the shock absorber.

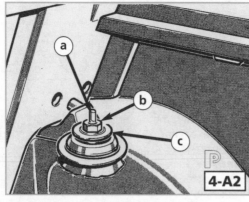

4-A2

→ Grip the flat (**a**) at the top of the shock absorber spindle to prevent it from turning while the nut (**b**) is undone.
→ Remove the cap washer and top rubber insulator (**c**) from the top of the shock absorber.

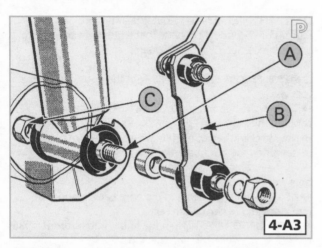

4-A3

❐ **STEP A3:** Disconnect the lower end of the shock absorber:
→ Remove the nut (**C**) and take the shock absorber off the through bolt (**A**).
→ This bolt is shared by the anti-roll bar link (**B**), when fitted.

❐ **STEP A4:** Disconnect the lower end of the shock absorber from the suspension:
→ Use a lever (**a**) to force the eye (**b**) on the arm on the shock absorber off the peg (**c**) on the suspension.

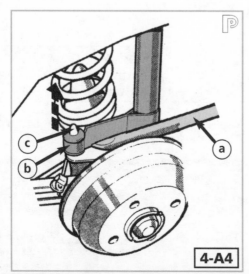

4-A4

❐ **STEP A5:** The shock absorber can now be removed from the vehicle.

❐ **STEP A6:** If the bushes (arrowed) in the shock absorber need to be replaced, the old ones can be pushed or pressed out and new ones fitted.

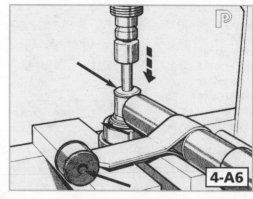

4-A6

→ Use plenty of soapy water to help the bush to slip out.
→ Cutting off one end of a rubber bush and then pushing against that end is often the best way of removing it.

REFITTING

❐ **STEP A7:** Start by refitting the eye onto the peg on the lower suspension.
→ Use a lever against one of the coil springs (position arrowed) and lubricate with plenty of soapy water.
→ You can now fit the

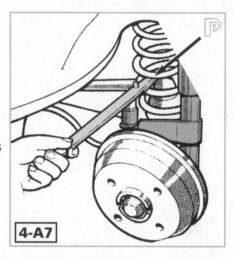

4-A7

bottom shock absorber mounting nut on the through bolt – see **Step A3**. Do not tighten the nut at this stage.

❐ **STEP A8:** Make sure that the components fitted to the top of the shock absorber are correctly positioned.
→ Refit the top washer and top nut but do not tighten.

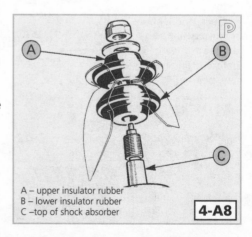

A – upper insulator rubber
B – lower insulator rubber
C – top of shock absorber

4-A8

❐ **STEP A9:** When the weight of the vehicle is back on the ground, the top and bottom shock absorber mounting nuts can be tightened to the correct torque.

Section B: Escort and Orion 1980 to 1989 (not including Van or Estate/Wagon).

☐ **STEP B1:** Working inside the vehicle, remove the plastic cap, nut, washer and rubber insulator from the top of the shock absorber. Use a

4-B1

suitable Allen key to hold the threaded section of the shock absorber to prevent it turning while the nut is undone.

4-B2

☐ **STEP B2:** Remove the brake line (arrowed) from the shock absorber, without separating the flexible hose from the pipe.
➜ Slacken the locking nut and slide the hydraulic line from the slot in the strut.

☐ **STEP B3:** Undo and remove the two bolts attaching the shock absorber to the axle carrier.
➜ In the background, you will see a Sykes-Pickavant hydraulic hose clamp.
➜ This is only necessary if you are removing the brake backplate and wheel cylinder.

4-B3

☐ **STEP B4:** Withdraw the shock absorber from the vehicle.

☐ **STEP B5:** Refitting is the reverse of the removal process.
➜ Where 'Nyloc' type nuts are fitted, new nuts must be used during reassembly.

Section C: Escort Van and Estate/Wagon.

☐ **STEP C1:** With the vehicle's weight supported off the ground and rear suspension hanging free:
➜ Place jacks under the rear axle and take part of the weight of the vehicle on the jacks - just enough to slightly compress the rear springs.

☐ **STEP C2:** Remove the lower shock absorber pivot bolt (arrowed).

4-C2

☐ **STEP C3:** Remove the two bolts (arrowed) attaching the top mounting bracket to the body.
➜ IMPORTANT NOTE: On later Van versions, there are four vertical bolts holding the shock absorber to the body.
➜ Remove the shock absorber from the vehicle.

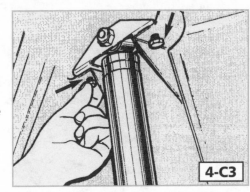

4-C3

☐ **STEP C4:** Refitting is the reverse of the removal process.
➜ Transfer the mounting bracket from the old shock absorber to the new.
➜ Where 'Nyloc' type nuts are fitted, new nuts must be used during reassembly.

JOB 5:	REAR SPRINGS – VEHICLES WITHOUT INTEGRAL STRUT – *remove, replace.*

Raise the vehicle off the ground and support it with the rear suspension hanging free. Place a jack underneath the end of the axle beam on the side you are working on ready to support the weight of the suspension as it is dismantled.

Section A: Fiesta 1976 to 1989.

☐ **STEP A1:** Remove the rear shock absorber – see *Job 4, Section A*.

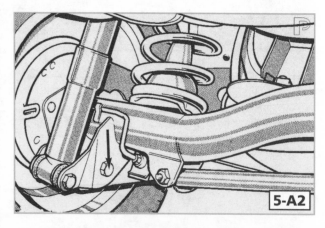

5-A2

☐ **STEP A2:** Remove the through bolt (arrowed) holding the end of the trailing arm to the rear suspension.

☐ **STEP A3:** Lower the jack beneath the axle so that the spring and the rubber insulator (arrowed) can be removed from the vehicle.

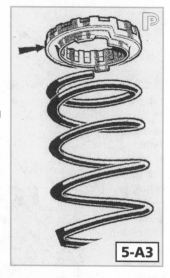

5-A3

☐ **STEP A4:** With the spring out of the way, it is now simple to replace the bump stop (**a**) if necessary.
➔ Cut through the bump stop (position **b**) using soapy water as a lubricant.
➔ A new bump stop can be pushed into place through the hole in the top of the spring support.

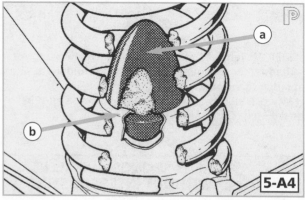

5-A4

☐ **STEP A5:** New springs should always be replaced in pairs and must have the same colour-code marking as each other.
➔ Make sure that the spring is seated correctly in the upper seat as the jack is raised to reposition the rear suspension
➔ Reconnect the rear suspension components as the reverse of the removal process.

Section B: Escort and Orion Estate/Wagon (not including Van).

Not all versions use the same layout but the principles are similar.

☐ **STEP B1:** Use a jack to support the appropriate suspension arm so that the spring is slightly compressed.

☐ **STEP B2:** Where applicable, lever the rear stabiliser bar from the top of each shackle – see *Job 7*.

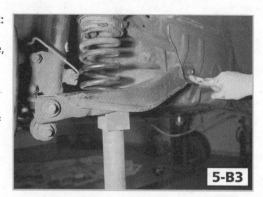

5-B3

☐ **STEP B3:** Remove the lower suspension arm inboard pivot bolt, pointed out here.

☐ **STEP B4:** Carefully lower the jack. Remove the spring and rubber insulator pad.

5-B4

☐ **STEP B5:** Refitting is the reverse of the removal process, bearing in mind the following points.
➔ Where 'Nyloc' type nuts are fitted, new nuts must be used during reassembly.
➔ Where applicable, the spring must be refitted with the plastic sleeved-end uppermost.
➔ Tighten all nuts and bolts to the correct torque when the wheels are back on the ground.

☐ **STEP B6:** This is the type fitted to later models.

5-B6

Section C: Escort Van/leaf-springs.

❑ **STEP C1:** With the weight of the vehicle supported separately, allow the rear suspension to hang free.
➜ Now support the rear axle on jacks or stands.

❑ **STEP C2:** Unscrew and remove the 'U'- bolts (arrowed – viewed from above) attaching the spring 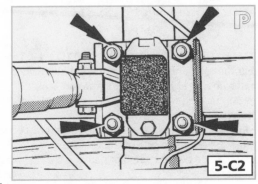 to the axle. Remove the rubber bump stop along with the shock absorber lower attachment.

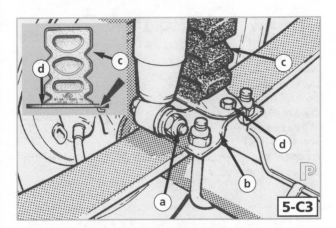

❑ **STEP C3:** Remove the following:
➜ The shock absorber lower bolt (**a**).
➜ The U-bolt plate (**b**) complete with bump stop (**c**).
➜ The bump stop can now be removed by undoing bolt (**d**).
➜ If the bump stop is to be replaced, note the location hook (inset, arrowed).

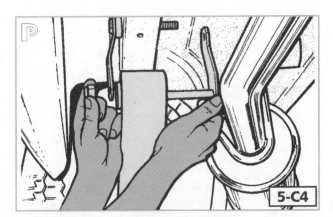

❑ **STEP C4:** Support the spring, to prevent it dropping, and remove the bolt from the rear spring shackle.

❑ **STEP C5:** If necessary, pull the spring down and away from the rear shackle and axle.

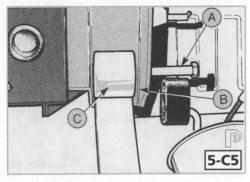

➜ Remove the front bolt (**A**) from the mounting (**B**) and withdraw the spring (**C**) from the vehicle.

❑ **STEP C6:** Refitting is the reverse of the removal process, bearing in mind the following points.
➜ Do not fully tighten the spring attachment nuts until the weight of the vehicle is on the wheels.
➜ Check and adjust the setting of the load sensing valve - see *Chapter 12, Part G*

Section D: Fiesta Courier and Combi Models.

See illustration in *Part A, Type 15*.

Torsion bar springs are used on the Fiesta Courier and Combi models.
➜ Although these springs can be removed on their own, special tools are needed to set vehicle ride height and suspension geometry during refitting.
➜ The rear suspension, including torsion bars - can be removed as a unit.
➜ If it is necessary to remove the torsion bars separately, have the work carried out by a suitably equipped Ford dealer.

JOB 6: REAR STRUT – *remove, replace*.

❑ **STEP 1:** Use a jack or stand to support the relevant trailing arm.
➜ Do not use excessive force along the trailing arm - these components are relatively easily damaged.

❑ **STEP 2:** Remove the strut attachment bolt at the lower end of the trailing arm.

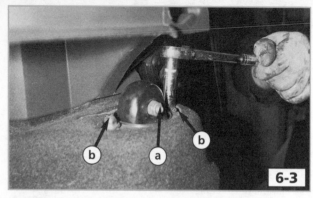

6-3

☐ **STEP 3:** Detach the top of the shock absorber.
→ IMPORTANT NOTE: On models with two upper attachment nuts, do not attempt to remove the through bolt (**a**) until the strut has been removed from the vehicle and a suitable spring compressor has been fitted.
→ Working inside the rear of the vehicle, remove any plastic protective caps and undo the two strut top mounting nuts (**b**) or, depending on type...

☐ **STEP 4:**
...the single central nut (arrowed) - you will need to hold the top of the threaded section of the strut while the nut is undone.

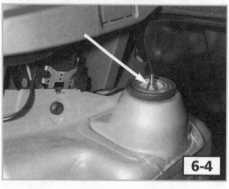

6-4

→ The strut should remain supported on the trailing arm but you may need to have someone else hold the strut from outside the vehicle while the top is being undone.

☐ **STEP 5:** Lower the trailing arm while supporting the strut and withdraw the strut from the vehicle.

☐ **STEP 6:**
The procedure for dismantling, inspecting and reassembling the rear strut is similar to that used for the front strut - see *Part C, Job 4*.

6-6

→ With spring compressors fitted this is the nut and bolt holding the strut top in place.

☐ **STEP 7:** Refitting the rear strut is the reverse of the removal process, bearing in mind the following points.
→ Where 'Nyloc' type nuts are fitted, new nuts must be used during reassembly.
→ Fully tighten the strut mounting nuts to the correct torque but only when the weight of the vehicle is on its wheels.

JOB 7:   REAR ANTI-ROLL BAR – *remove, replace.*

☐ **STEP 1:** Disconnect the ends of the anti-roll bar from the suspension trailing arms.
→ In some cases, the anti-roll bar is bolted directly to the trailing arm and in others it is connected via a link arm.
→ If link arms are fitted, they will have bushes in them and these should be checked for wear.

☐ **STEP 2: ESCORT AND ORION 1980 TO 1989:** The anti-roll bar cannot be removed from these models without removing, or at least lowering the fuel tank.
→ Support the fuel tank and remove the three attachment bolts.
→ Lower the tank so that the anti-roll bar can be removed from the left-hand side of the vehicle.
→ Take care not to stretch or damage the fuel pipes and hoses.

☐ **STEP 3:** The anti-roll bar is bolted to the vehicle's body (**A**).
→ Remove the attachment nut or nuts and take off the bracket (**D**).
→ Remove the anti-roll bar (**C**) complete with the rubber bushes (**B**). Check and replace the bushes if necessary.

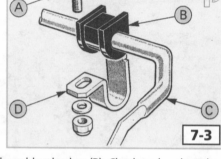

7-3

JOB 8:   REAR AXLE ASSEMBLY – *dismantle, overhaul, replace.*

See *Part A* for an explanation of where the various components described here are fitted.
→ Shock absorber and spring removal are covered in *Jobs 4 and 5*.
→ Hub and hub bearing removal are covered in *Jobs 2 and 3*.

Section A: Fiesta 1976 to 1989

☐ **STEP A1:** To disconnect the trailing arm from the body, remove the through bolt (arrowed) from the bracket on the body.

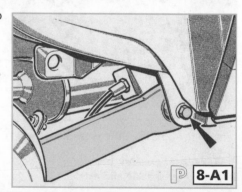

8-A1

→ If the trailing arm is to be removed from the vehicle, it can now be unbolted from the axle – see *Job 5, Step 2*.
→ If the trailing arm is being disconnected so that the whole rear axle can be removed, there is no need to disconnect it from the axle mounting bracket.

❑ **STEP A2:**
The Panhard rod is disconnected from the body mountings by removing the nut and through bolt (a) and from the axle mountings by removing the bolt (b).

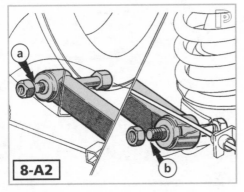
8-A2

❑ **STEP A3:** If the whole rear axle assembly is being removed, disconnect the parking brake, the brake hydraulics and fuel system components.

Section B: Escort and Orion 1980 to 1990 – not leaf-spring models.

See *Part A* for an explanation of where the various components described here are fitted.
→ Shock absorber and spring removal are covered in *Jobs 4 and 5*.
→ Hub and hub bearing removal are covered in *Jobs 2 and 3*.

❑ **STEP B1:** Each trailing arm is located at the body with a through bolt and nut...

8-B1

❑ **STEP B2:** ...and at its front end it is supported by a nut, washers and bushes at the base of the suspension arm.

❑ **STEP B3:** If the lower arm is to be removed, it is best to detach the brake hydraulic components (a) to avoid any risk of damage.

8-B2

→ The system will need to be bled after reassembly – see *Chapter 12, Brakes*.
→ The outer lower suspension arm nut and through bolt are shown here (b).
→ For reference, this is the tie bar fixing nut (c).

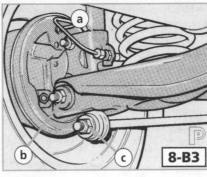
8-B3

❑ **STEP B4:** Disconnect where necessary, the following:
→ **MODELS WITH ABS BRAKES:** The load proportioning valve from the rear suspension.
→ **MODELS WITH REAR ANTI-ROLL BARS:** The anti-roll bar link from the suspension arm – see *Job 7*.

❑ **STEP B5:** Place a jack beneath the lower suspension arm and just take the pressure off the coil spring.

❑ **STEP B6:**
Remove the inner pivot bolt (both bolts arrowed).

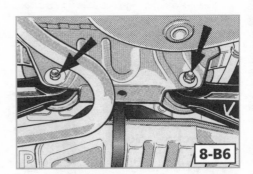
8-B6

❑ **STEP B7:** Remove the outer pivot bolt.

❑ **STEP B8:** Carefully lower the lower arm so that the tension is removed from the coil spring. Remove the arm and coil spring from the vehicle.

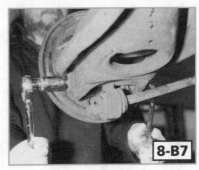
8-B7

❑ **STEP B9:** Refitting is the reverse of the removal process but do not fully tighten nuts and bolts until the weight of the vehicle is on its wheel.

Section C: Fiesta, Escort and Orion from 1989 and Ka.

❑ **STEP C1:** Disconnect the parking brake cables at each rear wheel - see *Chapter 12, Part K*.
→ Disconnect the rear brake flexible hoses from the brackets on the axle - see *Chapter 12, Part C*.
→ **MODELS WITH MODULATOR TYPE ABS:** Remove the retaining nuts and disconnect the load proportioning valve links from the axle - see *Chapter 12, Part G*. The load proportioning valves should not be removed.

➜ **MODELS WITH ELECTRONIC ABS:** Disconnect the battery negative lead and separate the two sections of the rear wheel sensor cable connector at the bracket under the vehicle. Remove the connector from the bracket - see *Chapter 12, Part I*.

❐ **STEP C2:** Place a suitable support, such as a trolley jack, under the centre of the rear axle (arrowed).

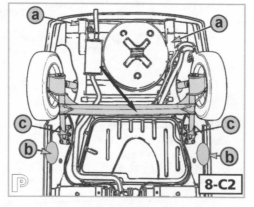

8-C2

➜ Use a block of wood between the jack and axle to prevent damage.

➜ ONLY USE THE JACK TO SUPPORT THE WEIGHT OF THE AXLE - you will damage the axle if you attempt to lift the vehicle or raise the axle against the springs.

➜ Use points **(b)** as lifting points, and points **(a)** for chassis stands.

➜ These are the pivot bracket locations – **(c)**.

❐ **STEP C3: EITHER:** Remove the four pivot mounting bracket bolts (arrowed) on each side of the vehicle.

❐ **STEP C4: OR:** You can remove just the pivot bolts.

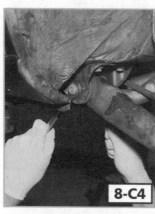

8-C4

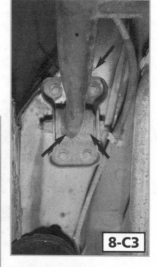

8-C3

❐ **STEP C5:** Remove the suspension strut to axle attachment bolt on each side - see *Job 6*.

➜ **ESTATE/WAGON VERSIONS:** These are the attachment points (arrowed). As you lower the axle assembly, the tension will be released from the coil springs.

❐ **STEP C6:** Lower the jack and withdraw the axle.

8-C5

❐ **STEP C7:** Refitting is the reversal of removal:

➜ Attach the pivot bush mounting brackets first, making sure that the locating cones are seated correctly.

➜ If disconnected, refit the trailing arms to pivot bush mounting bracket - do not fully tighten bolts.

➜ Refit the axle to the suspension strut but do not fully tighten the attachment bolts.

➜ Reconnect the hydraulic pipes and hoses and bleed the hydraulic system - see *Chapter 12, Part K*.

➜ Adjust the parking brake.

➜ Fully tighten the attachment bolts to the correct torque figures when the weight of the vehicle is on the wheels.

Section D: Escort Van (leaf spring suspension).

❐ **STEP D1:** Disconnect the following (when fitted):

➜ The hydraulic hoses and pipes at the bracket on the axle tube.

➜ The load sensing valve from the rear axle - see *Chapter 12, Part G*.

➜ The parking brake cables at each rear wheel - see *Chapter 12, Part D*.

❐ **STEP D2:** Place suitable supports under the left and right-hand sides of the rear axle.

❐ **STEP D3:** Remove the shock absorber lower attachment bolts - see *Job 4*.

❐ **STEP D4:** Remove the 'U'-bolts attaching the spring to axle - see *Job 5*. Lower and withdraw the axle from vehicle.

❐ **STEP D5:** Refitting is the reversal of removal:

➜ Offer up the axle to the spring and refit the 'U'-bolts – see *Job 5*.

➜ Fit the lower shock absorber attachment bolts but do not fully tighten the nuts until the weight of the vehicle is on the wheels.

➜ Bleed the appropriate section of the hydraulic system. Adjust the parking brake.

Section E: Fiesta Courier and Combi Models.

Although the rear suspension can be removed as a unit, do not dismantle the suspension unless you have access to the special tools needed to set vehicle ride height and suspension geometry during refitting.

❐ **STEP E1:** Follow the procedures given in *Section D* as far as the end of *Step D3*.

❐ **STEP E2:** Remove the four bolts, two each side, attaching the axle assembly to the vehicle.

➜ Lower and withdraw the axle assembly from the vehicle.

❐ **STEP E3:** Refitting is the reverse of removal:

➜ Refit the four bolts attaching the axle assembly to the vehicle followed by the shock absorber attachment bolts. Do not fully tighten the bolts until the weight of the vehicle is on its wheels.

➜ Bleed the appropriate section of the hydraulic system. Adjust the parking brake.

CHAPTER 12: BRAKES

PLEASE READ **CHAPTER 2 SAFETY FIRST** BEFORE CARRYING OUT ANY WORK ON YOUR CAR.

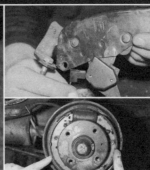

Part A: Front Brakes Inspection, Replacement, Overhaul

CONTENTS

SAFETY FIRST!

BRAKES AND BRAKING SYSTEMS

If you have not been trained in this work, but wish to carry it out, we strongly recommend that you have a garage or qualified mechanic check your work before using the car on the road.

• Always replace brake pads and shoes in sets of four, or discs and drums in pairs.

• After fitting new brake shoes or pads, avoid heavy braking - except in an emergency - for the first 150 to 200 miles (250 to 300 km).

• See *Chapter 2, Safety First!* for more brake and safety information.

JOB 1:   FRONT BRAKES - *pad replacement.*

Section A: All Fiesta models up to 1989, except XR2.

❏ **STEP A1:** This is an exploded view of the caliper type fitted to Fiestas up to 1989.

❏ **STEP A2:** After removing the road wheel, pull out the key-retaining split-pins (**P**) from each of the two keys (**O**); apply inwards pressure to the caliper and slide out the keys, as in the drawing.

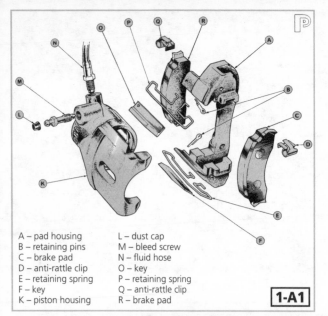

A – pad housing
B – retaining pins
C – brake pad
D – anti-rattle clip
E – retaining spring
F – key
K – piston housing

L – dust cap
M – bleed screw
N – fluid hose
O – key
P – retaining spring
Q – anti-rattle clip
R – brake pad

1-A1

❒ **STEP A3:** The caliper can now be lifted away from the pad housing (illustration *1-A1, item A*), leaving the pads behind – carefully lever sideways to free them, taking care not to lose the anti-rattle springs (*1-A1, item Q*) and (*1-A1, item D*) from the top and bottom edges of the pads as they will be needed for the new pads.

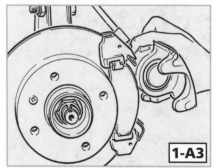

1-A2

1-A3

❒ **STEP A4:** The piston has to be retracted into its housing so that it will pass over the increased width of the new pads.
→ A special Ford tool is specified for this job (see illustration) but the job can be done using a woodworkers G-cramp, or a large pair of grips.
→ IMPORTANT NOTE: See *Step B16* before doing so.

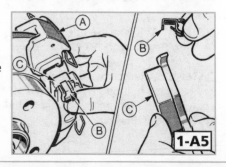

1-A4

1-A5

❒ **STEP A5:** Note how the caliper's (**A**) anti-rattle clips (**B**) fit onto the old pads (**C**), then transfer them to the new ones – this illustration will help you to position them.

❒ **STEP A6:** Fit the new pads into the housing, followed by the caliper. Replace the keys (*1-A1, item O*) and fit new retaining springs (*1-A1, item B and arrowed*).

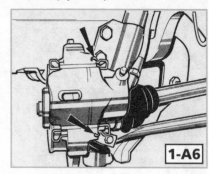

1-A6

❒ **STEP A7:** Pump the brakes several times to check that they work (!) and to expand the piston and push the pads against the disc, before using the vehicle on the road.

Section B: Escort to 1990; Fiesta from 1989 and all XR2; all Ka models.

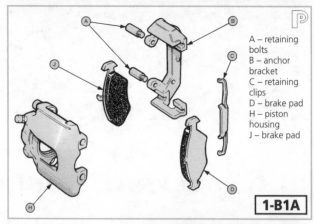

A – retaining bolts
B – anchor bracket
C – retaining clips
D – brake pad
H – piston housing
J – brake pad

1-B1A

❒ **STEP B1A:** This exploded diagram shows the layout of the 'Teves'-type caliper.

❒ **STEP B1B:** Note, on some late models the flat retaining spring (*1-B1A, item C*) has been replaced by a round-wire version, as shown here.

1-B1B

TOP TIP!

❒ **STEP B2:** • You will need some form of tool to retract the caliper piston into its bore.
• It can be improvised using a woodworking G-cramp or valve spring compressor tool and one of the old brake pads.

❒ **STEP B3:** First disconnect the brake wear indicator wiring, if fitted to your car, by pulling the connector (**A**) apart.

➜ The caliper is retained by two hollow bolts (**B**) for which an Allen key is required, either of the socket-adapter type shown at (**C**) or...

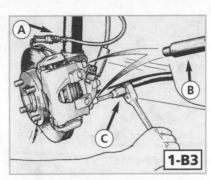

1-B3

❒ **STEP B4:** ...you could use the type shown here and available from your local accessory shop.
➜ IMPORTANT NOTE: Later models have plastic caps fitted to the bolt dust-excluding tubes which surround the bolts – remove them first. The bolts themselves are likely to be very stiff to turn initially, but take care as they often release quite suddenly, 'skinning' the knuckles of the unwary!

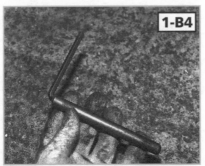

1-B4

❒ **STEP B5:** Remove both bolts completely, but don't remove the caliper until...

❒ **STEP B6:** ...the caliper assembly has been cleaned off with brake cleaner to prevent brake dust being disturbed into the atmosphere – or your lungs!

1-B5

❒ **STEP B7:** If a wear-ridge is present on the outer edge of the disc you may find it necessary to lever the caliper carefully against the disc to retract the piston slightly.
➜ Use a screwdriver as shown, or see *Step B12* if a large pair

1-B6

1-B7

1-B8

of grips are available. Note that you must never lever vigorously against the disc because of the risk of damaging it.

1-B9

❒ **STEP B8:** The caliper assembly can now be pulled forwards over the disc. Note that the outer pad may remain with the carrier bracket and require a sharp tap or two from a hammer to free it.

❒ **STEP B9:** The inner pad has a three-legged spring retaining it to the hollow piston – the pad usually comes away easily, but might need a tap from a hammer to free it if corroded.

1-B10

❒ **STEP B10:** Spray brake cleaner over the carrier bracket, paying particular attention to the pad seatings and those areas not accessible when the pads are fitted.

❒ **STEP B11:** Wire brush the pad seatings on the bracket, removing any hard scale or rust by scraping with an old screwdriver or chisel.

1-B11

❒ **STEP B12:** Retracting the piston is necessary before fitting new pads; this can be done earlier in the sequence when the caliper is still attached to the carrier as shown here, or at this stage, before cleaning. See *Step B16* regarding fluid level in the master cylinder reservoir.

1-B12

SAFETY FIRST!

❒ **STEP B13:** • NEVER allow the caliper to hang by the flexible brake hose. Unseen damage can occur to the hose that may not materialise until later, possibly when the brakes are needed in an emergency. Improvise a simple 'hook' from stout wire and suspend the caliper from the shock absorber/spring seat.

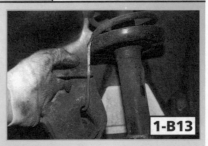

1-B13

STEP B14: Check the piston dust-excluder seal for splits, chafing or perishing. If any sign of brake fluid is present a leak is indicated, and you should renew the affected caliper.

1-B14

Put a **very thin** smear of special brake grease (NOT ordinary grease) on the steel backs of the brake pads to reduce the risk of noisy brakes. KEEP GREASE OFF ALL FRICTION SURFACES!

STEP B15: Re-assemble the new pads to their seats, fit the caliper and bolts, replace the pad retaining spring (if fitted) and reconnect the wear indicator wiring. Do not over-tighten the caliper bolts – firm hand pressure is sufficient.

1-B15

TOP TIP!

STEP B16: • As the piston is forced into its bore, the brake fluid it displaces will cause the master cylinder reservoir level to rise, possibly to the point of overflowing.
• Raise the bonnet so that the master cylinder can be observed as the piston is pushed home – it may be necessary to siphon a small quantity of fluid from the reservoir, for which purpose an old battery hydrometer is particularly useful to 'suck' fluid from the reservoir.

1-B16

STEP B17: Pump the brakes several times to check that they work (!) and to expand the piston and push the pads against the disc, before using the vehicle on the road.

Section C: Escort from 1990.

STEP C1: Remove the safety clip from the lower cross pin.

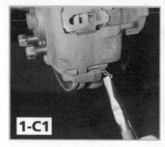

1-C1

STEP C2: Drift the pin from caliper.

1-C2

STEP C3: Swing the caliper upwards. Make sure that the flexible hose is not strained.
→ If necessary release the flexible hose from the strut.
→ Wash the caliper assembly with brake cleaner – see *Step B6*.

1-C3

STEP C4: Remove the pads from the pad housing.
→ A build up of dust and corrosion can mean that some force is needed.

1-C4

STEP C5: Check the visible portion of the piston and the dust cover for damage or leaks.
→ A damaged or incorrectly fitted dust cover will allow dirt and water onto the piston and bore resulting in wear or seizure.
→ If damage is found, fit a new or exchange caliper.

1-C5

STEP C6: Retract the piston using a tool such as this one available from Sykes-Pickavant, taking care not to damage the thin rubber dust cover.

1-C6

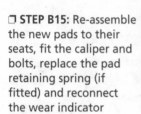

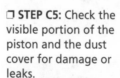

• Check when you are retracting the pistons to make sure that hydraulic fluid does not spill out of the master cylinder. See **Step B16**.

IMPORTANT NOTE: On Fiesta models from 1989 to 1995, Escort and Orion models from 1990 to 1997, Ford specify that the hydraulic master cylinder cap is not to be inverted when it is removed.

❑ **STEP C7:** Clean the pad housing paying particular attention to the pad supports. Some scraping to remove corrosion and dust build-up may be necessary.

FACT FILE

ADHESIVE BACKING ON PADS

• Depending on manufacturer, an adhesive material with protecting paper or foil may be applied to the pad backing plate.
• If the new pads have this feature remember to remove the protective covering before fitting.
• Follow the pad manufacturer's instructions.

❑ **STEP C8:** Lightly smear anti-seize grease on the pad supports and refit the pads.

❑ **STEP C9:** Slide the piston housing over the pads taking care not to damage the dust cover on the caliper piston.

❑ **STEP C10:** To complete the assembly:
→ Insert the cross pin and refit the safety clip.
→ Reconnect the brake wear warning wiring, if fitted.
→ Remount the flexible hose on the strut, if removed.

❑ **STEP C11:** Pump the brakes several times to check that they work (!) and to expand the piston and push the pads against the disc, before using the vehicle on the road.

JOB 2:   FRONT CALIPERS - *removal, replacement.*

• The brake hose may be difficult to undo from the piston housing and it is often best to loosen the connection before removing the piston housing, just sufficient to be sure that the connector will undo easily when the piston housing is removed. Take care not to twist the hose excessively.
• Use a properly designed brake hose clamp to prevent fluid leakage, do not use self gripping pliers such as 'Mole Grips' as these can damage flexible hoses.

❑ **STEP 1:** Place a brake hose clamp over the flexible hose as near to the caliper as possible.

❑ **STEP 2:** Loosen the flexible hose at the caliper (see illustration *2-3A, item 1*).
→ If fitted, disconnect the brake wear warning wiring.

❑ **STEP 3A: ESCORT FROM 1990:** Remove the spring clips (a) and drive out the pin (b) – see **Job 1, Section C**.
→ use a hexagonal wrench (c) to undo the caliper bolt (d).
→ Lift off the caliper (e).

❑ **STEP 3B: ALL OTHER MODELS:** See **Job 1, Section A or B**.

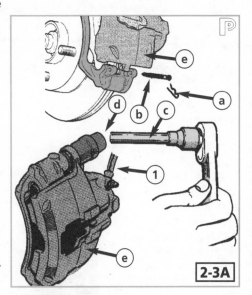

2-3A

❑ **STEP 4:** Unscrew the caliper from the flexible hose, leaving the hose in place.

❑ **STEP 5:** You can now move the caliper out of the way.
→ **EITHER:** Remove the fixed bracket separately.
→ **OR:** Leave the piston housing

2-5

attached to the fixed bracket and, after removing the two bolts holding the fixed bracket in place, lift the complete caliper assembly away from the disc.

❑ **STEP 6:** Reassembly and refitting is the reversal of dismantling and removal process.
→ Make sure the seal is not damaged as the piston is refitted.

❑ **STEP 7:** Make sure the hydraulic connections are tight, then bleed the brakes. See **Part I**.

JOB 3:   FRONT DISCS – *remove, replace.*

FACT FILE

FIXING TYPES

• **MODELS WITH WHEEL BOLTS:** The disc is held in place with a screw.
• **MODELS WITH WHEEL STUDS:** There is usually a spring clip fitted over one of the studs to hold the disc in place after a wheel has been removed.

❏ **STEP 1:** Raise the front of the vehicle and remove the appropriate wheel.

❏ **STEP 2:** Remove the piston housing and pads. See *Job 1*

❏ **STEP 3:** Remove the caliper support. See *Job 2, Step 4.*

❏ **STEP 4A: EITHER:** Remove the disc retainer – the spring washer should be on a stud (arrowed). It is often missing!

3-4A

→ The dust cap has been removed.

❏ **STEP 4B: OR:** Undo the disc retaining screw.

❏ **STEP 5:** If the disc doesn't come away easily, tap carefully around the periphery – ONLY with a soft-faced mallet.

3-4B

❏ **STEP 6:** Clean the areas on which the disc will seat and fit a new disc.
→ A smear of anti-seize compound should make any future removals a little easier.

3-5

❏ **STEP 7:** Refit the pads and piston housing. See *Job 2.*

Part B: Rear Brakes
Inspection, Replacement, Overhaul

CONTENTS

SAFETY FIRST!

• See *SAFETY FIRST!, BRAKES AND BRAKING SYSTEMS* at the beginning of this Chapter.

JOB 1:   REAR BRAKE DRUM/HUB – *remove, inspect brakes, replace.*

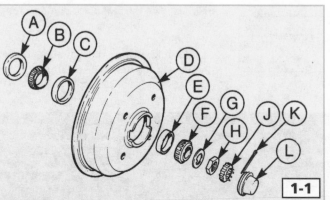

A – grease retainer
B – bearing cone
C – inner cup
D – drum and hub
E – outer cup
F – bearing cone
G – tab washer
H – locknut
J – nut retainer
K – split pin
L – grease cup

1-1

❏ **STEP 1:** This is an exploded view of the rear drum/hub assembly.

❏ **STEP 2:** Fully release the parking brake lever and, on all models except the early Fiesta described below, slacken the parking brake cable at the adjuster.

• Rocking the drum from side to side can help with its removal.
• **HOWEVER:** If, when you remove the outer bearing, you find it is has a nylon cage, TAKE GREAT CARE.
• These nylon cages are very easily damaged, particularly if the hub has to be rocked over the linings during removal.

DRUM AND HUB COMBINED - BEARING DISTURBED

❏ **STEP 3:** Lever off the grease cap taking care not to cause any damage.

❏ **STEP 4:** Remove and discard the split pin; remove and retain the castellated cap (arrowed).

1-3

❏ **STEP 5:** Unscrew the hub nut.
➔ On earlier models this is handed i.e. left-hand thread on the left-hand near-side and right-hand thread on the right-hand side.
➔ On later models, both sides have a right-hand washer. Look carefully at the thread on the stub axle if you are not sure which type is fitted.

1-4

❏ **STEP 6:** Slide the brake drum off the stub axle, catching the thrust washer and outer race, shown here separately.

1-6

MODELS WITH DRUM AND HUB COMBINED - BEARING NOT DISTURBED

❏ **STEP 7:** • For later cars, Ford changed the design of the integral rear hubs and drums, and recommend that the hub bearings are not disturbed.
• For this reason, many find it easier to remove the hub and leave the stub axle attached, as with earlier cars.

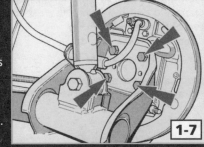
1-7

❏ **STEP 8:** Undo the four bolts holding the stub axle to the carrier and remove the brake drum and stub axle from carrier.

1-8

MODELS WITH SEPARATE DRUM

❏ **STEP 9: MODELS WITH WHEEL BOLTS:** Undo the retaining screw.
➔ The screw head is easily damaged so, if it is difficult to remove, use an impact screwdriver such as the Sykes-Pickavant type shown here.

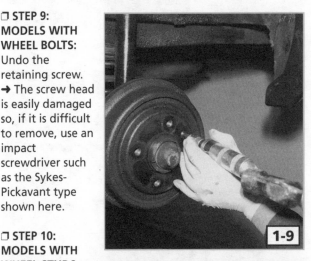
1-9

❏ **STEP 10: MODELS WITH WHEEL STUDS:** Remove the spring clip retainer fitted to one of the studs. This clip is identical to the one used on the front discs – see *Part A, Job 3, Step 4A*.

1-10

☐ **STEP 11:** Remove the drum from the hub.

☐ **STEP 12:** Inspect the brake shoes for lining thickness and for uneven wear, contamination and scoring.
→ The brake shoes should be replaced if the friction material thickness, at any point, is less than 1.0 mm or if it is expected that the shoes will wear below this figure before the next service.

TOP TIP!

• Once the brake shoes are removed, residual pressure in the brake hydraulic system will result in one, or both, pistons being pushed from the wheel cylinder.
• An elastic band or soft wire can be wrapped around the wheel cylinder to stop the pistons from popping out.

☐ **STEP 13:** Note whether the hub nut had a left-hand or right-hand thread.
→ Tighten the hub nut as shown in the following Fact File.
→ Refit the dust cap and road wheel.
→ Apply the brakes firmly, several times, before driving the vehicle. This expands the auto. adjuster – and checks that the brakes work!
→ Check the brake fluid level.

1-13

FACT FILE
TIGHTENING REAR HUB NUTS

Procedures differ for different models. Use the procedure applicable to the vehicle you are working on:

FIESTA TO 1980 AND ESCORT TO 1990 (Adjustable taper – roller bearings)
• Tighten nut to 20 to 25 Nm (15 to 18 lbf. ft) while turning drum anti-clockwise.
• Slacken nut by 180 degrees and check that hub/drum can spin.
• Fit road wheel. Grasp top and bottom of wheel and rock the wheel. There MUST be a small perceptible movement. If not, repeat process and recheck.
• Fit nut retainer, a NEW split-pin (turn ends over and around nut) and dust cap.

FIESTA FROM 1989 AND ESCORT FROM 1990 (Non-adjustable)
• Tighten the hub nut to 250 to 290 Nm (184 to 214 lbf. ft.).
• Hub nuts must be loosened and tightened with vehicle on wheels.
• Use a new hub nut each time. Stake as shown in *Chapter 11, Steering, Suspension.*

JOB 2: REAR BRAKE SHOES – *replace.*

Section A: Fiesta to 1983.

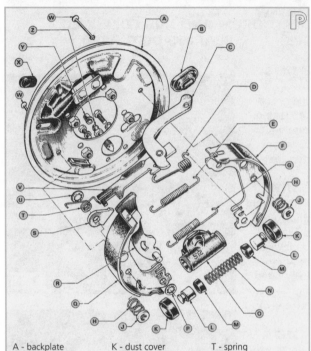

A - backplate	K - dust cover	T - spring
B - rubber boot	L - piston	U - spring retaining
C - parking brake	M - piston seal	washer
operating lever	N - wheel cylinder	V - spacer strut
D - lever return spring	spring	W - pin
E - shoe return spring	O - wheel cylinder	X - inspection hole
F - trailing brake shoe	P - spring retaining	grommet
G - shoe return spring	washer	Y - dust cover
H - hold down spring	Q - leading shoe	Z - bleed nipple
J – shoe holding down	R - large ratchet	
washer	S - small ratchet	2-A1

☐ **STEP A1:** Note the positions of shoes, springs and the parking brake operating mechanism. The right-hand brake is shown here.

A – clevis pin
B – parking brake cable
C – parking brake lever
D – washer
E – spring clip

2-A2

☐ **STEP A2:** Undo the parking brake cable clevis at the appropriate wheel.

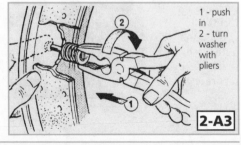

1 - push in
2 - turn washer with pliers

2-A3

☐ **STEP A3:** Release and remove the leading shoe hold down spring.

→ Support the pin from the rear of the brake back plate;
→ Push the cup washer towards the brake shoe (**1**) to compress the spring;
→ Rotate the cup washer (**2**) through 90 degrees.

☐ **STEP A4:** Rotate the leading shoe away from the back plate:
→ Release the springs;
→ Remove the leading shoe.

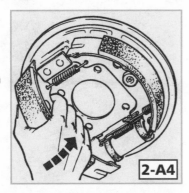
2-A4

☐ **STEP A5:** Release and remove the trailing shoe hold down spring. See *Step A3*.

☐ **STEP A6:** Slide the lower end of the spacer strut (**A**) out from the slot (**B**) in the back plate.

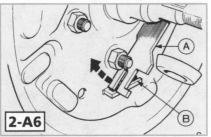
2-A6

☐ **STEP A7:** Lift the trailing shoe (**A**) and strut (**C**) away, withdrawing the parking brake operating lever (**D**) through the back plate (**B**).

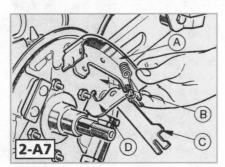
2-A7

☐ **STEP A8:** Dismantle the leading shoe assembly (**B**).
→ Lever off and discard the two spring clips (**A, C**), remove the two ratchet arms (**E, F**) and the spring (**D**).

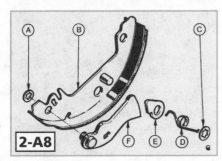
2-A8

☐ **STEP A9:** Twist the spacer strut (**B**) and parking brake operating lever from the trailing shoe (**A**) by rotating the spacer strut and releasing the spring (**C**).

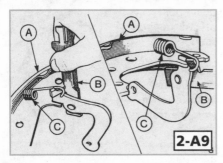
2-A9

☐ **STEP A10:** Clean the brake back plate – wash off with spray-on brake cleaner, such as Wurth spray - and check that the pistons have not seized in the wheel cylinder. See *Job 3*.

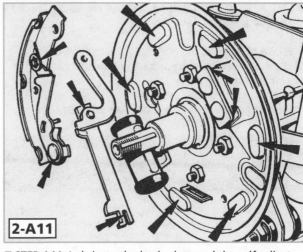
2-A11

☐ **STEP A11:** Lubricate the back plate and the self-adjust linkage at the points indicated with a smear of Wurth anti-seize grease.

☐ **STEP A12:** Reassembling the following is the reverse of the removal procedure:
→ The strut spacer.
→ The parking brake operating lever and spring to the new trailing shoe.
→ Refitting the trailing shoe to the back plate.

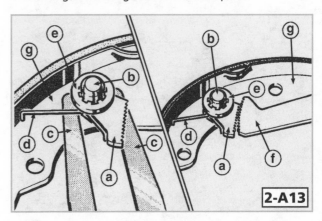
2-A13

☐ **STEP A13:** Reassemble the leading shoe (**g**):
→ Place the small ratchet (**a**) on its post (**b**) with two 0.2 mm (0.008 in.) feeler gauges (**c**) between the ratchet and the shoe.
→ Refit the return spring (**d**), a new retaining clip (**e**) and check for free operation of the ratchet.
→ Fit the large ratchet (**f**) to the shoe (**g**) and press on a new retaining clip making sure there is almost no clearance between the ratchet and the shoe.
→ Position the ratchets relative to each other with the overlap shown.

☐ **STEP A14:** Fit the stronger of the two pull-off springs to the leading and trailing shoes at the pivot ends, i.e. opposite to the wheel cylinder position. See *Step A4*.
→ Hook the leading shoe under the fixed pivot, press the shoe against the back plate and locate the shoe on the wheel cylinder piston.
→ Make sure that the long ratchet is engaged in the spacer strut.
→ Refit the hold down spring to the leading shoe.
→ Fit the weaker pull-off spring to the leading shoe and, using suitable pliers, the trailing shoe.

STEP A15: Using a suitable hook, pull the spring loaded ratchet back against its spring.

STEP A16: Replace the boot over the parking brake operating lever and re-assemble the parking brake clevis assembly – see *Step A2*.

STEP A17: Refit the brake drum. See *Steps B12-on*.

Section B: All other models with rear drum brakes.

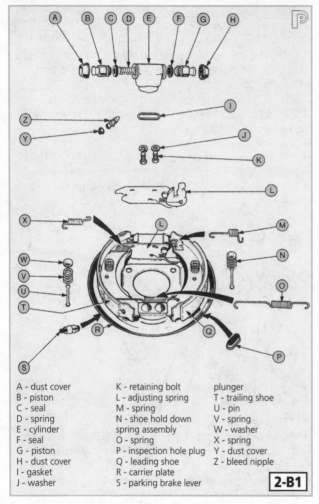

A - dust cover
B - piston
C - seal
D - spring
E - cylinder
F - seal
G - piston
H - dust cover
I - gasket
J - washer

K - retaining bolt
L - adjusting spring
M - spring
N - shoe hold down spring assembly
O - spring
P - inspection hole plug
Q - leading shoe
R - carrier plate
S - parking brake lever

plunger
T - trailing shoe
U - pin
V - spring
W - washer
X - spring
Y - dust cover
Z - bleed nipple

2-B1

STEP B1: Note the positions of shoes, springs and the parking brake operating mechanism. This is a typical arrangement for vehicles manufactured before 1983.

STEP B2: Note the positions of shoes, springs and the parking brake operating mechanism. This is a typical arrangement for vehicles manufactured after 1983.

STEP B3: Remove the brake shoe hold down springs.
→ **EARLY MODELS:** Push the clip towards the brake shoe and release the shoe by rotating the clip or retaining pin through 90 degrees.
→ **MORE RECENT MODELS:** A spring clip (arrowed) slides out of engagement.

STEP B4: Lever first one then the other brake shoe away from the fixed pivot (a) in the direction of the arrows, and

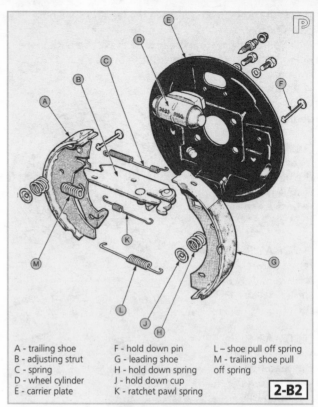

A - trailing shoe
B - adjusting strut
C - spring
D - wheel cylinder
E - carrier plate

F - hold down pin
G - leading shoe
H - hold down spring
J - hold down cup
K - ratchet pawl spring

L – shoe pull off spring
M - trailing shoe pull off spring

2-B2

pull them – lower-ends only – over the pivot to take tension off the spring.
→ Remove the lower pull-off spring.
→ **SEPARATE DRUM MODELS:** You will find it easier to remove the lower pull-off spring before unhooking the brake shoes from the fixed pivot.

2-B3

STEP B5: Disengage the shoes from the wheel cylinder and remove the upper pull-off/strut support springs.

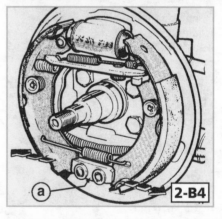

2-B4

STEP B6: Remove the adjusting strut from the trailing shoe and, by releasing the adjuster to its maximum extent, from the leading shoe.

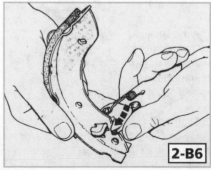

2-B6

☐ **STEP B7:** Detach the parking brake cable from the trailing shoe lever.

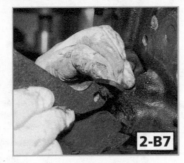

2-B7

☐ **STEP B8:** Lubricate the back plate at the points indicated with a smear of anti-seize grease. See *Section A, Step A11*.

☐ **STEP B9:** Reassembling and refitting the brake shoes to the back plate is the reverse of the dismantling procedure.

☐ **STEP B10:** Refit the brake drums. See *Step B12-on*.

☐ **STEP B11:** Refit the parking brake adjuster.

REFITTING DRUMS

☐ **STEP B12:** Inspect the drum before refitting.
→ Brush or, preferably, wash out dirt and dust from the drum with Wurth brake cleaner fluid.
→ Examine the drum for any signs of scoring, cracking, corrosion, uneven or excessive wear.
→ Remember to replace both drums at the same time.

☐ **STEP B13:** Check the drum for normal wear and fit new drums if the maximum diameter has been exceeded, or is likely to be exceeded before the rear brakes are next checked.
→ Ford specify a 1 mm (0.040 in.) limit for wear measured across the diameter.

☐ **STEP B14:** Refit the drum, adjusting the position of the brake shoes on the wheel cylinders and pivot point so that the drum slides easily into place.

SEPARATE DRUM

☐ **STEP B15:** Clean the surfaces that mate together on the drum and hub flange.

☐ **STEP B16:** Fit the drum over the brake shoes, making sure it butts squarely against the flange, and refit the retaining screw or spring clip.

DRUM AND HUB COMBINED - BEARING NOT DISTURBED

☐ **STEP B17:** Fit the drum over the brake shoes and bolt the hub to the back plate and torque the bolts to specified figure - see *Chapter 1, Facts and Figures*.

☐ **STEP B18:** If necessary, adjust the parking brake. See *Part C, Job 1*.

JOB 3:   REAR WHEEL CYLINDER - *remove, replace*.

☐ **STEP 1:** Remove the brake shoes.

TOP TIP!
• It may be possible to use the auto. expander to hold the brake shoes apart sufficiently for you to remove the wheel cylinder.
• If not, the shoes will have to come off.

☐ **STEP 2:** Fit a brake hose clamp to the flexible hose.

TOP TIP!

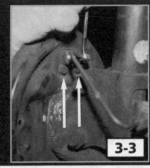

3-3

☐ **STEP 3:** • Take out the bleed nipple. This will enable you to 'get at' the hose connector.
• Note the positions of the wheel cylinder retaining bolts (arrows).

☐ **STEP 4:** Disconnect the hydraulic line from the back of the wheel cylinder.
→ This is a Sykes-Pickavant brake connector spanner and is less likely to round off the flats than an ordinary open-ended spanner.
→ Take out the two bolts holding the wheel cylinder to the backplate.

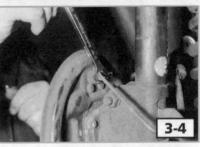

3-4

☐ **STEP 5:** Remove the wheel cylinder from the backplate.
→ It may be held in place with rust and need to be tapped free.

3-5

☐ **STEP 6:** Fit a new wheel cylinder as the reverse of removal.
→ Remove the hose clamp and bleed the brakes.

JOB 4:   REAR DISC BRAKES - *pad replacement*.

☐ **STEP 1:** Rear disc brakes consist of a caliper operating on a disc which also contains a brake drum for the parking brake.

4-1

a – pad retaining pin
b – anti-rattle plate
c – pads
d – caliper
e – retaining bolt
f – brake shoe steady pins
g – backplate
h – brake shoes
i – return springs
j – steady pin springs
k – steady pin retaining cups
l – brake disc and drum assembly

4-2

☐ **STEP 2:** These are the components of the rear disc brake assembly.

☐ **STEP 3:** To inspect the pads:
➜ Use a narrow punch to drift out the retaining pins.
➜ Take off the anti-rattle plate.
➜ Extract the pads.

IMPORTANT NOTE: In all other respects, removing and replacing brake pads is the same as for front disc brakes. See *Part A*.

JOB 5:   REAR BRAKE DISC – remove, replace.

☐ **STEP 1:** With the caliper removed, use a Torx bit to remove the screw (**a**) holding the disc/drum in place.

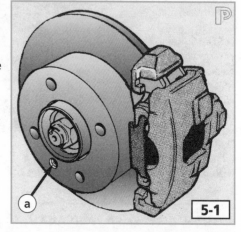

5-1

☐ **STEP 2:** Release the parking brake. The disc/drum assembly can now simply be lifted away.

IMPORTANT NOTE: For information on checking and replacing a brake disc - see *Part A*.

5-2

JOB 6:   REAR DISC BRAKE - PARKING BRAKE SHOES - *inspection, replacement.*

☐ **STEP 1:** Remove the disc/drum assembly – see *Job 5*.

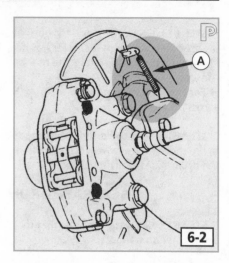

6-2

☐ **STEP 2:** If the shoes are to be replaced:
➜ Detach the parking brake return spring (**A**) and disconnect the cable from the operating lever.

☐ **STEP 3:** Note the parking brake components shown here:

☐ **STEP 4:** Remove and replace brake shoes by following closely the information in *Part A*.

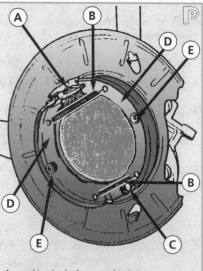

A – parking brake lever mechanism
B – pull-off springs
C – adjusters
D – brake shoes
E – brake shoe steady pins

6-3

Part C: Parking Brake Inspection, Adjustment, Repair

CONTENTS

JOB 1: PARKING BRAKE - *check, adjust.*

IMPORTANT NOTE:
• The parking brake is normally kept in adjustment by the rear brake automatic adjusters, so adjustment should only be necessary when new components have been fitted or any of the cables have stretched.

SAFETY FIRST!

• Before starting work, see *SAFETY FIRST!, BRAKES AND BRAKING SYSTEMS* at the beginning of this *Chapter and Chapter 2, Safety First!*

Section A: Early Fiesta (to 1983).

☐ **STEP A1:** Check the operation of the parking brake.
➔ The lever should move six or seven notches to fully apply the parking brake and it should not be possible to turn the rear wheels with the parking brake fully on.
➔ When the parking brake is released both rear wheels should rotate freely without any signs of the brakes binding.

☐ **STEP A2:** Raise the rear of the vehicle and release the parking brake.

☐ **STEP A3:** Apply the foot brake several times to fully take up the auto adjuster mechanism.
➔ Slacken the adjuster locknut (**B**).

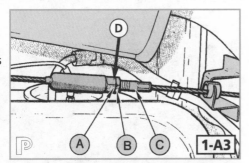

➔ Loosen off the adjuster (**A**) to slacken the cable (**C**).
➔ Tighten the adjuster until the slack is just taken out of the cable.
➔ Tighten the adjuster a further three complete turns.
➔ Tighten the locknut.
➔ When adjustment is complete, the machined section (**D**) should not protrude beyond the locknut.

☐ **STEP A4:** Check the operation of the parking brake - see *Step 1*.

Section B: Fiesta from 1989 to 1995.

☐ **STEP B1:** Check the movement of the adjustment plungers (arrowed) on the backplate.
➔ Adjustment is correct when the total in-and-out movement of

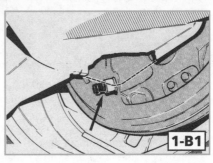

both plungers added together is between 0.5 and 2.0 mm (0.02 and 0.08 in.).
➔ If plunger movement is outside the specified limits the parking brake should be adjusted.

☐ **STEP B2:** If the parking brake needs adjusting:
➔ The adjuster is found beneath the vehicle under the left-hand side floor.
➔ **LATER MODELS:** Pull out the plastic locking pin (arrowed).

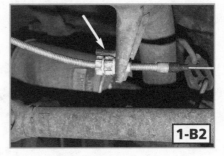

➔ Slacken the plastic locknut and turn the inner nut to adjust the cable.
➔ Turning the inner nut clockwise – against the bracket – reduces parking brake lever travel; loosening it increases the travel.
➔ Retighten the outer locknut and refit the pin, if fitted, after carrying out the adjustment.

Section C: Escort 1990 to 1995 and Ka models.

☐ **STEP C1:** The adjuster is located behind the parking brake lever and is accessed after removing the parking brake lever trim – see illustration *1-D1*.

☐ **STEP C2A: ESCORT:** There is a parking brake plunger on the brake backplates as described in *Section B*. Adjust the parking brake as described in that section.

❏ **STEP C2B: KA MODELS:** Adjust the parking brake so that it operates on the rear wheels as described in **Section D**.

Section D: Fiesta and Escort 1995-on.

❏ **STEP D1:** The parking brake adjuster is beneath the rear of the parking brake lever trim.
→ The adjuster is a vertical nut on a threaded rod as indicated here.

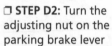

1-D1

❏ **STEP D2:** Turn the adjusting nut on the parking brake lever until there is no tension in the parking brake cable.
→ Now apply and release the parking brake lever three times.

❏ **STEP D3:** Raise and support the rear of the vehicle.
→ Pull the parking brake lever on by one notch and turn the adjusting nut until you can feel the rear brakes just starting to rub on the drums when the rear wheels are rotated.
→ Pull the parking brake lever on a further four or five notches and it should not now be possible to turn the rear wheels.
→ When the parking brake lever is fully released, both rear wheels must be able to rotate freely without any signs of the brakes binding.

Section E: Models with rear disc brakes.

❏ **STEP E1:** Raise and support the rear of the vehicle and release the parking brake.
→ Remove the rubber plug from the brake backplate (position arrowed).

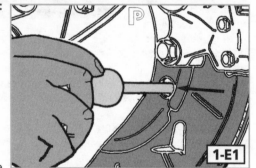

1-E1

→ Use a flat-bladed screwdriver to rotate the adjuster wheel seen inside the backplate until the road wheel is just gripped and prevented from turning.
→ Now back off the adjuster but only by enough until the road wheel rotates without binding.

❏ **STEP E2:** Repeat the process for the other road wheel.

❏ **STEP E3:** Check that the parking brake brake operation is now correct:

→ It should not be possible to turn the rear wheels with the parking brake fully on.
→ When the parking brake is released, both rear wheels must be able to rotate freely without any signs of the brakes binding.
→ Refit the rubber plugs on the back of the backplates.

JOB 2: PARKING BRAKE CABLE - *replacement*.

Refer to the illustrations in **Job 1**, in connection with this Job.

IMPORTANT NOTE: **VEHICLES WITH HEAT SHIELDS:** On many vehicles, there is a heat shield which prevents you from gaining access to the parking brake cable. In such cases, the heat shield screws will have to be taken out and the heat shield removed.
• On some models, it may be necessary to lower the exhaust pipe slightly by freeing the rear-end from its mounting rubbers – see **Chapter 9, Ignition, Fuel, Exhaust**. DO NOT put strain on the rest of the system!

To remove the parking brake cables you will need to:
→ Slacken the cables at the adjuster.
→ Remove the cables as described in the following Steps.
→ Refit and adjust – see **Job 1**.
→ Disconnecting the ends of the cables is as follows:

❏ **STEP 1:** To remove the cable from the parking brake lever you will need to:
→ Remove the split pin (or circlip on later models) at the pivot (A).

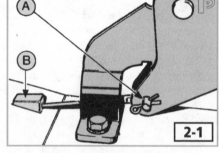

2-1

→ Drift out the pivot pin.
→ Disconnect the guide (B) and remove the cable.

TOP TIP!

❏ **STEP 2: BRAKES WITH SINGLE SECONDARY CABLE:** Follow the same process for removing the pivot from the equaliser.
• Place a suitable socket between the equaliser and the vehicle's body so that the pivot pin can be drifted up into the space inside the socket.

2-2

❏ **STEP 3: BRAKES WITH TWIN SECONDARY CABLES:** Remove the front end of the cables from the equaliser depending on which type is fitted to the vehicle you are working on.

→ ESCORT: To detach the outer cable from the support, you will have to pull out the horseshoe shaped clip holding the outer to the support.

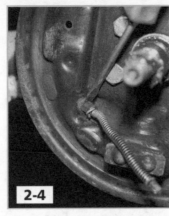

2-4

❏ **STEP 4:** To remove the parking brake cables from the backplate, you will first have to remove the brake shoes – see *Part A*.

→ The rear end of the cable is either held to the backplate with a clip which must first be levered off or is a friction fit into the backplate and needs to be drifted out.

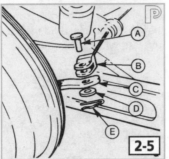

2-5

❏ **STEP 5:** On other models, the cable is fitted to a lever on the inside of the backplate.

→ Pull out the spring clip (**E**) take off the washer (**D**) drift out the clevis pin (**A**) and remove the end of the cable (**B**) from the parking brake lever (**C**).

❏ **STEP 6:** Insert cable guide clevis pin through mounting bracket and locate pin through transverse cable.

→ Mount roller and cable guide

A - cable guide
B - equaliser bracket
C - secondary cable
D - cable rolller
E - spring clip
F - transverse cable

2-6

onto clevis pin and secure with spring clip.
→ Connect cable to rear carrier plate, and secure with clevis pin and spring clip.
→ Adjust cable at parking brake lever.

JOB 3: PARKING BRAKE LEVER AND SWITCH - *remove, refit.*

See also *Job 1*.

❏ **STEP 1:** Before dismantling, disconnect the battery negative (-) earth/ground terminal. See *Chapter 10, Electrical, Dash, Instruments, Fact File: Disconnecting the Battery* BEFORE doing so!

→ You now need to gain access to the base of the parking brake lever. The degree of difficulty depends on the model you are working on.

❏ **STEP 2: FIESTA TO 1995:** Try easing the carpet away from the base of the parking brake lever.

→ If this does not give sufficient access you can try removing the front seats, which may free the carpet enough to allow sufficient access - see *Chapter 14, Interior, Trim*.

→ If it is still not be possible to gain access you will have to remove the carpet or cut it carefully.

❏ **STEP 3: FIESTA FROM 1995 AND KA:** Remove the parking brake lever gaiter.

❏ **STEP 4: ESCORT AND ORION:** If a long central console is fitted it will need to be removed - see *Chapter 14, Interior, Trim*.
→ You may still need to ease the carpet away from the base of the parking brake lever.

❏ **STEP 5: ESCORT, ORION AND FIESTA TO 1995:** Remove the pin or clip from the parking brake cable clevis and withdraw the clevis pin.

❏ **STEP 6: FIESTA FROM 1995 AND KA:** Completely undo and remove the parking brake adjuster nut. See *Job 1*.

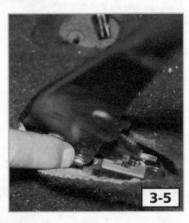

3-5

TOP TIP!

• Removing the adjuster nut on the parking brake lever allows the 'T' bar to fall out of engagement with the equaliser plate, when fitted. If this happens you will have to get under the car and re-engage the 'T' bar with the equaliser plate - removing and refitting the exhaust heatshields to gain access.

❏ **STEP 7:** Unscrew the two parking brake lever retaining bolts/nuts (**A**) and lift away the parking brake lever.
→ Remove the switch cover, if fitted.
→ EITHER: Disconnect the parking brake switch connector (**B**)

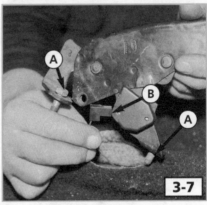

3-7

❏ **STEP 8: OR:** Remove the parking brake warning switch from the lever.

❏ **STEP 9:** Refitting the parking brake lever is the reverse of the removal process.

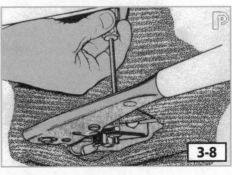

3-8

Part D: Hydraulic Reservoir and Master Cylinder Removal, Replacement

CONTENTS

SAFETY FIRST!

• Before starting work make sure you are aware of the health and safety precautions that need to be taken when working with braking systems.

• In particular you should be aware of the dangers associated with asbestos, hydraulic fluid and working under a raised vehicle.

• See *SAFETY FIRST!, BRAKES AND BRAKING SYSTEMS* at the beginning of this Chapter.

• When fitting new safety related components, follow any specific instructions issued by the component manufacturer.

• Ford specify in their servicing procedures that the vacuum in the servo must be released before the master cylinder or servo are removed - see *Job 2, Step 1.*

JOB 1:   HYDRAULIC RESERVOIR - *removal, refitting.*

❏ **STEP 1:** Exhaust the vacuum in the servo:
➜ **EITHER:** By disconnecting the vacuum pipe at the servo end, (see *Part E, Job 2), Step 2.*
➜ **OR:** By repeatedly pressing on the brake pedal with the engine turned off.

❏ **STEP 2:** Before dismantling, disconnect the battery negative (-) earth/ground terminal. See *Chapter 10, Electrical, Dash, Instruments, Fact File: Disconnecting the Battery* BEFORE doing so!

❏ **STEP 3:** Where fitted, disconnect the electrical connection to the fluid level warning transmitter and pressure differential switch.

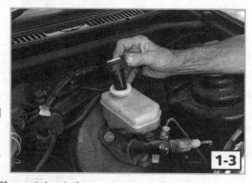

➜ The pressure differential switch was only fitted to some early Fiesta variants but most models have a fluid level warning transmitter.

IMPORTANT NOTE: On Fiesta models from 1989 to 1995, Escort and Orion models from 1990 to 1997, Ford specify that the hydraulic fluid master cylinder cap must not be inverted when it is removed.

TOP TIP!

HYDRAULIC CYLINDER AND MASTER CYLINDER DRAINING
❏ **STEP 4:** • Before removing the reservoir and master cylinder remove as much fluid as possible from the reservoir with a small syringe.
• Alternatively, you can drain the reservoir and master cylinder through the front bleed nipples. Follow the procedure for bleeding the front brakes but do not top up the master cylinder - see *Part I.*
• Use plenty of rags or wipes to absorb unavoidable leakage.

❏ **STEP 5: FIESTA AND KA FROM 1995 WITH HYDRAULIC CLUTCH:** Release the hose clip and remove the clutch supply hose from the reservoir - be prepared for some spillage from the hose. Plug or cover the open connections to reduce the chances of contamination.

❏ **STEP 6: FIESTA, ESCORT AND ORION WITH EARLY MODULATOR-TYPE ABS:** Disconnect the hydraulic return pipes (arrowed) that run from the modulator units to the reservoir.
➜ The connectors at the reservoir end will either be flexible hoses with jubilee-type clips (Escort and Orion models) or push-on fittings (Fiesta models).

➜ To release the push-on types, push the outer boss towards the reservoir while pulling the pipe away from the reservoir.

TOP TIP!

• If you are removing the master cylinder as well as the reservoir, they can be separated later on the workbench as we have done here.

STEP 7: Detach the reservoir by rocking carefully from side to side and pulling it off the two stubs (arrowed).

1-7

STEP 8: Check the two rubber seals for deterioration or damage and fit new seals if necessary.

STEP 9: Refitting the reservoir is the reverse of the removal process.

STEP 10: Refill the reservoir with hydraulic fluid and bleed the complete hydraulic system - see *Part I*.

1-8

JOB 2: HYDRAULIC MASTER CYLINDER - *removal, refitting.*

STEP 1: Before dismantling, disconnect the battery negative (-) earth/ground terminal. See *Chapter 10, Electrical, Dash, Instruments, Fact File: Disconnecting the Battery* BEFORE doing so!
→ Drain the reservoir and master cylinder - see *Job 1*.

STEP 2: On the appropriate vehicles disconnect the hydraulic connections to the reservoir - see *Job 1, Step 5*.

STEP 3: Detach the hydraulic unions.

STEP 4: KA MODELS WITH ABS: The hydraulic pipes are made from nylon.

2-3

STEP 5: VEHICLES WITH SERVO ASSISTED BRAKES: Remove the two nuts holding the master cylinder to the servo.

2-5

STEP 6: Lift the master cylinder, and the reservoir if still attached, away from the servo.

STEP 7: VEHICLES WITHOUT SERVO ASSISTED BRAKES: Working in the front footwell on the driver's side at the top of the brake pedal:
→ Remove the clip (**A**) from the operating rod clevis pin (**B**) and withdraw the pin.

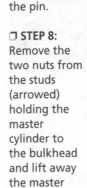

2-6

STEP 8: Remove the two nuts from the studs (arrowed) holding the master cylinder to the bulkhead and lift away the master cylinder.

2-7

STEP 9: Refitting, or fitting a new master cylinder, is the reverse of the removal procedure.
→ Use a new gasket between the master cylinder and the servo.

2-8

STEP 10: Refill the reservoir with hydraulic fluid and bleed the complete hydraulic system - see *Part I*.

Part E: Brake Servo
Test, Remove, Replace

CONTENTS

SAFETY FIRST!

• See *SAFETY FIRST!, BRAKES AND BRAKING SYSTEMS* at the beginning of this *Chapter and Chapter 2*, Safety First!

• Ford specify in their servicing procedures that the vacuum in the servo must be released before the master cylinder or servo are removed - see *Job 1, Step 1.*

• Disconnect the battery BEFORE disconnecting the electrical connections to the hydraulic fluid level warning transmitter and brake pressure differential switch, if fitted,

JOB 1: BRAKE SERVO NON-RETURN VALVE - *testing.*

❒ **STEP 1:** Disconnect the vacuum pipe from both the servo, (see *Job 2, Step 2*), and the engine.

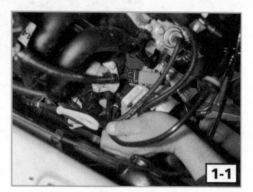
1-1

❒ **STEP 2:** Inspect the sealing grommet at the servo end of the vacuum pipe.

❒ **STEP 3:** Try blowing (don't suck - hydraulic fluid danger!) through the pipe from each end:
→ Air should flow easily in the servo to engine direction but not the other way.
→ If the valve is not working correctly the complete pipe must be replaced.

❒ **STEP 4:** Refit the vacuum pipe.

JOB 2: BRAKE SERVO – *removal, replacement.*

❒ **STEP 1:** Remove the master cylinder. See *Part D, Job 2*.

❒ **STEP 2:** Remove the vacuum hose from the servo.

❒ **STEP 3: FIESTA 1.25L AND 1.4L, FROM 1996:** Disconnect the electrical connectors (arrowed) to the emission control components on the bracket directly above the servo unit.
→ Undo and remove the bracket retaining screw, unclip and remove the bracket.
→ On these models you will also have to remove the fuel pipe support bracket on the right-hand side of the servo.

2-2

2-3

❒ **STEP 4:** On models fitted with the later electronically controlled four-wheel ABS, disconnect the electrical connector from the ABS hydraulic unit - see *Part H.*

2-5

❒ **STEP 5:** Remove the four nuts holding the servo unit to its mounting bracket and move the servo forward sufficiently to gain access to the push-rod clevis pin.

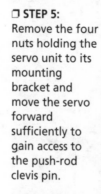

2-6

❒ **STEP 6:** On Escort and Orion models in particular, if you cannot gain sufficient access to remove the push-rod clevis pin, loosen and remove the servo bracket mounting nuts (arrowed) in the front passenger footwell. You will need to peel back the carpet.

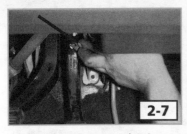

2-7 **2-8**

❏ **STEP 7:** On Escort and Orion models it may also be necessary to release the push-rod from the brake pedal.
➜ The clip (arrowed) is easily released from the push-rod with pliers.

❏ **STEP 8:** Remove the servo clevis pin retaining clip...

❏ **STEP 9:** ...and the clevis pin. The servo can now be removed.

❏ **STEP 10:** Refitting is the reversal of removal.

2-9

Part F: Brake Pressure Control Valves Removal, Replacement, Adjusting

CONTENTS

SAFETY FIRST!

• The early type of pressure control valve uses a moving ball inside the valve to sense vehicle deceleration. Fitting the right valves for the vehicle, and in the correct location and orientation, is essential if this type of valve is to work properly.

JOB 1: PRESSURE REGULATING VALVES - remove, refit.

❏ **STEP 1:** Note the positions of the brake pipes fitted to the pressure control valve unit so that they can be refitted in the correct locations.

❏ **STEP 2:** Undo the hydraulic connectors.
➜ Remove the bolts securing the valve unit to the mounting bracket and lift away the valve unit.

❏ **STEP 3:** Refitting is the reverse of removal:
Ensure that the valve unit is orientated correctly.
➜ Bleed the brakes. See *Part 1.*

JOB 2: LOAD SENSING VALVES - remove, refit.

❏ **STEP 1:** Load sensing valves are fitted to Escort vans, Fiesta Courier and Fiesta Combi models.
➜ The valve fitted to the Escort van is shown here. This type of valve is located at the rear of the vehicle close to the rear axle.

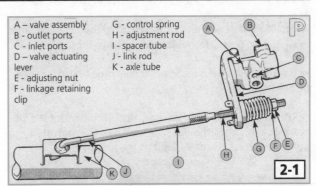

A – valve assembly
B - outlet ports
C - inlet ports
D – valve actuating lever
E - adjusting nut
F - linkage retaining clip
G - control spring
H - adjustment rod
I - spacer tube
J - link rod
K - axle tube

2-1

❏ **STEP 2:** Undo and remove the four hydraulic connections (arrowed) from the valve.

❏ **STEP 3:** Undo two bolts (**A**) holding valve to bracket.
➜ Item (**B**) is the adjusting nut.

2-2

❏ **STEP 4: FIESTA COURIER AND COMBI:** Unhook the linkage from the rear axle and lift away the valve.

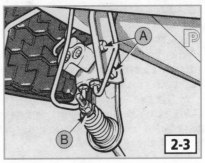

2-3

STEP 5: ESCORT VAN: Slide the spacer tube (*2-1, item I*) off the link rod (*2-1, item J*) and lift away the valve.
→ Unhook the link rod from the axle bracket - see *Step 4*.
→ On later van models the link rod is held in place by a spring clip.

STEP 6: Refitting is the reversal of removal:
→ Bleed the disturbed sections of the hydraulic system, (see *Part K*), and adjust the light laden valve - see *Job 4*.

JOB 3:   LOAD SENSING VALVES - *adjust*.

Section A: Fiesta Courier 1989 to 1995.

STEP A1: To adjust the load sensing valve you will need to get underneath the rear of the vehicle while the weight is still on the rear wheels.

STEP A2: Load the vehicle:
→ **FIRST:** So that the rear axle weight is 400 kg.
→ **LATER:** So that the rear axle weight is now 850 kg.

STEP A3: Measure the distance between the indicated points on the linkage.
→ At 400 kg rear axle weight the distance should be 147 mm
→ At 850 kg rear axle weight the distance should be 166 mm.
→ If either distance is incorrect the linkage length should be adjusted.

STEP A4: To adjust the linkage, slacken the locknut and move the rod until the distance between the indicated points is correct. Securely tighten the locknut.

Section B: Fiesta Courier and Combi from 1996.

IMPORTANT NOTE: Ford no longer give adjustment settings but specify the use of a setting tool. Have the work carried out by an approved Ford dealer.

Section C: Escort Van pre-1990 - check and adjust

IMPORTANT NOTE:
• When checking and adjusting the load sensing valve fitted to Escort Vans the vehicle must be unladen, with the fuel tank less than half full.

STEP C1: To adjust the load sensing valve you will need to get underneath the rear of the vehicle while the weight is still on the rear wheels.

STEP C2: Check the dimension (**C**) between the link rod (**A**) and the spacer tube (**B**).
→ If this is not within the specified range of 18.5 to 20.5 mm (0.76 to 0.84 in.), the linkage should be adjusted.

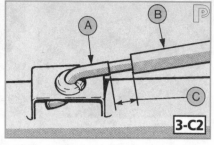

3-C2

STEP C3: Use the flats on the threaded adjustment rod to prevent it from rotating.
→ Turn the adjusting nut, to increase or decrease the dimension as appropriate.

Section D: Escort Van pre-1990.

STEP D1: See *Section C* up to *Step C1*.

STEP D2: Use the flats on the threaded adjustment rod to prevent it rotating and turn the adjusting nut until the groove (**B**) in the link rod (**A**) is aligned with the end of the spacer tube (**C**).

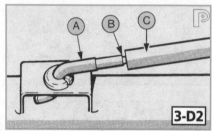

3-D2

Section E: Escort Van pre-1990.

STEP E1: See *Section C* up to *Step C1*.

STEP E2: Check the indicated dimension (**X**) and, if necessary, adjust the position of the nut until this is in the range 10 mm (0.4 in.) to 12 mm (0.5 in.).

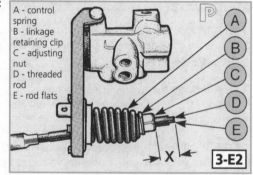

A - control spring
B - linkage retaining clip
C - adjusting nut
D - threaded rod
E - rod flats

3-E2

STEP E3: If necessary, rotate the spacer tube until the dimension (**C**) - see *Section C*, is within the range 18.5 mm to 20.5 mm.

STEP E4: Crimp the end of the spacer tube nearest the knurled section to prevent further rotation.

Section F: Escort Van post-1990.

❏ **STEP F1:** See *Section C* up to *Step C1*.

❏ **STEP F2:** Check the position of the rubber seal fitted to the end of the spacer tube. The end face of the seal should be within the width of the setting groove.

❏ **STEP F3:** If necessary adjust the position of the seal by holding the flats on the end of the rod, to prevent it rotating, and turning the adjusting nut to bring the end face of the seal within the width of the setting groove.

❏ **STEP F4:** New Valve: When the end face of the rubber seal is in the correct position, crimp the end of the spacer tube (the end next to the knurled section) onto the threaded rod.

JOB 4: LOAD PROPORTIONING VALVES - *removal, refitting, adjusting.*

Load proportioning valves are fitted to vehicles with the front-wheel-only ABS systems. These valves are fitted at the rear of the vehicle close to the rear axle or rear suspension components.

IMPORTANT NOTE: Correct adjustment of the load proportioning valves is essential if the vehicles brakes are to work properly. Ford do not give adjustment settings but specify the use of a setting tools and gauges. We recommend that the checking, removal, refitting and adjusting of the load proportioning valves is undertaken by an suitably equipped Ford dealer.

Part G: Stop Light Switch Adjusting, Replacement

CONTENTS

Page No.

Before dismantling, disconnect the battery negative (-) earth/ground terminal. See *Chapter 10, Electrical, Dash, Instruments, Fact File: Disconnecting the Battery* BEFORE doing so!

Two different types of stop light switch may be encountered:
➜ On early vehicles the stop light switch was held in place by locknuts.
➜ Later vehicles used a twist-to-lock type of stop light switch.
➜ The changeover date varies depending on model but, generally, after 1990 the twist-to-lock switch was used exclusively.

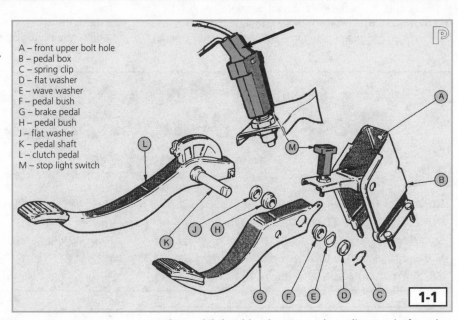

A – front upper bolt hole
B – pedal box
C – spring clip
D – flat washer
E – wave washer
F – pedal bush
G – brake pedal
H – pedal bush
J – flat washer
K – pedal shaft
L – clutch pedal
M – stop light switch

1-1

JOB 1: STOP LIGHT SWITCH - *check, adjust.*

The stop light switch is located in the driver's footwell at the top of the brake pedal. On some vehicles it is necessary to unclip and remove the lower fascia panel to gain access to the stop light switch.

❏ **STEP 1:** Switch on the ignition and press down on the brake pedal.

➜ The pedal should only move a short distance before the brake lights come on.
➜ If the lights do not come on, you should check the operation of the switch and, if necessary, carry out a check of the stop light switch electrical circuit - see *Chapter 10, Electrical, Instruments*.

TOP TIP!

• If the stop lights do not work it may not be the switch that is faulty - other problems, such as a poor connection or bad earth in the electrical circuit or a blown fuse can prevent the stop lights working.

□ **STEP 2:** It is possible to check the switch while it is still fitted but access is difficult. We recommend that the switch is removed and tested on the bench.

LOCKNUT TYPE SWITCH

□ **STEP 3:** The brake pedal (*1-1, item G*) should move a minimum of 5.0 mm (0.2 in) and a maximum of 20 mm (0.8 in) before the stop lights come on - this measurement 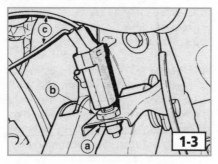 should be made at the centre line of the brake pedal footpad.

→ If necessary, loosen the locknut (**a**) and adjust the switch position using nut (**b**).
→ Retighten locknut (**a**) when complete.

□ **STEP 4: TWIST-TO-LOCK TYPE SWITCH:** No pedal movement figures are specified for the twist-to-lock type switch. If the switch is thought to be incorrectly adjusted, it is simply refitted in the correct position.
To remove the switch:
→ Unlock the switch by turning the switch body anti-clockwise and remove it from its bracket.
To fit the switch:
→ Hold the brake pedal in its normal position (against its return stop) so that it cannot move and push the switch downwards until the switch barrel contacts the brake pedal.

→ Turn the switch body clockwise to lock it in place and check for correct operation of the stop lights.
→ Make sure the switch is secure and not free to move in and out.

□ **STEP 5:** If adjusting the stop light switch does not cure the problem and an electrical check has not shown any problems with the stop light circuit, the stop switch should be removed for testing.

JOB 2: STOP LIGHT SWITCH - *remove, refit.*

□ **STEP 1:** Before dismantling, disconnect the battery negative (-) earth/ground terminal. See *Chapter 10, Electrical, Dash, Instruments, Fact File: Disconnecting the Battery* BEFORE doing so!

□ **STEP 2A: LOCKNUT TYPE SWITCH:** Remove the electrical connectors – see illustration *1-3, c*.
→ Loosen and remove the lower locknut.
→ The stop light switch can be withdrawn upwards and away from its retaining bracket.

□ **STEP 2B: TWIST-TO-LOCK TYPE SWITCH:** Remove the electrical connectors.
→ Rotate the switch body anti-clockwise and withdraw the switch upwards and away from its retaining bracket.

□ **STEP 3:** Refitting is the reverse procedure remembering to adjust the switch and refit the electrical connections.

Part H: ABS Components
Checking, Removal, Replacement

CONTENTS

JOB 1: ABS - *checking.*

Section A: Modulator type ABS (SCS system).

Each modulator unit is fitted with a belt-break warning switch. In the event of broken or very loose drive belt, an arm on the switch moves and the warning light on the instrument panel will illuminate.

□ **STEP A1:** Before dismantling, disconnect the battery negative (-) earth/ground terminal. See *Chapter 10, Electrical, Dash, Instruments, Fact File: Disconnecting the Battery* BEFORE doing so!

□ **STEP A2:** With the parking brake applied, switch on the ignition (key position II). If the ABS warning light does not illuminate the bulb should be tested and renewed. See *Chapter 10, Electrical, Instruments*.

□ **STEP A3:** Release the parking brake. If the warning light remains on with the parking brake off, there is probably a fault with the ABS. You should check modulator drive belt condition and tension.

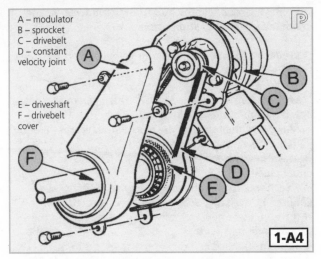

A – modulator
B – sprocket
C – drivebelt
D – constant velocity joint

E – driveshaft
F – drivebelt cover

1-A4

□ **STEP A4:** Working underneath the vehicle, locate the modulator units, which are fitted above the inner CV joints.
→ Some vehicles have an undertray which must be removed to gain access to the modulator units.
→ On Fiesta XR2i models you will also have to remove the front suspension crossmember - see *Chapter 11, Steering, Suspension*.

□ **STEP A5:** Remove the broken-belt warning switch from the modulator cover. See illustration *1-A6, positon a* for switch location.
→ Press the locking lever towards the switch body and carefully pull the switch clear.
→ Watch out for the operating arm catching on the drivebelt cover.

□ **STEP A6: ESCORT AND ORION, RIGHT-HAND MODULATOR COVER:** To remove the right-hand modulator cover undo the two nuts or bolts (arrowed)
→ On models from 1987, there is a third bolt holding the modulator cover in place.

1-A6

1-A7

□ **STEP A7: ESCORT AND ORION, LEFT-HAND MODULATOR COVER:** Left-hand modulator covers are held in place by three bolts (arrowed) - two at the top and one at the bottom.

□ **STEP A8: FIESTA:** Remove the two bolts holding the modulator covers in place - see *Step A6*.

□ **STEP A9:** Remove the modulator covers, taking care to prevent damage to the driveshaft CV boots.
→ Check the condition of the modulator drive belt.
→ If the belt is broken, cracked or obviously worn, it should be replaced - see *Job 3*.
→ Irrespective of condition, these belts should be replaced every 30,000 miles (48,000 km).

□ **STEP A10:** Check the tension of the drive belt:
→ Apply moderate finger pressure at a point mid-way between the two sprockets.
→ The belt should deflect 5.0 mm.
→ Adjust the tension if necessary - see *Job 2*.

Section B: Two-and four-wheel electronic ABS.

□ **STEP B1:** A dashboard warning light that does not go out indicates a fault with the ABS and it is recommended that you have the vehicle checked by an approved Ford dealer.

TOP TIP!

□ **STEP B2:** Check each wheel sensor and examine the wiring for signs of damage.
→ Check that the gap is not bridged by dirt, brake dust, mud or snow. These often cause sensor malfunction.

JOB 2: MODULATOR DRIVE BELTS - *adjusting, replacing.*

Section A: Modulator drive belt - adjusting.

□ **STEP A1:** Remove the modulator cover - see *Job 1, Section A*.

□ **STEP A2:** To adjust the modulator:
→ Slacken the modulator adjuster bolt (4) and move the modulator (3) to tension the belt.

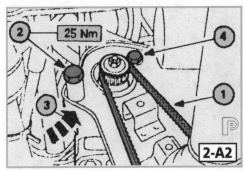

2-A2

→ Tension is correct when moderate finger pressure at a point (1) mid-way between the two sprockets results in 5.0 mm deflection – also see *Job 1, Step A10*.
→ If the modulator unit does not move easily you should also loosen the pivot bolt (2) and, if necessary, use a lever against the modulator unit.

➔ A wooden lever is preferred as components in this area, the transmission case in particular, can be damaged by excessive force.

❒ **STEP A3:** Retighten the adjuster bolt and, if loosened, the pivot bolt to the specified torques.
➔ Before tightening the adjuster bolt, smear copper grease on the exposed threads.

❒ **STEP A4:** Re-check drive belt tension once the bolts have been tightened.

❒ **STEP A5:** Refit the following:
➔ The drive belt cover.
➔ The broken-belt warning switch.
➔ Any splash or protection guards that may have been fitted.

Section B: Modulator drive belt - replacing.

TOP TIP!

• To remove the modulator drive belt you will have to separate the drive shaft from the transmission.
• Make sure you have a new circlip for the drive shaft and, if necessary, a splitpin for the steering arm ball joint before starting work.

❒ **STEP B1:** Remove the modulator cover - see *Job 1*.

❒ **STEP B2:** Slacken the modulator adjuster and pivot bolt (arrowed) and release the tension in the belt

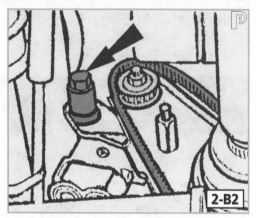

2-B2

so that the drive belt can be slipped off the sprockets.

❒ **STEP B3:** Disconnect the steering arm ball joint - see *Chapter 11, Steering, Suspension*.

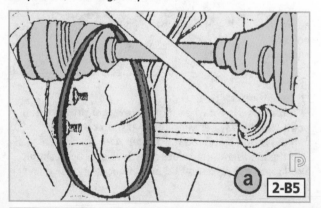

a   2-B5

❒ **STEP B4:** Disconnect the hub from the hub carrier - see *Chapter 11, Steering, Suspension*.

❒ **STEP B5:** Slide the modulator drive belt (**a**) off the drive shaft.

❒ **STEP B6:** Refitting is the reversal of the removal process, bearing in mind these points:
➔ Make sure the teeth on the modulator sprocket and CV joint are clean, dry and undamaged.
➔ Make sure the splines on the CV joint are clean and undamaged.
➔ Fit a new circlip to the splines on the CV joint - see *Chapter 11, Steering, Suspension* for driveshaft refitting.
➔ If fitted, use a new split pin when re-assembling the steering arm ball joint.
➔ Tighten all nuts and bolts to the specified torques.
➔ Top up the transmission lubricant to the correct level.
➔ Adjust drive belt tension - see *Job 2, Section A*.

JOB 3:   MODULATOR UNITS - *removal, refitting.*

Section A: Modulator units.

❒ **STEP A1:** Before dismantling, disconnect the battery negative (-) earth/ground terminal. See *Chapter 10, Electrical, Dash, Instruments, Fact File: Disconnecting the Battery* BEFORE doing so!
➔ Remove the cap from the hydraulic fluid reservoir.

IMPORTANT NOTE: On Fiesta models from 1989 to 1995, Escort and Orion models from 1990 to 1997, Ford specify that the hydraulic fluid master cylinder cap must not be inverted when it is removed.

❒ **STEP A2:** Drain as much fluid as possible from the reservoir - see *Part D, Job 1, Step 3*.

❒ **STEP A3: ESCORT MODELS:** Loosen the appropriate return-hose clip (arrowed) at the reservoir and disconnect the hose (LHD shown).
➔ The hose nearest the servo unit is from the right-hand modulator unit - the hose furthest from the servo is from the left-hand modulator unit.

3-A3

□ **STEP A4: FIESTA MODELS:** Disconnect the appropriate modulator return hose from the reservoir.
→ Push the hose towards the reservoir and then hold the collar while pulling the hose away.
→ The hoses and connectors are colour coded - the left-hand side is black and fits to the forward connection on the reservoir, the right-hand side is grey and fits to the rear connection on the reservoir.

□ **STEP A5:** Remove the drive belt cover - see *Job 1, Section A*. Slacken the adjuster and slide the drive belt off the modulator sprocket - see *Job 2, Section B*.

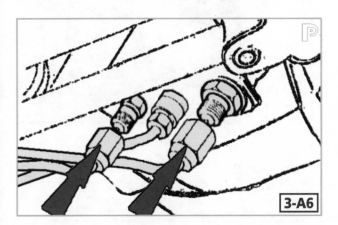

□ **STEP A6: ESCORT MODELS:** Disconnect the appropriate hydraulic pipes and hoses (arrowed) at the support bracket on the transmission crossmember.
→ Right-hand pipes and hoses should have yellow identifying bands.
→ Left-hand pipes and hoses should have white identifying bands.
→ Plug or cover the open hydraulic connections to prevent contamination.
→ Have a suitable container ready to collect any remaining hydraulic fluid.

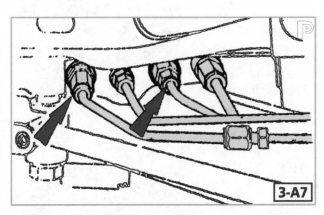

□ **STEP A7: FIESTA MODELS:** Disconnect the brake pipes (two arrowed) at the modulator unit.
→ Plug or cover the open hydraulic connections to prevent contamination.
→ Have a suitable container ready to collect any remaining hydraulic fluid.

□ **STEP A8:** Undo and remove the modulator adjuster and pivot bolts. Lift the modulator away.

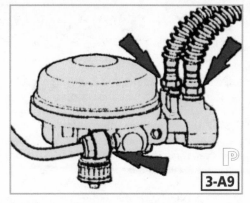

□ **STEP A9:** Disconnect the hydraulic pipes (arrowed) from the modulator.

□ **STEP A10:** Refitting is the reversal of removal:
→ The modulator units are not interchangeable from side to side. Right-hand units should have a part number with an 'A' suffix and a yellow arrow on the cover. Left-hand units should have a part number with a 'C' suffix and a white arrow on the cover. The arrows should point forward when the modulator units are fitted.
→ Adjust drive belt tension - see *Job 2, Section A*.
→ Fill the hydraulic reservoir and bleed the appropriate section of the braking system - see *Part I*.

JOB 4: HYDRAULIC UNIT - *removal, refitting.*

IMPORTANT NOTE: This Job is only applicable to ESCORT vehicles with a two-wheel electronically controlled ABS. Because of the need for specialist bleeding equipment it is recommended that removal of a hydraulic unit from vehicles with four-wheel electronically ABS is entrusted to a specialist Ford dealer.

□ **STEP 1:** Disconnect the battery and drain as much fluid as possible from the reservoir - see *Part D, Job 1, Step 3*.

□ **STEP 2:** Disconnect the hydraulic return lines from the master cylinder.
→ To release these connectors, push the pipe and collar towards the reservoir and then hold the collar while pulling the pipe away.
→ Unscrew and disconnect the unions at the master cylinder.

□ **STEP 3:** Disconnect the electrical multi-plug at the hydraulic unit.

□ **STEP 4:** Unscrew and disconnect the unions, two of which are at the rear of the hydraulic unit.

□ **STEP 5:** Unscrew the nut securing the multi-plug connector bracket and remove the bracket from the hydraulic unit.

□ **STEP 6:** Remove the retaining nut and bolt and lift the hydraulic unit away from the vehicle.

□ **STEP 7:** Refitting is the reversal of removal, except that you need to bleed the brakes.

JOB 5: ABS ELECTRONIC MODULE - *removal, refitting*

IMPORTANT NOTE: This Job is only applicable to ESCORT vehicles with a two-wheel electronically controlled ABS.

❒ **STEP 1:** Before dismantling, disconnect the battery negative (-) earth/ground terminal. See *Chapter 10, Electrical, Dash, Instruments, Fact File: Disconnecting the Battery* BEFORE doing so!

❒ **STEP 2:** Disconnect the wiring multi-plug, unscrew the three retaining bolts and lift away the ABS module.

❒ **STEP 3:** Refitting is the reversal of removal.

JOB 6: WHEEL SENSOR - *removal, refitting.*

❒ **STEP 1:** Before dismantling, disconnect the battery negative (-) earth/ground terminal. See *Chapter 10, Electrical, Dash, Instruments, Fact File: Disconnecting the Battery* BEFORE doing so!

6-2

❒ **STEP 2: FRONT WHEELS:** Unscrew the retaining bolt and remove the sensor from the hub carrier.

6-3

❒ **STEP 3: REAR WHEEL:** These are typical rear wheel fixings.

❒ **STEP 4:** Disconnect the sensor lead from the wiring loom, release the lead from the retaining clips and remove the sensor along with the lead.

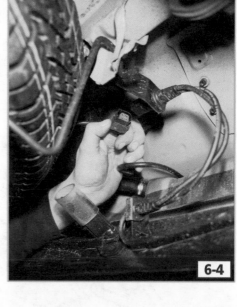

6-4

❒ **STEP 5:** Refitting is the reverse of removal.

JOB 7: WHEEL SENSOR RING - *removal, refitting.*

IMPORTANT NOTE: This Job is only applicable to ESCORT vehicles with a two-wheel electronically controlled ABS.

❒ **STEP 1:** Remove the hub carrier - see *Chapter 11, Steering, Suspension*.

❒ **STEP 2: SCREW-FIT SENSOR RING:** Unscrew and remove the bolts (arrowed) holding the sensor ring to the hub.

7-2

❒ **STEP 3: PRESS-FIT SENSOR RING:** If damaged, the press fitted sensor ring cannot be replaced separately, but must be renewed complete with the hub.

❒ **STEP 4:** Refitting is the reversal of removal:
➜ Make sure that the surfaces on which the sensor ring will seat are clean.
➜ Tighten the bolts to the correct torque.

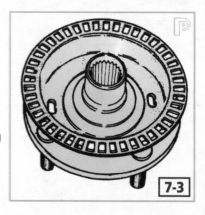

7-3

Part I: Bleeding the Brakes

CONTENTS

➜ If air enters the hydraulic unit on vehicles fitted with a four-wheel electronically controlled ABS, specialist equipment is needed to bleed the system. The vehicle should be taken to an approved Ford dealer.

SAFETY FIRST!

• See *Chapter 2, Safety First!.*

JOB 1:   HYDRAULIC SYSTEM – *brake bleeding.*

When bleeding the brakes:
➜ Start with the bleed nipple furthest away from the fluid reservoir, then its opposite on the same axle.
➜ Continue with the front wheel furthest from the reservoir, and finally the one nearest to it.

☐ **STEP 1:** Kits are available which make brake bleeding a simple one-man task. There are two basic equipment types. (Illustration, courtesy Sykes-Pickavant)

1-1

ONE-WAY VALVE KITS:
One-way valve kits use, as the name suggests, a non-return valve in the tube that fits over the bleed valve.
➜ When the bleed valve is opened and the brake pedal depressed, fluid and any trapped air flow out of the system.
➜ The non-return valve prevents the expelled fluid and air being sucked back into the system when the pedal is released, fresh fluid is drawn in from the reservoir so it is important to keep an eye on fluid level during this operation.

AIR PRESSURE KITS: Pressure kits use air pressure, normally from the spare tyre, to pressurise the hydraulic fluid reservoir.
➜ To reduce the chance of a fluid falling below the minimum level a pressurised fluid filled container is fitted to the hydraulic fluid reservoir.

☐ **STEP 2:** Remove the hydraulic reservoir cap and top up with the correct fluid to the maximum level. If you are using a one-man brake bleeding kit you should now follow the manufacturer's instructions for the particular kit. (Illustration, courtesy Sykes-Pickavant)

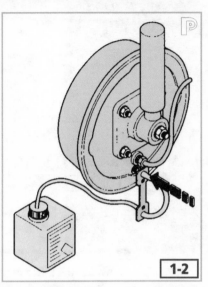

1-2

IMPORTANT NOTE: On Fiesta models from 1989 to 1995, Escort and Orion models from 1990 to 1997, Ford specify that the hydraulic fluid master cylinder cap must not be inverted when it is removed.

☐ **STEP 3:** If you are not using a brake bleeding kit you will need:
➜ A clean container, preferably glass or metal as hydraulic fluid attacks some plastics;
➜ Rubber or plastic tubing that is a tight fit over the bleed valve;
➜ A spanner for the bleed valve – preferably a purpose-made brake spanner or ring spanner is preferred;
➜ And an assistant.

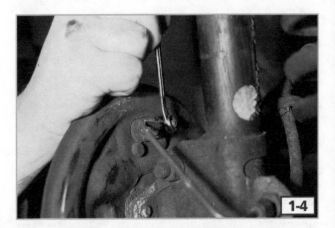

1-4

TOP TIP!

• If only part of the hydraulic system has been disturbed and you have taken care to minimise fluid loss it should not be necessary to bleed the whole system.
• If the complete system is being bled, bleed both rear brakes first followed by the front brakes.

STEP 4: Clean any dirt away from the bleed valve and, if fitted, remove the rubber dust cover.
→ If you are using a ring spanner, fit this to the bleed valve before fitting the tube over the bleed valve.
→ Place the free end of the tube in the container and put enough hydraulic fluid in the container to cover the end of the tube.

TOP TIP!

STEP 5: Ford recommend that the container is raised 300 mm (12 in.) above the bleed valve to reduce the chance of air seeping into the system around the threads of the open bleed valve.

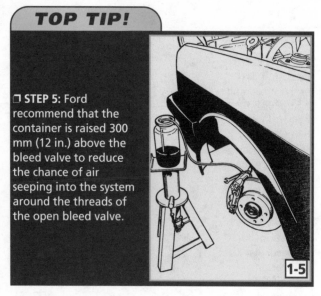

1-5

STEP 6: Press down on the brake pedal at the same time as your assistant loosens the bleed valve - the pedal should go all the way to the floor.
→ Tighten the bleed valve and release the brake pedal.
→ Repeat this operation until the fluid coming out of the bleed screw is clean and free from any air.
→ Make sure the level in the reservoir does not fall below the minimum mark during this operation otherwise air may be drawn into the system.

STEP 7: When clean fluid, free from air, comes from the bleed valve, securely tighten the bleed valve and remove the tube and spanner.

STEP 8: Repeat for the other bleed valves, as necessary.

STEP 9: Check the operation of the brake pedal to make sure that it feels firm.
→ Repeat the bleeding operation if there is any hint of sponginess.

JOB 2: HYDRAULIC SYSTEM - modulator (SCS) type ABS bleeding.

STEP 1: Make sure the reservoir is topped up to the maximum mark.

STEP 2: Slacken the by-pass valve Torx screw (arrowed) by one to one-and-a-half turns.

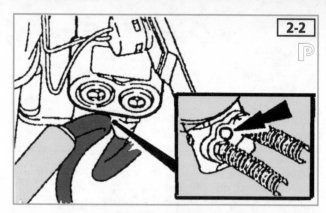
2-2

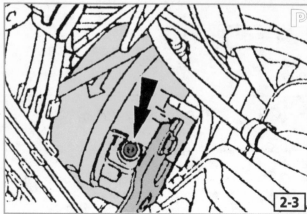
2-3

STEP 3: Press down on the modulator automatic bleed plunger (arrowed) until the plunger circlip contacts the modulator body.
→ Hold the plunger fully down and slowly pump the brake pedal at least 20 times.
→ Continue pumping until the hydraulic fluid returning to the reservoir is free from air.

STEP 4: Release the plunger and, if it does not move out to its original position, pull it out manually.

STEP 5: Tighten the by-pass Torx screw – see *Step 2*.

STEP 6: Repeat, if necessary, for the other modulator.

STEP 7: You can now bleed the system conventionally - see *Job 1*.

JOB 3: BRAKE FLUID – changing.

SAFETY FIRST!
• See *Chapter 2, Safety First!*.

STEP 1: Bleed the hydraulic system - see *Job 1*.
→ The aim is to flush old hydraulic fluid from the system replacing it with fresh fluid from the reservoir.
→ Bleed sufficient fluid through the bleed valves until you see fresh fluid come out of each bleed nipple.

CHAPTER 13: BODYWORK

*PLEASE READ **CHAPTER 2 SAFETY FIRST** BEFORE CARRYING OUT ANY WORK ON YOUR CAR.*

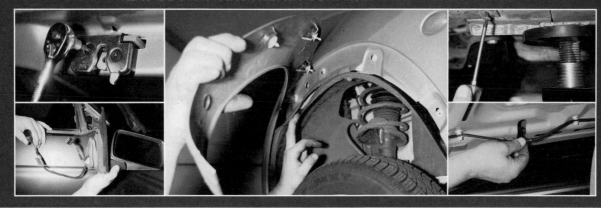

CONTENTS

JOB 1: RADIATOR GRILLE - *removal, replacement.*

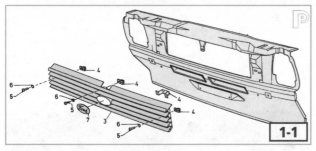

1-1

☐ **STEP 1:** Grilles are commonly held either by screws or clips – or both!
➡ Screws (**5**) and washers (**6**) are used on the *Fiesta 1976 to 1983, Escort and Orion 1990 to 1993* (with locating pegs at the rear): *Escort and Orion 1990 to 1993: Escort 1993 to 1996: Escort from 1996:*

☐ **STEP 2:** If screws are used remove them and lift away the grille.
➡ On other models covered by this manual, the grille is held solely by clips.

☐ **STEP 3:** On versions where, there are also screws holding the grille in place, remove if necessary.
➡ Locate the clips (**A** and **B**) and spring them free to remove the grille.

☐ **STEP 4: ESCORT AND ORION 1988 TO 1990:** The radiator grille is part of the front bumper and cannot be removed separately, see *Job 7*.

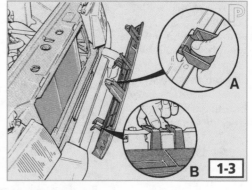

1-3

☐ **STEP 5: KA:** Remove the front bumper, see *Job 7* and unclip the radiator grille panels.

TOP TIP!

☐ **STEP 6:** Refitting is the reverse of the removal process, bearing in mind the following points.
➡ **FIESTA 1976 TO 1983:** Make sure the special nuts are fitted correctly in the front body panel apertures and the spire clip is in position on the mounting tab on the upper edge of the grille aperture. Fit the grille, check the alignment and tighten the attachment screws.
➡ **FIESTA 1989 TO 1995:** If the radiator grille is being fitted to a new bumper, you will have to make a 12.0 mm square hole in the middle of the new bumper and drill two 8.0 mm holes for the grille locating pegs.

JOB 2: BONNET - *removal, replacement, adjustment.*

❑ **STEP 1: FIESTA 1976 TO 1983:** Remove the radiator grille - see *Job 1*.

❑ **STEP 2:** Mark the outline of the bonnet hinges on the front panel.

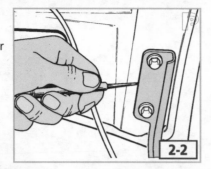

TOP TIP!

BONNET ALIGNMENT
• Mark the position of the hinges before bonnet removal so that you can refit the bonnet very close to the correct position. A fine felt pen or soft pencil are ideal.

❑ **STEP 3: FIESTA 1976 TO 1989:** Remove the bonnet stay attachment screws.

❑ **STEP 4:** Where necessary, disconnect the windscreen washer jet tube.
→ If you cannot separate the tube at a suitable connector, such as the non-return valve you will have to cut the tube, inserting a connector piece during refitting.

❑ **STEP 5: ESCORT AND ORION:** Where fitted, separate the earth/ground lead (arrowed) and/or other electrical connections such as radio interference suppressor, from the hinge.

❑ **STEP 6:** Have an assistant hold the bonnet while you remove the hinge attachment nuts or bolts.

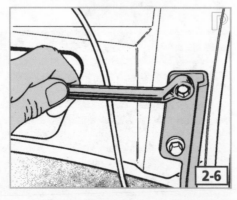

❑ **STEP 7:** Carefully lift the bonnet away from the vehicle.

❑ **STEP 8:** Refitting is the reverse of the removal process, bearing in mind the following points.
→ Make sure the hinges are aligned with the marks before fully tightening the attachment bolts.
→ Carefully lower the bonnet into position – one person standing each side of the vehicle - see *Step 9*.

❑ **STEP 9:** To adjust the alignment, partly undo the attachment bolts so that the bonnet can be moved relative to the body or hinges.
→ Close the bonnet and adjust the position so that there is an even gap all around - on Fiesta models from 1976 to 1989, Ford recommend 6.0 mm (0.25 in) at the rear and 4.0 mm (0.16 in) at each side but even spacing and aligning the rear of the bonnet with the body panel is more important than precise measurement.
→ If necessary, adjust the position of the lock or rubber stops so that the bonnet lies flush with the body.

❑ **STEP 10:** Tighten the attachment bolts, making sure the bonnet remains aligned and the bonnet release operates satisfactorily, see *Job 3*.

JOB 3: BONNET RELEASE MECHANISM - *removal, replacement.*

IMPORTANT NOTE: When you refit a cable and release mechanism, you should make sure the cable and release mechanism operate correctly before closing the bonnet. Otherwise, you might have great difficulty in opening it again!

❑ **STEP 1:** Open the bonnet.
→ Where necessary, remove the steering column shroud so that you have access to the bonnet release lever.
→ On some models you may also have to separate the choke control from the shroud.

❑ **STEP 2: FIESTA 1976 TO 1983:** Inside the vehicle, remove the two screws attaching the release cable to the cowl side panel.

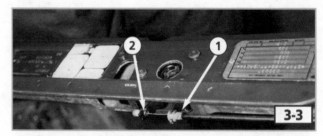

❑ **STEP 3: FIESTA FROM 1983, ESCORT AND ORION FROM 1990:** Disengage the cable nipple (**1**) and outer (**2**) from the bonnet release lever and the abutment to which they are clipped.
→ There should be sufficient slack in the cable for the nipple to slide out of the lever without difficulty.

❑ **STEP 4: ESCORT 1980 TO 1990:** Undo the screw and remove the cable bracket from the steering column.

☐ **STEP 5:** Note the route of the release cable, separate the release cable from any support clips and pull the cable through the bulkhead into the vehicle.

➜ On later versions, pull the cable into the engine bay.

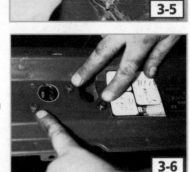
3-5

☐ **STEP 6:** If necessary, undo the screws shown here and remove the release mechanism from the vehicle.

➜ On some models you will have to remove the radiator grille for access to the release mechanism, see *Job 1*.

➜ Mark the position of the release mechanism before removal, so it can be refitted in the correct position.

3-6

☐ **STEP 7:** Refitting is the reverse of the removal process. If necessary, adjust the position of the release mechanism before fully tightening the attachment bolts - the bonnet should close without excessive force and lie flush with the body.

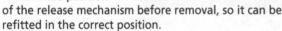

JOB 4: DOORS, DOOR GEAR - *removal, stripdown.*

Section A: Door removal and refitting.

SAFETY FIRST!

• If you do not have an assistant supporting the door there is a chance of the door toppling off the supports when the hinges are unbolted or the pins removed - be ready to prevent the door toppling.

FACT FILE

HINGE TYPES

Three types of hinge pins have been used on the models covered by this manual.

• The door can easily be separated from some vehicles by drifting out the roll pin or clip-retained solid pin.

• Ford recommend that a special tool is used to remove the door hinge pins. The tool fits over the head of the hinge and pulls the pin through the hinge. With care, a suitable drift can be used instead of the recommended tool.

• On vehicles with the non-removable solid pin, the hinge has to be unbolted from the vehicle - the side trim panel and the lower facia panel have to be removed for access to the hinge attachment bolts.

☐ **STEP A1: FIESTA 1976 TO 1989:** Identify the type of hinge used on the vehicle and, if necessary, remove the trim panels for access to the hinge attachment bolts. Have an assistant support the door in the open position.

➜ Alternatively, support the door on jacks or blocks, taking care not to damage the paintwork or door frame.

➜ Unbolt the hinges or, where appropriate, remove the plastic plugs or clips from the hinge pins and use a suitable drift to knock the pins out of the hinges.

➜ Remove the door from the vehicle.

☐ **STEP A2: FIESTA FROM 1989:** On models with electrical components in the door, disconnect the multi-plug (a) from the 'A' pillar, where fitted, or remove the door trim panel, see *Section B*, and disconnect each component, pulling the grommet and wiring through the hole in the front of the door.

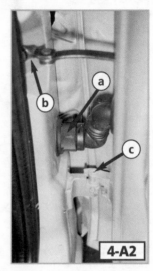
4-A2

➜ Unbolt the door check strap (b) from the 'A' pillar.

➜ Remove the retaining clips from the hinge pins.

➜ Support the door and use a suitable drift to knock the pins (c, lower hinge shown) out of the hinges – see *FACT FILE: HINGE TYPES*.

➜ Remove the door from the vehicle.

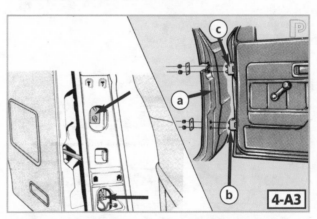
4-A3

☐ **STEP A3: ESCORT AND ORION DOORS 1980 TO 1986:**

➜ **FRONT DOORS:** Remove the scuff plate from the sill, lower cowl trim panel, radio speaker where fitted, and heater duct.

➜ On vehicles with electrical equipment in the doors, disconnect the multi-plug and feed the cable through the hole in the 'A' pillar.

➜ Unbolt the door check strap from the 'A' pillar (a) and support the door - see *Step 1*.

➜ From inside the vehicle, unbolt the lower hinge (b) followed by the upper hinge (c). Remove the door from the vehicle.

➜ **REAR DOORS:** See text for **FRONT DOORS** but remove the centre pillar trim panels to expose the hinge mountings (arrowed).

STEP A4: ESCORT AND ORION FRONT DOORS 1986 TO 1990: See *Step A3* but note that the upper hinge is not unbolted.

➜ Remove the retaining clip and use a suitable drift to knock out the upper hinge pin – see *FACT FILE: HINGE TYPES*. Remove the door from the vehicle.

STEP A5: ESCORT AND ORION FRONT AND REAR DOORS FROM 1990, KA: Disconnect the multi-plug and check strap from the 'A' or 'B' pillar, as appropriate.

➜ Support the door (see *Step 1*) and unscrew the hinge retaining bolt from each hinge.

➜ If necessary, use a suitable drift to assist removal of the hinge pins from the hinge and lift the door away from the vehicle.

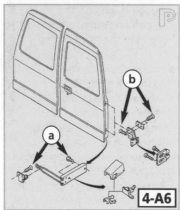

4-A5

STEP A6: VAN REAR DOORS: Remove the check mechanism fixings (a).

➜ Open and support the door.

➜ Remove the hinge fixings (b) and lift away the door.

4-A6

Section B: External door handles removal and refitting.

STEP B1: Remove the door trim panel (see *Chapter 14, Interior, Trim*) and the plastic waterproofing shield. Take care not to cut or tear the shield.

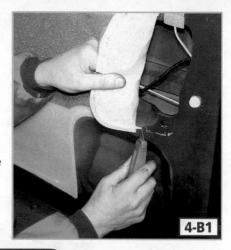

4-B1

TOP TIP!

• Early Fiestas, up to 1983, have a separate operating lever fitted to the handle side of the handle.
• On all other models the operating lever is moulded as part of the handle.

STEP B2: FIESTA FROM 1995, KA: Remove the two screws (Fiesta,) or drill out the rivets (Ka) attaching the lock shield/window upper guide rail to the door. Manoeuvre the lock shield/window upper guide rail from the door, breaking the sealant attaching the lock shield to the door skin.

STEP B3: Note the position of the external handle to door lock operating rod and separate the rod from the lock by prising or twisting off the retaining clip.

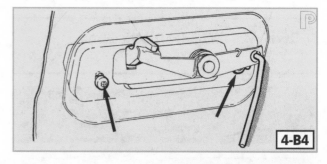

4-B4

FACT FILE

DOOR HANDLES AND LOCKS

Although door locking assemblies vary across the range of vehicles covered by this manual, the basic layout of the components is similar.

a - exterior handle
b - interior handle
c - barrel
d - lock
e - striker
f - interior lock button

g - The inset shows a lock with central locking solenoid.

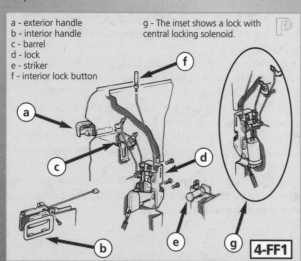

4-FF1

a - exterior handle
b - interior handle
c - lock

d - interior lock button
e - central locking solenoid

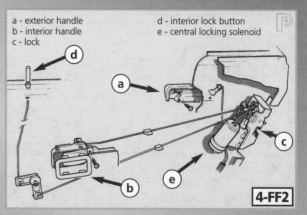

4-FF2

STEP FF1: This the a typical front door locking assembly.

STEP FF2: This is a typical rear door lock assembly.

☐ **STEP B4: FIESTA 1976 TO 1983:** Undo the two screws (arrowed) and remove the handle, along with the operating rod, from the door. If necessary, you can now separate the rod from the operating lever.

☐ **STEP B5: ALL OTHER MODELS:** Separate the rod from the lever on the handle, undo the two screws and remove the handle from the door. On Escort and Orion rear doors you will have to remove a rubber blanking plug for access to one of the screws.

TOP TIP!

☐ **STEP B6:** Refitting is the reverse of the removal process, bearing in mind the following points.
→ **FIESTA 1976 TO 1983:** The handle bush should be warmed in hot water before refitting and the hooked end of the operating rod should point to the rear when the rod is refitted to the handle. Lightly smear each end of the operating rod with a suitable lubricant, such as petroleum jelly.
→ **FIESTA FROM 1995, KA:** Re-seal the lock shield to the door skin, using new sealant if necessary.

Section C: Door lock cylinder removal and refitting.

☐ **STEP C1:** Remove the door trim panel, see *Chapter 14, Interior, Trim*, and plastic waterproofing shield. Take care not to cut or tear the shield.

☐ **STEP C2: ESCORT CABRIOLET FROM 1993:** Remove the door window glass.
☐ **STEP C3: ESCORT AND ORION 1986 TO 1990:** Remove the exterior door handle, see *Section B*.

☐ **STEP C4: FIESTA FROM 1989, ESCORT AND ORION FROM 1990 KA:** Drill out the rivets (Fiesta 1989 to 1995, Ka) or undo the screws (Fiesta from 1995, Escort and Orion) and remove the lock shield (Escort and Orion) or lock shield/door glass guide (Fiesta, Ka) above the lock cylinder. On Fiesta and Ka models you will have to break the sealant between the lock shield and door skin.

☐ **STEP C5:** Lever off the retaining clip and separate the rod connecting the lock cylinder to the lever on the lock.

☐ **STEP C6: FIESTA 1976 TO 1995, ESCORT 1980 TO 1990:** Slide out the retaining clip (1) and remove the lock cylinder (2), complete with rod (3) from the door.

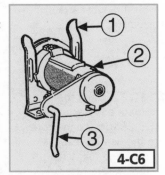
4-C6

☐ **STEP C7: FIESTA 1976 TO 1983:** If necessary, the cylinder can be dismantled. Undo the screw (1) and, after noting their positions, remove the end cap (2), lever (3) and cylinder spring (4). Put the key into the lock (5) and withdraw the barrel. The outside sealing pad (6) and internal 'O' ring can also be removed.

☐ **STEP C8: FIESTA FROM 1995:** On vehicles equipped with central locking, disconnect the battery negative connection - make sure you have the radio code or take precautions to prevent data loss. Disconnect the electrical plug and unclip the microswitch from the lock cylinder.

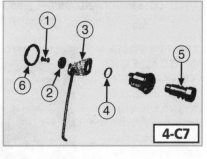
4-C7

☐ **STEP C9: FIESTA FROM 1995, KA:** Use a suitable tool, such as a punch or section of rod, and tap the retaining plate anti-clockwise to release the lock cylinder. Remove the retaining plate.

☐ **STEP C10:** Refitting is the reverse of the removal process, bearing in mind the following points.
→ **FIESTA 1976 TO 1983:** Make sure the barrel is inserted into the cylinder with the tab in the barrel in the cylinder groove. The spring should be fitted with the legs around the small lug on the cylinder. After fitting the lever, make sure the end cap is fitted with the tab between the spring legs.
→ The cylinder should be refitted with lever pointing towards the front of the car.
→ Make sure the gasket between the cylinder outer surround and door skin is fitted correctly.
→ **KA:** The 'V'-shaped cut-out in the retaining plate should be at the bottom.
→ **FIESTA 1989 TO 1995:** After securely riveting the door glass guide, make sure the door window winds up and down correctly.
→ **FIESTA FROM 1995, KA:** Re-seal the lock shield to the door skin, using new sealant if necessary.

Section D: Door lock removal and refitting.

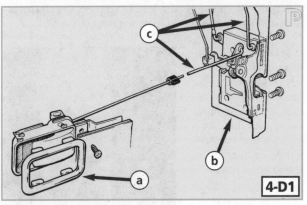
4-D1

☐ **STEP D1:** This is a typical door lock arrangement of interior handle (a), lock (b) and operating rods (c).

☐ **STEP D2:** Remove the door trim panel (see *Chapter 14, Interior, Trim*) and plastic waterproofing shield. Take care not to cut or tear the shield.
→ Where appropriate, unscrew and remove the internal lock knob.

❏ **STEP D3: ESCORT AND ORION 1986 TO 1990:** Remove the exterior door handle - see *Section B*.

❏ **STEP D4: FIESTA 1989 TO 1995 WITH CENTRAL LOCKING:** On rear doors, undo the two screws and remove the rod guard.
→ Disconnect the battery negative connection - make sure you have the radio code or take precautions to prevent data loss.

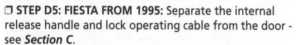

4-D4

→ On front and rear doors, disconnect the multi-plug and pull the section of wiring loom attached to the motor into the door cavity.
→ Separate the internal release handle from the door, see *Chapter 14, Job 2*.

❏ **STEP D5: FIESTA FROM 1995:** Separate the internal release handle and lock operating cable from the door - see *Section C*.
→ If necessary, remove the foam padding from the side impact protection bar so that you have sufficient room to remove the door lock.
→ Note the position of the padding so that it can be refitted in the correct position.
→ Remove the lock shield/window guide, see *Section C, Step 4*.

❏ **STEP D6: FIESTA 1976 TO 1995, ESCORT AND ORION 1980 TO 1990:** Lever the clips from the exterior handle, lock cylinder (front doors) and remote control rods. Separate the rods from the lock.

❏ **STEP D7: FIESTA FROM 1995:** On vehicles equipped with central locking, disconnect the battery negative connection - make sure you have the radio code or take precautions to prevent data loss. Disconnect the electrical plug and unclip the wiring from the door.

❏ **STEP D8:** Undo the three attachment screws (arrowed). Remove the lock/motor assembly, along with the internal lock rod and, where appropriate, the internal release handle.

❏ **STEP D9: ESCORT AND ORION 1980 TO 1990 WITH CENTRAL LOCKING:** As the lock assembly is being removed, release the

4-D8

wiring from the clips, undo the attachment screws and separate the solenoid from the lock.

❏ **STEP D10: FIESTA FROM 1995:** Where applicable, unclip the door open switch from the top of the lock assembly and, on vehicles equipped with central locking, disconnect the wiring plug from the lock motor.
→ If necessary, remove internal release cable from the lock

❏ **STEP D11:** If necessary, remove the internal lock rod, retaining clips and the bushes from the lock.

❏ **STEP D12:** Refitting is the reverse of the removal process, bearing in mind the following points.
→ If necessary, soften the bushes in hot water to ease refitting.
→ Use a suitable lubricant, such as petroleum jelly, to lubricate the bushes.
→ **FIESTA FROM 1995, KA:** Re-seal the lock shield to the door skin, using new sealant if necessary.

❏ **STEP D13: ESCORT CABRIOLET:** Escort Cabriolets were fitted with riveted door locks. These locks are no longer available and the later type of lock, along with a threaded plate and striker plate must be fitted.
→ To accommodate the later type of lock, drill the door at points (**a**) and remove the shaded area (**b**) from the threaded plate.

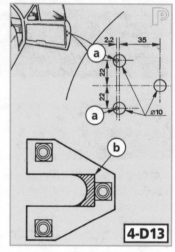

4-D13

❏ **STEP D14:** The threaded plate must be modified by removing the shaded section.
→ Where a screwed-on lock is replacing the riveted type, corrosion-protect the bare metal, and remove the shaded portion of the threaded plate.

JOB 5:   TAILGATE - stripdown, *remove, replace*.

❏ **STEP 1:** This is a typical tailgate lock assembly.

a - exterior push button/barrel
b - lock
c - central locking solenoid

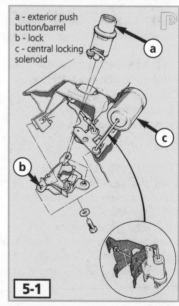

5-1

❏ **STEP 2:** Open the tailgate and disconnect the electrical connectors to the heated rear screen and rear screen wiper, where fitted.
→ Support the tailgate and disconnect the gas strut at the tailgate end.

❏ **STEP 3:** Remove the rubber seal (**a**) and peel back the headlining (**b**), sufficient to gain access to the tailgate hinges at the top of the tailgate aperture.

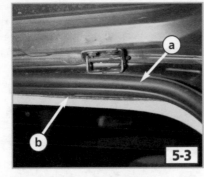

5-3

❏ **STEP 4:** Mark the outline of the hinges - see *Job 2, TOP TIP, BONNET ALIGNMENT*.
→ Unscrew the nuts and remove the tailgate from the vehicle.

❏ **STEP 5: TAILGATE LOCK:** Open the tailgate and remove the tailgate trim panel.
→ Unclip the rod (**a**) from the clip. Slide the retainer (**c**) along so that the cylinder (**b**) can be removed from the door.
→ Refitting is the reverse of the removal process.

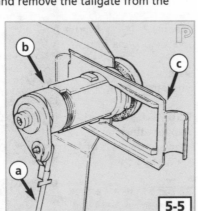

5-5

❏ **STEP 6: TAILGATE MANUAL LATCH:** Remove the tailgate trim panel and rod - see *Step 5*.
→ Undo the screws and remove the latch along with the lever and rod.
→ Refitting is the reverse of the removal process, making sure that the lever and rod are aligned with the end of the lock cylinder.

5-6

❏ **STEP 7: TAILGATE SOLENOID:** Remove the latch assembly, see *Step 6*. Undo the attachment screws, unhook the operating rod, disconnect the electrical connections and remove the latch solenoid assembly. Refitting is the reverse of the removal process, making sure the operating rod is securely engaged in the nylon actuator – see illustration *5-1*.

❏ **STEP 8: STRIKER:** Open the tailgate and mark the outline of the striker, see *Job 2, TOP TIP, BONNET ALIGNMENT*.
→ Undo and remove the attachment bolts, washers and striker.

5-8

→ Refitting is the reverse of the removal process, making sure that the striker plate is aligned with the outline marks.

JOB 6:   GAS STRUT - *removal, replacement.*

The method used to attach the gas strut to the tailgate and body depends on model and date of manufacture.
→ On early vehicles, the strut was locked to the sliding pivot by a peg, later vehicles used a metal clip.

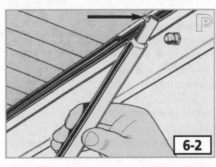

6-2

❏ **STEP 1:** Raise and support the tailgate.

6-3

❏ **STEP 2:** Using a suitable lever, lever out the peg (arrowed)...

❏ **STEP 3:** ...or lever off the metal clip (arrowed).

❏ **STEP 4:** Repeat at the other end and remove the strut (arrowed) from the vehicle.

6-4

JOB 7:   BUMPERS - *removal, replacement.*

Section A: General.

❏ **STEP A1:** If any bumper-mounted electrical equipment is fitted, disconnect the battery negative (-) earth/ground terminal. See *Chapter 10, Electrical, Dash, Instruments, Fact File: Disconnecting the Battery* BEFORE doing so!

❏ **STEP A2:** Disconnect the headlamp washer hose, where appropriate.

STEP A3: On models with moulded bumpers it is necessary to remove the radiator grille panel (see *Job 1*) the splash seal from the underside of the car, and the headlights - see *Chapter 10, Electrical, Instruments*.
→ On Escort and Orion from 1996 it is also necessary to support the radiator and remove its lower supports.

STEP A4: The bumpers on nearly all of the models covered by this manual are simply bolted on.

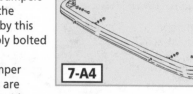

7-A4

→ The front bumper front fixing nuts are accessible from inside or underneath the engine bay.
→ The rear bumper fixing nuts are accessible from the luggage bay.
→ The side fixings are accessible from within the wheelarch - after the wheelarch liners have been removed where fitted.
→ Remove the fastenings and slide the bumper off.

STEP A5: Some bumpers comprise a centre section and quarter sections which are normally jointed together.

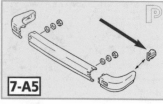

7-A5

→ Many bumpers have slotted section which slide into retainers (arrowed).
→ If you remove the quarter section retainer or renew the wing, attach the quarter section retainer with new rivets.
→ The sections can be separated if necessary, though the tangs break easily.
→ Reassemble the quarter sections to the centre section before fitting to the vehicle.

STEP A6: BUMPER OVER-RIDERS: Where fitted, separate the headlamp washer hose from the front over-rider (2).

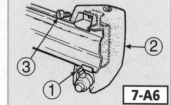

7-A6

→ Remove the clamp screws (3 - two per over-rider) and separate the over-rider from the bumper.
→ Refitting is the reverse of the removal process - front over-riders with headlamp washers should be fitted central to the headlamp and the washer jets aligned after tightening the clamp screws.

STEP A7: To refit a bumper, push the bumper into position and make sure the quarter sections fully engage where appropriate.

> **TOP TIP!**
> • Do not fully tighten any of the attachments until you are happy with bumper alignment.

STEP A8: COURIER AND COMBI: Remove the two bolts each side attaching the bumper mounting bracket to the body. If necessary, you can remove the mounting brackets from the bumper and unlock the clips to separate the end mouldings. Additionally, you can also remove the attachment screws (two screws at the front and one at the rear) and remove the rear quarter mouldings

Section B: Ka - front bumper.

STEP B1: Raise the front of the vehicle (see *Chapter 2, Safety First*) and remove the front wheels.
→ Remove the wheelarch liners.

7-B2

STEP B2: Remove the bumper attachment screws at the base of the wheelarches.

STEP B3: Remove the front number plate and the screws as follows.
→ Screws around the number plate area.
→ Screws at the upper edge of the front bumper.

STEP B4: Carefully lever the front bumper away from the wheelarch/wing.
→ The four clips (arrowed) each side are tight, fragile and easily broken.

7-B4

> **TOP TIP!**
> • You may find it easier to remove the headlight units so that you have better access to the bumper attachment points.
> • Because the plastic clips are fragile, it can be worthwhile having spares available before starting work.

STEP B5: Release the plastic clips at the front of the bumper - you will have to press in the bumper and lower the clips.

STEP B6: To remove the rear bumper, first raise the rear of the vehicle - see *Chapter 2, Safety First*.

STEP B7: Remove the attachment screws at the wheelarch. These are likely to be rusty with the slots blocked with dirt, especially on older vehicles.

STEP B8: Drill out the attachment rivets (arrowed) as follows.
→ Three upper and one lower rivet beneath each wheelarch.

→ Two rivets at the centre of the bumper, underneath the vehicle.
→ Three rivets at the top of the bumper, work from the luggage compartment.

❑ **STEP B9:** Remove the rear light clusters and the number plate lamp.

❑ **STEP B10:** Remove the clips from the brackets in the rear light apertures and the clips in the wheelarches.

❑ **STEP B11:** Pull the bumper away from the vehicle to the rear.

7-B8

JOB 8: SPOILERS - *removal, replacement*.

The operations described here only relate to spoilers fitted as original equipment - we have not covered the removal and replacement of the many types of 'non-original' spoilers which may have been fitted to these models.

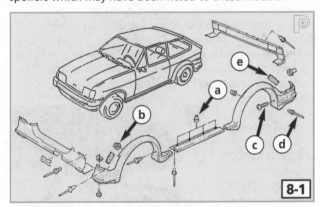
8-1

❑ **STEP 1:** Spoilers and other exterior panels are attached to the vehicle and to each other by various studs (**a**), nuts (**b**), screws (**c**) and rivets (**d**).
→ However, some panels are partly held in place with double-sided adhesive tape (**e**).

❑ **STEP 2:** Remove all visible fittings.
→ Pop rivets have to be drilled out.

❑ **STEP 3:** If the panel is still securely held, check whether there are any studs securing it.
→ Studs should spring apart under gentle leverage.

❑ **STEP 4:** Typical positions of screw (**A**) and stud/nut (**B**).

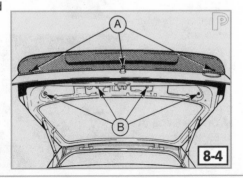
8-4

❑ **STEP 5:** Front spoiler fixings, screws (**A**) and retaining pegs (**B**).

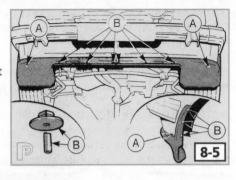
8-5

TOP TIP!

❑ **STEP 6:** If the panel is still held then there will be adhesive tape between it and the bodyshell.
→ It is very easy to damage paintwork when removing adhesive tape.
→ Gentle heat can soften the adhesive.
→ Clean all traces of adhesive away and fit replacement adhesive tape in the same position as the original.

JOB 9: BODY MOULDINGS AND BADGES - *replacement*.

Most body mouldings and badges are held in place by adhesive and we have covered removal and refitting of these components in *Section B*. Where there are differences we have covered these in *Section A*.
→ Where fixings other than adhesive are used, the fixings can be hidden under clipped-in strips or caps. Find and remove the fixings – don't be surprised if the mouldings still prove to be bonded as well!

Section A: Body mouldings.

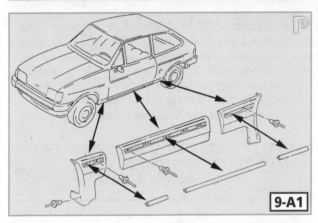
9-A1

❑ **STEP A1: BODY SIDE MOULDING:** Some are held by rivets, hidden under filler strips. Carefully lever out the insert strip, working along the lower edge, then drill out the side moulding attachment rivets and remove the side moulding.

❑ **STEP A2: DOOR WEATHERSEAL MOULDING:** Remove the exterior mirror, see *Job 10*. Taking care not to bend or kink the moulding, lever it up and remove it from the vehicle. Refit the moulding by aligning the rear end and carefully tapping it into position.

STEP A3: DRIP RAIL MOULDING (EXCEPT COURIER): Carefully raise the forward end of the drip rail moulding from its retaining flange and carefully pull it from the retaining flange. Make sure you do not kink or bend the moulding. Refitting is the reverse of the removal process, start at the rear and gently tap moulding into place.

STEP A4: DRIP RAIL MOULDING (COURIER): Lift the inside edge of the moulding and rotate the complete moulding towards the outside of the vehicle. Refitting is the reverse of the removal process making sure that the moulding outboard edge properly engages the roof lip.

Section B: 'Stuck On' badges and mouldings.

STEP B1: Before attempting to remove a badge or moulding, use masking tape as an alignment guide so that the replacement can be fitted in the correct position.

STEP B2: Use a suitable hot air blower to warm the component but do not use excessive heat. Flexible badges can be peeled off and methylated spirits  used to remove all traces of old adhesive. Rigid badges can be levered off but a better method is to use thin nylon cord (in cheesewire fashion) to separate the badge from the body - again use methylated spirits to remove all traces of old adhesive.

STEP B3: Apply adhesive primer and warm the component, if required. Press the component into the correct position and remove the masking tape.

STEP B4: BODY SIDE MOULDING: Before attempting to remove the side moulding, apply masking tape along the side of the body as an alignment guide. Carefully lift the side moulding away from the body using a knife or thin cord, such as nylon fishing line, to break the adhesive seal. Use methylated spirits to remove all traces of the old adhesive and fit the new body side moulding.

JOB 10: DOOR MIRRORS - removal, replacement.

SAFETY FIRST!

• On vehicles with electric mirrors, you should disconnect the battery negative lead before removing the mirror glass or mirror assembly.

STEP 1: MIRROR GLASS REMOVE/ REPLACE:
→ The mirror glass can be removed quite easily on the pre-1989 Fiesta by levering the retainer from the mirror body and lifting the glass away. Refitting is the reverse of the removal process but make sure the retainer is fully engaged.

→ **FIESTA FROM 1989:** The mirror glass is removed by carefully levering the upper outer corner of the glass away from the mirror body to disengage 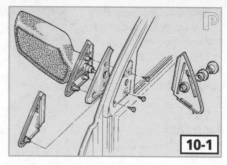 the outer pivot, disengaging the inner pivot and separating the glass from the operating link. Refitting is the reverse of the removal process - make sure the outer pivot is fully engaged.

→ The mirror glass is removed from the Fiesta from 1995 and the Ka by pushing the inner side (nearest the vehicle) forward into the assembly so that the outer side can be pulled outwards and away from the assembly to disengage the glass from the mirror. Where appropriate, disconnect the wiring from the glass. Refitting is the reverse of the removal process - make sure the outer edge of the glass clicks into place and locks in position.

→ On the Escort and Orion to 1989, two types of non-remote control mirror may be encountered - on higher specification models the mirror glass assembly is levered outward to disengage from the balljoint mounting, on lower specification models the cover must be unclipped and the securing screw removed. Where remote control mirrors are fitted the glass is removed by moving the locking tang towards the door - the tang is accessed through a hole in the base of the mirror.

→ The mirror glass is removed from later Escort and Orion by levering the glass from the mirror assembly. Where appropriate, disconnect the wiring from the glass. Refitting is the reverse of the removal process.

STEP 2: MIRROR ASSEMBLY – REMOVE, REPLACE:
→ In short, remove the adjustment knob and the interior mirror trim panel.

STEP 3: Undo the mirror fixings and disconnect the wiring plug where appropriate.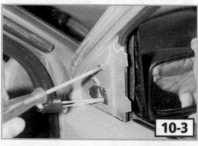

STEP 4: The mirror can now be removed.

STEP 5: There are minor design variations between models:
→ On the Fiesta to 1989, the mirror can be removed as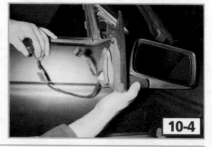

a complete unit by levering the plastic cover from adjustment knob, removing the knob, trim panel and mirror attachment nuts - support the mirror as the nuts are removed. Refitting is the reverse of the removal process.

➜ On the Fiesta from 1989, the mirror can be removed as a complete unit by removing the door trim panel sufficient to gain access to the mirror attachment screws, see *Job 4*, the operating knob and surrounding trim and the three mirror attachment screws - support the mirror as the screws are removed. Refitting is the reverse of the removal process. On models with electric mirrors, disconnect the mirror lead and separate it from the door. Remove the operating knob, where applicable, and the three mirror attachment nuts - support the mirror as the nuts are removed. Refitting is the reverse of the removal process.

➜ On the Ka, where appropriate, carefully lever the operating stalk grommet from the inner trim panel and, working from the top, lever the mirror trim panel from the door. Remove the locking screw, support the mirror assembly and undo the attachment nut. If necessary, the outer trim panel can be removed from the door. Refitting is the reverse of the removal process.

➜ On early Escort and Orion models use a suitable 'C' spanner to remove the mirror actuator bezel, on later models remove the circlip and the remote control handle. Removal is now the same as for the non remote type.

❑ **STEP 6:** Refitting all types is the reverse of the removal process. On models with electric mirrors you should check mirror operation before refitting the door trim panel.

JOB 11: SUN ROOF - *removal, replacement.*

Section A: Non-sliding sun roof.

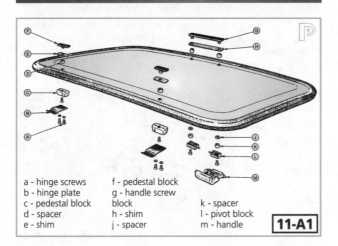

a - hinge screws
b - hinge plate
c - pedestal block
d - spacer
e - shim
f - pedestal block
g - handle screw block
h - shim
j - spacer
k - spacer
l - pivot block
m - handle

11-A1

❑ **STEP A1:** Disengage the handle pins from the bracket by pressing in the pins on each side.

➜ Remove the stop clip and lift the sun roof glass from the vehicle.

➜ On later models, press in the red locking bar on the handwheel to release the sunroof panel.

❑ **STEP A2:** If necessary, the hinge blocks and handle can be separated from the sun roof panel.

➜ Remove the hinge block attachment screws and the handle pivot attachment screws.

➜ Lift off the blocks, pivot and handle.

❑ **STEP A3: HINGE RETAINER REMOVAL AND REFITTING:** Remove the sun roof panel and the aperture rubber seal.

➜ Pull the headlining from the front edge of the sun roof aperture, remove the headlining clips, and pull down the headlining sufficient for access.

➜ Remove the retainer screws and withdraw the retainer and seal.

➜ Refitting is the reverse of the removal process - you should use a new retainer seal.

❑ **STEP A4:** Refitting the sun roof components and sun roof panel is the reverse of the removal process, bearing in mind the following points.

➜ When a new aperture seal is being fitted, the join should be in the middle of the rear flange. Carefully cut the seal to the correct length, making sure the mating faces are square to each other.

➜ Fit the shim to the handle screw block, insert the screw block spigots into the holes in the sun roof panel and fit the washers to the spigots.

➜ Adjust the hinge plates as necessary by sliding in the hinge backwards or forwards before fully tightening the screws.

➜ Close the sun roof and check the fit. If necessary, adjust the sun roof panel so that it is flush with the roof by adding or removing washers under the handle.

IMPORTANT NOTE: Depending on model, an electric sliding cloth type sun roof or a solid panel type sun roof may be fitted. The sliding cloth type is complex and, in the following section, we have covered the solid panel type - if you are working on the sliding cloth type, we recommend that you consult an approved Ford dealer.

Section B: Manual sliding sun roof.

❑ **STEP B1:** Removing the glass panel is not difficult. Close the sun roof and move the sun blind to the rear. Wind the operating handle one turn anti-clockwise and remove the three screws and clips that attach the glass and lower frame.

11-B1

❑ **STEP B2:** Now close the sun roof and remove the three glass to sliding gear attachment screws on each side.

❑ **STEP B3:** You can now lift the panel from the vehicle.

11-B2

STEP B4: Refitting is the reverse of the removal process, bearing in mind the following points.
→ Align the glass with the roof and locate the lower frame to glass brackets.

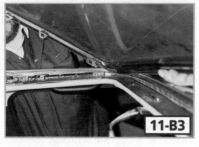

11-B3

→ Insert the clips through the brackets.
→ Insert the centre retaining screw followed by the screws on each side.

STEP B5: The sun roof panel can be adjusted for alignment with the roof as follows.
→ The panel to aperture gap can be adjusted by bending the weatherstrip flange as necessary - the gap should be even around the circumference and be between 7.73 mm and 8.73 mm.
→ Adjust panel height at the front by loosening the corner screws and raising or lowering the panel as necessary. Alignment is correct when the panel is flush with the roof or, at most, 2.0 mm below the roof. Tighten the screws.
→ Adjust the panel at the rear by loosening the screws on the link assemblies and move the links up or down as necessary. Alignment is correct when the panel is flush with the roof or, at most, 2.0 mm above the roof. Tighten the screws.

STEP B6: To remove the sliding gear, remove the panel, see *Steps B1 to B3*.

STEP B7: Place the operating handle in the fully closed position. Remove the three screws, operating handle and guard.

11-B7

STEP B8: Remove the four screws each side which attach the sliding gear to the roof. You can now withdraw the sliding gear from the roof.

11-B8

STEP B9: Refitting is the reverse of removal. See *Step B5* for adjustment details.

Section C: Electrically operated sun roof.

STEP C1: Close the sun roof and disconnect the battery negative lead.

STEP C2: Starting at the corners, very carefully lever the surround panel from the headlining.

STEP C3: Disconnect the electrical connection from the motor, remove the screws and the motor.

STEP C4: Remove the screw and the relay bracket.

STEP C5: Remove the screws on each side and lift the glass from the vehicle.

STEP C6: If necessary, undo the screws in the sequence shown and remove the clamp frame from the roof.

STEP C7: You can now remove the mainframe, weatherstrip and foam seal.

STEP C8: Refitting is the reverse of removal. Ford recommend that a new foam seal is fitted during reassembly.

JOB 12:   FRONT SCREEN – *replacement.*

Section A: Screen held in with rubbers.

It is possible to fit a new screen yourself where an early Fiesta or Escort has its screen held in place with windscreen rubbers. However, we don't recommend it! A company such as Autoglass will be able to supply and fit a screen for little more than the cost of buying one. The risk of breaking a screen when you fit it yourself is high.

STEP A1: Mel from Autoglass removed the old screen from the vehicle and cleaned off all the old sealant from the aperture.

12-A1

→ The screen is pushed out from the inside so use an old blanket or similar to protect the bonnet.
→ Check to see whether you have a toughened or laminated windscreen. A toughened screen may shatter completely if it is chipped or cracked, spreading broken glass inside the car. A laminated windscreen will normally come out in one piece.

→ Allow time for de-rusting and painting any affected areas.

→ The new rubber has been fitted to the glass.

→ Fitting string into the groove on the rubber which will fit over the lip in the windscreen aperture.

→ The loose ends seen here have simply been tucked in to the upper edge of the rubber so that they are out of the way as the glass is being fitted.

→ Soapy lubricant is applied to the rubber to help it slip in to place.

□ **STEP A2:** If you are doing this yourself, it's best to have two people offer up the new glass with rubber. The rubber must be seated evenly in to the aperture all the way around.

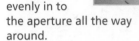

12-A2

□ **STEP A3:** As the fitting string is pulled out of the rubber, the inner lip is eased over the windscreen aperture. Particularly on an older, brittle rubber, you have to take great care not to pull the string through the rubber.

12-A3

□ **STEP A4:** There is always a little tidy up of rubber flanges to carry out, to make sure that they are all sitting evenly. If the screen is pushed in too far, the rubbers will start to recess in to the seating around the windscreen aperture. The outer lip should lie more or less flush with the bodywork.

12-A4

Section B: Bonded glass.

It is best to have a windscreen specialist replace a bonded windscreen because of the equipment required. Autoglass have demonstrated how they replaced a bonded windscreen on an Escort, the Fiesta and Ka are similar.

TOP TIP!

□ **STEP B1:** • Mel from Autoglass recommends putting masking tape over the screen vent outlets to prevent debris from falling into the vents - although a laminated windscreen can usually be removed in one piece, fragments of glass can break away from damaged windscreens.

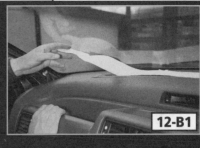

12-B1

• If debris – or worse still, shards of broken glass – fall into the vent, it could be thrown into the eyes of the car's occupants next time the screen vent fan is turned on.

□ **STEP B2:** There will inevitably be interior trim to remove from around the screen. In this case, the trim is partly screwed and partly clipped into place.

→ Use an upholstery lever for freeing the trim clips.

→ Take special care where, as in this case, an alarm sensor is fitted on the trim. Be sure not to disturb the wiring.

12-B2

□ **STEP B3A:** In cases where a trim cover is fitted at the base of the screen, remove the wipers and unscrew or clip off the trim cover.

12-B3A

□ **STEP B3B:** On this Ford Escort, the trims which clip on to the A-pillars are easily destroyed as they are pulled away and, if this happens, would have to have to be replaced with new. Similar trim is used on other vehicles covered by this manual and, although not expensive to replace, there is no guarantee that a local Ford dealer will hold stock of these items.

12-B3B

TOP TIP!

□ **STEP B3C:** Where a vehicle is fitted with a heated front screen, be sure to disconnect the wiring and free it from the position of the wiring plug right back to the screen. You should also take care to prevent damage to the wiring when cutting out the old windscreen.

12-B4

12-B5

☐ **STEP B4:** Mel wears protective goggles and gloves for this stage of the work. If a power cutter is being used you should also wear ear protection.
→ The bonded glass has to be cut from the screen aperture.
→ This special tool has a blade which reaches behind the glass and cuts through the sealant as Mel pulls it around the perimeter of the screen.
→ Positioning blocks are placed at the base of the screen. The old blocks should be cut out and new blocks fitted.

☐ **STEP B5:** The old glass can now be lifted away.

☐ **STEP B6:** Mel spends quite a considerable amount of time cleaning up the screen aperture before applying the adhesive hardener to the aperture frame. It is vitally important the aperture is completely dry - the bonding filler will not stick to wet areas.
→ On anything more than a few years old, there will almost inevitably be rust found behind the glass or glass trim.
→ In worst cases, some welding may be necessary; in almost all cases it will be necessary to clean off the rust, apply a product such as Wurth Rust Killer and then prime and paint the metal.

12-B6

12-B7

☐ **STEP B7:** As with the screen frame, Mel uses a panel wipe to clean all traces off the surface of the glass (where it will touch the screen frame) before wiping hardener on to the surface of the glass.

☐ **STEP B8:** The glass seals are now fitted in place around the edge of the glass – only applicable to certain types of screen.

12-B8

☐ **STEP B9:** A very thick bead of

12-B9

bonding filler is now applied by Mel all the way around the screen frame. Check the manufacturer's recommendations - some sealants will not set properly below 10 degrees C.

12-B10

12-B11

☐ **STEP B10:** Note the special suction lifting pads that Mel uses to grip the glass so that he can lower it accurately in to position on the screen frame. Note also the tabs of masking tape fitted ready in place on top of the screen...

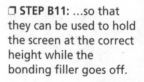

12-B12

☐ **STEP B11:** ...so that they can be used to hold the screen at the correct height while the bonding filler goes off.

IMPORTANT NOTE: If you close the vehicle doors with the windows closed before the bonding filler has set it is possible to pop the windscreen out - take the precaution of opening the windows.

☐ **STEP B12:** Where the rear view mirror is fitted to the glass, use special double-sided mirror fixing tape but be sure to clean both the mounting pad on the mirror and the area of the glass to which it is fitted with panel wipe so that there are no traces of grease on either.

TOP TIP!

• The screen that Mel took from this vehicle was cracked right down the middle, starting from the rear view mirror mounting position.
• The crack was caused by someone having previously fitted the mirror using 'Superglue' or epoxy resin.
• Either of them will cause differential expansion to take place in the glass and will, in every case, cause it to crack.

☐ **STEP B13:** A properly fitted screen will be free from leaks and also free from crack-inducing stresses.

12-B13

TOP TIP!

• Be sure to clean the windscreen wiper blades and, if necessary, replace them so that the new screen is not instantly marked with disfiguring scratches.

CHAPTER 14: INTERIOR TRIM

PLEASE READ CHAPTER 2 SAFETY FIRST BEFORE CARRYING OUT ANY WORK ON YOUR CAR.

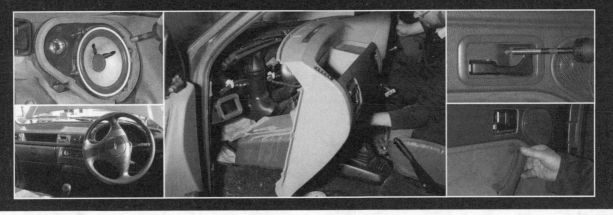

CONTENTS

SAFETY FIRST!

ALL INTERIOR TRIM AREAS:

• Before carrying out any work on any part of the interior, read *Job 13: Airbags and Pre-Tensioners - essential Safety First!*

• There are very important safety hazards attached to working on, OR IN THE VICINITY OF these components.

The information given in this chapter is applicable to all of the vehicles covered in this manual.
➔ There are many detail variations both between different models and between different versions and ages of the same models - too many to cover here in detail.
➔ The details given here may well need to be related to the specific fixtures that you may find on a vehicle, but are designed to be applied to the variations you are likely to come across when working on these vehicles.

SAFETY FIRST!

• Do not dismantle any body or trim components in the region of an airbag.

• Read and follow the instructions in *Jobs 13 and 14 first*.

• Note the location of all airbags before starting work.

JOB 1:   TRIM FIXINGS – *mysteries explained.*

At first sight, it may look as though interior trim was never designed to be removed! But with a little thought and the certain knowledge that all the fixings *can* be found once you know where to start looking for clues, you'll find yourself able to work through the whole proceedings, step-by-step.
➔ Start with the outer fixings first. Work patiently and methodically.
➔ Pull carefully on plastic trim - you'll be able to see where it flexes and this often tells you where fixings are located and whether panels are separate, with a concealed join, or all-in-one.
➔ If you are certain that there are no fixings that can be unscrewed, try pulling carefully - the trim may be held with concealed clips.

❏ **STEP 1:** In some cases, self-tapping screws are used to hold trim in place.
Whenever you see a cap or other type of finisher, you can assume that it's there to cover something up. In this case, the cap is levered off, exposing the screw head beneath.

1-1

STEP 2: Similar at first sight, but in fact much flatter, is this type of plastic clip. To remove it, all you need to do is carefully lever under the head of the clip.

1-2

STEP 3: Some similar looking clips (1) have a peg under the head, rather like a plastic nail, which pushes into a plastic socket mounted in the bodywork. The peg is pulled out first and then the socket (sometimes still attached to the peg; sometimes not) pulls out after it. On these later-type door aperture trims (2), the cover is also clipped down to spring clips (3) on the body.

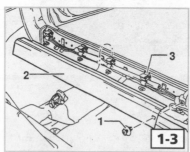

1-3

STEP 4: Door seals are simply pushed on to the edge of the door and tread plates are either clipped or screwed down. Replacement door seals are remarkably expensive so, if yours are in good condition, do your best to save them.

1-4

STEP 5: On some models, the tread plates may be held in place with metal clips which stayed on the body seam after the trim has been removed and need to be levered off separately.

1-5

STEP 6: Door trim and rear side trim is often fitted with concealed spring clips which push into the bodywork. If there is no evidence of any other type of clip, try easing the trim carefully back and see if it springs away.

STEP 7: Two fixing types shown here:
→ Another version of the hidden clip (3) may pull

1-6

out of the trim panel, or might stay in the body. Whichever - before refitting, make sure it's first properly clipped into the trim panel.
→ The

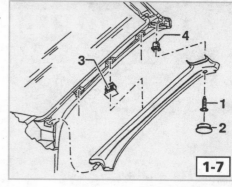

1-7

threaded screw (1) is covered by a cap (2) which has to be carefully levered out with a flat-bladed screwdriver. The screw goes into an expanding plastic plug (4) which is pushed into a square hole in the body. On some versions, the cap is a softer material and is flush-fitting to the trim.

STEP 8: On some older models trim is held in place with sections of double sided tape, like this Fiesta pillar trim. Take great care when

1-8

levering these free as it is easy to damage the trim irreparably.

STEP 9: Some sections of plastic trim and, more often, carpet are glued down. Take the very greatest care when pulling them off because the carpet is shaped and

1-9

will be impossible to replicate from a flat piece.

STEP 10: On models with a fuel cut-off valve behind the passenger side trim, the trim panel is removed after using a coin to turn these two turnbuckles (arrowed) to release them.

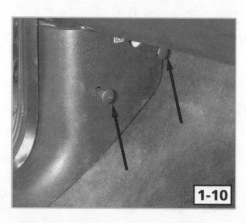

1-10

JOB 2: INTERIOR TRIM PANELS - *remove, replace.*

TOP TIP!

TRIM REMOVAL
• The clips used to attach many trim panels are fragile and easily broken.
• Additionally, panels themselves can be easily damaged.

Section A: Door panels.

TRIM REMOVAL

❐ **STEP A1:** This is a standard trim-removal tool recommended by Ford for removing and refitting door trim panels.

❐ **STEP A2:** Where fitted, remove the door trim panel capping.
→ Carefully slide the trim panel capping retaining clips (A) sideways and out of their location on the door inner panel.

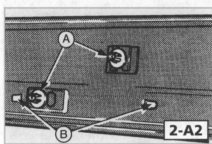

→ Items (B) are locating tangs to be lined up when refitting the moulding.

❐ **STEP A3: OLDER MODELS OR MODELS OF LOWER TRIM SPECIFICATION:** Remove the door pull/arm rest, by where necessary, levering open the screw head covers and removing the two fixing screws.

❐ **STEP A4A: OLDER MODELS OR MODELS OF LOWER TRIM SPECIFICATION:** Remove the manual window regulator by removing the plastic insert (a), centre screw (b) and the window winder handle (c) and...

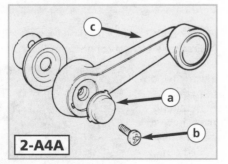

❐ **STEP A4B: MODELS WITH ELECTRIC WINDOWS:** ...lever out the switches (arrowed) and label the connecting terminal. Where necessary remove the door pocket finisher to gain access to the arm rest securing screws.

❐ **STEP A5:** On some models, such as this Escort, screws through the door pocket (arrowed) are part of the trim panel fixing and will need to be released.

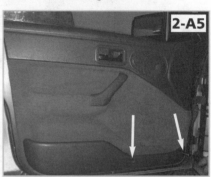

❐ **STEP A6:** Undo the retaining screw and release the door handle bezel from its lugs by sliding the bezel rearwards. Although styles have changed, the attachment method remains the same.

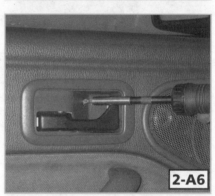

❐ **STEP A7:** On more modern models you may need to lever away the door handle trim cover...

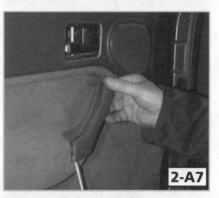

❐ **STEP A8:** ...to access the concealed screws behind (arrowed).

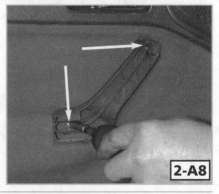

❒ **STEP A9A:** On some models it will be necessary to locate the door panel retaining clips by feeling around the periphery of the panel.

➜ Carefully lever out each door panel retaining clip, preferably using the special tool (see *Step 1*) and remove the door panel.

❒ **STEP A9B:** On other models the door panel is retained by screws in the rim of the panel indicated by the screwdriver and arrows.

➜ This 1990 Escort has 6 screws....

2-A9B

❒ **STEP A9C:** ......this Ka has three retaining screws. Remove these and lift the panel away.

2-A9C

❒ **STEP A10:** At this point on the earlier models, the pockets can be separated from the door panels by removing the screws or clips.

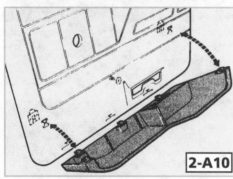
2-A10

However, on the more recent models, the pockets are moulded as part of the door panel

PROTECTIVE SHEETING REMOVAL

❒ **STEP A11:** Remove and disconnect the speaker (three screws, arrowed)...

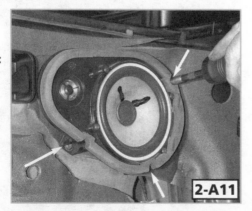
2-A11

❒ **STEP A12:** ...and unscrew the inner door handle (indicated by the screwdriver). You can now slide it forwards to release it from the door.

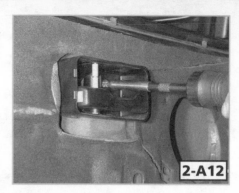
2-A12

COMPONENTS INSIDE DOOR

TOP TIP!

❒ **STEP A13:** •To work on components inside the door the protective sheeting must be peeled away.
• You can carefully remove the whole sheet taking care not to touch the self-adhesive surfaces or re-bonding will be difficult.
• The vehicle illustrated here had been worked on before and the sheet had been cut to allow access and re-sealed with tape.
• It's best to face up to the (low) cost of fitting a new sheet.

2-A13

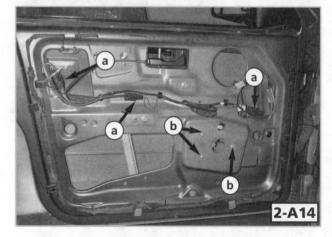
2-A14

❒ **STEP A14:** This picture shows a stripped down door indicating electrical connections (**a**) and the rivets (**b**) securing the electric window regulator.

➜ Retaining rivets have to be carefully drilled out, without damaging panels or components.

2-A15

STEP A15: Refitting is the reverse of the removal process.

→ Ensure that the rivets and electrical connections mentioned in *Step A14* are secure before refitting the protective sheet.

→ Where appropriate – locate the panel firmly on the lugs in the door…

→ …or make sure the door panel attachment clips are lined up correctly and press the panel into position.

Section B: Tailgate panel.

STEP B1: On models with rear wash/wipe, remove the motor cover section by turning the retaining clips through 90 degrees.

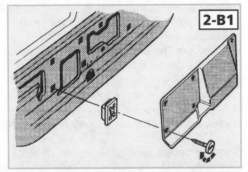

2-B1

STEP B2: Remove the screws from the panel. These will vary in number and position in each model.

→ There are seven on this Escort tailgate – positions arrowed.

2-B2

STEP B3: …and two (one each side) in this Ka.

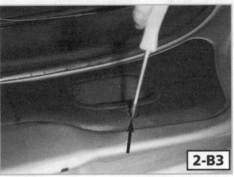

2-B3

STEP B4: Carefully lever out any remaining panel clips.

STEP B5: Refitting is the reverse of the removal process

JOB 3: CENTRE CONSOLE - *remove, refit.*

STEP 1: Before dismantling, disconnect the battery negative (-) earth/ground terminal. See *Chapter 10, Electrical, Dash, Instruments, Fact File: Disconnecting the Battery* BEFORE doing so!

STEP 2: Where switches are fitted to the centre console, carefully lever these out, disconnect the plugs from the switches and label them. If the switches do not come away easily then remove them as the console is lifted away.

STEP 3: B5 and iB5 MANUAL TRANSMISSIONS: Unscrew the gear lever knob. → **MTX 75 TRANSMISSION:** Pull off the gear knob.

STEP 4: AUTOMATIC TRANSMISSION: Undo the securing screw and lift off the selector handle.

STEP 5: Remove the gear lever gaiter.

→ **'LEATHER' TYPE GAITER:** Carefully lever the surround from the base of the gear lever gaiter.

→ **ESCORT/ORION:** Separate the gaiter and bezel from the console and lift them off the gear lever.

STEP 6: AUTOMATIC TRANSMISSION: Put the selector in the Park ('P') position. Carefully lever free the indicator panel and bezel and lift them off the gear lever.

STEP 7A: The console fixings vary from model to model.

→ **SHORT CONSOLES:** Most have four retaining screws, like this Escort.

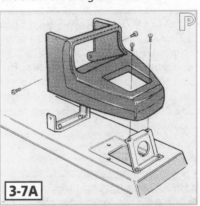

3-7A

STEP 7B: LONG CONSOLE, PRE-1996: Remove (typically) the four nuts beneath the gear shaft (**positions, a**), and screws (**b**) in the rear storage box – numbers of fixings may vary.

STEP 7C: LONG CONSOLE, FROM 1996: Remove the four nuts, the gear lever inner gaiter, retaining plate and 'O' ring.

→ Remove the screw (**a**) in the rear storage box or, on models without a storage box, the screw under a trim cap at the rear of the console.

→ Separate the parking brake gaiter from the console.

→ Lift the centre console up and over the gear lever.

→ If any wiring is still connected to console switches, disconnect it now.

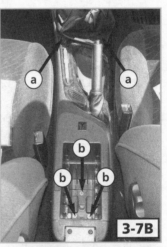

3-7B

3-7C

STEP 8: LONG CONSOLE: Lift the parking brake lever up as far as it will go and try to manipulate the console over the parking brake lever and gear lever.
➜ If you have difficulty manoeuvring the console over the parking brake lever, it may be necessary to disconnect the parking brake cable or slacken the adjuster - see *Chapter 12, Brakes*.

STEP 9: On models with a clock and radio fitted to the centre console you will have to manoeuvre the console so that you can get access to disconnect the clock and radio.

STEP 10: Refitting is the reverse of the removal process.

JOB 4:   DASHBOARD - *remove, refit.*

SAFETY FIRST!

VEHICLES WITH PASSENGER AIR BAGS
• **There is a risk of serious injury if an air bag inflates unintentionally. It is, therefore, vital that you fully understand the dangers and take the necessary precautions before attempting to remove the dashboard on vehicles equipped with passenger air bags. Read *Jobs 13 and 14* in full before removing the dashboard.**

IMPORTANT NOTE:
• It is impossible to document here the wide variety of dashboard design and fitting that are found in the range.
➜ The steps indicated here are a general pattern of removal with some reference to specific models.
➜ We suggest that you read the section and then scrutinise your dashboard to establish the exact operation.
➜ See **Job 1** for further advice on fixings.
➜ See *Chapter 10, Electrical, Instruments* for instrument panel removal.

SAFETY FIRST!

• **Do not disconnect any hoses or connections on an air conditioning system.**

STEP 1: Disconnect the battery negative connection. On vehicles equipped with air bags you should wait at least 30 minutes before starting work. See *Jobs 13 and 14* for additional safety information.

STEP 2: Remove the steering wheel - see *Chapter 11, Steering, Suspension*.
➜ Undo the retaining screws, and remove the upper and lower steering column shrouds.

STEP 3: Remove any cover trim panels and disconnect wiring plugs underneath.
➜ The placement of cover panels varies from model to model.

STEP 4: Remove any switches from the steering column and disconnect the multi-plug from the ignition switch.

➜ On some Escort and older Fiesta models undo the bolt and disconnect the earth/ground lead from the panel beneath the dashboard on the driver's side.

STEP 5: Remove the instrument panel. See *Chapter 10, Electrical, Instruments*.

STEP 6: PRE-1990 ESCORTS, POST-1989 FIESTAS AND KA: The steering column should be removed or loosened to lower onto the front seat. See *Chapter 11, Steering, Suspension*.

STEP 7: ADDITIONAL ELECTRICAL COMPONENTS: Locate, disconnect and/or remove, where fitted.
➜ The auxiliary warning system indicator control unit and fuel computer - see *Chapter 10, Electrical, Instruments*.
➜ **PRE-1986 MODELS:** Disconnect the loudspeaker cable.
➜ Remove the radio or radio/cassette and radio mounting bracket - see *Chapter 10, Electrical, Instruments*.
➜ Remove the ashtray and cigarette lighter mounting panel. Disconnect the cable from the cigarette lighter.
➜ Where fitted. Remove the clock.
➜ Remove the footwell lights from both sides of the dashboard - see *Chapter 10, Electrical, Instruments*.

STEP 8: Where applicable disconnect cable connections such as the choke or bonnet release.

STEP 9: Disconnect the heater controls, multi-plugs and switches. Remove the heater control knobs and the control panel - see *Chapter 9, Ignition, Fuel, Exhaust*.
➜ **LATER MODELS:** Pull off the fan speed knob and move the control levers fully right. Unclip and remove the heater trim panel towards the left, disconnecting the light as it is removed. You will normally need to remove the sliding control knobs as well.
➜ Unscrew the screws at the top of the heater control unit, release the clips at the sides and pull the control panel from the dashboard. Disconnect the electrical connections, the control cable and withdraw the unit from the dashboard.

STEP 10: On some models it will be necessary to remove the centre console - see **Job 3**.

STEP 11: On most model it will be necessary to remove the glove box:
➜ Remove the screws attaching the glove box to the dashboard.
➜ Remove the screws attaching the glove box latch and on some models the screw inside the top of the glove box, which attaches the glove box to the bracket or the hinges holding the lid.
➜ Disconnect the switch wiring and courtesy light where fitted.

STEP 12: Remove the fuse box cover and the fuse box attachment screws. Separate the fuse box from the dashboard.

4-12

STEP 13: Separate the hoses and ducts from the heater, if it can be done at this stage.

STEP 14: Depending on model it may be necessary to undo the side vent retaining screws, remove the side vent panel, and disconnect the wiring from the panel mounted switches.

STEP 15: Remove the door seals from the front pillars, the front pillar trim panels and, where fitted, the dashboard side trim panels. Disconnect any multi-plugs behind the A-pillar trim and label them.

STEP 16: Where fitted, remove the passenger side airbag. If it has been possible to disconnect it at this point. See *Job 13*.

STEP 17A: Locate and identify the type and number of dashboard attachment clips and screws. This shows the variety of fixings used by Ford.

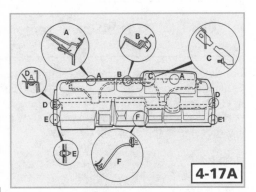

4-17A

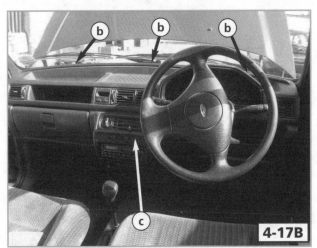

4-17B

STEP 17B: Screws (**b**), often three in number are usually found along the top of the dash board, usually with trim covers . Screws or retaining nuts are often found in area (**c**) in the ashtray or other fascia cavities.

STEP 17C: Screws (**a**) are found behind the door weatherstrip (arrowed).

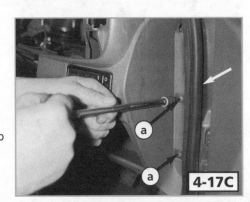

4-17C

IMPORTANT NOTE: On the Ka the bulkhead safety bar should be left attached to the dashboard and separated, if necessary, after dashboard removal. You should not undo the screws attaching the bulkhead safety bar at this stage.

STEP 18: KA: Additional steps:
→ Remove the windscreen wiper arms - see *Chapter 10, Electrical, Instruments*.
→ Open the bonnet and remove the screws attaching the vent to the bulkhead.
→ Remove the left and right vents and disconnect the screen washer supply pipe.

> **TOP TIP!**
> • Removing the dashboard is easier if you have an assistant.
> • Mark or make a note of the location of the electrical connectors so they can be refitted correctly.
> • Make a note of the location of the loom clips and supports.

STEP 19: Undo the dashboard attachments.

STEP 20: Pull the dashboard to the rear so that you have access to the space between the bulkhead and dashboard.

4-20

STEP 21: At this point check that all disconnections have been made if they were not done at an earlier stage, examples being:
→ Disconnect the cigarette lighter and clock.
→ On models with a passenger airbag, disconnect the two wires.
→ Disconnect the airbag control module multi-plug. Press the lock tag upwards and pull over the retaining strap.
→ Remove the screws and heater ducting from under the front of the dashboard.
→ Disconnect speedometer cable and wiring loom clips.

> **TOP TIP!**
> • Label all connections and note the path of cable and wiring loom routes.

STEP 22: Manoeuvre the dashboard to the rear and withdraw it from the vehicle. If necessary, move the gear lever out of the way by engaging second or fourth gear.

STEP 23: Remove the dashboard complete with crash padding - the crash padding can be separated from the dashboard after removal from the vehicle.

STEP 24: Refitting is the reverse of the removal process.
→ Ensure that wiring and cables are correctly routed and securely located.
→ Use new clips and ties.

JOB 5: INTERIOR MIRROR – *remove, refit.*

IMPORTANT NOTE:
• All models covered by this manual have interior rear view mirrors that are attached to the inside of the windscreen by self-adhesive pads.
• Normally, the interior rear view mirror will only need to be removed when the windscreen is being replaced or the mirror has been broken. It is important that the correct adhesive pads are used to attach the mirror. Using the wrong adhesive, such as 'superglue' or epoxy can result in the windscreen cracking.

❒ **STEP 1:** Remove the mirror by holding it with both hands and pushing forwards to break the adhesive bond.

❒ **STEP 2:** If the base comes adrift from the screen:
→ Mark the outside of the screen with felt pen to show where the mirror is to be relocated.
→ Use ONLY a proprietary mirror base adhesive for relocating the base.

→ Other types of adhesive may 'work' but will probably cause the screen to crack.
→ Clean off all traces of old adhesive from screen and base with a sharp blade.
→ Wipe the base and screen with degreaser and allow to dry.

❒ **STEP 3:** The Wurth mirror adhesive we used comes in two parts:
→ Break the phial of green adhesive and use the integral applicator to wipe adhesive onto the base pad.
→ Some types of mirror adhesive involve special double-sided tape – the principles are the same. Follow instructions on the pack.

❒ **STEP 4:** Use the markings on the outside of the screen. Apply hardener to the area of the screen where the base is to be fixed.

❒ **STEP 5:** Hold the base into position. It will stick into place very quickly, but will need to be allowed to cure before reattaching the mirror – see instructions on the pack.

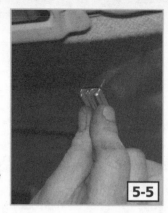

JOB 6: SUN VISORS - *remove, refit.*

The sun visors may be swivelling, or non-swivelling. Generally, the older and lower specification vehicles have the non-swivelling type.
→ Higher specification models have a vanity mirror incorporated in the passenger sun visor.

❒ **STEP 1:** Remove the single screw (non-swivelling) or two screws (swivelling) from the outer attachment points.

❒ **STEP 2:** Slide the sun visor from the inner pivot (non-swivelling) or unclip the sun visor (swivelling) from the inner attachment point. Remove the sun visor from the vehicle.

❒ **STEP 3:** If necessary, undo the single screw from the inner pivot (non-swivelling) or retaining pivot (swivelling)

and remove these items from the vehicle.

❒ **STEP 4:** Refitting is the reverse of the removal process.

JOB 7: GRAB HANDLES - *remove, refit.*

❑ **STEP 1:** Carefully lever out the 'snap in' covers at the front and rear of the grab handle.

7-1

❑ **STEP 2:** On Ka models where coat hooks only are fitted in the rear, carefully lever out the single 'snap in' cover.

❑ **STEP 3:** Undo the attachment screws and remove the grab handles or coat hooks from the vehicle

7-3

❑ **STEP 4:** Refitting is the reverse of the removal process.

JOB 8: HEADLINING - *remove, refit.*

There are two distinct types of headlining fitted to the vehicles covered by this manual. The early type of headlining is of one piece design with one (sunroof) or four (non-sunroof) support wires. It is held by adhesive and clips at the door and window openings. Later head linings are one piece moulded components.
→ Fitting a fabric heading is a highly skilled job that should be entrusted to a vehicle upholsterer.
→ Fitting a moulded headlining is possible, though it is recommended that the work is entrusted to an upholsterer. These are the steps.

❑ **STEP 1:** Remove the following components.
→ Sun visors - see *Job 6*.
→ Passenger grab handles on all models and rear coat hooks on the Ka - see *Job 7*.
→ The 'A' pillar trims on all models, the 'B' pillar trims on Escorts and the 'C' pillar trims on Escorts and Fiestas - see *Job 2*.
→ The sunroof - on models with electrically operated sunroofs, remove the sunroof motor - see *Chapter 13, Bodywork*.
→ The interior light - on Escort and Fiesta models you must remove the complete overhead console - see *Chapter 10, Electrical, Instruments*.
→ The head rests - these pull upwards out of the seats.

Additionally, lowering the front and rear seats as well will improve access and make headlining removal easier.
→ The rubber seals at the top of the door openings.
→ **ESCORT AND FIESTA:** Remove the two plugs on either side above the driver and passenger doors.

❑ **STEP 2:** Lever out the retaining clips (three on Ka, two on Escort and Fiesta) at the rear of the headlining.

❑ **STEP 3:** Pull away the tailgate rubber seals from the headlining.

❑ **STEP 4:** Carefully remove the headlining through the open tailgate. On four door Escort models the headlining can be removed through one of the rear doors. Make sure the headlining is not bent excessively or soiled during removal and storage.

❑ **STEP 5:** Refitting is the reverse of the removal process.

JOB 9: SEAT BELTS - *remove, refit.*

SAFETY FIRST!

• Some models covered by this manual are equipped with seat belt pre-tensioners.

• These may be mechanical or pyrotechnic, depending on model and year of manufacture. Inadvertent activation of the seat belt pre-tensioners can result in serious injury. You must take the necessary safety precautions.

• **MECHANICAL PRE-TENSIONERS:** See *Job 10, Safety First at start of Job.*

• **PYROTECHNIC PRE-TENSIONERS:** See *Job 13* for vital safety information before working on vehicles equipped with seat belt pre-tensioners.

• If you are not sure which type is fitted – or if pre-tensioners are fitted – consult a Ford dealer before carrying out any work on the vehicle.

❑ **STEP 1:** On vehicles fitted with pyrotechnic seat belt pre-tensioners, (arrowed) disconnect the battery negative connection and wait 30 minutes, before starting work.

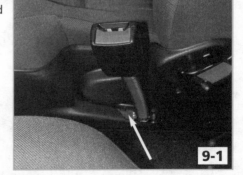

9-1

❑ **STEP 2:** On vehicles fitted with mechanical pre-tensioners, fit the transit safety clip before starting work.

STEP 3: FRONT AND REAR SEAT BELTS - UPPER PILLAR MOUNTING POINTS: Lever free the plastic cover from the upper seat belt mounting point.

→ Using a suitable socket, remove the upper mounting bolt - the bolt (arrowed) will be a hexagon or Torx type.
→ Make a note of the order in which the spacers and washers are fitted.

STEP 4: FRONT AND REAR SEAT BELTS - INERTIA REEL MOUNTING POINTS: Where necessary, remove the trim panels (arrowed) or rear seats so that you have access to the inertia reel mechanism.
→ On two-door models you will need to release bolt (a) to free the belt from the sliding rod.

STEP 5: Using a suitable socket, remove the mounting bolt - the bolt will be a hexagon or Torx type.
→ Note the

routing of the seat belt through the trim panels and the order in which the spacers and washers are fitted.

TOP TIP!

• There is a risk of serious injury if seat belt pre-tensioners are inadvertently operated. We recommend that, where pre-tensioners are fitted, any work on the seat belt stalk is carried out by an approved Ford dealer.

STEP 6: ONLY VEHICLES WITHOUT SEAT BELT PRE-TENSIONERS:
→ **FRONT SEAT BELT STALK:** Remove the front seat belt stalk from the floor or front seat.
→ Again, the bolt will be a hexagon or Torx type.

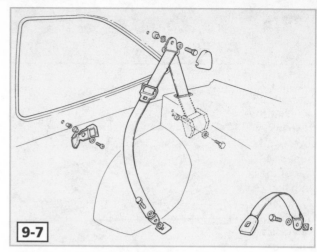

STEP 7: REAR SEAT BELTS: Remove or fold down the rear seats so that you can access the rear seat belt mountings. This is a typical rear seat belt layout.
→ Note the routing of the seat belts through the seat and remove the attachment bolts.

STEP 8: Refitting is the reverse of the removal process, bearing in mind the following points:
→ Make sure the seat belts are not twisted and are routed correctly through the trim panels and rear seats.
→ Make sure the washers and spacers are fitted in the correct sequence. Tighten the attachment bolts to the correct torque.

JOB 10: FRONT SEATS - *remove.*

SAFETY FIRST!

• READ *Job 13* IN FULL BEFORE WORKING ON SEATS FITTED WITH PYROTECHNIC SEAT BELT PRE-TENSIONERS.

MECHANICAL SEAT BELT PRE-TENSIONERS

• Before attempting to remove the seat or seat belt mechanism on a vehicle fitted with mechanical pre-tensioners, you must fit a transit safety clip, available from an approved Ford dealer.

• Unless you are familiar with the correct method of using the transit clip, you should seek the advice of an approved Ford dealer before attempting to fit the clip.

• Make sure the transit safety clip is removed after the seat belts and seat have been refitted.

You may come across several different front seat mounts on the early Fiesta. Very early sliding and non-sliding seats share the same mounting points but later seat designs, similar to the type used on early Escorts, have different mountings.

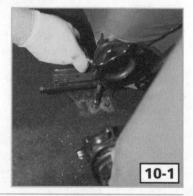

STEP 1: If necessary, slide the seat as far forward as it will go so that you can undo the rear mounting bolts. The rear bolts on the early sliding and non-sliding seats fit through the seat rails.

STEP 2A: Later Escort-style seats have pedestal brackets at the rear. On later vehicles you will have to remove the carpet so that you can get at the bolts.

10-2A

STEP 2B: On Ka models, the smaller brackets bolt down to the floorpan.

10-2B

STEP 3: If necessary, slide the seat as far to the rear as it will go and undo the front bolts.

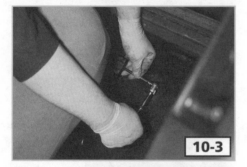

10-3

STEP 4: Again you will have to remove the carpet so that you can get at the bolts, as shown on this Ka.

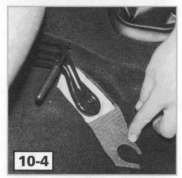

10-4

STEP 5: Manoeuvre the seat from the vehicle.

10-5

STEP 6: Refitting the seat is the reverse of the removal process, bearing in mind the following.
→ Tighten the attachment bolts to the correct torque - see *Chapter 1, Facts and Figures*. To ensure correct seat alignment, tighten the front bolts first.
→ See *Chapter 13, Bodywork* for details of reconnecting pyrotechnic seat belt pre-tensioners.

JOB 11: **REAR SEAT** - *remove, adjust, replace.*

Section A: Fiesta Hatchback, Ka, Escort hatchback and estate, Orion from 1990.

STEP A1: Unlock and fold the seat back forward. Depending on vehicle spec. and age, the seat back will be in one or two sections.

STEP A2: FIESTA PRE-1983: Pull the spring pins from each rear seat back pivot. Lever the pivot bushes from their brackets and slide them along the pivots until clear of the brackets. Lift the seat back from the vehicle.

STEP A3: FIESTA FROM 1989, KA: Remove the seat back to hinge attachment screws/ bolts (there may

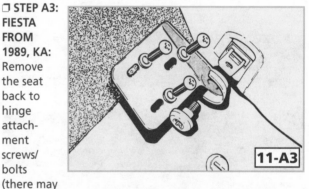

11-A3

be three or four) and lift the seat back out of the vehicle.
→ After removing the seat back you can also remove the hinges. Mark around them so they can be refitted in the correct position, undo the attachment screws/bolts and remove the hinges.

STEP A4: REAR SEAT CUSHION: Peel back the trim and remove the screws at the front of the seat cushion.
→ There are usually two screws, except on Fiesta models from 1989 which have three screws.

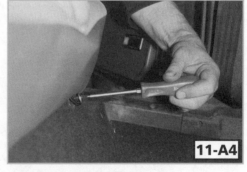

11-A4

STEP A5: Push to the rear and unhook the rear of the cushion from the floor pan tabs - see *Section C, Step C1*. Where appropriate, feed the seat belts through the cushion while it is lifted out of the vehicle.

STEP A6: Refitting is the reverse of the removal process, bearing in mind the following points.
→ Make sure the seat cushion engages with the floor pan tabs.
→ Make sure the hinges are refitted in their original positions.
→ Make sure the seat back panels engage the retaining catches.

Section B: Fiesta Courier and Combi.

The rear seat can be removed as an assembly.

STEP B1: Fold down the seat back and tilt the complete seat assembly forward.

STEP B2: Release the locking catches and remove the complete seat assembly from the vehicle.

STEP B3: Refitting is the reverse of the removal process.

Section C: Orion pre-1990.

STEP C1: Remove the screws from the seat cushion hinges at each side - you will need a Torx type

11-C1

screwdriver or socket. Push the cushion to the rear to disengage the hook and lift the cushion from the vehicle.

STEP C2: Remove the seat back attachment screws on the cushion side, followed by...

11-C2

STEP C3: ...the attachment nuts in the luggage bay. Remove the seat back from the vehicle.

11-C3

STEP C4: Refitting is the reversal of the removal process.

Section D: Escort Cabriolet.

STEP D1: Remove the seat belt inertia reel attachment bolts. You will need to move the seat cushion out of the way to gain access.

STEP D2: Remove the two seat back upper section attachment screws.

STEP D3: Fold down the seat back - the release is in the luggage bay. Pull away the seat back cover, sufficient to gain access, and remove the two top section attachment screws.

STEP D4: Separate the seat belt guide from the seat back and feed the inertia reel anchor plate through the seat back.

STEP D5: Remove the lower seat back hinge bolts on each side and remove the seat back from the vehicle.

A power operated soft-top was available as an option from 1987. Hydraulic pressure from an electrically driven pump opens or closes the soft-top via two hydraulic rams. The hydraulic pump is located on the left-hand side of the luggage bay floor and the rams are mounted on each side of the vehicle, close to the wheel arches.
→ The control switch for the power operated soft-top is located on the centre console. Opening a by-pass valve on the pump allows manual operation of the power operated soft-top.
→ The power operated soft-top hydraulic system is sealed and, apart from checking the fluid level, no other maintenance is needed.
→ We strongly recommend that work on the soft-top is carried out by an approved Ford dealer or specialist coach trimmer.

JOB 12: SOFT-TOP.

STEP 1: This is the manual soft-top frame and gas struts.
→ Some versions have a powered-soft top with hydraulic rams.

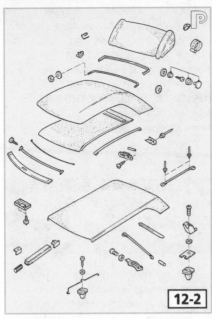

12-2

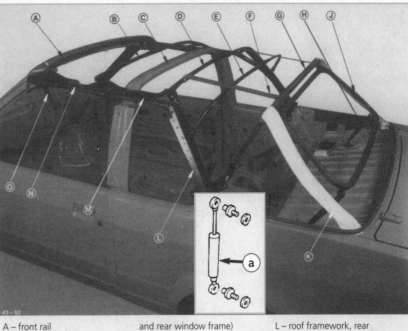

A – front rail	and rear window frame)	L – roof framework, rear
B – tubular bow	G – rear bow	M – roof framework, centre
C – roll over bar	H – rear window frame guide	N – roof framework, front
D – main bow	J – rear window frame	O – locking catch
E – auxiliary bow	K – webbing strap (between rear	a – gas strut
F – strap (between main bow	bow and bodywork)	

12-1

☐ **STEP 2:** These are typical soft-top trim components.
➔ Details vary on later models.

A seat belt pre-tensioner is a device which is designed to pull the seat belt tight in the event of a frontal crash.
➔ Air bags and seat belt pre-tensioners all normally contain a pyrotechnic (explosive) charge.
➔ It is MOST IMPORTANT that the whole of this Job is read and understood before you consider how to deal with air bags and seat belt pre-tensioners and the components surrounding them.
➔ The risks of harm from these items are not extreme, but they are real and must be acted upon in an appropriate way.

JOB 13:	**AIRBAGS AND SEAT BELT PRE-TENSIONERS** - *essential Safety First!*

SAFETY FIRST!

• **THE WHOLE OF THIS JOB IS *'SAFETY FIRST!'***

• **Read ALL of the information in this Job before working ON OR NEAR air bags and seat belt pre-tensioners.**

Section A: Essential safety notes.

☐ **STEP A1:** Note the location of all airbags and seat belt pre-tensioners before starting work.
➔ **AIR BAGS:** These may be fitted, for example, in the steering wheel, in front of the passenger seat, in the door or in the side of the seat. There is normally an embossed label at the position of an air bag.
➔ **SEAT BELT PRE-TENSIONERS:** These may not easily be visible until the seat is partly dismantled. See the vehicle's handbook and also see *Job 10: Front Seats* and *Job 9: Seat belts* in this Chapter.

➔ If you are not sure whether or not a vehicle is fitted with air bags or pre-tensioners, or which type you are dealing with, or you are not fully competent to carry out any of the work described here, consult with, or take the vehicle to the vehicle manufacturer's dealership.

☐ **STEP A2:** All manufacturers recommend that air bags and seat belt pre-tensioners are worked on only by their own, trained personnel.
➔ IF FOR ANY REASON, YOU ARE UNABLE TO COMPLY EXACTLY WITH THE INSTRUCTIONS AND WARNINGS GIVEN HERE, DO NOT HANDLE OR WORK ON THE AIR BAG OR SEAT BELT PRE-TENSIONER COMPONENTS - leave it to the vehicle manufacturer's dealership.

☐ **STEP A3:** You may choose to have a dealer carry out the removal and replacement of air bag and/or pre-tensioner components so that you can carry out other work on the vehicle.
➔ If you choose to drive the vehicle to or from a main dealer with any of the pyrotechnic safety devices removed or disarmed, you will be taking a risk. In the event of a crash, you and/or your passengers will not be able to benefit from the normal function of the safety devices.
➔ Take care not to commit an offence or illegal act. For instance, in the UK, the seat belts must be functional and used by those in the vehicle. Do not contravene any laws or regulations by using the vehicle with safety devices disabled.

☐ **STEP A4:** If a tensioner device or airbag needs to be renewed:
➔ Remember that levering an airbag can cause it to be triggered.
➔ If an airbag or seatbelt tensioner receives a voltage across its terminals it can deploy. Almost any voltage is enough, even the very low current from a test meter or one inducted from an electric welder. Disconnect the

battery and the airbags and controller before welding the body shell. Never use a test meter on any airbag circuit.
→ Make sure the new unit is supplied in its correct safety packaging. It must be kept in its packaging at all times until fitted to the vehicle.
→ Place the old unit in the safety packaging after removing and fitting the new one.
→ Immediately take the old unit to the vehicle's main dealer and have them dispose of it.
→ Make sure that you carry out the work when you have access to the main dealer's premises - do not store new or old pyrotechnic safety devices.
→ If air bags or pre-tensioners have to be moved in a motor vehicle, they should be placed in the (closed) luggage compartment and EMPHATICALLY NOT in the passenger compartment.

☐ **STEP A5:** It must not be assumed that a replaced air bag or seat belt pre-tensioner will work properly.
→ Take the vehicle to the vehicle's main dealer to have the unit checked and, if necessary, re-programmed.
→ Take note of the warning in *Step A3*.

☐ **STEP A6: IMPORTANT GENERAL NOTES:** The following notes apply to all seat belt pre-tensioners and air bags, where relevant.
→ Both air bags and pre-tensioners are referred to as 'safety devices' in the following notes.
→ Where a safety device has a safety locking mechanism, the safety device should not be removed from a vehicle or handled unless the locking mechanism is used, activated or fitted, as described in the relevant part of this manual.
→ A belt tensioner which has been dropped on the floor, or dented or damaged in any way must not be used.
→ On some vehicles, a seat belt on which the tensioner has been 'fired' is not safe to use. On those vehicles, the seat belt cannot be checked for locking once 'fired'.
→ Do not subject safety devices to blows, drilling, mechanical working or heating.
→ DO NOT drop safety devices or subject them to impacts. If one is accidentally dropped, it should not be used but returned to the main dealership.
→ If the safety devices have been activated, ALWAYS wait for at least 30 minutes after the activation before carrying out any operations to it - it may be hot enough to burn skin.
→ If a safety device which has been activated has to be handled, use protective gloves and goggles.
→ Wash your hands with soap and water after handling a safety device.

☐ **STEP A7: WHEN WORKING ON THE VEHICLE:**
→ Both air bags and pre-tensioners are referred to as 'safety devices' in the following notes.
→ Do not subject an area surrounding the safety device to strong impacts. When, during bodywork repairs, for example, the use of a hammer is necessary, remove the complete unit.
→ If it is necessary to heat the area surrounding any of the safety devices or to carry out welding or brazing, then the complete safety devices in that area MUST be removed.
→ Safety devices have been designed to be fitted only on the type and model of vehicle for which they are intended. They cannot be adapted, reused or fitted on

other vehicles, but only on those for which they were designed and produced. Any attempts to reuse, adapt or fit safety devices on different types of vehicles could cause serious or fatal injuries to the occupants of the vehicle, either in the case of an accident or in normal usage.

☐ **STEP A8: IN THE DEPLOYMENT AREA OF THE AIRBAG:**
→ NEVER fit accessories or store objects.
→ Use ONLY seat covers approved by the vehicle's manufacturer.

Section B: Airbags and seat belt pre-tensioners - handling and storage.

This Section is taken from general information on how to handle and store airbags and seat belt pre-tensioners aimed originally at garages and workshops which handle and store only limited numbers, i.e. up to three or four, at any one time.
→ *Anyone working in domestic premises is strongly advised to follow the guidelines laid down here.*
→ This information is reproduced from the leaflet INDG280 10/98 C400 produced by the British Health & Safety Executive (HSE), and contains notes on good practice which are not at the time of publication compulsory in the UK but which you may find helpful in considering what you need to do.
→ Users in other territories must consider laws and regulations which may apply to them.
→ This information is current at August 1998 and is reproduced with thanks to HSE.

More and more vehicles are being fitted with a range of airbags and seat belt pre-tensioners. There is therefore an increasing likelihood that you will come across these devices at work.
Even though these devices are designed to save lives, there is the possibility of:
• *physical injury; and*
• *poisoning;*
if they are not handled correctly. While the likelihood of an accident involving an airbag or seat belt pre-tensioner is low, a few simple precautions can be taken to reduce the risks further.

☐ **STEP B1: WHAT TO DO:**
→ Find out from your supplier the UN hazard classification of the airbags and seatbelt pre-tensioners that you may handle.
→ **If any are classed as UN Hazard Class 1 (the explosives class) and you want to keep them on the premises,** you will need to register for a **Mode B Registered Premises** with your local authority under the Explosives Act 1875. The department dealing with registration varies from region to region, but it is usually the:
• fire brigade;
• trading standards; or
• environmental health

☐ **STEP B2: REGISTRATION:** The HSE recommend that, as a garage or workshop, you should register even if you don't plan to keep these devices, as delays in fitting them to the vehicle may mean they need to be kept on the premises, overnight, for example.

TOP TIP!

• For airbags or seat belt pre-tensioners which are classed as **UN Hazard Class 2** or **UN Hazard Class 9**, the HSE recommend that you keep them under similar conditions to those required for Mode B registration.

❏ STEP B3: STORING AIRBAGS AND SEAT BELT PRE-TENSIONERS:

→ You can buy cabinets or containers which meet the requirements for Mode B registration. In general terms, these requirements are for a substantial container which:
• has no exposed steel;
• is easy to keep clean; and
• can be closed and locked.
→ You should keep the container away from:
• oils, paints and other flammable material;
• areas where hot work, such as welding or brazing, is taking place; and
• electricity cables, sockets, distribution boards etc.
→ Also make sure the container is:
• secured to the wall or floor if possible; and
• kept dry at all times.

❏ STEP B4: HANDLING AIRBAGS AND SEAT BELT PRE-TENSIONERS:

→ **It is essential that the manufacturer's or supplier's information is checked before starting work on vehicles containing airbags, as procedural differences will occur from make to make.**
→ Never place your head or body close to the front of an un-deployed airbag, especially when fitting it, or removing it from a vehicle.
→ Always carry the airbag module with the trim cover facing away from you.
→ Never place an airbag module, or steering wheel assembly fitted with an airbag, face (trim side) down or with the trim against a hard surface.
→ Never attempt to repair or modify airbag modules.
→ Never expose airbag modules to excessive heat (over 90 degrees C), impact, electrical current (including static electricity) or radio transmitters.
→ Always use new components. Return any modules which are damaged or appear suspect to your supplier, **except** where the damage has resulted in the contents of the inflator cartridge being exposed or spilt, in which case obtain specialist advice from your supplier.
→ Return undeployed airbags to your supplier using the packaging the replacement device is supplied in. If for any reason this packaging is not available, contact your supplier and ask them to provide you with it.
→ Airbags should only be deployed by appropriately trained personnel working to the manufacturer's procedures.
→ Seek the advice of your supplier before disposing of any deployed airbags and seat belt pre-tensioners. Some manufacturers advise that their deployed airbags or seat belt pre-tensioners can be disposed of, or recycled, as normal waste; others recommend that they are treated as hazardous waste.

→ It is illegal to dispose of explosives as normal waste and domestic/commercial waste bins **must not** be used for disposing of **undeployed** airbags or seat belt pre-tensioners in Class 1.

❏ STEP B5: TO SEEK MORE COMPREHENSIVE INFORMATION:

→ Comprehensive guidance for those handling, storing or transporting larger numbers of these devices is provided in the HSE publication: *The handling, storage and transport of airbags and seat belt pre-tensioners* **HSG184 HSE Books 1998 ISBN 0 7176 1598 7.**
→ HSE priced and free publications are available by mail order from: HSE Books, PO Box 1999, Sudbury, Suffolk CO10 6FS. Tel: 01787 881165 Fax: 01787 313995.
→ HSE priced publications (i.e. those for which a charge is made) are also available from good booksellers.
→ For other enquiries, ring HSE's InfoLine on 0541 545500, or write to HSE's Information Centre, Broad Lane, Sheffield S3 7HQ.

JOB 14: AIRBAG SYSTEM – *deactivating, reactivating.*

DEACTIVATING THE AIRBAG SYSTEM

❏ **STEP 1:** Turn off the ignition, disconnect the battery and remove it from the vehicle so that there is no possibility of the battery leads accidentally contacting the terminals.

❏ **STEP 2:** Leave the vehicle for 30 minutes to ensure that any stored electrical energy in the airbag/pre-tensioner has been dispersed.

❏ **STEP 3:** If the vehicle body shell is to be welded, disconnect all airbags, airbag control units, pyrotechnic seat belt pre-tensioners and control unit wiring harness leads.

RECONNECTING THE BATTERY

❏ **STEP 4:** As the battery is reconnected, there is a small risk that an airbag may deploy.

❏ **STEP 5:** Before reconnecting the battery, close the vehicle's doors and leave a side window open by a small amount.

❏ **STEP 6:** Park the vehicle out of doors and make sure that no-one is standing closer than 10 metres to the vehicle. Reconnect the battery.

JOB 15: AIRBAGS – *remove, refit.*

IMPORTANT INFORMATION:
• Read *Jobs 13* and *14* IN FULL before working on any part of the airbag system.

Section A: Driver's-side airbag removal and refitting

❐ **STEP A1:** Deactivate the airbag system - see *Job 14*.

❐ **STEP A2:** Remove the upper and lower steering column shrouds so that you have access to the rear of the steering wheel boss.

15-A2

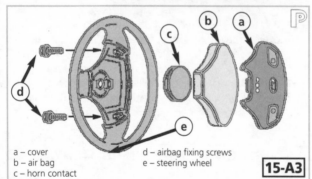

a – cover
b – air bag
c – horn contact
d – airbag fixing screws
e – steering wheel

15-A3

❐ **STEP A3:** Pull off the cover (a) and remove the horn contact (c) to reveal the airbag (b) beneath.

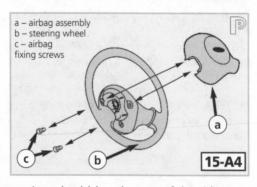

a – airbag assembly
b – steering wheel
c – airbag fixing screws

15-A4

→ Turn the steering wheel (e) so that one of the airbag attachment screws (d) can be accessed behind the steering wheel at the top.
→ Undo the screw using a Torx type socket (Fiesta shown).

❐ **STEP A4:** Move the steering wheel so that the second airbag retaining screw can be removed (Ka shown).

❐ **STEP A5:** After noting the wiring routing, disconnect the multi-plug from the airbag and, if necessary, the two electrical connectors from the steering wheel.
→ Lift the airbag from the steering wheel.

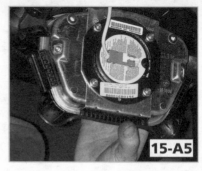

15-A5

❐ **STEP A6:** Remove and safely store the airbag - see *Job 13*.

❐ **STEP A7:** Refitting is the reversal of the removal process, bearing in mind the following points.
→ Tighten the airbag retaining screws to the correct torque.
→ See *Job 14, Step 4* for important safety notes regarding battery reconnection.

Section B: Passenger airbag removal and refitting.

IMPORTANT INFORMATION:
• Read *Jobs 13* and *14* IN FULL before working on any part of the airbag system.

❐ **STEP B1:** Deactivate the airbag system - see *Job 14*.

❐ **STEP B2: FIESTA TO 1995:** Remove the dashboard - see *Job 4*.
→ Remove the attachment screws and remove the airbag from the dashboard.

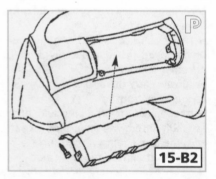

15-B2

❐ **STEP B3: FIESTA FROM 1995:** Release the air bag cover clips.
→ Undo the airbag cover strap attachment.
→ Lift the cover and strap away from the dashboard and remove the three Torx type bolts attaching the airbag.

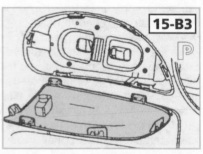

15-B3

❐ **STEP B4: KA:** Use a lever to release

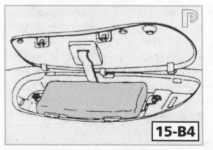

15-B4

the two clips on the rear edge of the airbag cover, taking care not to damage the cover.
→ Lift the rear of the cover and release the three clips at the front.
→ Using a Torx type socket, remove the two rear airbag retaining screws and the screws at each side.

❑ **STEP B5:** Lift out the airbag and cover. Note the wiring routing and disconnect the two connectors from the airbag.

❑ **STEP B6:** Remove and safely store the airbag - see *Job 13*.

❑ **STEP B7:** Refitting is the reversal of the removal process, bearing in mind the following points.
→ Make sure the cover retaining strap is not twisted.
→ Tighten the airbag retaining screws to the correct torque - see *Chapter 1, Facts and Figures*.
→ Check that the electrical connections have been made correctly and are secure.
→ Check that the electrical wiring has been routed correctly.

Section C: Airbag control unit removal and refitting.

IMPORTANT INFORMATION:
• Read *Jobs 13* and *14* IN FULL before working on any part of the airbag system.

❑ **STEP C1:** Deactivate the airbag system - see *Job 13*.

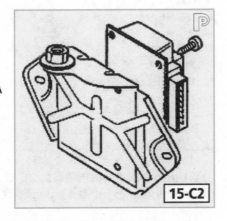
15-C2

❑ **STEP C2: FIESTA TO 1995:** Remove the control unit cover from the rear of the glove box and disconnect the multi-plug.
→ Remove the dashboard - see *Job 4* – and remove the control unit attachment bolts.

❑ **STEP C3: FIESTA FROM 1995:** Access to one of the control unit attachment screws is very difficult and there is a risk of damaging the airbag during removal. We recommend that the control unit module is removed by an approved Ford dealer.

❑ **STEP C4: ESCORT:** Remove the six screws and the lower panel from below the steering column.
→ Remove the instrument panel, see *Chapter 10, Electrical, Instruments* and undo the control unit attachment screws.

❑ **STEP C5: KA:** The airbag control unit is fitted beneath the centre of the dashboard. Lift back the carpets sufficient for access and remove the attachment screws.

❑ **STEP C6:** Lift the unit away and disconnect the multi-plug.

❑ **STEP C7:** Refitting is the reversal of the removal process, bearing in mind the following points.
→ Tighten the airbag control unit screws to the correct torque - see *Chapter 1, Facts and Figures*.
→ Check that the electrical connections have been made correctly and are secure.
→ Check that the electrical wiring has been routed correctly.

Section D: Airbag 'clockspring' removal and refitting.

IMPORTANT INFORMATION:
• Read *Jobs 13* and *14* IN FULL before working on any part of the airbag system.

❑ **STEP D1:** Deactivate the airbag system - see *Job 13*.

❑ **STEP D2:** Remove the driver's airbag - see *Section A*.

❑ **STEP D3:** Remove the steering wheel - see *Chapter 11, Part B, Job 12*.
→ Where appropriate, disconnect the horn connections, after noting the location and routing of the electrical wires.

❑ **STEP D4: ESCORT, ORION AND PRE-1995 FIESTA:** Undo the three screws. Note the routing of the wiring and remove the clockspring.

❑ **STEP D5: FIESTA FROM 1995 AND KA:** Disconnect the wiring connectors. Use a suitable lever to release the three tangs from the steering wheel. Note the routing of the wiring and remove the clockspring.

❑ **STEP D6:** Before fitting or refitting, the clockspring must be centralised.
→ Press in and hold the red locking pin.
→ Rotate the inner rotor fully anti-clockwise against the outer rotor.
→ Rotate the inner rotor 3.75 turns clockwise and release the locking pin.
→ Make sure the inner rotor is locked.

❑ **STEP D7:** Refitting is now the reverse of the removal process, bearing in mind the following points.
→ Tighten the airbag attachment screws to the correct torque.
→ Check that the electrical connections have been made correctly and are secure.
→ Check that the electrical wiring has been routed correctly.

CHAPTER 15: WIRING DIAGRAMS

HOW TO USE FORD WIRING DIAGRAMS

We don't pretend to include every wiring diagram for every model of Ford covered in this manual. It simply can't be done in a single workshop manual.
· To show every wiring diagram for all of the vehicles covered by this manual would, we estimate, take well over a thousand pages!
· The wiring diagrams shown here are a selection aimed at the (generally more complex) later vehicles. We concentrate on providing you with a selection that might prove useful to you.
· If you need a wiring diagram specific to the vehicle you are working on, you might be able to persuade the Parts Department of your local Ford dealership to do you a print-out of the relevant section from the Ford manual on CD Rom, called TIS.

EARLY DRAWINGS - PAGES 15-3 TO 15-6

Many of the codes and symbols used on these drawings are aimed at the auto-electrician or Ford mechanic with a complete set of wiring diagrams. The wiring diagrams shown here can be used by following the notes shown for later drawings. You can, in effect, ignore all the other code numbers shown.

DRAWINGS FOR LATER MODELS - PAGES 15-7-on.

❑ **WIRING 1: WIRING CONNECTIONS:** Each dotted line represents an electrical wire. At the ends, and sometimes within each line are symbols, and they have the following meanings:
a. male connector
b. female connector
c. connection
d. wires cross with connection
e. wires cross, no connection
f. splice
g. detachable connection
h. earth/ground connection

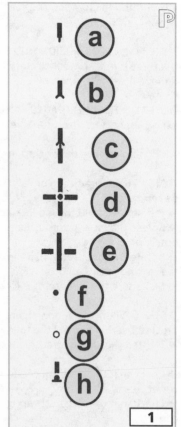

❑ **WIRING 2: COMPONENTS (1):** These are the main components shown in each diagram:
a. battery
b. fuse
c. circuit breaker

d. fusible link
e. component case directly connected to earth/ground
f. component with screw terminals
g. diode - current flows in direction of arrow
h. LED - light-emitting diode
i. capacitor
j. variable capacitor
k. piezoelectric sensor
l. wire resistance
m. heating element, or resistor
n. potentiometer - pressure or temperature
o. potentiometer - adjustable

❑ **WIRING 3: COMPONENTS (2):** Main components have their names printed alongside them.

❑ **WIRING 4: WIRE COLOURS AND SIZES:**
The colour codes and size of each wire are printed alongside the line for each wire.
➔ At the start, you will see a number. For example **0.35**, means that the wire cross section is **0.35 mm²**.
➔ Sometimes there is just one colour code, which is used for single-colour wire.
➔ Usually there are two codes, such as **BN/WH**.
➔ When you look up the colour (see the following list of colour codes) you'll see that **BN** stands for **brown** (the main colour) and **WH** stands for **white** (the secondary, or 'trace' colour).

WIRE COLOUR CODES

BK	Black	**LG**	Light green	**VT**	Violet
BN	Brown	**OG**	Orange	**WH**	White
BU	Blue	**PK**	Pink	**YE**	Yellow
GN	Green	**RD**	Red	**NA**	Natural
GY	Grey	**SR**	Silver		

☐ **WIRING 5:** Numbers on the wiring diagrams (in some instances) and colour codes relate to the following functions:

NUMBER DESCRIPTION COLOUR

4	Data link bus - positive	GY
5	Data link bus - negative	BU
7	Voltage D.C. supplied at all times (sensor)	YE
8	Sensor signal	WH
9	Sensor signal return	BN
14	Voltage supplied in Start and Run (overload protected)	VT
15	Voltage, ignition switch in Start or Run (not overload protected)	GN
29	Voltage supplied at all times (overload protected)	OG
30	Voltage supplied at all times (not overload protected)	RD
31	Earth/Ground	BK
32	Switch output supplies battery voltage, earth/ground or open-circuit to motor. Positive voltage output is for front-down, open, mirror leftward, unlock-on	WH
33	Switch output supplies battery voltage, earth/ground or open circuit to motor. Positive voltage output is for front-up, close, mirror rightward, lock off	YE
49	Pulsed power feed (overload protected)	BU
50	Voltage, ignition switch in Start (not overload protected)	GY
59	AC Power	GY
63	Variable D.C. voltage (over-load protected)	WH
64	Variable D.C. voltage (not overload protected)	BU
74	Voltage in Run or Accessory (overload protected)	BU
75	Voltage: Ignition switch in Accessory or Run	YE
89	Voltage supplied at all times (overload protected electronic module)	OG
90	Voltage supplied at all times (not overload protected electronic module)	RD
91	Earth/Ground	BK
94	Voltage, ignition switch in Start or Run (overload protected electronic module)	VT
95	Voltage, ignition switch in Start or Run (not overload protected electronic module)	GN

FUSES AND RELAYS

☐ **WIRING 6:** There are many different types and locations - see vehicle handbook for details.

→ In the type of fuse box show, relays are located in the same box. In this set-up, item **(A)** is the overload circuit breaker for the central locking system. Item **(B)** is the overload circuit beaker for the electrically operated windows.

→ You can remove the earlier type of flat fuse with fingers - the later type are removed by using the extractor clipped inside the fusebox.

→ **LATER MODELS:** The fusebox is situated beneath the fascia - remove the fixing screws - see *Chapter 14, Interior and trim*.

→ On these models, the relays are found on the back of the fuse board.

→ Later models also have a 'main' fuse box adjacent to the battery.

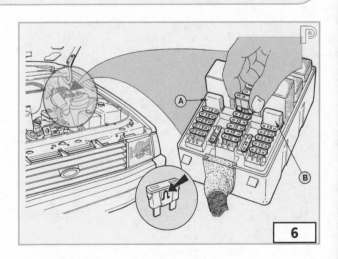

6

CHAPTER 15 Wiring Diagrams

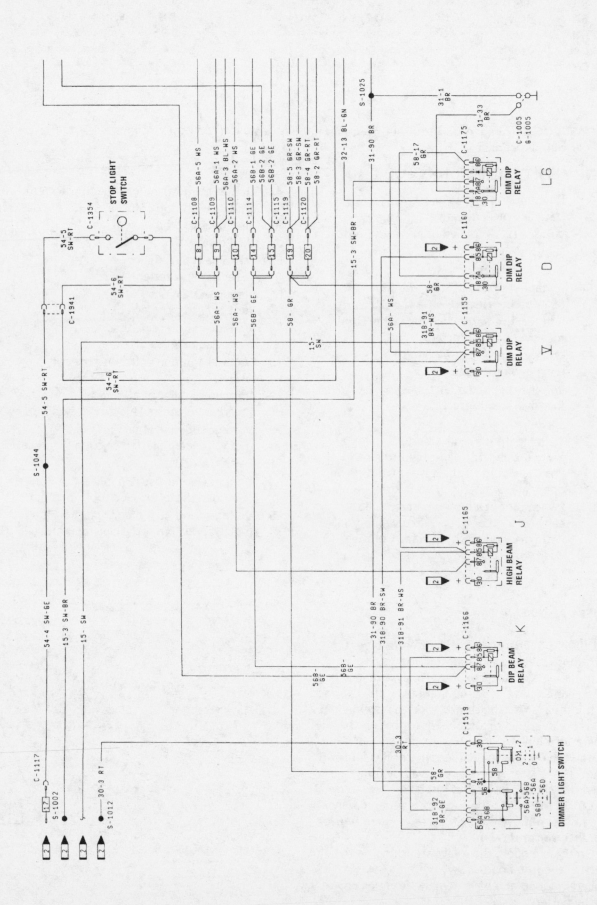

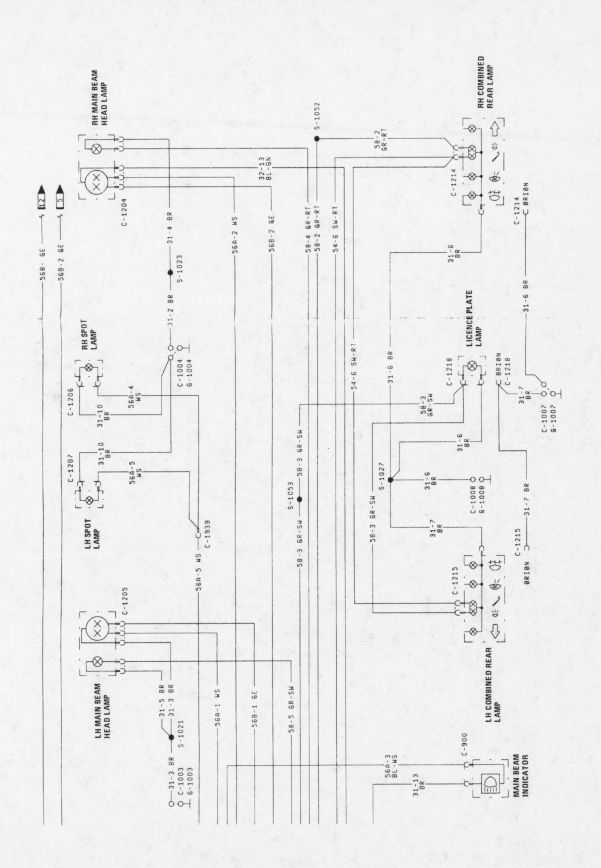

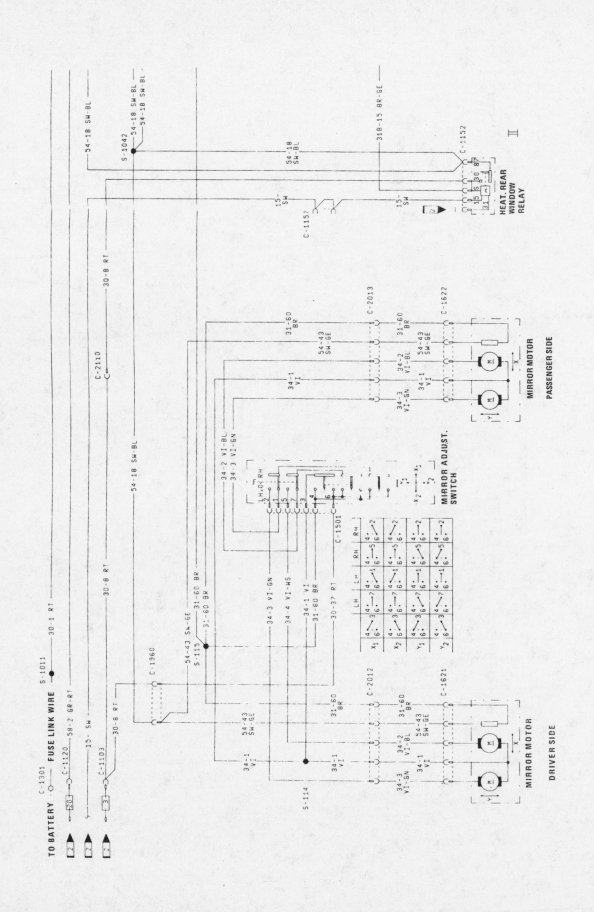

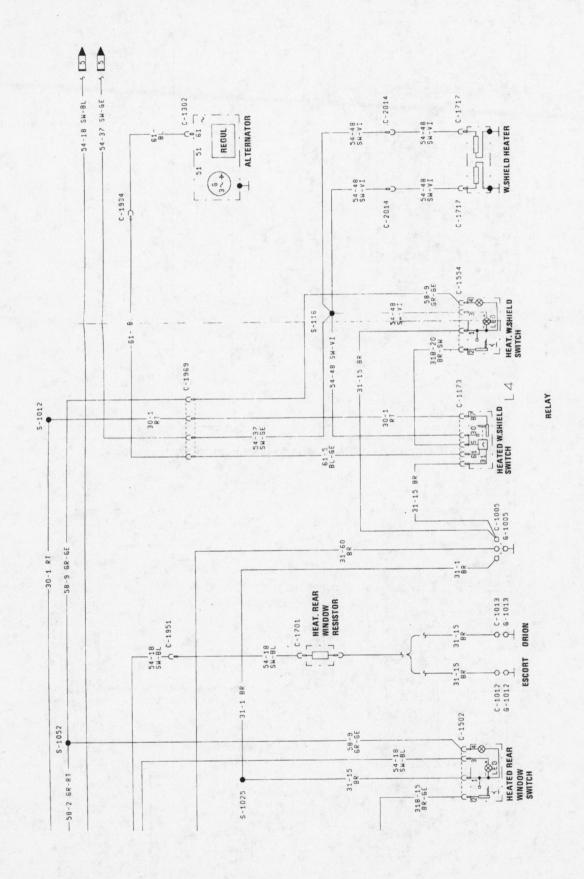

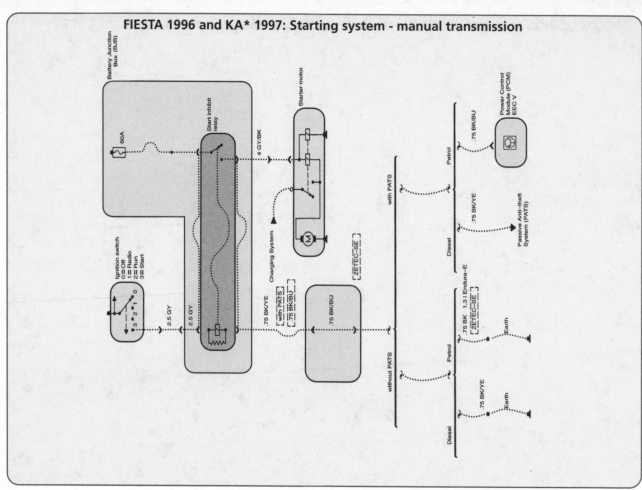

FIESTA 1996 and KA* 1997: Starting system - manual transmission

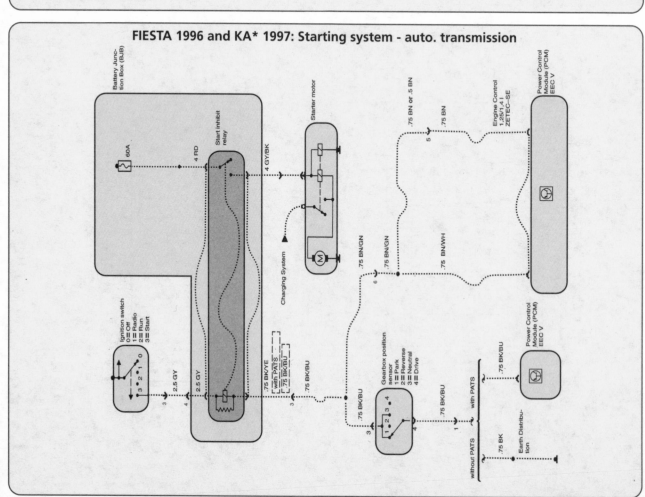

FIESTA 1996 and KA* 1997: Starting system - auto. transmission

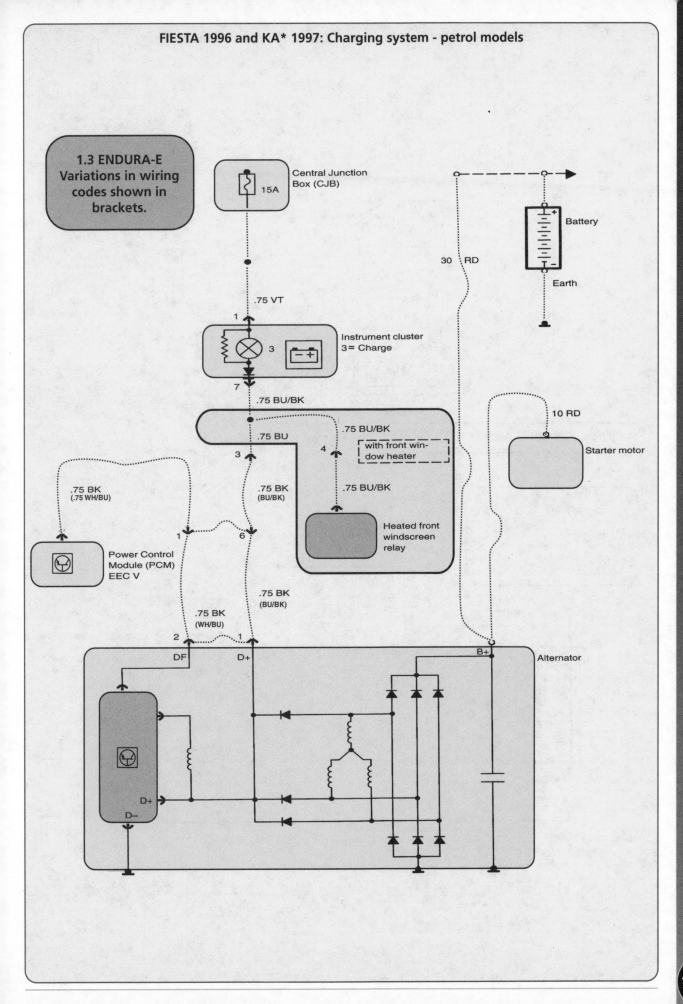

FIESTA 1996 and KA* 1997: Charging system - diesel

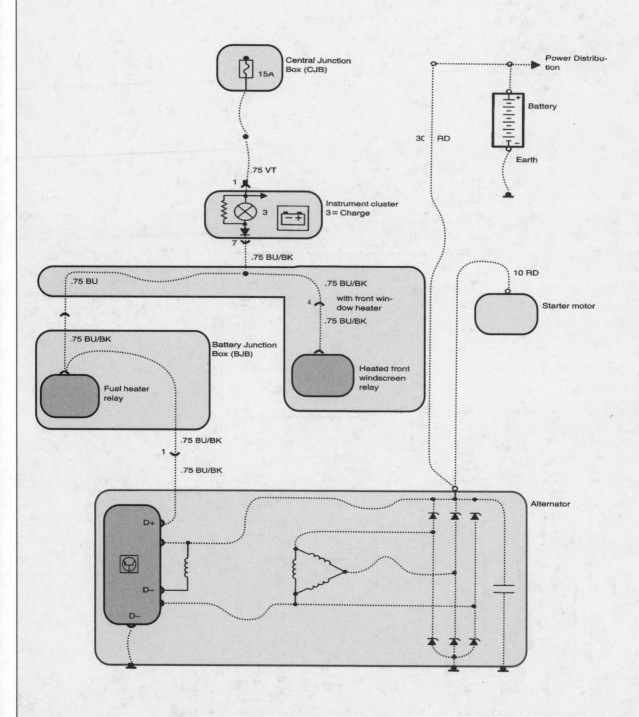

FIESTA 1996: Headlights operating system - page 1 of 2

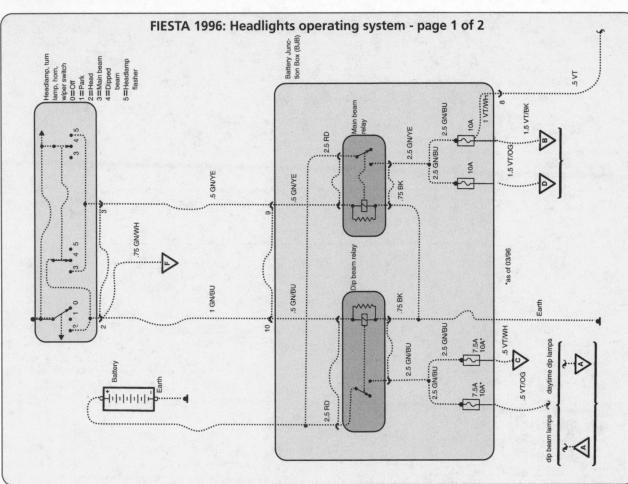

FIESTA 1996: Headlights operating system - page 2 of 2

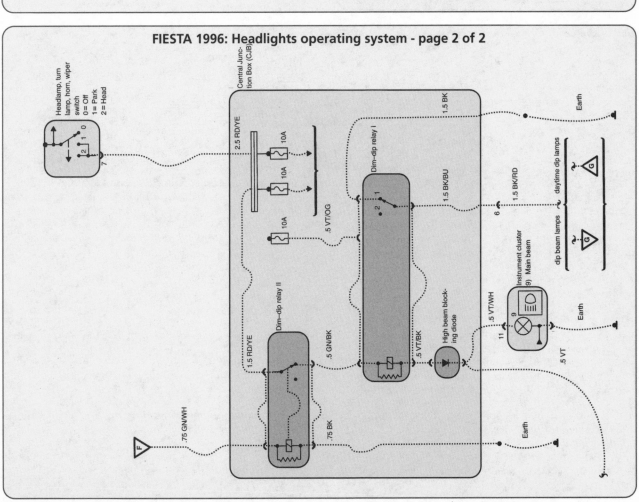

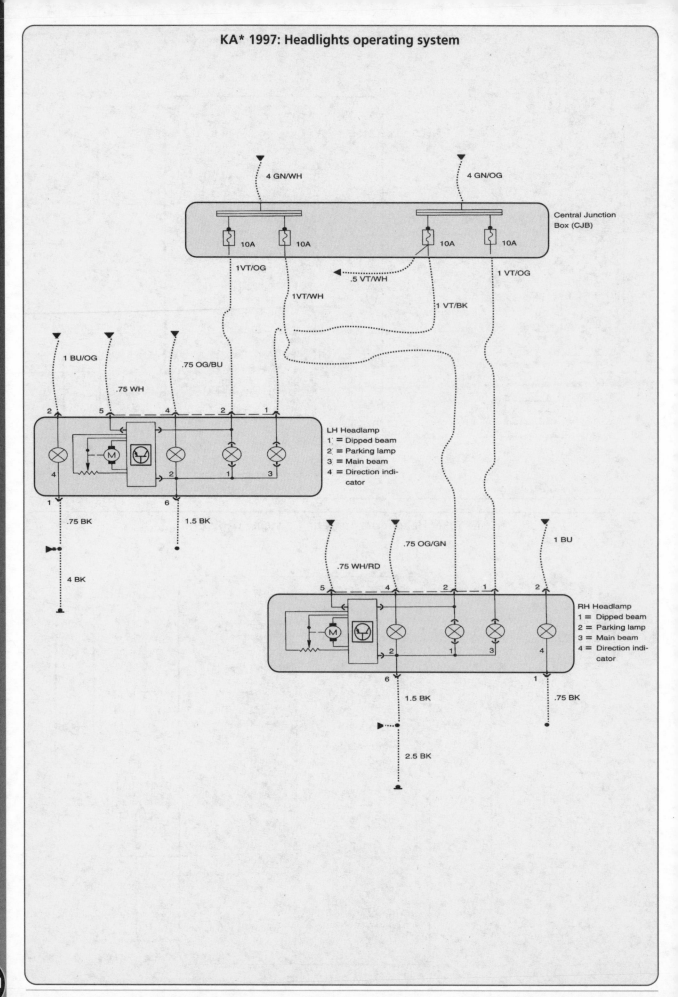

KA* 1997: Headlights operating system

FIESTA 1996 and KA* 1997: Stop lights

FIESTA 1996 and KA* 1997: Reversing lights

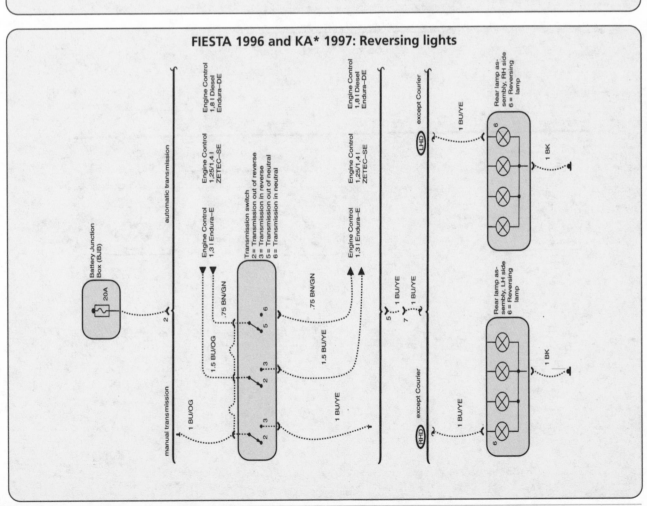

FIESTA 1996 and KA* 1997: Rear fog lights

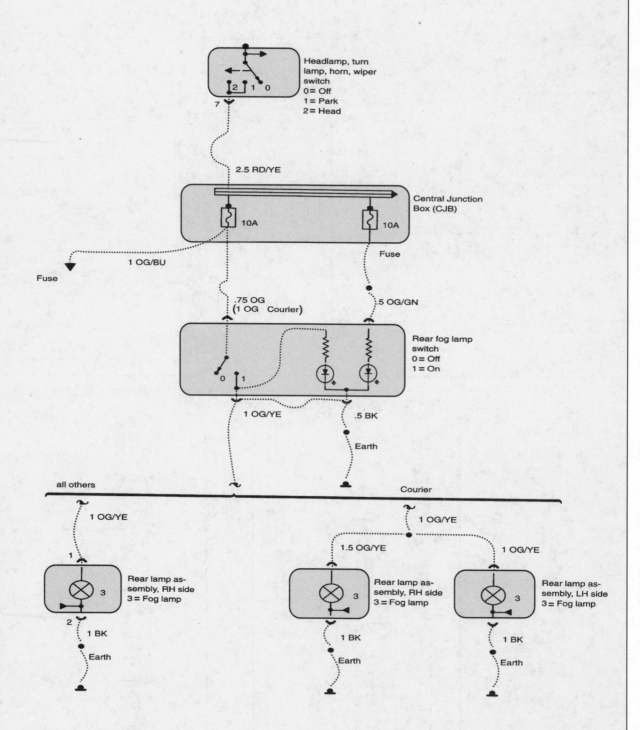

Headlamp, turn
lamp, horn, wiper
switch
0 = Off
1 = Park
2 = Head

2.5 RD/YE

Central Junction
Box (CJB)

10A

10A

Fuse

Fuse

1 OG/BU

.75 OG
(1 OG Courier)

.5 OG/GN

Rear fog lamp
switch
0 = Off
1 = On

1 OG/YE

.5 BK

Earth

all others

Courier

1 OG/YE

1 OG/YE

1.5 OG/YE

1 OG/YE

Rear lamp as-
sembly, RH side
3 = Fog lamp

Rear lamp as-
sembly, RH side
3 = Fog lamp

Rear lamp as-
sembly, LH side
3 = Fog lamp

1 BK

1 BK

1 BK

Earth

Earth

Earth

FIESTA 1996 and KA* 1997: Turn indicators and hazard lights

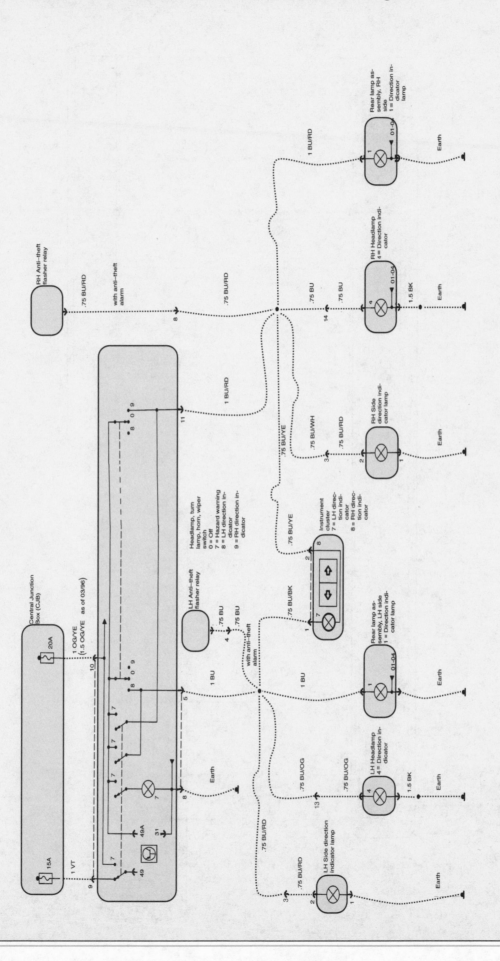

FIESTA 1996 and KA* 1997: Front screen wipers and washers

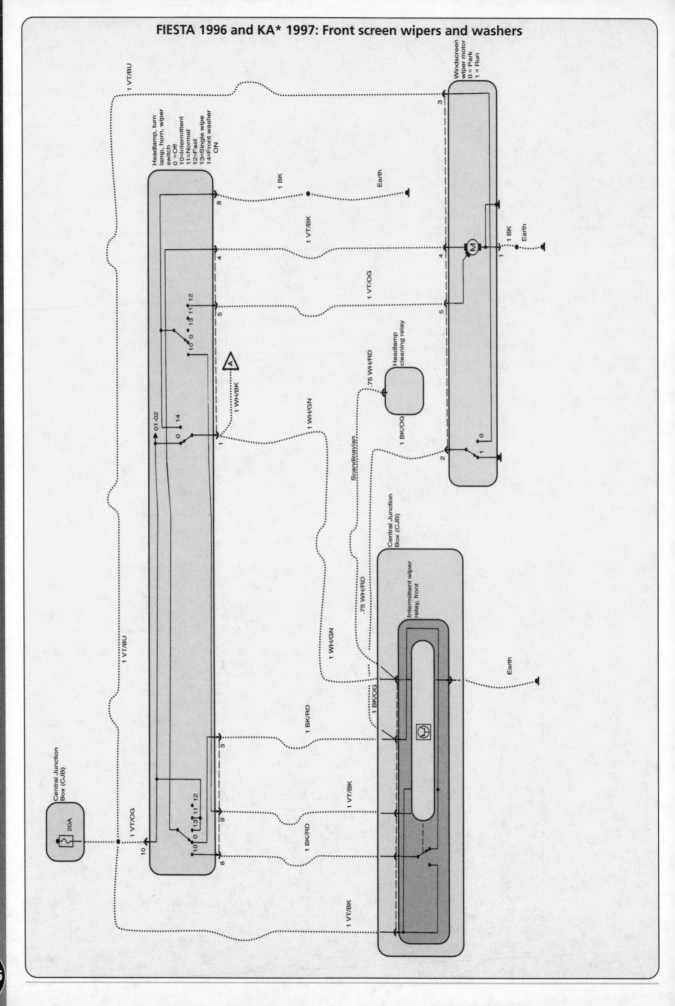

FIESTA 1996 and KA* 1997: Rear screen wipers and washers

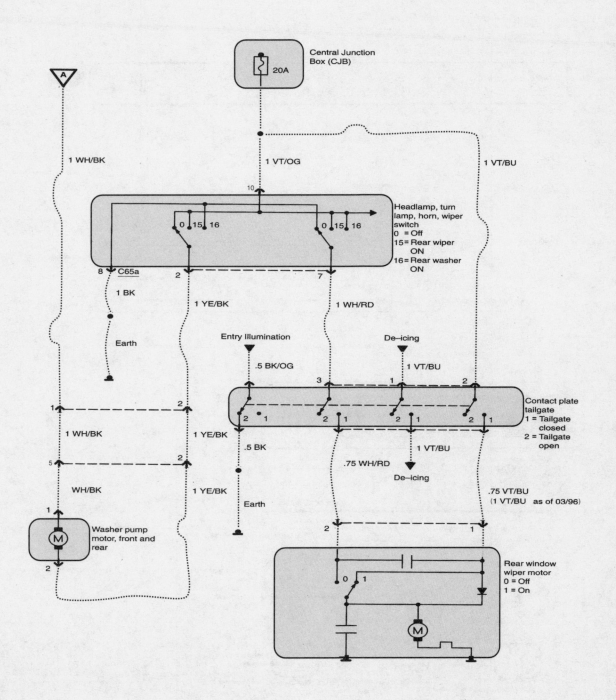

Central Junction Box (CJB)
20A

A

1 WH/BK

1 VT/OG

1 VT/BU

10

Headlamp, turn lamp, horn, wiper switch
0 = Off
15= Rear wiper ON
16= Rear washer ON

0 15 16   0 15 16

8 C65a   2   7

1 BK   1 YE/BK   1 WH/RD

Earth

Entry Illumination   De–icing

.5 BK/OG   1 VT/BU

3   1   2

1   2   1   2   1   2   1

Contact plate tailgate
1 = Tailgate closed
2 = Tailgate open

1   2   1   2   1   2   1

1 WH/BK   1 YE/BK   .5 BK   .75 WH/RD   1 VT/BU

5   2   De–icing

WH/BK   1 YE/BK   Earth   .75 VT/BU
(1 VT/BU as of 03/96)

1   2   1

M

Washer pump motor, front and rear

2

Rear window wiper motor
0 = Off
1 = On

0 1

M

FIESTA 1996 and KA* 1997: Heated rear screen

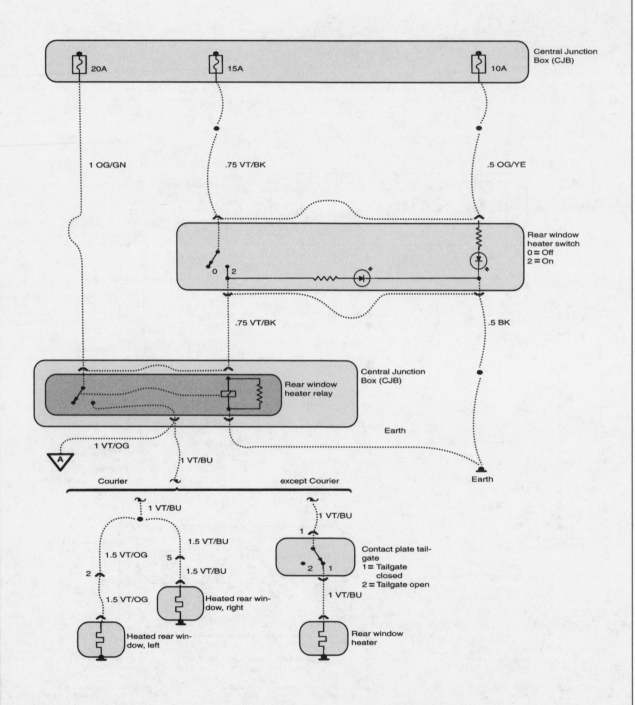

Central Junction Box (CJB)

20A   15A   10A

1 OG/GN   .75 VT/BK   .5 OG/YE

Rear window heater switch
0 = Off
2 = On

0 2

.75 VT/BK   .5 BK

Central Junction Box (CJB)

Rear window heater relay

Earth

1 VT/OG

1 VT/BU

A

Courier   except Courier

1 VT/BU

1 VT/BU   1 VT/BU

1.5 VT/OG   1.5 VT/BU

Contact plate tail-gate
1 = Tailgate closed
2 = Tailgate open

1

2   1

2   1.5 VT/BU

1.5 VT/OG   Heated rear win-
                   dow, right

1 VT/BU

1.5 VT/OG

Heated rear win-
dow, left

Rear window
heater

Earth

FIESTA 1996 and KA* 1997: Heating and ventilation - Part 1

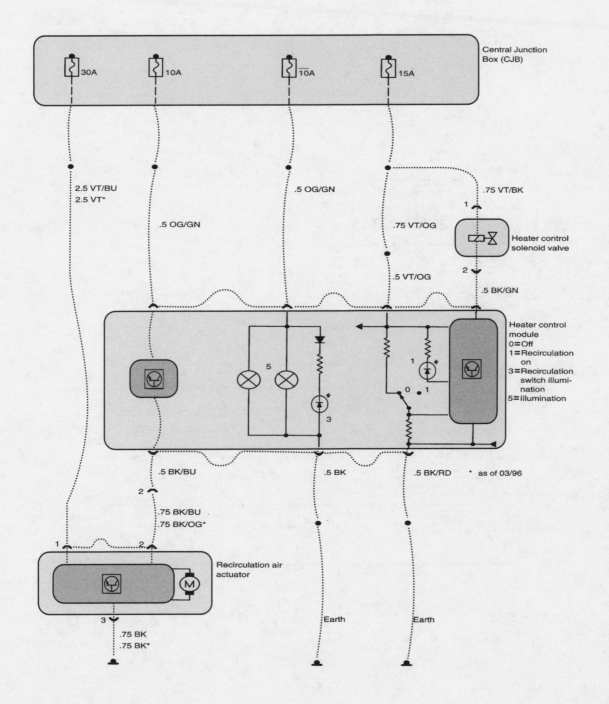

Central Junction Box (CJB)

30A 10A 10A 15A

2.5 VT/BU
2.5 VT*

.5 OG/GN

.5 OG/GN

.75 VT/OG

.5 VT/OG

.75 VT/BK

Heater control solenoid valve

.5 BK/GN

Heater control module
0 = Off
1 = Recirculation on
3 = Recirculation switch illumination
5 = Illumination

5

3

1

0 1

.5 BK/BU

2

.75 BK/BU
.75 BK/OG*

.5 BK

Earth

.5 BK/RD

Earth

* as of 03/96

1 2

Recirculation air actuator

3

.75 BK
.75 BK*

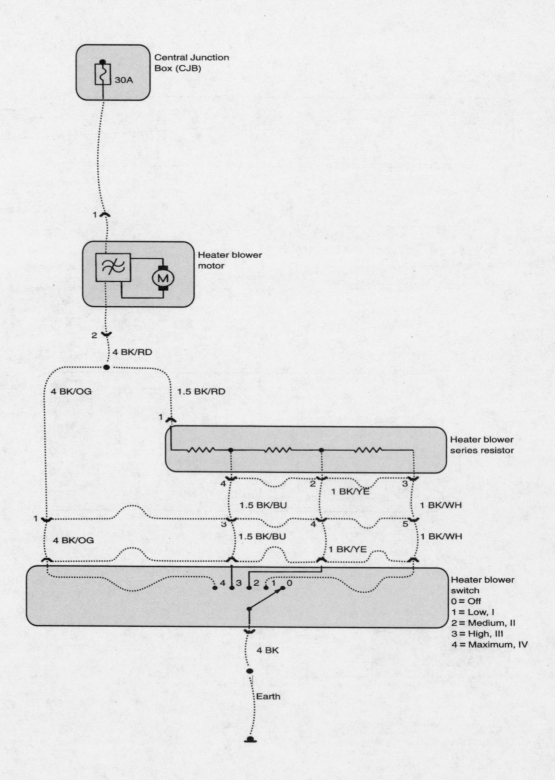

Central Junction
Box (CJB)

30A

Heater blower
motor

1

2

4 BK/RD

4 BK/OG

1.5 BK/RD

1

Heater blower
series resistor

4 · · 2 · · 3

1 BK/YE

1.5 BK/BU

1 BK/WH

1

3 · · 4 · · 5

4 BK/OG

1.5 BK/BU

1 BK/YE

1 BK/WH

Heater blower
switch
0 = Off
1 = Low, I
2 = Medium, II
3 = High, III
4 = Maximum, IV

4 · 3 · 2 · 1 · 0

4 BK

Earth

KA 1997: Electrically operated windows

Driver side

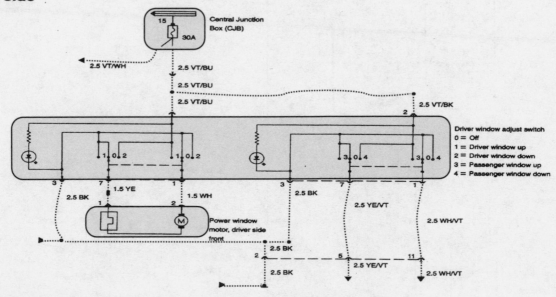

Passenger side

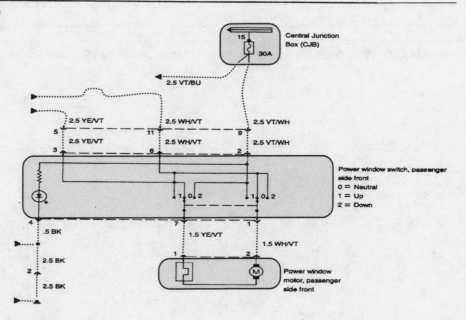

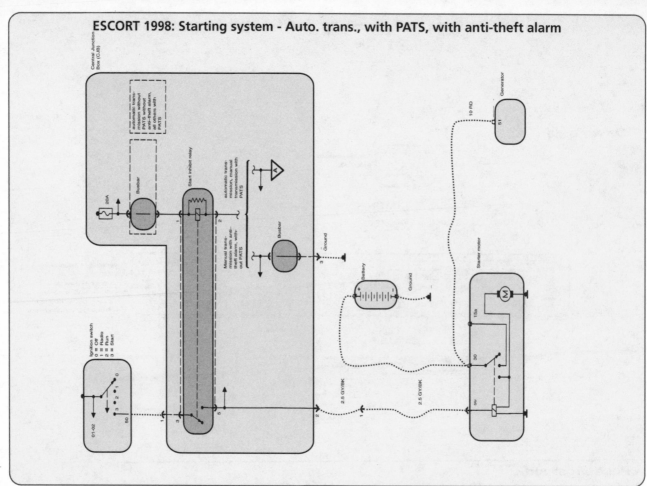

ESCORT 1998: Starting system - Auto. trans., with PATS, with anti-theft alarm

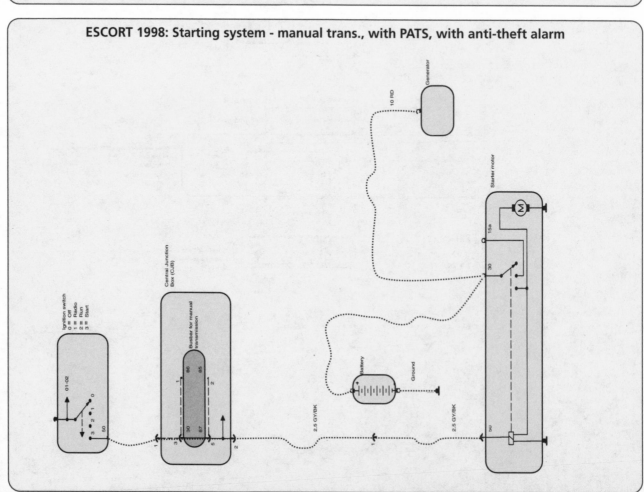

ESCORT 1998: Starting system - manual trans., with PATS, with anti-theft alarm

ESCORT 1998: Charging system - Petrol engines with EEC modules IV and V

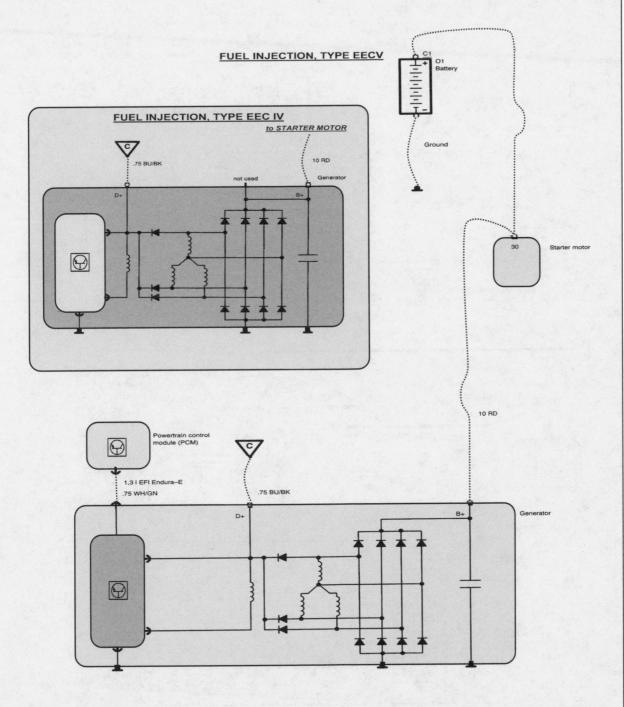

FUEL INJECTION, TYPE EECV

FUEL INJECTION, TYPE EEC IV

to STARTER MOTOR

ESCORT 1998: Charging system - Diesel engines

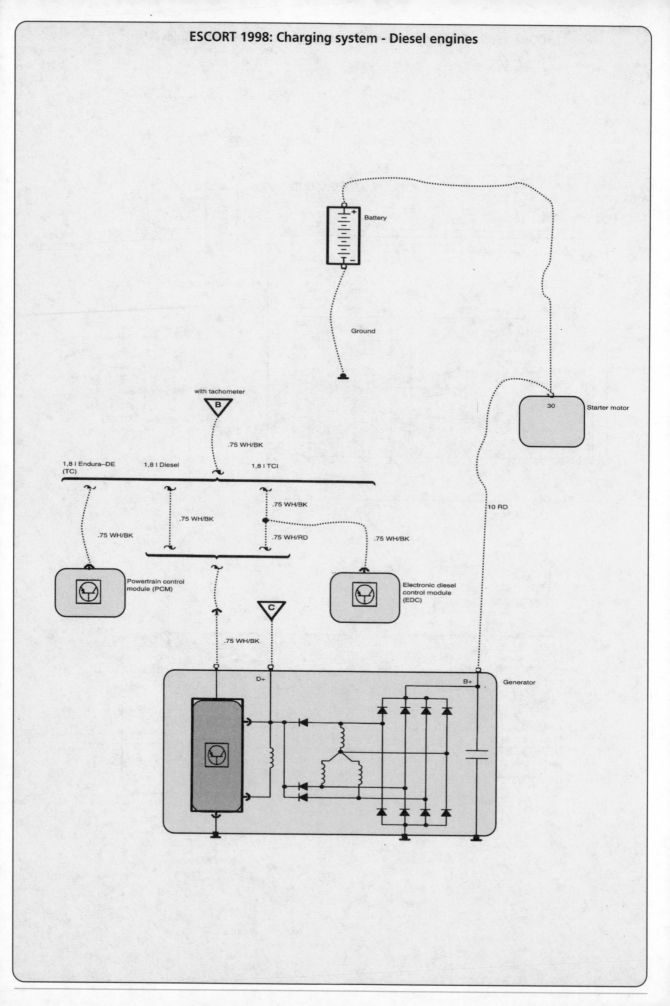

ESCORT 1998: Headlights, operating system

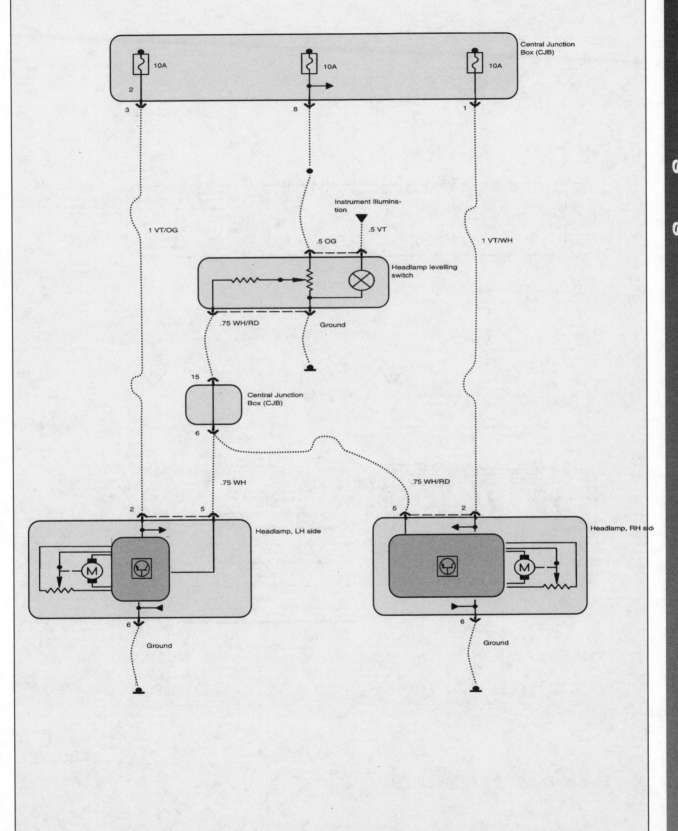

Central Junction Box (CJB)

10A

10A

10A

2

3

8

1

1 VT/OG

Instrument Illumina-tion

.5 OG

.5 VT

1 VT/WH

Headlamp levelling switch

.75 WH/RD

Ground

15

Central Junction Box (CJB)

6

.75 WH

.75 WH/RD

2   5

Headlamp, LH side

5   2

Headlamp, RH side

M

M

6

Ground

6

Ground

ESCORT 1998: Headlights units - with leveling

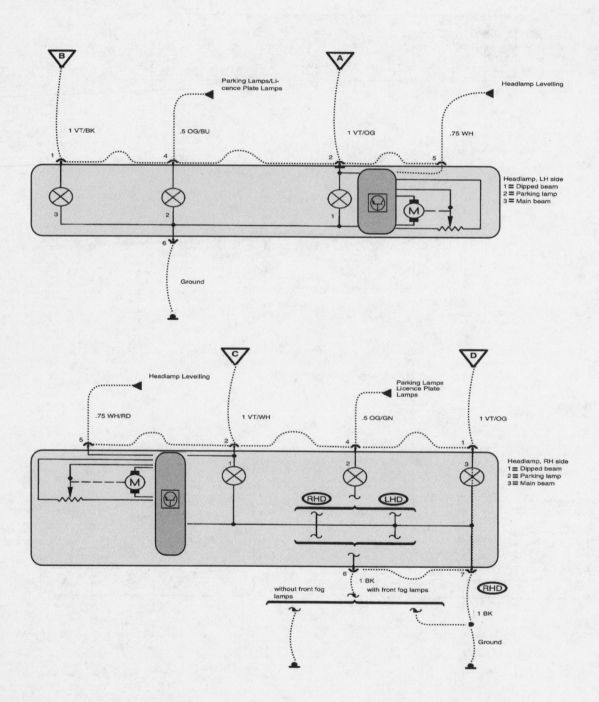

ESCORT 1998: Stop lights

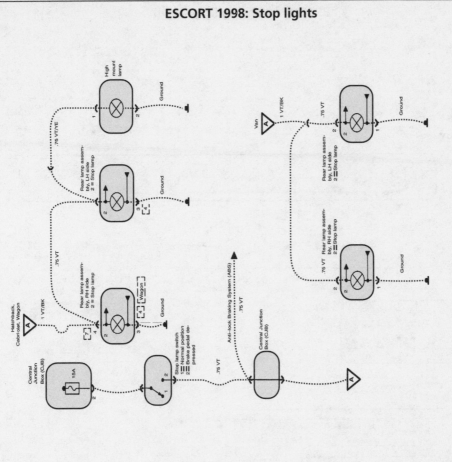

ESCORT 1998: Reversing lights

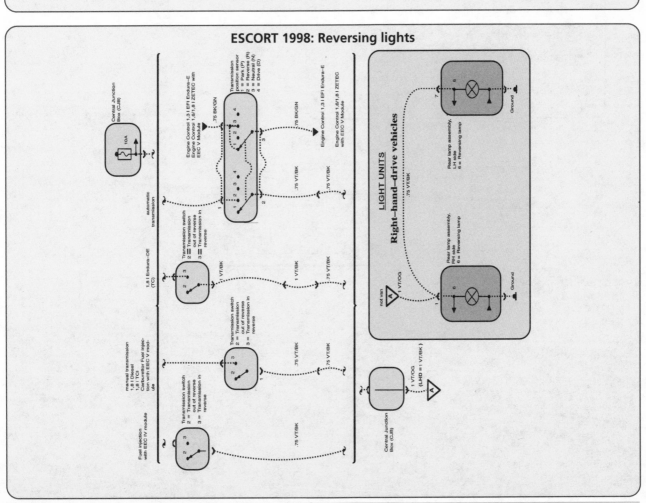

ESCORT 1998: Fog lights, rear

Rear fog lamps

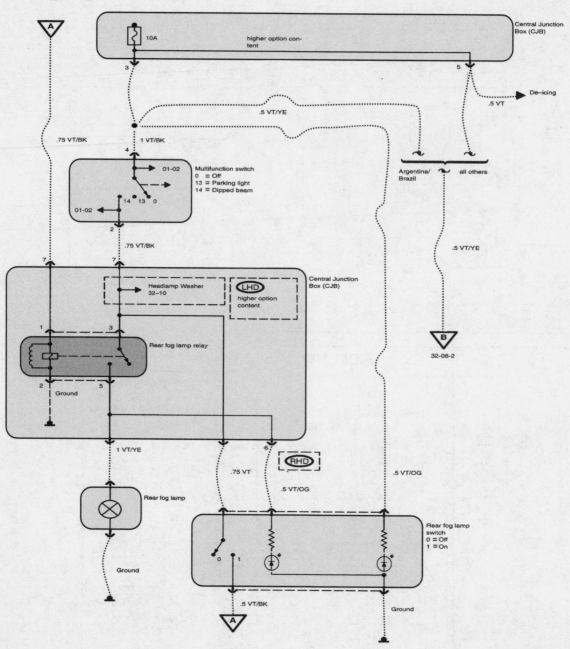

ESCORT 1998: Fog lights, front

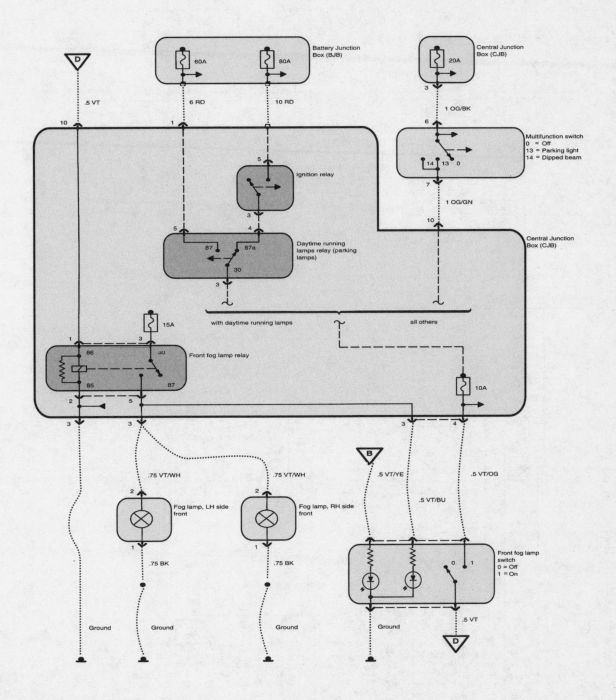

ESCORT 1998: Turn indicator and hazard lights

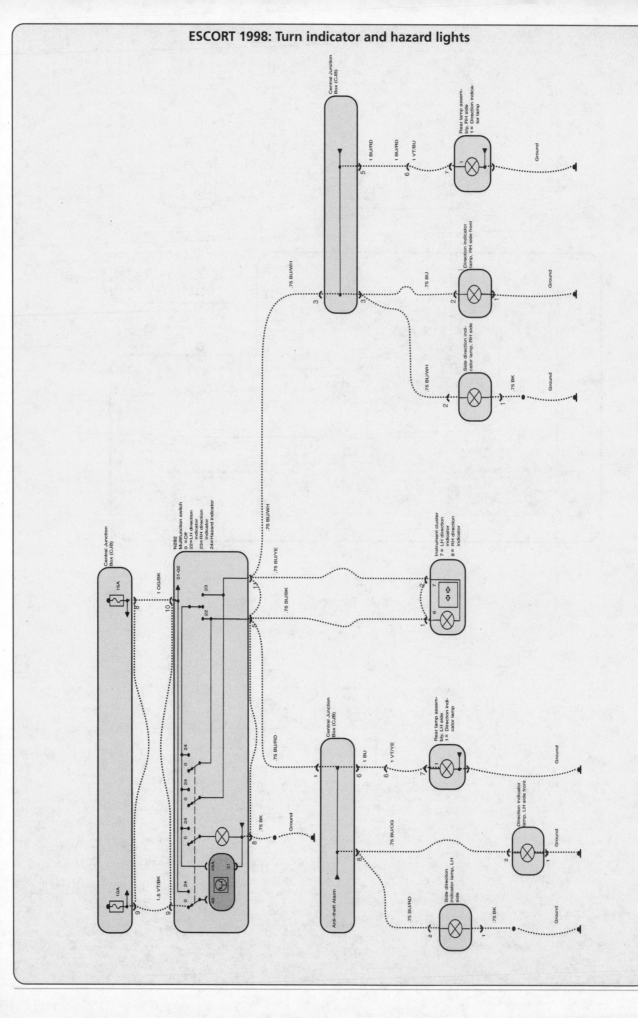

Escort 1998: Front screen wipers and washers

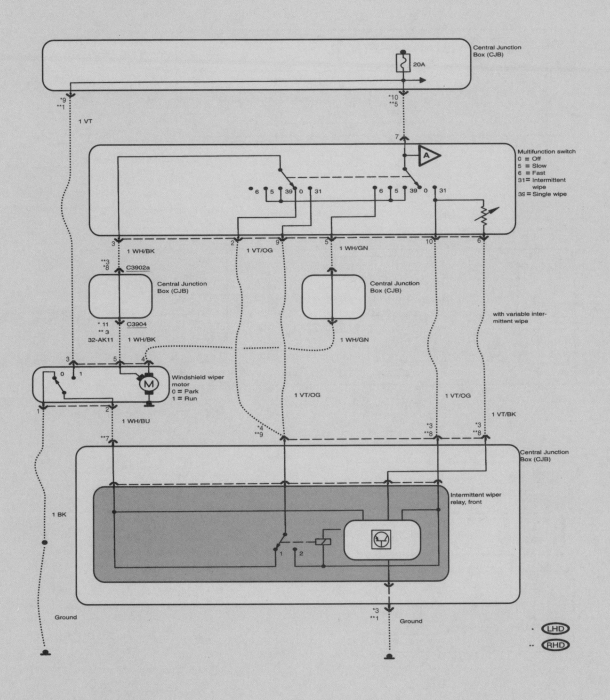

Central Junction Box (CJB)

20A

*9
**1

1 VT

*10
**5

7

A

Multifunction switch
0 = Off
5 = Slow
6 = Fast
31 = Intermittent wipe
39 = Single wipe

6   5   39   0   31   6   5   39   0   31

3   2   9   5   10   6

1 WH/BK   1 VT/OG   1 WH/GN

**3
*8   C3902a

Central Junction Box (CJB)

Central Junction Box (CJB)

with variable intermittent wipe

* 11   C3904
** 3
32-AK11   1 WH/BK   1 WH/GN

3   5   4

0   1

M

Windshield wiper motor
0 = Park
1 = Run

1   2

1 WH/BU   1 VT/OG   1 VT/OG

1 VT/BK

*3   *3
**8   **8

**7   *4
**9

Central Junction Box (CJB)

1 BK   Intermittent wiper relay, front

1   2

Ground   *3
**1   Ground

LHD

RHD

Escort 1998: Rear screen wipers (not intermittent) and washers

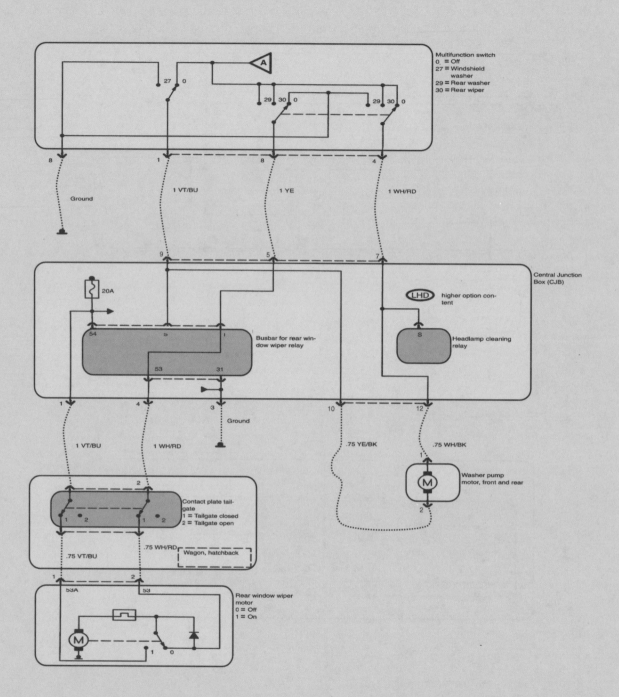

Multifunction switch
0, = Off
27 = Windshield washer
29 = Rear washer
30 = Rear wiper

Ground

1 VT/BU

1 YE

1 WH/RD

Central Junction Box (CJB)

20A

LHD higher option content

Busbar for rear window wiper relay

Headlamp cleaning relay

Ground

1 VT/BU

1 WH/RD

.75 YE/BK

.75 WH/BK

Washer pump motor, front and rear

Contact plate tailgate
1 = Tailgate closed
2 = Tailgate open

.75 VT/BU

.75 WH/RD

Wagon, hatchback

Rear window wiper motor
0 = Off
1 = On

Escort 1998: Heating and Ventilation

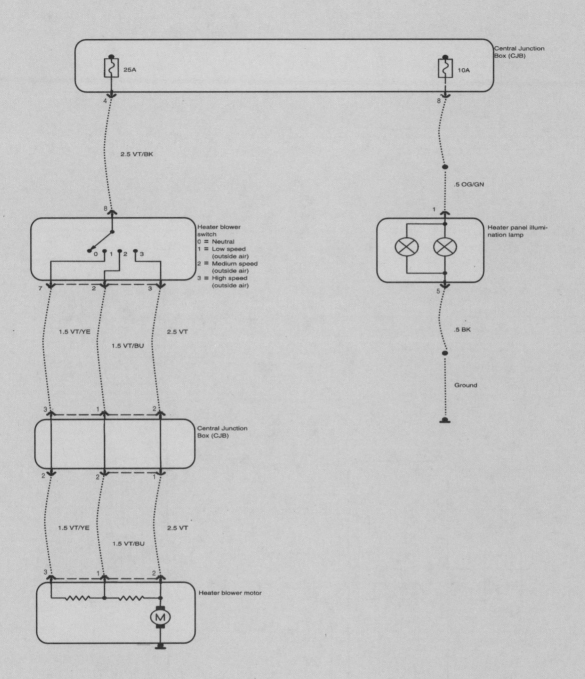

Central Junction Box (CJB)

25A

10A

4

8

2.5 VT/BK

.5 OG/GN

8

1

Heater blower switch
0 = Neutral
1 = Low speed (outside air)
2 = Medium speed (outside air)
3 = High speed (outside air)

0   1   2   3

Heater panel illumination lamp

7   2   3

5

1.5 VT/YE   2.5 VT

.5 BK

1.5 VT/BU

Ground

3   1   2

Central Junction Box (CJB)

2   2   1

1.5 VT/YE   2.5 VT

1.5 VT/BU

3   1   2

Heater blower motor

M

Escort 1998: Heated rear screen

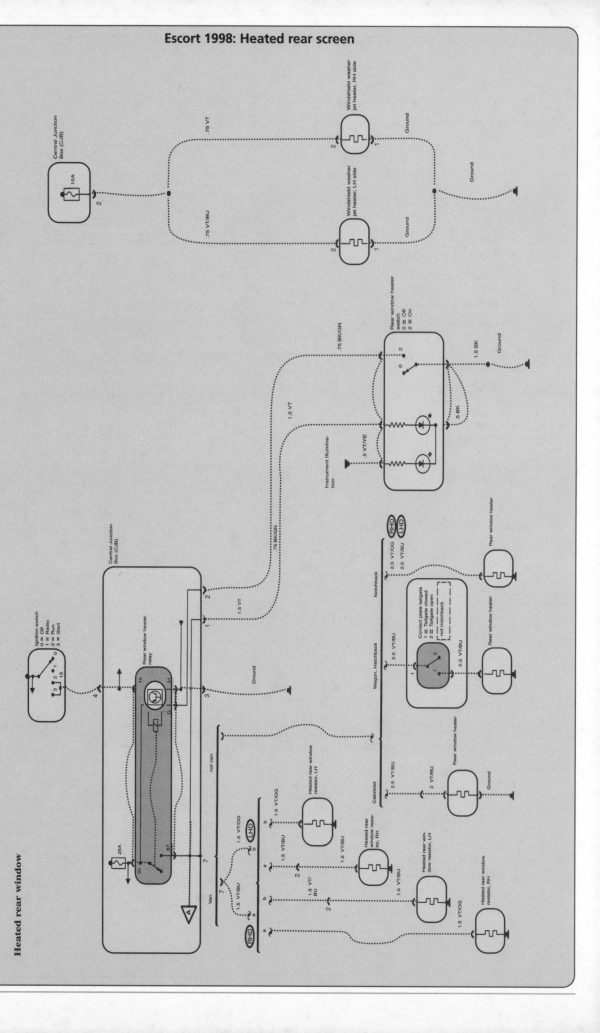

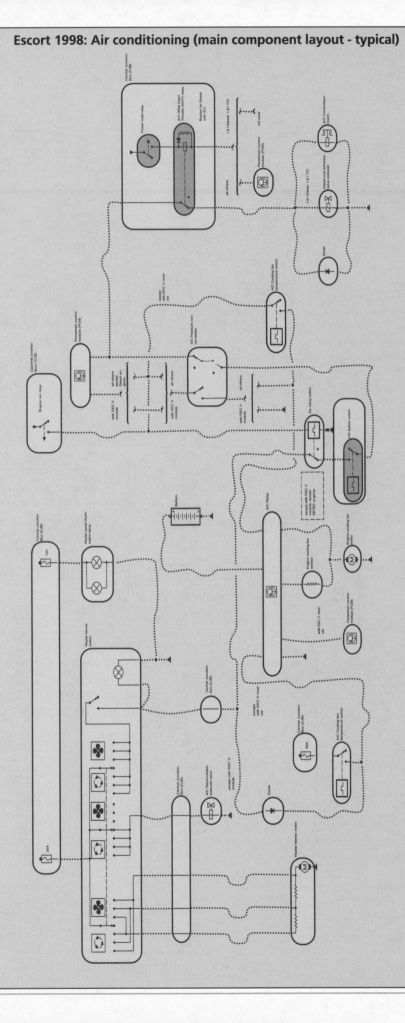

Escort 1998: Air conditioning (main component layout - typical)

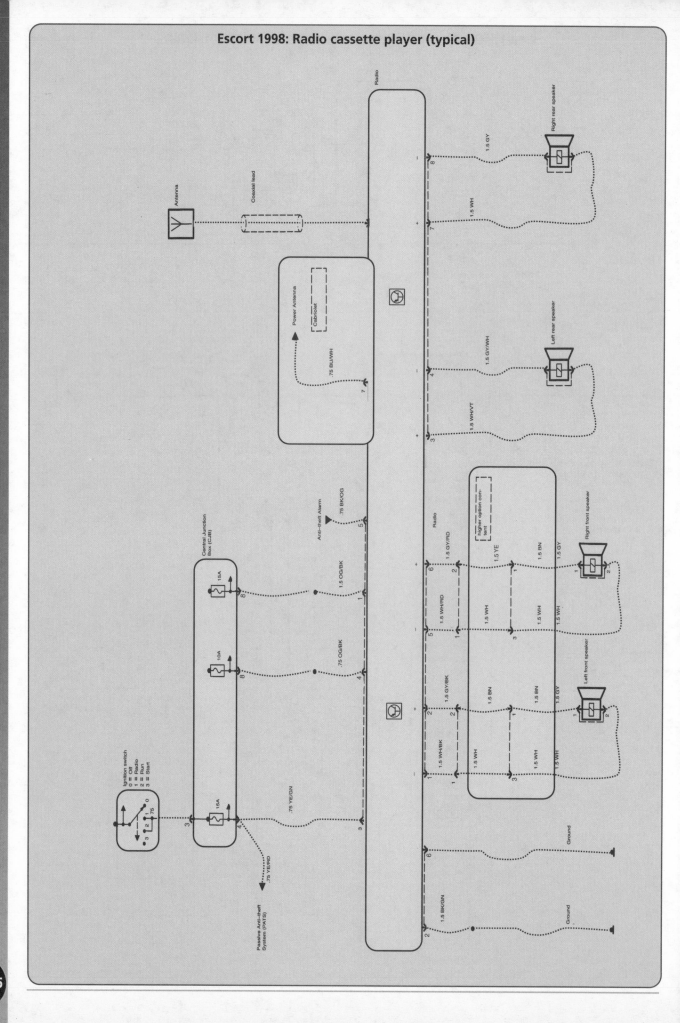

Escort 1998: Radio cassette player (typical)

Escort 1998: Central locking (4- and 5-door models - typical)

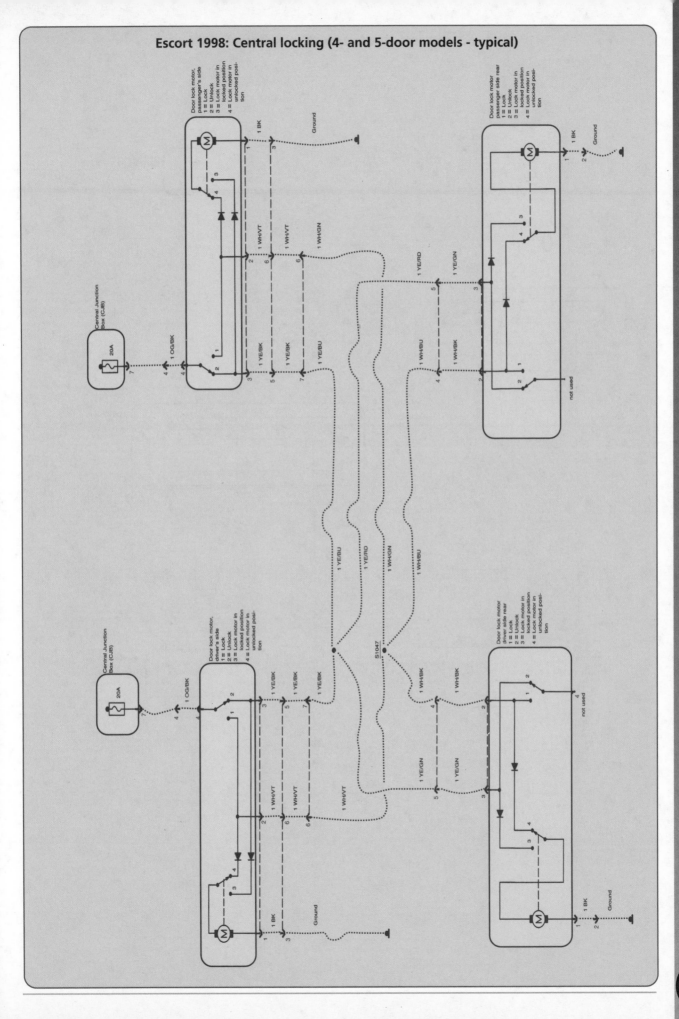

Escort 1998: Power windows (lower option version)

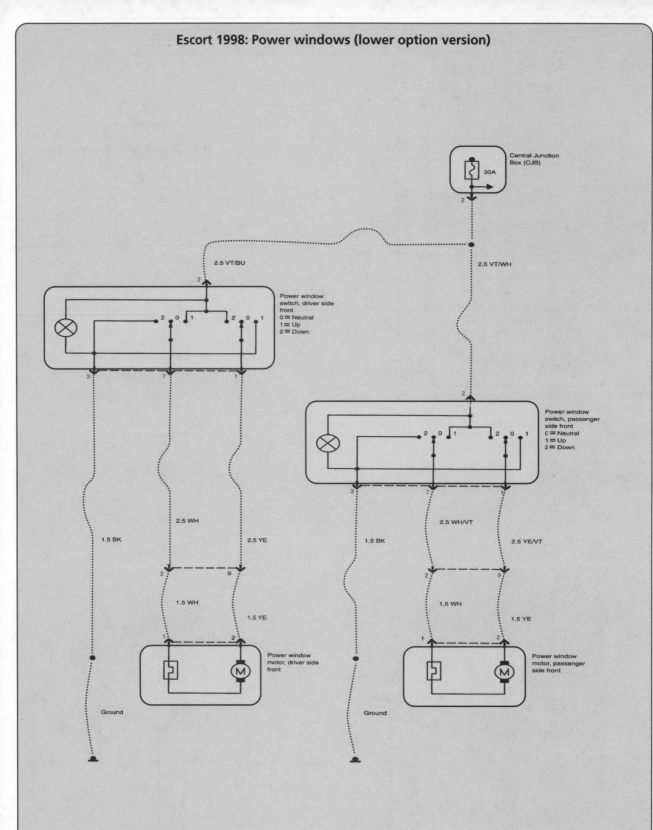

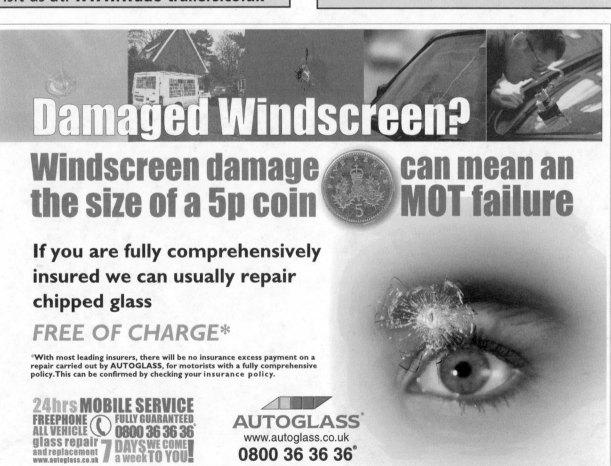

WÜRTH

THE ASSEMBLY PROFESSIONALS

Würth UK has been supplying the automotive repair and refinishing trade for over 25 years. With over 7,000 product lines and over 250 sales consultants covering every inch of Great Britain, Würth UK are able to offer the highest level of service.

The product range includes hi-spec chemical products including additives, brake cleaner, carburettor cleaner, greases, lubricants, valeting sprays, screenwash and electrical cleaning, lubrication and protection sprays. Würth also stocks a full range of DIN and ISO standard fasteners, electrical terminals, bulbs and fuses, trim clips, and vehicle wire.

Würth products meet strict DIN standards and Würth have been ISO 9002 certified since 1996 . Due to this high level of support and service, Würth are the preferred supplier to over 15 vehicle manufactures including BMW, Saab and Vauxhall, in excess of 30 dealer groups, and over 1000 independent vehicle repairers.

Würth UK Limited
1 Centurion Way
Erith
Kent
DA18 4AE

Tel. 0870 5 98 78 41
Fax. 0870 5 98 78 42

web: www.wurth.co.uk
email: sales@wurth.co.uk

Simple Solutions in a Complex World

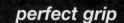

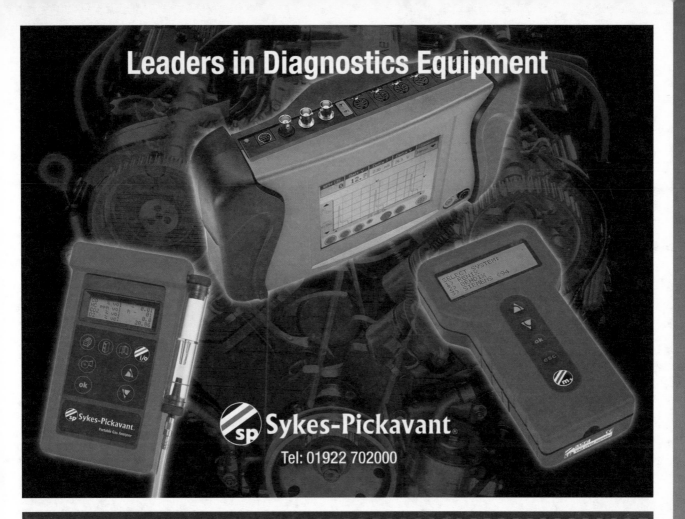

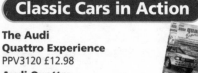

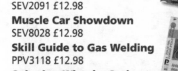
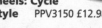

INDEX